*Additional Praise for*

EXPLORATIONS IN ORGAN.

"W     le he                                                         irliest

and     xploratio                                             1, insti-

tutional logics, and                                          themes

of organizations in                                          l and

given shape. Explorations of each                                ;aniza-

tions as complex, rule-based, imperf               ~w as vital and

vibrant in organization studies today as when it helped found the fie   half century ago."

JOEL BAUM,

CANADIAN NATIONAL CHAIR IN STRATEGIC MANAGEMENT,

ROTMAN SCHOOL OF MANAGEMENT, UNIVERSITY OF TORONTO

"In an age in which scholarship is increasingly commodified, *Explorations in Organizations* reminds us that it is possible to pursue ideas across what others see as boundaries. This volume presents several well-defined windows onto the garden of organization theory that March has done a great deal to create, suggesting some directions for growth. As March notes in his introduction to the volume, the somewhat chaotic nature of the garden may be an important part of the vitality of the field."

MARTHA S. FELDMAN,

JOHNSON CHAIR FOR CIVIC GOVERNANCE AND PUBLIC

MANAGEMENT, UNIVERSITY OF CALIFORNIA, IRVINE

"In this third collection of papers (which, together, span five decades!), Jim March continues to inspire—not just with his ideas, but also by being 'unremittingly exuberant about the pursuit of [them].' In all three collections, economists may find greatest connection to the idea of an 'organization as a decision-making process' proposed by Cyert and March (1963). In each successive decade, March and co-authors have elaborated on this theme; more recently, so have organizational economists. But, whereas Coase (1972) described his 1937 article as 'much cited and little used,' the reverse might be said of March's work: in organizational economics, we use his ideas every day, often without recalling their inception."

ROBERT GIBBONS,

SLOAN SCHOOL OF MANAGEMENT AND

DEPARTMENT OF ECONOMICS, MIT

# EXPLORATIONS IN ORGANIZATIONS

## James G. March

WITH INTRODUCTIONS BY

Zur Shapira

Daniel Levinthal

Johan P. Olsen

Mie Augier

Ellen S. O'Connor

STANFORD BUSINESS BOOKS

An Imprint of Stanford University Press

Stanford, California

Stanford University Press
Stanford, California

Printed in the United States of America on acid-free, archival-quality paper

Library of Congress Cataloging-in-Publication Data

Explorations in organizations / James G. March.
  p. cm.
Includes bibliographical references and index.
 ISBN 978-0-8047-5897-0 (cloth : alk. paper)—ISBN 978-0-8047-5898-7 (pbk. :
alk. paper)
1.  Organization. 2.  Management. I. March, James G.
 HD31.E875 2008
 302.3'5—dc22
 2008011551

Typeset by at Stanford University Press in 9.25/14 Sabon

# Contents

# Foreword

I WANT TO EXTEND MY THANKS to the Stanford University Press (as represented in human form by Margo Beth Crouppen, Judith Hibbard, Sarah Ives, and Jessica Walsh) for publishing this collection of articles; to Mie Augier, Markus Becker, Diane Coutu, Richard Cyert, Jerker Denrell, Thorbjørn Knudsen, Johan P. Olsen, Herbert A. Simon, and Bilian Ni Sullivan for their collaboration on the articles and their willingness to have them appear here; and to Daniel Newark for preparing the index. I am also much in debt to Mie Augier, Daniel Levinthal, Ellen O'Connor, Johan P. Olsen, and Zur Shapira for writing introductory essays to the various sections of the book. Their essays provide a freshness of perspective and force of insight that grace the book. All of these colleagues demonstrate once again that scholarship is a collective, not an individual, activity.

I also wish to thank the following publishers for granting permission to reprint pieces originally published by them:

Chapter 1: "Ideas as Art: A Conversation with James G. March" (with Diane Coutu), from *Harvard Business Review*, 84:10 (October 2006), 82–89.

Chapter 2: "Introduction to the Second Edition" (with Herbert A. Simon), from pp. 1–19 in James G. March and Herbert A. Simon, *Organizations*, 2nd edition. Oxford, UK: Blackwell, 1993.

Chapter 3: "An Epilogue" (with Richard M. Cyert), from pp. 214–246 in Richard M. Cyert and James G. March, *A Behavioral Theory of the Firm*, 2nd edition. Oxford, UK: Blackwell, 1992.

Chapter 4: "Learning and the Theory of the Firm," from *Economia e Banca—Annali Scientific* (Trento), 5 (1992), 15–35.

Chapter 5: "Understanding Organizational Adaptation," from *Society and Economy*, 25 (2003), 1–10.

Chapter 6: "Adaptation as Information Restriction: The Hot Stove Effect" (with Jerker Denrell), from *Organization Science*, 12 (2001), 523–538.

Chapter 7: "Schumpeter, Winter, and the Sources of Novelty" (with Markus C. Becker and Thorbjørn Knudsen), from *Industrial and Corporate Change*, 15 (2006), 353–371.

Chapter 8: "Rationality, Foolishness, and Adaptive Intelligence", from *Strategic Management Journal*, 27 (2006), 201–214.

Chapter 9: "The New Institutionalism: Organizational Factors in Political Life" (with Johan P. Olsen), from *American Political Science Review*, 78 (1984), 734–749.

Chapter 10: "The Institutional Dynamics of International Political Orders" (with Johan P. Olsen), from *International Organization*, 52 (1998), 943–969.

Chapter 11: "A Learning Perspective on the Network Dynamics of Institutional Integration," from pp. 129–155 in Morten Egeberg and Per Lægreid, eds., *Organizing Political Institutions: Essays for Johan P. Olsen*. Oslo: Scandinavian University Press, 1999.

Chapter 12: "Research on Organizations: Hopes for the Past and Lessons from the Future," from *Nordiske Organisasjonsstudier*, 1 (1999), 69–83.

Chapter 13: "Parochialism in the Evolution of a Research Community: The Case of Organization Studies," from *Management and Organization Review*, 1 (2004), 5–22.

Chapter 14: "Notes on the Evolution of a Research Community: Organization Studies in Anglophone North America, 1945–2000" (with Mie Augier and Bilian Ni Sullivan), from *Organization Science*, 16 (2005), 85–95.

Chapter 15: "The Study of Organizations and Organizing since 1945," from *Organization Studies*, 28 (2007), 9–19.

Chapter 16: "Scholarship, Scholarly Institutions, and Scholarly Communities," from *Organization Science*, 18 (2007), 537–542.

Chapter 17: "The Pursuit of Relevance in Management Education" (with Mie Augier), from *California Management Review*, 49 (2007), 129–146.

Chapter 18: "Literature and Leadership" (French: "Littérature et leadership"), from *Revue Économique et Sociale* (Lausanne), 59 (2001), 301–308.

Chapter 19: "Poetry and the Rhetoric of Management: *Easter 1916*," from *Journal of Management Inquiry*, 15 (2006) 70–72.

Chapter 20: "Ibsen, Ideals, and the Subornation of Lies," from *Organization Studies*, 28 (2007), 1277–1285.

James G. March
Stanford, California
January, 2008

# INTRODUCTION

JAMES G. MARCH

THIS BOOK is the third in a trilogy of collected papers that I have authored or coauthored. The earlier volumes were published in 1988 (March, 1988) and 1999 (March, 1999). Although the 1999 volume included four articles published before 1988, and the present volume includes five articles published before 1999, to a substantial extent, the three books represent three different periods in publication and in the age of the author.

A thoughtful reader may detect ways in which the present volume differs from earlier ones and perhaps even contains symptoms of moral maturation and intellectual decay conventionally attributed to aging, including reflections on intellectual and institutional history and excursions into literature. Nevertheless, the questions being addressed and the general spirit of their examination have remained fairly constant over the years.

The spirit is appropriately cautious about proclamations of momentous discovery but unremittingly exuberant about the pursuit of ideas that might illuminate organizational life, contribute to believable stories about organizations, or augment the recognition and creation of truth, beauty, and justice in organization studies and organizations. The spirit is as grand as the questions are mundane: How is information processed and used? How do decisions happen? What is the role of institutions? How do organizations, collections of organizations, and studies of organizations learn and evolve? How do we construct comprehensible stories about organizational life? How do we make organizations better in a sense that matters?

There are several well-known issues surrounding attempts to answer such questions: Are organizational attributes the stable equilibrium outcomes of organizational histories, or the transitory outcomes of dynamic processes of change? Are organizations choice based, or rule based? Are organizations typified by clarity and consistency, or by ambiguity and inconsistency? Are the activities of organizations instrumental or interpretive in character? Are organizational phenomena due to the independent actions of autonomous actors, or to the systemic properties of an interacting ecology?

The papers and books I have written generally reflect perspectives that are a bit less oriented to visions of organizations as stable, choice based, coherence seeking, instrumental, and autonomous, and a bit more oriented to visions of organizations as changing, rule based, incoherent, interpretive, and ecologically embedded. Insofar as the field as a whole wanders in the same directions over the coming years, it will, among other things, become more concerned with representing processes of complexity, paradox, contradiction, conflict, chaos, ambiguity, ritual, and mythology. If it does so, it is likely to give more attention to complex ideas involving more interactions, more elaborate models, and more complicated analyses and simultaneously more attention to humanistic and qualitative efforts to understand the confusions and paradoxes of social life. Studies of organizations in such a spirit seek to combine analytical complexity and precision with aesthetic sensitivity and grace. They are not always successful.

The papers in the present book are organized into five main sections, each with an introductory essay written by a distinguished colleague and friend:

- Explorations in theories of organizational action, an examination of efforts to develop ideas about decision making in organizations (with an introduction by Zur Shapira)
- Explorations in the role of novelty in organizational adaptation, an examination of the tendency of learning to extinguish novelty, and a consideration of the search for mechanisms that overcome that tendency (with an introduction by Daniel Levinthal)
- Explorations in institutions and logics of appropriateness, an examination of the role of rules, identities, and institutions in organizational behavior (with an introduction by Johan P. Olsen)
- Explorations in the modern history of organization studies, an examination of the institutional and intellectual evolution of the field (with an introduction by Mie Augier)
- Explorations in organizations through literature, an examination of the possibilities for finding ideas relevant to organization studies in classics of literature (with an introduction by Ellen O'Connor)

The present brief introduction to the book does not attempt to say anything specific about the individual sections, leaving that to the section introductions. Rather, it consists in minor ruminations about ideas in organization studies as they have developed in the years since World War II. The ruminations are presented here both as a ritual introduction to the papers in the book and as a gentle reminder of the continued existence of their author.

## THE PURSUIT OF ORGANIZATION THEORY

For many years I toyed with the idea of writing a book on "organization theory" without ever coming close to doing so. Over the years, the vision of a somewhat coherent and moderately powerful introduction to organization theory has remained a recurrent hope. However, like other fantasies of aging men, it has become increasingly more a pleasant dream than a plausible aspiration.

Some future scholar will undoubtedly provide a definitive invention or exegesis of organization theory, and I apologize for leaving the task undone. The obvious primary reason for this deterioration of ambition into fantasy is the lure of other things. Someone less enchanted by other scholarly projects and by other pleasures of life would undoubtedly have found time to translate a desire for organization theory into some kind of realization.

To some extent, however, my laziness can be rationalized by uncertainty about what a book on organization theory might plausibly contain. It clearly could not contain the derivations from a single axiomatic foundation shared widely among organization scholars. Even the most romantic imagination about the field would have difficulty in justifying an attempt to describe such a thing. It might be possible for someone with energy, imagination, and chutzpah to identify a collection of key propositions as a basis for thinking about organizations, but any such collection requires enough qualification to discourage a "theory" metaphor.

In particular, the search for a theory of organizations has to confront the many ways in which context matters. The context of history matters: Many of the phenomena observed in organizations are tied powerfully to their times, as are the ideas scholars use to talk about them. The context of locale matters: Organizations are embedded in local cultures that shape them and our interpretations of them profoundly. The context of institutions matters: Organizations and organizational scholars exist in complex networks of legal, political, economic, and social institutions and must be understood as co-evolving with those institutions and the rules that inhabit them.

The contextual dependence of organizational phenomena has implications for the kinds of research that students of organizations pursue, for the methods they use, for the ways in which they construct stories about organizations, for the nature of the knowledge to which they aspire, and for the advice they render. For example, although students of organizations use effectively the full panoply of quantitative and statistical tools of social science, some of their more important studies are richly "ethnographic" or "historiographic" descriptions of the fine detail of organizational anatomy or functioning in a specific time and place.

Context dependence clearly constrains organization theory. Insofar as context matters, the "universal" propositions of organization theory are mostly restricted to three kinds of assertions, none totally satisfactory. The first kind of assertion consists in what might be called "taxonomies" of ideal types. These assertions seek to arrange organizations into categories. For example, organizations may be categorized as "public" or "private" and cross-classified as "centralized" or "decentralized," thus yielding one of the classificatory tables beloved by social science. The taxonomies ordinarily have implicit theoretical bases for the distinctions; but the main point is to provide a way of sorting organizations into categories that group together institutions that might be treated as being, in some sense, "similar."

The second kind of assertion consists in what might be called "big ideas." These are ideas that provide very general notions that can be used to frame observations and thinking. They claim enough generality to apply across contexts and across a very broad class of phenomena. Partly because of their pursuit of universality, big ideas are generally difficult to disconfirm through observations. The variables they specify and the predictions they yield are at a level of generality that tends to make them tautologically true or confirmable primarily through transparent tricks of definition or measurement.

The third kind of assertion consists in what might be called "little ideas." These are ideas of much more limited scope. They generalize from specific descriptions of specific times and places to provide propositions about a small set of phenomena within a small set of contexts. The more interesting of these little ideas represent speculations about dynamic mechanisms of moderate power capable of clarifying small corners of organizational phenomena.

Organization theory, if it exists, is a garden of such ideas evolving into a shifting ecology of varieties through a mix of self-fertilization, cross-fertilization, and the migration of seeds. Thanks to the usual human disposition to attribute history to human intervention, that evolution is often attributed to contributions from specific scholars and specific pieces of scholarship; but it probably could be modeled reasonably well by an idea-centric, rather than scholar-centric, theory of the reproduction, elaboration, survival, and spread of ideas.

## A FEW BIG IDEAS

Big ideas in studies of organizations are taken from the international bookshelf of big ideas. They are not unique to organization studies. They have been developed primarily outside of the field and have invaded organization studies through the usual epidemiological mechanisms. The big ideas that have come to shape the thinking of scholars in organizations studies include (but are not limited to):

*The pursuit of rationality.* The idea is that human beings act by making choices and make choices by anticipating the consequences of alternative actions and choosing actions that will, if the anticipations are fulfilled, lead to consequences subjectively judged favorably.

*The pursuit of identity and rules.* The idea is that behavior is rule based, that organizations (and societies) are collections of identities and rules associated with them, and that individuals and organizations seek to match situations with rules appropriate to an evoked identity.

*The class struggle.* The idea is that history is a story of conflict between social groups in which the poor (and many) confront the rich (and few), conflicts that may or may not lead to some ultimate equilibrium but along the way are characterized by changing outcomes traceable to the inevitabilities of history and variations in the self-corruption of the rich and the self-organization of the poor.

*The struggle with self.* The idea is that individual behavior in organizations and consequent organizational attributes are understood as stemming from efforts to comprehend the self and to deal with the contradictions within the self and between the self and the organization.

*Creating and living in social structures.* The idea is that social structures are codes of rights and duties organized within systems of stratification, differentiation, and subdivision, and that those structures co-evolve with behavior that is manifested within them.

*Creating and using networks.* The idea is that the elementary components of a system (e.g., cells, individuals, groups) are connected by relationships (e.g., communication links, friendship, authority, mobility chains). The properties of the resulting web of relations are primary determinants of organizational phenomena.

*The distribution and exercise of power.* The idea is that power is distributed unequally among groups and individuals, and the possession of power gives control over organizational actions and over individuals. This control contributes to the achievement of objectives and is, therefore, valuable for any individual or group that has it but problematic for any individual or group that does not.

*Adaptation through learning.* The idea is that individuals, groups, and organizations modify their beliefs and behaviors by observing their own and others' experiences, possibly making inferences about the causes of those experiences, but in any event adjusting propensities to favor the replication of actions and beliefs that have been associated with favorable outcomes in the past.

*Adaptation through natural selection.* The idea is that the behavior of fundamental elements (e.g., genes, routines) is unchanging but that the mix of different behavioral propensities within a population changes as a result of differential survival and reproductive success of the basic elements in a competitive environment.

*The spread of things.* The idea treats organizational forms, practices, and actions as spreading through imitation and invasion within a population of organizations. It relaxes some of the more standard assumptions of epidemiology, in particular the notions that an object of diffusion and the network of contacts through which it spreads are unchanged by the process.

*The pursuit of meaning.* The idea is that human behavior is organized by the construction, reproduction, and communication of meaning. These interpretations are critical both for shaping individual action in an ambiguous environment and for maintaining the human myths and illusions of comprehension that underlie organization.

Big ideas are primarily the first paragraphs of knowledge. They provide a set of assumptions that can orient an analysis and provide useful frames and rhetorical templates. Many of the arguments in the literature of organization studies are arguments over which big ideas to use. Those arguments are replete with various levels of epistemological and ontological sophistication, as well as eloquent proclamations of faith and assertions of fact that sometimes seem to seek confirmation more by repetition than by demonstration.

### A FEW LITTLE IDEAS

Although much of the rhetoric in organization studies is about big ideas, many of the more serious contributions of the field are manifested in little ideas that infuse big ideas with less grand but more operational meaning. Little ideas identify and explore small mechanisms of limited scope capable of producing notable effects and possibly susceptible to empirical verification.

To illustrate, I list a few little ideas that have been of some importance in areas in which I have worked. They are familiar examples, not exemplars. A more serious effort to identify key little ideas from organization studies would result in a list that was considerably longer and much less self-referential.

*Satisficing.* The basic idea is that preference functions are not continuous but are bi-valued. Decision makers distinguish between alternatives that are "good enough" and those that are not, but do not make distinctions within the two categories. From this came several derivative ideas: Experiential learning. Organizations learn to reproduce action associated with outcomes above aspirations and to extinguish actions associated with outcomes below aspirations. This leads to improvements sometimes, but it also leads to superstitious learning and the learning of other false lessons. Adaptive aspirations: The definition of good enough shifts over time, rising with success and declining with failure, and tracking the performance of others. As a result, fluctuations in search are less than might be expected from fluctuations in performance, and improvements through learning are confounded by changes in aspirations. Variable risk preferences: Inclinations to take risks vary with position relative to aspirations, with risk taking more characteristic of poor positions than of good positions.

*Attention allocation.* The basic idea is that attention is a scarce good. Organizations do not attend to all alternatives, all possible consequences of alternatives, all possible problems or solutions, or all dimensions of preferences, but to only a subset of those. As a result, the mechanisms for evoking attention are critical. Among other things, this leads to ideas of the sequential attention to goals, the notion that only a subset of organizational goals are evoked at a time and thus that conflict and inconsistencies are sometimes maintained by shifting patterns of attention. It also leads to ideas of problemistic search, the notion that search is more intense when performance is below aspirations than when it is above them and that it is directed first to the temporal and spatial near-neighborhood of the problem. In turn, this leads to ideas about organizational slack: In good times, organizations fail to discover good alternatives that they can subsequently discover in poorer times. As a result, organizational performance varies less over time than the fluctuations in the environment. It also leads to ideas of garbage can processes in which problems, solutions, and decision makers are brought together less by their mutual relevance than by their simultaneous availability, and to ideas of the separation of talk and action into different arenas of attention.

*Low sampling of failure.* The idea is that learning involves reducing the sampling rate of alternatives associated with poor outcomes. This leads to systematic errors that are not routinely corrected. In particular, learning leads to abandoning alternatives that have a record of poor results historically. If a poor history is unrepresentative of the long-run possibilities of an alternative, the normal processes of learning will not discover that fact. This feature of learning is implicated in competence traps. It is quite possible to be trapped by learning into using an inferior technology because competence in using the technology depends on experience with it, and poor early results terminate experience with an apparently inferior technology. It is also implicated in risk aversion. Risky alternatives require patience with failure in order to realize their value. Learning encourages impatience with failure and consequently is biased against risky alternatives.

*Exploration and exploitation.* The idea is that an adaptive system engages in two kinds of activities—exploiting and refining what is known and exploring what might come to be known. Exploitation has returns that tend to be relatively certain and relatively near in terms of time and space. Exploration has returns that tend to be relatively uncertain and relatively distant in time and space. Both are necessary. Exploitation alone leads to obsolescence. Exploration alone leads to frivolity. The optimal mix is difficult to specify and depends on the time and space horizons assumed. The issues are confronted in slightly different forms in several parts of the literature: Bandit problems. In a situation in which information about an alternative is secured only by trying it, how do we balance between the choice of an alternative with the highest expected value and the choice of a different alternative in order to learn more about its possible value? Structural holes. How do we organize linkages among individuals so as to facilitate the intense exploitation of ideas within tightly connected groups without losing the bridges among such groups that facilitate cross-fertilization and the exploration of new ideas?

These are illustrations, intended to suggest the character of little ideas. They comprise neither a complete list of those ideas nor even a list of the more important ones. Other little ideas include ideas about absorptive capacity, density dependence, institutional isomorphism, hypocrisy, loose coupling, robust action, transaction costs, vacancy chains, and a host of others.

Most of the justification for the claim that organization studies has added to theoretical knowledge since World War II lies in little ideas such as these. They are embedded in different big ideas and only by a definitional legerdemain can they be made to yield a single integrating theory that treats them all as derivations from a single set of axioms. Collectively, however, they and others like them provide a set of tools for organization studies and provide modest substance to a claim of knowledge.

## A SERIOUS FIELD

My grandmother was born in 1862, and, for her, the world largely regressed after that date. She conceded that time had given her a life of increasing affluence and technological abundance; but she felt that in more personal and communal ways, life had become worse. My parents had similar feelings about the early twentieth century, and I suppose my own childhood memories are of a world more appealing to me in important ways than are the worlds of my grandchildren, as seen by me. The usual interpretation of this phenomenon of sweet nostalgia for the past has something to do with a combination of resistance to change and faulty memories attributable to senility; and I suppose such things are as likely in recalling the history of a scholarly field as they are in recalling lives.

When I look at organizations scholarship, however, nostalgia for the good old days gives way to a recognition of the many ways in which the present is manifestly better than it was when I entered graduate school in 1949. The number of scholars who identify with the field of organization studies increased enormously in the decades after World War II. So also did the number of journals specializing in organization and management studies. The field differentiated itself to some degree from the disciplines of economics, political science, psychology, and sociology within which it had originally developed and created a new quasi-discipline, located within traditional disciplines to some degree but increasingly located in professional schools such as business schools. It established its own professional associations. To some extent, it gained control over the training of succeeding generations of organizations scholars.

This institutional consolidation of a field was not accompanied by any significant paradigmatic consolidation. The last sixty years have seen little sign of convergence to a single core paradigm in organization studies. Rather the field has spawned numerous smaller domains, distributed non-homogeneously across the regions, disciplines, and institutions of the world, in each of which there has been the development of a few moderately powerful ideas and some modest tendency to converge on understandings, but among which there has been, at most, mutual tolerance spawned by ignorance or indifference.

Nevertheless, in almost every meaningful sense, the intellectual position of the field is stronger than it was sixty years ago. It has become a serious field of study. From a small collection of ideas found in the writings of a handful of scholars scattered among the disciplines, the corpus of organization studies and the community of scholars have grown immensely. One of my friends has complained to me that the giants of scholarship have disappeared, that contemporary scholars contain no Herb Simon, no Jim Thompson. Insofar as that is true, I think it is largely because there are now too many distinguished scholars for any two or three to stand out in the same way.

As a long-time observer of it all, I celebrate the many ways in which organizations scholarship has improved and salute the scholarly rigor, imagination, and dedication, not to mention the baby booms and the persistence of prosperity in developed nations that have contributed to that outcome. I also record with equally unabashed pleasure the happy terror associated with the inexorable personal process of becoming a lost footnote to the development of knowledge.

### REFERENCES

March, James G. 1988. *Decisions and Organizations*. Oxford, UK: Blackwell.
March, James G. 1999. *In Pursuit of Organizational Intelligence*. Oxford, UK: Blackwell.

# CHAPTER I

# Ideas as Art

## *A Conversation with James G. March*

DIANE COUTU

IN THESE PAGES, three years ago, consultants Laurence Prusak and Thomas H. Davenport reported the findings of a survey of prominent management writers who identified their own gurus. Although his is an unfamiliar name to most readers of this periodical, James G. March appeared on more lists than any other person except Peter Drucker.

March is a writer to whom the experts turn when they want to engage new ideas. He is a polymath whose career over the past five decades has encompassed numerous disciplines. A professor emeritus in management, sociology, political science, and education at Stanford University, he has taught courses on subjects as diverse as organizational psychology, behavioral economics, leadership, rules for killing people, friendship, decision making, models in social science, revolutions, computer simulation, and statistics.

March is perhaps best known for his pioneering contributions to organization and management theory. He has coauthored two classic books: *Organizations* (with Herbert A. Simon) and *A Behavioral Theory of the Firm* (with Richard M. Cyert). Together with Cyert and Simon, March developed a theory of the firm that incorporates aspects of sociology, psychology, and economics to provide an alternative to neoclassical theories. The underlying idea is that although managers make decisions that are intendedly rational, the rationality is "bounded" by human and organizational limitations. As a result, human behavior is not always what might be predicted when rationality is assumed.

In addition to this work, March has been a leading contributor to the study of political institutions, particularly through the books *Rediscovering Institutions* and *Democratic Governance* (both coauthored with Johan P. Olsen); the study of leadership, through *Leadership and Ambiguity* (with Michael D. Cohen) and *On Leadership* (with Thierry Weil); and the study of decision making, through his books *A Primer on Decision Making* and *The Pursuit of Organizational Intelligence*.

This chapter originally appeared in *Harvard Business Review*, 84:10 (October 2006), 82–89.

March's influence on students of organizations and management and his accomplishments in other areas of social science have conferred on him an almost unprecedented reputation as a rigorous scholar and a deep source of wisdom. In the academic literature, it has become de rigueur to cite his articles. Professor John Padgett of the University of Chicago wrote in the journal *Contemporary Sociology* that "Jim March is to organization theory what Miles Davis is to jazz. . . . March's influence, unlike that of any of his peers, is not limited to any possible subset of the social science disciplines; it is pervasive."

Despite his renown in the social sciences, March has not confined his interests to those fields. Besides his professional and scholarly articles and books, he has made one film (*Passion and Discipline: Don Quixote's Lessons for Leadership*), is currently working on another, and has written seven books of poetry. His poetic sensibility can be felt in the metaphors he has created over the years: the "garbage can theory" of organizational choice, the "technology of foolishness," the role of consultants as "disease carriers," and the "hot stove effect."

In a recent interview with *Harvard Business Review* senior editor Diane Coutu at his home in Portola Valley, California, March shared his thinking on aesthetics, leadership, the usefulness of scholarship, the role of folly, and the irrelevance of relevance when it comes to the pursuit of ideas. The following is an edited version of that interview.

*How did you come to have such influence on management thinking without being as public a figure as Peter Drucker?*
I don't claim to have any notable impact, partly because I question the methodology by which such an impact is assigned to me, and partly because I suspect it is easier to infiltrate the idea consciousness of the business community if you do not worry about attribution, reputation for significance, or direct communication. And even if that is not true, I fear that my own enjoyments come more from playing with ideas than from selling them. I am a scholar; I do what scholars do. I think about things, conduct research studies, and write up my thoughts and research in professional journals. The writing is probably more a way of understanding my thoughts than of communicating them.

That sounds more reclusive than I believe I am. I am hardly so perverse as to resist having my writings read by others. The articles I write are accessible to any manager who chooses to read them. I don't write obscurely—at least not deliberately—and the ideas are not exceptionally arcane. Dull, maybe, but not arcane.

*You liked to begin your classes at Stanford each year saying, "I am not now, nor have I ever been, relevant." What did you mean by that?*
It was a signal to students that it would not be fruitful to ask me about the immediate usefulness of what I had to say. If there is relevance to my ideas, then it is for the people who contemplate the ideas to see, not for the person who produces them. For me, a feature of scholarship that is generally more significant than relevance is the beauty of the ideas. I care that ideas have some form of elegance or grace or surprise—all the things that beauty gives you. The central limit theorem, for example, is one of the more important theorems in classical statistics; it allows you to say things about sampling errors. But for me, the theorem is primarily a thing of extraordinary beauty. I think that anyone who teaches the central limit theorem should try to communicate that aesthetic joy to students.

Charlie Lave and I wrote *Introduction to Models in the Social Sciences*. Among the books I've written, it is one of my favorites. It introduces students to the rudiments of four very fundamental models in social science. It treats modeling as an art form. Scholarship will always have an element of aestheticism, because scholars are obliged to advance beauty as well as truth and justice.

*This seems to be your artistic sensibility. How do you justify such a sensibility in a world where business is so desperately in need of practical solutions?*
No organization works if the toilets don't work, but I don't believe that finding solutions to business problems is my job. If a manager asks an academic consultant what to do and that consultant answers, then the consultant should be fired. No academic has the experience to know the context of a managerial problem well enough to give specific advice about a specific situation. What an academic consultant can do is say some things that, in combination with the manager's knowledge of the context, may lead to a better solution. It is the combination of academic and experiential knowledge, not the substitution of one for the other, that yields improvement.

*Have you ever consulted to businesses?*
When I was younger—younger and poorer, I suppose—I used to do some relatively technical consulting about things involving statistics or research methods. I don't do that any longer. I still occasionally do something I humorously call "consulting" but probably is better seen as getting someone to buy lunch for me. If someone calls me up and says a manager would like to talk to me, I'm inclined to respond that I almost certainly don't have anything useful to say. But if the answer is that it doesn't matter, that the manager still wants to have

lunch with me, then I am happy to have lunch. I think that it would ordinarily be difficult to discover any practical use for such conversations, but I may occasionally have a way of looking at things that is sufficiently different to help a manager in some marginal way. Usually, managers are sensible enough not to ask me to lunch, and I end up paying for most of my lunches myself.

*Leadership has become a big concern and a big industry in recent years. What is happening in leadership research?*
I doubt that "leadership" is a useful concept for serious scholarship. The idea of leadership is imposed on our interpretation of history by our human myths, or by the way we think that history is supposed to be described. As a result, the fact that people talk about leaders and attribute importance to them is neither surprising nor informative. Although there is good work on several aspects of asymmetric relations in life, broad assertions about leadership are more characteristic of amateurs than of professionals. Unless and until a link to significant scholarship can be made, the thinking on leadership will produce more articles in popular journals than in professional ones, more homilies and tautologies than powerful ideas. In the meantime, in order for leadership scholarship to generate some good ideas, it needs to build buffers to protect itself from the temptations of immediate relevance.

*What kinds of questions do you think are important for leaders?*
In my course on leadership and literature, I ended up with a list of about ten topics—for example, power, dominiation, and subordination; ambiguity and coherence; gender and sexuality; the relation between private and public lives. Not a unique list, and hardly a complete one. Each of the topics can draw illumination from social science, but I think they often are more profoundly considered in great literature. One issue, which I used to talk about by looking at George Bernard Shaw's *Saint Joan,* is how madness, heresy, and genius are related. We often describe great leaders as having the drive, vision, imagination, and creativity to transform their organizations through daring new ideas. Retrospectively, of course, we sometimes find that such heresies have been the foundation for bold and necessary change, but heresy is usually just crazy. Most daring new ideas are foolish or dangerous and appropriately rejected or ignored. So while it may be true that great geniuses are usually heretics, heretics are rarely great geniuses. If we could identify which heretics would turn out to be geniuses, life would be easier than it is. There is plenty of evidence that we cannot.

*In your film on Don Quixote and leadership, you say that if we trust only when trust is warranted, love only when love is returned, and learn only when learning is valuable, then we abandon an essential feature of our humanity. How do we lose part of our humanity?*

We justify actions by their consequences. But providing consequential justification is only a part of being human. It is an old issue, one with which Kant and Kierkegaard, among many others, struggled. I once taught a course on friendship that reinforced this idea for me. By the end of the course, a conspicuous difference had emerged between some of the students and me. They saw friendship as an exchange relationship: My friend is my friend because he or she is useful to me in one way or another. By contrast, I saw friendship as an arbitrary relationship: If you're my friend, then there are various obligations that I have toward you, which have nothing to do with your behavior. We also talked about trust in that class. The students would say, "Well, how can you trust people unless they are trustworthy?" So I asked them why they called that trust. It sounded to me like a calculated exchange. For trust to be anything truly meaningful, you have to trust somebody who isn't trustworthy. Otherwise, it's just a standard rational transaction. The relationships among leaders and those between leaders and their followers certainly involve elements of simple exchange and reciprocity, but humans are capable of, and often exhibit, more arbitrary sentiments of commitment to one another.

*You've said that scholars and managers do fundamentally different things. Can you elaborate on that?*

You need both academic knowledge and experiential knowledge, but they are different. The scholar tries to figure out, What's going on here? What are the underlying processes making the system go where it's going? What is happening, or what might happen? Scholars talk about ideas that describe the basic mechanisms shaping managerial history—bounded rationality, diffusion of legitimate forms, loose coupling, liability of newness, competency traps, absorptive capacity, and the like. In contrast, experiential knowledge focuses on a particular context at a particular time and on the events of personal experience. It may or may not generalize to broader things and longer time periods; it may or may not flow into a powerful theory; but it provides a lot of understanding of a particular situation. A scholar's knowledge cannot address a concrete, highly specific context, except crudely. Fundamental academic knowledge becomes more useful in new or changing environments, when managers are faced with the unexpected or the unknown. It provides alternative frames for looking at problems rather than solutions to them.

*Along with Richard Cyert and Herb Simon, you laid the groundwork for the field of behavioral economics. Do you think you started a revolution?*
Scholarship is a communal activity. No one comes first; and no one stands alone. Insofar as there has been a behavioral economics "revolution," it is a revolution started by many. Nowadays, economists and others do talk a fair amount about bounded rationality. But the economists are more inclined to see the limits on rationality as minor perturbations, easily accommodated within some variation of neoclassical economic theory, than as fundamental challenges. I once wrote a paper on the tendency of economists to maintain neoclassical theory by reinterpreting its definitions and constraints. I called the paper "The War Is Over, and the Victors Have Lost," to note the way economics has tended to become so tautological as to "explain" everything at the cost of abandoning predictive power. At times, economics as a theory threatens to become economics as a faith.

*You've been unusually interdisciplinary in your life's work. Is there some overarching question that you've tried to answer?*
I don't think it's been that grand. It just happens that the disciplines are organized in ways that distribute my rather narrow areas of research focus across standard disciplinary lines. I've studied problem solving and decision making, risk taking, information processing, innovation and change, learning, selection, and the creation and revision of rules and identities. In a very loose way, I think, you could say my main focus has been on the cognitive aspects of organizations, as long as you include in the term "cognitive" such things as conflict, bias, rule following, and confusion.

*Much of your research has focused on learning in one way or another. How is this tied to the hot stove effect?*
That term comes from an article by Jerker Denrell and me, but it is stolen from some of Mark Twain's wisdom. Twain said that if a cat ever jumps on a hot stove, he will never jump on a hot stove again. And that's good. But he will also never jump on a cold stove again—and that may not be good.

The hot stove effect is a fundamental problem of learning. Learning reduces your likelihood of repeating things that got you in trouble, as you hope it will. But that means you know less about the domains where you've done poorly than about the domains where you've done well. You might say, "Well, why should that cause problems?" It causes problems whenever your early experience with an alternative is, for whatever reason, not characteristic of what subsequent experience would be. It clearly causes problems in domains where practice makes a difference. For example, you are likely to abandon an approach or a technology prematurely.

One form of the hot stove effect is the competency trap, where learning encourages people to stick to and improve skills they have already honed to a fine degree rather than spend time gaining new ones. Some of my grandchildren say to me, "We're not very good at mathematics, so we're not going to take any more mathematics." I say, "Wait a minute. Mathematics is a practice sport. If you're not very good at it, you take more of it." That's counterintuitive, and it goes against the main logic of experiential learning, not to mention grandchildren's sentiments about control over their own lives. It has also been demonstrated that the hot stove effect leads experiential learners to be risk averse. It is possible to limit the hot stove effect by slowing learning so that you increase the sample of alternatives that have poor results. That obviously has the cost of incurring short-run losses and consequently is hard for an adaptive system to do.

*You've written about the importance of a "technology of foolishness." Could you tell us a little about it?*

That paper sometimes gets cited—by people who haven't read it closely—as generic enthusiasm for silliness. Well, maybe it is, but the paper actually focused on a much narrower argument. It had to do with how you make interesting value systems. It seemed to me that one of the important things for any person interested in understanding or improving behavior was to know where preferences come from rather than simply to take them as given.

So, for example, I used to ask students to explain the factual anomaly that there are more interesting women than interesting men in the world. They were not allowed to question the fact. The key notion was a developmental one: When a woman is born, she's usually a girl, and girls are told that because they are girls they can do things for no good reason. They can be unpredictable, inconsistent, illogical. But then a girl goes to school, and she's told she is an educated person. Because she's an educated person, a woman must do things consistently, analytically, and so on. So she goes through life doing things for no good reason and then figuring out the reasons, and in the process, she develops a very complicated value system—one that adapts very much to context. It's such a value system that permitted a woman who was once sitting in a meeting I was chairing to look at the men and say, "As nearly as I can tell, your assumptions are correct.

And as nearly as I can tell, your conclusions follow from the assumptions. But your conclusions are wrong." And she was right. Men, though, are usually boys at birth. They are taught that, as boys, they are straightforward, consistent, and analytic. Then they go to school and are told that they're straightforward, consistent, and analytic. So men go through life being straightforward, consistent, and analytic—with the goals of a two-year-old.

And that's why men are both less interesting and more predictable than women. They do not combine their analysis with foolishness.

*How do you encourage people to be foolish?*
Well, there are some obvious ways. Part of foolishness, or what looks like foolishness, is stealing ideas from a different domain. Someone in economics, for example, may borrow ideas from evolutionary biology, imagining that the ideas might be relevant to evolutionary economics. A scholar who does so will often get the ideas wrong; he may twist and strain them in applying them to his own discipline. But this kind of cross-disciplinary stealing can be very rich and productive. It's a tricky thing, because foolishness is usually that—foolishness. It can push you to be very creative, but uselessly creative. The chance that someone who knows no physics will be usefully creative in physics must be so close to zero as to be indistinguishable from it. Yet big jumps are likely to come in the form of foolishness that, against long odds, turns out to be valuable. So there's a nice tension between how much foolishness is good for knowledge and how much knowledge is good for foolishness.

Another source of foolishness is coercion. That's what parents often do. They say, "You're going to take dance lessons." And their kid says, "I don't want to be a dancer." And the parents say, "I don't care whether you want to be a dancer. You're going to take these lessons." The use of authority is one of the more powerful ways to encourage foolishness. Play is another. Play is disinhibiting. When you play, you are allowed to do things you would not be allowed to do otherwise. However, if you're not playing and you want to do those same things, you have to justify your behavior. Temporary foolishness gives you experience with a possible new you—but before you can make the change permanent, you have to provide reasons.

*What role would there be for foolishness in business education?*
We have some foolishness already, though we dress it up as fairly serious activity. For example, we have students play roles. We have them pretend they are the CEO of IBM, and that's foolishness. They aren't, and they can't be, and they won't be. But if you are encouraged to think of yourself as somebody else, you

start acting the way you imagine such a person ought to act and experimenting with who you might become.

On the whole, I think that American management education is so deeply embedded in a rational mystique that pressure toward foolishness often has to become extreme in order to have even a minor effect. At the same time, I don't think any of us would want to live in a world of foolishness that ignored the fact that one of the major glories of the human estate is the capability to practice intelligent rationality.

It's all a question of balance. Soon after I wrote my paper on the technology of foolishness, I presented it at a conference in Holland. This was around 1971. One of my colleagues from Yugoslavia, now Croatia, came up and said, "That was a great talk, but please, when you come to Yugoslavia, don't give that talk. We have enough foolishness." And I think he may have been right.

*You're famous for your garbage can theory of organizational choice. Can you sum up the theory for us?*
The original article on the garbage can theory was written jointly with Michael Cohen and Johan Olsen, so they have to share in whatever fame or shame there is in it. A fair number of people took the organized-anarchy notion that life is ambiguous and said, "The garbage can is really a label for confusion." That wasn't quite what we meant.

We were operating at two levels. On one level, we were saying that choice is fundamentally ambiguous. There is a lot of uncertainty and confusion that isn't well represented by standard theories of decision making. Opportunities for choice attract all sorts of unrelated but simultaneously available problems, solutions, goals, interests, and concerns. So a meeting called to discuss parking lots may become a discussion of research plans, sexual harassment, managerial compensation, and advertising policies. Time is scarce for decision makers, though, and what happens depends on how they allocate that time to choice opportunities.

On the second level, we tried to describe the way in which organizations deal with flows of problems, solutions, and decision makers in garbage can situations. The central ideas were that a link between a problem and a solution depends heavily on the simultaneity of their "arrivals," that choices depend on the ways in which decision makers allocate time and energy to choice opportunities, that choice situations can easily become overloaded with problems, and that choices often can be made only after problems (and their sponsors) have moved to other decision arenas and thus typically are not resolved.

In our minds, the garbage can process is a very orderly process. It looks a little peculiar from some points of view, but it isn't terribly complex, and it isn't terribly jumbled. The good thing, I think, is that our perspective has opened up the possibility for people to say, "That's a garbage can process"—meaning it's an understandable process in which things are connected by their simultaneous presence more than by anything else, even though they look all mixed up.

*Does it concern you that people sometimes misunderstand your ideas?*
In a real sense, there is no such thing as "my" ideas. Scholarship and notions of intellectual property are poor bedmates. I have often read things, both by critics and by enthusiasts, that seem to me to be based on a less than precise reading of what I have written; but once you publish something, you lose special access to it. The interpretations of others have as much legitimacy, if they can be defended, as yours do. In the best of all worlds, others will generate interpretations that are more interesting than the ones you had in your mind. In fact, a basic goal in writing is to choose words that can evoke beautiful and useful meanings that were not explicit in your own mind. Some very good writers resist that idea. They want to be their own interpreters. I think that is a mistake. The evocative ambiguities of language are sources of creativity.

*You've said that the numbers of women coming into the workforce have changed the sexual character of organizations but that many people will pine for the simplicity of the old order.*
Oh, sure. But I'm also committed to the notion that a lot of happiness comes from dealing with complexity. We may regret the passing of a simple life—a simple division of labor between the sexes or a work world without hetero-sexuality—but we wouldn't like it if that life were restored to us. I think the problems of wrestling with the issues of gender and sexuality have been, for my generation, very important. They've obviously been important to women, and, as a result, they've been important to men. Many of the beauties we now see in people have come out of that struggle, and the struggle is by no means over. Nor am I sure you would want to have it over. For example, life might be much less interesting if you actually took sex and sexuality out of management. It would be easier, and it might, in some ways, be less prone to atrocity—but it surely wouldn't be as much fun.

*Are there any practitioners you admire?*
I guess I admire all of them, even the scoundrels. Modern organized life poses problems that are not trivial; and anyone who is prepared to try to function

meaningfully in a modern organization has my respect. Dealing with the simultaneous demands for self-respect, autonomy, control, coordination, order, freedom, imagination, discipline, and effectiveness that are essential parts of modern organizations seems to me worthy of respect, even when it is done in a less than perfect way. I know there is some sense in the observation that hierarchies and competition can make monsters out of ordinary, good people. They often do, and I think we have an obligation to recognize that problem. The business firm is one of the few contemporary institutions in which the arbitrary and gratuitous cruelty of the powerful in dealing with the weak is tolerated, even encouraged. Even so, most of the executives I've met seem to be trying to do as decent a job as they can. Of contemporary figures, probably the one I know best is John Reed, the longtime CEO of Citibank and recently the supervisor of reforms in the New York Stock Exchange. I admire John. I think he has a sense of what it means to be a human being.

I think practicing managers are sometimes less reflective than they might be. The rhetoric of management requires managers to pretend that things are clear, that everything is straightforward. Often they know that managerial life is more ambiguous and contradictory than that, but they can't say it. They see their role as relieving people of ambiguities and uncertainties. They need some way of speaking the rhetoric of managerial clarity while recognizing the reality of managerial confusion and ambivalence. In a recent paper, I argued that reading poetry helps, but I fear that is a small response to a large problem.

*You are a poet yourself. Why do you write poetry?*
I'm not sure why I write poetry. I'm not always sure that it is poetry. It has something to do with an affection for the beauties and grace of life, along with an affection for its efficiency or effectiveness. I think it is the beauty of rationality, as well as its utility, that attracts me to it. It is the beauty of emotions and feelings that makes them compelling for me. Poetry is a way of contemplating and augmenting those beauties, as well as the absurdities of their presence in the dustbins of life. Poetry celebrates the senses; it celebrates the feelings in ways that other things don't. It's also a place where you can play with the splendor, sound, and combinatorics of words. And you don't usually do that in other genres.

*You began your courses by denying claims to your relevance. How did you end them?*
It depended on the course; but quite often I would end with a quote from a French writer, Étienne Pivert de Senancour. Even in English, it provided a patina of culture to an otherwise midwestern sensibility: "Man is perishable. That may

be; but let us perish resisting, and, if nothingness is what awaits us, let us not act in such a way that it would be a just fate."

In the end, you know, we are very minor blips in a cosmic story. Aspirations for importance or significance are the illusions of the ignorant. All our hopes are minor, except to us; but some things matter because we choose to make them matter. What might make a difference to us, I think, is whether in our tiny roles, in our brief time, we inhabit life gently and add more beauty than ugliness.

PART I

# EXPLORATIONS IN THEORIES OF ORGANIZATIONAL ACTION

*An Introductory Essay*

ZUR SHAPIRA

THE ROOTS OF ORGANIZATION THEORY include, among other sources, the field of operations research. Prescriptions of early approaches in operations research called for setting objective functions for firms. The idea was that once such objectives were set firms could allocate the most appropriate resources with the minimal costs to attain such objectives. In other words, optimization was the name of the game. Several mathematical techniques were developed to help firms achieve their objectives, and indeed many examples show that mathematical methods can help firms complete complex projects and obtain their objectives. Yet, the organizations that are imagined under the operations research paradigm are somewhat different from many of the organizations one observes. Real organizations tend to be less fully informed about alternatives and their consequences, less guided by clear, consistent goals, and less able to implement coherent policies than are the organizations imagined by optimizing models. The chapters in this section point at a much richer and more valid description of organizations where preferences may be ambiguous, goals can change in a dynamic manner, and conflicts are pervasive without many mechanisms that can resolve them.

Another field that influenced organization theory at its infancy was economics. Early economic theories of the firm that emphasized efficient resource allocation processes with no conflict were questioned by Berle and Means (1932) who cautioned economists that modern firms were going to be run by professional managers who were not the firm's owners. This, according to Bearle and Means (1932) created a major problem that was later referred to as agency costs (see, e.g., Jensen and Meckling, 1976). Thus, unlike the operations research paradigm, the economics approach conceived of conflict as a major feature of organizations. Yet, in addition to the assumption that people behave in a rational manner, economists' dealing with agency theory made additional simplifying assumptions about behavior in organizations that allowed them to arrive at elegant solutions to the agency problem. For example, they assume that employees are inherently lazy and always attempt to shirk. Such an assumption is not based necessarily on systematic studies but is rather "required" by the model. In addition, the fact that principals have information that they do not disclose to the employees is not considered an issue, while the reverse condition is of major importance. Agency theorists are mainly focused on designing optimal incentive contracts for the main agents (such as CEOs) and are generally silent on similar treatment of employees. In contrast, Simon's (1951) notion of the employment contract is much more symmetric, arguing that a mere contract cannot guarantee anything but the exertion of minimal effort by employees. Unfortunately, economic analysis of the employment relation as a reciprocal relation, as in Akerlof's (1982) gift exchange idea, is an exception rather than the rule.

The above brief description of the economic roots of modern organization theory is not complete without acknowledging the influence that neoclassical economics had on organization theory. From its inception, the Carnegie school (i.e., Cyert, March, Simon) rejected the basic premise of the theory of the firm that individuals are rational actors who make decisions under uncertainty by maximizing their expected utility (see for example, Marshall, 1936, Stigler, 1946) The discrepancy between the image of decision makers in neoclassical economics and decision making in the real world drew a reaction from Simon (1947), who observed, at the time, the way city officials in Milwaukee were making decisions. Simon claimed that the way these officials made decisions was a far cry from rationality. Simon (1955) argued that neither maximization nor optimization were good candidates for describing human decision behavior. To maximize or optimize, humans had to have all the available information and the capability to process it according to the theory. In contrast, Simon (1955) proposed the idea of satisficing, which argues that since people do not have all of the information in making most choices, they actually examine only a subsample of all the available alternatives. Once they have done so, they select the best alternative that meets a criterion that is defined as being "good enough." It can clearly be shown that this process may be at odds with the ideas of maximization and optimization, but it has a clear advantage: it is much more valid as a descriptive model of human decision making. Simon (1952–1953) emphasized that in contrast with the focus of the theory of the firm on optimizing, organization theories were more concerned with the issue of finding viable solutions that can help organization survive. The seeds of the behavioral theory of the firm were sown and their sprouts emerged in 1958 with the publication of *Organizations* by March and Simon (1958) and in 1963 with the publication of the *Behavioral Theory of the Firm* by Cyert and March (1963).

The behavioral theory of the firm intended to provide a behaviorally realistic view of organizational decision making. In so doing Cyert, March, and Simon engaged in a debate with economists who, at the time, conceived of the firm as a black box. Consequently, most economists developed rational models of the individual (consumer or manager) and applied them to the aggregate level, whether at the organizational level or at a more macro level. Simon himself often treated these levels of analysis similarly as March (1978, p. 859) noted: "He [Simon] obscured a distinction one might make between individual and organizational decision making proposing for the most part the general ideas for both." Yet, Simon argued that realistic assumptions about the behavior of both individuals and organizations were required to make economic theories of the firm palatable.

The behavioral theory of the firm (Cyert and March, 1963, 1992) portrayed organizations as consisting of different people with multiple goals that lead to conflicts that may not be resolved. The characteristics of conflict and the eventual non-resolution or quasi-resolution of conflicts is an important aspect of the chapters in this section and they provide a behaviorally realistic perspective on life in organizations. The chapters suggest that the main way conflicts are resolved is by bargaining and coalition formation but not necessarily in a rational manner. March's perspective on bounded rationality, the importance of targets, the quasi-resolution of conflict, and the different logics of action leads to a refreshing approach to organization theory—culminating in a new approach to organizational action. I discuss some issues related to these topics.

## THE SIGNIFICANCE OF TARGETS
### FOR DECISION MAKING

Classical economic models of decision making, whether by individuals or firms, emphasize outcomes at the expense of processes. Expected utility theory proposes that, when choosing between alternatives, decision makers should focus on the final asset positions associated with each choice alternative. Psychological analysis shows, in contrast, that relative changes are the drivers of choice behavior rather than final asset positions. Kahneman and Tversky's (1979) prospect theory demonstrates that people are more sensitive to relative gains and losses than to final wealth positions. Furthermore, the idea of framing (Tversky and Kahneman, 1981) suggests that describing essentially identical choice alternatives, while framing them differently as either gain or loss situations, may lead to a reversal of preferences.

In agreement with the above, March and Simon (1958, 1993) write about the importance of targets and Cyert and March (1963, 1992) elaborate on this concept. Organizations have to set targets to be able to evaluate how they make progress toward reaching their goals. Such goals provide feedback that tells managers whether they succeeded or failed in reaching their targets and such successes or failures have consequences. Consider the accusation that leaders of modern corporations are shortsighted. Such an accusation fails to take into account the fact that quarterly reports are mandated by shareholders in public corporations as a means of tracking managerial performance. These quarterly reports are a hindrance to setting long-term strategic goals, which is much more in line with ideas of normative economics. However, the "long term" that is recommended by normative theory does not have much power in describing managerial behavior. March's portrayal of the importance of targets is much more valid as a descriptive model. It fits the results of empirical studies showing how reaching targets may depart from conventional notions of utility maximization.

For example, Camerer, Babcock, Lowenstein, and Thaler (1997) studied the number of hours New York City taxi drivers choose to drive on different days. Their daily wage fluctuates because on rainy days many customers look for a cab, but on summer weekends the demand for cabs is likely to be low. The standard theory assumes that drivers would plan ahead and drive a lot on high-revenue days, saving up so they can quit early on low-revenue days. The data show contrary results: Inexperienced drivers work as if they set a daily income target and quit when they reach it. This means that they drive a lot on low-revenue days and quit early on high-revenue days. It appears that the drivers could have earned about 15 percent more if they had switched their hours around and driven longer on high-revenue days. Experienced drivers, however, drive a similar number of hours on good and bad days and end up earning more than the inexperienced drivers, though less than they could with an optimal strategy. Shapira (2007) studied government bond traders and found that once they were close to the end of the year, when bonus decisions are made, they stopped taking risks if they were above their target but took enormous risks if they were below their targets. Such patterns of behavior can probably be explained by a zealous believer in utility maximization who can invent exotic utility functions at the cost of parsimony. March's view is that these are realistic samples of the behavior of people who try to reach their goals without the need to assume maximization. Such attempts may not result in achieving optimal outcomes but reaching one's goals is an important aspect of human behavior, whether or not it is optimal according to the rational model.

## ASPIRATIONS, SURVIVAL, ATTENTION, AND MANAGERIAL RISK TAKING

Managers have substantive targets in making decisions. A major target is survival; any living system signals survival as its main goal. Managers also have targets in the form of aspiration levels that in many cases are set for them. Following the basic arguments of the behavioral theory of the firm, March and Shapira (1987, 1992) argued that risk preference varies with context. They argued that risky choice depends on the relation between the dangers and opportunities reflected in the choice alternative and some critical benchmark or targets for the decision maker. Thus, the variation in risk taking may emerge from a change in focus among a set of inconsistent and perhaps even ambiguous preferences (March, 1978) than from the revision of a coherent preference for risk (March, 1988). As a result of changing assets or aspirations, focus may shift away from the dangers involved in a particular alternative and toward its opportunities (Lopes, 1987; March and Shapira, 1987).

The tendency to focus on a few aspects of a decision problem at a time is evident in the discussion of the "elimination by aspects" by individual decision makers (Tversky, 1972), the "sequential attention to goals" by organizational decision makers (Cyert and March, 1963, 1992), or "garbage can models of choice" (Cohen, March, and Olsen, 1972). These examples suggest that decision-making activity is often interpreted as being driven by preferences, and changes in those preferences can be explained by ideas about attention. Theories that emphasize the sequential consideration of a relatively small number of alternatives (March and Simon, 1958, 1993; Simon, 1955), and those that treat slack and search as stimulated by a comparison of performance with aspirations (Cyert and March, 1963), or those that point at the significance of order of presentation and agenda effects (Cohen, March, and Olsen, 1972; Dutton, 1997) suggest that understanding decision making under conditions of incomplete information may depend more on processes of attention allocation than on choice processes.

In many of these theories, there is often a single critical focal value for attention, such as the reference point that divides subjective success from subjective failure. The ideas about shifting focus of attention in risk seem to confirm the importance of two focal values rather than a single one (Lopes, 1987; March and Shapira, 1987, 1992). Managers in Shapira's (1995) study evoked reference points relating to performance target such as breakeven, and a survival level. These two reference points divide possible states into three outcome regions: success, failure, and extinction. The added focus value associated with extinction changes somewhat the predictions about attention to risk as a function of success. If one is above a performance target, the main focus is on avoiding choices that might place one below it. The dangers of falling below the target dominate attention; the opportunities for gain are less salient. This leads to relative risk aversion among successful managers, particularly those who are barely above the target. Since dangers are more salient than opportunities, the latter are less important to the choice. For managers who experience success, attention to opportunities and thus risk taking is stimulated only when performance exceeds the target by a substantial amount.

Decision makers who are below the performance target and strive to reach it, focus on it in a way that generally leads to risk taking especially if they are close to reaching this point. In this case attention is focused on the opportunities for gain, rather than the dangers. However, when decision makers are close to the survival point they tend to pay a close attention to that level. If performance is well above the survival point, the focus of attention results in a preference for relatively high variance alternatives, or risk-prone behavior. If performance is close to the survival point, the emphasis on high variance alternatives is moderated by a heightened awareness of their dangers. Thus, in line with the satisficing principle, attention is focused on only a part of the alternatives and can therefore lead to a choice that departs from what would be expected under the model of rational choice.

## DYNAMIC PREFERENCES AND THE QUASI-RESOLUTION OF CONFLICT

Classical theories of choice argue that preferences are stable. A famous treatise on the subject is Stigler and Becker's (1977) paper that argued that changes in preferences are just responses to price changes. In a famous contrarian article, March (1978) argues that while decisions are made on the basis of current tastes, the consequences of most of those decisions are going to be in the future and we have only ambiguous ideas about our future preferences. Economic studies of the time dimension of preferences have shown a consistent discounting effect of future outcomes (Strotz, 1956). March's (1978) argument goes even further by suggesting that preferences are dynamic, inconsistent, and unstable. More than that, he argues that we strategically manipulate our preferences, confound them, avoid them, and suppress them. March's (1978) dictum was probably the first statement about the construction of preferences, now an established theme in behavioral decision theory. Furthermore, March's notion of history-dependent preferences goes far beyond the account of myopia described by Strotz (1956). Preferences are also history dependent and when viewed in a longitudinal evolutionary manner they may not be as inconsistent as they may appear. Changes in tastes, when considered along a history-dependent path may reflect real underlying values and inclinations rather than the precise conception of price-induced changes in a narrowly conceived world marked only by consistent tastes (i.e., Stigler and Becker, 1977).

The ambiguity of preferences is also partially due to exogenous changes. It fits the image of humans portrayed by March and Simon (1958, 1993) and Simon (1955, 1967) that people basically act on their immediate environment and do not consider the entire sample of alternatives available to them. In the same vein, Shapira (1981) showed that when making trade-offs among job attributes, managers conceive of only small changes on those attributes, much in line with the idea of satisficing. Furthermore, these managers, in line with the idea of simplification (March and Simon, 1958; Simon, 1955), often ended up preferring one attribute while ignoring the others in a way that leads them to choose what economists call corner solutions that do not extract all the potential trade-offs among attributes. These observations are based at least in part on March and Simon's (1958) idea of bounded rationality and the sequential attention to goals (Cyert and March, 1963). Instead of consistency and coherent behavior, it describes decision makers as switching their attention among goals.

In developing the idea of satisficing further, Radner (1975) proposed a model of satisficing that is based on the notion of thermostat behavior and portrayed decision makers as attending to alternatives in a stochastic rather than a fully disorganized manner. Seshadri and Shapira (2001) described the behavior of a manager who needs to attend to both short-term and long-term goals and cannot do so simultaneously. Their model that follows on the ideas of March and Simon (1958), Radner (1975), and Simon (1955) shows that in attempting to survive in a dynamic environment where attention is interrupted, managers often need to resort to rationing their time commitment and to follow attention allocation rules in order to manage and stay on top of things. Perfect matching to the environment is impossible (cf., March, 1992) and learning can only offer modest help. These studies suggest that the model of action initiated by March and Simon (1958) and Cyert and March (1963) goes further than the decision-making model they developed. It describes a much larger domain of human behavior for which their decision-making framework offers a very useful descriptive model.

## UNDERSTANDING ORGANIZATIONAL ACTION

Imagine an important meeting of the board of a firm that gathers to decide how to allocate resources to different activities under budget constraints. Executives get up one after the other and preach their position in an elegant and convincing manner. Debates rage as the board considers the different alternatives and the conflicting views and positions that were presented. At the end some decisions are made and funds are allocated to some initiatives. The curtain falls, so to speak, on the saga. Two observers who were present at the meeting describe it later. One observer who proceeds from a rational inclination describes the process as an orderly debate that culminated in an agreed-upon good solution. Borrowing from the world of the movies, such an ending is in line with what is preferred by Hollywood directors who often create a few possible endings to a movie and screen the film with those different endings to a "randomly" selected audience in some town in the United States. The ending that the audience selects usually portrays a happy ending, but, even more often, the audience demands that the ending be decisive and unambiguous.

The other observer offers a different perspective on what happened, and in narrating the meeting he resorts to an explanation that describes decision makers, problems, streams of solutions, and decision opportunities much in line with the garbage can model (Cohen, March, and Olsen, 1972). For this narrator, no coherent unique solution was achieved at the end of the meeting, rather, it was one episode in a continuous conflict among different parties, each of which told a different story, and it is not clear what the real outcome of the meeting will be even though some final statements were made. This observer knows that it is also possible that nothing practical was achieved in the meeting in terms of operational goals. In borrowing from the world of the movies again, the story he tells fits another story told by a director from outside of Hollywood. In his acclaimed movie *Rashomon*, the great Japanese director, Akira Kurosawa, describes a murder trial where each of four witnesses tells a different story and no resolution is attained at the end of the film. For Kurosawa, ambiguity is a natural aspect of decision making, and tolerance to ambiguity is an important aspect of life; those aspects of ambiguity are equally important for March. His theories provide us with a dialectical analysis of decision making that points at coherence as well as at ambiguity, that highlights the consequences of planning as well as the posterior discovery of intention from one's own choices. This dialectical analysis reflects real decision contexts and their complexities since rarely in life can we observe coherent solutions for continuous conflicts as they are portrayed in the ending of a Hollywood-style film. Those of us who cherish the dialectical analysis and the understanding of organizational action it provides have the same feeling when reading March's writing as when watching a movie directed by the legendary Kurosawa; they leave us with a deeper understanding and with a desire to taste more. The three chapters that make this section clearly have this flavor.

### REFERENCES

Akerlof, G. 1982. "Labor contracts as partial gift exchange," *Quarterly Journal of Economics*, 97, 543–569.

Berle, A. and G. Means. 1932. *The Modern Corporation and Private Property*. New York: Harcourt, Brace and World.

Camerer, C., L. Babcock, G. Lowenstein, and R. Thaler. 1997. "Labor supply of New York City cab drivers: One day at a time," *Quarterly Journal of Economics*, 112, 407–441.

Cohen, M., J. G. March, and J. Olsen, (1972). "A garbage can model of organizational choice," *Administrative Science Quarterly*, 17, 1–25.

Cyert, R. M. and J. G. March. 1963. *A Behavioral Theory of the Firm*. Englewood Cliffs, NJ: Prentice Hall.

Cyert, R. M. and J. G. March. 1992. *A Behavioral Theory of the Firm*, 2nd ed. Oxford, UK: Blackwell.

Dutton, J. 1997. "Strategic agenda building in organizations." In Z. Shapira (ed.), *Organizational Decision Making*. New York: Cambridge University Press.

Jensen, M. and W. Meckling. 1976. "Theory of the firm: Managerial behavior, agency costs and ownership structure," *Journal of Financial Economics*, 3, 305–360.

Kahneman, D. and A. Tversky. 1979. "Prospect theory: An–291.

Kurosawa, A. 1950. *Rashomon* (a film).

Lopes, L. L. 1987. "Between hope and fear: The psychology of risk," *Advances in Experimental Social Psychology*, 20, 255–295.

March, J. G. 1978. "Bounded rationality ambiguity, and the engineering of choice," *Bell Journal of Economics*, 9, 587–608.

March, J. G. 1988. "Variable risk preferences and adaptive aspirations," *Journal of Economic Behavior and Organization*, 9, 5–24.

March, J. G. 1992. "Learning and the theory of the firm," *Economia e Banca-Annali Scientific*, 5, 15–35.

March, J. G. and Z. Shapira. 1987. "Managerial perspectives on risk and risk taking," *Management Science*, 33, 1404–1418.

March, J. G. and Z. Shapira. 1992. "Variable risk preferences and the focus of attention," *Psychological Review*, 99, 172–183.

March, J. G. and H. A. Simon. 1958. *Organizations*. New York: Wiley.

March, J. G. and H. A. Simon. 1993. *Organizations*, 2nd ed. London: Blackwell.

Marshall, A. (1936). *Principles of Economics*, 8th ed. London: Macmillan.

Radner, R. 1975. "A behavioral model of cost reduction," *Bell Journal of Economics and Management Science*, 6, 196–215.

Seshadri, S. and Z. Shapira. 2001. "Managerial allocation of time and effort: The role of interruptions," *Management Science*, 47, 647–662.

Shapira, Z. 1981. "Making tradeoffs between job attributes," *Organizational Behavior and Human Performance*, 28, 331–355.

Shapira, Z. 1995. *Risk Taking: A Managerial Perspective*. New York: Russell Sage Foundation.

Shapira, Z. 2007. "Organizational control of their market actors: Managing the risk of government bond traders." Working paper. New York University.

Simon, H. A. 1947. *Administrative Behavior*. New York: Macmillan.

Simon, H. A. 1951. "A formal theory of the employment relation," *Econometrcia*, 19, 293–305.

Simon, H. A. (1952–1953). "A comparison of organization theories," *Review of Economic Studies*, 20, 40–49.

Simon, H. A. 1955. "A behavioral model of rational choice," *Quarterly Journal of Economics*, 69, 99–118.

Simon, H. A. 1967. "Motivational and Emotional Controls of Cognition," *Psychological Review*, 74, 1, 29–39.

Stigler, G. 1946. *The Theory of Price*. New York: Macmillan.

Stigler, G. and G. Becker. 1977. "Des Gustibus Non Est Disputandum," *American Economic Review*, 67, 76–90.

Strotz, R. 1956. "Myopia and inconsistency in dynamic utility maximization," *Review of Economic Studies*, 23, 165–180.

Tversky, A. 1972. "Elimination by aspects: A theory of schoice," *Psychological Review*, 143–151.

Tversky, A. and D. Kahneman. 1981. "The framing of decisions and the psychology of choice," *Science*, 211, 453–458.

# CHAPTER 2

# Introduction to the Second Edition

JAMES G. MARCH AND HERBERT A. SIMON

MORE THAN A THIRD OF A CENTURY AGO, we undertook, together with Harold Guetzkow, a "propositional inventory" of theory about organizations. The intent was to list generalizations (preferably true ones) and to assess the empirical evidence supporting them. Of course, to inventory propositions one has to organize them, and so the book that evolved from this exercise also proposed a structure of organization theory.

Our book has continued to attract attention and interest over the intervening years. For some, it has provided a guide to the research on organizations published prior to 1958. For others, it has been a useful source of propositions about organizations, to be cited, emended, enlarged upon, and criticized. For still others, it has become an icon of a prehistoric age.

Sufficient interest continues in the book to suggest the usefulness of a new edition, retaining the original text, but adding some comments, stimulated by the text, about events in the world of organizations and organization theories during the 35 years since the first edition appeared. We are happy to add those comments, along with the warning that we are today probably not much wiser than we were then. It is perhaps an unfortunate symptom of authorship that we still enjoy reading the book from time to time and are surprised more often by the things we knew then, but have forgotten, than by the things we know now but did not know then.

If there were any general pronouncement we would want to utter today, it would be that no events during this long period have shaken the foundations of organizations or organization theory so roughly as to make them unrecognizable, or even greatly distorted. The years since 1958 have witnessed considerable change in the social context of organizations, particularly in the rhetoric, ideology, and reality of relations among ethnic and gender groups. They have witnessed considerable change in the technological context of organizations,

---

This chapter originally appeared as "Introduction to the Second Edition," pp. 1–19 in James G. March and Herbert A. Simon, *Organizations*, 2nd edition. Oxford, UK: Blackwell, 1993.

particularly in information technology and robotics. The years since 1958 have also produced an impressive array of research findings on organizations; we are much better off with respect to both the amount of research being done on organizations and its quality than we were in the 1950s. Nevertheless, the new phenomena we have observed, and perhaps most of the new concepts as well, fit without too much Procrustean squeezing or folding into the earlier framework that was designed to hold them. That is one reason (among many) why we limit ourselves to these comments instead of rewriting the book.

## WHAT THE BOOK IS ABOUT

This book is about the theory of formal organizations. Organizations are systems of coordinated action among individuals and groups whose preferences, information, interests, or knowledge differ. Organization theories describe the delicate conversion of conflict into cooperation, the mobilization of resources, and the coordination of effort that facilitate the joint survival of an organization and its members.

These contributions to survival are accomplished primarily through control over information, identities, stories, and incentives. Organizations process and channel information. They shape the goals and loyalties of their participants. They create shared stories—an organization ethos that includes common beliefs and standard practices. They offer incentives for appropriate behaviors.

Effective control over organizational processes is limited, however, by the uncertainties and ambiguities of life, by the limited cognitive and affective capabilities of human actors, by the complexities of balancing trade-offs across time and space, and by threats of competition.

As organizational actors deal with each other, seeking cooperative and competitive advantage, they cope with these limitations by calculation, planning, and analysis, by learning from their experience and the experience and knowledge of others, and by creating and using systems of rules, procedures, and interpretations that store understandings in easily retrievable form. They weave supportive cultures, agreements, structures, and beliefs around their activities. This melange of organizational behaviors is the focus of this book. We try to understand how collections of individuals and groups coordinate themselves in relatively systematic ways.

Most of the organizations with which we deal are conventionally seen as hierarchies. Hierarchical descriptions of organizations are common, partly because hierarchy is often efficient, partly because hierarchical orderings fit more general cultural norms for describing social relations in terms of domination and subordination. Hierarchy has two, nearly independent, aspects. First, it refers to the boxes-within-boxes structure that characterizes most organizations, with generally more intensive communication within boxes at any level than between different boxes at that level. Second, hierarchy refers to the common pyramidal arrangement of formal authority relations, stepwise from the "top" to the "bottom" of an organization.

The boxes-within-boxes character of hierarchy permits specialization of subunits, keeping within bounds the amount of interaction and coordination among subunits that is needed. At the same time, hierarchy facilitates the use of formal authority as a directing and coordinating mechanism.

Organizational processes are, however, not consistently hierarchical. They also involve networks of other types. They include flows of influence and control that go up and sideways as well as down. They reflect ecologies of interconnecting activities within which simple ideas of linear causal order and power are hard to sustain. They defy sharp definitions of organizational boundaries. There are some senses in which there are "principals" and "agents," or "insiders" and "outsiders," but such conceptions make an organization appear neater than it is.

The central unifying construct of the present book is not hierarchy but decision making, and the flow of information within organizations that instructs, informs, and supports decision-making processes. The idea of "decision" can also be elusive, of course. Defining what a decision is, when it is made, and who makes it have all, at times, turned out to be problematic. Nevertheless, the concept seems to have served us reasonably well.

Several kinds of decisions are important for organizations. First there are decisions of individuals to participate in organizations (as employees, members, supporters, managers, customers, owners) or to leave them, and decisions as to what degree of effort and enthusiasm they will invest in their participation. Second, there are decisions that direct the organization's business, determine how to organize, what goals to proclaim, how to coordinate tasks to reach those goals, when to change directions or structure.

Although the central construct is decision making, much of the theory developed in the book is less a theory of choice than a theory of attention. Decision makers do not attend to all of their goals at once, nor all of their alternatives, nor all of the consequences of the alternatives. Particular goals are high on the agenda at particular times, and off the agenda at other times. Attention may be restricted to alternatives known from past experience, or to a few specific alternatives generated by a product development or a design process. Attention may focus on one set of consequences (e.g., liquidity) under one set of circumstances, and another set of consequences (e.g., share of market) under another.

Since, to indulge in understatement, not everything is attended to, understanding the ways in which attention is allocated is critical to understanding decisions. As a result, much of our own attention in the book is devoted to theories of search: to examining when, where, and how organizations search for information about urgent problems, alternatives, and their consequences.

The theories of organizational attention reflected in this book are built on two little ideas that have proven to have considerable power and appeal. The first is satisficing: the idea that organizations focus on targets and distinguish more sharply between success (meeting the target) and failure (not meeting the target) than among gradations in either. The second idea is that organizations devote more attention to activities that are currently operating below their own targets than they do to activities that are achieving their targets. In the years since 1958, these two ideas (along with their close correlates) have yielded a fairly rich harvest of implications for decision making.

Conceiving organizations and decision making as reflecting limits on rationality and an orderly pattern of attention-constrained action and search does not, of course, capture all of the things the book says, but it encompasses perhaps the central core.

### WHAT THE BOOK SAID SOFTLY

Readers of the book have generally seemed to find our ideas on organizations useful, and we have the standard authors' conceit that most of the truths we did not write down explicitly can be seen as implicit in those we did. However, there are at least four broad features of our treatment that would be a little different if we were writing the book for the first time now:

1. We would give more attention to empirical observations as opposed to theoretical speculations;
2. We would place relatively less emphasis on analytically rational, as opposed to rule-based, action;
3. We would less often take the premises of decisions as given exogenously;
4. We would accord a greater role to the historical, social, and interpretive contexts of organizations.

Although we think the book anticipates much of what we say here about these points, it did not deal with any of them in as much detail as would be required if we were undertaking a comparable project today.

## Speculations and Data

In our present view of the matter, the greatest deficiency in the book is its treatment of empirical evidence. Matters are not so bad in the first five chapters where we were able to draw upon a large body of literature. Of course there are many more such studies today, which could be used to buttress our case further or to amend it where our claims appeared to be speculative. The development of multivariate statistical techniques, improved training in research design and analysis, and the diligence of researchers in generating useful data have combined to provide a reasonably solid empirical base for the topics considered in those chapters.

The difficulties are greater when we deal somewhat less with individuals, and somewhat more with systems. Most of the relevant evidence we found took the form of monographic studies of particular organizations—case studies—and there was nothing in the extant literature on scientific methodology that told us how to make case studies into the sort of objective, reproducible, representative evidence that we were taught science is founded on. Even identifying the potentially relevant cases and collecting them turned out to be a virtually impossible job.

We were quite aware that to find and test hypotheses about organizational decision-making processes, someone would have to examine such processes in real organizational contexts. Almost the only scholars who had done so had studied particular organizations over shorter or longer periods of time, operating largely in the mode of social historians or ethnographers. Their samples were samples of opportunity, representing no definable universe. Their data consisted largely of historical narratives, the causal connections induced by a liberal application of common sense and organizational shrewdness. There were few quantitative data.

Someone trying to repeat our undertaking today (if there were anyone so foolish) would be much better off in certain respects. There has been a considerable proliferation of studies of decision behavior, both in laboratory settings and in the field. Some of these studies have used archival data on decisions; others have placed experienced organizational participants in quasi-laboratory situations for observation; others have observed actual decision processes in organizations. Our empirical understanding of such things as risk-taking behavior in organizations, for example, is substantially more precise than it was in 1958.

There has been a considerable development, in sociology and psychology, of methods for dealing with nonquantitative verbal data in systematic ways. For example, in research on problem solving in cognitive science, we now have methods for using as data the verbal thinking-aloud protocols of subjects performing problem-solving tasks. In sociology, there have been parallel developments in methods for analyzing the content of verbal texts of many kinds. We know a good deal today about how to encode and process such data, and how to use them to test hypotheses, including hypotheses in the form of computer programs that simulate the phenomena being studied.

There has perhaps been less progress in solving the problems of sampling populations of organizations or of organization members, and the problems of aggregating individual data or data from small units in ways that cast light on the behavior of the larger systems to which the individuals or units belong. Almost surely, however, these problems would at least bend and possibly yield if addressed vigorously enough and often enough. The increasing attention being paid by social scientists today to the work of social historians and ethnographers is a good omen of greater willingness to take case studies and historical narratives seriously as data for discovering and testing theories of organization.

Finally, there has recently been an upsurge, especially in economics departments, business schools, and psychology departments, of laboratory studies of decision making, markets, and small organizations. This work still seems to us to be too much dominated by ideas drawn from the formal structures of neoclassical economics and the mathematical theory of games; but exposure to the data coming from these laboratory experiments will almost inevitably confront experimenters with surprises and new ideas, leading them in time to conceptual frameworks and explanations that will suit the phenomena better than those used at present.

Perhaps the most critically needed and least advanced methodological development is reconstructing statistical theory to deal with the kinds of data that are beginning to be gathered, and the kinds of models that are being tested. Statistics for data analysis are not adapted to theories of organizations, with the result that the more sophisticated analyses of data are informed only by the crudest of theoretical models (e.g., linear regression) and the empirical status of the more interesting theoretical ideas is left uncertain. That situation has improved to a modest degree since 1958, but not much.

## Logics of Action
### Analysis-Based Action

The basic idea that humans make choices and that these choices are informed by assessing alternatives in terms of their consequences underlies much of contemporary social science, not to mention "common sense." This idea, particularly as it is manifested in the dogmas of neoclassical economics, has often been criticized as providing neither an accurate nor an attractive portrayal of the human spirit. Many authors have suggested that human beings are not capable of achieving perfect rationality. Fewer, but with compensating fervor, have suggested that the pursuit of rationality leads systematically to less intelligent behavior than do other decision methods.

Although those who criticize obsession with rationality will find many more tempting targets than our book, it is probably fair to place it in the "rational" section of the library. For the most part, we portray behavior as resulting from, and organized around, choices. And we interpret choices as depending on an evaluation of their consequences in terms of preferences. In those senses at least, this book is about rationality.

Its rationality is, however, a considerably qualified rationality. The people who inhabit the book are imagined to have reasons for what they do. Those reasons inform both their choices and their justifications (whether explanations or rationalizations) for their choices. Thus, they provide a basis for predicting both behavior and explanations of behavior.

The reasons reflect two related logics of action. The first, an analytic rationality, is a logic of consequences. Actions are chosen by evaluating their probable consequences for the preferences of the actor. The logic of consequences is linked to conceptions of anticipation, analysis, and calculation. It operates principally through selective, heuristic search among alternatives, evaluating them for their satisfactoriness as they are found.

The second logic of action, a matching of rules to situations, rests on a logic of appropriateness. Actions are chosen by recognizing a situation as being of a familiar, frequently encountered, type, and matching the recognized situation to a set of rules (sometimes called a performance program in the present book). The logic of appropriateness is linked to conceptions of experience, roles, intuition, and expert knowledge. It deals with calculation mainly as a means of retrieving experience preserved in the organization's files or individual memories.

The book explores both kinds of reasoning behavior, but it devotes more attention to the first than to the second. It is built heavily on the assumption that there are consequential reasons for action: that we can predict behavior in and by organizations by assessing the expected subjective value of alternative courses of action. This general frame is used to examine a wide variety of decisions.

Rationality (in the consequential or analytic sense) does not assure intelligence. To assume that people often have consequential reasons for what they do is quite different from assuming that they reliably select actions that would be objectively optimal in the light of their goals. The organizations portrayed in the book are rational in intent and in the ways in which they justify their choices (they are procedurally rational), but their pursuit of rationality does not assure either coherent or intelligent action (often their actions are not substantively rational).

Ambiguity of goals and goal conflict, as well as human ignorance and error, are significant parts of the picture of behavior in organizations. The actions of individuals in an organization may aim at the official organizational goals, or some quite different and wholly personal goals. Their actions may be well adapted to their goals, or poorly adapted, for people are often misinformed, or lack information, or are unable to predict or even compute the consequences of their actions. Their goals may sometimes be well specified and stable, but often they are unclear, inconsistent, and changing.

Nor does the assumption of intended, limited rationality, in this realistic sense, ignore the important role of emotions in behavior.

Still less does it omit the wide range of human wants and desires—pushed sometimes by greed, sometimes by altruism, sometimes by egoism, sometimes by loyalty to groups—that motivate human action.

The idea of limited, consequential rationality found in the book has become more or less standard in modern theories of decision making, at least outside the hard core of orthodox neoclassical economic theory. Economics today pays continually increasing attention to the incomplete knowledge of economic actors, their uncertainties about the future, and the limits on their ability to discover optimal actions. Limited rationality underlies contemporary theories of the firm, behavioral decision theory, and many theories derivative of these. Except for some relatively minor deviants (e.g., rational expectations theory), it has become the received doctrine. No received doctrine is received forever, so it is natural to ask whether we still hold to this one. The answer is yes, we do.

We believe that limited rationality still provides a powerful basic framework for examining organizations despite the elaboration of information technology, as embodied in computers, operations research, and management science. Modern information and decision technology, with its disciplines of management science, decision science, operations research, and information engineering, had just begun to make inroads into organizational consciousness when this book was published. Those disciplines undertook to apply a new technology to organizational decision making, using the conceptual framework of optimization theory and empowering it with mathematical tools that, fed with appropriate numerical data and powerful new computational equipment, could carry out calculations previously beyond imagination. Using the new technologies, the new disciplines sought to reduce or eliminate the restrictions on rationality imposed by the cognitive and calculative limitations of individuals and organizations. Since human informational and computational limitations are the fundamental premises of bounded rationality, improvements in information technology might plausibly be viewed as providing a major challenge to the idea.

These new tools have had a substantial impact on many kinds of decisions: For example, inventory and manufacturing control, and record and information management. The total impact upon organizations has been limited, however, by the fact that the new tools apply mainly to situations that can be described without too much distortion in mathematical form, and for which numerical data appropriate to the formulation can be gathered.

These conditions have restricted applications largely to middle-management and lower-management decisions. In general, the work of managers at higher levels has not been much changed despite frequent proclamations of an information technology revolution. Efforts to use modern technology to develop new forms of management information systems for organizations have been pursued in many organizations, but they have commonly produced systems that seem to match rather poorly the actual decision processes and managerial needs in organizations.

Electronic communication has also undergone extremely rapid development since the first edition of the book was published. Telefaxing was unknown as a commercial product in 1958, as was electronic mail. Although the former is now generic and the latter is spreading slowly, they do not yet seem to have changed the fundamental nature of the processes discussed in this book.

The matter is a little different with artificial intelligence and so-called "expert systems," and this for three reasons. First, they are not as limited as are the operations research and management science models to quantitative methods. Second, they take more fully into account the "boundedness" of human rationality, and its requirements for radical approximation and satisficing. Third, they combine the logic of consequences (heuristic search) with the logic of appropriateness (recognition and rule-based action). Consequently, artificial intelligence and the expert systems it has begun to spawn may in time penetrate further into the central core of managerial tasks than operations research and management science have. As yet, however, that possibility is far from realization. None of these developments in decision engineering has yet required a major rethinking of the application of the principles of limited rationality to management.

## Rule-Based Action

The book probably understates the role of rule-based, or recognition-based, forms of action. Although we discuss performance programs, roles, and other forms of rule-based action, such discussions are generally subordinated to ideas of analysis-based action (as they are for the most part in other modern treatments of organizations). Recent work reasserts the pervasiveness of logics of appropriateness and raises the possibility that consequential, calculative logics may not capture important human techniques for acting intelligently.

Modern understanding of the cognitive bases of expert behavior has considerably clarified the respective roles in the decision-making process of systematic (and sometimes quantitative) consequential analysis, on the one hand, and the matching of appropriate action to recognized situations, on the other. The latter appears to be an important component of phenomena such as "intuition" that are frequent in the behavior of experienced decision makers.

The distinctive earmarks of intuition are rapid response (a matter of seconds) and inability of the respondent to report a sequence of steps leading to the result—even denial of awareness of any such steps. The response is not always right, but what impresses observers about intuition is that responses, especially those of experts, are frequently correct even though they seem to have required almost no processing time or effort. When we are especially impressed by intuition, we sometimes apply other honorific terms to it: "insight" or "creativity." When we are less impressed, we are more likely to call it "blind spots" or "jumping to conclusions."

The role and nature of intuition are illustrated by studies of chess playing. It has often been demonstrated that a grandmaster can play simultaneous games against 50 or more opponents, going from board to board and taking only a few seconds for each move, and still win virtually all of the games—provided that the opponents are no stronger than experts (400 or more Elo rating points below the grandmaster). In contrast with tournament games, where players often look ahead to the consequences of moves, sometimes exploring as many as 100 branches of the game tree, there is almost no time for such analysis in simultaneous play. When asked how they select moves with such speed, the grandmasters are likely to reply that they do it "intuitively."

Research on this performance has shown that a grandmaster's intuition is achieved by noticing cues on the board, cues—very familiar from past experience with many thousands of chess positions—that signal weaknesses the opponent has created in his or her arrangement of pieces. Intuition is simply skill in recognizing those things that have become familiar through past experience.

A typical grandmaster, it has been shown, carries in memory at least 50,000 such cues (usually called "chunks")—familiar patterns of pieces that occur often in games—and, together with these cues, has stored rules indicating how they should be exploited to gain an advantage.

What does this research say about the relation between analysis and intuition? It says that intuition is synonymous with the familiar phenomenon of recognition. It says that when there is substantial time available for making decisions, the skilled chess player does a great deal of analysis (assisted, to be sure, by intuition in choosing the lines of play to analyze and in evaluating them). In rapid play there is no time for analysis, and the grandmaster relies almost wholly on intuition (that is, upon recognition). When moving rapidly, he or she does not play as well as under tournament conditions, but plays formidably enough to demonstrate that a substantial fraction of chess skill is encapsulated in intuition, that is, in the capacity to recognize familiar significant cues, and to retrieve stored knowledge about how to use them.

This story of chess skill has been duplicated in many other domains where expert behavior has been studied and experts interrogated in the course of designing so-called expert systems for computers. There is no reason to suppose that managerial skill is different along these dimensions from the other skills that have been studied. Expert managers use both consequential analysis and rule-based intuition (recognition) to reach their decisions. The experience of expert managers will often lead them to correct decisions without explicit, conscious calculation. Intelligent managers manage not by analysis alone, but by analysis thoroughly interwoven with the rich intuitions (capabilities for recognition) and rules for action acquired through years of training and experience in the managerial domain.

This process of gaining individual expertise by coding experience into recognition/action pairs is paralleled by organizational processes for developing pairings between rules and situations. In the book, we talk of performance programs. Organizations are collections of roles and identities, assemblages of rules by which appropriate behavior is paired with recognized situations. Some of these assemblages are imported into an organization by employing professionals; accountants do what accountants are trained to do. Other assemblages are developed in an organization through collective experience and stored in the organizational memory as standard procedures.

The processes of identification and socialization, by which individuals associate themselves with an identity and learn a role, are mechanisms for routinizing responses to the recognition of a situation. Organizations turn their own experience, as well as the experience and knowledge of others, into rules that are maintained and implemented despite turnover in personnel and without necessary comprehension of their bases. As a result, the processes for generating, changing, evoking, and forgetting rules become essential in analyzing and understanding organizations.

Although organizational action is driven by matching appropriate behavior to situations, the action is not uniquely determined by such performance programs, professional codes, or expert intuitions. Participants follow rules, but it is not always clear precisely which rules are appropriate. Different identities with different rules intrude on a single situation. Situations are unclear; they cannot always be recognized unambiguously; appropriate rules are difficult to specify; executing a rule may require skill and will that are not always forthcoming.

Rule-based action founded on a logic of appropriateness is discussed in the book, but is probably not given as much attention as we would now give it. Intuition at the individual level and rules at the organizational level play a more important part than the book accords them. This is true in two senses: First, much of the behavior we observe in organizations is "intuitive" in the sense that it occurs immediately upon recognition of a situation. The relevant cognitive and organizational processes are recognition and categorization processes more than they are processes of evaluating consequences.

Second, much of the intelligence we observe in organizational action comes not from explicit analysis but from rules. Rule-based action can, of course, lead to foolishness. Coding experience into rules by no means guarantees optimal or even suitable behavior. But any account of the ability of an organization to act intelligently toward its own goals must attend to the role of logics of appropriateness as well as logics of consequence.

## Autonomous Preferences

Theories of choice, including the theories outlined in this book, tend to treat preferences as autonomous and antecedent to decisions. Individual choices are seen as being made in the service of individual preferences, but the process by which those preferences are shaped is treated as exogenous to the choice. The resulting theories tend to describe decision makers as autonomous individuals and decision making as proceeding in two, strictly sequential stages—setting goals, then making choices.

The book is explicit in treating the social character of decision makers and their preferences. People in organizations are not viewed as isolates whose wants, identities, and ideas are formed in independence of the other people who surround them. Organization members are social persons, whose knowledge, beliefs, preferences, and loyalties are all products of the social environments in which they grew up, and the environments in which they now live and work. Because of these complex loyalties to a variety of groups and subgroups—including the self and family, organizations and their subunits—intrapersonal and interpersonal conflicts are omnipresent features of organizational life.

These loyalties develop and shape the actions of organization members. In particular, the strong loyalties to organizational units, global or parochial, that people acquire constitute a basic mechanism for securing adherence to organizational goals. The book does not deny the important role of monetary and other incentives, but it suggests that these latter motives are not capable, by themselves, of securing the level of attachments to organizational goals that are actually observed.

Devotion to organization goals, rather than to personal selfish interests, can be viewed as a form of altruism. If we wish to account for organizational identification, we must make the case for the robustness of altruism in the face of the apparently imperious Darwinian demands for individual "fitness" as a condition for survival. That case is not made in the present book, but it has become a central concern for students of population biology, as well as for students of decision making. It has been examined by one of us in a paper published in December 1990 in *Science*.

The decision makers we portrayed in 1958 were unabashedly social. On the other hand, they were somewhat more static than perhaps they should have been. The book might well have attended more explicitly to the significance of the changing character of organizational goals in response to social and environmental influences. Organizations are sometimes described as instruments of purpose, that is, it is imagined that they are created to accomplish some collective purpose. There may often be truth in such a description, but it is misleading if it leads to ignoring the tendency of organizations to endure long after their original "purposes" are accomplished or forgotten.

When polio vaccine destroys the *raison d'être* of The March of Dimes, that society finds a new goal in the prevention and treatment of birth defects. A company, IBM, that grew with the applications of punched-card tabulating systems, first to the Census, then to Social Security, and then to business accounting systems, sees electronic computers on the horizon and embraces them, with all the new and unforeseen applications that have come with them.

Universities are prime examples of organizations that survive long after their initial goals have vanished, transforming them almost beyond recognition: the

University of Paris in the 12th century and today, Carnegie Institute of Technology which became Carnegie Mellon University, innumerable normal schools and teachers' colleges that became universities.

The book does not pay much attention to this fluidity of goals. Nor does it pay much attention to the fact that links between problems and solutions, or between goals and decisions, may be constructed by organizational processes rather than being embedded in objective reality. The linkages may be imposed by an organizational structure that associates goals and actions by virtue of their organizational proximity. (A law enforcement agency may regard criminalizing an activity as the obvious way of eliminating it.) They may be imposed by a temporal structure that associates goals and actions by their simultaneity: if home ownership has increased while incomes are rising, promote home ownership to increase incomes further.

The idea that opportunities for choice attract all sorts of unrelated (but simultaneously available) problems, solutions, goals, interests, concerns—just as garbage cans attract garbage—was labeled by one of the authors and his colleagues the "garbage-can theory of decision making." He apologizes for introducing this pungent phrase into the organizational literature, but the phenomenon is real enough and important (and it is probably too late to banish the label). So a meeting called to discuss parking lots may become a discussion of sexual harassment, compensation policies, and football.

But perhaps the most conspicuous way in which we would elaborate the conception of goals found in this book is to recognize more explicitly the fact that actions may produce goals as readily as goals produce actions. It is convenient to think of goals as existing prior to organizations, shaping and directing them. The prior existence of utilities is one of the most treasured axioms of traditional theories of choice. But the conception is misleading. The process runs in both directions.

If we ask someone learned in music how we can advance our musical tastes, we will probably be told to listen to more music. In the same way, we learn what we want from life (whether we be organizations and communities or individuals) by living. By living, that is by producing and selling goods and services, business firms encounter problems and opportunities that are transformed into preferences and desires. New products swallow up their markets (autos for carriages; hand calculators for slide rules); inflation hikes their costs; social changes produce new markets (women's liberation and restaurants, the automobile and suburban shopping marts); government regulations condition their goals (health and safety rules, environmental regulations); new legal rules permit or exclude organizational forms (anti-trust, geographical limits on banks). We create our wants, in part, by experiencing our choices.

Closely related to the idea that actions generate their goals is the fact that action is itself an important goal in the lives of many people. The goal of a cruise ship is not to reach port, but to cruise. So in understanding organizations we must take into account that activity is one of the goods that organization members, perhaps managers especially, wish to consume. Being part of a "live-wire" organization is exhilarating. The power game can be a fun game, especially for the winners. Being an executive who makes decisions is empowering not only in giving control over resource allocation but also in encouraging a strongly positive conception of self. The pleasures are often in the process rather than in the outcome.

### Historical and Social Contexts

In many respects, this book was a response to a classical point of view denying the significance of decision processes for decision outcomes. Such a view, once dominant in economic theories of organization and very general elsewhere, argued that organizational actions were instantaneous and unique adaptations to an external environment. Decisions were seen as uniquely determined by the constraints, thus predictable without attention to any features of the process by which decisions happened.

The implicit response in the present book was that decision outcomes are not uniquely determined by the context but depend in important ways on organizational and decision processes. Limitations on rationality introduce massive unpredictability; there are multiple equilibria; in any event, the time to equilibrium is rather slow relative to the changes in the context; external environments are not really exogenous but are (partly) created by the organization and its decisions. These elements of indeterminacy in action make organizational decisions impossible to predict simply from a knowledge of "objective" constraints.

We think the position of the book was well taken, but it may have resulted in understating the significance of the historical and social context of action. If action depends on expectations and preferences, then we need to ask where the expectations and preferences come from. If action depends on matching rules to situations, then we need to ask how the matches are defined and interpreted. If the realized branches of history transform the distributions from which future histories are drawn, then we need to be conscious of aspects of timing in action.

To answer such questions we must recognize the ways in which any particular organization is tied into a history and a collection of organizations from which it draws aspirations, beliefs, technologies, and personnel. We must become conscious of how ecologies of action, including cooperation and competition, affect the premises of action. We must see how the organization fits into a pattern of resource exchanges and dependencies with other organizations. We must model the extent to which features of an organization may be invariant, selected by convention rather than subject to intentional choice. We must attend to the social context of meaning within which deliberate action takes place.

Implicitly, the book concedes that not everything can be studied at once by everyone. Students of organizations make distinctions among micro-, meso-, and macro-organizational studies, corresponding to the individual, organizational, and societal levels of analysis. This book has elements of all three, but there is no doubt that it lies more fully in the first two levels than in the third. The book is written mainly from the viewpoint of someone seeking to understand organizations and the behavior of people in them, rather than someone trying to characterize a social system containing organizations. Thus, it is, for the most part, written from the perspective of understanding how an organization responds to changes in its (exogenous) environment. Studies of the external environment are essential in that view, but they can be carried out without simultaneous attention to studies of decision making, and vice versa. A proper division of labor.

Modern efforts to model adaptive systems suggest that life is not that simple. Processes within an organization shape the external world, even as it is being shaped by that world. Technology is not just adopted and adapted to, it is changed. Information received includes echoes of information sent. Preferences mold the world, which molds preferences. The code word is co-evolution. Ours is a path-dependent world in which small steps are easily escalated into irreversible, or nearly irreversible, commitments. Contemporary results in evolutionary studies, organizational learning, and population biology all indicate that it is more difficult to separate the internal processes of organizational decision making from their historical and social contexts than we might previously have believed.

Finally, studies of organizations since the publication of the book have placed considerable emphasis on the symbolic and interpretive context of organizational behavior. Meaning makes a difference, and meaning is socially constructed and communicated through an interpretive language that permeates organizational life. In a society in which rational ideology is dominant, decision making is (in part) a sacred ritual by which that ideology is confirmed and communicated. Organizations gather information and conduct analyses because that is what proper organizations and proper decision makers do. At a different time and in a different society, decision makers consulted oracles and prayed for revelations. As ideologies and worldviews change, organizations change, and vice versa.

Organizations organize themselves within a context of socially recognized metaphors. When a society induces a museum to describe its holdings as "products" and its patrons as "customers," it imposes a collection of meanings associated with those metaphors. When a society labels an institution of higher education a "community college" instead of a "junior college," it encourages a transformation of identity and purpose, the details of which are hard to anticipate. When a society imagines a business firm to be an instrument of stockholders, the firm becomes something different from what it becomes when it is imagined to be a producer of goods and services, or a source of support for its workers.

Some contemporary students of meaning in organizations would go further to assert that it is interpretation, rather than choice, that is central to life. Within such a view, organizations are organized around the requirement to sustain, communicate, and elaborate interpretations of history and life—not around decisions. Decisions are primarily instruments to interpretation, rather than the other way around. Although we think an interpretive perspective yields important insights into organizations, we would not go that far, even in retrospect. But we suspect that a 1992 book on organizations, even while reaffirming that there is a real world out there to which organizations are adapting and which they are affecting, would need to pay somewhat more attention than a 1958 book did to the social context of meaning within which organizations operate.

The historical, social, and interpretive contexts of organizations are pervasive and important. At the same time, however, it is possible to exaggerate the difficulties they create for the construction of the theory of organizations. That everything is (more or less) connected to everything else does not make all research impossible. The world of organization studies is still partially decomposable. It is just not quite as decomposable for all purposes as we might have once thought.

## FINAL THOUGHTS

We have tried to indicate a few things that we might say differently now than we do in the main body of the book. They are, we think, mostly things that are anticipated in the book and are consistent with it, rather than things that require a radically different perspective. On the whole—and without much qualification—we are content to let the original text speak for itself.

Yet, in contemplating the past 35 years, we note that the study of organizations has expanded its scope and improved its quality. In 1958 almost none of the current research journals specializing in research on organizations existed. Now there are several of high quality. In 1958 students of organizations in the United States were almost entirely cut off from students of organizations in other countries. Now the international ties are rich with considerable cross-fertilization. In 1958 the study of organizations represented an insignificant part of economics, psychology, and sociology. Now organizational economics, organizational psychology, and organizational sociology are major subfields of their respective disciplines. In 1958 the systematic study of organizations was a small part of management departments in business schools. Now it is a large part of those departments and an important part of departments of strategy, human resources, industrial organization, and labor relations.

The point is not that organization research and theory represent uniquely expanding domains, nor that this particular book was especially significant to that expansion. The growth of the study of organizations over the past 35 years has been part of a phenomenal growth of the behavioral and social sciences generally. Nevertheless, part of the growth has probably come from the vitality and salience of the ideas. And if this book has contributed to making those ideas accessible, we are pleased.

When we wrote the book we thought the kinds of questions that it addressed were important ones. We still do. We hoped that a foundation had been laid for significant future research. We think those hopes have been justified. We imagined that by now we could both retire. That imagination proved illusory. There are still a few things to be done, and despite our great enthusiasm and affection for our colleagues, we are not yet prepared to let them have all the fun.

# CHAPTER 3

# An Epilogue[1]

RICHARD M. CYERT AND JAMES G. MARCH

IN THE YEARS SINCE *A Behavioral Theory of the Firm* was first published, both the economic theory of the firm and the behavioral study of decision making in organizations have prospered. In this chapter, we attempt to place that book into a context of developments subsequent to the original publication.

## CORE IDEAS OF THE BEHAVIORAL THEORY OF THE FIRM

Much of *A Behavioral Theory of the Firm* is built around three related but largely independent ideas. The first idea is *bounded rationality*, the observation that rational actors are significantly constrained by limitations of information and calculation. Because of those limitations, explicit and timely calculations of optimality are costly or impossible. In neoclassical theories of the firm, organizations identify, choose, and implement optimal alternatives. In behavioral theories, organizations simplify the decision problem in a number of ways. They set targets and look for alternatives that satisfy those targets, rather than try to find the best imaginable solution. They allocate attention by monitoring performance with respect to targets. They attend to goals sequentially, rather than simultaneously. They follow rules-of-thumb and standard operating procedures.[2]

The second idea is *imperfect environmental matching*, the observation that the rules, forms, and practices used by economic actors are not uniquely determined by the demands of the environmental setting in which they arise. In neoclassical theories of the firm, it is assumed that competition leads to the prevalence of rules and forms that have unique survival advantage. Thus, differences among organizations in the rules they follow or forms they use are seen as stemming from differences in their environments, and certain organizational forms (e.g., hierarchy, division of labor) are assumed to come to dominate because they provide very general advantages. In contrast, behavioral theories

---

This chapter first appeared as "An Epilogue," pp. 214–246 in Richard M. Cyert and James G. March, *A Behavioral Theory of the Firm*, 2nd edition. Oxford, UK: Blackwell, 1992.

emphasize the inefficiencies of history, the ways in which the match between an environment and the rules followed by organizations may be slow to evolve or indeterminate, thus the importance of specifying the process of organizational adaptation.[3]

The third idea is *unresolved conflict*, the assumption that economic organizations involve multiple actors with conflicting interests not entirely resolved by the employment contract. Neoclassical theories of the firm recognized the principle that economic actors are self-interested, but conflicts of interest internal to the firm were ignored or assumed to be resolved through a prior contract by which employees agreed to pursue the interests of an entrepreneur. The alternative assumption, pursued in behavioral theories, is that the relation between the "interests" of the organization and the interests of subgroups and individuals is continually being negotiated and renegotiated, that consistency is rarely achieved and difficult to sustain.[4]

None of these ideas was novel in 1963. Writers such as Coase, Simon, and Marschak anticipated one or more of them, and the ideas were familiar to many others.[5] Nevertheless, at that time, the theory of the firm was substantially a theory of unlimited, conflict-free rationality, and efficient adaptation. The process of environmental matching was maximization of expected utility. The internal problems of the firm were problems of efficient coordination among cooperating team members. Insofar as behavioral treatments of organizational decision making have made contributions to economic theories of the firm, it has been by identifying the limitations of such visions and providing clues for alternative formulations.

## DEVELOPMENTS IN ECONOMIC
## THEORIES OF THE FIRM

Significant parts of the story of economic theories of the firm over the past 28 years can be written as a history of elaboration of the core ideas sketched above. This is not to say that the elaboration was conscious or that the behavioral theory of the firm "transformed" economic thinking. Economic thought changed in the direction of the ideas found in this book, but the mechanisms of change were by no means so direct.[6] The book itself was part of a gradual reconstruction of the theory of the firm in which the genesis and influence of specific ideas are hard to identify. Through the mysteries of intellectual development and fashion, deviant concepts have been given greater precision, have been integrated into the main corpus of economic thought, and have been extended to form the heart of contemporary microeconomics.[7]

## Theory of Teams

If we consider the firm as having a coherent preference function, conflict of interest is subordinated, but information problems remain. This is the essential strategy of several modern treatments of the firm and information economics. One of the best developed versions is the economic theory of teams developed by Jacob Marschak and Roy Radner.[8] In this formulation, the team (and by extension the firm) is viewed as an organization in which all organizational participants share a common interest. The theory of teams examines issues of optimal decision rules, given specified information structures and payoff functions, as well as the optimal size of groups within teams. The emphasis is on the problems of information and its utilization under conditions of shared interests but limited rationality.

For example, Marschak and Radner observe:

The limitations of available men and machines explain why it pays to process information . . . it may not be feasible to assign to the same man or machine the task of reading original reports (that are relatively fine or relatively errorless), and also the task of computing optimal decisions on the basis of such reports; thus it may be necessary to insert intermediaries and, hence, coarsen or garble the report. Similarly, the constraints on available resources may also make it impossible to take full advantage of information pooling. A man (or machines) able to absorb messages from two sources and to make optimal decisions on the basis of this information may not exist for the type of messages and actions considered.[9]

Thus, the theorems of the theory of teams are concerned with optimal ways of organizing and processing information in the face of human and organizational limitations on rationality. The spirit is one of optimizing within constraints.

## Control Theories of the Firm

Where the theory of teams emphasizes calculation of optimal strategies under conditions of bounded rationality, control theories of the firm emphasize the idea that a firm deals with cognitive limitations by adapting incrementally to its environment.[10] Like other modern economic theories of the firm, control theory attempts to bring descriptive and prescriptive theories of the firm closer together by accepting some aspects of behavioral observations of the firm as inherent in the firm (e.g., limited rationality, targets) or the situation (e.g., uncertainty). It then relates other observations of the firm to the prescriptive requirements of rational action, in this case sequential Bayesian estimation.

Within a control framework, adaptation takes place through a sequence of actions, observations of their consequences, and modification of the decision rules from which subsequent actions are derived. A firm is assumed to have a collection of control variables that can be varied and can be presumed to produce some effect on performance, conditional on the state of the environment and the actions of competitors. These control variables include some that are primarily designed to influence revenue, for example, price, marketing strategy, external relations. They also include others primarily designed to affect cost, for example, output, internal organizational structure, labor policy. The firm tries to use the control variables to accomplish two things: First, it seeks to achieve its current targets with respect to things like profitability and sales by increasing revenue and reducing costs. The actions taken by a firm (e.g., raising price, increasing output) are intended to achieve a goal (e.g., a particular level of profit, a certain market share). Second, it seeks to learn something about the world in which it operates.[11] The results of actions are analyzed to generate information that might be useful in the future.

As a result of a series of observations of actions and their apparent consequences, estimates (e.g., of demand or cost curves) begin to take form in the organization. For example, if price is increased on a number of different occasions and demand does not slacken, the demand curve is likely to be seen as inelastic. The feedback can take many different kinds of forms, but some of the most important come from routine monthly financial, production, and sales statements. In a typical firm, the comparisons of such results with targets is the focus of discussions and analyses designed to explain discrepancies between realizations and targets. This social, interactive process continues over time and results in a gradual modification of beliefs about the firm and its environment.

The firm operates under conditions in which the probability distribution of observable random variables depends on unknown values of various parameters. Under these conditions, the true values of the parameters cannot usually be learned with certainty. The classical problems of statistics apply: the firm cannot be sure that it has correctly specified the model (the specification problem); it cannot be sure that its observations are correctly recorded (the measurement problem); and it cannot be sure that it has correctly estimated the parameters within a model (the estimation problem). In practice, the data available to a firm to solve such problems fall considerably short of what is required.[12] In addition, the firm has only a limited capability to process information. As a result, firms may well come to accept estimates that are incorrect and decision rules that are less than optimal. Nevertheless, much of the time, ordinary adaptive learning serves the firm reasonably well.

In observations of firms from a control perspective, the goals that drive the process do not vary much from firm to firm, though the aspiration levels with respect to the goals may vary from firm to firm as well as over time. This commonality of goals is not an assumption of the theory, but simply an empirical observation. Business firms seem regularly and generally to care about profits, sales, market shares, productivity, and the like. They exist within a normative structure that substantially homogenizes goals.[13] The theory does not rule out the possibility that new goals may be acquired over time, or old ones may be discarded. Nor does the theory rule out conflict of interest in goals. The usual assumption is that targets are established by some kind of prior interactive, bargaining process, thus can be treated as exogenous to the adaptive process. The theory focuses on the ways in which a firm adapts to feedback from its experience.

## Transaction Cost Economics

In the same general spirit as the theory of teams and control theory, but from a tradition less imbued with decision theory, is transaction-cost economics. Primacy in the development of transaction-cost economics is generally credited to John R. Commons and Ronald Coase. Commons argued that transactions were the natural basic units of analysis for economics and that transactions should be studied through the study of contracts.[14] Coase identified transaction-cost economizing as a primary reason for the existence of the firm (as an alternative to the *ad hoc* purchasing of services within a market).[15]

Much of the credit for the modern development of transaction-cost economics is due to Oliver Williamson and his associates.[16] According to Williamson:

Transaction-cost economics adopts a contractual approach to the study of economic organization. Questions such as the following are germane: Why are there so many forms of organization? What main purpose is served by alternative modes of economic organization and best informs the study of these matters? Striking differences among labor markets, capital markets, intermediate product markets, corporate governance, regulation, and family organization notwithstanding, is it the case that a common theory of contract informs all? What core features—in human, technology, and process respects—does such a common theory of contract rely on?[17]

Transaction-cost economics seeks to link the idea of information limitations with the idea of conflict of interest to generate a two-stage theory of the firm, essentially a theory of contracts. Williamson makes two behavioral assumptions about "contracting," as opposed to "maximizing." The first assumption is bounded rationality, the notion that not everything can be known, that there are limits to the capabilities of decision makers for dealing with information and anticipating the future. The second assumption is opportunism, the notion that there is conflict of interest within, as well as between, organizations, that participants in an organization will lie, cheat, and steal in their own self-interest if they can.

Opportunism becomes particularly significant when some assets, or capabilities, that are exceptionally valuable to the firm are controlled by a small group of participants, and those participants, in turn, have only a small number of firms for which the assets are valuable. Those members of the coalition whose assets are highly specific to the firm are unusually valuable to the others and can seek to exploit that advantage. For example, if a firm makes an investment that is dependent on an input controlled by another firm, it risks having its dependence exploited once the investment has been made.[18] At the same time, however, the coalition is also unusually valuable to members with firm specific assets and may seek to exploit that advantage. This general situation, now most commonly called "asset specificity" in the economics literature[19] and "resource dependence" in the organizations literature,[20] has long been of interest to students of the firm, primarily because of the indeterminacy of terms of trade resulting from the bilateral monopoly and the risks of exploitation of one party by another.

The emphasis in transaction-cost approaches is on discovering contractual arrangements that keep the parties from inducing one-way asset specificity (e.g., a sole supplier who has multiple customers) and then exploiting it. Organizational forms are seen as implicit or explicit solutions to the problems of decision and control created by limited rationality and opportunism. Thus, it is possible to interpret the prevalence of particular forms of organization, or contracts, in particular situations as reflecting calculated or evolved solutions to these problems.[21]

The transaction-cost framework can be illustrated by Williamson's stylized analysis of the conditions under which a firm will be financed through debt, rather than equity.[22] In the case of corporate financing, the general argument is that where asset specificity is low, debt financing is likely. Low asset specificity means that the assets of the firm can be redeployed through the market, thus that the pre-emptive claims of bondholders are protected by the market value of the assets. On the other hand, where asset specificity is high, bondholders are at greater risk. As a result, the costs of debt financing will have to grow to cover the risk. At the same time, the gains from closer internal oversight also grow. Equity financing, which is linked to more managerial control and oversight, is a response to this situation.

The spread of transaction-cost ideas not only through economics but into organization theory[23] suggests some of the power of the framework, as do efforts to provide empirical tests.[24] It has become a basis for substantial parts of contemporary industrial economics and has made inroads into the economics of law.[25] The framework is evocative. For some of the same reasons that have plagued most theorizing in economics, including our own, it is also somewhat difficult to disconfirm. The flexibility of the definition of transaction costs tends to make the concept a more powerful tool for interpreting historical outcomes than for predicting future ones.

## Agency Theory

An approach similar in spirit to transaction-cost economics, but one that gives a much smaller weight to limited rationality, as opposed to conflict, is found in agency theory.[26] One of the oldest problems of political philosophy is understanding the relation between the "master" who is given socially legitimate control over certain actions and the "servant" who controls the information on which the "master" acts.[27] In 1932 Berle and Means called attention to the problem in the context of the firm,[28] as did Burnham in 1941.[29] And in 1951 W. W. Cooper identified the weakness of entrepreneurial theories of the firm:

. . . the entrepreneur is regarded as operating directly on (more or less) "will-less" factors of production. . . . In short, there is no organization; there are no agents, as distinct from entrepreneurs and factors. This despite the fact that the characteristic firm is, by its very nature, an organization and does work, generally, through agents.[30]

These ideas were not much developed by economists until the 1970s, when articles by Alchian and Demsetz[31] and Jensen and Meckling[32] signaled renewed interest. As these ideas have been shaped into agency theory by subsequent contributors, attention to bounded rationality has tended to fade into the background, and attention to conflict of interest has become paramount. Indeed, as Williamson has pointed out, much of agency theory is closer in spirit to an unbounded rationality tradition than to limited rationality.[33] The informational problems of the firm are seen as the product of willful strategic misrepresentation by actors in conflict, rather than as inherent in the cognitive or organizational limitations of individuals and organizations. Agency theory has become a branch of game theory, while retaining a traditional orientation to the asymmetry between "principal" and "agent."

The prototypic example of the principal-agent relation in modern economic theory is the relation between equity holders in a corporation (principals) and management (agents). The formulation is, at heart, a classic one of an employment contract. The basic idea is that principals and agents enter voluntarily into mutually binding contracts governing their future relations. The theory emphasizes informational problems with such contracts. There are numerous future contingencies that cannot now be anticipated, and there are numerous ways in which one or the other of the contracting partners might be able to control information relevant to the implementation of the contract. Since these problems can be anticipated by each of the contracting parties, the contract has to be designed to reflect them.

In such a formulation, of course, the theory is symmetric. A solution to the contract problem is one that is jointly acceptable—given full knowledge of the complications of incompleteness in information. In practice, the theory is written from the point of view of one side of the contract. It is a convention of modern economic writing that the "principals" are the equity holders in a corporation. Thus, the problem is couched as a problem in control of the management and other employees by the owners—rather than the other way around. From this perspective, there is a cascade of principal-agent relations in a firm beginning with stockholders and passing through the board of directors and the top management to lower levels of employees.

All participants in this chain have some discretion and function in ways that are not known entirely to their principals. In such a situation, the costs to the principal of monitoring the behavior of the agent may be high. Each agent has the potential for misleading the principal, for implementing the contract in a way that serves the agent's interests beyond the rights specified under the contract. Assuming that principals and agents, in full awareness of each other's potential for falsification and shirking, try to find a mutually acceptable contract, the theory seeks to identify an incentive system that will lead agents, in their own self-interest, to exert full effort on behalf of the principal.[34]

By emphasizing features of internal conflict of interest, transaction-cost economics and agency theory yield new perspectives on the theory of the firm. By emphasizing issues of contracts and internal governance, they have raised a set of questions distinct from the classical questions of the theory of the firm. The theory of the firm was originally oriented primarily to explaining price and output decisions in economic enterprises. Transaction-cost economics and agency theory attend to a much broader set of concerns. Agency theory has stimulated a closer examination of incentive compensation schemes, and transaction-cost economics has provided an economic frame for considering issues of corporate governance and organization structure. Both yield predictions of interest to anyone interested in understanding why economic organizations take the forms they do.

## Evolutionary Theories

Since World War II, economic theories of the firm have not been much concerned with imperfect matching between organizational forms and environmental demands. The general inclination has been to assume that competition drives economic practices to unique equilibria. Thus, the standard style of analysis has been to explain outcomes as being the implicit equilibrium solution to a properly specified joint optimization problem. Different organizational forms and practices are explained by assuming different environmental conditions (e.g., different cost structures). Interest in the processes by which organizations adapt to changing environments has been limited to some relatively general observations on the forces of selection or learning. These features of economic thought are as typical of the modern forms (e.g., transaction-cost analysis, agency theory) as they are of earlier efforts. They also characterize a large fraction of management and sociological discussions of comparative organizational forms.[35]

There are, however, some recent exceptions. On the one hand, game theoretic students of the firm have come to recognize the numerous game theory situations that have multiple equilibria and the difficulty of specifying the conditions under which one equilibrium, rather than another, will be realized.[36] At the same time, students of learning and evolution in economics have tried to specify more precisely the conditions for and consequences of history dependent change.[37]

One example of the latter approach is the evolutionary theory developed by Nelson and Winter.[38] In company with other theorists who emphasize differential survival as a primary basis for changing populations of firms, they see firms as being selected upon by virtue of their fit to the environment. But they explicitly reject both profit maximization as a primary motive of the firm and the identification of an equilibrium as the ultimate goal of a theory of the firm. They draw two key concepts from behavioral theories of the firm. The first is the idea that organizations develop, stabilize, and follow routines. The routines may change over time, but in the short run they function as carriers of knowledge and experience. The second idea is a conception of search. In the Nelson and Winter formulation, organizations are not strictly invariant but change as a result of search for new solutions when old ones fail to work. Search follows routines and in that way is similar to other activities in the firm, but the outcomes of search are subject to stochastic variation.

Differential outcomes from search result in differential rates of survival and growth in firms. These differences, in turn, effect the distribution of activities and interactions at the industry level. The idea of search-based change makes the Nelson and Winter theory a bit more Lamarckian and a bit less Darwinian than most modern theories of biological evolution. They argue:

Search and selection are simultaneous, interacting aspects of the evolutionary process: the same prices that provide selection feedback also influence directions of search. Through the joint action of search and selection, the firms evolve over time, with the condition of the industry in each period bearing the seeds of its condition in the following period.[39]

The emphasis on the historical path by which organizational forms are achieved finds echoes in a number of other developments in economic history.[40] Recent research on path dependent theories ranges from careful studies of specific historical paths in the development of a specific technology[41] to general analytical investigations of non-linear dynamic systems of chaos.[42] Their characteristic feature is doubt about the possibility of predicting attributes of a social institution, such as the firm, simply from attributes of the environment in which it is found.

## DEVELOPMENTS IN BEHAVIORAL STUDIES OF ORGANIZATIONAL DECISION MAKING

As we have seen, the primary effort in economics has been to render ideas of limited rationality and unresolved conflict within an enriched but relatively conventional framework of economic theory. These theoretical consolidations of earlier ideas have occurred in parallel with a continuing research tradition of observing the real behavior of organizations as they make decisions.[43] Since 1963, research on how decisions happen in organizations has been clustered around four interrelated visions:

The first vision sees decisions as resulting from intentional, consequential action. This vision is elaborated by considering developments associated with problems of uncertainty, ambiguity, risk taking, and conflict. It is particularly concerned with the problematic nature of objectives, the implications of preferences that are unstable, inconsistent, and endogenous.

The second vision sees decisions as driven not by a logic of consequence but by a logic of appropriateness implemented through a structure of organizational rules, roles, and practices. The discussion of rules and rule-following is extended by considering the ways in which rules of behavior evolve through strategic choice, experience, and selection, and particularly to an examination of the ways in which the coevolution of organizations and their environments produce multiple suboptimal equilibria.

The third vision sees decisions as heavily influenced by the interactive ecological character of decision making. What happens in that ecology depends on the ways in which multiple actors, events, and demands fit together in networks, systems of imitation, and temporal orders.

The fourth vision sees the outcomes of decisions as artifactual rather than as central to understanding decision making. This vision is exemplified by discussions of the social development of interpretation, the extent to which organizations and the decision processes in them are better understood in terms of their links to a system of meaning and symbols than in terms of their links to output, price, and internal resource allocation.[44]

For the most part, these treatments extend, rather than contradict, the major themes of the behavioral theory of the firm, but the extensions are significant. The result has been for behavioral and economic theories of the firm to maintain a significant distance from each other, even as microeconomic theory has converged to important elements of earlier behavioral perspectives.[45]

## Decision Making as Intentional, Consequential Action

Virtually all of modern economics and large parts of the rest of social science, as well as the applied fields that build upon them, embrace the idea that human action is the result of human choice.[46] Standard theories of choice view decision making as intentional, consequential action based on a knowledge of alternatives and their consequences evaluated in terms of a consistent preference ordering.

### Ambiguous Preferences

Theories of rational choice presume two guesses about the future: a guess about the future consequences of current actions and a guess about future preferences with respect to those consequences. Classical versions of theories of rational choice assumed that both guesses were improbably precise. Actual decision situations often seem to make each of them problematic.

The first guess—about the uncertain future consequences of current action—has long attracted attention from both students of decision making and choice theorists. Even if decisions are made in a way generally consistent with choice theories—that is, even if estimates of the consequences of alternative actions are formed and action is *intendedly* rational—there are informational and computational limits on human choice. There are limits on the number of alternatives considered, and limits on the amount and accuracy of information that is available.[47]

These ideas are strongly reflected in the behavioral theory of the firm and need not be further elaborated here. Within that tradition, theories of choice have placed considerable emphasis on ideas of search and attention, and these efforts—in combination with concern for the problems of incomplete information and information and transaction costs—have turned substantial parts of recent theories of choice into theories of information and attention, that is, into theories of the first guess.[48]

The second guess—about the uncertain future preferences for the consequences of current actions—has been less considered, yet poses, if anything, greater difficulties. Preferences as they appear in standard theories of choice are stable, consistent, and exogenous. Often enough to be troublesome, each of these features of preferences seems inconsistent with observations of decision making by individuals and organizations. Preferences change over time in such a way that predicting future preferences is often difficult. Preferences are inconsistent. And while preferences are used to choose among actions, it is also often true that actions and experience with their consequences affect preferences.[49]

Behavioral research on preferences has taken two major directions. The first direction is the experimental investigation of limits to the axioms of rational choice as descriptors of individual human behavior. These studies have indicated substantial, consistent deviation from the consistency assumptions of standard theory.[50] The second direction is the study of the development of preferences in actual organizations. These studies have identified considerable reasons for a theory that allows the endogenous construction of preferences.[51]

## Risk Taking

Because of its role both in rational theories of choice and in theories of organizational learning, risk taking is a major concern of recent studies of decision making.[52] In classical theories of choice, risk preference is characteristically treated as a fixed trait of a decision maker or organization, embedded in the utility function. In this tradition, some individuals and organizations are described as risk averse and others as risk seeking. Empirical research on risk taking indicates that such individual and organizational differences exist but that they account for less of the variation in risk taking than do situational factors. Preferences for high variance alternatives are not constant but are responsive to changing fortune.

The behavioral phenomena of risk taking are familiar to empirical students of decision making:

First, risk taking appears to be affected (inconsistently) by threats to survival. On the one hand, increasing threats to survival have been observed to stimulate greater and greater risk taking, presumably in an effort to escape the threats. On the other hand, danger has been portrayed as leading to rigidity, to extreme forms of risk aversion.

Second, risk taking appears to be affected by the presence of resources in excess of current aspirations. Where organizational slack is plentiful, it tends to lead to relaxation of controls, reduced fears of failure, institutionalized innovation, and increased experimentation, thus to relatively high levels of risk taking. Where slack is limited (or negative), tight controls and efforts to improve productive efficiency with known technologies and procedures lead to relatively low levels of risk taking.

Third, risk taking appears to be affected by the size of the gap between aspirations and realizations. As long as risk takers are close to a target, they appear to be risk seeking below the target, risk averse above it.

Fourth, risk takers seem to be sensitive to whether they interpret the resources that they risk as "their resources." Greater risks are taken with new resources than with resources held for a longer time. Managers appear to be more inclined to take risks with an organization's resources than with their own.

Fifth, risk taking is affected by illusions of control. Successful risk takers seem to accept some mixture of a belief that their past successes are attributable to their special abilities, a belief that nature is favorable to them, and a belief that they can beat the odds.[53]

These phenomena have become the bases for models of risk preferences in individuals and organizations, as well as of risk-taking populations in competitive situations.[54] They cast some light on possible underlying behavioral mechanisms, but the determination of an optimal level of risk taking remains elusive.[55]

## Conflict among Rational Actors

In standard choice theory, conflict among objectives is treated as a problem of assessing tradeoffs, establishing marginal rates of substitution among goods. The process *within* individuals is mediated by an unspecified mechanism by which individuals are imagined to be able to make value comparisons among alternatives. The process *among* individuals is mediated by an explicit or implicit price system. In classical theories of organization, for example, a firm is transformed into an individual by assuming that markets (particularly markets for labor, capital, and products) convert conflicting demands into prices. In this perspective, entrepreneurs are imagined to impose their goals on an organization in exchange for mutually satisfactory wages paid to workers, rent paid to capital, and product characteristics paid to customers.[56]

Such a process can be treated as yielding a series of contracts by which decision making is divided into two stages. At the first stage, each individual negotiates the best possible terms for agreeing to pursue another's preferences, or securing such an agreement from another. In the second stage, individuals execute the contracts. In more sophisticated versions, of course, the contracts are designed so that the terms negotiated at the first stage are self-enforcing at the second. As we have seen above, this two-stage vision is characteristic of much of the modern work in agency theory and applications of game theory to economic behavior, as it is of much of classical administrative theory.

Seeing participants as having conflicting objectives is also a basic feature of the political coalition visions of decision making found in the present book. In political treatments, however, the emphasis is less on discovering or designing a system of contracts between principals and agents, or partners, than it is on understanding a political process that allows decisions to happen without necessarily resolving conflicts among the parties. Such processes are often badly understood within an intendedly rational frame.[57]

Insofar as decisions involve rational action, the decision processes we observe seem to be infused with strategic actions and politics at every level and every point. The machinations of strategic actors produce a complicated concatenation of maneuver.[58] In such conflict systems, alliances involve ambiguous agreements across time, informal loose understandings and expectations. As a result, decision making often emphasizes trust and loyalty, in parallel with a widespread belief that they are hard to find and sustain, and power comes from being thought to be trustworthy. Modern research on organizations, as well as on games of repeated interaction and iterated calculation among rational actors, has moved reputation to a central position in theories of rational bargaining.[59]

## Decisions as Rule-Based Action

Most of the developments described thus far are built on a conception of decision making that is consequential and—within the limits imposed by information constraints and conflict—intendedly rational. That is, theories of limited rationality are, for the most part, theories of rational decision making by organizations with consistent preferences. Theories of conflict in organizational decision making are, for the most part, also rational theories. They add the complication of multiple actors, each rationally pursuing self-interested objectives and constrained or facilitated by the similar rational pursuit of self-interested objectives by others.

Such theories of rational, anticipatory, calculated, consequential action underestimate both the pervasiveness and the intelligence of an alternative decision logic—the logic of appropriateness, obligation, identity, duty, and rules. Much of the decision making behavior we observe reflects the routine way in which people do what they believe they are supposed to do. Much of the behavior in an organization is specified by standard operating procedures, professional standards, cultural norms, and institutional structures. Decisions in organizations, as in individuals, seem often to involve finding "appropriate" rules to follow. The terminology is one of duties, scripts, identities, and roles rather than anticipatory, consequential choice.[60]

The logic of appropriateness differs from the logic of consequence. Rather than evaluating alternatives in terms of the values of their consequences, a decision maker asks: (1) What kind of a situation is this? (2) What kind of a person am I? (3) What is appropriate for a person such as I in a situation such as this? Such rule-following is neither willful nor consequential in the normal sense. It does not stem from the pursuit of interests and the calculation of future consequences of current choices. Rather, it comes from matching a changing (and often ambiguous) set of contingent rules to a changing (and often ambiguous) set of situations.

Rule-following can be viewed as contractual, an implicit agreement to act appropriately in return for being treated appropriately. Such a contractual view has led game theorists to an interest in interpreting norms and institutions as meta-game agreements.[61] To some extent there certainly appear to be such implicit "contracts," but socialization into rules and their appropriateness is ordinarily not a case of willful entering into an explicit contract. It is a set of understandings of the nature of things, of self-conceptions, and of images of proper behavior that evolve over time and become part of the fabric of the organization. The existence and persistence of rules, combined with their relative independence of idiosyncratic concerns of individuals, make it possible for societies and organizations to function reasonably reliably.[62]

Because they develop over time, rules can be seen as storing information generated by previous experience and analysis. As a result, studies of organizational decision making have led to research on the ways in which rules change and develop and to questions of the long-run intelligence of rule-following, thus to some classical puzzles of culture, history, and population biology. Three major processes by which rules develop are commonly considered. First, we can see rules and roles as being chosen and negotiated strategically by rational actors.[63] That is, the process by which rules are created can be seen as being a deliberate, calculated process falling within the broad frame of rational action outlined above. Second, we can see an organization or society as learning from experience, modifying the rules for action incrementally on the basis of feedback from the environment.[64] Third, we can see the mix of rules as changing through a process of selection among invariant rules. As in the case of experiential learning, choice is dependent on history, but the mechanism is different. Individual rules are invariant, but the population of rules changes over time through differential survival and extension.[65]

Ideas about the strategic, learned, and selective bases of decision rules are sometimes used to justify an assumption that decision makers maximize expected utility. The argument is simple: competition for scarce resources results in differential survival of rules that produce decisions that are, in fact, optimal. Thus, it is argued, we can assume that surviving rules (whatever their apparent character) are optimal. Although the argument has a certain charm to it, most close students of models of adaptation have suggested that neither strategic choice, nor learning, nor selection will reliably guarantee a population of rules that is optimal at any arbitrary point in time.[66]

In general, the intelligence of rules depends on a fairly subtle intermeshing of rates of change, consistency, and experimentation. Insofar as rules are strategic choices, we expect to observe a conscious effort to match organizational forms and procedures to environmental conditions. But errors are made, particularly when environmental conditions are changing or when their effects are distributed unevenly around an organization. Similarly, experiential learning is often adaptively rational. That is, it allows organizations to find good, even optimal, rules for many choices they are likely to face. However, learning from experience can produce surprises. Learning can be superstitious, and it can lead to local optima that are quite distant from the global optimum. If goals adapt rapidly to experience, outcomes that are good may be interpreted as failures, and outcomes that are poor may be interpreted as successes. If technological strategies are learned quickly relative to the development of competence, an organization can easily adopt technologies that are intelligent given the existing levels of competence, but may fail to invest in enough experience with a suboptimal technology to discover that it would become the dominant choice with additional competence. Such anomalies are frequent and important.[67]

## The Ecological Structure of Decision Making

Classic ideas of order in organizational decision making involve two related concepts. The first is that events and activities can be arranged in chains of means and ends, causes and effects. Thus, consequential relevance arranges the relation between solutions and problems, as well as the participation of decision makers. The second concept is that organizations are hierarchies in which higher levels control lower levels, and policies control implementation.

Portrayals built on such conceptions of order seem, however, to underestimate the confusion and complexity surrounding actual decision making. The observations are familiar. Many things are happening at once; technologies are changing and poorly understood; alliances, preferences, and perceptions are changing; problems, solutions, opportunities, ideas, people, and outcomes are mixed together in ways that make their interpretation uncertain and their connections unclear; actions in one part of an organization appear to be only loosely coupled to actions in another; solutions seem to have only modest connection to problems; policies are not implemented; decision makers seem to wander in and out of decision arenas.[68]

As we have seen in the resurgence of interest in game theory, contemporary students of organizations tend to emphasize the ways in which the events of organizational life are produced by the complex ecological character of organizational existence. Modern firms are often large systems of intermeshing parts embedded in large, complex industries and markets. The outcomes they generate are due more to their properties as systems than to any easily traced interests or intentions of individual actors.[69] Moreover, firms function within a complex environment. As a firm changes by internal developments and by interaction with its environment, the environment is simultaneously changing through interaction with the firm (as well as other firms). Outcomes are produced not by a process of decision making within a single firm but by complicated networks of interacting organizations and parts of organizations. Ideas about ecological interactions are, of course, present in theories of strategic action, learning, selection, and diffusion. They are seen in relatively pure form in recent work on networks and attention mosaics.

### Networks

One of the oldest observations about organizations is that we tend to describe them as hierarchies but they tend to function as less hierarchical networks of relations.[70] Recent research on decision making in organizations has considered both sides of this anomaly. On the one hand, students of organizations, particularly feminist scholars, have asked why the hierarchical description persists in the face of persistent disconfirmation. Their general answer is that hierarchies fit a (mostly male) world-view of human order as organized around relations of domination and subordination, that such a world-view tends to create real and imagined hierarchies in order to provide opportunities for defining domination and subordination.[71]

At the same time, students of organizational networks have tried to develop more powerful instruments for analyzing the network structure of complex diffusion and decision systems.[72] These techniques, which marry traditional technologies of socio-metric diagrams to modern computational capabilities of computers and to theories of complex structures have reinforced earlier observations that standard organization charts are inadequate and misleading representations of organizations, but they have not, as yet, yielded a generally accepted alternative conception of the basis for network structures. They suggest, however, that a simple rationalization of organizational decisions is unlikely to be possible. Decisions arise from multiple interactions within a relatively elaborate structure.[73]

One conspicuous example of the impact of networks on organizational decision making is found in the way actions, procedures, rules, and forms diffuse from one organization to another. Decisions can be seen as spreading through a group of organizations like fads or measles, or in response to institutional pressures.[74] Decision makers copy each other. Imitation is a common feature of ordinary organizational adaptation. If we want to account for the adoption of accounting conventions, for example, we normally would look to ways in which standard accounting procedures diffuse through a population of firms.[75] We would observe that individual accountants rather quickly adopt those rules of good practice that are certified by professional associations and implemented by opinion leaders. This ability to learn from others is one of the most powerful of adaptive tools available to individuals and economic organizations. It depends, however, on a structure of linkages among firms. In addition, it depends on a capability for absorbing the lessons, a capability that may often not be present.[76] As a result, sometimes, the processes by which knowledge diffuses and the processes by which fads diffuse are remarkably similar.

## Attention Mosaics

Observations of the apparent disorderliness in organizational decision making have led to a claim that there is very little order to it, that it is best described as bedlam. A more common position, however, is that the ways in which organizations bring order to disorder is less through hierarchies and means-ends chains than is anticipated by conventional theories. There is order, but it is not a conventional order. In particular, it is argued that any decision process involves a collection of individuals and groups who are simultaneously involved in other things. Any particular decision process combines different moments of different lives, and understanding decisions in any one arena requires an understanding of how those decisions fit into the lives of participants.[77] From this point of view, the loose coupling that we observe in a specific decision situation is a consequence of our theories. The apparent confusion results from a shifting intermeshing of the demands on the attention and lives of the whole array of actors.

A more limited version of the same fundamental idea focuses on the allocation of attention. The idea is simple. Individuals attend to some things, and thus do not attend to others. The attention devoted to a particular decision by a particular potential participant depends on alternative claims on attention.[78] Since those alternative claims are not homogeneous across participants and change over time, the attention any particular decision receives can be both quite unstable and remarkably independent of the properties of the decision. The apparently erratic character of decision making is made somewhat more explicable by placing it in this context of multiple, changing claims on attention.[79]

These ideas of attention mosaics have been generalized to deal with temporal flows of solutions and problems, as well as participants, in what has come to be called a garbage can decision process.[80] In a garbage can process, there are exogenous, time-dependent arrivals of choice opportunities, problems, solutions, and decision makers. The logic of the ordering is temporal rather than hierarchical or consequential. Problems and solutions are attached to choices, and thus to each other, not only because of their means-ends linkages but also because of their simultaneity. At the limit, almost any solution can be associated with almost any problem—provided they are contemporaries. This limiting case is, however, normally not observed in pure form. The process functions, but it functions within a structure of constraints on linkages between problems and solutions.[81]

## Decisions as Artifacts

In the theoretical frames we have described thus far, it is imagined that decision making is concerned with making decisions. Ideas built around either an intendedly rational frame, a rule-based action frame, or an ecological interaction frame tend to treat the outcomes of decision processes as central to their character and interpretation. An interest in decision making leads to organizing history as a series of choices. In this spirit, theories of decision making usually assume that a decision process is to be understood in terms of its outcomes, that decision makers enter the process in order to affect outcomes, and that the point of life is choice.

Increasingly in recent years, behavioral students of organizations have questioned the primacy of choice. Studies of decision arenas seem often to describe a set of processes that make little sense from a choice-centered point of view. Information that is ostensibly gathered for decisions is often ignored.[82] Contentiousness over the policies of an organization is often followed by apparent indifference about their implementation.[83] Individuals fight for the right to participate in decision processes, but then do not exercise the right. Studies of managers consistently indicate very little time spent in making decisions. Rather, managers seem to spend time meeting people and executing managerial performances.[84]

Such observations have moved behavioral theories of decisions somewhat toward a conception of choices as artifacts, as being not as central to an understanding of decision making (and vice versa) as might be expected. In particular, emphasis is placed on the many ways in which decision making is an arena for developing and enjoying an interpretation of life and one's position in it.[85] A business firm is a temple and a collection of sacred rituals as well as an instrument for producing goods and services. The rituals of choice tie routine events to beliefs about the nature of things. They give meaning. The meanings involved may be as global as the central ideology of a society committed to reason and participation. They may be as local as the ego needs of specific individuals and groups. As a result, recent research on organizations has introduced concepts of decisions and decision making that highlight the role of decisions and decision making in the development of meaning and interpretations. The focus has shifted from the "substantive" to the "symbolic" components of decisions.

Some treatments of symbols in decision making portray them as perversions of the decision process. They are presented as ways in which the gullible are misled into acquiescence.[86] Although there is no question but that symbols are often used strategically, it is hard to imagine a society with modern ideology that would not exhibit a well-elaborated and reinforced myth of choice, both to sustain social orderliness and meaning and to facilitate change. From this point of view, business firms are classic symbolic systems, particularly in contemporary western countries where the rituals of markets and firms confirm important ideological beliefs about the way things are and ought to be. On the one hand, the processes of choice reassure those involved that the choice has been made intelligently, that it reflects planning, thinking, analysis, and the systematic use of information; and that the choice is sensitive to the concerns of relevant people, that the right people are involved. At the same time, the processes of choice reassure those involved of their own significance. The symbols of decision making reinforce the idea that managers (and managerial choices) affect the performance of firms, and do so properly.

Thus, students of symbolic action are led to a perspective that challenges the first premise of many theories of choice, the premise that life is choice. They argue that life is not primarily choice; it is interpretation. In this view, outcomes are generally less significant—both behaviorally and ethically—than process. It is the process that gives meaning to life, and meaning is the core of life. The reason that people involved in decision making devote so much time to symbols, myths, and rituals is that they (appropriately) care more about them.[87] These ideas, once quite alien to research on the firm have become considerably more important in recent years. They are, however, still largely absent from economic treatments of business behavior and choice.[88]

### POSTSCRIPT

The modern business firm is an impressive social creation. Since the nineteenth century, it has been credited with major contributions to economic progress and growth, as well as to human misery and degradation. Perhaps because it is a relatively modern invention compared with other major social institutions, because it is often seen in ideological terms, and because it requires integrated attention from several different perspectives and disciplines, the firm is well understood neither by practitioners nor by social scientists.

*A Behavioral Theory of the Firm* was published as a modest attempt to improve that understanding. It used political, economic, organizational, psychological, and sociological concepts to comprehend empirical observations of the behavior that actually takes place within firms. The book anticipated some subsequent developments in economic and behavioral research on the firm. Modern economic theories of the firm assume that rational action in a firm is subject to limited rationality and conflicts of interest. Modern behavioral theories of organizations have been built on somewhat less rationalized versions of the same ideas.

There are times when we would like to imagine that tomorrow's theory of the firm will reflect both a continuation of such developments and attention to the newer ideas outlined in this chapter. It is a nice thought, but it is easier to tell history than to predict it. Just as we could not easily have predicted in 1963 the flowering of interest in ambiguity, inefficient histories, and interpretation, or the resurgence of game theory that are conspicuous features of the last twenty-nine years, we cannot really tell the details of where we are going from where we are.

All of which suggests one of the advantages of publishing a second edition of a book almost thirty years after the first: the authors are forced to admit that they may not have it all quite right. Yet.

## NOTES

1. This chapter draws from James G. March, "How decisions happen in organizations," *Human-Computer Interaction*, 6 (1991), 95–117.

2. The classic references for bounded rationality are two articles by H. A. Simon: "A behavioral model of rational choice," *Quarterly Journal of Economics*, 69 (1955), 99–118; and "Rational choice and the structure of the environment," *Psychological Review*, 63 (1956), 129–38. Early elaborations of the ideas can be found in J. G. March and H. A. Simon, *Organizations* (New York: Wiley, 1958); and C. E. Lindblom, "The 'science' of muddling through," *Public Administration Review*, 19 (1959), 79–88.

3. See H. E. Aldrich, *Organizations and Environments* (Englewood Cliffs, NJ: Prentice-Hall, 1979); J. G. March, "Decisions in organizations and theories of choice," in A. Van de Ven and W. Joyce, eds., *Assessing Organization Design and Performance* (New York: Wiley, 1981), 205–44; J. G. March and J. P. Olsen, *Rediscovering Institutions: The Organizational Basis of Politics* (New York: Free Press/Macmillan, 1989).

4. See J. von Neumann and O. Morgenstern, *Theory of Games and Economic Behavior* (Princeton: Princeton University Press, 1944); D. B. Truman, *The Governmental Process* (New York: Knopf, 1951); R. A. Dahl and C. E. Lindblom, *Politics, Economics, and Welfare* (New York: Harper, 1953); March and Simon, *op. cit.*; J. G. March, "The business firm as a political coalition," *Journal of Politics*, 24 (1962), 662–78.

5. R. H. Coase, "The nature of the firm," *Economica*, 4 (1937), 368–405; H. A. Simon, *Administrative Behavior* (New York: Macmillan, 1947); J. Marschak, "Elements for a theory of teams," *Management Science*, 1 (1955), 127–37.

6. For some speculations on the development of ideas in the theory of the firm see K. Arrow, "Reflections on the essays," in G. Feiwel, ed., *Arrow and the Foundations of the Theory of Economic Policy* (New York: NYU Press, 1987), 727–34; O. E. Williamson, "Chester Barnard and the incipient science of organization," in O. E. Williamson, ed., *Organization Theory: From Chester Barnard to the Present and Beyond* (New York: Oxford University Press, 1990), 172–206.

7. See B. R. Holmstrom and J. Tirole, "The theory of the firm," in R. Schmalensee and R. D. Willig, eds., *Handbook of Industrial Organization*, vol. 1 (New York: Elsevier Science Publishers B.V., 1989), 61–133; O. Hart, "An economist's perspective on the theory of the firm," in O. E. Williamson, ed., *Organization Theory: From Chester Barnard to the Present and Beyond* (New York: Oxford University Press, 1990), 154–71.

8. J. Marschak and R. Radner, *Economic Theory of Teams* (New Haven: Yale University Press, 1972).

9. *Ibid.*, 305.

10. R. M. Cyert and M. H. DeGroot, "Toward a control theory of the firm," in R. Wolff, ed., *Organizing Industrial Development* (Berlin: Walter de Gruyter, 1986), 342–86; R. M. Cyert and M. H. DeGroot, "The maximization process under uncertainty," in L. S. Sproull and P. D. Larkey, eds., *Advances in Information Processing in Organizations* (Greenwich, CT: JAI Press, 1984), 47–61; R. M. Cyert and M. H. DeGroot, *Bayesian Analysis and Uncertainty in Economic Theory* (Totowa, NJ: Rowman and Littlefield, 1987).

11. J. G. March, "Exploration and exploitation in organizational learning," *Organization Science*, 2 (1991), 71–87.

12. Cyert and DeGroot, *Bayesian Analysis and Uncertainty in Economic Theory, op. cit.*; J. G. March, L. S. Sproull, and M. Tamuz, "Learning from samples of one or fewer," *Organization Science*, 2 (1991), 1–13.

13. P. DiMaggio and W. W. Powell, "The iron cage revisited: Institutional isomorphism and collective rationality in organizational fields," *American Sociological Review*, 48 (1983), 147–60.

14. J. R. Commons, *Institutional Economics* (Madison, WI: University of Wisconsin Press, 1934).

15. Coase, *op. cit.*

16. O. E. Williamson, *Markets and Hierarchies* (New York: Free Press, 1975); O. E. Williamson, *The Economic Institutions of Capitalism* (New York: Free Press, 1985).

17. O. E. Williamson, "Transaction cost economics," in R. Schmalensee and R. D. Willig, eds., *Handbook of Industrial Organization*, vol. 1 (New York: Elsevier Science Publishers, 1989), 136–82.

18. A. Marshall, *Principles of Economics*, 8th edn (London: Macmillan, 1936), 453–54.

19. A. A. Alchian and S. Woodward, "The firm is dead; long live the firm," *Journal of Economic Literature*, 26 (1988), 65–79.

20. J. Pfeffer and G. Salancik, *The External Control of Organizations: A Resource Dependence Perspective* (New York: Harper and Row, 1978).

21. See also, D. North, *Structure and Change in Economic History* (New York: Norton, 1981); N. Fligstein and K. Dauber, "Structural change in corporate organization," *Annual Review of Sociology*, 15 (1989), 73–96.

22. Williamson, "Transaction cost economics," *op. cit.*; see also O. E. Williamson, "The logic of economic organization," *Journal of Law, Economics, and Organization*, 4 (1988), 136–82.

23. O. E. Williamson, "The economics of organization: The transaction economics approach," *American Journal of Sociology*, 87 (1981), 548–77; O. E. Williamson and W. Ouchi, "The market and hierarchies and visible hand perspectives," in A. Van de Ven and W. Joyce, eds., *Perspectives on Organizational Design and Behavior* (New York: Wiley, 1981), 347–70.

24. See for example, P. Joskow, "Vertical integration and long term contracts: The case of coal-burning electric generating plants," *Journal of Law, Economics, and Organization*, 1 (1985), 33–80; C. Helfat and D. Teece, "Vertical integration and risk reduction," *Journal of Law, Economics, and Organization*, 3 (1987), 47–68.

25. See for example, O. E. Williamson, "Transaction-cost economics: The governance of contractual relations," *Journal of Law and Economics*, 22 (1979), 233–61.

26. E. F. Fama, "Agency problems and the theory of the firm," *Journal of Political Economy*, 88 (1980), 288–302; K. J. Arrow, "The economics of agency," in J. Pratt and R. Zeckhauser, eds., *Principals and Agents* (Boston: Harvard Business School Press, 1985), pp. 37–51; D. A. Levinthal, "A survey of agency models of organization," *Journal of Economic Behavior and Organization*, 9 (1988), 153–85.

27. See, for example, E. Barker, *The Politics of Aristotle* (Oxford: Clarendon, 1946), Book I.

28. A. A. Berle, Jr., and G. C. Means, *The Modern Corporation and Private Property* (New York: Macmillan, 1932).

29. J. Burnham, *The Managerial Revolution* (New York: John Day, 1941).

30. W. W. Cooper, "A proposal for extending the theory of the firm," *Quarterly Journal of Economics*, 65 (1951), 87–109, at 90.

31. A. Alchian and H. Demsetz, "Production, information costs, and economic organization," *American Economic Review*, 62 (1972), 777–95.

32. M. Jensen and W. Meckling, "Theory of the firm: managerial behavior, agency costs, and capital structure," *Journal of Financial Economics*, 3 (1976), 305–60.

33. O. E. Williamson, "Corporate finance and corporate governance," *Journal of Finance*, 43 (1988), 567–91, at 570.

34. O. Hart and B. Holmstrom, "The theory of contracts," in T. Bewley, ed., *Advances in Economic Theory* (Cambridge, England: Cambridge University Press, 1987).

35. See for example, P. R. Lawrence and J. W. Lorsch, *Organization and Environment* (Boston: Harvard Business School, 1967).

36. D. M. Kreps, *A Course in Microeconomic Theory* (Princeton, NJ: Princeton University Press, 1990), 402–43.

37. See, for example, P. A. David, "The hero and the herd in technological history: Reflections on Thomas Edison and 'The battle of the systems'," in P. Higgonet and H. Rosovsky, eds., *Economic Development Past and Present: Opportunities and Constraints* (Cambridge, MA: Harvard University Press, 1990).

38. R. R. Nelson and S. G. Winter, *An Evolutionary Theory of Economic Change* (Cambridge, MA: Harvard University Press, 1982).

39. *Ibid.*, 19.

40. See, for example, P. A. David and J. A. Bunn, "The economics of gateway technologies and network evolution," *Information Economics and Policy*, 3 (1987), 165–202.

41. See, for example, P. A. David, "Clio and the economics of QWERTY," *American Economic Review,* 75 (1985), 332–37.

42. W. J. Baumol and J. Benhabib, "Chaos: Significance, mechanism, and economic applications," *Journal of Economic Perspectives*, 3(4) (1989), 77–105.

43. A. Grandori, *Perspectives on Organization Theory* (Cambridge, MA: Ballinger, 1987); W. R. Scott, *Organizations: Rational, Natural, and Open Systems*, 2nd ed. (Englewood Cliffs, NJ: Prentice-Hall, 1987).

44. J. G. March, *Decisions and Organizations* (Oxford: Basil Blackwell, 1988); March and Olsen, *Rediscovering Institutions, op. cit.*

45. J. G. March and G. Sevón, "Behavioral perspectives on theories of the firm," in W. F. van Raaij, G. M. van Veldhoven, and K. E. Wärneryd, eds., *Handbook of Economic Psychology* (Dordrecht, Netherlands: Kluwer, 1988), 369–402.

46. See, for example, P. C. Ordeshook, *Game Theory and Political Theory: An Introduction* (Cambridge, England: Cambridge University Press, 1986); J. S. Coleman, *Individual Interests and Collective Action* (Cambridge, England: Cambridge University Press, 1986); J. S. Coleman, *Foundations of Social Theory* (Cambridge, MA: Harvard University Press, 1990).

47. March and Simon, *op. cit.*; G. T. Allison, *Essence of Decision* (Boston: Little Brown, 1971); I. L. Janis, *Decision Making* (New York: Free Press, 1977).

48. March, *Decisions and Organizations, op. cit.*

49. R. M. Cyert and M. H. DeGroot, "Adaptive utility," in R. Day and T. Groves, eds., *Adaptive Economic Models* (New York: Academic Press, 1975), 223–46; J. G. March, "Bounded rationality, ambiguity, and the engineering of choice," *Bell Journal of Economics*, 9 (1978), 587–608.

50. P. J. H. Schoemaker, "The expected utility model: Its variants, purposes, evidence and limitations," *Journal of Economic Literature*, 20 (1982), 529–63; M. J. Machina, "Choice under uncertainty: Problems solved and unsolved," *Economic Perspectives*, 1(1) (1987), 121–54.

51. March, *Decisions and Organizations, op. cit.*; March and Olsen, *Rediscovering Institutions, op. cit.*; M. S. Feldman, *Order without Design: Information Production and Policy Making* (Stanford, CA: Stanford University Press, 1989).

52. D. Kahneman and A. Tversky, "Prospect theory: An analysis of decision under risk," *Econometrica*, 47 (1979), 263–91; J. G. March and Z. Shapira, "Managerial perspectives on risk and risk taking," *Management Science*, 33 (1987), 1404–18; P. Bromiley, "Testing a causal model of corporate risk-taking and performance," *Academy of Management Journal*, in press (1991).

53. This summary is taken from J. G. March and Z. Shapira, "Variable risk preferences and the focus of attention," *Psychological Review*, in press (1992).

54. *Ibid.*; Bromiley, *op. cit.*; J. G. March, "Variable risk preferences and adaptive aspirations," *Journal of Economic Behavior and Organization*, 9 (1988), 5–24.

55. March, "Exploration and exploitation in organizational learning," *op. cit.*

56. C. I. Barnard, *Functions of the Executive* (Cambridge, MA: Harvard University Press, 1938); Simon, *Administrative Behavior, op. cit.*; Alchian and Demsetz, *op. cit.*

57. J. P. Olsen, *Organized Democracy* (Bergen, Norway: Universitets-forlaget, 1983); J. G. March and J. P. Olsen, *Rediscovering Institutions, op. cit.*

58. J. Pfeffer, *Power in Organizations* (Marshfield, MA: Pitman, 1981); H. Mintzberg, *Power in and around Organizations* (Englewood Cliffs, NJ: Prentice-Hall, 1983).

59. D. Kreps and R. Wilson, "Reputation and imperfect information," *Journal of Economic Theory*, 27 (1982), 253–79; P. Milgrom and J. Roberts, "Predation, reputation, and entry deterrence," *Journal of Economic Theory*, 27 (1982), 280–312.

60. The classic text on rules and procedures as bases for organizational action is M. Weber, *The Theory of Social and Economic Organization* (Oxford: Oxford University Press, 1947). More recent discussions are in A. Stinchcombe, *Creating Efficient Industrial Administration* (New York: Academic Press, 1974); and R. P. Abelson, "Script processing in attitude formation and decision making," in J. S. Carroll and J. W. Payne, eds., *Cognition and Social Behavior* (Hillsdale, NJ: Erlbaum, 1976), 33–46.

61. See, for example, K. Shepsle and B. Weingast, "The institutional foundations of committee power," *American Political Science Review*, 81 (1987), 85–104.

62. J. Elster, *The Cement of Society* (Cambridge, England: Cambridge University Press, 1989); J. G. March and J. P. Olsen, *Rediscovering Institutions, op. cit.*

63. A. Chandler, *Strategy and Structure* (Cambridge, MA: MIT Press, 1962).

64. B. Levitt and J. G. March. "Organizational learning," *Annual Review of Sociology*, 14 (1988), 319–40.

65. Nelson and Winter, *op. cit.*; G. R. Carroll, ed., *Ecological Models of Organization* (Cambridge, MA: Ballinger, 1988); M. T. Hannan and J. Freeman, *Organizational Ecology* (Cambridge, MA: Harvard University Press, 1989).

66. J. V. Singh and C. J. Lumsden, "Theory and research in organizational ecology," *Annual Review of Sociology*, 16 (1990), 161–95.

67. See S. R. Herriott, D. A. Levinthal, and J. G. March, "Learning from experience in organizations," *American Economic Review*, 75 (1985), 298–302; J. G. March, "Exploration and exploitation in organizational learning," *op. cit.*

68. J. G. March and J. P. Olsen, *Ambiguity and Choice in Organizations* (Bergen, Norway: Universitets-forlaget, 1976); K. Weick, "Educational organizations as loosely coupled systems," *Administrative Science Quarterly*, 21 (1976), 1–19; N. Brunsson, *The Irrational Organization* (Chichester, England: Wiley, 1985).

69. See for example, C. Perrow, *Normal Accidents* (New York: Basic Books, 1984).

70. See for example, F. J. Roethlisberger and W. J. Dickson, *Management and the Worker* (Cambridge, MA: Harvard University Press, 1939); W. L. Warner and J. O. Low, *The Social System of the Modern Factory* (New Haven, CT: Yale University Press, 1947); C. R. Walker and R. H. Guest, *The Man on the Assembly Line* (Cambridge, MA: Harvard University Press, 1952).

71. R. M. Kanter, *Men and Women of the Corporation* (New York: Basic Books, 1977); M. French, *Beyond Power: On Women, Men and Morals* (New York: Ballantine, 1985); K. E. Ferguson, *The Feminist Case against Hierarchy* (Philadelphia: Temple University Press, 1984).

72. J. Galaskiewicz and R. S. Burt, "Interorganizational contagion in corporate philanthropy," *Administrative Science Quarterly*, 36 (1991), 88–105.

73. P. Marsden, *Social Structure and Network Analysis* (Beverly Hills, CA: Sage, 1982); R. S. Burt, *Applied Network Analysis* (Beverly Hills, CA: Sage, 1983); L. C. Freeman, D. R. White, and A. K. Romney, eds., *Research Methods in Social Network Analysis* (Fairfax, VA: George Mason University Press, 1989).

74. P. DiMaggio and W.-W. Powell, "The iron cage revisited," *op. cit.*; W. R. Scott, "The adolescence of institutional theory," *Administrative Science Quarterly*, 32 (1987), 493–511; L. G. Zucker, "Institutional theories of organization," *Annual Review of Sociology*, 13 (1987), 443–64.

75. S. Mezias, "An institutional model of organizational practice: Financial reporting at the Fortune 200," *Administrative Science Quarterly*, 35 (1990), 431–57.

76. W. M. Cohen and D. A. Levinthal, "Absorptive capacity: A new perspective on learning and innovation," *Administrative Science Quarterly*, 35 (1990), 128–52.

77. See, for example, S. Krieger, *Hip Capitalism* (Beverly Hills, CA: Sage, 1979).

78. R. M. Cyert, "Defining leadership and explicating the process," *Nonprofit Management and Leadership*, 1 (1990), 29–38.

79. March, *Decisions and Organizations, op. cit.*; J. W. Kingdon, *Agendas, Alternatives, and Public Policies* (Boston: Little, Brown, 1984).

80. M. D. Cohen, J. G. March, and J. P. Olsen, "A garbage can model of organizational choice," *Administrative Science Quarterly*, 17 (1972), 1–25.

81. J. G. March and J. P. Olsen, "Garbage can models of decision making in organizations," in J. G. March and R. Weissinger-Baylon, eds., *Ambiguity and Command: Organizational Perspectives on Military Decision Making* (Cambridge, MA: Ballinger, 1986); B. Levitt and C. Nass, "The lid on the garbage can: Institutional constraints on decision making in the technical core of college-text publishers," *Administrative Science Quarterly*, 34 (1989), 190–207.

82. M. S. Feldman and J. G. March, "Information in organizations as signal and symbol," *Administrative Science Quarterly*, 26 (1981), 171–86.

83. V. E. Baier, J. G. March, and H. Sætren, "Implementation and ambiguity," *Scandinavian Journal of Management Studies*, 2(1986), 1978–212; K. Kreiner, "Ideology and management in a garbage can situation," in J. G. March and J. P. Olsen, *Ambiguity and Choice in Organizations, op. cit.*, 156–73; S. Christensen, "Decision making and social-

ization," in J. G. March and J. P. Olsen, *Ambiguity and Choice in Organizations*, *op. cit.*, pp. 351–85.

84. M. D. Cohen and J. G. March, *Leadership and Ambiguity*, 2nd ed. (Boston: Harvard Business School Press, 1986); J. Hannaway, *Managers Managing* (New York: Oxford University Press, 1989).

85. J. G. March and G. Sevón, "Gossip, information, and decision making," in L. S. Sproull and J. P. Crecine, eds., *Advances in Information Processing in Organizations*, vol. 1 (Greenwich, CT: JAI Press, 1984), 95–107.

86. M. Edleman, *The Symbolic Uses of Politics* (Urbana, IL: University of Illinois Press, 1964).

87. March and Sevón, "Gossip, information and decision making," *op. cit.*; J. G. March, "Ambiguity and accounting: The elusive link between information and decision making," *Accounting, Organizations, and Society*, 12 (1987), 153–68; N. Brunsson, *The Organization of Hypocrisy* (Chichester, England: Wiley, 1989).

88. But see D. McCloskey, *The Consequences of Economic Rhetoric* (Cambridge, England: Cambridge University Press, 1988).

# CHAPTER 4

# Learning and the Theory of the Firm

JAMES G. MARCH

## EARLY DEVELOPMENTS IN BEHAVIORAL
## THEORIES OF THE FIRM

At the risk of providing only a highly sketchy account of intellectual history, we can summarize behavioral approaches to the study of the firm in terms of three key ideas.

The first idea is what I will call here imperfect environmental matching. In most traditional economic theories of the firm, as well as in many theories of organization, it is presumed, either explicitly or implicitly, that the environment drives an organization inexorably and relatively rapidly to a form or strategy that matches the organization's environment. As a result, we can predict an organization's behavior from knowledge of its environment. The contrary notion, developed in the early days of behavioral theorizing, was that a perfect match between an organization and its environment was not guaranteed, thus that organizational forms and strategies could not be predicted simply from a knowledge of environmental conditions. As a result, one had to know something about the processes of choice and adaptation that occurred inside the firm.

The second idea was actually a set of ideas normally grouped under the heading of limited or bounded rationality. Bounded rationality encompassed the ideas that organizations and individuals in them have limited capacities for information processing, that they do not know all of their alternatives, that they do not possess all the relevant information about the consequences of those alternatives, that they approach the problem of choice by satisficing rather than maximizing, that is that they distinguish between alternatives that are good enough and those that are not, and that they follow a search strategy that increases the intensity of search whenever results fall below the aspiration level. Bounded rationality was pictured as leading to sequential attention to goals.

This chapter is based on a talk given at the Department of Economics of the University of Trento in September 1992 and appeared in *Economia e Banca—Annali Scientific* (Trento), 5 (1992), 15–35. The research has been supported by the Spencer Foundation and the Stanford Graduate School of Business.

Rather than making trade-offs among value dimensions, organizations attend to demands or desires sequentially. It was also pictured as leading to the use of rules and standard operating procedures to make choice processes consistent with the limited information processing capabilities of the organization.

The third idea was unresolved conflict. Even after employment contracts have been negotiated, even after coalitions have been formed and side payments arranged, conflict remains in an organization. The classical view acknowledged that individuals in an organization might have different values, thus were in actual or potential conflict with each other. This conflict was imagined to be resolved through a two-stage process. In the first stage a contract was negotiated. This contract was imagined to transform a conflict of interest into a collection of compatible interests. Then, at the second stage, the contract was implemented by an employer providing wages and other contractually agreed inducements in return for an employee undertaking to pursue the preferences of the employer. The contrary idea was that conflict was endless. Contracts do indeed account for some forms of goal coordination and conflict reduction, but they seem to be incomplete and incompletely enforceable. Members of an organization never seem to reach a conflict-free point.

These three ideas—the idea of imperfect matching between the firm and its environment, the idea (or collection of ideas) that is called bounded rationality, and the idea of unresolved conflict in organizations—have now become central parts of contemporary theories of the firm. Although they retain a basic kernel of belief in rationality, modern economic theories of the firm are strikingly different from the theories of thirty or forty years ago. And those differences can be described in terms of the extent to which the theories have adopted one or more of the ideas.

Early revisions of the theory of the firm in economics emphasized cognitive and information limits on rationality only. Marschak and Radner's team theory accepted the notion of bounded rationality but avoided conflict of interest by assuming a coherent common objective and did not worry about the incomplete matching between the firm and its environment. Similarly, control-theoretical models of the firm accepted the information assumptions of bounded rationality, though they ignored the possibilities of conflict and incomplete matching.

More recent revisions have gone in slightly different directions. Transaction cost analysis clearly adopts the ideas of bounded rationality and unresolved conflict—called "opportunism," by Oliver Williamson. Transaction cost versions of theories of the firm do not attend to incomplete matching, relying on a comparative statics strategy that infers organizational form from environmental conditions.

Agency theory and related game-theoretic formulations make conflict issues the main focus of analysis, though they do not, in most forms, do much with bounded rationality. They are a little ambivalent about imperfect matching. Although early game-theoretic versions tended to assume uniqueness in "solutions," the problem of multiple equilibria has become more conspicuous in more recent treatments.

Overall, although there is no contemporary economic theory of the firm that adopts all three of the major ideas of the earlier behavioral critique, the notions that were current in organization studies of the 1950s and 1960s have now rather thoroughly penetrated standard microeconomics and have been rather elegantly developed, formalized, and elaborated. Some forms of bounded rationality and unresolved conflict have become more or less standard in economic theories of the firm. The idea that history is inefficient—that environments do not uniquely determine firm structure or strategy—is less standard.

## LATER DEVELOPMENTS IN BEHAVIORAL STUDIES OF ORGANIZATIONS

In the last twenty years or so, behavioral theories of organizations have evolved in directions which, we might imagine, might also become standard topics for microeconomic theory—in another twenty or thirty years.

The attention of behavioral students of organizations has been directed, first, to the role of ambiguity in preferences. In classical choice theory, as carried over into classical microeconomics, preferences are assumed to be consistent, stable, and exogenous. Preferences as we encounter them in real organizations appear instead to be inconsistent, unstable, and endogenous.

The second cluster of problems which have attracted attention among behavioral students of organizations are those associated with a recognition of the logic of appropriateness as a basis for action. In classical theories of the firm, as in most of contemporary social science, we imagine that individuals (or firms) act by identifying the consequences of various alternatives for some antecedent preferences, and then choosing that alternative that has the best anticipated consequences. The alternative vision of action is one that sees behavior not as following a logic of consequences but a logic of appropriateness. The relevant questions are: "What kind of a person am I? What is my identity? What kind of a situation is this? What does a person of my kind do in a situation like this?" The logic of appropriateness leads to a renewed focus on rules and a substantial re-emergence of institutionalism—the notion that much of behavior is dictated by broadly accepted norms, standards, and rules.

The third focus of recent behavioral studies of organization is on history-dependent conceptions of organizational action and forms. In much of our thinking in choice theory and economics, we imagine that the present is implicit in the future. The present enacts the future: Individuals and organizations match present actions to expectations of their future consequences. Recent work in the behavioral tradition places a somewhat greater emphasis on the ways in which the present enacts the past. Rules and norms develop through history and are projected into the present. This shift of emphasis has made the theories much more attentive to how history is encoded into rules, thus a focus on history-dependent models such as evolutionary models of variation and selection and models of experiential and knowledge-based learning.

The fourth focal point for research in behavioral studies of organizations in the last twenty years is what could be called the ecological structure of organizational action. One of our problems in understanding organizations is that we have usually imagined individuals and groups acting, taking decisions, learning, etc., within an environment that is exogenous to them. But what actors actually face is an environment that consists heavily in other actors simultaneously acting. In standard microeconomic discussions, this consideration is reflected in the contrast between partial equilibrium and general equilibrium formulations, a difference that depends on the role of anticipations and reactions of competitors in the model. But the relation among competitors is only part of a more general concern with the ecological interaction among actors and environments. A focus on the ecology of connections makes the study of linkage networks critical, and recent research emphasizes the ways in which organizations are connected, the ways in which information spreads within a population of organizations, the ways in which aspirations spread, and the consequences of competitive and cooperative interactive effects.

The fifth theme of recent behavioral studies of organizations is the important role of interpretation and meaning. Organizations can be seen less as decision-making systems than as systems of meaning. The social construction of belief is clearly relevant to standard theories of choice. Anticipations are a central concern. And if the social construction of beliefs about consequences can be accepted as important, then alternatives and preferences need also to be treated as socially constructed too. The challenge is, however, more fundamental than simply observing that the premises of choice are socially constructed. In some recent behavioral studies of organizations, the development of interpretation and meaning is seen as the primary organizing processes in an organization, more significant to understanding organizations than are decisions or resource allocations. The argument is that a theory of the firm cannot hope to comprehend the behavior of the firm until it accommodates the fact that the allocative decisions it makes and the resources that it distributes are secondary to its activities in constructing an interpretation of an ambiguous world.

## A FOCUS ON THE LEARNING OF RULES
## IN ECOLOGIES OF ORGANIZATIONS

I think these five themes capture a fair amount of what has been going on in recent studies of organizations. And I think each of them has implications for economic theories of the firm. I will, however, focus on the implications of only some aspects of three of them. Developing the implications of two others will be left to the listener as an exercise. The idea that the fundamental activities of the firm are construction of meaning and elaboration of interpretation has some profound importance for economic theories of the firm, but I suspect that idea will not penetrate economics very rapidly. Questions about preferences and how they are formed, and especially the problems of endogenous, unstable preferences, are clearly significant for modern economic theory and are subject to rather intense effort currently, both within and outside of economics, but I will not deal with it here.

My concerns are with a conception of action in organizations as being based on a logic of appropriateness implementing rules that store and code an organization's historical experience within an ecology of learning organizations. I think that the economic theory of the next few decades will increase the amount of attention devoted to rule following, learning, and the ecological context of history.

The argument that rules evolve through a history of experience in an environment is part of a long tradition in economics and much of social science. One of the most conventional ideas we have in social science is the idea that instigations (or organizations) and their environments adapt to each other, coming to match each other in important ways. What I call the efficient history hypothesis—one that runs through much of social science—is that such a matching process has a unique optimal equilibrium. As I pointed out earlier, if we believe that history is efficient then understanding the processes of history is unnecessary for predicting its outcomes. Almost all modern studies of adaptive processes, on the contrary, identify important elements of inefficiency in history, and almost all modern theories of evolution, learning, or adaptation in general are theories in which there is no presumption of a stable, optimal, unique equilibrium.

On the one hand, institutional change is generally slow relative to environmental change, so that even though there may exist a single equilibrium, the process rarely reaches it before the conditions change. On the other hand, slowness is not the most critical problem. Many of the processes that we observe have multiple path-dependent equilibria. For example, there are typically many different solutions to the survival problems of an ecology of species. There is no way of inferring from an existing distribution of organizational forms anything about the efficiency, optimality, appropriateness, or whatever, of those forms. The adaptive outcomes in these theories depend heavily upon the specific processes that are involved and the specific realized course of history.

History dependence is in many ways a discouraging phenomenon. At the least it implies that the processes of adaptation have to be understood in a fair amount of detail. We cannot presume that if organizations follow analytic choice procedures, they will be driven inexorably to some particular unique optimum. We cannot presume that if organizations imitate each other, they will be led to a single unique outcome or solution. We cannot presume that if we have a full-blown evolutionary system of variation and selection, it will produce a unique distribution of forms. And we cannot presume that, if we have a learning process making incremental improvement, it will lead to a single optimal outcome. These theories suggest that outcomes cannot be predicted from preconditions or current conditions, that where the system goes tomorrow depends not only on where it is today but on how it got there.

### LEARNING PROCESSES IN THE FIRM

To explore some aspects of these new developments, I will look at ideas about learning. The choice of learning is, to some extent, arbitrary. Many of the observations I will make could also be made about other models of adaptation, for example, variation and selection models.

### Two Meanings of Learning

One of the problems in the economic (and other) literature on learning, as in the literatures on other forms of adaptation, is that learning has two rather different meanings. We sometimes use the word "learning" to refer to improvement in outcomes. In this usage we say that a person has learned if he or she has improved his or her capabilities for doing something. That is essentially the definition of learning that is used in conventional learning curves in economics. Learning is defined as a reduction in the cost of producing a unit of output.

The other definition of learning refers to a particular process of reacting to information. Usually we define learning as a process involving a sequence of steps: beginning with the taking of an action, followed by the monitoring of the outcomes of the action, their interpretation, and then some modification of the propensity to repeat the action. It is usually assumed that if the outcomes of an action are evaluated as successful or satisfactory ones, then the likelihood of doing the action at a future date is increased. If the outcomes are evaluated as unsatisfactory, then the probability of doing the action at a future date is decreased.

Either of these meanings of learning can be used. Both have led to important studies of adaptation. The problem is that the two meanings are sometimes confused. Students of improvement sometimes presume that improvement has stemmed from a particular learning process, and students of learning processes sometimes presume that they are describing a process that necessarily leads to improvement. Neither presumption is warranted in general.

I will discuss learning from a process perspective. That is, I will speak of learning theories as theories that specify a particular process for monitoring experience and producing changes in behavioral propensities as a result of that monitoring. Whether that process leads to improvement will be treated as a question to be addressed rather than a linguistic assumption.

There are three broad clusters of questions that we ask about learning from experience in organizations. I will devote most of the rest of this essay to looking at a few aspects of each of those three clusters. The first cluster of questions concerns the nature of the learning process: How do organizations learn from their experience? How do they interpret history and apply those interpretations to the future? How do they record and retrieve those interpretations? The second cluster of questions regards the ecological character of learning: How is the learning path of an organization affected by its interaction with other simultaneously learning organizations? How does the environment learn from the organization as the organization learns from the environment? The third cluster of questions concerns the intelligence of the learning process: Under what conditions do learning processes lead to intelligent or unintelligent outcomes? What mistakes does learning make and is there anything that can be done about them?

### Learning from Ambiguous Histories

Organizations cope with the problems of historical inference by building interpretations of history. They tend to move toward reliable—that is shared—interpretations of history. Not necessarily valid interpretations, but shared ones. In the face of historical ambiguity, actors gain confidence from the fact that several share the same interpretation, and tend to treat agreement as equivalent to validity. These pressures toward consistency of beliefs are constrained by the formation of subcultures of belief, subcultures which are sustained by conflict and competition within the organization. The pressures toward consistency and diversity produce learning in which many of the lessons of history are shared broadly but some important ones vary from one subculture to another.

There are as many limitations of information processing and inference making in learning as there are in rational analysis. If we have bounded information capabilities with respect to rational choice, we have to expect to have bounded information capabilities with respect to experiential learning. In order to learn, organizations need to know what happened, why it happened, and whether what happened was satisfactory. Typically they have to extract that information from very small samples of ambiguous history. God is a miserable designer of experiments, leaving many variables uncontrolled, correlated, or unobserved.

Research in psychology provides us with ample evidence on human limitations in interpreting history. Human observers tend to over-attribute historical events to human intention. If something happens, someone must have wanted it to happen. Humans tend to interpret history as a set of necessary outcomes, rather than as draws from a distribution of possible outcomes. It is hard for them to treat events that actually occur as having a probability, possibly a rather low probability, rather than being necessary outcomes. Human observers use very simple rules for interpreting history. They believe, for example, that big effects must have big causes, although most of our research teaches us that many big effects are actually produced by small causes amplified through positive feedback loops. They believe that causes will be found in the neighborhood of their effects, although our research tells us that effects often have remote causes.

Human beings seem to over-interpret single events. They seem to extract more meaning from a single case study than most experts believe they should. For example, it is clear that individuals learn from the process of acting as well as from the ultimate outcomes of the action. They will repeat decisions because of the pleasures of the process rather than because the outcomes were good. They learn from anticipations of consequences. They treat anticipations as though they were outcomes, so that high expectations often seem to have the same learning effect as successful outcomes.

Ingmar Björkman observed that the Finnish firms he observed tended to take a long time deciding to make their first overseas investment, worried about it, thought deeply about it, analyzed a lot of data. After they finally made the decision to invest, and long before they had any information as to whether the investment was a good one, they made several more of the same kind. Björkman attributed this to the sense of self that the decision makers had achieved: They were the kind of people who made such decisions, and they enjoyed making them.

The bridge between history and learning is interpretation, but the bridge between history and action is the development of rules. Rules encode history. They accumulate knowledge. Rules reflect experience. They reflect the peace treaties for organizational wars. They reflect the incremental refinement of practice. Because of their crucial importance to the study of organizations and learning in organizations, understanding the ways in which rules are evoked and applied is particularly important. Rules tell an actor what to do, but they rarely fit a situation precisely. As a result, there is considerable ambiguity in determining exactly which rule applies to a particular situation or exactly what any particular rule commands.

Rules encode history, and they change as a result of experience. Those changes make studies of the long-term dynamics of rules essential to a new behavioral theory of the firm. Martin Schulz and Xueguang Zhou, for example, have analyzed the historical development of rules in one organization in terms of hazard functions and event history analysis. The central questions are: If an organizational rule is modified at one time, does that change increase or decrease the chance of a subsequent change? And does it increase or decrease the amount of time before the next change? It is easy to imagine reasons why a change in a rule would decrease subsequent pressure for a change. It is also easy to imagine reasons why a change in a rule increases the likelihood of later changes. The latter case, for example, might be true of computer software, as in other systems characterized by high degrees of interdependence among constituent parts. In such cases, changes are likely to introduce more problems than they solve, so each correction that is made increases the probability of needing another correction later.

### Learning in an Ecology of Learners

The basic idea of ecological learning is that learning is embedded in a mosaic of learning: On the one hand, any one unit is learning simultaneously on several different dimensions, and those dimensions interact in a complex way. At the same time, any one organization is a collection of individuals, each of whom is learning, and their learnings interact. And any one organization is part of a community of organizations whose learning processes interact as well.

One of the more standard consequences of the ecological nature of learning is what has come to be called the "competency trap." Individuals and organizations learn from experience what strategies or technologies to use. But at the same time, they gain competence in the strategies and technologies they use. Suppose an individual or organization uses a strategy or technology and experiences favorable outcomes. This will lead to using the strategy or technology again. The more a particular strategy or technology is used, the more competent the individual or organization becomes in using it. As a result of becoming more competent at it, the likelihood of a favorable outcome increases, which in turn increases the likelihood of repeating the same strategy or technology and so on. Thus, the actor becomes very quickly firmly committed to a particular strategy or technology, which may or may not be the best. It is the best for the actor, given his competence at it, but he is likely to be trapped at an inferior technology or strategy by the positive feedback loop of his own competence. This kind of competency, or specialization, trap is one of the more common path-dependent suboptimalities of adaptive systems.

Another important aspect of the ecological character of learning concerns the network structure of contacts among actors. Organizations, and individuals in them, do not exist in isolation but form networks through which knowledge is exchanged and effects of action diffused. Organizations learn from the experience of others, imitate each other, or simply steal ideas from each other. This process of diffusion is mediated by professional networks, by educational institutions, and by personal contacts. It makes the development of cultures of ideas highly sensitive to the structure of the networks.

The networks are not simply communication systems but also are networks of causal effects. The actions of one organization affect the likelihood of actions by others. Competition and cooperation both feed on the network structure. One effect is what is usually called "network externalities," the way in which the return and learning from the use of one strategy, technology, or action depends on what strategy, technology, or action characterizes others. Communication technologies are the obvious case in cooperative networks; strategies are the obvious case in competitive networks. Within interactive networks, what is learned by one actor depends on what others are doing, which in turn depends on what others are learning, which depends on what the original actor is doing.

## The Intelligence of Learning

The lessons of history, embedded in rules, are disconnected from the history which generated them. Rules translate the lessons of history into prescriptions for action, but they ordinarily do not carry their historical justifications with them.

Appropriate behavior tends to become disjointed from the experiential learning that generated it. The fact that the experiential basis for rules is not retrievable makes the argument between classical conservatives—who believe that existing social rules have accumulated experience in an intelligent manner—and classical radicals—who believe that rational calculation is more intelligent than rules—a difficult argument to resolve.

One of the main claims for learning as a process is that it has elements of intelligence. In fact, this is really how we first approached learning in the theory of the firm. When ideas of consequential, analytical, rational action were made problematic as routes to intelligence by observations of the limits on rationality, learning appeared as a possible alternative route to intelligence that demands less heroic information assumptions. It is a useful idea and has stimulated considerable work that suggests that learning may often be intelligent but sometimes leads us astray.

At the outset, however, it should be observed that the meaning of "intelligence" is not well defined in this context. What does it mean to say a process is intelligent? In some general sense, it means that it leads to better outcomes. But if social welfare theory has taught us anything, it is that the notion of better outcomes is an obscure one when it involves complicated trade-offs across time, space, and social agents. Actions that lead to better outcomes in the short run do not necessarily lead to better outcomes in a longer run, and vice versa. What is good for one person is not necessarily good for another. What is good for an individual is not necessarily good for the organization of which he is a member. What is good for one organization may not be good for another or for the community of organizations as a system.

Studies of learning and other forms of adaptation may permit us to engineer changes, to affect the course of history without giving us much confidence that the outcomes we produce will be viewed, ultimately, as desirable ones. In standard biological evolution, we have known for a long time how to engineer species, with breeding and now with genetic engineering. What we do not know is whether any particular change we make will ultimately be a good or bad one.

Despite these difficulties, it is possible to say some things about learning as an instrument of intelligence. For the most part, what we can say emphasizes the limitations of learning from experience. Experience is ambiguous. As a result, it makes a poor teacher. There are sample design problems: Learners are dealing with small samples of poorly designed experiments. There are observational problems: The methods for observing history are poorly specified and excessively subjective. There are inference problems: The environments we try to understand are complicated, changing, and endogenous to our own actions.

When these problems are combined with human tendencies toward conserva-
tion of belief, experience tends to lead to social agreement about history much
more commonly than it does to a valid representation of history.

One typical example of a systematic error in experiential learning is the
degradation of performance that experience brings in a new employee. When
an organization acquires a new member, he or she will act on the basis of some
combination of educated beliefs and experience. The more experience the individual has, the greater the weight given to the lessons from that experience, as we
would expect. Thus, the employee gains two things from experience: knowledge
about the world and confidence in the experiential knowledge. Fairly frequently,
I think, the gains in confidence are more rapid than the gains in knowledge.
As a result, when individuals start accumulating experience in a new situation,
they gain confidence in the lessons of experience much more quickly than that
experience teaches them anything. The consequent substitution of experientially
learned "knowledge" for education knowledge leads to at least a short-run dec-
rement in performance.

Another example of problems in learning arises when actors are learning from
situations involving very low probability events of high consequence. Nuclear
safety is an example of such a situation. In a reasonably engineered nuclear fa-
cility, the likelihood of an accident is extremely low. But if it happens, it is likely
to be a disaster. In such a situation, most participants never experience the low
probability event. Participants who never experience the low probability event
tend to "learn" that it is less likely than it actually is. Therefore, experience creates a threat. The more experience people have in a high reliability system, the
more likely they are to underestimate the risk.

In the nuclear safety example, the very low probability event is a bad one.
There are also situations involving good low probability events of great consequence. Examples would be dramatic scientific discoveries or radical product
innovations. Most people in research and development laboratories never experience such events. Therefore, most people learn from direct experience that
the likelihood of such discoveries is lower than it actually is. The more experience people have in a rare discovery system, the more likely they are to underestimate the opportunities.

Some strategies have been suggested for coping with some of these problems
in experiential learning. One somewhat counterintuitive idea that arises in several forms is that a relatively slow rate of learning may frequently be more effective than a rapid rate. The problem with a rapid rate of learning is the higher
likelihood that it will lead to being trapped into a tight suboptimization by the

positive feedback that is typical of adaptation. Slow learning facilitates greater accumulation of information prior to commitment, with a lower chance of being trapped in inefficient behavior.

Other suggestions involve an improvement in the sample design of experience by minimizing the number of simultaneous changes and by increasing the scale of those changes. From this perspective at least, incrementalism is not particularly recommended. The problem with incrementalism from the point of view of learning is that the signal tends to be lost in the noise. If we act in a complicated world, in order to isolate the effects of our actions, we require relatively dramatic action along a single dimension, otherwise the effects are lost in the complexities of the situation.

There are other, less conventional, strategies that can be followed. Organizations can experience history more richly: They can consider a single case more intensely, rather than try to have additional cases. They can interpret experience in more ways: They can try to reduce measurement error rather than sampling error.

But the strategy that organizations seem more frequently to follow is to try to experience events that did not actually happen: They construct hypothetical histories. Michal Tamuz has studied the ways in which air traffic control systems in the United States gather information on near accidents, the accidents that almost happened but did not. It is, of course, a rather complicated thing to learn from accidents that did not happen, because it remains highly uncertain whether we should learn from such cases that what looked like a dangerous situation really was a safe one, or that what turned out to be a safe situation really was a dangerous one. As organizations (and historians) seek to construct hypothetical histories, they begin to tamper with one of the more important principles of classical theories of historical inference—the distinction between theory and evidence.

There are also some strategies for improving the capabilities for learning from others. Wesley Cohen and Daniel Levinthal, for example, argue that an organization wishing to use new discoveries by others must have command of some fairly fundamental knowledge.

Without this "absorptive capacity," it cannot imitate. Perhaps the most interesting feature of the Cohen and Levinthal model is the way it produces two stable industry equilibria. One equilibrium is characterized by low investments in R&D, a low rate of discovery, and a low rate of copying.

In this equilibrium there are no incentives for any firm to engage in R&D because the main payoff from R&D is not the return to one's own inventions

but the return from copying other people's inventions. Since no one is investing in R&D, there are no inventions to be copied, and no reason for any firm
to invest in R&D. The other equilibrium is characterized by high investment in
R&D, a high rate of discovery, and a high rate of copying. There is no incentive for any one firm to decrease investment in R&D, because the investment is
required to take advantage of the inventions that are produced within the industry. R&D is sustained not by the initial inventions it produces—which may
be too infrequent to justify the investment—but by the capabilities for utilizing
inventions it develops.

## Balancing Exploration and Exploitation

Lurking beneath many of these complications in the intelligence of learning is
an issue central to all adaptive theories: the balance between exploration and
exploitation. There are two kinds of activities that an organization can engage
in. One of them is exploitation, using what is already known, possibly improving on it, doing it more efficiently. The other activity is exploration, examining new possibilities, experimenting with things that are not known but might
become known.

Any kind of long-run adaptive or learning process requires a mix of exploitation and exploration. If the system engages in exploitation alone, it will find
itself trapped in some suboptimal state, failing to discover new directions or
to develop competence in them. If the system engages in exploration alone, it
never secures the advantages of its discoveries, never becomes good enough at
them to make them worthwhile.

It is extremely difficult—in general impossible—to specify the optimum balance between exploitation and exploration. That optimum involves trade-offs
across time and across space. Because returns to exploitation are distributed
across time in a different way from returns to exploration, the optimum mix
depends on the time horizon considered. Because the returns are distributed
differently among social groups or parts of an organization, the optimum mix
depends on the constituency of actors considered.

Not only is it difficult to specify the optimum, it is also difficult to sustain
a favorable balance. Adaptive systems appear to be dynamically unstable in
the neighborhood of the optimum mix. There are at least two fairly obvious
dynamics. A first dynamic is one in which exploitation tends to drive out exploration. Since the returns to exploitation tend to be closer in time and space
than returns to exploration, they tend to come to dominate. A second dynamic
is one in which exploration tends to drive out exploitation. When new things

are tried, they usually fail. Even if they are good ideas, they ordinarily require developing competence in them before they work well. When they fail, there is a tendency to abandon them and try something else—which, in turn, fails. The system runs from one new idea to another without success. These two dynamics—one leading to more exploitation, the other leading to more and more exploration—make it hard to maintain a reasonable balance.

Some empirical studies of the exploitation/exploration balance have focused on risk taking. Behavioral studies of risk taking have generally noted that the level of risk taking is not a trait of individuals or organizations but is situationally determined. That is to say, there appears to be relatively little reliable variation in risk taking due to stable properties of individuals or organizations. Rather, the differences in risk taking seem to be mainly the result of differences in the situations in which decision makers find themselves.

In particular, the level of risk taken seems to be related systematically to the relation between current performance and aspirations for that performance. This result is reminiscent of earlier treatments of bounded rationality. In discussions of bounded rationality and satisficing, it has been observed that many of the key features of search behavior stem from the fact that individuals have aspiration levels and make sharp distinctions between outcomes that are above and outcomes that are below the aspiration level. Some of the more interesting dynamics of bounded rationality come about because those aspirations are not fixed but change over time in response to experience.

A similar phenomenon is observed in learning. An experiential learning model requires some mechanism for assessing outcomes, for determining whether an outcome is good (and thus "reinforcing") or poor (and thus "extinguishing"). The aspiration level serves that function, and the adaptiveness of the aspiration level is extremely important in shaping the speed and direction of learning. If actors have high aspiration levels, they are likely to have experiences that they define as failures and thus lead them not to repeat the behavior. If aspirations are low, experiences are likely to lead to a repetition of the behavior. Thus, learning from experience becomes highly subjective, and what one individual learns from a particular environment may differ greatly from what another individual learns.

These characteristics of adaptive aspirations are carried over into studies of risk taking. Since the level of risk assumed seems to be affected by the relation between performance and aspirations, risk taking is affected by the process by which aspirations are changed in response to experience. Some models of risk taking indicate that the long-term survival of a community of risk takers can be affected by varying the rate of adaptation of aspiration levels.

## CONCLUSIONS

Much of what I have said can be summarized in two general observations: First, economic theories of the firm have been profoundly affected by behavioral observations of firms beginning in the 1950s and 1960s. To be sure, the central axiom of economics—the idea that behavior is driven by rational calculation—has been retained. Bounded rationality has been rationalized. Satisficing has been rationalized. Conflict has been rationalized. But the new microeconomics is radically different from the microeconomics of thirty or forty years ago. It is a microeconomics that embraces bounded rationality, conflict, and inefficient histories. It is a microeconomics that considers things such as rules and institutions and worries about learning. The rational axioms play a role similar to that played by Marxist assumptions in a Marxist society—something that must be recited rather than believed.

Second, learning processes have become more prominent in our thinking about firm behavior. Organizations use learning as a basis for changing behavior. In the course of making learning a more prominent feature of our thinking, we have discovered some rather complicated aspects of learning that deserve particular attention. Learning is not perfect. The outcomes of learning processes depend on the interactions among learners. History is path dependent, thus generally inefficient in discovering unique, stable outcomes. The pursuit of intelligence through learning is problematic, as is the concept of intelligence itself.

There is still some work to do. We are just beginning to understand how rules are created, modified, and eliminated, how institutions evolve. We need to understand how rules are transformed into action, and how rule following intertwines with other logics of action. For example, the argument that individuals and organizations follow rules is not an argument that consequences are never considered. Quite the contrary. They are considered, but their consideration enters as a set of constraints on the more fundamental logic of appropriateness. This reverses the usual formulation of classic decision theory in which actors are seen as acting consequentially (maximizing expected utility), subject to normative constraints. The newer perspective assumes that individuals follow normative rules of appropriateness, subject to some constraints of consequentiality.

As we look at how normative rules are translated into action in concrete situations, we see a rather subtle intertwining of several logics. The logic of appropriateness provides actors with a set of rules which tell them, more or less, what to do. But in order to determine which rule among several might be used, and what the precise meaning of the rule is in a particular situation, some consequential considerations are often invoked. And there are other kinds of logic:

The logic of congruence by which people imitate other people, asking "Is this what other people are doing in this situation?" And the logic of coincidence, sometimes called the garbage can theory of action, by which problems and solutions are mixed because of their simultaneity. In particular, it has been observed that actions often seem to be driven more by capabilities than by objectives. If I know how to do something, I will do it. It is not that I decide what I want to achieve and then build necessary capabilities. It is more that I decide what I want to achieve by contemplating what I know how to do.

All of this will lead us, I think, to a better understanding of rules, their development, and their utilization. It will also lead us to research on how path-dependent histories can be understood and managed, and to some clearer comprehensions of the ways in which individual and organizational actors are served by exploitation and exploration.

PART II

# EXPLORATIONS IN THE ROLE OF NOVELTY IN ORGANIZATIONAL ADAPTATION

*An Introductory Essay*

DANIEL LEVINTHAL

NOVELTY WOULD SEEM TO BE THE LIFEBLOOD of the process of organizational adaptation. Adaptation suggests change and the notion of change, in turn, suggests a shift to a new form or set of practices—not a return to the familiar. However, March notes a deep irony of adaptive processes: feedback driven learning mechanisms will generally shift attention, energy, and resources to the relatively familiar and established grounds of existing or closely related organizational practices. Actions that are most clearly associated with positive outcomes are most strongly reinforced and these associations are likely to occur with respect to actions that generate outcomes near in time and that engage and draw on the organization's existing capabilities.

This pathology of the process of organizational adaptation poses the question of how adaptive, learning entities may sustain elements of novelty as they evolve in order to sustain their long-run viability and to identify initiatives that may be of value that are not local in a temporal sense or with respect to the organization's existing capabilities. An important related, and somewhat understudied, question is what constitutes the metric of "localness." Intelligent action with respect to novel initiatives, unless informed by oracles or divine inspiration, must still draw on some experiential basis. For instance, analogical reasoning (Gavetti, Levinthal, and Rivkin, 2005), where the experience base is outside the current context, or population learning (Miner and Haunschild, 1995), where the experience base is outside the focal organization, are mechanisms of experiential learning that use past experience to guide an organization into novel domains.

Differential rewards, whether survival rates among organizations or payoffs to individual organizational actors, acknowledge apparent success. What actions, in turn, are likely to yield apparent success? These will tend to be actions involving initiatives with which the organization has some existing level of competence. They are also likely to be actions with which the organization has some familiarity; a random choice of action is unlikely, on average, to compare favorably with actions that have survived either a prior selection process or have been identified as attractive through prior experience. Apparent success also requires that the link between action and observed outcome be made by participants. As a result, initiatives that set the stage for subsequent success are likely to be undervalued, and actions that yield favorable immediate outcomes but possibly adverse long-run consequences (e.g., pushing sales to the current quarter, reducing employee benefits, rushing products to market) tend to be overvalued.

Thus, mechanisms that differentially reward organizations and individual actions within them will tend to promote initiatives that are close to the organization's experience base. In that sense, learning processes can be said to be myopic (Levinthal and March, 1993). There is an important exception to this tendency. Differential rewards that only reward extreme outliers, winner-take-all reward schemes or survival of only the fittest and not merely the fitter, will tend to engender risk taking and, as a consequence, novelty. Operating in the zone of the familiar and of existing competence is likely to yield better than average outcomes, but less assuredly extreme positive outcomes. Consider the stylized example of a gambling house offering games of chance with different odds of success. An even money bet offers a good chance of walking out of the gambling house whole, while a 100–1 shot is likely to yield an empty wallet but offers a small chance at substantial wealth.

Indeed, while feedback-driven learning processes may tend to engender a high degree of conservatism, business press accounts of extreme success stories, such as the college dropout who now heads a wildly successful enterprise, provide encouragement for dramatic risk taking and the pursuit of novelty. Bill Gates, Steve Jobs, and Michael Dell may not be representative of the fates of college dropouts, but they are surely among the most well known of college dropouts.

Modern organizational theorists have become quite sensitive to the possible dangers of drawing inferences about the attractiveness of an action (dropping out of school to pursue an entrepreneurial initiative; betting the company on a single high-risk initiative) based only on the successful experiences associated with the practice. This has become known as the sample selection problem and both statistical techniques and data sampling strategies have been devised to address this danger.

Naive social scientists, including the business press and potential entrepreneurs, are less likely to correct for this bias. Attributes associated with a subpopulation of wildly successful companies may be irrelevant to their success, and hence may be a possible basis of superstitious learning. For instance, successful companies may offer similar platitudes in their mission statement, but there may be no causal link between these statements and the companies' success and unsuccessful companies may be equally, or even more likely to offer such statements. Alternatively, these attributes may be associated with initiatives that generate tremendous variability in possible outcomes, though not attractive expected values. In this sense, the experience base of a set of highly skewed success stories provides encouragement for risk taking and novelty.

## RECONCEPTUALIZING EXPLORATION:
## DOING VERSUS SEEING[1]

Discussions of the lack of novelty presuppose a definition of what constitutes novelty. Clearly actions that are not in the organization's existing repertoire are reasonably viewed as being novel. But how is an organization or an individual actor to choose among the vast sea of novel acts, should the motivation to do so present itself. In analytical treatments of this problem, the norm has been to conceive of the identification of novel acts as akin to pulling balls blindly from an urn.

While images of "long jumps" or "drawing from urns" may capture mathematical representations of exploratory activities, they serve not only as stylized but also arguably misleading suggestions of actual exploratory processes. Consider one of the paradigmatic examples of exploratory activity: 3M's fabled policy of allowing scientists to allocate 15 percent of their time and resources according to their individual discretion. This policy has been identified as an important example of slack search. While the policy clearly illustrates the idea of slack search, we need to be more careful in how we interpret exactly what this means.

The policy provides "slack" in the sense that the scientist's efforts are not required to be evaluated according to the performance benchmarks of any of the firm's existing initiatives. However, it also important to note what these scientists are not doing. They are not boating on Lake Superior, nor are they sitting idle in their offices and labs 15 percent of the time waiting for lightening to strike. Rather, these engineers and scientists are working to solve particular puzzles and problems, testing various hunches and hypotheses. The critical feature of these activities is that these initiatives are not undirected but rather that they are "other" directed where the modifier "other" connotes the notion that the goals and objectives of these discretionary activities need not correspond to the current objectives of the firm. These researchers are pursuing dimensions of progress that, while possibly not orthogonal to the organization's performance objectives, may not be highly collinear with them. However, these efforts do not correspond to "spinning one's wheels." Rather, these efforts correspond to the actor's attempting to climb dimensions of performance not fully sanctioned or recognized by the broader organization.

From the perspective of the entrepreneurial scientist his or her colleagues are flatlanders (Abbott, 1884).[2] They are living on the lower-dimensional surface of the officially sanctioned goals of the organization and are sensitive to indicators of progress only on this plane. While the entrepreneur is engaged in highly directed activity, these efforts push him or her further along a performance dimension that is largely unseen or unvalued by those around them. If the entrepreneur is to validate these efforts, he must, in turn, find a way to validate this novel dimension of performance. Of course, individuals may perceive possible dimensions of performance that are unlikely ever to have any mapping to any pragmatic "real-world" flat land. Poets and dreamers may climb "castles in the sky" or "tilt at windmills."

Thus, an important organizational challenge remains: The firm must ultimately sort through initiatives that pursue novel but potentially pragmatic dimensions, and those that may only have relevance in terms of the dimension that is forming the basis of exploration. Thus, theologians may make progress on the question of how many angels may reside on the head of a pin and, in its own terms, there can be meaningful progress on this agenda. However, that agenda is unlikely to cast shadows on other goals or dimension of progress. Further, there can be substantial delay in the forming of such shadows. For instance, the question of measuring the magnetic resonance of the atom was an interesting question in physics in the late 1940s (Bloch, Levinthal, and Packard, 1947) and the bases for awarding of a Nobel Prize to Felix Bloch in 1952. It was not until many decades later that the solution to this puzzle in physics cast a "shadow" on the quest for better diagnostic images of soft tissues, resulting in the development of nuclear magnetic resonance (NMR) devices. However, again, it is important to note that Felix Bloch and his students where very much engaged in goal-directed, problem-solving research, not random walks.

The problem remains to clarify how organizations distinguish those initiatives that correspond to climbing toward "castles in the sky" from those that may be unearthing promising new veins of technological progress and product initiatives. Inspiration and lunacy, as March has noted, are not ex-ante so clearly distinguishable. The challenge for the entrepreneur, whether of the "corporate" or "start-up" variety is to provide some validation for the allocation of resources to his or her initiative beyond what discretionary slack (perhaps 15 percent of their workday in the former case and the carrying capacity of their credit card debt in the latter) provides. In the corporate context, one important mechanism is to reframe a nonconforming initiative in a way that fits within the official strategy, that is, to identify ways in which progress along the 'other' dimension results in a projection of progress along the legitimated dimensions. Burgelman's (1991) discussion of Intel's venture into reduced instruction set computing (RISC) is a classic example. The venture required the allocation of precious development resources away from the legitimated approach of complex instruction set computing (CISC). The reallocation was accomplished by justifying the RISC effort as a complementary project of developing a math coprocessor to the core CISC processor and thereby hiding its true nature as a substitute platform for CISC. More generally, the garbage can nature of organizational decision-making processes (Cohen, March, and Olsen, 1972)—which results in a potentially loose coupling of solutions, problems, and decision contexts—provides rich opportunities for such justification efforts.

Such subterfuge is required when an initiative is targeting illegitimate dimensions because, as in the Flatland tale, describing the existence of a new dimension requires a language and a perspective that is unavailable to participants before they are presented with the definitive, visceral proof of the validity of the new perspective. It is only after a Flatlander is confronted with the reality, rather than the promise, of the new dimension that they find the justification to adjust their preexisting map of reality.

## POINTS OF RECONCILIATION

While, as noted, there is an inherent tension between the novel and routine, there are important, and often overlooked, respects with which these attributes are rendered consonant with one another.

### Routinization and Novelty

Routinization and novelty are naturally viewed as opposed constructs. However, theories of search, and process perspectives on firms more generally, offer an important sense in which the attributes may be tightly linked. An important fact, a fact that much of the recent discussion of so-called dynamic capabilities in the strategy literature obscures, is that relatively stable and enduring processes may generate distinct and arguably novel products. Intel, as it proceeds along a trajectory of developing and building smaller, more powerful, and cheaper microprocessors, is leveraging and exploiting existing capabilities and search, or problem-solving, heuristics. At the same time, each new generation of microprocessor is a remarkable and innovative engineering feat. An important point made in the early work on the resource view of the firm is that there is not a one-to-one mapping from a firm's capability set to its product (or service) array. A "little d" notion of dynamic capabilities associated with novel products and services need not be at odds with relatively fixed and exploitive set of routine actions. Of course, a "big D" notion of dynamic capabilities that connotes a shift in a firm's capability set, for instance the move from a chemical base of scientific discovery in pharmaceuticals to the manipulation of large molecules and genetic engineering, does pose a tension between a quest for novelty and the leveraging of existing capabilities.

A process perspective on the question of novelty poses further possible consistencies between routinization and novelty. Consider the set of learning heuristics associated with Kanban and the Toyota Production System more generally. These processes of measurement—the elimination of slack at adjacent stages of production or norms of local autonomy for local experimentation—are relatively constant. However, the particular production processes that they generate are continually changing, yielding ever-increasing productivity and reliability.

In the same vein, consider other administrative arrangements, 3M's or Google's rules providing some degree of slack for researcher-defined initiatives, or even structural properties such as a commitment to a decentralized organizational form, which (until recent years) had been a hallmark property of Hewlett-Packard. These administrative arrangements are enduring properties of these organizations. Presumably, over time, the organization refines the manner in which they manage these particular practices. Such refinements of existing practices could reasonably be viewed as conservative and exploitive; however, the outcomes of these relatively fixed processes may offer tremendous elements of novelty.

## Recombinations

While lay accounts of evolutionary dynamics, including many of those in the management literature, point to the role of mutations in generating novelty into an evolutionary system, more sophisticated accounts in the biology literature note the important role of recombination. A fundamental fact about evolution for biologists is why we observe the predominance of sexual reproduction in higher order, multicellular creatures. Asexual reproduction is a viable option and indeed an option observed in a large number of life forms. The important property of sexual reproduction, quite apart from its possible appeal to the participants, is that it offers a conservative, in some sense exploitive, mechanism to introduce a significant degree of novelty in the gene pool. Random change via mutation is unlikely to offer a beneficial change in the genetic structure of the recipient. Macromutations, random change over a significant segment of the genetic code, is even more unlikely to be salutary. In contrast, recombination through sexual reproduction offers as building blocks well working prototypes from the two parties. The ensuing changes need not be local, but lack the unstructured random quality of a macromutation.

In the organizational context, we observe at least loose analogues of recombinatoric change. The merger of two organizations, the transfer of one individual familiar with a set of practices to a new organizational context, the reorganization of organizational subunits all offer the prospect of some recombinatoric change. In the context of technological change, it is well recognized that an important property of modular designs and architectures is that they offer the possibility of mixing and matching of component elements, which not only allows for a high level of variety of overall systems at a point in time but also allows for dramatic rates of change and technological progress as well.

Indeed, Schumpeter's classic statement of the fundamental forms of entrepreneurial initiative hinges on the notion of recombination. He argues that entrepreneurs engage in making novel linkages of existing technologies, linking existing technologies to new markets, or providing a link of existing means of production or marketing to new contexts. Building on the last of these linkages, entrepreneurs often reason by analogy and attempt to conceive of business plans to be the "Dell" of industry x or to export the retail concept of a "category killer" from one domain to another (Gavetti et al., 2005).

## CONCLUSION

A basic irony of the dynamics of experiential learning is their tendency to focus attention and energy on the familiar and the relatively immediate. However, while there is no reason to believe that organizations will achieve some optimal mix of exploration and exploitation, it is plausible that practices emerge to counter the myopic tendencies of the direct feedback of experiential learning. As a further irony, while a forward-looking calculus of consequential reasoning is typically heralded on the basis of the use of normatively favored tools of rationality, such technologies of choice are important mechanisms by which novel, not necessarily profitable or wise, actions are justified. Underlying consequential reasoning, beneath the trappings of spreadsheets and projected cash flows, is faith and belief in a particular future. As a consequence, rational decision making in complex and highly uncertain worlds can arguably serve as technologies of foolishness providing justifications for exploratory initiatives that only faith and scenario planning could justify. Of course, boundedly rational expressions of rational choice behavior are also capable of editing out positive ramifications of initiatives across spheres of the organization or temporal boundaries and thereby reject potentially valuable exploratory behavior.

As March has argued, the pursuit of intelligent action on the part of organizations is just that, a pursuit, and any particular mechanism, whether it be feedback-driven learning or an explicit calculus of consequential actions, is a process whose possibly beneficial or less benign consequences must be analyzed and not assumed. Learning is a fundamental property of adaptive entities. That its consequences are not entirely benign should not be regarded as a surprise or a disappointment, but rather a puzzle to be cherished and explored.

## NOTES

1. This section draws from Adner and Levinthal (*Strategic Entrepreneurship Journal*, forthcoming), "Doing versus seeing: Acts of exploitation and observations of exploration."

2. In Abbott's (1884) allegorical tale a stranger from "Spaceland" (a world that recognizes three dimensions) attempts to convince an inhabitant of "Flatland" (a world that only recognizes two dimensions) of the existence of a third dimension that he refers to as height. Discovering that it is impossible to discuss meaningfully the existence of the third dimension using the Flatland's language and metrics (which, of course, have no spatial constructs that extend beyond length and width), the Spacelander's only way to convince the Flatlander of the validity of the third dimension is to demonstrate its existence by lifting "up." Upon viewing Flatland from this raised position, in which he could observe both the two dimensions of the plane, as well as witness the new perspective of these that was offered by the "raised" position, the Flatlander becomes convinced of the existence and potential offered by the new dimension. (When the Flatlander returns and tries to convince others of his world about the existence of height, but without the ability to demonstrate its existence by raising them above the plane, he is branded a lunatic and sent off to isolated confinement.)

## REFERENCES

Abbott, E. 1884. *Flatland: A Romance of Many Dimensions*. Seely & Co: London, UK.

Adner, R. and D. Levinthal. Forthcoming. Doing versus seeing: Acts of exploitation and observations of exploration. *Strategic Entrepreneurship Journal*.

Bloch, F., E. C. Levinthal, and M. E. Packard. 1947. Relative nuclear moments of H1 and H1. *Physics Review*, 72, 1125–1126.

Burgelman, R. 1991. Intraorganizational ecology of strategy making and organizational adaptation: Theory and field research. *Organization Science*, 2, 239–262.

Cohen, M. D., J. G. March, and J. G. Olsen. 1972. A garbage can model of organizational choice. *Administrative Science Quarterly*, 17(1), 1–25

Gavetti, G., D. Levinthal, and J. Rivkin. 2005. Strategy-making in novel and complex worlds: The power of analogy. *Strategic Management Journal*, 26, 691–712.

Levinthal, D. and J. March. 1993. The myopia of learning. *Strategic Management Journal*, 14, 95–112.

Miner, A. and P. Haunschild. 1995. Population level learning in L. L. Cummings and B. M. Staw (eds.), *Research in Organizational Behavior*, Greenwich, CT: JAI Press, 115–166.

# CHAPTER 5

# Understanding Organizational Adaptation

JAMES G. MARCH

Recent enthusiasms have emphasized particularly ideas of "learning organizations," calling attention both to the ways organizations learn and to the possibilities for improving organizational intelligence through increasing the rate and precision of learning. These enthusiasms have often encouraged the too easy assumption that learning processes necessarily lead to organizational improvement. The usefulness of learning as an instrument of organizational intelligence has to be demonstrated, not assumed. Adaptive processes such as learning are not guaranteed to reach or sustain a global maximum on an outcome surface. In order for proposals for "learning organizations" to be more than vague wishes for improvement, learning must be defined in terms of some specific process and the conditions under which that process does or does not lead to improvement must be established.

This essay is built around six simple propositions, a kind of catechism for consideration of learning as an instrument of intelligence.

SÁNDOR MÁRAI'S brilliant short novel translated into English under the title *Embers* (Márai 2002) tells the story of a friendship elaborated and enriched by experiences together, broken through treachery and cowardice, and fossilised by hate into an obsession. It is a story of one man who retreats to the country, another who retreats to seclusion, and a woman who retreats to death. It is a story of passion that destroys three lives while giving them meaning. It is a story of a man tormented not by doubt but by certainty. Most of all, it is a story of self-destructive adaptation, the shriveling of a soul through the refinement of focused knowledge.

Márai tells the story through his interlocutor, the General, a man who is probably incapable of understanding, and certainly indifferent to, the dynamics of personal history that have produced the tragedies and triumphs that define

This essay was given as a talk at the Budapest University of Economic Sciences and Public Administration on April 2, 2003, on the occasion of conferring an honorary doctorate on the author, and appeared in *Society and Economy*, 25 (2003), 1–10. The essay is based on research supported by the Spencer Foundation.

his life. We, the readers, however, can see how great passions and great obsessions are unfortunate residues of everyday efforts to comprehend incomprehensible experience. Dramas of pain and pretense are produced by ordinary people adapting to ordinary events in ordinary ways.

The Márai novel is a caution. It is a warning about the dangers of a compulsion for interpreting history and of excessive emphasis on learning from experience. It is a caution that has echoes in recent work on organizations. Organizations evolve over time in response to experience. They change their structures, procedures, rules, practices, and rhetorics. The processes by which organizations change include rational processes of consequential choice, political processes of negotiation among conflicting interests, learning processes of reaction to experience or appropriating the knowledge of others, and selection processes of differential reproduction and survival. These various processes of change are both frames for interpreting organizational change and instruments for improving organizational intelligence.

Recent enthusiasms have emphasized particularly ideas of "learning organizations," calling attention both to the ways organizations learn and to the possibilities for improving organizational intelligence through increasing the rate and precision of learning.

These enthusiasms have often encouraged the too easy assumption that learning processes necessarily lead to organizational improvement. The usefulness of learning as an instrument of organizational intelligence has to be demonstrated, not assumed. Adaptive processes such as learning are not guaranteed to reach or sustain a global maximum on an outcome surface. In order for proposals for "learning organizations" to be more than vague wishes for improvement, learning must be defined in terms of some specific process and the conditions under which that process does or does not lead to improvement must be established.

This essay is built around six simple propositions, a kind of catechism for consideration of learning as an instrument of intelligence.

## CONFUSIONS OF LEARNING

PROPOSITION 1: *Experience can be a poor teacher, not only because of limitations of human cognition and the complexity of history but also because adaptive processes are subject to systematic error.*

There are good reasons for hesitation in embracing an unconditional zeal for learning. A recent book on the adaptation of rules puts it this way:

. . . learning is an indispensable tool for organizational intelligence, but it is also an unreliable tool. Learning is hampered by errors in interpreting history, by its own myopia, by its tendency to eliminate the variation that it requires, and by the intricate relations among different levels of a nested and conflictual learning system. Rules, as instruments of learning, encapsulate all of these features. They record and reinforce erroneous interpretations of experience. They adapt locally in time and space to the detriment of the more distant. They accumulate competence in ways that reduce experimentation. And they develop with local autonomy sufficient to assure inconsistencies and conflict. (March et al. 2000: 199)

Understanding organizational adaptation involves examining these problems and dilemmas.

## Exploitation and Exploration

PROPOSITION 2: *A fundamental requirement for intelligent adaptation is to maintain a balance between the exploitation of things already known and the exploration of things that might come to be known.*

This enduring problem of adaptation occurs in slightly different forms in different adaptive processes—rational choice, learning from experience, learning from others, and competitive selection. It is the starting point for a theory of adaptation.

Consider a classic problem in rational choice, the so-called "bandit" problem. In simple bandit problems we imagine a person choosing between two alternatives, each of which offers returns that are draws from an unknown probability distribution. A decision maker who wants to maximize expected return would put all of his investment into the alternative offering the highest expected value if he knew which one did, but he does not know. Consequently, he must use some of his investment to explore the outcome distribution. Of course, he does not want to spend too many resources exploring the two alternatives because he wants to invest as much as possible in the better alternative. On the other hand, he does not want to invest all of his resources in the alternative that appears to be better unless he is certain that it is the better alternative.

The bandit problem is to specify an optimal strategy for dividing resources between investing in the apparently best alternative and exploring other alternatives on the chance they might prove to be better. The basic problem can be made more realistic as a portrayal of real decision problems, if we generalize to cases involving $n$ alternatives, to cases in which new alternatives may appear, and to cases in which the payoff distributions may be changing (either exogenously or endogenously).

The results in the study of bandit problems fill a very large literature. Various heuristics to deal with the problem have been generated, but general solutions to the optimality question exist only in the simplest situations. Determining optimal strategies in bandit problems is, indeed, a difficult thing, although ordinary human beings often act in bandit situations.

The bandit problem is a metaphor for the general problem of balancing exploitation and exploration, a problem that lies at the heart of adaptation. In learning from experience, it is the problem of balancing the exercise of old competencies and the development of new ones. In learning from others, it is the problem of balancing seeking knowledge from established sources and experimenting with new ones. In selection, it is the problem of balancing tightening competitive pressures to eliminate the less successful and encouraging new variations. Balancing exploitation and exploration is involved in balancing unity and diversity, just as in balancing competence and imagination, or in balancing reliability and risk.

It is clear that a strategy of exploitation without exploration is a route to obsolescence. It is equally clear that a strategy of exploration without exploitation is a route to elimination. But it is not clear where the optimum lies between those two extremes. The problem is partly one of ignorance about the distribution of costs and benefits, but it is only partly that. A deeper problem is that specifying the optimum requires comparing costs and returns across time and space.

An exploitation/exploration balance that is good in the short run is likely not to be good in the long run. And a balance that is good for the individual actor is likely not to be good in the long run for the community of actors. Thus, although we cannot specify the optimum balance, we know that that optimum depends on the time and space perspective taken. More specifically, the longer the time horizon and the broader the space horizon, in general, the more the optimum moves toward exploration.

## BIAS IN FAVOR OF EXPLOITATION

PROPOSITION 3: *Because returns to exploitation are systematically more certain, sooner, and closer than are the returns to exploration, exploitation has a fairly general advantage within adaptive processes.*

Although it is not possible to specify the optimal balance between exploitation and exploration, we can be reasonably confident that organizations usually give greater attention to exploitation and less attention to exploration than would be optimal, that is, adaptive processes are biased.

Adaptive processes in organizations are implicitly local in their time and space perspectives. The main mechanism of organizational choice, learning, and selection are all local. Adaptive processes give a favored position to alternatives whose benefits are local in time and space and whose costs are distant in time and space. Alternatives with distant benefits and local costs are disadvantaged.

This feature of adaptive processes is well known. It leads to substantial literature on the difficulties of imposing self-control (offsetting current costs with future benefits) and altruism (offsetting individual costs with community benefits) in a system of rational choice; on the learning difficulty in persisting in an alternative that does poorly in local feedback; and on the ways in which short-run selection pressures eliminate alternatives that would be particularly fit in a longer run.

For example, one of the classical problems of democracy involves matching the current democratic constituency with the long-run interests that will develop in a society. Who cares about the long run? Who cares about the larger political system? How in a democratic system do we represent the unborn? Or the interests that are affected but are domiciled outside the political boundaries?

The bias against distant time and space is also a bias against exploration. The benefits of exploitation are systematically more certain and nearer in time and space than are the benefits of exploration. Conversely, the costs of exploration are systematically more certain and nearer in time and space than are the costs of exploitation.

This feature of adaptive processes depends substantially on the sequential sampling character of organizational adaptation. Actions that appear to be locally successful tend to be reproduced; actions that appear to be locally unsuccessful tend not to be reproduced. Most of the positive consequences of adaptation stem from this differential reproduction of actions associated with successes. For example, experience eliminates "losers" at a faster rate than "winners." This sampling is biased. It leads, for example, to underestimation of the risks of disaster by airline pilots, operators of nuclear facilities, and managers who are promoted to higher ranks in an hierarchical organization.

The problem is compounded by practice effects. If performance is a product of the potential of an alternative and the competence of an operator, and competence is a function of experience, organizations are vulnerable to two kinds of traps. The first can be called a failure trap and is an example of a situation in which exploration actually drives out exploitation. Inexperience leads to failure which leads to changing alternatives which leads to failure again, an endless cycle of failure and trying new things. The organization fails to gain enough experience to become competent at anything. The pursuit of novelty (exploration) drives out competence, thus makes adaptation more difficult in the long run. The second trap is probably more common. It is a success or competency trap. Success at an alternative leads to repeating it. The additional experience increases competence and increases the likelihood of success. Over time, however, the organization becomes so competent at a current alternative that it is difficult for an adaptive process to switch to another alternative, even to one with greater potential. The pursuit of efficiency (exploitation) has driven out exploration, thus made adaptation more difficult in the long run.

By not reproducing actions that have been associated with failures, adaptive processes are likely not to correct mistaken local impressions. And therein lies a major difficulty with learning and selection as instruments of intelligence. Three kinds of actions are particularly troublesome in this respect. The first is action that involves a new technology or idea. New things characteristically require development and practice in order to achieve their potential. Early local feedback is likely to be negative. Adaptive organizations are likely not to repeat the action, thus failing to accumulate the competence and experience that would reveal the true value of the action. The second is risky action that involves a small chance of a very good, but a large chance of a mediocre return. Once again early local feedback is likely to be negative, and the failure to repeat the action leads most such organizations not to discover the true potential of the action. The third is action that has good consequences for the organization as a whole but poor consequences for the part of the organization executing the action. Local negative feedback is likely to extinguish the action before its more distant positive consequences can be realised.

Adaptive processes are self-destructive in the sense that they tend to reject the new ideas that are critical to exploration. The reasons are not mysterious. Most new ideas are bad ones, and particularly bad in the temporal and spatial neighborhood. It is impossible to distinguish good new ideas from bad new ideas. The more deviant the idea the more likely it is to be rejected, and the greater its value if it turns out to be right. In particular, knowledge tends to discriminate (sensibly) against new ideas, and adaptive systems have difficulties in sustaining new ideas long enough to determine their value—if they have any.

These problems are not particularly due to cognitive limitations of human beings. They are, for the most past, structural limitations of adaptive processes. They are accentuated by increasing the rate and precision of adaptation, thus by pressures toward local efficiency. The processes of adaptation will not reliably locate global optima.

## ALTRUISM AND SELF-CONTROL

PROPOSITION 4: *In order to compensate for the adaptive bias against exploration, it is generally necessary to stimulate altruism (the sacrifice of local advantage for global advantage) and self-control (the sacrifice of immediate advantage for long-run advantage).*

The adaptive bias against exploration stems in large part from the myopia of adaptive processes. They attend more to outcomes that are local in time and space than to ones that occur at some distance. The bias is well known from ordinary experience. When dealing with children or students, it is often necessary to encourage "self-control" to protect adaptation from short-run feedback, or selection pressure in order to support longer-run adaptation. When dealing with soldiers or sales agents, it is often necessary to encourage "altruism," to protect adaptation from local feedback or selection pressure in order to favor system-wide adaptation.

An organization that is conscious of the myopic bias against exploration may seek to compensate for that bias by redefining the consequences of action or the obligations of key identities. The first tries to increase the exploration rate and patience with new ideas by making exploration more rational. The second tries to increase the exploration rate and patience with new ideas by making exploration an obligation of personal or social identities.

The strategy of changing incentives is a familiar one in the modern era. It is generally understood that the exploration rate can be increased by improving the immediate, local returns for "wild ideas" that turn out to be right and by providing insurance protection for wild ideas that turn out poorly. Such awareness is the basis of many strategies for tying incentives to success and providing bankruptcy protection. Unfortunately, the strategy of providing large rewards for ideas that ultimately prove exceptionally valuable suffers from its dependence on results that are often quite distant in time and space. Since adaptation responds to local feedback, distant consequences must be both estimated and given salience at the time of learning.

The strategy of building identities that demand exploration is also familiar. It is not hard to imagine that the identity of a "fighter pilot," a "revolutionary," or an "entrepreneur" supports risk taking that exploration involves. The willingness to take risks is not tied to expectations of consequences but to the understanding of what it means to embrace a particular identity. Toward that end, organizations create subcultures and roles with clear risk-taking (or risk-avoiding) expectations. These identities serve to shift attention from the consequences of an action to its consistency with an accepted identity.

Such conscious attempts to modify the exploration rate are part of a larger picture that includes several factors which are generally less deliberate but may be subject to some conscious management. Organizations and the people in them exhibit risk preferences that vary depending on the relation between their past successes and failures relative to an aspiration level and to a survival point. The variation is relatively complex, depending on which reference point is considered, the extent to which the reference points are themselves adapting to past experience or the experience of others, and differences in the rate of adaptation to failure and success.

Moreover, for a consequential actor, the exploration of an alternative depends on estimates of the expected consequences, and erroneous estimation of risk is common. In particular, accurate estimations of risk are inhibited by the differential reporting of successes and failures, through illusions of efficacy that lead to the attribution of success to skill rather than luck and thus the underestimation of risk by successful actors, and by biases in the transfer of knowledge from experienced actors to new ones. Organizations contribute systematically to such phenomena through hierarchical promotion systems, through buffering parts of the organization from external and internal knowledge, and by slowing learning through buffers on feedback stemming from ideology, imagination, fashions in action, and social legitimacy.

Perhaps the greatest problem for sustaining exploration is the way in which adaptation encourages patience with old ideas and impatience with new ones. If an organization is to escape the traps of learning, it needs to be impatient with old ideas, which tend to be relatively good on average, but patient with new ideas, which tend to be relatively poor on average. The central problem is that feedback on exploration is likely to be negative; the central strategy is to shield exploration from that feedback. Organizations shield exploration by creating interpretations of negative feedback that make it appear positive. They interpret failure as success. They embrace models or ideologies that cannot be disconfirmed. They encourage the hubris of leaders. They create pressures to conceal failures and segregate subunits so they cannot learn from one another.

Organizations can also try to change the bias against exploration by trying to change time horizons. Typically, the stresses of management lead to shortening time horizons, especially through an emphasis on short-run efficiencies and accountability, through tying incentives tightly to immediately measurable outcomes. The positive consequences obtained through such measures have to be weighed against their negative effects on exploratory activity, and organizations sometimes seek ways of extending horizons. A long forward time perspective is linked to a connection to the past, to the idea of a history that extends into the distant past and therefore into the distant future. Thus, it is linked to enduring social establishments—families, communities, and institutions.

Alternatively, it has been suggested that ideas of organizational adaptation should accept the basic fact that individual organizations will necessarily be myopic, and that their adaptation will respond to things that are close in time and space. From this perspective, established organizations will always specialise in exploitation, in becoming more efficient in using what they already know. Such organizations will become dominant in the short run, but will gradually become obsolescent and fail in the long run.

New organizations, in this perspective, will provide the only exploration. Most new organizations will fail. Most new ideas are bad ones. However, a few will succeed in discovering a new product or process. At that point, they stop exploring and start exploiting; but they have provided innovation for the population of organizations. This adaptive system of disposable organizations has some attractions, but a system built on semi-permanent organizations cannot be quickly overturned without major problems. Moreover, a system of disposable organizations works only if there is a steady flow of new organizations that are exploring new options.

## NO FREE LUNCH

PROPOSITION 5: *Exploration can be increased through stimulating altruism and self-control, but the resulting increase in the number and persistence of good new ideas is accompanied by an unavoidable increase in the number and persistence of bad new ideas.*

Exploration is necessary, but it is costly, and increasing exploration through altruism or self-control increases the costs. This would not be true if it were possible to distinguish good new ideas from bad ones with some validity. In practice, it is not possible. When knowledge filters the flow of ideas, it eliminates novelty, as it should at least on an actuarial basis. And when it does so, it eliminates not only the disastrous crazy ideas, but also the brilliant ones.

There is no magic solution to this dilemma. Great new ideas are crazy from the point of view of established knowledge, but only a tiny fraction of crazy new ideas will prove to be great ones, and usually only after some period of time.

Although much effort has gone into discovering reliable routes to creativity and to making the early identification of good ideas feasible, most of that effort has been unrewarding. We can increase or decrease the rate of creation and persistence in new ideas; but any reduction in the creation of and persistence in *bad* new ideas also reduces the creation and persistence in *good* new ideas. And any increase in the creation and persistence in *good* new ideas also increases the creation and persistence in *bad* new ideas.

## LIMITS TO ADAPTATION

PROPOSITION 6: *The first step toward understanding organizational adaptation involves recognising that adaptiveness will sometimes solve problems and sometimes create them; and slow, imprecise adaptation is often better than fast, precise adaptation, particularly in the long run.*

Recent enthusiasms for organizational change emphasize the possibility of creating organizations that learn effectively and have proclaimed the importance of making organizations learn more rapidly and more precisely. The proclamations may seem obvious, but they are actually misleading.

There are structural problems that cause confusion and mistakes, as well as intractable problems of balancing exploitation and exploration. An organization can increase exploitation and persistence by various means, but thereby it also increases the risk of becoming obsolescent. An organization can increase exploration by various means, but thereby it also increases the risk of being stupid. An organization can try to make the trade-offs intelligently, but intelligence involves improbable calculations including some that depend critically on intertemporal and interpersonal comparisons of utility.

Enthusiasts for learning organizations have to recognise that although adaptation is a powerful instrument of intelligence in organizations, there is no magic.

## REFERENCES

Márai, S. 2002. *Embers* (*A gyertyák csonkig égnek,* Budapest, 1942), translated by Carol Brown Janeway. New York: Vintage.

March, J. G., Schulz, M., and Zhou, X. 2000. *The Dynamics of Rules: Change in Written Organizational Codes.* Stanford, CA: Stanford University Press.

CHAPTER 6

# Adaptation as Information Restriction

## *The Hot Stove Effect*

JERKER DENRELL AND JAMES G. MARCH

Individuals and social systems are often portrayed as risk averse and resistant to change. Such propensities are characteristically attributed to individual, organizational, and cultural traits such as risk aversion, uncertainty avoidance, discounting, and an unwillingness to change. This paper explores an alternative interpretation of such phenomena. We show how the reproduction of successful actions inherent in adaptive processes, such as learning and competitive selection and reproduction, results in a bias against alternatives that initially may appear to be worse than they actually are. In particular, learning and selection are biased against both risky and novel alternatives. Because the biases are products of the tendency to reproduce success that is inherent in the sequential sampling of adaptation, they are reduced whenever the reproduction of success is attenuated. In particular, when adaptation is slowed, made imprecise, or recalled less reliably, the propensity to engage in risky and new activities is increased. These protections against the error of rejecting potentially good alternatives on inadequate experiential evidence are costly, however. They increase the likelihood of persisting with alternatives that are poor in the long run as well as in the short run.

We should be careful to get out of an experience only the wisdom that is in it—and stop there; lest we be like the cat that sits down on a hot stove lid. She will never sit down on a hot stove lid again—and that is well; but also she will never sit down on a cold one. (Twain 1897, p. 124)

INDIVIDUALS AND SOCIAL SYSTEMS are often portrayed as risk averse and resistant to change. A standard interpretation of such propensities attributes them to individual, organizational, and cultural traits. Within this interpretation, risk aversion and change aversion are fundamental properties of individuals and

---

A complete list of short definitions of the symbols used in the models is provided in the appendix to this chapter. The chapter originally appeared in *Organization Science*, 12 (2001), 523–538.

organizations. The tendencies reflected in these traits may vary among individuals and groups and may be augmented or overcome by incentives, norms, selection, or situational factors (March 1994, pp. 40–55), but the traits themselves are fixed and unexplained. This paper explores an alternative interpretation of risk taking and change in social systems, one that pictures these predispositions as evolving from experience at the individual or population level. In particular, we show how the reproduction of success, inherent in the sequential sampling of adaptive processes, results in a bias against both risky and novel alternatives.

## ADAPTATION AS SEQUENTIAL SAMPLING

Modern treatments of organizational development over time are primarily variations on two themes of adaptation. The first theme is experiential learning, the idea that organizations and the people in them modify their actions on the basis of an evaluation of their experiences (Cyert and March 1963, Huber 1991, Haleblian and Finkelstein 1999). The second theme is competitive selection and reproduction, the idea that organizations and the people in them are essentially unchanging, but survive and reproduce at different rates depending on their performance (Hannan and Freeman 1977, Nelson and Winter 1982, Aldrich 1999).

Traditionally, both forms of adaptation have been presented as instruments for improving the fit between organizations (or populations of organizations) and their environments. Indeed, presumptions of the efficiency of learning and competitive selection in reaching optimal solutions have been portrayed as justifications for theories of rational choice (Friedman 1953). Such a portrayal is misleading. Although there is no question that both forms of adaptation can lead to major transformations of organizations (Yelle 1979, Haveman 1992, Greve 1996, Usher and Evans 1996, Sutton and Barto 1998), neither learning nor competitive selection and reproduction can guarantee the discovery and adoption of optimum practices. Explicit models of adaptation have demonstrated that adaptive processes are prone to settling into stable suboptima (Levinthal and March 1981, Herriott et al. 1985, Kauffman 1993, Carroll and Harrison 1994, Levinthal 1997). Except in a tautological sense, the fittest do not necessarily survive (Nelson and Winter 1982, Carroll and Harrison 1994, Barnett 1997, Gimeno et. al. 1997), and learning from experience does not necessarily locate global maxima (Busemeyer et al. 1986, Levinthal and March 1993, Miner and Mezias 1996, Levinthal 1997). In this paper we demonstrate that the sequential character of adaptation implies two specific kinds of suboptimality that are important for organizational development.

An adaptive process can be seen as a process of sequential sampling. At each point in a sequential sampling process, one alternative is sampled from a set of alternatives; the probability of sampling any particular alternative depends on the past history of observations (Wald 1947, Feller 1968). An adaptive process is a sequential sampling process in the sense that alternatives that have experienced relatively good outcomes in the past are more likely to be sampled than are alternatives that have experienced relatively poor outcomes (Holland 1975). Several models have been developed to explore optimal stopping rules in this kind of situation (Rothschild 1974, Easley and Kiefer 1988, Goldberg 1989, Kaelbling 1993, Blume and Easley 1995). The focus here is different. We examine the behavioral consequences of the sequential sampling character of adaptation.

In general, sequential sampling processes lead to improvement in performance as alternatives with good outcomes in previous samples come to dominate future samples. However, the differential reproduction of successful alternatives not only affects the returns to action but also the accumulation of information. Because alternatives that do well are reproduced, adaptation will generate further information about their potential. The additional information tends to correct any errors involving alternatives that initially appear better than they actually are. On the other hand, alternatives that do poorly are likely to be avoided. As a result, it is less likely that additional information about their potential will be obtained. Consequently, adaptation will often fail to correct errors involving alternatives that initially appear worse than they actually are. In deference to Mark Twain and his homily about cats with which we began this paper, we call this phenomenon the hot stove effect. The hot stove effect refers to the asymmetry in the capability of adaptive processes to correct early sampling errors.

The hot stove effect leads to a bias against new alternatives that require practice and against alternatives involving risk. Consider new alternatives. There are numerous reasons why new alternatives fare poorly in comparison with the status quo. We address here a particular feature of adaptive processes that operates to sustain the status quo—the so-called "competency trap." Most new alternatives require practice to realize their full potential reliably. As a result, the outcomes of new alternatives tend initially to be lower than their potential and unreliable (high variability). With repeated experience, average performance improves and variability is reduced. However, even a new alternative that has the potential to improve with practice and eventually to surpass existing alternatives is initially likely to perform poorly in comparison with old and established alternatives. The short-run disadvantage leads to avoidance, which restricts the practice that would develop the performance. As a result, the error is unlikely to be corrected.

On average, and without any particular individual or organizational resistance to change, this leads to a bias against new alternatives in competition with established ones (David 1985, Levitt and March 1988, Arthur 1989).

The same mechanism produces a bias against risky alternatives. When early experiences are more favorable to a risky alternative than its true average value warrants, the probability of sampling the risky alternative will increase and subsequent sampling will correct the error. However, when early experiences are less favorable to a risky alternative than its true average value warrants, the probability of choosing the risky alternative will decrease. As a result, the error is less likely to be corrected. On average, this asymmetry of sequential sampling leads to a bias against risky alternatives. The bias is sometimes labeled "risk aversion" when it is observed, but it is not attributable to any trait-like risk preferences on the part of individuals or organizations. Adaptation itself produces behavior that can be described as risk averse (March 1996).

To demonstrate the effects more precisely, we consider two classic modes of adaptation—experiential learning and competitive selection—each of which exhibits reduced sampling of failures. Each of these domains is rich with models. The intricacies of their fine detail are essential, but we focus on their basic features to illustrate how those features are implicated in information restriction.

### EXPERIENTIAL LEARNING

In an experiential learning process, the propensity to select a particular alternative in period $t + 1$ is based on the outcome of choices in previous periods (Cyert and March 1963, Nelson and Winter 1982, Levitt and March 1988, Huber 1991, Miner and Mezias 1996). Although it is clear that such updating can lead to improvements (Yelle 1979, Argote and Epple 1990), analytical models of experiential learning have demonstrated that the process does not necessarily converge to a global optimum.

As a result of ambiguity, environmental turbulence, interdependency, and path dependency introduced by competence multipliers, experiential learning can produce superstitious learning (Lave and March 1975, Lounamaa and March 1987, Levitt and March 1988) and converge to inferior alternatives (Levinthal and March 1981, Herriott et al. 1985, Levitt and March 1988, Levinthal 1997). Although the idea that experiential learning is prone to mistakes is well known (Huber 1991, Levinthal and March 1993, Lant 1994, Miner and Mezias 1996), it is less commonly observed that the failures tend to be systematic. In this section we show more precisely how experiential learning leads to a bias against risky and new alternatives.

There is a long tradition of computer simulation models of experiential learning within organizational research (Levinthal and March 1981; Herriott et al. 1985; March 1991; Lant and Mezias 1990, 1992; Lant 1994). Although the models differ in their details, most of them assume that organizations repeat actions that appear successful and change actions that appear unsuccessful, and that performance is evaluated relative to an aspiration level that depends on the history of past performances (Cyert and March 1963, Lant 1992, Greve 1998).

A basic model consistent with this tradition is an experiential learning model of an individual or organization choosing between two alternatives. The probability that the first alternative is chosen in period $t$ is denoted $P_t$. Learning is assumed to change this probability on the basis of a comparison between the realized outcome from the choice of an alternative at a particular time and an aspiration level. The aspiration level summarizes past experience as a mix between the previous aspiration and the previously realized outcome, thus as an exponentially weighted average of past outcomes (Levinthal and March 1981). Formally, the aspiration level at $t + 1$ is given by:

$$L_{t+1} = L_t(1 - b) + O_t b, \tag{1}$$

where $L_t$ is the aspiration level and $O_t$ is the outcome at $t$. The mix between the most recent outcome and the most recent aspiration is controlled by $b$, a non-negative fraction that reflects the rate at which aspirations adjust to experience.

Consistent with stochastic learning models (Bush and Mosteller 1955, Coombs et al. 1970), we assume that positive experience with an alternative increases, and negative experience decreases, the probability that this alternative will be chosen in the future. The change in the probability is assumed to be proportional to the difference between $P_t$ and the learning limit (that is, one in the case of an increase and zero in the case of a decrease). Specifically, if the first alternative is tried and yields an outcome better than the aspiration at time $t$, or if the second alternative is tried and yields an outcome worse than the aspiration, the probability of choosing the first alternative in the next time period, $P_{t+1}$, increases in the following way:

$$P_{t+1} = P_t + a(1 - P_t) \tag{2}$$

Here, $a$ is a positive fraction parameter that defines the speed of learning. The higher the value of $a$, the more a single experience will affect the subsequent probability of choosing the risky alternative.

On the other hand, if the first alternative is tried and yields an outcome that is worse than the aspiration, or if the second alternative is tried and yields an outcome better than the aspiration, the probability of choosing the first alternative decreases in the following way:

$$P_{t+1} = (1 - a) P_t \qquad (3)$$

Regardless of which alternative is chosen, if the realized outcome is identical to the aspiration, the probability of choosing the risky alternative in the next time period remains unchanged.

## The Reproduction of Reliability through Experiential Learning

To demonstrate how the model of experiential learning specified above generates a bias against risky alternatives, we examine a two-alternative setting in which one alternative has a certain outcome, Y, and the other alternative involves risk. The risk of the latter alternative is measured by the variability in the probability distribution over possible outcomes conditional on its choice. In the remainder of the present treatment, we consider a risky alternative characterized by a normally distributed outcome distribution with mean X and standard deviation S, and we consider the effect of varying the value of S.

We define the probability that the risky alternative will be chosen at time t as $P_t$. We assume that initially a learner is equally likely to choose the risky alternative or the certain one ($P_0 = 0.5$) and that the initial aspiration is identical to the expectation at $t = 0$ ($L_0 = [P_0 X + \{1 - P_0\} Y]$), where X is the expectation of the risky alternative, and Y is the expectation of the certain alternative. Thus, the learner has no initial bias with respect to risk and has an initial aspiration that is equal to the expectation. Alternative assumptions about the initial aspiration level were explored. As long as they are not extreme, they do not affect the general results below.

We ask what happens to the likelihood of choosing the risky alternative over time in this learning situation. It seems reasonable to expect that the results might depend on the relation between the expected returns from the two alternatives, with a risky alternative becoming more likely to be chosen over time the greater its expected return. That expectation is correct. However, there is also a systematic bias in favor of reliability. Suppose that the risky alternative and the certain alternative have the same long-run expectation, X = Y. To examine the aggregate statistical properties of learning in such a situation, we simulate the learning of 5,000 learners over 50 time periods and record the fraction of the 5,000 who choose the risky alternative on the fiftieth choice,

$F_{50}$. As Figure 1 shows, the results indicate a clear learning bias against risky alternatives. The fraction of learners choosing the risky alternative at time 50 depends on the learning rate, $a$, but for all levels of $a$, the fraction choosing the risky alternative is less than one-half.

The effect is due to the natural learning tendency to avoid alternatives that produce poor outcomes and the high likelihood that a risky alternative will do so. The normal variation of a risky alternative produces periods of good returns and periods of poor returns. Whenever the risky alternative is chosen and generates a poor outcome, the probability of choosing it again decreases. This optional stopping feature of learning leads the learner to abandon a risky alternative that, at some point, has a run of bad luck and thus fails to experience any subsequent run of good luck. After some time, most individuals will have a low probability of choosing the risky alternative. In that sense, at least, learning produces behavior that might be classified as risk aversion (March 1996).

The bias against risky alternatives can be overcome if the risky alternative has a sufficient advantage in expected value. Suppose the expected value of the certain alternative $(Y)$ is equal to 10. What expected value for the risky alternative $(X^*)$ is required to make that alternative equally likely to be chosen after learning from the outcome of 50 choices? As might be anticipated, the expected value advantage required for the risky alternative depends on the standard deviation $(S)$ and the learning rate $(a)$. On the basis of simulations similar to

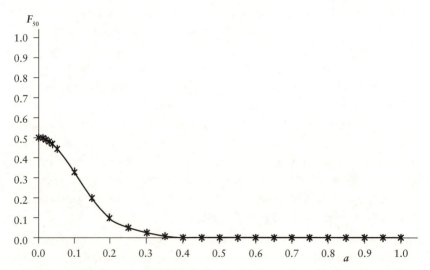

FIGURE I    The fraction of 5,000 individuals who choose the risky alternatives at the end of period 50 as a function of $a$. Based on averages from 25 sets of 5,000 simulations where $X = 10$, $Y = 10$, $S = 10$, $b = 0.5$.

TABLE 1A   The approximate value of X required for 50% of the choices at time 50 to be choices of the risky alternative, for various values of S. Each entry is based on 5,000 simulations where $Y = 10$, $a = 0.2$, and $b = 0.5$.

| S | 5 | 10 | 15 | 20 | 25 |
|---|---|----|----|----|----|
| X* | 13.7 | 17.2 | 21.7 | 25.1 | 28.8 |

TABLE 1B   The approximate value of X required for 50% of the choices at time 50 to be choices of the risky alternative, for various values of a. Each entry is based on 5,000 simulations where $Y = 10$, $S = 10$, and $b = 0.5$.

| a | 0.1 | 0.2 | 0.3 | 0.4 | 0.4 |
|---|-----|-----|-----|-----|-----|
| X* | 13.4 | 17.2 | 20.2 | 21.7 | 22.9 |

those above, we can estimate the expected value of the risky alternative that is required for the risky alternative to be chosen half of the time at trial 50. This estimate is given in Tables 1a and 1b for selected values of S and a. The expected value advantage required to compensate for the bias against risky alternatives can be quite large.

It should be noted that the bias against risky alternatives is sensitive to the aspiration level updating process assumed. If the updating function includes a positive constant (Lant 1992), the aspiration level will be above an exponentially weighted moving average of realized past outcomes; thus it is likely to be above the expected value of the alternatives. As a result, the bias will be attenuated. If the aspiration level is above the expected value of the alternatives, there will be a bias against the certain alternative unless the constant is so large as to make all outcomes failures and learning superstitious (Lave and March 1975). On the other hand, if the updating function includes a negative constant, the bias will be strengthened. The certain alternative is much more likely to be defined as a success than is the risky alternative, unless the negative constant is so large (in absolute terms) as to essentially make all outcomes successes and learning superstitious.

## The Reproduction of the Status Quo through Experiential Learning

New alternatives frequently require competence to realize their full potential. If competence depends on experience, experiential learning may converge to stable suboptima when the outcome of alternatives depends on their frequency of use (Levinthal and March 1981, Herriott et al. 1985). In this section we show that

the same learning model that produces a bias against risky alternatives also produces a bias against new alternatives that require practice.

Suppose there is an existing alternative with a certain return of $Y$ and a new
alternative with a payoff subject to risk. We assume that the risky alternative
generates an outcome with an average potential of $X$ ($X > Y$), subject not only to
the random fluctuations of risk but also the systematic fluctuations due to variations in competence. The realized outcome from the new alternative at $t$ is a draw
from a normal distribution with a mean equal to $c_t X$, where $c_t$ is the competence
at $t$ ($0 < c_t \leq 1$). The standard deviation of the outcome distribution at $t$ is $(S/c_t)^k$,
where ($0 < k \leq 1$. Competence at the new alternative increases each time that
alternative is chosen, thus increasing the expected performance and reducing
the variation (although the standard deviation always remains positive). Over
repeated choices of the new alternative, the outcome from using that alternative
approaches an expected return of $X > Y$ and a standard deviation of $S^k$, but in
the short run, when $c_t$ is relatively small, outcomes from the new alternative are,
on average, inferior to outcomes from the existing (certain) alternative.

Competence in using the new alternative increases with each utilization in
a way analogous to standard learning curves (Yelle 1979, Argote and Epple
1990). Thus,

$$c_{t+1} = c_t \text{ if the existing alternative is chosen}$$
$$c_{c_{t+1}} = c_t + d\,(1 - c_t) \text{ if the new alternative is chosen} \tag{4}$$

The learning parameter, $d$, is a non-negative fraction and reflects the competence learning rate.

In this modification of the original experiential learning model, the adapter
simultaneously learns which alternative to choose and gains competence on the
chosen alternative. As intuition might suggest, the probability of choosing the
new alternative frequently falls to a very low level. As the probability of choosing the new alternative becomes very low, it becomes unlikely that a learner will
experiment any further with it. As a result, competence remains low and the
probability of choosing the new alternative remains low. Only those individuals
who persist with the new alternative gain enough competence and eventually
increase the probability of choosing it.

The proportion of individuals who choose the new alternative depends on the
competence learning parameter, $d$, by which competence at the new alternative
increases with experience. The proportion of individuals who choose the new alternative also depends on the choice learning parameter. The smaller the value of
$a$, the larger the proportion of individuals who will choose the new alternative at

the end of 50 periods. Figure 2 shows that the fraction of all individuals choosing the new alternative as $a$ varies from 0.05 to 0.95 for several values of $d$, when $X = 15$ and $Y = 10$. As Figure 2 suggests, one way of avoiding a bias against alternatives that require practice is rapid learning of competence and slow learning of choices—longer experimentation with alternatives that seem poor. The latter would clearly be a good idea save for the obvious complication that in a world in which seemingly poor alternatives most often are poor, extended periods of experimentation with apparently poor alternatives is usually a very costly strategy.

## Robustness

The above simulations show that a behavioral model of organizational learning produces a bias against risky and new alternatives. The results are not limited to a narrow range of parameter values or to the specific models outlined above. For example, a bias against risky alternatives is also a property of learning models that select alternatives on the basis of the average outcome they have generated in the past (Sutton and Barto 1998), and also of models in which the magnitudes of learning effects depend on the magnitudes of success and failure. Among the models that we have considered, only those that insert an explicit preference for alternatives with a high variance (i.e., Kaelbling's Interval Estimation Method, Kaelbling 1993) avoid the bias against risky alternatives.

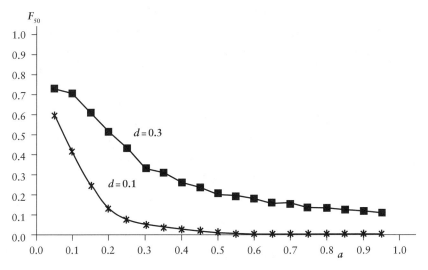

FIGURE 2    The fraction of 5,000 individuals who choose the new alternative at the end of period 50 as a function of $a$ and $d$. Each line is based on averages from 19 sets of 5,000 simulations where $X = 15$, $Y = 10$, $S = 5$, $k = 0.5$, $c_0 = 0.3$, and $b = 0.5$.

All these models are strictly models of autonomous experiential learning. In-dividuals and organizations also routinely learn from each other (Bandura 1977, Levitt and March 1988, Miner and Haunschild 1995, Miner and Raghavan 1999). Whether such imitation will attenuate or aggravate the above biases depends on the mode and sequence of imitation (Haunschild and Miner 1997, Miner and Raghavan 1999). If imitation involves observing both the actions of others and their associated outcomes, it is possible that the bias against risky alterna-tives will be weakened. If knowledge about a risky alternative is shared among several organizations, the false impressions gained from the limited sample of one organization can be corrected, provided the shared knowledge itself does not affect the individual actions. If poor outcomes in any organization lead to avoidance by all organizations, however, the bias against risky alternatives is likely to be strengthened, rather than weakened, by sharing. Finally, if imitation is based on the frequency of particular actions, but not on any observation of their consequences (DiMaggio and Powell 1983, Tolbert and Zucker 1983), a bias against risky or new alternatives may be aggravated through imitation.

## COMPETITIVE SELECTION AND REPRODUCTION

The actions in a population of organizations can be seen as the results of adaptive processes in which the characteristics of a population of actions in period $t + 1$ are a function of the relative performance of organizations exhibiting those actions in period $t$ (Hannan and Freeman 1977, Nelson and Winter 1982, Barnett 1997, Aldrich 1999). The population changes by virtue of selection—the differential survival of higher performers—and by reproduction (the differential adoption of the attributes of higher performers by new members of the population).

Although selection and reproduction can lead to major transformations of populations (Usher and Evans 1996, Baldwin 1998), they, like learning processes, do not necessarily lead to global optima. Competitive selection processes are history and frequency dependent and are prone to settling into stable subop-tima (Kauffman 1993, Carroll and Harrison 1994, Levinthal 1997). However, deviations from optima are not random. Processes of competitive selection and reproduction favor some alternatives over others. Here, we focus on the tendency for such processes to be biased against risky and new alternatives.

Most empirical studies of competitive selection examine selection and re-production as a function of characteristics of the population, such as density (Hannan and Carroll 1992) or the level of concentration (Baldwin 1998) and do not include explicit measures of individual or organizational performance. There are several simulation models, however, in which selection and reproduction are treated as a function of individual performance. These models range from stylized reduced form models, in which the probability of failure is assumed to be a decreasing function of relative or absolute performance (Lant and Mezias 1990, 1992; Levinthal 1991, 1997; Mezias and Eisner 1997), to detailed models of the competitive process and of capital markets (Nelson and Winter 1982).

To illustrate the bias against risky alternatives, we consider a reduced form model in which the probability of failure is assumed to be a decreasing function of relative performance. Specifically, we consider a population of unchanging organizations drawn from two distinct types. The types differ in their propensities to choose one or the other of two alternatives. As a result of their differing propensities to choose the two alternatives, the two types realize different outcomes. We assume that organizations with low performance relative to others fail to survive and are replaced. Because the two types survive and reproduce at different rates, the process generates a changing population of invariant types. There is, however, no mutation of types. The model is strictly a model of competitive selection and reproduction among invariant types.

We assume a constant population size of $N_{1,t} + N_{2,t}$ organizations, where $N_{j,t}$ is the number of organizations of type $j$. In the beginning each of the two types is equally represented in the population. Their representation in the population changes over time in response to differential survival and reproduction. Survival can be modeled in many different ways (Lant and Mezias 1990, 1992; Levinthal 1991; Mezias and Lant 1994; Mezias and Eisner 1997). To capture the importance of relative performance without relying upon an explicit model of the competitive process, we assume the probability of failure depends on a ranking of organizations according to performance. Specifically, we assume that lower ranked organizations fail and that some fraction, $w$, of the population is eliminated in each period.

Each eliminated organization is replaced by a new organization. Denote the probability that the replacement will be of type $j$ by $r_{j,t}$. Several different assumptions about $r_{j,t}$ are possible and have been used in the literature. First, reproduction may be random among the types. That is, the type of a new organization may be randomly selected from the set of surviving types without regard to the number of survivors of the several types.

Second, reproduction may be sensitive to the number of survivors (Lant and Mezias 1990, 1992; Hannan and Carroll 1992; Carroll and Harrison 1994). To reflect this we define:

$$r_{j,t} = N_{j,t}^{b}/(N_{j,t}^{b} + N_{i,t}^{b}). \tag{5}$$

The hypothetical process is one in which relative density confers legitimacy or in which new replacements are produced by survivors. Lower values of $h$ reduce the reproductive advantage of numbers. Higher values of $h$ increase the reproductive advantage of numbers.

A third feature of the surviving population that might affect $r_{j,t}$ is the aggregate performance of the survivors of each type (March and Shapira 1992). To reflect this, we define:

$$r_{j,t} = T_{j,t}^{h}/(T_{j,t}^{h} + T_{i,t}^{h}),\tag{6}$$

where $T_{j,t}$ is the aggregate performances of all survivors of the type $j$. The hypothetical process is one in which reproduction is driven by the total prior performance of a particular type. Prior performance of survivors provides the resources for reproducing their types. The exponent $h$ affects the sensitivity of reproduction to the aggregate performance of a type.

Finally, a fourth feature of the surviving population that might affect $r_{j,t}$ is the average performance of each type. To reflect this, we define:

$$r_{j,t} = A_{j,t}^{h}/(A_{j,t}^{h} + A_{i,t}^{h}),\tag{7}$$

where $A_{j,t}$ is the average performance of survivors of organizations of type $j$. The hypothetical process is one of imitation and diffusion. New organizations mimic existing types that have high average performance (Argote et al. 1990). The exponent $h$ affects the sensitivity of reproduction to the average performance of a type.

### The Reproduction of Reliability through Competitive Selection and Reproduction

To examine the reproduction of reliability we consider a situation in which the first type of organization consistently chooses a certain alternative, while the second type consistently chooses a risky alternative. The certain alternative is characterized by a reliable return, $Y$. The risky alternative is characterized by a normally distributed outcome distribution with mean $X$ and standard deviation $S$. Each organization realizes an outcome for each time period, resulting in a ranking of organizations according to their most recent performance. Higher ranked performers survive; poorer performers are eliminated. Each period, a fraction, $w$, of the population is eliminated.

As long as $w$ is less than one-half, the variability in the performances of the risky alternative assures that eliminated organizations will be drawn disproportionately from the type that chooses the risky alternative. If reproduction is random, selection thus leads to a steady decrease in the proportion of organizations of the risky type when $w$ is less than one-half and a steady increase in the proportion of organizations of the risky type when $w$ is greater than one-half. If reproduction is responsive to the number of survivors, or is randomly drawn from surviving organizations with positive performance (Lant and Mezias 1990, 1992), the bias is aggravated. The adaptive process (in both its "death" and "birth" processes) steadily increases the fraction of the population that avoids the risky alternative if $w$ is less than one-half, and steadily decreases that fraction if $w$ is more than one-half. The results after 50 trials, when reproduction is responsive to the number of survivors, are illustrated in Figure 3. The case shown is for $X = Y = 10$ and $S = 10$, and for various values of $w$ and $h$. As is clear from Figure 3, unless selection pressure eliminates a majority of the population each time period (i.e., $w > 0.5$), the selection process reproduces reliability. This result holds even if the alternatives vary less profoundly in their risk and (under some circumstances) even if the expected value for the risky alternative is greater than that of the certain alternative.

Suppose, next, that reproduction depends on the total aggregate performance of survivors of a particular type, that is, follows Equation (6). In general, the results are similar to the case involving numbers alone. The process usually reproduces reliability as long as selection eliminates less than one-half of

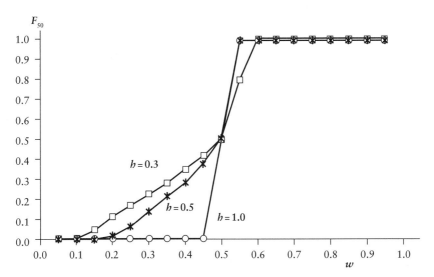

FIGURE 3    The fraction of the population who choose the risky alternative at the end of period 50 as a function of $w$ and $h$. Each line is based on averages from 19 sets of 1,000 simulations where $X = 10$, $Y = 10$, and $S = 10$. The constant population size is 100.

the population each time period (i.e., $w < 0.5$). However, dependence on total aggregate performance of survivors makes that result weaker. If reproduction depends on the aggregate performance of all actors who have existed in a particular time period (including those who are eliminated in that period), reliability is reproduced as long as $w < 0.5$. However, when reproduction depends only on survivors, the fact that the average performance of survivors of the risk-taking types will, in general, be greater than that of the risk-averse types assures that the reproduction of reliability will be moderated. This also holds if reproduction depends on average performance of the two types, that is, follows Equation (7). When reproduction responds to the average performance of the types, the risk-taking type continues to be eliminated in greater numbers than the risk-averse type; but it is favored in reproduction. As a result, it is possible (though not guaranteed) that the risk-taking type will maintain a substantial presence in the population even if $w < 0.5$. However, this can only occur if reproduction is based on the average performance of survivors, rather than the average performance of all organizations of each type.

## The Reproduction of the Status Quo through Competitive Selection and Reproduction

Competitive selection and reproduction processes are biased not only against unreliable alternatives but also against alternatives that require practice. The fundamental intuition is that since alternatives that require practice will initially be inferior to other alternatives, it is possible that they will be eliminated before their potential can be revealed (Nelson and Winter 1982, Elster 1984, Levitt and March 1988, Carroll and Harrison 1994). Whether this will happen depends on the rate of competence gain relative to the speed of selection and on the possibilities for reproductive transfer of competence (Argote et al. 1990).

To examine this, we assume that replacements are drawn from two types according to the number of survivors, as in Equation (5). As in the parallel case within the learning model, we assume that the established alternative generates a certain outcome of $Y$. The new alternative has a potential expected value of $X > Y$ but generates a realized outcome at $t$ that is a draw from a normal distribution with a mean equal to $c_t X$, where $c_t$ is the competence at $t$ ($0 < c_t \leq 1$). The standard deviation of the outcome distribution at $t$ is $(S/c_t)^k$, where $0 < k \leq 1$. Competence at the new alternative increases each time that the alternative is chosen according to Equation (4). Although the new alternative may initially only be represented by a few organizations, we examine the case where both types are equally represented in the initial population.

Consider, first, the case in which there is no within-type intergenerational reproductive transfer of competence. Learning affects reproduction rates within a generation by affecting competence, and thereby relative performance, but competence is not reproduced. In terms of the above model, this implies that whenever an organization is eliminated and replaced with another organization, the initial competence of the new organization is set at $c_0$.

Given these assumptions, it is clear that any organization choosing an alternative that requires practice will initially exhibit inferior performance. The longer it survives, the better its performance. If its potential is greater than that of the established alternative and it survives long enough, its performance will become reliably better than the established alternative. However, even though the potential of the new alternative is greater than the performance of the certain alternative, that is, $X > Y$, and thus could ultimately come to dominate, the new alternative can fail to survive in the population long enough to achieve the level of competence that leads to survival and reproduction. The likelihood of this outcome depends on $w$ and $d$, as illustrated in Figure 4. Only if competence is gained relatively quickly (i.e., $d$ is relatively large), or if strong selection pressure favors risky alternatives (i.e., $w$ is relatively large), will a new alternative be able to survive and dominate. The effect of $w$ is sensitive to the standard deviation of the alternative that requires practice. If the standard deviation (i.e., $S$) is low

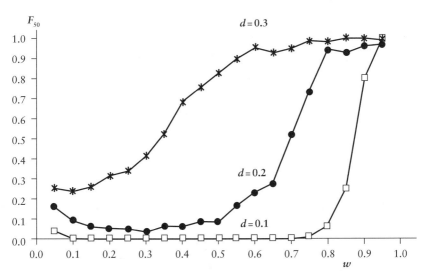

FIGURE 4 The fraction of the population who choose the risky alternative at the end of period 50 as a function of $w$ and $d$ when $h = 0.5$. Each line is based on averages from 19 sets of 100 simulations where $X = 15$, $Y = 10$, $S = 5$, $k = 0.5$, and $c_0 = 0.3$. The constant population size is 100.

(e.g., $S = 1$), organizations choosing the alternative that requires practice are reliably worse than the established alternative and are thus unlikely to survive for long, unless the selection pressure (i.e., $w$) is very low.

If $S$ is somewhat greater, however, there is always some chance that an organization choosing the alternative that requires practice will survive and be reproduced. If a sufficient number of organizations of that type survive, reproduction will increase the supply of organizations choosing the alternative that requires practice, which, if they survive, will also become reliably better, and so on until organizations choosing the alternative that requires practice will come to dominate (pending the arrival of a new competitor). This implies that the alternative that requires practice is quite likely to dominate, ultimately, if the total population is large enough. "Ultimately" is usually, however, an extremely long time in the future.

Suppose, on the other hand, that competence is transferred in reproduction. Specifically, suppose we assume that the initial competence of a new organization arriving in period $t + 1$ is equal to the average competence of all surviving organizations of the same type at the end of period $t$. As in the case without transfer of competence, the average performance of surviving organizations choosing the new alternative will surpass the performance of organizations choosing the certain alternative at some point, but they are at risk of becoming extinct before that occurs. Intergenerational transfer of competence reduces that risk, but the risk remains. The fraction of the population choosing the new alternative can go to zero even in the presence of intergenerational transfer of competence.

In general, although there are conditions under which new alternatives can overcome old ones through competitive selection and reproduction, the status quo has a fairly clear advantage, even in competition with alternatives that are, on average, considerably better. It may be worth noting that the effects are sensitive to the size of the population. If the population is large, it is less likely that all individuals choosing an initially inferior, but potentially better, alternative will fail to be reproduced. As a result, it is more likely that some individuals will survive and eventually attain a level of reliable competence sufficient to avoid being eliminated.

## ROBUSTNESS

Somewhat different assumptions about selection and reproduction could be made. Alternative assumptions about reproduction have been discussed above. It was demonstrated that the present results hold for a wide variety of assumptions regarding reproduction. With respect to selection, it should be clear that the results hold for a wide variety of models in which poor performers are unlikely to survive, while average performers and good performers are likely to survive. For example, suppose that organizations fail whenever their cumulative resources fall below some absolute level of performance (Nelson and Winter 1982; Lant and Mezias 1990, 1992; Levinthal 1991; Mezias and Eisner 1997), and this absolute level of performance is below the expected performance of the two types. In this case, because organizations of the risk-taking type will be more likely than organizations of the risk-averse type to generate a performance below the level required for failure, they will be less likely to survive. Similarly, organizations making use of a new alternative will be less likely to survive. These results would be weakened, however, if it were assumed that the expected performance of organizations of a given type was a decreasing function of the number of organizations of this type (Hannan and Carroll 1992). In this case, a high density of a particular type would decrease its expected performance, which eventually would reduce its density.

As noted above, the results are also sensitive to alternative assumptions about imitation and the diffusion of knowledge. If knowledge about the results achieved by others is diffused, it may eliminate the biases, depending on the speed with which it affects the abandonment of apparently inferior alternatives. If competencies are diffused, competence gains from experience are shared through a population, and there is less chance that a potentially good alternative will become extinct before its potential is discovered. A more refined model of diffusion and selection would have to take account of the network of linkages among organizations in a population (MacArthur and Wilson 1967, Rogers 1995). Some of the more relevant elaborations involve elements of "partially permeable membranes" that are found in networks of associations. In a typical network, different parts of the system evolve partly (but not completely) independently. By virtue of being partly separated, they are likely to evolve in different directions. By virtue of being partly connected, the favorable outcomes in one can spread ultimately, but not too rapidly, to another. In this case, there is some chance that risky or new alternatives that are discarded by most will be adopted by some—from whom others can ultimately adopt the alternative (Wright 1931, Weick 1976).

We have not explored elaborations that involve these considerations of the diffusion process, including variations that would attend to issues of legitimacy (DiMaggio and Powell 1983, Tolbert and Zucker 1983). Nor have we explored the effect imitation of a particular organizational behavior can have on the average performance of organizations exhibiting this behavior. In a behavioral model of risk taking and change, such changes in performance could also have systematic effects on risk taking and the probability of change (March 1988, March and Shapira 1992, Shapira 1995, Mezias and Eisner 1997, Greve 1998).

## IMPLICATIONS FOR RISK TAKING AND CHANGE IN ORGANIZATIONS

The simulations demonstrate that behaviors that are often labeled as conservatism or risk aversion may reflect biases in adaptive processes. Because the biases result from the tendency of learning and selection to reproduce successful actions, the biases will be weakened whenever failures are more likely to be reproduced. Thus, they will be reduced in situations where, for whatever reason, adaptation is slowed, made imprecise, or recalled less reliably. In this sense, the survival of risky and new alternatives will be associated with ineffective adaptation, and several forms of organizational ineffectiveness can increase the propensity of an organization to engage in risky and new activities.

### Speed of Adaptation

The results suggest that slow adaptation will increase the frequency of risky and novel activities. By reproducing successful alternatives, fast learners quickly eliminate poor-performing alternatives in favor of better ones. The very quickness that makes such a process particularly effective, however, also makes it biased against risky and new alternatives. By continuing to reproduce failures, slow learners are less likely than their quicker cousins to suffer from the hot stove effect.

In the case of the model of stochastic learning, slow adaptive response is represented by the learning parameter, $a$. Slow learning, where $a$ is relatively small, leads to more gradual adaptation of the probability of choosing different alternatives and thus less profound bias against risky and new alternatives. In the case of the model of competitive selection and reproduction, slow adaptive response is represented by the selection pressure, $w$, and the reproductive responsiveness parameter, $h$. Slow reproductive response, where $h$ is relatively small, leads to more gradual adaptation and thus less profound bias against risky and, in particular, new alternatives. The impact of variations in selection pressure, $w$, on the other hand, is mixed. Smaller selection pressures lead to less bias against new alternatives with low risk than do more substantial selection pressures, but they lead to greater bias against risky alternatives. The latter result stems from the way the outcomes from risky alternatives are arrayed at the extremes of the outcome space and thus are especially vulnerable if only a few actors are eliminated.

We ask whether there are features of organizational life that affect the rate of learning or selection. Of particular importance in this regard are features of organizational inertia (Hannan and Freeman 1984) that delay reactions to feedback about new alternatives. Adaptation is slowed by any rule, practice, norm, heuristic, or information processing bias that allows an alternative to survive for some number of observations regardless of what those observations are. Such inertia is likely to attach to new, untried alternatives in situations in which the organizational enthusiasm required to adopt a practice assures that early unfavorable results will be overlooked or ignored. This inclination to persist is likely to be augmented by individual and organizational biases toward confirming initial expectations (Rabin and Schrag 1999), and by the costs of political renegotiations required for changing organizational action. As a result, alternatives with poor initial performance may survive sufficiently long for their benefits (if any) to be discovered.

Similarly, in situations where a selection process, regardless of its intensity, operates on a type only after a period of time, types with low performance can survive for a considerable time. For example, poorly performing organizations endure into adolescence by drawing on their initial endowments of resources and expectations (Fichman and Levinthal 1991, Levinthal 1991), by locating themselves within the institutional protections of legal and political systems (Meyer and Zucker 1989), and by exploiting the informational limitations of the relevant financial, labor, and product markets. The longer the honeymoon (nonadaptive) period, the slower the adaptive process and the weaker the bias against risky and new alternatives.

Adaptation is also slowed by beliefs associated with such things as social legitimacy, ideology, and imagination. Strong beliefs with respect to a course of action systematically buffer individuals and organizations from learning, particularly from adverse evaluations of a course of action. Consider, for example, the role of management fashions. Communities of belief surrounding organizations allow types to survive (at least in the short run) if their actions fulfill expectations of appropriate behavior. Organizational practices that have become fashionable or socially legitimate within the culture of management persist in the face of adverse evidence about their effectiveness (Meyer and Rowan 1977, Meyer and Zucker 1989, Hannan and Carroll 1992, Abrahamson and Fairchild 1999). In the case of a potentially valuable practice, social legitimization allows survival long enough for the value to be developed or exhibited.

Ideology and imagination are similar belief-based sources of delay that can lead to avoiding the premature abandonment of an alternative that would ultimately prove valuable (Hirschman 1967, Kolakowski 1968). Because they are slow to learn from adverse experience, ideologues are likely both to do poorly on average and to be the first to discover valuable novel and risky innovations. Imagination plays a comparable role. The ability and will to deviate from established ways involve being able to conjure a different world, to see things with different eyes. This talent for deviance is, however, of little use by itself because a person or organization that easily rejects ideas will flit from one to another, abandoning each new idea long before it can become or be identified as a good one. The second component of imagination—the inclination to stick with an idea despite evidence of its inadequacy—is equally important. Without such tenacity, new ideas wither. Thus, it is necessary to combine a willingness to deviate from old ideas with an irrational pigheadedness in support of the new (slow learning). Imagination does this by substituting a fantastical world for an observed world, a substitution that usually leads to disaster but occasionally leads to discovery (March 1995).

## Precision of Adaptation

The results suggest that imprecise adaptation will increase the probability that an adaptive system will engage in risky and new activities. Imprecision in adaptation increases the probability of reproducing failures. The reproduction of actions that have led to failure results in all of the familiar adverse consequences (Levinthal and March 1981, Lant and Mezias 1990, Lant 1994), but it also results in reducing the bias against new and risky alternatives.

Suppose that information on the outcome of a learning trial is subject to random error. That is, suppose in the case of the stochastic learning model that the realized outcome is as indicated above, plus a draw from a normal distribution with mean zero and standard deviation, $E$. Then, the discriminations of learning are confused by noise in outcomes. Figure 5 compares the proportion of learners choosing the risky alternative over 50 periods for various values of $E$. Increasing the noise increases the fraction choosing the risky alternative in a learning situation. The sensitivity to $E$ is more gradual than that displayed in Figure 5 if learning depends on the magnitude of success or failure.

Suppose, similarly, that the performance that determines the elimination of less successful organizations in competitive selection and reproduction is subject to random error. As in the case of learning, the discriminations of selection are confused by noise in outcomes. Figure 6 compares the proportion of the population choosing the risky alternative over 50 periods for various values

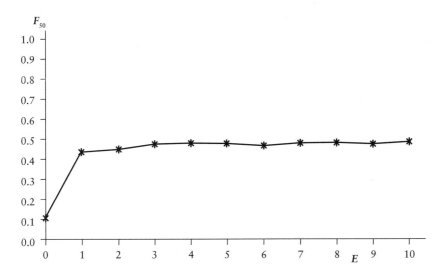

FIGURE 5    The effect of $E$ on the reproduction of reliability through experiential learning. Based on averages from 11 sets of 5,000 simulations where $X = 10$, $Y = 10$, $S = 10$, $a = 0.2$, and $b = 0.5$.

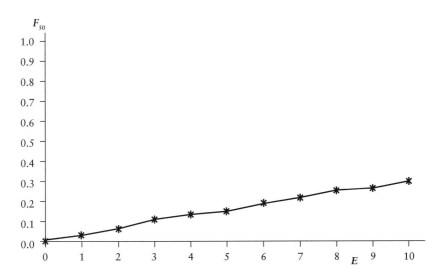

FIGURE 6    The effect of $E$ on the reproduction of reliability through competitive selection. Based on averages from 11 sets of 100 simulations where $X = 10$, $Y = 10$, $S = 10$, $w = 0.2$, $h = 0.5$. The constant population size is 100.

of $E$, where reproduction is according to the numbers of each type surviving as shown in Equation (5) and $h = 0.5$. Increasing the noise (reducing the precision of selection) increases the fraction choosing the risky alternative in a competitive selection situation.

The results exhibited in Figures 5 and 6 are not surprising, given what we have seen previously. Because the biases against risky and new alternatives are produced by learning and selection, making the feedback on which those processes depend less precise reduces the biases. If reducing the biases is important to long-run effectiveness, it is also important to reduce the short-run precision of learning and selection (Hedberg et al. 1976, Mezias and Glynn 1993). Noise generates errors in the feedback on which adaptation is based and produces failures (eliminations) and successes (survivals) that are arbitrary relative to the true potentials at the time. These arbitrary "mistakes" in adaptation can be destructive in the short run, but they reduce the biases of adaptation against risky and new alternatives, thus providing advantages in the long run under some conditions.

Organizational contexts of adaptation provide a variety of examples of common phenomena that result in such errors (Aldrich 1999). First, rather than being tied to past history, action can be remarkably arbitrary with respect to any history of successes or failures with previous actions. For example, action is disconnected from experience by a context of rules. Actors function within social structures that develop and impose rules that are independent of the learning or the selection history of the individual actor who executes them. As a result, alternatives may survive even though they have been unsuccessful in the past.

Second, even if action is responsive to historical experience, the interpretation of experience may be indeterminate. Histories are confounded by causal ambiguity, ignorance, and bias. If, as in the case of risky and new alternatives, accurate interpretation of past experience would indicate that the action has not been successful, causal ambiguity, ignorance, and bias may result in more exploration. Alternatives that might reasonably be rejected on the basis of clearer feedback can survive. Causal indeterminacy, complexity, and bias are also important factors in competitive selection. Individual attributes with negative performance implications can survive by "hitchhiking" in a package of attributes with good performance (Gould and Lewontin 1984, Barnett 1997).

Third, even if the interpretation of experience is straightforward, coding of outcomes as successes or failures is made indeterminate by the existence of multiple, incommensurable objectives and criteria. This ambiguity of objectives makes it possible for alternatives with poor performance on any one criterion to survive by exhibiting good performance on other criteria. An innovation survives by attaching itself to one set of criteria until it has developed capabilities with respect to a different set (Amabile 1988).

Finally, the coding of outcomes is made indeterminate by the fact that success and failure are often defined in relative terms. If success is measured relative to an aspiration level, higher aspirations will lead to more failures than lower aspirations and thereby to more and briefer experimentation. Similarly, a selection regime in which only a small fraction of the population survives each time period, and most individuals are eliminated, favors risky alternatives. The result is a variation on a familiar proposition that in a competition for primacy, the importance of variability relative to expected value increases (Lippman and Rumelt 1982, March 1991, Mezias and Glynn 1993, Frank and Cook 1995).

## *Memory of Adaptation*

The results also suggest that poor memory will increase the probability that an adaptive system will engage in risky and new activities. The hot stove effect stems from the stabilization of knowledge concerning alternatives that have resulted in early failures. Because such alternatives are not chosen subsequently, the early unfavorable impressions are not corrected. However, if memory is not perfect, or if the reputations of alternatives are not segregated from each other, the effect will be attenuated. Adaptation stores memories of experience in rules and reputations of alternative rules (Levitt and March 1988, Huber 1991, Walsh and Ungson 1991, March et al. 2000). The memory of failures tends to make their reproduction unlikely, and the lack of reproduction preserves the memory. On the other hand, if failures are remembered poorly, or if the reputation of a particular alternative is affected by experiences with other alternatives, an alternative that is initially unsuccessful can overcome its early bad reputation (March 1973, Nystrom and Starbuck 1984).

Two phenomena associated with adaptive memory are likely to increase the later reproduction of early failures. The first is the decay of memory of past experience. Decays in memory are a characteristic feature of human recall, but perhaps even more so in organizations (Huber 1991). Failures of the past are likely to be forgotten or remembered poorly. As a result, traces of early failure are likely to fade in recall. Organizations with imperfect memories are likely to repeat the failures of the past, with all the attendant negative consequences (Neustadt and May 1986), but they are also less likely to reproduce reliability and the status quo (Hedberg et al. 1976, Brunsson and Olsen 1993). Variations in turnover of personnel or authorities (March 1991, Carley 1992), in documentation of the past (Huber 1991), in departmentalization and fragmentation (Huber 1991), and in estimates of the rate of change in the world are all features of an organizational setting that are likely to lead to variations in the reliability of memory.

The second feature of adaptation that is likely to increase the later reproduction of early failures is the generalization of experience. Experiences (good or bad) with one alternative can spread to other alternatives. When this happens, differences among alternatives are muted, with consequent improvement in the relative position of alternatives that have themselves experienced failures. The most obvious mechanism is the generation of self-confidence (Miller 1993). Success with an alternative is presumably some mixture of the potential of the alternative, the capabilities of the individual or organization in executing that alternative, and good fortune. Individuals and organizations are likely to overestimate the contribution of their capabilities to the outcome and underestimate the contribution of the alternative and luck. Because capabilities can be imagined to transfer to other alternatives, success on one alternative tends to inflate expectations of success on other alternatives. The result is that the relative likelihood of choosing an alternative rejected early increases somewhat over time for actors who are successful in other domains.

### Managing Reactions to Risk and Change

Most proposals for managing reactions to risk and change start from the premise that individual and organizational propensities to take or avoid risk and to embrace or resist change are buried in their utility functions and are susceptible primarily to countervailing incentives. The fact that models of experiential learning and competitive selection can produce behavior that looks like risk aversion and resistance to change does not negate the role of individual, organizational, and cultural predispositions in producing observed risk taking and change behavior. However, it does suggest that the search for levers by which to control the taking of risks and resistance to change should include attention to adaptive processes and particularly to persistence with alternatives having poor early outcomes.

Because the bias against risky and new activities is a product of the tendency to reproduce actions that have been successful, the bias will be reduced whenever failures are more likely to be reproduced. Thus, the bias will be reduced in situations where, for whatever reason, adaptation is slowed, made imprecise, or recalled less reliably. By examining the sources of slow, imprecise adaptation and unreliable recall, we have implicitly suggested how several features of adaptive ineffectiveness can increase the propensity of organizations to engage in risky and new activities.

For example, to the extent that inertia and ideology lead to slow adaptation, inertia and ideology will be associated with increased propensities to engage in risky activities and persist in new ones. Similarly, to the extent that causal complexity and ignorance lead to imprecise adaptation, causal complexity and ignorance will be associated with increased propensities to engage in risky activities and persist in new ones. More generally, any organizational characteristic that leads to persistence with alternatives that exhibit poor early results will increase the likelihood of risk taking and change in that organization. Because adaptation is precisely a process for reproducing successes, these characteristics are, for the most part, characteristics of short-run inefficiency in adaptation.

## CONCLUSION

We have shown that biases against new and risky alternatives may be less properties of individuals, organizations, or cultures than of learning and of competitive selection and reproduction themselves. The basic adaptive mechanism that produces biases in favor of reliable alternatives and the status quo is the differential reproduction of actions that have led to success. Because alternatives with a record of good performance are reproduced, alternatives with high potential that initially do poorly are likely to be avoided in the future. Early misrepresentation of the relative values of alternatives can thus have a lasting effect.

Because they exhibit variability in results, risky alternatives are likely to be misestimated on the basis of small samples of experience. Because they are likely to require practice to realize their full potential, new alternatives are likely to be underestimated on the basis of small samples of experience. Thus, an adaptive system will exhibit behavior that looks like risk aversion and resistance to change even in situations in which the long-run expected returns from new alternatives and risky alternatives are notably higher than those from existing alternatives and reliable alternatives. Because the biases are a product of the tendency to reproduce successes, the biases will be smaller whenever failures are more likely to be reproduced. Thus, according to this argument, the survival of risky and new alternatives will be associated with slow and imprecise adaptation and unreliable recall, all classical characteristics of short-run inefficiency in adaptation.

These features of adaptation pose a difficult dilemma for organizations, one that is more likely to be confronted by an ecology of micro-organizational phenomena than by deliberate strategic calculation, particularly because the latter involves knotty intertemporal and interpersonal comparisons. Without resolving how that dilemma might be faced in detail, we can observe that the biases we have identified as stemming from rapid, precise adaptation are relatively easy to justify in a world in which risky and new alternatives are systematically and persistently poor ones. In such a world, the benefits of increasing risk taking and reducing resistance to change are likely to be smaller than the costs. On the other hand, in a world in which risky and new alternatives have a fair chance of being good ones, any unconditional enthusiasm for fast, precise learning is likely to place an organization at a longer-term competitive disadvantage.

## ACKNOWLEDGMENTS

The research has been supported by grants from the Spencer Foundation. The authors are grateful for the comments of Sidney Winter, participants at seminars at the Wharton School, the Prince Bertil Symposium, the Conference on Knowledge and Innovation in Helsinki, the editor, and two anonymous reviewers.

## APPENDIX. LIST OF SYMBOLS

$A_{i,t}$  The average performance (outcomes) for all survivors of type $j$ in period $t$

$E$  Noise in realized outcomes; the standard deviation of the normally distributed error

$F_t$  The fraction of the population having a particular property at period $t$

$L_t$  The aspiration level at period $t$

$N_{j,t}$  The number of organizations of type $j$ in period $t$

$O_t$  The performance (outcome) at period $t$

$P_t$  The probability of choosing the risky alternative (or the alternative that requires practice) at period $t$

$S$  The base line standard deviation of performance

$T_{i,t}$  The aggregate performance (outcomes) for all survivors of type $j$ in period $t$

$X$  The expected performance (outcome) of the risky alternative or the alternative that requires practice

$Y$  The expected performance (outcome) of the certain alternative or the established alternative

$a$  The rate of adjustment in the probability of choosing the risky alternative (or the alternative that requires practice)

$b$  The rate of adjustment in the aspiration level

$c_t$  The competence in period $t$

$d$     The competence learning rate

$h$     Parameter regulating the sensitivity of reproduction to the average performance (outcome) of a type

$k$     Parameter regulating the rate of reduction in the standard deviation

$r_{j,t}$     The probability in period $t$ that a replacement will be of type $j$

$w$     The proportion of the population eliminated in each period

## REFERENCES

Abrahamson, E., G. Fairchild. 1999. Management fashion: Lifecycles, triggers, and collective learning processes. *Admin. Sci. Quart.* 44(4) 708–740.

Aldrich, H. 1999. *Organizations Evolving.* Sage Publications Inc., Thousands Oaks, CA.

Amabile, T. M. 1988. A model of creativity and innovation in organizations. B. Staw, L. L. Cummings, eds. *Res. Organ. Behavior.* 10 123–167.

Argote, L., S. L. Beckman, D. Epple. 1990. The persistence and transfer of learning in industrial settings. *Management Sci.* 36(2) 140–154.

———, D. Epple. 1990. Learning curves in manufacturing. *Sci.* 247 (Feb.) 920–924.

Arthur, B. W. 1989. Competing technologies, increasing returns, and lock-in by historical events. *Econom. J.* 99(394) 116–131.

Baldwin, J. R. 1998. *The Dynamics of Industrial Competition: A North American Perspective.* Cambridge University Press, Cambridge, MA.

Bandura, A. 1977. *Social Learning Theory.* Prentice Hall, Englewood Cliffs, NJ.

Barnett, W. P. 1997. The dynamics of competitive intensity. *Admin. Sci. Quart.* 42(1) 128–160.

Blume, L. E., D. Easley. 1995. What has the rational learning literature taught us? A. Kirman, M. Salmon, eds. *Learning and Rationality in Economics.* Blackwell, Oxford, UK.

Brunsson, N., J. P. Olsen. 1993. *The Reforming Organization.* Routledge, London, UK.

Busemeyer, J. R., K. N. Swenson, A. Lazarte. 1986. An adaptive approach to resource allocation. *Organizational Behavior and Human Decision Processes* 38(3) 318–341.

Bush, R. R., F. Mosteller. 1955. *Stochastic Models for Learning.* John Wiley & Sons, New York.

Carley, K. 1992. Organizational learning and personnel turnover. *Organ. Sci.* 3(1) 20–46.

Carroll, G. R., R. J. Harrison. 1994. Historical efficiency of competition between organizational populations. *Amer. J. Sociology* 100(3) 720–749.

Coombs, C. H., R. M. Dawes, A. Tversky. 1970. *Mathematical Psychology: An Elementary Introduction.* Prentice-Hall, Englewood Cliffs, NJ.

Cyert, R. D., J. G. March. 1963. *A Behavioral Theory of the Firm.* Prentice-Hall, Englewood Cliffs, NJ.

David, P. A. 1985. Clio and the economics of QWERTY. *Amer. Econom. Rev.* 75(2) 332–337.

DiMaggio, P. J., W. W. Powell. 1983. The iron cage revisited: Institutional isomorphism and collective rationality in organizational fields. *Amer. Soc. Rev.* 48(2) 147–160.

Easley, D., N. M. Kiefer. 1988. Controlling a stochastic process with unknown parameters. *Econometrica* 56(5) 1045–1064.

Elster, J. 1984. *Ulysses and the Sirens: Studies in Rationality and Irrationality,* 2nd ed. Cambridge University Press, Cambridge, UK.

Feller, W. 1968. *An Introduction to Probability Theory and Its Applications,* vol. 1, 3rd ed. John Wiley & Sons, New York.

Fichman, M., D. A. Levinthal. 1991. Honeymoons and the liability of adolescence: A new perspective on duration dependence in social and organizational relationships. *Acad. Management Rev.* 16(2) 442–468.

Frank, R. H., P. J. Cook. 1995. *The Winner-Take-It-All Society: Why Few at the Top Get So Much More Than the Rest of Us.* The Free Press, New York.

Friedman, M. 1953. The Methodology of Positive Economics. *Essays in Positive Economics.* Chicago University Press, Chicago, IL.

Gimeno, J., T. B. Folta, A. C. Cooper, C. Y. Woo. 1997. Survival of the fittest? Entrepreneurial human capital and the persistence of underperforming firms. *Admin. Sci. Quart.* 42(4) 750–783.

Goldberg, D. E. 1989. *Genetic Algorithms in Search, Optimization, and Machine Learning.* Addison-Wesley, Reading, MA.

Gould, S. J., R. C. Lewontin. 1984. The spandrels of San Marco and the Panglossian paradigm: A critique of the adaptationist program. E. Sober, ed. *Conceptual Issues in Evolutionary Biology.* MIT Press, Cambridge, MA. 252–270.

Greve, H. R. 1996. Patterns of competition: The diffusion of a market position in radio broadcasting. *Admin. Sci. Quart.* 41(1) 29–60.

———. 1998. Performance, aspirations, and risky organizational change. *Admin. Sci. Quart.* 43(1) 58–86.

Haleblian, J., S. Finkelstein. 1999. The influence of organizational acquisition experience on acquisition performance: A behavioral learning perspective. *Admin. Sci. Quart.* 44(1) 29–56.

Hannan, M. T., G. R. Carroll. 1992. *Dynamics of Organizational Populations.* Oxford University Press, Oxford, UK.

———, J. Freeman. 1977. The population ecology of organizations. *Amer. J. Soc.* 82(5) 929–964.

———, ———. 1984. Structural inertia and organizational change. *Amer. Soc. Rev.* 49(2) 149–164.

Haunschild, P. R., A. S. Miner. 1997. Modes of interorganizational imitation: The effects of outcome salience and uncertainty. *Admin. Sci. Quart.* 42(3) 472–500.

Haveman, H. A. 1992. Between a rock and a hard place: Organizational change and performance under conditions of fundamental environmental transformation. *Admin. Sci. Quart.* 37(1) 48–75.

Hedberg, B. L., P. C. Nystrom, W. H. Starbuck. 1976. Camping on seesaws: Prescriptions for a self-organizing organization. *Admin. Sci. Quart.* 21(1) 41–65.

Herriott, S. R., D. A. Levinthal, J. G. March. 1985. Learning from experience in organizations. *Amer. Econom. Rev. Proc.* 75(2) 298–302.

Hirschman, A. O. 1967. *Development Projects Observed.* The Brookings Institution, Washington, DC.

Holland, J. H. 1975. *Adaptation in Natural and Artificial Systems.* The MIT Press, Cambridge, MA.

Huber, G. P. 1991. Organizational learning: The contributing processes and the literatures. *Organ. Sci.* 2(1) 88–115.

Kaelbling, L. P. 1993. *Learning in Embedded Systems.* The MIT Press, Cambridge, MA.

Kauffman, S. A. 1993. *The Origins of Order: Self-Organization and Selection in Evolution*. Oxford University Press, Oxford, UK.

Kolakowski, L. 1968. *Toward a Marxist Humanism: Essays on the Left Today*. Grove Press, Inc., New York.

Lant, T. K. 1992. Aspiration level updating: An empirical exploration. *Management Sci.* 38(5) 623–644.

———. 1994. Computer simulations of organizations as experiential learning systems: Implications for organizational theory. K. Carley and M. Prietula, eds. *Computation Organizational Theory*. Erlbaum Associates, Hillsdale, NJ. 195–216.

———, S. J. Mezias. 1990. Managing discontinuous change: A simulation study of organizational learning and entrepreneurship. *Strategic Management J.* 11 (summer) 147–179.

———, ———. 1992. An organizational learning model of convergence and reorientation. *Organ. Sci.* 3(1) 47–71.

Lave, C. A., J. G. March. 1975. *An Introduction to Models in the Social Sciences*. Harper & Row, New York.

Levinthal, D. A. 1991. Random walks and organizational mortality. *Admin. Sci. Quart.* 36(3) 397–420.

———. 1997. Adaptation on rugged landscapes. *Management Sci.* 43(7) 377–415.

———, J. G. March. 1981. A model of adaptive organizational search. *J. Econom. Behavior Organ.* 2(4) 307–333.

———, ———. 1993. The myopia of learning. *Strategic Management J.* 14(2) 95–112.

Levitt, B., J. G. March. 1988. Organizational learning. *Ann. Rev. Soc.* 14 319–340.

Lippman, S. A., R. Rumelt. 1982. Uncertain imitability: An analysis of interfirm differences in efficiency under competition. *Bell J. Econom.* 13 (Autumn) 418–438.

Lounamaa, P., J. G. March. 1987. Adaptive coordination of a learning team. *Management Sci.* 33(1) 107–123.

MacArthur, R. H., E. O. Wilson. 1967. *The Theory of Island Biogeography*. Princeton University Press, Princeton, NJ.

March, J. G. 1973. Model bias in social action. *Rev. Ed. Res.* 42(4) 413–429.

———. 1988. Variable risk preferences and adaptive aspirations. *J. Econom. Behavior and Organ.* 9(1) 5–24.

———. 1991. Exploration and exploitation in organizational learning. *Organ. Sci.* 2(1) 71–87.

———. 1994. *A Primer on Decision Making*. The Free Press, New York.

———. 1995. The future, disposable organizations, and the rigidities of imagination. *Organ.* 2 427–440.

———. 1996. Learning to be risk averse. *Psych. Rev.* 103(2) 309–319.

———, Z. Shapira. 1992. Variable risk preferences and the focus of attention. *Psych. Rev.* 99(1) 172–183.

———, M. Schulz, X. Zhou. 2000. *The Dynamics of Rules: Change in Written Organizational Codes*. Stanford University Press, Stanford, CA.

Meyer, J. W., B. Rowan. 1977. Institutionalized organizations: Formal structure as myth and ceremony. *Amer. J. Sociology* 83(2) 340–363.

Meyer, M. W., L. G. Zucker. 1989. *Permanently Failing Organizations*. Sage, Newbury Park, CA.

Mezias, S. J., A. B. Eisner. 1997. Competition, imitation, and innovation: An organizational learning approach. *Adv. Strategic Management* 14 261–294.

————, M. A. Glynn. 1993. Three faces of corporate renewal: Institution, revolution, and evolution. *Strategic Management J.* 14(2) 77–101.

————, T. K. Lant. 1994. Mimetic learning and the evolution of organizational populations. J. A. C. Baum, J. V. Singh, eds. *Evolutionary Dynamics of Organizations.* Oxford University Press, New York. 179–198.

Miller, D. 1993. The architecture of simplicity. *Acad. Management Rev.* 18(1) 116–138.

Miner, A. S., P. R. Haunschild. 1995. Population level learning. L. L. Cummings, M. Barry, eds. *Research in Organizational Behavior* 17 115–166.

————, S. J. Mezias. 1996. Ugly duckling no more: Pasts and futures of organizational learning research. *Organ. Sci.* 7(1) 88–99.

————, S. V. Raghavan. 1999. Interorganizational imitation: A hidden engine of selection. B. McKelvey, J. A. C. Baum, eds. *Variations in Organization Science: In Honor of Donald T. Campbell.* Sage Publications, London, UK. 35–62.

Nelson, R., S. G. Winter. 1982. *An Evolutionary Theory of Economic Change.* Harvard University Press, Cambridge, MA.

Neustadt, R. E., E. R. May. 1986. *Thinking in Time: The Uses of History for Decision-Makers.* Free Press. New York.

Nystrom, P. C., W. H. Starbuck. 1984. To avoid organizational crises, unlearn. *Organ. Dynam.* 12 (Spring) 53–65.

Rabin. M., J. L. Schrag. 1999. First impressions matter: A model of confirmatory bias. *Quart. J. Econom.* 114(1) 37–82.

Rogers, E. M. 1995. *Diffusion of Innovations,* 4th Ed. The Free Press, New York.

Rothschild, M. 1974. A two-armed bandit theory of market pricing. *J. Econom. Theory* 9(2) 185–202.

Shapira, Z. 1995. *Risk Taking: A Managerial Perspective.* Russell Sage, New York.

Sutton, R. S., A. G. Barto. 1998. *Reinforcement Learning: An Introduction.* The MIT Press, Cambridge, MA.

Tolbert, P. S., L. G. Zucker. 1983. Institutional forces of change in the formal structure of organizations: The diffusion of civil services reform, 1880–1935. *Admin. Sci. Quart.* 28(1) 22–39.

Twain, M. 1897. *Following the Equator: A Journey Around the World.* American Publishing Co., Hartford, CT.

Usher, J. M., M. G. Evans. 1996. Life and death along gasoline alley: Darwinian and Lamarckian processes in a differentiating population. *Acad. Management J.* 39(5) 1428–1466.

Wald, A. 1947. *Sequential Analysis.* John Wiley & Sons, New York.

Walsh, J. P., G. R. Ungson. 1991. Organizational Memory. *Acad. Management Rev.* 16(1) 57–91.

Weick, K. E. 1976. Educational organizations as loosely coupled systems. *Admin. Sci. Quart.* 21(1) 1–19.

Wright, S. 1931. Evolution in Mendelian populations. *Genetics* 16(1) 97–159.

Yelle, L. E. 1979. The learning curve: Historical review and comprehensive survey. *Decision Sci.* 10(2) 302–328.

# CHAPTER 7

# Schumpeter, Winter, and the Sources of Novelty

MARKUS C. BECKER, THORBJØRN KNUDSEN,

AND JAMES G. MARCH

This article examines what Joseph Schumpeter said on the emergence of novelty in economic institutions, what Sidney Winter did to build on and deviate from that foundation, and what puzzles remain. Winter built a framework for answers to a puzzle that Schumpeter could not solve—how novelty emerges in a system based on routines. He identified two major sources of novelty: the combinatorics of routines and the unreliability of routine imitation. As possible inspirations for further progress in evolutionary thought, the article points to ideas from chemistry, linguistics, and the diffusion of fashion for elaborations of these key Winterian insights.

## INTRODUCTION

In his brilliant and pioneering paper on a neo-Schumpeterian theory of the firm, Sidney Winter anticipated many of the subsequent developments of an evolutionary approach to understanding firms and markets (Winter, 2006). On this occasion, we want to acknowledge the debt of the field to Sidney Winter by reviewing briefly what Joseph Schumpeter said, what Winter did to build on and deviate from that foundation, and what puzzles the two of them have left for the rest of us. It is a journey worthy of considerably more elaboration than we can provide here. The resolution of all unresolved issues is left to the reader as an exercize.

## A ROUTINE-BASED FIRM OF LIMITED RATIONALITY

### Behavior as Following Routines

A conception of a routine-based, limited rationality is fundamental to an understanding of firms as developed by both Schumpeter and Winter. As Winter noted and applauded, Schumpeter saw the firm as embedded in a history and future with dimensions of space and time that make talk of an optimum frivolous and rational calculation of little value. As an alternative to assuming that firms were

---

This chapter originally appeared in *Industrial and Corporate Change*, 15:2 (2006), 353–371.

guided by explicit rational calculations, Schumpeter saw most of the behavior in business firms of his time as following routines, rules, and procedures that provided reliable responses to environmental changes. In his view, actions stemmed not from calculated rationality on the part of individuals but from a pattern of recognizing a situation and applying a routine developed through history to it. Thus, he asks himself how a farmer knows what to plant and when. His answer (Schumpeter, 1934: 6) was

[L]ong experience, in part inherited, has taught him how much to produce for his greatest advantage; experience has taught him to know the extent and intensity of the demand to be reckoned with. To this quantity he adheres, as well as he can, and only gradually alters it under the pressure of circumstances.

## Schumpeter's Conception of Routines

A comparison of the three editions of *Theory of Economic Development*—the first (1911) and the second (1926) German editions, and the English translation (1934)—shows that between each edition, Schumpeter made systematic changes that reflect some combination of changes in his thinking and changes in his relationship to the English language. For instance, he introduced the term "routine" in added passages in the 1926 edition and further expanded his use of this term in the 1934 translation, a translation with which he was very actively involved (Stolper, 1988).

Schumpeter does not simply translate the German term "routine" into English. Rather, he captures a variety of German expressions in the English word "routine," even though in each case, a straightforward translation of the German expression exists. The record provides an insight into Schumpeter's evolving understanding and use of the idea of a "routine."

| Second German edition (1926), Theorie der wirtschaftlichen Entwicklung | Literal translation | English edition (1934), Theory of Economic Development |
|---|---|---|
| in der Wirklichkeit (1926: 150) | In reality | In the ordinary routine of established business (1934: 104) |
| Automatismus eines ausbalancierten Kreislaufs (1926: 112) | Automatism of a balanced circular flow | The routine of the circular flow (1934: 75) |
| Veränderung seiner Bahn (1926: 112) | Change of his trajectory | Changes in his routine (1934: 98) |

| Bloß Verwaltungsarbeit (1926: 113) | Mere administrative work | Merely routine work (1934: 76) |
| das Erledigen von Qualifi-kationslisten (1926: 115) | Running down checklists | Routine work (1934: 77) |
| Basis des Gewohnten (1926: 119 n.) | Base of what one is used to | Routine (1934: 81 n.) |
| Bahn des Ablaufs (1926: 121) | Trajectory of the process | The channels of economic routine (1934: 82) |
| Alltäglichkeiten (1926: 123) | Everyday things | Routine (1934: 84) |

Winter has a more specific idea of routines, and he sees them as the fundamental building block for an evolutionary theory of the firm. In particular, he has decision rules and standard operating procedures in mind (Winter, 1971, 1975, 1984; Nelson and Winter, 1973, 1982). In Nelson and Winter (1982), "routine" is also used in the sense of an abstract "way of doing things," a performance program. In their treatment, a link to organizational memory is established by seeing routines as a coding of lessons from experience (Becker, 2004).

## The Efficiency of Routines

Both Schumpeter and Winter explore the efficiency of routines, their relation to procedures that would be in some sense "optimal." Without specifying the process in detail, both of them assume some process of incremental learning of routines that improves their efficiency. Schumpeter is inclined to think that although the time required to achieve optimality makes the point largely irrelevant, the learning process could lead to an efficient match between routines and their environments if given sufficient time.

The assumption that conduct is prompt and rational is in all cases a fiction. But it proves to be sufficiently near to reality, if things have time to hammer logic into men. . . . But this holds good only where precedents without number have formed conduct through decades and, in fundamentals, through hundreds and thousands of years, and have eliminated unadapted behavior. (Schumpeter, 1934: 80)

Winter appears to be somewhat less confident than Schumpeter that the adaptations of a learning process, as it meanders over a rough landscape, would ever reliably converge to optimal procedures:

No guardian angel stands watch over the firm's identity, and a sufficiently long sequence of incremental changes can make two initially similar firms dissimilar, or two dissimilar ones converge. (Winter, 2006: 140)

Nevertheless, he sees the learning process as generally improving the fit of routines to their environments as long as the environments are reasonably stable. It is a vision that is consistent with some studies of the birth, revision, and death of organizational rules (March et al., 2000).

## SCHUMPETER AND NOVELTY

The central concern of both Schumpeter and Winter is not primarily with the normal functioning of a well-run, rule-based firm, reacting to changes in its environment by following routines that improve slowly with experience. Their interest is in more dramatic and innovative changes, what Schumpeter called "development." Schumpeter defined development as a change from one equilibrium, cost curve, or norm to another in such a way that the transition cannot be decomposed into infinitesimal steps (Schumpeter 1934, 1939, 2005). He insisted that incremental change and discontinuous change are completely different phenomena:

Development in our sense is a distinct phenomenon, entirely foreign to what may be observed in the circular flow or in the tendency towards equilibrium. (Schumpeter, 1934: 64)

Schumpeter puzzled over how a theory of routines might comprehend novelty. It was an issue to which he returned frequently. How can novelty arise endogenously in a routine-based system? In the first German edition (1911) of the *Theory of Economic Development*, the character traits of the entrepreneur provided the answer: while hedonic, rule followers merely adapt to changing circumstances, the energetic entrepreneur identifies new combinations and "pushes them through."

As he revised the book for subsequent editions in German (1926) and English (1934), Schumpeter apparently changed his views. Gradually, he shifted to a position that de-emphasized the dichotomy between incremental improvement and the introduction of novelty, blending these into a continuum. In the 1934 version of *Theory* known to most English-speaking readers, innovation is no longer attributed to a distinctive character trait of the entrepreneur. Rather, innovation originates in a depersonalized function of "carrying out new combinations," a function anyone can fulfill, which indeed can be a consequence of a sequence of operations within the firm by different people. Schumpeter, in fact, moved toward the idea of production functions, which could at certain times produce new combinations.

In his article *Development* (2005), Schumpeter identified the explanation of novelty as the greatest unmet scientific challenge. He considered three explanatory routes but did not find any of them entirely satisfactory: (i) character traits of entrepreneurs, as mentioned above; (ii) new combinations generated by production functions. He briefly considered interaction effects between different spheres of the social realm as possible causes of novelty but did not elaborate; and (iii) turning to theories of evolution for inspiration. Schumpeter's opinion of Darwin's evolutionary theory is not entirely clear, because it depends on an interpretation of the few remarks he made on the subject in his writings. As he clarified in *Development*, Schumpeter acknowledged the value of both Darwin's and Mendel's theories as explanations of incremental change. He did, however, dismiss both theories as explanations of novelty and discontinuity:

[D]evelopment is a problem, not simply of the facts but of our mental apparatus. This raises a difficulty, not for empirical research but for logic. This circumstance can be demonstrated for any domain you please, as for any domain of the social sciences. The theory of descent is particularly close at hand. Be it of the Darwinian type, with adaptation—which in a wider sense also includes decay—or according to the Mendelian type, with mixtures of constant elements. It always fails when it comes to the inaccessibility and indeterminacy of novelty and of the leap, even more so when such a theory of descent acknowledges the leap and names it, e.g. sport or mutation. It always runs into logical limits, or in other words, the fact that our logic is a logic of the adaptation process which can only *deny* or dismiss development. And precisely *that* explains what remains unsatisfactory about the matter, as can easily be seen. (Schumpeter, 2005: 117–118)

Schumpeter saw clearly that "mutation," as that term is normally used in Darwinian evolutionary theories, is less an explanation than a label for the inexplicable. He tried, without much success, to identify "the process by which innovation—technological and organizational change—is generated" (Ruttan, 1959: 599). He emphasized the impact of new combinations on competition. Famously, he identified five types of new combinations that mattered in this regard: new products, new production methods, new forms of organization, new markets, and new sources of supply. However, he was never able to link his typology of new combinations to an understanding of the processes generating novelty.

Thus, although Schumpeter saw combinations as involved in novelty, he found it difficult to provide any description of an inheritance mechanism that is any more precise than the word "combination." His interest in Mendel (and Mendel's discoverer de Vries; interview with Wolfgang Stolper, 4 August 2001, at his home in Ann Arbor, MI) might indicate that he hoped for the identification of some regularity underlying replications, such as the Mendelian combinatorics of reproduction. Neither he nor subsequent scholars have been able to find such regularities. Much as he tried throughout his career, he failed to generate any explanation of novelty (a fact that did not escape his critics, cf. Solo, 1951; Ruttan, 1959). In *Development*, Schumpeter himself also arrived at the conclusion that he could not provide such an explanation.

## WINTER AND NOVELTY

Whereas Schumpeter flirted with evolutionary ideas but, for the most part, found them uncongenial, Winter embraced the fundamental ideas of evolutionary thought but bent them to fit economic life and thinking. Partly, the difference reflects the evolving nature of the biological theory of evolution, changes that made the theory more palatable to an economist of Winter's generation than to an economist of Schumpeter's (Mayr, 1982). Partly, it reflects a difference between seeing the evolutionary glass as half-full (as Winter has) rather than half-empty (as Schumpeter did).

Like Schumpeter, Winter has rejected the standard interpretation of "mutation" as an unpredictable random event that is inexplicable. He has viewed such a formulation as unacceptably defeatist, much as Einstein is reputed to have viewed quantum mechanics (Pais, 1982). In attempting to develop a conception of novelty in the firm, Winter has taken a route hinted at, but not pursued, by Schumpeter—paying explicit attention to the actual decision processes of a firm. Although Schumpeter (2000) had an interest in "technique[s] of production and the methods and ways of commerce," and "ways of doing things" (letter to S. Colum Gilfillan, May 18, 1934), he did not particularly focus on them in discussing sources of novelty. Without elaborating on the components of the firm, Schumpeter used the description of routines as a general foundation for a theory of prices that extended to the possibility of both disrupting and generating equilibria.

In contrast, Winter has seen studies of the processes firms actually use as fundamental to understanding novelty in firms. He has tried consistently to unpack the black box of the firm, the production function. He has focused on routines as (the most) important building block(s) for an evolutionary theory of economic change and development, making explicit the link between routines and genes (Winter, 1975: 101) that was carried over into the classic work with Richard Nelson:

routines in general play the role of genes in our evolutionary theory (Nelson and Winter, 1982: 400)

The evolutionary framework has thus been harnessed for explaining change and development, and how novelty arises.

Behavioral routines do change over time, in both desired and undesired ways. Such changes correspond to mutations in the biological theory, and without them there could be no long-term evolutionary change. In so far as these changes are unintended and undirected, as many of them certainly are, the biological analogy is very close, and perhaps it can be extended to the realm of theoretical results. (Winter, 1975: 102)

Along the way, Winter has largely ignored conventional distinctions between learning and evolution and between processes of variation and processes of selection. In doing so, he has made a fruitful link between students of novelty (variation) and students of search over landscapes (adaptation and selection).

Recent advances in the description of selection environments suggest a coupling between variation and selection that supports Winter's tack. NK models depend on the number of genetic components (to be recombined) and their interdependencies (Kauffman, 1993); and they have been widely employed in the study of organizations (Levinthal, 1997; Sorenson, 2002; Rivkin and Siggelkow, 2003). These models produce a mapping of components onto fitness values that constitute the selection environment. Increasing the number of interdependencies among components increases cross-sectional variation in fitness, thus linking the combinatorics of components to the generation of variation.

Where Schumpeter thought mutations could not explain novelty, Winter has been more optimistic. His optimism, however, has depended on abandoning a central tenet of the classical biological theory of mutations, the idea that mutations are inexplicable, random events, and replacing it with ideas that associate "mutations," for the most part, with intentional, motivated change. Although the processes that Winter has emphasized are analogous in a very general way to those found in biological evolution (particularly some of its modern developments), by being attentive to the specifics of economic life, they deviate significantly from their biological forbears[1]:

[W]hile the decision rules themselves are the economic counterpart of genetic inheritance, the failure-stimulated search process apparently has no analogue in biological evolution—it would correspond to a mechanism that automatically generates a burst of mutations when they are needed. (Winter, 1971: 245)

[A] slavish pursuit of the biological analogy would be counterproductive, for it is quite clear that the bulk of what we count as interesting long-term change in business behavior is not the product of blind chance. Rather, it is deliberate innovation, the product of directed effort, typically undertaken in response to identifiable economic stimuli, and motivated by profit consideration. Thus, with a considered step away from the bio-logical theory, it is proposed that deliberate innovations, large and small, be counted as the most significant subset of the changes in routine behavior. (Winter, 1975: 102)

Winter (1964, 1971) drew ideas of failure-induced search from work on a behavioral theory of the firm (Cyert and March, 1963) and proposed that a theory of innovation emphasizes such motivations for intentional change.

When the firm is doing well, it will not expend time and money on "search activity." Thus if a firm is behaving according to a routine that is actually viable, given the exist-ing competition of other organization forms and the character of the environment, it will not be inclined to depart from the routine. (Winter, 1964: 264)

Continuing that line, Nelson and Winter argued that

the observed role of simple decision rules as immediate determinants of behavior, and operation of the satisficing principle in the search process of new rules, provided the required genetic mechanisms. (Nelson and Winter, 1982: 42)

The direction was cheered by Redlich, who contrasted it with Schumpeter's ideas:

The dead hand of Schumpeter's prestige should not keep us from recognizing that which his model veils, namely the great importance of failure in economic develop-ment. (Redlich in März 1991, 26)

Thus, "mutation" of routines, that is, the production of novelty in organizations, came to be pictured as driven by processes of failure-induced search:

Our concept of search obviously is the counterpart of that of mutation in biological evolutionary theory. . . . And our treatment of search as partly determined by the rou-tines of the firm parallels the treatment in biological theory of mutation as being deter-mined in part by the genetic makeup of the organism. (Nelson and Winter, 1982: 18)

In the Winter formulation, search stimulated by the experience of failure has been supplemented by imitative search, the copying of routines used by other firms.

The second type of search process is an imitation mechanism: The firm is more likely to consider a given technique the greater the percentage of current industry output produced with that technique. (Nelson and Winter, 1973: 442)

In this way, Winter has addressed Edith Penrose's (1952) critique of the use of biological analogies in economics. She had noted the problem of identifying an economic counterpart of genetic inheritance. Winter found the counterpart in failure-induced search and the imitative replication of successful routines. To some extent, the Winter approach had been anticipated by Alchian (1950: 215–216), who emphasized "reproduction" via imitation of rules of behavior.

By framing the mutation process as involving failure-induced search for new routines, and the attempted replication of routines used by others, Winter opened the door to a consideration of the imperfections of search and imitation. Other researchers have identified relevant systematic cognitive biases and errors that agents have and commit (Kahneman and Tversky, 1973; Reason, 1990; Fiske and Taylor, 1991) and the systematic variation introduced by such biases and errors (Hogarth and Einhorn, 1992; Denrell, 2005). Within such a perspective, it is possible to ask the much more concrete question: What are the sources of variation arising in the replication process, and what are their effects on a history of change? Answering those questions has, however, proven to be difficult.

### THE THORNY PROBLEMS OF NOVELTY

As Winter has consistently recognized, a neo-Schumpeterian theory of the firm requires a theory of changes in routines that accommodates three rather different kinds of changes: (i) incremental changes in existing routines on the basis of experience; (ii) inter-firm and intra-firm diffusion of routines; and (iii) endogenous generation of new, distinctively novel routines.

The incremental change of routines seems reasonably well comprehended within a theory of experiential learning (Levitt and March, 1988; Greve, 2003). Some of the relevant properties of experiential learning have been documented in recent work (Gavetti and Levinthal, 2000; Denrell and March, 2001; Denrell, 2005). In particular, it is clear that experiential learning is myopic (Levinthal and March, 1993) and is vulnerable to errors attributable both to human biases and to the conflicts within an organization (Lounamaa and March, 1987; Reason, 1990; Denrell, 2005).

The diffusion of routines seems reasonably well comprehended within an epidemiological theory such as modern versions of "institutionalization" in sociology. Some of the relevant properties of the diffusion of routines have also been documented in recent work (Attewell, 1992; Westphal et al., 1997; Strang and Soule, 1998; Miner and Raghavan, 1999). In particular, it is clear that a theory of the diffusion of routines has to relax two common assumptions of conventional epidemiological models—the assumption of reproductive reliability and the assumption of network exogeneity (Anderson and May, 1991; March, 1999).

Diffusion research casts some light on the way the incremental spread of routines sometimes leads to wide adoption and notable persistence in routines (Fischer, 1989; Vincenti, 1994; Nelson et al., 2004). Accounting for the reliable spread of more complex routines is a challenge, but recent work indicates how it can happen. One example is the "McDonald's approach" where a common template with a proven track record facilitates reliable replication of a large number of similar outlets that deliver a product or perform a service (Winter and Szulanski, 2001).

Accounting for the reliable spread and differential adoption of routines is only part of the puzzle, however. What is missing is a theory of the endogenous generation of distinctively novel routines. For Schumpeter and Winter, as well as others, the problem seems to be: Where do we look for mechanisms of such variation? Some of Winter's most important contributions lie in his attempts to illuminate two such mechanisms: first, the combinatorics of routines and, second, the unreliability of routine replication.

## Combinatorics of Routines

Winter has tried persistently to identify regularities in combining routines (similar in a very general way to Mendelian combinatorics).

The canonical question of evolutionary theory is this: Consider a group of firms, operating according to specified routines—subject to modification by specified search rules—in a specified market environment. Which classes of routine behavior are capable of protracted coexistence with each other, without producing, out of their own dynamic logic, pressures for change? What classes are mutually incompatible or antagonistic, and in what time frame is the clash likely to become acute? (Winter, 1975: 108–109)

To command explanatory and predictive power similar to Mendel's laws in the realm of biology, however, we need to respond to questions such as: What are the basic phenomena resulting from combinations of routines? What new routines are generated by the coming together of routines? To some extent, this is consistent both with Schumpeter's interest (interview with Wolfgang Stolper, 4 August 2001, at his home in Ann Arbor, MI) in the ideas of de Vries (1901–1903) and with Winter's emphasis on the role of reliable routines in producing novelties (Winter and Szulanski, 2001; Winter, 2006). The study of the combinatorics of routines is, however, in its infancy. How and with what success it will develop is unclear.

## Unreliability in the Imitation of Routines

Most ideas about the diffusion of ideas, routines, or technologies proceed, sometimes explicitly, from a conception of "progress." They assume processes that make at least local discrimination between what apparently leads to failure and what apparently leads to success. The vision is one of processes subject to error but basically tending toward improvement.

Although Winter is reasonably comfortable with such a vision, he qualifies it in two important ways. First, he is quite conscious of the meandering character of history and the many occasions on which adaptive processes fail to achieve global maxima (Nelson and Winter, 1964, 1982; Winter, 1971). Second, he understands the potential for variation found in the unreliability of the replication of routines as they spread to new places and activities. Attributing the origin of novelty to unreliability in replication, however, begs for a better explanation of such error. Without it, unreliability becomes an instance of mutation, an unpredictable random event perturbing a routine when it is imitated or reproduced. For Winter, the goal is to discover comprehensible sources of novelty in the mechanisms of imitation.

In his work on routine replication, Winter pointed to incompleteness in a template for routine imitation as a source of copying error (Winter and Szulanski, 2001).

[T]he template provided by the existing routine may not yield a good copy. There will be some mutation of the routine as it is transferred to the new plant. Of course, perfect replication is not more of an ultimate objective than perfect control. What matters is not that the plant be the same, but that it work with overall efficiency comparable to the old one. (Nelson and Winter, 1982: 121)

In Winter's view, such incompleteness in a template is often linked to the underlying combinatorics of its components. This is the case when the intricate combination of personnel and equipment involved in a routine is hard to grasp (Nelson and Winter, 1982; Winter and Szulanski, 2001). Reproduction on the basis of a few controlled components in a routine will be a random walk over combinations of uncontrolled attributes. With interdependencies among components (as opposed to unrelated components), the walk will exhibit more variation. In his search for an explanation of the emergence of distinctively novel routines, Winter thus pointed to the linking of properties that arise from the combinatorics of a routine's components to the generation of new variation in its reproduction.

## TOWARD AN EVOLUTIONARY ECONOMICS

The original core ideas of evolutionary models in biology and economics emphasized adaptation to an exogenous environment through differences in the survival rate of genes (routines) and through differences in the replication rate of genes (routines) that reproduce precisely except for rare, random mutations. Variation in survival and birth rates are described as fitness components that reflect differences in the adaptiveness of traits to the environment, and traits are thought to reflect genetic variation reliably.

Variation among genes is produced by mutations, and variation among genetic combinations is produced by reproductive combinatorics. Selection among genes is produced by selection among genetic combinations. Selection feeds on variation in trait differences to produce genetic distributions that better reflect the requirements of the environment. Insofar as the selection process involves reproductive combinatorics, it also reproduces the variation it feeds on. The process is imagined to be relatively efficient in matching gene pools to environments.

Modern evolutionary models fit generally within that structure, but they fiddle with it considerably:

- They are inclined to portray environments as endogenous. They emphasize the effects of competition and the coevolution of species in an interactive ecology.
- They are inclined to picture selection processes as relatively complex, operating at multiple levels of biological (social) organization, and involving multiple interdependent selection criteria (fitness components).
- They are inclined to attach greater importance to genetic and trait combinations and interactions as factors in the survival of genes and traits, noting such phenomena as mutualisms and "hitchhiking."
- They are inclined to view the correspondence between genetic variation and trait variation as imperfect and stress the role of the latter in producing evolutionary outcomes.
- They are inclined to see evolutionary processes as inefficient in the sense that they have multiple equilibria and do not reliably discover optima.
- They are inclined to view mutations less as inexplicable random error than as changes caused by comprehensible processes.
- At least in economic versions, they are inclined to introduce cognitive and organizational mechanisms of conscious behavior such as anticipatory, intentional search and choice, internal conflict, and deliberate imitation into both selection processes and the processes of mutation.

The result has been that the models have become both considerably more consistent with observations of evolutionary histories and processes and considerably less tractable. The observed phenomena are more complex than our representations and understandings of them. It is an old story, from which it is possible to draw either pain or pleasure, but the latter seems more consistent with the celebration of Sid Winter. In that spirit, we might suggest two possible elaborations of the key Winterian insights. The first is a set of possible directions for pursuing the combinatorics of routines. The second is a set of possible directions for pursuing the diffusion of routines.

### COMBINATORICS OF ROUTINES

Consideration of Mendelian reproductive combinatorics is an obvious stimulus to a search for understanding the combinatorics of routines as a factor in economic evolution. The problem with using Mendel as a model, however, is that Mendel's theory was developed on the basis of an enormous number of empirical, especially experimental, studies of the replications of genetic combinations. There is nothing even remotely similar in studies of routines in firms and the reproductions ensuing from mixing them. There are, however, some starts that suggest the Winter vision may not be entirely unreasonable.

For example, Brian Pentland has pioneered an analysis that involves decomposing observable routines into constituent components, thus portraying routines as sequences of "moves" (Pentland, 1995, 2003). He has identified possible combinations of routine components but only observed some of these empirically. For our purpose, one interesting question addressed in Pentland's research is: Why are some theoretically possible combinations not observed in practice? Pentland's answer is that interdependencies among routine components prevent some of the theoretically possible combinations from being implemented in practice (for instance, the text must be prepared before it can be printed).

In further pursuit of the basic perspective, Pentland has followed the lead from evolutionary studies of language (Bloom, 1973; Bickerton, 1981, 1990; Chomsky, 1986; Pinker, 1994) in focusing on rules that comprise a "grammar of action" (Pentland and Rueter, 1994). Grammar is an evolved system of rules governing how words combine to produce meaning. Historically, poetry has served as a domain of grammatical experimentation, as has the process of learning the rules by children and by persons acquiring a new language. A grammar of language tolerates only rather modest violations, however. Swapping two words in a sentence can produce poetic novelties or utter nonsense. Linguistic combinatorics stimulates error correction by providing positive feedback to word combinations that are consistent with grammar and negative feedback to word combinations that violate it.

Grammar provides an error threshold that facilitates the reliable reproduction of word combinations, a process that tends to reinforce the use of particular simple word combinations. As simple word combinations become stable, they can be substituted for words, thus generating a nested hierarchy of word combinations that produce meaning. The length of meaningful sentences is testimony to the level of reproductive reliability achieved in linguistic combinatorics.

The similarity between language grammar and the regularity underlying the Mendelian combinatorics of reproduction has been noted in recent work (Maynard Smith and Szathmáry, 1999). Grammar increases reproductive reliability by constraining variation in word combination (novelty). The effect of increasing the reliability (and force) of reproduction by constraint is a well-known phenomenon in epidemiological studies that take immune response into account. Extending this vision to the production of stable behavioral combinations is a start, however far the reliability of routine replication may be from Mendelian precision.

Considering a combinatorics of routines that preserves reproductive reliability in ways similar to a grammar of language also points to a few missing items in such a vision. It is presently unclear how we account for the ability to acquire grammar; we do not know how grammar evolves; and it is hard to explain the spread of grammatical novelties—as opposed to new words (Bickerton, 1981, 1990; Maynard Smith and Szathmáry, 1999; Pinker, 1994).

Another possible clue to a theory of combinatorics is provided in the observation that the combinatorics of language shares some features with the laws of chemistry (Maynard Smith and Szathmáry, 1999). For example, well-understood physical principles explain how chemical components combine to make stable or unstable compounds. Some chemical compounds can also reproduce by generating autocatalytic cycles, that is cycles of systematic transformation that multiply their constituent compounds. Generally, the limited reproductive reliability of autocatalytic cycles tends to spawn combinations that yield degenerate cycles and instability. In some cases, however, physical laws facilitate the emergence of stable complex autocatalytic cycles by constraining the interaction among chemical compounds (and by exploiting catalytic stimulants, such as enzymes), much in the way that grammar facilitates reliable reproduction of word combinations. Perhaps, similar structuring principles within economic institutions are required for the emergence of stable cycles of self-reproducing routines that exhibit some level of complexity.

In recent work, John Padgett and coworkers have pursued a chemical perspective in accounting for economic production as an instance of routine combinatorics. As in the origin-of-life problem, Padgett et al. (2003) are concerned with the formation of stable cycles of compounds (routines) from a "soup" of random components. Their work on production as chemistry confirms prior work (Hofbauer and Sigmund, 1988) by identifying a threshold that limits the size of viable cycles to a very few components (five or less) in the absence of constraints on component interaction. Only if exogenous constraints on component interaction are present, do more complex production cycles become stable (Padgett et al., 2003). The level of complexity in the cycles produced in this work is not comparable to the level of complexity observed in DNA, English sentences, rules governing social institutions, or routines in a shop floor; but the research provides a possible approach to studying and understanding the combinatorics of routines in economic life.

In a related but quite different direction, Padgett has sought to understand the evolution of a political system in Florence (Padgett and Ansell, 1993; McLean and Padgett, 1997; Padgett, 2001). This work also indicates that the emergence and evolution of complex rules and routines that characterize exchange in a market economy and political system are facilitated by structuring principles that limit interaction among actors.

Padgett and his coworkers suggest that understanding the emergence and evolution of routines may be informed by understanding the principles that account for the emergence and evolution of chemical compounds. A similar conclusion is reached by Maynard Smith and Szathmáry (1999) in suggesting that any system capable of generating increasingly complex cycles that continue to feed on the variation they produce can be informed by an understanding of chemistry. The genetic code and human language are canonical examples of such systems. It seems imaginable that emergent cycles of rules and routines have a similar role in explaining the evolution of social institutions.

## Diffusion of Routines

By noting some of the ways in which imitation is an imperfect replicator of routines, Winter anticipates recent work emphasizing that diffusion involves systematic transformation of routines in association with their transfer (Czarniawska and Sevón, 1996, 2005). Such an interest might well lead Winter to theories of fashion (Abrahamson, 1991; Kieser, 2002; Czarniawska, 2005). The fundamental difference between theories of fashion and most theories of learning or evolution in economics is that there is no idea of progress in theories of fashion. It is what Young called "evolution without destination" (Young, 1973: 109). Fashions cycle without (for the most part) becoming better, or better "fit," to their environments. They are, in that respect, different from the usual conception of diffusing technologies or knowledge; but the difference shrinks almost to the vanishing point in a Winterian formulation.

A fundamental problem for theories of fashion, as for theories of learning or evolution, is to account simultaneously for the incremental spread of an idea, practice, style, or enthusiasm, and for its discontinuous displacement by another.

Fashion is the imitation of a given example and satisfies the demand for social adaptation. . . . At the same time, it satisfies in no less degree the need of differentiation, the tendency for dissimilarity, the desire for change and contrast. (Simmel, 1971: 296)

What Winter's insights suggest (though not explicitly to him) is that understanding novelty in business firms may be informed by understanding novelty in fashion. Because theories of fashion fit the political and epistemological worldviews of most sociologists better than they do the political and epistemological worldviews of most economists, they are more common in sociology than in economics. However, as Winter implicitly recognizes, the difference between sociological theories of fashions and economic theories of technological change appear to be greater than the difference between processes affecting the distribution of skirt lengths and processes affecting the distribution of production technologies.

Fashion seems capable of generating increasingly complex cycles that feed on the variation they produce. If fashion cycles are indeed captured by such a description, we would expect them to be governed by a "grammar of fashion," a structuring principle that constrains interaction among fashion components. A grammar of fashion would increase the reliability (and force) of reproduction by constraint as would infections that are countered by immune response. Although specific equations would be highly speculative at this point, it is possible that immune response to fashion (infection) is driven by periodic variations in susceptibility that can be captured by a system of (three or more) equations exhibiting chaotic variation (Anderson and May, 1991). Such a perspective is likely to help understand novel combinations of skirt length and color (as well as novel combinations of routines) in response to variations in local taste, even though it may fall short of accounting for a gradually evolving complexity in fashion cycles (routines).

The point is not that these particular directions are strikingly more promising than all others. They illustrate possibilities that owe debts both to Schumpeter and to Winter for their persistence in pursuing an understanding of the sources of novelty in economic institutions. Sidney Winter might well have relaxed after elaborating the Schumpeterian vision of economic development into an articulate linking of ideas of rule-based actions in firms with ideas of evolutionary change and after noting the difference between incremental improvement and the introduction of novelty. However, he did not. Without contradicting the Schumpeterian vision significantly, he built a framework for answers to the part of the puzzle that Schumpeter could not solve—how novelty emerges in a system based on routines. He identified two major sources of novelty: the combinatorics of routines and the unreliability of routine imitation. Winter's ideas that evolutionary economics might seek to capture critical features of the reproductive unreliabilities generated through combinations of routines and their diffusion are noble, even Nobel, thoughts. Building on those should keep the rest of us busy for another fifty years or so, if Sid does not beat us to it.

## ACKNOWLEDGMENTS

The research has been supported by grants from the Sloan Foundation and the Fulbright Scholar Program.

## NOTES

1. Over the last two decades, molecular biology has begun uncovering some sources of mutationally defined genes, in terms of their molecular identities and mechanisms of regulation (Haag and True, 2001). However, any connection between these results and the Winter emphasis on intention and motivation is obscure.

## REFERENCES

Abrahamson, E. (1991), "Managerial fads and fashions: The diffusion and rejection of innovations," *Academy of Management Review, 16,* 586–612.

Alchian, A. A. (1950), "Uncertainty, evolution, and economic theory," *Journal of Political Economy, 58,* 211–221.

Anderson, R. M. and R. M. May (1991), *Infectious Diseases of Humans.* Oxford University Press: Oxford.

Attewell, P. (1992), "Technology diffusion and organizational learning: The case of business computing," *Organization Science, 3,* 1–19.

Becker, M. C. (2004), "Organizational routines: A review of the literature," *Industrial and Corporate Change, 13,* 643–677.

Bickerton, D. (1981), *Roots of Language.* Karona: Ann Arbor, MI.

Bickerton, D. (1990), *Species and Language.* Chicago University Press: Chicago, IL.

Bloom, P. (1973), *One Word at a Time: The Use of Single Word Utterances Before Syntax.* Cambridge University Press: Cambridge.

Chomsky, N. (1986), *Knowledge of Language: Its Nature, Origin and Use.* Praeger: New York.

Cyert, R. M. and J. G. March (1963), *A Behavioral Theory of the Firm.* Prentice Hall: Englewood Cliffs, NJ.

Czarniawska, B. (2005), "Fashion in organizing," in B. Czarniawska and G. Sevón (eds), *Global Ideas: How Ideas, Objects and Practices Travel in the Global Economy.* Liber AB and Copenhagen Business School Press: Malmö, Copenhagen, pp. 129–146.

Czarniawska, B. and G. Sevón (eds) (1996), *Translating Organizational Change*. De Gruyter: Berlin.

Czarniawska, B. and G. Sevón (eds) (2005), *Global Ideas: How Ideas, Objects and Practices Travel in the Global Economy*. Liber AB and Copenhagen Business School Press: Malmö, Copenhagen.

Denrell, J. (2005), "Why most people disapprove of me: experience sampling in impression formation," *Psychological Review, 112,* 951–978.

Denrell, J. and J. G. March (2001), "Adaptation as information restriction: the hot stove effect," *Organization Science, 12,* 523–538.

Fischer, D. H. (1989), *Albions Seed. Four Brittan Folkways in America*. Oxford University Press: New York, Oxford.

Fiske, S. T. and S. E. Taylor (1991), *Social Cognition*. McGraw Hill: New York.

Gavetti, G. and D. A. Levinthal (2000), "Looking forward and looking backward: Cognitive and experiential search," *Administrative Science Quarterly, 45,* 113–137.

Greve, H. R. (2003), *Organizational Learning from Performance Feedback*. Cambridge University Press: Cambridge.

Haag, E. S. and J. R. True (2001), "Perspective: from mutants to mechanisms? Assessing the candidate gene paradigm in evolutionary biology," *Evolution, 55,* 1077–1084.

Hofbauer, J. and K. Sigmund (1988), *Dynamical Systems and the Theory of Evolution*. Cambridge University Press: Cambridge.

Hogarth, R. M. and H. J. Einhorn (1992), "Order effects in belief updating: The belief-adjustment model," *Cognitive Psychology, 24,* 1–55.

Kahneman, D. and A. Tversky (1973), "On the psychology of prediction," *Psychological Review, 80,* 237–251.

Kauffman, S. A. (1993), *The Origins of Order: Self-Organization and Selection in Evolution*. Oxford University Press: New York.

Kieser, A. (2002), "Managers as marionettes? Using fashion theories to explain the success of consultants," in M. Kipping and L. Engwall (eds), *Management Consulting: Emergence and Dynamics of a Knowledge Industry*. Oxford University Press: Oxford, pp. 167–183.

Levinthal, D. A. (1997), "Adaptation on rugged landscapes," *Management Science, 43,* 934–950.

Levinthal, D. A. and J. G. March (1993), "The myopia of learning," *Strategic Management Journal, 14,* 95–112.

Levitt, B. and J. G. March (1988), "Organizational learning," *Annual Review of Sociology, 14,* 319–340.

Lounamaa, P. H. and J. G. March (1987), "Adaptive coordination of a learning team," *Management Science, 33,* 107–123.

March, J. G. (1999), "A learning perspective on some dynamics of institutional integration," in M. Egeberg and P. Lægreid (eds), *Organizing Political Institutions: Essays for Johan P. Olsen*. Scandinavian University Press: Oslo, pp. 129–155.

March, J. G., M. Schulz, and X. Zhou (2000), *The Dynamics of Rules: Change in Written Organizational Codes*. Stanford University Press: Stanford, CA.

März, E. (1991), *Joseph Schumpeter. Scholar, Teacher and Politician*. Yale University Press: New Haven and London.

Maynard Smith, J. and E. Szathmáry (1999), *The Origins of Life. From the Birth of Life to the Origins of Language*. Oxford University Press: Oxford.

Mayr, E. (1982), *The Growth of Biological Thought. Diversity, Evolution, and Inheritance.* The Belknap Press of Harvard University Press: Cambridge, MA and London.

McLean, P. and J. F. Padgett (1997), "Was Florence a perfectly competitive market? Transactional evidence from the Renaissance," *Theory and Society, 26,* 209–244.

Miner, A. S. and S. V. Raghavan (1999), "Interorganizational imitation. A hidden engine of selection," in J. A. C. Baum and B. McKelvey (eds), *Variations in Organization Science. In Honor of Donald T. Campbell.* Sage: Thousand Oaks, CA, pp. 35–62.

Nelson, R. R., A. Peterhansl, and B. Sampat (2004), "Why and how innovations get adopted: A tale of four models," *Industrial and Corporate Change, 13,* 679–699.

Nelson, R. R. and S. G. Winter (1964), "A case study in the economics of information and coordination: The weather forecasting system," *The Quarterly Journal of Economics, 78,* 420–441.

Nelson, R. R. and S. G. Winter (1973), "Toward an evolutionary theory of economic capabilities," *American Economic Review (Papers and Proceedings), 68,* 440–449.

Nelson, R. R. and S. G. Winter (1982), *An Evolutionary Theory of Economic Change.* Harvard University Press: Cambridge, MA.

Padgett, J. F. (2001), "Organizational genesis, identity and control: The transformation of banking in renaissance Florence," in J. E. Rauch and A. Casella (eds), *Networks and Markets.* Russell Sage: New York, pp. 211–257.

Padgett, J. F. and C. K. Ansell (1993), "Robust action and the rise of the Medici, 1400–1434," *American Journal of Sociology, 98,* 1250–1310.

Padgett, J. F., D. Lee, and N. Collier (2003), "Economic production as chemistry," *Industrial and Corporate Change, 4,* 843–878.

Pais, A. (1982), "Max Born's statistical interpretation of quantum mechanics," *Science, 218,* 1193–1198.

Penrose, E. T. (1952), "Biological analogies in the theory of the firm," *American Economic Review, 42,* 804–819.

Pentland, B. T. (1995), "Grammatical models of organizational processes," *Organization Science, 6,* 541–556.

Pentland, B. T. (2003), "Conceptualizing and measuring variety in organizational work processes," *Management Science, 49,* 857–870.

Pentland, B. T. and H. H. Rueter (1994), "Organizational routines as grammars of action," *Administrative Science Quarterly, 39,* 484–510.

Pinker, S. (1994), *The Language Instinct.* William Morrow: New York.

Reason, J. (1990), *Human Error.* Cambridge University Press: Cambridge.

Rivkin, J. W. and N. Siggelkow (2003), "Balancing search and stability: interdependencies among elements of organizational design," *Management Science, 49,* 290–311.

Ruttan, V. W. (1959), "Usher and Schumpeter on invention, innovation, and technological change," *Quarterly Journal of Economics, 73,* 596–606.

Schumpeter, J. A. (1911), *Theorie der wirtschaftlichen Entwicklung,* 1st edn. Duncker & Humblot: Leipzig.

Schumpeter, J. A. (1926), *Theorie der wirtschaftlichen Entwicklung,* 2nd edn. Duncker & Humblot: Leipzig.

Schumpeter, J. A. (1934), *The Theory of Economic Development. An Inquiry into Profits, Capital, Credit, Interest, and the Business Cycle.* Harvard University Press: Cambridge, MA.

Schumpeter, J. A. (1939), *Business Cycles. A Theoretical, Historical, and Statistical Analysis of the Capitalist Process.* McGraw Hill Books: New York.

Schumpeter, J. A. (2000), "Letter to Colum Gilfillan, 18. Mai 1934," in U. Hedtke and R. Swedberg (eds), *Joseph Alois Schumpeter. Briefe/Letters. Ausgewählt und herausgegeben von Ulrich Hedtke und Richard Swedberg.* Mohr Siebeck: Tübingen, pp. 265–266.

Schumpeter, J. A. (2005), "Development," *Journal of Economic Literature, XLIII,* 104–116 (Entwicklung) [Translated by M. C. Becker and T. Knudsen].

Simmel, G. (1971), "Fashion," in D. N. Levine (ed.), *Georg Simmel on Individuality and Social Forms.* University of Chicago Press: Chicago, IL, pp. 294–323.

Solo, C. S. (1951), "Innovation in the capitalist process: a critique of the Schumpeterian theory," *Quarterly Journal of Economics, 65,* 417–428.

Sorenson, O. (2002), "Interorganizational learning," in J. A. C. Baum (ed.), *Companion to Organizations.* Blackwell: Oxford, pp. 664–685.

Stolper, W. F. (1988), "Schumpeters *Theorie der wirtschaftlichen Entwicklung*—eine kritische Exegese," in H. C. Recktenwald, F. M. Scherer, and W. F. Stolper (eds), *Schumpeters monumentales Werk—Wegweiser für eine dynamische Analyse.* Verlag für Wirtschaft und Finanzen: Düsseldorf, pp. 35–74.

Strang, D. and S. A. Soule, 1998. "Diffusion in organizations and social movements: From hybrid corn to poison pills," *Annual Review of Sociology, 24,* 265–290.

Vincenti, W. G. (1994), "The retractable airplane landing gear and the Northrop 'anomaly': Variation-selection and the shaping of technology," *Technology and Culture, 35,* 1–34.

Vries, H. de (1901–1903), *Die Muthationstheorie.* Veit & Co: Leipzig.

Westphal, J. D., R. Gulati, and S. M. Shortell (1997), "Customization or conformity? An institutional and network perspective on the content and consequences of TQM adoption," *Administrative Science Quarterly, 42,* 366–394.

Winter, S. G. (1964), "Economic 'natural selection' and the theory of the firm," *Yale Economic Essays, 4,* 225–272.

Winter, S. G., Jr. (1971), "Satisficing, selection and the innovating remnant," *Quarterly Journal of Economics, 85,* 237–261.

Winter, S. G. (1975), "Optimization and evolution in the theory of the firm," in R. H. Day and T. Groves (eds), *Adaptive Economic Models.* Academic Press: New York, pp. 73–118.

Winter, S. G. (1984), "Schumpeterian competition in alternative technological regimes," *Journal of Economic Behavior and Organization, 5,* 287–320.

Winter, S. G. (2006), "Toward a Neo-Schumpeterian theory of the Firm," *Industrial and Corporate Change, 15,* 1.

Winter, S. G. and G. Szulanski (2001), "Replication as strategy," *Organization Science, 12,* 730–743.

Young, A. B. (1973), "Recurring cycles of fashion," in G. Wills and D. Midgley (eds), *Fashion Marketing.* Allen & Unwin: London, pp. 107–124

# CHAPTER 8

# Rationality, Foolishness, and Adaptive Intelligence

JAMES G. MARCH

Technologies of model-based rationality are the core technologies of strategic management, having largely replaced earlier technologies that placed greater reliance on traditional practice or on communication either with the stars or with the gods. The technologies used by organizations in their pursuit of intelligence can be imagined to change over time as a result of responding to the successes and failures associated with the technologies. Although technologies of rationality seem clearly to be effective instruments of exploitation in relatively simple situations and to derive their adaptive advantage from those capabilities, their ventures in more complex explorations seem often to lead to huge mistakes and thus unlikely to be sustained by adaptive processes. Whether their survival as instruments of exploratory novelty in complex situations is desirable is a difficult question to answer, but it seems likely that any such survival may require hitchhiking on their successes in simpler worlds. Survival may also be served by the heroism of fools and the blindness of true believers. Their imperviousness to feedback is both the despair of adaptive intelligence and, conceivably, its salvation.

## INTRODUCTION

Organizations pursue intelligence. That is, they can be described as seeking to adopt courses of action that lead them over the long run to outcomes that they find satisfactory, taking into account any modifications of hopes, beliefs, preferences, and interpretations that occur over time, as well as conflict over them. The pursuit of intelligence is an ordinary task. It is neither mysterious nor unusually difficult. It is carried out by ordinary organizations in ordinary ways every day in ways that permit most of them to survive from day to day. Since the earliest recorded times, however, the pursuit of intelligence has been pictured, particularly by the intelligentsia, as requiring exquisite talents and considerable

This chapter originally appeared in *Strategic Management Journal*, 27 (2006), 201–214.

training. In the view of academic theorists of organizational intelligence, the task involves trying to understand a complex and changing system of causal factors on the basis of incomplete, ambiguous, and contested information. It involves anticipating and shaping an environment that consists of other actors who are similarly and simultaneously anticipating and shaping their environments. It involves confronting inconsistencies in preferences across groups and across time and making interpersonal and intertemporal comparisons of desires (March, 1994: Ch. 6).

Over the years, the pursuit of intelligence in organizations, like other organizational activities (Gavetti and Rivkin, 2004), has increasingly become the responsibility of people with special competencies. It has been organized around concepts and functions such as strategic management, planning, and economic and decision analysis that professionalize the making of policies and decisions. This professionalization has been buttressed by the development of elaborate tools for guiding organizations toward favorable outcomes. These tools comprise the technologies of rationality that have come to be recognized as a major post-enlightenment contribution to Western civilization, supplementing and to a large extent replacing earlier technologies that placed greater reliance on traditional practice or on communication either with the stars or with the gods. The basic rational rubric has become an almost universal format for justification and interpretation of action and for the development of a set of procedures (e.g., budgeting, planning, economizing, operations analysis, strategic analysis, and management) that are accepted as appropriate for organizations pursuing intelligence (Odiorne, 1984; Buffa and Sarin, 1987).

The preeminence of rationality as an interpretation of human action is obvious, but so also are complaints about it. Not everyone agrees that rational models comprehend human behavior adequately. They are seen as ignoring the limits to rationality, the emotionality of human existence, and alternative logics of actions (Langlois, 1986; Halpern and Stern, 1998; Elster, 1999; March and Olsen, 2005). The position of rationality as a norm of intelligent behavior is less subject to criticism, but it has not escaped entirely (March, 1978; Elster, 1983, 1984; Arrow, 1992: 46, 50). Indeed, criticism of purveyors of rational technologies fills history and literature. Tolstoy (1869) satirized the rational pretensions of German and French military strategists, and Camus (1951) argued that more evil has been based on rationality than on convention or religion.

This paper explores some aspects of experience with rational technologies in the pursuit of intelligence and the place of those technologies within a framework of feedback-based adaptive intelligence. In particular, it examines the role of rationality in the balance between exploitation and exploration by which adaptive systems sustain themselves.

## RATIONALITY AND ITS CRITICS

The notion that human action is, or should be, rational in the sense of being derived from a model-based anticipation of consequences evaluated by prior preferences permeates contemporary Western thinking. The notion builds on a set of Western European ideas that trace in a general way to Plato and Aristotle, were resurrected by scholars and writers in the 16th and 17th centuries and made into the scripture of modernity by Voltaire, Descartes, Bentham, and Mill, and were converted in the 20th century into a technology of operational procedures by Savage, Morgenstern, and von Neumann and by contributors to the elaboration of operations, policy, and systems analysis and the microeconomics of choice in the second half of the 20th century (Gal, Stewart, and Hanne, 1999).

Throughout modern history, the primacy of this technology of rational analysis and choice has been challenged, most conspicuously with respect to large system decision making in the debate over planning and rational system design in the 1930s (Hayek, 1935; Popper, 1966) and in the shadow of the collapse of the Soviet Empire (Campbell, 1992; Solnick, 1998), but also with respect to individual or organizational choice more generally (Sen, 2002) and the functioning of complex technical and organizational systems (Perrow, 1984). Nevertheless, these procedures, in various degrees of elaboration, are commonly seen as being both common and desirable bases for making choices as varied as those of public policy, consumer goods, mates, careers or jobs, investments, military strategies, and education. The technology and ideology of rationality jointly sustain standard procedures of action in modern Western organizations. They are the bases for justifications of action, teaching of decision making, and management of organizations. They are the conventional commandments of policy making, planning, strategy formation, risk taking, asset and attention allocation, decision making, and the management of life (Davis and Devinney, 1997; Lichbach, 2003).

For example, most discussions of strategic action in business firms emphasize the use of a model-based rational logic to assess alternative strategies for changes in product, process, market, resource, or capability mix in response to information about expectations, threats, opportunities, and goals in a competitive environment in which others are making decisions similarly (Porter, 1998; Walker, 2004). Modern academic treatments of strategic action sometimes subordinate a conception of strategic planning based on the comparison of expected values across pre-specified alternatives to a conception of designing methods for assuring capabilities to deal flexibly with an unfolding future, but the underlying notion is that strategic choices should be made by some kind of model-based assessment of the likelihoods of different possible future outcomes and of preferences among them (Vertinsky, 1986; Rumelt, Schendel, and Teece, 1991; Barnett and Burgelman, 1996; Williamson, 1999).

The technologies of rationality involve three components: first, *abstractions,* models of situations that identify sets of variables, their causal structures, and sets of action alternatives; second, collections of *data* capturing histories of the organization and the world in which it acts; third, *decision rules* that consider alternatives in terms of their expected consequences and select the alternative that has the best expected consequences from the point of view of the organization's values, desires, and time perspectives. The technologies are embedded in an ideology that holds that action should be a product of mind and choice, not tradition, rule, routine, or revelation; that choice should be derived from carefully considered expectations of future consequences, not from the dictates of habit, custom, identity, intuition, or emotion; that insight into the dynamics of histories can be obtained from abstract models of them; and that levels of intelligence superior to those produced by other procedures can be achieved through model-based rationality.

This combination of theory, ideology, technology, and theology has shaped thinking in the social and behavioral sciences in the last 100 years, as well as applications to fields such as medicine, law, and management. In particular, it has become the bedrock of modern economic theory (Arrow, 1974: 16) and of both the derivatives of economic theory in other disciplines, including strategic management, and of important critiques of the use of that theory (Lippman and Rumelt, 2003a, 2003b).

Rational models are common; but for many parts of the social science intellectual scene, rationality is less a sacred belief than a convenient bête noire, organizing those who reject it as much as those who accept it. This includes the three incomparable figures of the history of the social and behavioral sciences—Sigmund Freud, Karl Marx, and Charles Darwin—all of whom provided bases for challenges to the centrality of rationality. Modern critics of rationality generally eschew the grander critiques made by those giants in order to make two, not self-evidently consistent, complaints. On the one hand, rationality has been characterized as overly conventional, lacking in creative imagination except within the narrow confines of received knowledge, too tied to established institutions and creeds, thus incapable of generating revolutionary approaches or novel ideas (Steuerman, 1999). The analytical rigidity of rationality is seen as limiting it to refinements on what is already known, believed, or existent and is contrasted with the imaginative wildness of various forms of creativity. The argument is that a technology of rationality has to be balanced by other technologies that free action from the constraints of conventional knowledge and procedures and introduce elements of foolishness into action (March, 1988: Ch. 12).

On the other hand, technologies of rationality have been described as sources of huge mistakes, habitually misspecifying or encouraging the misspecification of situations and thereby producing disasters of major scope (Sagan, 1993; Vaughan, 1996; Albin and Foley, 1998). Although it is possible to demonstrate that actions taken within such technologies are effective in achieving desired outcomes in a wide range of simple decision situations, ranging from textbook problems to short-run investment decisions, it is harder to show empirically that applications of such procedures are reliably beneficial in the more complicated problems with which they sometimes deal.

The list of difficulties noted by critics of the theory is long and includes:

- *Uncertainty.* The future consequences are often quite obscure, and estimating them is confounded by inadequacies of information and biases introduced by desires, prejudices, and the limitations of experience (Knight, 1921; Shackle, 1961; Weick, 1969).

- *Causal complexity.* The systems being modeled and analyzed are substantially more complex than can be comprehended either by the analytical tools or the understandings of analysts. As a result, important variables and interactions among them are invariably overlooked or incorrectly specified (Albin and Foley, 1998).

- *Confound of measurability and importance.* Some things are more easily measured or estimated than others. Variables that can be measured tend to be treated as more "real" than those that cannot, even though the ones that cannot be measured may be the more important (Halberstam, 1972; Wildavsky, 1979).

- *Preference ambiguity.* Preferences, in the sense of the values, wants, or utilities that are served by action, are unclear and inconsistent. Their summary and combination appear to demand metrics and procedures that are elusive (March, 1978; Winter, 2000; Greve, 2003). They change, partly endogenously (Lowenstein, Read, and Baumeister, 2003). Since consequences unfold over time, intelligence requires intertemporal trade-offs that are neither trivially specified nor easily accomplished.

- *Interpersonal trade-offs.* Different participants have different preferences and combining them requires some way of making interpersonal trade-offs. Such trade-offs are major problems for theories of multi-actor choice (Arrow, 1951; Pfeffer and Salancik, 1978).

- *Strategic interaction.* Outcomes, and therefore choices, of one organization depend on the choices of other organizations whose outcomes and choices are, in turn, simultaneously dependent on the first organization (Luce and Raiffa, 1957; Tirole, 1988; Gibbons, 1992; Ghemawat, 1997).

This partial disenchantment with rational models as a basis of intelligence in complex situations has come in parallel with a change in the adversaries of rationality within the social and behavioral sciences. Freud and Marx have been moved, temporarily perhaps, to those parts of the academic theater more closely allied with the humanities and critics of contemporary social and political regimes. Within social science, the principal current alternatives to rational models are more closely connected to Darwin. The metaphors, and to some extent the theories, of evolutionary change are as familiar to social and behavioral scientists today as those of Oedipus and the class struggle once were; and one of the primary discourses involves exploring how to think about processes of adaptation and theories that emphasize reacting to feedback from experience, rather than anticipating the future (Selten, 1991; Levinthal and Myatt, 1994; Börgers, 1996; Gregorius, 1997; Gavetti and Levinthal, 2000).

### THEORIES OF FEEDBACK-BASED ADAPTATION

Contemporary theories that emphasize reacting to feedback include theories of:

- *Experiential learning.* A process by which the propensities to use certain procedures (or to have certain attributes) depend on the history of outcomes associated with previous uses in such a way that successes associated with a procedure in the past increase the propensity to use that procedure in the present (Cohen and Sproull, 1996; Lomi, Larsen, and Ginsberg, 1997; Greve, 2003).

- *Learning from others (diffusion, imitation).* A process by which procedures or attributes of one unit are reproduced in another, and the likelihood of reproducing a particular procedure depends (positively) on the successes of the units using it (Abrahamson, 1991; Mezias and Lant, 1994; Miner and Haunschild, 1995; Strang and Soule, 1998; Miner and Raghavan, 1999).

- *Variation/selection.* A process by which the procedures used by particular units are unchanging but more successful units are more likely to survive, grow, and reproduce than are less successful ones (Nelson and Winter, 1982; Hannan and Freeman, 1989; Aldrich, 1999).

Each of these is a theory of feedback-based change over time. They posit that procedures or attributes associated with successes are more likely to survive and to replicate at a more rapid rate than procedures or attributes associated with failures. The reproductive history is sensitive to variety and change in the environments, including parts of the environment that are simultaneously co-evolving. The adaptation may be imagined to occur at the individual unit (individual, rule, procedure, or organization) level or at the level of a population of units. The extent to which adaptation is seen as involving consciousness of its processes and opportunities for mindful intervention in them varies from one variant on the adaptive theme to another (Feldman, 2003).

Such feedback-based adaptive processes have long been noted as relevant to the pursuit of human intelligence and to organizations (Cyert and March, 1963). However, it is also well known that they do not necessarily result in the timely achievement of global optima (Brehmer, 1980; Carroll and Harrison, 1994; Barron and Erev, 2003). There are numerous potential complications in using feedback-based adaptation to pursue intelligence. Some of those complications stem from properties of the settings in which adaptation occurs. Environments are often complicated, endogenous, subjective and contested. Some of the complications stem from properties of human actors. They are limited in their cognitive, attention, and memory capabilities and are dependent on a variety of well-known simplifications in historical interpretation and heuristics of judgment and action (Kahneman and Tversky, 2000; Camerer, Lowenstein, and Rabin, 2004). Some of the complications stem from properties of adaptive processes. Adaptive histories are inefficient in the sense that they proceed slowly and with error and can easily lead to stable equilibria that are far from global maxima. Except tautologically, the fittest do not always survive (Gould, 2002).

In discussions of these complications in recent years, one conspicuous difficulty has been noted repeatedly: the problem of maintaining adequate experimentation. Empirical observations of adaptive systems seem to suggest that they commonly fail to generate or adopt new ideas, technologies, strategies, or actions that would provide long-run survival advantages. That issue arises in the context of discussions of innovation and the problems of stimulating it (Garud, Nayyar, and Shapira, 1997; Van de Ven, Angles, and Poole, 2000); in the context of discussions of entrepreneurship and new enterprises (Lant and Mezias, 1990); and in the context of discussions of diversity in species (Potvin, Kraenzel, and Seutin, 2001), work groups (Janis, 1982), and cultures (Martin, 1992).

The common observations are empirical, but it is not hard to derive the problem also from adaptive theory (Campbell, 1985; Baum and McKelvey, 1999). The first central requirement of adaptation is a reproductive process that replicates successes. The attributes associated with survival need to be reproduced more reliably than the attributes that are not. The second central requirement of an adaptive process is that it generate variety. Opportunities to experiment with new possibilities need to be provided. In order to meet these two requirements, adaptive processes engage in activities associated with exploitation—the refinement and implementation of what is known—and exploration—the pursuit of what might come to be known. Exploitation involves the application of established competence to problems. It yields reliable, good, standard answers, particularly in a stable world. Exploratory activities are sources of novel, unconventional, improbable, wild ideas and actions. Such ideas and actions become the bases for major innovations and responses to change when they prove to be right; they can lead to major disasters when they prove to be wrong.

In the face of an incompletely known and changing environment, adaptation requires both exploitation and exploration to achieve persistent success (Holland, 1975; March, 1991). Exploitation without exploration leads to stagnation and failure to discover new, useful directions. Exploration without exploitation leads to a cascade of experiments without the development of competence in any of them or discrimination among them. Specifying the optimal mix of exploitation and exploration is difficult or impossible (March, 1994: Ch. 6). In addition to the complications of dealing with a highly uncertain set of possibilities, determining an optimum involves trade-offs across time and space that are notoriously difficult to make. Although it can be shown that, everything else being equal, lower discount rates and longer time horizons make investment in exploration in standard bandit problems more advantageous than do higher discount rates or shorter time horizons (DeGroot, 1970: 398–399; Gittens, 1989: 82), such knowledge provides little precision in the identification of an optimum.

Furthermore, achieving a desirable mix of exploitation and exploration is made difficult by the local character of adaptation. Adaptive mechanisms are myopic (Levinthal and March, 1993; Denrell and March, 2001). Learning from others, experiential learning, and differential reproduction and survival all privilege outcomes, threats, opportunities, and preferences in the temporal and spatial neighborhoods of an adaptive agent. There are cognitive, motivational, and physical necessities that dictate this myopia. It is not something that can be routinely abandoned. Moreover, it makes considerable adaptive sense. For the most part, a local focus contributes to organizational survival. An organization cannot survive in the long run if it fails to survive in the short run, and the circumstances under which the self-sacrificing failure of a local component contributes positively to global success are fairly special.

It is well known that the myopia of adaptive processes poses a problem for exploration and therefore for long-run viability. Since the outcomes from novel initiatives generally have greater variability, longer lead times, and lower average expectations than do outcomes from known best alternatives, feedback-based adaptation favors exploitation over exploration, and thus favors technologies that yield observable, short-run returns (March 1991). In the name of adaptation, exploitation eliminates exploration; efficiency eliminates foolishness; unity eliminates diversity. As a result, adaptive processes are biased against alternatives that require practice or coordination with other alternatives before realizing their full potential, a bias that leads to the well-known competency trap (David, 1985; Levitt and March, 1988; Arthur, 1989). The myopia of adaptation also results in a bias against risky alternatives—those alternatives that have a relatively large variance in the probability distribution over possible outcomes (Denrell and March, 2001; Hertwig et al., 2004). Adaptive agents learn to be risk averse (March, 1996); and although not all risky alternatives involve exploration, exploration almost always involves variability in possible outcomes. A bias against risk is effectively a bias against exploration.

Adaptive myopia underlies two classic sets of problems recognized in studies of collective choice. Within a myopic process, alternatives that provide benefits that are local in time or space and costs that are more distant are likely to be chosen more often than they should be. This leads to concerns about stimulating "self-control," the foregoing of local benefits because of more distant costs—something that adaptive systems have difficulty in accomplishing (Postrel and Rumelt, 1992; Elster, 2000). Conversely, alternatives that provide costs that are local and benefits that are more distant are likely to be chosen less often than they should be. This leads to concerns about stimulating "altruism," the acceptance of local costs in anticipation of subsequent or more global benefits—something that adaptive systems also have difficulty in accomplishing (Badcock, 1986; Cronin, 1991). The stimulation of altruism and self-control, when it is possible, counteracts problems stemming from the myopia of adaptive systems, but it introduces knotty conundrums of intertemporal and intergroup exchange and equity. Similar problems exist with other forms of diversity or variation, and efforts to shape adaptive processes to counteract their limitations often both conflict with other desires and are hard to implement.

## THE SEARCH FOR MECHANISMS OF VARIATION

The ways in which adaptation itself extinguishes the exploration on which it depends are well understood; but theories of adaptation typically do not provide powerful understandings about the generation of new ideas, attributes, or actions, or about the ways in which persistence in novelty is supported. Adaptive theory generally leaves the endurance of exploratory initiatives and the mechanisms that produce them unexamined and unexplained. To a large extent, explorations in actions, attributes, and ideas, with their notorious low success rates, are accomplished by errors in the process. The underlying proposition is that nothing is perfect, that there will always be errors in the reproduction of success in any complex adaptive process, and that errors yield variation.

In most evolutionary theories, for example, variety is produced by sampling variation (e.g., the genetic combinatorics of mating) or arbitrary random error (e.g., mutation) (Harrison, 1988; Ayala, Fitch, and Clegg, 2000). In a similar way, students of organizational adaptation identify as sources of variation various forms of relatively random errors in adaptation (e.g., ignorance, failures of memory, emotion-based irrationalities). In addition, however, students of exploration in organizational settings have described several less random mechanisms. These include incentives that link exploration to immediate and near-neighborhood returns (e.g., competition for position), buffers of action from immediate feedback (e.g., organizational slack, inattention), and modes of action that are unresponsive to feedback on consequences (e.g., intuition, commitments to identities, and the tying of success to an adaptive aspiration level) (March and Shapira, 1992; Winter, 2000; Greve, 2003).

A more general basis for the endurance of exploratory mechanisms in a myopic adaptive process is found in the crudeness of adaptive discrimination. Adaptive processes operate on bundles of attributes rather than individual attributes. Organizational adaptation deals both with elementary components of action and with technologies that are amalgams of such components. It is possible that attributes associated with exploitation are so intermixed with attributes associated with exploration that the latter can be sustained by the replications fostered by the former. Surviving exploratory mechanisms are linked to instruments of selective efficiency.

For example, sexual reproduction is a fundamental instrument of mammalian replication of what is known to be related to success. Successful individuals mate, so the mating has elements of selective breeding; but successful individuals do not clone themselves exactly. There is substantial variation introduced by the arousal-based selection of mates and the sampling of genes. Since sexual arousal and receptivity are relatively unselective, they are simultaneously two of the main engines of the exploitative reproduction of success and sources of exploratory variation. The mechanisms of arousal and receptivity in mating among corporations, as well as those of reproduction, are different in detail from those associated with mammalian evolution; but it is easy to predict that selection among business firms is likely to have an imprecision comparable to that found among mammals.

Although it is recognized that mechanisms of variation can arise in these ways without conscious planning or intent, the designers of adaptive systems often proclaim a need for deliberately introducing more of them to supplement exploration. In their organizational manifestations, they advocate such things as foolishness, brainstorming, identity-based avoidance of the strictures of consequences, devil's advocacy, conflict, and weak memories (George, 1980; George and Stern, 2002; Sutton, 2002). They see potential advantages in organizational partitioning or cultural isolation, the creation of ideological, informational, intellectual, and emotional islands that inhibit convergence to a single world view (March, 2004). Whereas the mechanisms of exploitation involve connecting organizational behavior to revealed reality and shared understandings, the recommended mechanisms of exploration involve deliberately weakening those connections.

### EXPLORATION AND TECHNOLOGIES OF RATIONALITY

Technologies of rationality are implicated in such stories. Organizations use a variety of technologies to generate actions. Some of those technologies are tied to rules and routines and depend on matching action appropriate to a particular identity or role to a particular situation. Some of those technologies accumulate knowledge through experience and attention to others and encode that knowledge in the form of action propensities. Some of those technologies use confrontation among contending interests and dialectical processes of conflict. Some of those technologies are based on logics of consequences, modeling, and rationality. The mix of technologies used by any particular organization or by families of organizations can be imagined to change over time as a result of some mix of adaptive processes, responding to indications of success or failure with the technologies (Chandler, 1962; Dutton, Thomas, and Butler, 1984).

The widespread replication of model-based rational choice as a technology of action and the sanctification of rational choice as a technique of problem solving testifies, in part, to a record of successes of rationality as an instrument of intelligence. There seems little question that technologies of rationality are often effective instruments of exploitation. Model-based rational analysis has led to numerous improvements, for example the introduction of slippery water in the New York Fire Department, the development of single queues in multiple server facilities, the design of auctions, and the implementation of flexible timing of traffic signals and other regulators of queues. Rational technologies are now used routinely to solve numerous problems of focused relevance, limited temporal and spatial perspectives, and moderate complexity (*RAND Review*, 1998). Rationality and its handmaiden, well-established knowledge, both increase average return and reduce variance (unreliability). A feedback-based adaptive process supports and replicates technologies exhibiting such exploitative capabilities; and model-based rationality has been widely replicated as a technology of action.

These successes have, however, not been repeated reliably in more complex situations. As complexity is increased and temporal and spatial perspectives are extended, returns (both of alternatives that are adopted and of those that are rejected) are likely to be misestimated by huge amounts. This means that those alternatives that are adopted are likely to have been overestimated by huge amounts. There are many instances in which the use of a technology of rationality in a relatively complex situation has been described as leading to extraordinary, even catastrophic, failures. These include the extensive efforts of the Soviet Union to manage an economy through planning and rational analysis (Campbell, 1992; Solnick, 1998); the attempts of various American firms to use learning curves as a basis for investment, pricing, and output strategies (Ghemawat, 1985, 2002); the attempt by the American political and military establishment to use rational analysis to develop strategies for war in Vietnam (Halberstam, 1972); the attempt by Long-Term Capital Management to use rational theories to make money in the options market (Warde, 1998); and the wave of corporate mergers in the United States from 1998 to 2001 (Moeller, Schlingemann, and Stulz, 2003, 2005).

To some extent, the poor record of rational technologies in complex situations has been obscured by conventional gambits of argumentation and interpretation. The failures have been pictured as stemming not from the technologies but from some features of misguided use of them. It is sometimes claimed that the schemes generated by such technologies are good ones but have been frustrated by implementation problems, by the perversities or incompetence of individuals involved in bringing them to fruition. It is sometimes claimed that although the rhetoric justifying a particular action is explicitly rational, a rational technology has actually been used only as a justificatory vocabulary not as a basis, thus did not produce the disaster. It is sometimes claimed that although the record is poor, it is at least as good as alternative technologies for dealing with complex situations.

Argumentation and interpretation cannot, however, conceal the essential problem: the unintended exploration produced through technologies of rationality in complex situations seems clearly to produce many more disasters than it produces glories of successful discovery. There is no magic by which this fundamental dilemma of adaptation can be eliminated. The use of rational technologies in complex situations may very well be maintained by generalization from successes in simpler worlds, by the enthusiasm of the industry that has grown up around it, and by the hubris and limited memories of decision makers (McMillan, 2004), but it seems unlikely to be sustained by experience in complex situations and feedback-based adaptation stemming from that experience.

This result, however, can be seen as a possibly unfortunate reflection of one of the more persistent problems associated with learning from history. Adaptation responds to the recorded events of history, not to the underlying distribution of possible events. In effect, adaptive processes treat realized outcomes of history as necessary ones. As a result, they essentially exaggerate the likelihood of what has happened and underestimate the likelihood of things that might have happened. If history is seen not as a fixed outcome of determinate forces but as a draw from a probability distribution over possibilities, then the lessons to be drawn from history are not contained simply in its realizations but extend to the hypothetical histories that might be imagined from simulating the inferred underlying historical process (Brenner, 1983; March, Sproull, and Tamuz, 1991; Ferguson, 1999; Tetlock, 1999). Any probabilistic historical process is subject to sampling error in its realizations, and historical processes involving small samples, highly skewed underlying distributions (such as those hypothesized to exist with respect to novel ideas), and sampling rates that are affected by sampling experience are particularly prone to being poorly represented by their realizations (Denrell and March, 2001; Hertwig et al., 2004; Denrell, 2005). The misrepresentation leads to faulty adaptation.

In the present case, historical interpretations are likely to ignore the extent to which the legendary mistakes of rational technologies may be symptoms of exploratory power. History is filled with cases where the technologies of rationality have initiated or supported experimentation with new actions or strategies that offer novel approaches of great predicted value. Characteristically, the predicted values have failed to materialize. The same methods that identify new possibilities also contribute to substantial errors of estimation. The technology depends on abstract models of reality that reduce the complexity of any particular context to what are believed to be its essential components and relations. The models depend on strong assumptions about the extent to which present knowledge encompasses the causal structure of the world and the preference structures of human actors. Within such abstractions, the forecasts of rational calculation compound so that small errors or oversights multiply into large ones and multiply at an increasing rate as complexity increases. These errors are often costly, even deadly, in their consequences.

In a world in which great ideas are unlikely draws from a pool of apparently crazy ideas, the capability of rational abstractions to generate huge mistakes in their exploratory gambles is a potential gauge of their capability to discover dramatically useful surprises. Although it would be perverse to interpret all disasters as stemming from imagination, frequent cases of ventures that have turned out to be hugely misguided are one of the possible signs of a potential for generating a rich cache of wild ideas. The evidence from failures of rationality in complex situations, such as those identified above, suggests that imagination thrives on the power of rational technology and on the ambitions of utopian rational modelers. By a sophisticated (and optimistic) invocation of counterfactual histories, one can picture the capabilities of rational technologies for producing huge disasters as symptomatic of their capabilities for producing great discoveries. Thus, it is possible to imagine that the exploratory power of rational technologies might be sustained in an adaptive process. The sophistication, however, comes at a price that plagues counterfactual thinking. Learning from counterfactual histories blurs the distinction between data and theory. It thereby compromises the integrity of evidence and inferences from it. It solves one problem but creates another.

By this reading of history, however, technologies of rationality are not so much enemies of foolishness and exploration, as they are agents of them. Those who seek instruments of variation, exploration, and radical change in organizations are often inclined to scorn rational technologies, seeing them as allies of conventionality and of the institutions, disciplines, and professions of the status quo. It is argued that the link between rationality and conventional knowledge keeps rational technologies reliable but inhibits creative imagination. This characterization seems plausible, but it probably underestimates the potential contribution of rational technologies to foolishness and radical visions. Technologies of rational choice, and the technologists of model-based rationality are not simple instruments of exploitation but (partly) instruments of exploration hiding behind a façade of exploitation: revolutionaries in pin-stripe suits. As such, they should perhaps be seen less as stodgy agents of conventional knowledge than as dangerous fools, joining thereby the pool of dreamers out of which come great ideas as well as monstrous and idiotic ones.

Seeing the use of technologies of rationality in complex situations as a source of exploration, however, still leaves unresolved a classical normative question of exploration—whether the brilliant discoveries that might occasionally be achieved are adequate recompense for the many egregious stupidities committed. The mysteries of hypothetical histories and the conundrums of trade-offs across time and space make the answer to that question conspicuously indeterminate; but the outcome provided by adaptive processes is much less problematic. Whatever the potential value of rational technologies as a source of exploration, their adverse record in solving complex problems cannot be expected to sustain them in a myopic adaptive process that reproduces practices associated with local success and extinguishes practices that lead to local failure. Insofar as they have survived, they have done so because alternative technologies are not conspicuously better in complex situations and because of the effectiveness of rational technologies in simpler situations. The exploratory activities of rationality have hitchhiked on its exploitative successes.

As with all hitchhiking phenomena, and for the same reasons that exploration is disadvantaged by a myopic adaptive process, this kind of hitchhiking solution to the exploration problem is potentially ephemeral. The same adaptive process that selects among technologies also shapes the applications of the technologies, matching applications to situations of success. The differentiation among situations may be slow, but it seems reasonable to expect that in the long run, and in the absence of some other mechanism, organizations will learn to use technologies of rationality for simple problems, but not for complex ones. Learning to differentiate simple problems from complex problems and using the technologies only for the former would eliminate most of the exploratory output of rational technologies. There are folkloric indications of such a differentiation. Decision makers now frequently comment that technologies of rationality are not particularly useful in major complex decisions but should be focused on "more narrowly defined problems" (*RAND Review*, 1998: 5). One of the architects of the attempt to model the competition between the United States and the USSR during the Cold War era described the complications in these terms:

If we really are to understand the nature of the competition, the nature of their interaction process, we will need to understand much better than we do now the decision making processes within both the U.S. and Soviet political-military-industrial bureaucracies. We need an understanding of the processes that lead to the selection of specific R&D programs, to R&D budgets and their allocations, to procurement decisions, to the operation of the whole of the weapon system acquisition process. We would need to understand how the perceptions of what the other side is doing come about in various places within these complicated bureaucracies, and how these perceptions influence the behavior of the various organizations and the decision makers involved in the complex decision processes that drive the evolution of the several defense programs involved. (Marshall, 1971: 7)

Such an understanding is likely to be elusive within models of rational technology. As a result, attention to feedback from experience in complex situations discourages the use of the technology (Popper, 1961: Myrdal, 1971; Hirschman, 1981). For example, the imaginative and provocative set of ideas pioneered by John von Neumann and Oskar Morgenstern (1944) under the rubric of game theory has proven to be enormously useful in analyzing simple forms of conflict but arguably less powerful in more complex situations. From the late 1940s to the mid 1960s, academic scholars working at the RAND Corporation, including such luminaries as Kenneth Arrow, Merrill Flood, John Nash, Thomas Schelling, Martin Shubik, and Lloyd Shapley, produced research memoranda on game theory, its possible applications, and its pitfalls. By the end of that period, game theory was well established as a domain, and its applications to some (but not all) relatively simple situations were viewed as successful (Ghemawat, 1997); but the relevance of game theory for dealing with complex situations such as that involved in the confrontation of the United States and the USSR was widely questioned. This negative adaptive experience with game theory as a basis for dealing with international conflict is not unique. It appears not to be a product of any particular application of any specific rational technology but an inherent characteristic of the technology itself.

It is possible to imagine that the feedback disadvantages of the wild ideas of rationality might be reduced by reshaping organizational experience. The most obvious possibility is to discover ways, at an early stage, to distinguish novel ideas that will be spectacularly successful from those that will be disasters, thus to change the success rate of experience. This possibility has supported considerable research on creativity. The evidence is strong, however, that such early discriminations are almost impossible to make, particularly when the novel ideas deviate substantially from received truths—precisely the case of interest. Historically, new ideas that have subsequently been shown to change things dramatically have generally looked distinctly unpromising initially (Aronson, 1977; David, 1990). Most attempts to distinguish creative instances of craziness from useless or dangerous ones at an early stage impose criteria of conventionality on craziness and thereby impose self-defeating filters that reduce novelty.

Alternatively, if it were possible to make small experiments with wild ideas, while retaining the possibility of diffusing those that prove to be good ones, the adaptive position of exploration would be strengthened (Romano, 2002; Holahan, Weil, and Wiener, 2003). Since structures that protect the system from the catastrophic consequences of wild ideas generally also inhibit the transfer of major discoveries (Cohen and Levinthal, 1989, 1990), there is no perfect solution to the problem. However, two kinds of strategies seem to have appeal: the first involves controlling the "bet size" of developing ideas. If small-size experiments can be devised to examine an idea, and if they can be scaled up without loss of validity subsequently, bad ideas can be sorted from good ones at a cost that is less than the return generated by the few good ones when they are scaled up. There are difficulties associated with the problems of scaling up from small experiments to large implementations, particularly when one of the common complications is the failure to capture the full complexity of the system, but small experiments are a classic device.

A second strategy involves partitioning the audience into subgroups. Technologies of action spread so that practitioners and theorists share a common sense of what is true, just, and beautiful. The community is often fractured, however, into segregated subgroups pursuing different practices and ideas. Experience with the good or bad consequences of those practices is localized to the subgroups, and the resulting smaller sample sizes of experience increase the possibilities for a locally favorable result from a practice having a poor expected value (Dubins and Savage, 1965), and thus for local persistence in pursuing technologies that generate wild ideas. Although most of that persistence will turn out to be unproductive, the segregation of subgroups sustains experimentation in a few cases that are ultimately deemed successful. Provided the segregation of groups is not complete, these successes can spread more widely (March, 2004). There is, however, an obvious complication: subgroup segregation contributes to local differentiated persistence with ideas, but it also inhibits the diffusion of good ideas to groups other than the ones that originally discovered them. As a result, the optimum level of segregation is difficult to specify.

### THE HEROISM OF FOOLS

Enthusiasts for rational technologies in complex situations, like other enthusiasts for variation in adaptive systems, generally proclaim an unverifiable confidence in two propositions. The first proposition is that the current level of exploration is less than would be optimal. The second proposition is that, in a long-term and global perspective, the threats to survival posed by the disasters of rational technologies applied to complex situations are less than those posed by failure to discover and exploit the beneficial ideas generated by the technologies. Neither proposition is obvious, nor is it obvious how one might easily confirm or disconfirm either of them.

We do know something, however. Exploratory foolishness may sometimes be desirable, and technologies of rationality may be important sources of exploration; but the use of rational technologies in complex situations is unlikely to be sustained by the main events and processes of history. Technologies and practices that produce wild ideas have large variances in their returns and relatively low means. Their positive returns are disproportionately realized at temporal and spatial distances from the point of action. These properties make them vulnerable to a myopic adaptive process. Some ameliorations of the dilemma are possible, but it cannot be eliminated. In the end, foolishness and exploration are the natural (and largely unlamented) victims of adaptive processes. Their sustenance requires errors of adaptation, in particular the errors produced by the heroism of fools and the blindness of faith.

A commitment to rationality as an instrument of exploration might be imagined to be proper for academic scholars of strategic management. Persistence in such a commitment is not, however, a likely product of experience outside the world of the mind. Foolishness in the service of exploration will usually turn out to be dangerously unwise: it is unlikely to be rewarded by the histories recorded in the temporal or spatial neighborhoods of the craziness, nor can it be guaranteed to be justified in a longer or broader perspective. Belief in the exploratory value of rational technologies requires a leap of faith about the virtue, joy, and beauty of imagination, the contribution of abstract thinking to fostering it, and the pleasures of deriving surprising implications from unrealistic assumptions. Such enthusiasm for exploratory rationality fulfills academic obligations to defend a utopia of the mind against the realism of experience, and academic purities of belief can endure within a relatively closed community of similar academics. Such faith-based imperviousness to feedback is both the despair of adaptive intelligence and, occasionally but only occasionally, its salvation.

### ACKNOWLEDGMENTS

This paper was originally presented as the 2004 Viipuri Lecture at the Lappeenranta (Finland) University of Technology, 26 May 2004. I am grateful for comments by the participants at that lecture and by Mie Augier, Jerker Denrell, Hans Hvide, W. Richard Scott, and two anonymous referees.

## REFERENCES

Abrahamson E. 1991. Managerial fads and fashions: The diffusion and rejection of innovations. *Academy of Management Review* 16: 586–612.

Albin PS, Foley DK. 1998. *Barriers and Bounds to Rationality: Essays on Economic Complexity and Dynamics in Interactive Systems.* Princeton University Press: Princeton, NJ.

Aldrich H. 1999. *Organizations Evolving.* Sage: London.

Aronson SH. 1977. Bell's electrical toy: What's the use? The sociology of early telephone usage. In *The Social Impact of the Telephone,* de Sola Pool I (ed). MIT Press: Cambridge, MA; 15–39.

Arrow KJ. 1951. *Social Choice and Individual Values.* Yale University Press: New Haven, CT.

Arrow KJ. 1974. *Limits of Organization.* W. W. Norton: New York.

Arrow KJ. 1992. I know a hawk from a handsaw. In *Eminent Economists: Their Life and Philosophies,* Szenberg M (ed). Cambridge University Press: Cambridge, UK; 42–50.

Arthur BW. 1989. Competing technologies, increasing returns, and lock-in by historical events. *Economic Journal* 99: 116–131.

Ayala FJ, Fitch WM, Clegg MT (eds). 2000. *Variation and Evolution in Plants and Microorganisms: Toward a New Synthesis 50 Years after Stebbins.* National Academy Press: Washington, DC.

Badcock CR. 1986. *The Problem of Altruism: Freudian-Darwinian Solutions.* Blackwell: Oxford, UK.

Barnett WP, Burgelman RA. 1996. Evolutionary perspectives on strategy. *Strategic Management Journal,* Summer Special Issue 17: 5–19.

Barron G, Erev I. 2003. Small feedback-based decisions and their limited correspondence to description-based decisions. *Journal of Behavioral Decision Making* 16: 215–233.

Baum JAC, McKelvey W (eds). 1999. *Variations in Organization Science: Essays in Honor of Donald D. Campbell.* Sage: Thousand Oaks, CA.

Börgers T. 1996. On the relevance of learning and evolution to economic theory. *Economic Journal* 106: 1374–1385.

Brehmer B. 1980. In one word: Not from experience. *Acta Psychologica* 45: 223–241.

Brenner R. 1983. *History: The Human Gamble.* University of Chicago Press: Chicago, IL.

Buffa ES, Sarin RK. 1987. *Modern Production Operations Management* (8th edn). Wiley: New York.

Camerer CF, Lowenstein G, Rabin M (eds). 2004. *Advances in Behavioral Economics.* Princeton University Press: Princeton, NJ.

Campbell BG. 1985. *Human Evolution: An Introduction to Man's Adaptations* (3rd edn). Aldine: Chicago, IL.

Campbell RW. 1992. *The Failure of Soviet Economic Planning: System, Performance, Reform.* Indiana University Press: Bloomington, IN.

Camus A. 1951. *L'Homme Révolté.* Gallimard: Paris, France.

Carroll GR, Harrison JR. 1994. Historical efficiency of competition between organizational populations. *American Journal of Sociology* 100: 720–749.

Chandler AD. 1962. *Strategy and Structure: Chapters in the History of the Industrial Enterprise.* MIT Press: Cambridge, MA.

Cohen MD, Sproull LS (eds). 1996. *Organizational Learning.* Sage: Thousand Oaks, CA.

Cohen WM, Levinthal DA. 1989. Innovation and learning: The two faces of R&D. *Economic Journal* 99: 569–590.

Cohen WM, Levinthal DA. 1990. Absorptive capacity: A new perspective on learning and innovation. *Administrative Science Quarterly* 15: 128–152.

Cronin H. 1991. *The Ant and the Peacock: Altruism and Sexual Selection from Darwin to Today.* Cambridge University Press: New York.

Cyert RM, March JG. 1963. *A Behavioral Theory of the Firm.* Prentice-Hall: Englewood Cliffs, NJ.

David PA. 1985. Clio and the economics of QWERTY. *American Economic Review* 75: 332–337.

David PA. 1990. The hero and the herd in technological history: reflections on Thomas Edison and "The Battle of the Systems." In *Economic Development Past and Present: Opportunities and Constraints,* Higgonet P, Rosovsky H (eds). Harvard University Press: Cambridge, MA; 72–119.

Davis JG, Devinney TM. 1997. *The Essence of Corporate Strategy: Theory for Modern Decision Making.* Allen & Unwin: St. Leonards, Australia.

DeGroot MH. 1970. *Optimal Statistical Decisions.* McGraw-Hill: New York.

Denrell J. 2005. Why most people disapprove of me: Experience sampling in impression formation. *Psychological Review* 112 (in press).

Denrell J, March JG. 2001. Adaptation as information restriction: The hot stove effect. *Organization Science* 12: 523–538.

Dubins LE, Savage LJ. 1965. *How to Gamble if You Must: Inequalities for Stochastic Processes.* McGraw-Hill: New York.

Dutton JM, Thomas A, Butler JE. 1984. The history of progress functions as a managerial technology. *Business History Review* 58: 204–233.

Elster J. 1983. *Sour Grapes: Studies in the Subversion of Rationality.* Cambridge University Press: Cambridge, UK.

Elster J. 1984. *Ulysses and the Sirens: Studies in Rationality and Irrationality* (2nd edn). Cambridge University Press: Cambridge, UK.

Elster J. 1999. *Alchemies of the Mind: Rationality and the Emotions.* Cambridge University Press: Cambridge, UK.

Elster J. 2000. *Ulysses Unbound: Studies in Rationality, Precommitment, and Constraints.* Cambridge University Press: Cambridge, UK.

Feldman MS. 2003. A performative perspective on stability and change in organizational routines. *Industrial and Corporate Change* 12: 727–752.

Ferguson N (ed). 1999. *Virtual History: Alternatives and Counterfactuals.* Basic Books: New York.

Gal T, Stewart TJ, Hanne T (eds). 1999. *Multicriteria Decision Making: Advances in MCDM Models, Algorithms, Theory, and Applications.* Kluwer Academic: Boston, MA.

Garud R, Nayyar PR, Shapira ZB. 1997. *Technological Innovation: Oversights and Foresights.* Cambridge University Press: Cambridge, UK.

Gavetti G, Levinthal D. 2000. Looking forward and looking backward: Cognitive and experiential search. *Administrative Science Quarterly* 45: 113–138.

Gavetti G, Rivkin JW. 2004. On the origin of strategy: Action and cognition over time. Manuscript, Harvard Business School.

George AI. 1980. *Presidential Decision Making in Foreign Policy: The Effective Use of Information and Advice.* Westview: Boulder, CO.

George AL, Stern EK. 2002. Harnessing conflict in foreign policy making: From devil's to multiple advocacy. *Presidential Studies Quarterly* 32: 484–508.

Ghemawat P. 1985. Building strategy on the experience curve. *Harvard Business Review* 63(2): 143–149.

Ghemawat P. 1997. *Games Businesses Play: Cases and Models.* MIT Press: Cambridge, MA.

Ghemawat P. 2002. Competition and business strategy in historical perspective. *Business History Review* 76: 37–42.

Gibbons R. 1992. *Game Theory for Applied Economists.* Princeton University Press: Princeton, NJ.

Gittens JC. 1989. *Multi-armed Bandit Allocation Indices.* Wiley: New York.

Gould SJ. 2002. *The Structure of Evolutionary Theory.* Harvard University Press: Cambridge, MA.

Gregorius H-R. 1997. The adaptational system as a dynamical feedback system. *Journal of Theoretical Biology* 189: 97–105.

Greve H. 2003. *Organizational Learning from Performance Feedback: A Behavioral Perspective on Innovation and Change.* Cambridge University Press: Cambridge, UK.

Halberstam D. 1972. *The Best and the Brightest.* Random House: New York.

Halpern J, Stern RN (eds). 1998. *Debating Rationality: Nonrational Aspects of Organizational Decision Making.* Cornell University Press: Ithaca, NY.

Hannan MT, Freeman J. 1989. *Organizational Ecology.* Harvard University Press: Cambridge, MA.

Harrison GA. 1988. *Human Biology: An Introduction to Human Evolution, Variation, Growth, and Adaptability.* Oxford University Press: Oxford, UK.

Hayek FA (ed). 1935. *Collectivist Economic Planning: Critical Studies on the Possibilities of Socialism.* G. Routledge: London.

Hertwig R, Barron G, Weber EU, Erev I. 2004. Decisions from experience and the effect of rare events in risky choices. Manuscript. University of Basel.

Hirschman AO. 1981. *Essay in Trespassing: Economics to Politics and Beyond.* Cambridge University Press: Cambridge, UK.

Holahan J, Weil A, Wiener JM (eds). 2003. *Federalism and Health Policy.* Urban Institute Press: Washington, DC.

Holland JH. 1975. *Adaptation in Natural and Artificial Systems.* University of Michigan Press: Ann Arbor, MI.

Janis IL. 1982. *Groupthink: Psychological Studies of Policy Decisions and Fiascoes* (2nd edn). Houghton Mifflin: Boston, MA.

Kahneman D, Tversky A (eds). 2000. *Choice, Values, and Frames.* Cambridge University Press: Cambridge, UK.

Knight FH. 1921. *Risk, Uncertainty, and Profit.* Harper & Row: New York.

Langlois R. 1986. Rationality, institutions and explanation. In *Essays in the New Institutional Economics*, Langlois R (ed). Cambridge University Press: New York; 225–255.

Lant TK, Mezias SJ. 1990. Managing discontinuous change: A simulation study of organizational learning and entrepreneurship. *Strategic Management Journal*, Summer Special Issue 11: 147–179.

Levinthal DA, March JG 1993. The myopia of learning. *Strategic Management Journal*, Winter Special Issue 14: 95–112.

Levinthal DA, Myatt J. 1994. Co-evolution of capabilities and industry: The evolution of mutual fund processing. *Strategic Management Journal,* Winter Special Issue 15: 45–62.

Levitt B, March JG. 1988. Organizational learning. *Annual Review of Sociology* 14: 319–340.

Lichbach MI. 2003. *Is Rational Choice All of Social Science?* University of Michigan Press: Ann Arbor, MI.

Lippman SA, Rumelt RP. 2003a. The payments perspective: Micro-foundations of rational analysis. *Strategic Management Journal,* Special Issue 24(10): 903–927.

Lippman SA, Rumelt RP. 2003b. A bargaining perspective on resource advantage. *Strategic Management Journal* 24(11): 1069–1086.

Lomi A, Larsen E, Ginsberg A. 1997. Adaptive learning in organizations: A system dynamics-based exploration. *Journal of Management* 23: 561–582.

Lowenstein G, Read D, Baumeister R (eds). 2003. *Time and Decision: Economic and Psychological Perspectives on Intertemporal Choice.* Russell Sage Foundation: New York.

Luce RD, Raiffa H. 1957. *Games and Decisions.* Wiley: New York.

March JG. 1978. Bounded rationality, ambiguity, and the engineering of choice. *Bell Journal of Economics* 9: 587–608.

March JG. 1988. *The Pursuit of Organizational Intelligence.* Blackwell: Oxford, UK.

March JG. 1991. Exploration and exploitation in organizational learning. *Organization Science* 2: 71–87.

March JG. 1994. *A Primer on Decision Making: How Decisions Happen.* Free Press: New York.

March JG. 1996. Learning to be risk averse. *Psychological Review* 103: 308–319.

March JG. 2004. Parochialism in the evolution of a research community. *Management and Organization Review* 1: 5–22.

March JG, Olsen JP. 2005. The logic of appropriateness. In *The Oxford Handbook of Public Policy,* Rein M, Moran M, Goodin RE (eds). Oxford University Press: Oxford, UK. (in press).

March JG, Shapira Z. 1992. Variable risk preferences and the focus of attention. *Psychological Review* 99: 172–183.

March JG, Sproull LS, Tamuz M. 1991. Learning from samples of one or fewer. *Organization Science* 2: 1–13.

Marshall A. 1971. Long term competition with the Soviets: A framework for strategic analysis. *RAND Paper P-21542.* RAND Corporation: Santa Monica, CA.

Martin J. 1992. *Cultures in Organizations: Three Perspectives.* Oxford University Press: New York.

McMillan J. 2004. Avoid hubris: And other lessons for reformers. *Finance and Development* 41 (September): 1–4.

Mezias SJ, Lant TK. 1994. Mimetic learning and the evolution of organizational populations. In *Evolutionary Dynamics of Organizations,* Baum JAC, Singh JV (eds). Oxford University Press: New York; 179–198.

Miner AS, Haunschild P. 1995. Population level learning. In *Research in Organizational Behavior,* Vol. 17, Cummings LL, Staw BM (eds). JAI Press: Greenwich, CT; 115–166.

Miner AS, Raghavan SV. 1999. Interorganizational imitation: A hidden engine of selection. In *Variations in Organization Science: In Honor of Donald T. Campbell,* McKelvey W, Baum JAC (eds). Sage: London; 35–62.

Moeller SB, Schlingemann FP, Stulz RM. 2003. Do shareholders of acquiring firms gain from acquisitions? National Bureau of Economic Research Working Paper Number 9523.

Moeller SB, Schlingemann FP, Stulz RM. 2005. Wealth destruction on a massive scale? A study of acquiring-firm returns in the recent merger wave. *Journal of Finance* 60: 757–782.

Myrdal G. 1971. [1957]. *Economic Theory and Underdeveloped Regions*. Harper & Row: New York.

Nelson RR, Winter SG. 1982. *An Evolutionary Theory of Economic Change*. Harvard University Press: Cambridge, MA.

Odiorne GS. 1984. *Strategic Management of Human Resources*. Jossey-Bass: San Francisco, CA.

Perrow C. 1984. *Normal Accidents: Living with High-risk Technologies*. Basic Books: New York.

Pfeffer J, Salancik G. 1978. *The External Control of Organizations: A Resource Dependence Perspective*. Harper & Row: New York.

Popper KR. 1961. *The Poverty of Historicism*. Harper & Row: New York.

Popper KR. 1966. *The Open Society and Its Enemies* (5th edn). Princeton University Press: Princeton, NJ.

Porter ME. 1998. *Competitive Strategy: Techniques for Analyzing Industries and Competitors*. Free Press: New York.

Postrel S, Rumelt RP. 1992. Incentives, routines, and self command. *Industrial and Corporate Change* 1: 397–425.

Potvin C, Kraenzel M, Seutin G (eds). 2001. *Protecting Biological Diversity: Roles and Responsibilities*. McGill-Queen's University Press: Montreal.

RAND Review 1998. 50 years of looking forward. *RAND Review*, Fall.

Romano R. 2002. *The Advantages of Competitive Federalism for Securities Regulation*. American Enterprise Institute Press: Washington, DC.

Rumelt RP, Schendel D, Teece DJ. 1991. Strategic management and economics. *Strategic Management Journal*, Winter Special Issue 12: 5–29.

Sagan SD. 1993. *The Limits of Safety: Organizations, Accidents, and Nuclear Weapons*. Princeton University Press: Princeton, NJ.

Selten R. 1991. Evolution, learning and economic behavior. *Games and Economic Behavior* 3: 3–24.

Sen AK. 2002. *Rationality and Freedom*. Harvard University Press (Belknap): Cambridge, MA.

Shackle GLS. 1961. *Decision, Order and Time in Human Affairs*. Cambridge University Press: Cambridge, UK.

Solnick SL. 1998. *Stealing the State: Control and Collapse in Soviet Institutions*. Harvard University Press: Cambridge, MA.

Steuerman E. 1999. *The Bounds of Reason: Habermas, Lyotard, and Melanie Klein on Rationality*. Routledge: London.

Strang D, Soule SA. 1998. Diffusion in organizations and social movements: From hybrid corn to poison pills. *Annual Review of Sociology* 24: 265–290.

Sutton RI. 2002. *Weird Ideas That Work: 11½ Practices for Promoting, Managing, and Sustaining Innovation*. Free Press: New York.

Tetlock PE. 1999. Theory-driven reasoning about possible pasts and probable futures: Are we prisoners of our preconceptions? *American Journal of Political Science* 43: 335–366.

Tirole J. 1988. *The Theory of Industrial Organization*. MIT Press: Cambridge, MA.

Tolstoy L. 1869. (2000). *Voina i Mir*. Zakharov: Moscow.

Van de Ven AH, Angles HL, Poole MS. 2000. *Research on the Management of Innovation: the Minnesota Studies*. Oxford University Press: Oxford, UK.

Vaughan D. 1996. *The Challenger Launch Decision: Risky Technology, Culture, and Deviance at NASA*. University of Chicago Press: Chicago, IL.

Vertinsky I. 1986. Economic growth and decision-making in Japan: The duality of visible and invisible guiding hands. In *Organizing Industrial Development*, Wolff R (ed). Walter de Gruyter: Berlin; 41–57.

Von Neumann J, Morgenstern O. 1944. *The Theory of Games and Economic Behavior*. Princeton University Press: Princeton, NJ.

Walker G. 2004. *Modern Competitive Strategy*. McGraw-Hill: New York.

Warde I. 1998. Crony capitalism: LTCM, a hedge fund above suspicion. *Le Monde Diplomatique* 5 November. http://mondediplo.com/1998/11/05warde2 [15 August 2005].

Weick KE. 1969. *The Social Psychology of Organizing*. Random House: New York.

Wildavsky A. 1979. *Speaking Truth to Power: The Art and Craft of Policy Analysis*. Little Brown: Boston, MA.

Williamson OE. 1999. Strategy research: Governance and competence perspectives. *Strategic Management Journal* 20(12): 1087–1108.

Winter SG. 2000. The satisficing principle in capability learning. *Strategic Management Journal*, Special Issue 21(10–11): 981–996.

# PART III

# EXPLORATIONS IN INSTITUTIONS AND LOGICS OF APPROPRIATENESS

## *An Introductory Essay*

JOHAN P. OLSEN

## A PERSPECTIVE ON POLITICAL LIFE

This section presents three landmark articles that are part of a research agenda launched more than twenty years ago. Then, "The New Institutionalism: Organizational Factors in Political Life" invited a reappraisal of how political institutions could be conceptualized, to what degree institutions have independent and endurable implications, the kinds of political phenomena they impact, the mechanisms through which they do so, and the processes through which institutions emerge, are maintained, and change. Since then, the original contribution has been elaborated in several publications.[1] In contrast to much of the work in organization studies, the focus has been on political, rather than economic, organizations.

"The new institutionalism" offers a perspective on how political life is organized, functions, and changes in contemporary democracies. The term includes a set of theoretical ideas, assumptions, and hypotheses concerning the relations among institutional characteristics, political agency, performance, and institutional change, and the wider social context of politics. In contrast with an older institutionalism that used formal-legal rules as proxies for political action, the new institutionalism is behavioral. Theoretical ideas are required to be consistent with empirical observations.

The institutional approach supplements and competes with two other interpretations of democratic politics and government. The first is a rational actor perspective that sees political life as organized by exchange among calculating, self-interested actors maximizing their expected utility. The second is a society-centered perspective that sees political institutions and behavior as arising from societal forces, rather than society as being governed by politics. One version gives primacy to macroeconomic, technological, and social change. Another interprets politics as organized by shared worldviews in a community of culture, history, and fate.

These perspectives focus attention on different actors, mechanisms, and explanatory factors, and they differ when it comes to what contribution to the flow of history is attributable to political institutions and actors. The key distinctions are (a) the extent to which political institutions are seen as having some degree of autonomy and independent effects, and (b) the extent to which a perspective pictures institutionalized rules and identities as being reproduced with some reliability, at least partly independent of deliberate design and reform efforts, as well as of environmental stability or change.

## BASIC IDEAS

Core assumptions of the new institutionalism are that political institutions create elements of order and predictability in political life, have durable and independent effects, and some robustness toward individual actors and environments.

An institution is an enduring collection of rules and organized practices, embedded in structures of meaning and resources that are relatively invariant in the face of turnover of individuals and changing external circumstances. Constitutive rules and repertoires of standard operating procedures prescribe appropriate behavior for specific actors in specific situations. Structures of meaning, involving standardization, homogenization and authorization of common purposes, vocabularies, ways of reasoning and accounts give direction to, explain, justify, and legitimate behavioral rules. Structures of resources create capabilities for acting. Resources are routinely tied to rules and worldviews, empowering and constraining actors differently and making them more or less capable of acting according to behavioral codes.

The logic of appropriateness is a perspective on human action. To act appropriately is to proceed according to the institutionalized practices of a collectivity and mutual understandings of what is true, reasonable, natural, right, and good. Actors seek to fulfil the obligations and duties encapsulated in a role, an identity, and a membership in a political community. Rules are followed because they are perceived to be adequate for the task at hand and to have normative validity.

The new institutionalism assumes that political life is not solely organized around policy making, aggregation of predetermined preferences and resources, and regulation of behavior and outcomes through external incentives and constraints. Consistent with an old strand in the study of politics, institutionalism holds that politics involves a search for collective purpose, direction, meaning, and belonging. In contrast with standard equilibrium models, assuming that institutions reach a unique organizational form conditional on current functional and normative circumstances, and thus independent of their historical path, institutionalism holds that history is "inefficient." The matching of institutions, behaviors, and contexts takes time and has multiple, path-dependent equilibria.

In sum, the basic units of analysis of the new institutionalism are internalized rules and practices, identities and roles, normative and causal beliefs, and resources; not micro-rational individuals or macro forces. Institutionalism assumes that the organization of political life has an independent explanatory power and emphasizes the endogenous nature and social construction of institutions.

A challenge is to provide better understanding of the processes that translate institutionalized rules into political action and consequences, and of the processes that translate human action into rules and institutions. Institutionalists need to explain how such processes are stabilized or destabilized and identify factors that sustain or interrupt ongoing processes.

### IMPACTS ON ACTION, POLICIES, AND PEOPLE

Over the last twenty years debates about the significance of formally organized political institutions has turned into a concern with to what extent, in what respects, through what processes, under what conditions, and why institutions make a difference. The organization of political life affects the motivations and capabilities of collectivities and individuals. Institutions prescribe how authority and power are constituted, exercised, legitimated, controlled, and redistributed. They empower and constrain actors, define basic rules for resolving conflicts, and impact the allocation of advantages and burdens. Institutions create and select actors. They integrate a community and develop affective ties among its members (Weaver and Rockman 1993; Egeberg 2003, March and Olsen 2006a, 2006b).

To the degree that institutions generate beliefs in a legitimate order, they simplify politics by ensuring that many things are taken as given. Rules and practices specify what is normal, must be expected, can be relied on, and what makes sense in a community. While the blessings of rules are mixed, some of the capabilities of modern institutions come from their effectiveness in substituting rule-bound behavior for individually autonomous behavior. Institutions also facilitate sense-making, guide and stabilize expectations, and dampen conflicts over resource allocations.

This "established wisdom" about the effects of political institutions has, however, been described as fragile (Rothstein 1996). Causal chains are often complex, long, and contingent (Weaver and Rockman 1993) and the legitimacy of democratic institutions is partly based on the expectation that they will provide open-ended processes without determinate outcomes (Pitkin 1967). Institutions do not determine political action and results in detail. They constrain and enable outcomes without being an immediate or direct cause of them. The same organizational arrangement can have different consequences under different conditions, and different arrangements can produce the same effects. Two issues arise for the new institutionalism: How are rules of appropriateness translated into behavior and how do actors become carriers of rules and practices?

## Impacting Behavior and Policies

A key task is to improve the understanding of the conditions under which actors are motivated and capable of complying with rules of appropriateness, the processes through which rules are translated into behavior and the factors that strengthen or weaken the relation between rules and actions.

In routine situations, rule-based action may reflect in an almost mechanical way prescriptions embedded in constitutions, laws, institution-specific rules, or professional norms. Defining a role or identity and achieving it can, however, require time and energy, thought and capability. It is well known, for example from courts of law that following rules can be a complicated cognitive process involving thoughtful, reasoning behavior.

Such reasoning is not primarily connected to the anticipation of consequences. Actors use criteria of similarity and congruence, rather than likelihood and expected value. The core behavioral proposition of the new institutionalism is that, most of the time humans take reasoned action by trying to answer three elementary questions: What kind of a situation is this? What kind of person am I (are we)? What does a person such as I (we) do in a situation such as this—what kind of behavioral prescriptions follow from matching the facts of the situation with the relevant rules (March and Olsen 1989)?

The clarity and consistency of rules and identities are variables, and so are the familiarity with and understanding of situations and the behavioral implications of matching rules. There may be more or less time for analysis and decision making; and when prescriptions are straightforward, institutionalized authority and resources may be adequate, or overpowered by noninstitutionalized resources and informal processes.

Therefore, actors may have a difficult time interpreting which historical experiences are relevant for current situations. They may struggle with how to classify themselves and others—who they are, and what they are—and what the classifications imply in a specific situation. The problems are particularly challenging when several institutions structured according to different principles and rules provide competing analyses and behavioral prescriptions for the same area of action.

For example, diplomats face competing expectations because diplomacy as an institution involves a tension between being the carrier of the interests of a specific state and being a defender of transnational principles, norms, and rules maintained and enacted by representatives of the states in mutual interaction (Bátora 2005). In a Weberian bureaucracy, often seen as the archetype hierarchical organization, there are also competing claims to authority and logics of appropriateness, such as following command rooted in formal position, rule following based on laws, and behavior dictated by professional knowledge, truth claims, or axioms of enlightened government.

Furthermore, adjudication involves an intricate interweaving of rule application, creation, and reinterpretation as new and unfamiliar situations arise (Magnussen 2006). Policy situations can be defined in different ways that call forth different legitimate rules, actors, and arguments (Ugland 2002), and global prescriptions of administrative reform have consistently been interpreted and responded to differently depending on national institutional arrangements, resources, and historical traditions (Christensen and Lægreid 2007).

The possible indeterminacy of rules, roles, identities, and situations requires detailed observations of the processes through which rules are translated into behavior through constructive interpretation and available resources. This includes how institutions affect exposure to and search for information, deliberation and interpretation, codification and validation of evidence, and memory building and retrieval, as well as the mechanisms through which institutions distribute resources and enable actors to follow rules, across a variety of settings and situations (March and Olsen 1995). There is also a need to understand how actors become rule bound.

## Fashioning People

The effects of external opportunity and incentive structures on behavior are directed and limited by institutions. Institutions are carriers of a polity's character, history, and visions, and institutions have a potential for fashioning actors' character, preferences, and commitments. Identification is a fundamental mechanism in group integration, based on an internalized acceptance of obligations and duties (March and Simon 1958). Actors internalize culturally defined purposes to be sought as well as modes of appropriate procedures for pursuing purposes, and there is no perfect positive correlation between political effectiveness and normative validity (Merton 1938). Legitimacy, therefore, depends not only on showing that actions accomplish appropriate objectives but also that actors behave in accordance with appropriate procedures ingrained in a culture (Meyer and Rowan 1977).

As a result, students of institutions need to study the types of humans selected and formed by different types of institutions and specify the mechanisms by which different rules of appropriateness evolve and become legitimized, reproduced, modified, and replaced. In democratic contexts, there is a special need to explore which mechanisms and institutional settings transform individuals into law-abiding and consensus- and compromise-seeking citizens; how elected representatives, bureaucrats, and judges are turned into office holders with an ethos of self-discipline, impartiality, and integrity; and how different institutions create different balances between the requirements of offices and individual calculated interests.

Internalized rules are lessons from experience, encoded by actors drawing inferences from their experiences, or by differential survival or reproduction rates (March, Schultz, and Zhou 2000). Identities may be strong or weak and there may be competing institutional and group belongings. Internalization takes place through processes of education, socialization, explanation, and justification in a variety of institutional settings, such as ordinary work situations, political institutions, civil society, and institutions of higher education. Possibly, the processes and determinants of identification are not much different from those relevant for interpreting rules, or institutional dynamics in general.

## DYNAMICS OF CHANGE

Institutions are not static. Change is a constant feature of institutions as they respond to experience. The scopes and modes of institutionalized activity vary across political systems, policy areas, and historic time. There are shifts within an existing repertoire of rules and practices and change of repertoires.

Why then are institutions what they are? Through what processes do institutions and rules emerge or change and what factors lead to different forms of institutional integration? What is the role of human action and how do existing institutional arrangements affect the emergence, reproduction, and transformation of institutions? Which institutional characteristics favor change or make institutions resistant to change? The new institutionalism approaches these issues by arguing, first, that history is "inefficient" and that a task is to identify factors that create inefficiencies in adaptation; and second, that change is not driven solely by external processes and shocks but that there is a need to explore intra- and inter-institutional sources of change.

### HISTORICAL INEFFICIENCY

A standard argument in the literature is that institutions survive and flourish because they are well adapted to their functional (Goodin 1996, Stinchcombe 2001) or normative environments (Meyer and Rowan 1977). A democratic ideal is that citizens and their representatives should be able to design political institutions at will. However, this democratic ideal is frustrated by *Rechtsstaat* principles and by limited human capacity for understanding and control. In practice, actors show limited willingness and ability to adapt rules and identities on the basis of experience.

Rules develop in response to history, but that development is not uniquely optimal in any meaningful sense. The new institutionalism argues that key behavioral mechanisms encoding experience into rules and routines are history dependent and neither guarantee improvement nor increasing survival value. Observation and interpretation of experience and institutional memories, retrieval, and responses are affected by institutional arrangements, and adaptation is less continuous and precise than assumed by standard equilibrium models (March 1981, March and Olsen 1989). A better understanding of historical inefficiency requires detailed exploration of possible frictions in processes of institutional design and reform, institutional abilities to adapt spontaneously to changing circumstances, and environmental effectiveness in eliminating suboptimal institutions and identities (Olsen 2001).

Reformers are institutional gardeners more than architects and engineers. They reinterpret codes of behavior, impact causal and normative beliefs, foster civic and democratic identities and engagement, develop organized capabilities, and improve adaptability. Still, institutions are defended by insiders and validated by outsiders and cannot be changed arbitrarily. The more institutionalized an area, the more robust are institutional structures against reform efforts and environmental change, and resistance is strongest when change threatens institutional identities (March and Olsen 1983, 1989, Olsen 2007: Ch.8). This does not imply that institutions always favor continuity over change, but that the processes of adaptation can sometimes be fast and direct but often are tortuous.

### Intra- and Inter-Institutional Dynamics

Institutions prescribe and proscribe, speed up and delay change, and the assumption that structures persist unless there are external irritants or shocks underestimates intra- and inter-institutional dynamics and sources of change. Change can be driven by explicit rules, pressures from institutional ideals that can never be fulfilled in practice, internal loss of faith in institutions and interpreters of appropriateness, and by intra- and inter-institutional tensions between organizational and normative principles.

While concepts of institution and order assume some internal coherence and consistency, tensions and disputes are endemic. The principles and rules on which an institution is constituted are never fully accepted by the entire society and political orders are never perfectly integrated (Eisenstadt 1965, Goodin 1996). Order is created by a collection of institutions that fit more or less into a coherent system and most political systems function through a mix of coexisting, partly inconsistent organizational and normative principles, behavioral logics, and legitimate resources (Orren and Skowronek 2004, Olsen 2007). The coherence of political institutions and orders varies over time through processes of institutionalization, de-institutionalization, and re-institutionalization.

Institutionalization implies:

1. Increasing clarity and agreement about behavioral rules, including allocation of formal authority. Standardization and formalization of practice reduce uncertainty and conflict concerning who does what, when and how. As some ways of acting are perceived as natural and legitimate there is less need for using incentives or coercion in order to make people follow prescribed rules.

2. Increasing consensus concerning how behavioral rules are to be explained and justified, with a common vocabulary, expectations and success criteria. There is a decreasing need to explain and justify why modes of action are appropriate in terms of problem solving and normative validity.

3. The supply of resources becomes routinized and "taken as given." It takes less effort to obtain or mobilize the resources required for acting in accordance with prescribed rules of appropriate behavior.

Thus, *de-institutionalization* implies that institutional identities, roles, authority, borders, explanations and justifications, and resources are contested. There is increasing uncertainty, disorientation, and conflict. New actors are mobilized. There are demands for new explanations and justifications of existing practices. Outcomes are more uncertain, and it is necessary to use more incentives or coercion to make people follow prescribed rules.

The coherence of an institution or a political order can be threatened by strong identifications with subunits or roles, and institutions organized on competing principles can create problems for each other. Still, one hypothesis is that democratic systems work comparatively well *because* their political orders are not well integrated. In everyday life inconsistencies and tensions are buffered by institutional specialization, separation, autonomy, sequential attention, local rationality, and conflict avoidance (Cyert and March 1963). Arguably, these mechanisms help democracies cope with conflicts that create confrontations and stalemates at constitutional moments when demands for consistency and coherence are stronger (Olsen 2007: Ch.9).

Certain periods are characterized by institutional confrontations (Weber 1978). There are radical intrusions and attempts to achieve control over other institutional spheres, as well as stern institutional defense against invasions of alien norms. Changing patterns of power follow from inter-institutional processes of separation and integration, de-coupling or re-coupling, as new bridges or walls are built between institutions.

An improved understanding of the dynamics of institutions and identities requires attention to several "imperfect" and disjointed processes of change, not a focus on a single mechanism and coherent and dominant process; and the second chapter in this section explores institutional integration and disintegration by means of an experiential learning model. Networks transform themselves as participants learn from local experience and adjust local linkages, rather than as a result of some global rationality achieved through rational choice or competitive selection. Learning is myopic and meandering, rather than optimizing. It is "inefficient" in the sense of not reaching a uniquely optimal arrangement, and different learning rates from successes and failures have important consequences for integration and disintegration (March 1999).

## PURIFICATION AND RECONCILIATION

The basic ideas of the "new institutionalism" have fared fairly well. The "logic of appropriateness" and "historical inefficiency" still are promising rather than outdated ideas, and there have been important advances. Nevertheless, many theoretical challenges remain and there is need for detailed empirical studies testing the quality of theoretical speculations.

Further theoretical exploration of the role of institutions in political life may take two different avenues. One is to purify the competing conceptions of political institutions, action, and change and make further efforts to specify the conditions under which each provides a good approximation to important empirical phenomena. Within this approach, the new institutionalism needs to identify processes and determinants that increase or hamper the autonomy and ordering effect of political institutions, facilitate or hinder political action according to a logic of appropriateness, and make history more or less inefficient and maintain stability or promote institutional change.

Another avenue is to explore how competing perspectives interact and impact each other. The spirit of the new institutionalism is to supplement rather than reject alternative approaches. The recognition of an autonomous role for institutions does not deny the importance of political agency and environmental imperatives.

In this spirit, the last chapter in this section makes an effort to clarify relations between a logic of appropriateness and a logic of consequentiality. The chapter discusses which factors determine the salience of different logics and the institutional conditions under which each is likely to dominate (March and Olsen 1998). Political actors may subsume one logic as a special case of the other. They may establish a hierarchy among logics, or be governed by the relative prescriptive clarity of different logics. The resources available for acting in accordance with different logics may be decisive. Actors may use different logics for different purposes. There may be a sequential ordering of logics of action, and change between logics of action may result from specific experiences.

## LITERATURE

Bátora, J. 2005. Does the European Union transform the institution of diplomacy? *Journal of European Public Policy*, 12 (1): 1–23.

Christensen, T. and P. Lægreid. 2007. *Transcending New Public Management. The Transformation of Public Sector Reform*. Aldershot: Ashgate.

Cyert, R. M. and J. G. March. 1963. *A Behavioral Theory of the Firm*. Englewood Cliffs, NJ: Prentice-Hall. 2nd ed. 1992. Oxford: Basil Blackwell.

Egeberg, M. 2003. How bureaucratic structure matters: An organizational perspective. In B. G. Peters and J. Pierre (eds.) *Handbook of Public Administration*: 116–126. London: Sage.

Eisenstadt, S. 1965. *Essays on Comparative Institutions*. New York: Wiley.

Goodin, R. E. 1996. *The Theory of Institutional Design*. Cambridge: Cambridge University Press.

Magnussen, A.-M. 2006. *Domstolskapt rett. En institusjonell analyse av utviklingen av regelen om ulovfestet objektivt ansvar fra 1866 til 2003*. Bergen: Universitetet i Bergen. Institutt for administrasjon og organisasjonsvitenskap: Rapport nr. 92.

March, J. G. 1981. Footnotes to organizational change. *Administrative Science Quarterly* 16: 563–77.

March, J. G. 1999. A learning perspective on the network dynamics of institutional integration. In M. Egeberg and P. Lægreid (eds.) *Organizing Political Institutions*: 129–155. Oslo: Scandinavian University Press.

March, J. G. and J. P. Olsen. 1983. Organizing political life: What administrative reorganization tells us about government. *American Political Science Review* 77: 281–297.

March, J. G. and J. P. Olsen. 1984. The new institutionalism: Organizational factors in political life. *American Political Science Review* 78 (3): 734–749.

March, J. G. and J. P. Olsen. 1989. *Rediscovering Institutions*. New York: Free Press.

March, J. G. and J. P. Olsen. 1995. *Democratic Governance*. New York: Free Press.

March, J. G. and J. P. Olsen. 1998. The institutional dynamics of international political orders. *International Organization* 52: 943–969.

March, J. G. and J. P. Olsen. 2006a. The logic of appropriateness. In M. Rein, M. Moran, and R. E. Goodin (eds.), *The Oxford Handbook of Public Policy*: 689–708. Oxford: Oxford University Press.

March, J. G. and J. P. Olsen. 2006b. Elaborating the "New Institutionalism." In R. A. W. Rhodes, S. Binder, and B. Rockman (eds.): *The Oxford Handbook of Political Institutions*: 3–20. Oxford: Oxford University Press.

March, J. G. and H. A. Simon. 1958. *Organizations*. New York: Wiley. 2nd ed. 1993. Cambridge, MA: Blackwell.

March, J. G., M. Schultz, and X. Zhou. 2000. *The Dynamics of Rules. Change in Written Organizational Codes.* Stanford CA: Stanford University Press.

Merton, R. K. 1938. Social structure and anomie. *American Sociological Review* 3: 672–682.

Meyer, J. and B. Rowan. 1977. Institutionalized organizations: Formal structure as myth and ceremony. *American Journal of Sociology* 83: 340–63.

Olsen, J. P. 2001. Garbage cans, new institutionalism, and the study of politics. *American Political Science Review* 95 (1): 191–198.

Olsen, J. P. 2007. *Europe in Search of Political Order.* Oxford: Oxford University Press.

Orren, K. and S. Skowronek. 2004. *The Search for American Political Development.* Cambridge: Cambridge University Press.

Pitkin, H. F. 1972 (1967). *The Concept of Representation.* Berkeley: University of California Press.

Rothstein, B. 1996. Political institutions: An overview. In R. E. Goodin and H.-D. Klingemann (eds.): *A New Handbook of Political Science*: 133–166. Oxford: Oxford University Press.

Stinchcombe, A. L. 2001. *When Formality Works. Authority and Abstraction in Law and Organizations.* Chicago: University of Chicago Press.

Ugland T. 2002. *Policy Recategorization and Integration—Europeanization of Nordic Alcohol Policies.* Oslo: Arena Report 02/3.

Weaver, R. K. and B. A. Rockman (eds.). 1993. *Do Institutions Matter? Government Capabilities in the United States and Abroad.* Washington, DC: Brookings.

Weber, M. 1978. *Economy and Society.* Berkeley: University of California Press.

### NOTES

1. "Institutionalism" means different things to different people. Here it refers to the approach initiated by March and Olsen 1984 (the first chapter in this section, Chapter 9) and elaborated in March and Olsen 1989, 1995, 1998, 2006a, 2006b. I draw on these publications and nearly forty years of cooperation and friendship with James G. March.

# The New Institutionalism

## *Organizational Factors in Political Life*

JAMES G. MARCH AND JOHAN P. OLSEN

Contemporary theories of politics tend to portray politics as a reflection of society, political phenomena as the aggregate consequences of individual behavior, action as the result of choices based on calculated self-interest, history as efficient in reaching unique and appropriate outcomes, and decision making and the allocation of resources as the central foci of political life. Some recent theoretical thought in political science, however, blends elements of these theoretical styles into an older concern with institutions. This new institutionalism emphasizes the relative autonomy of political institutions, possibilities for inefficiency in history, and the importance of symbolic action to an understanding of politics. Such ideas have a reasonable empirical basis, but they are not characterized by powerful theoretical forms. Some directions for theoretical research may, however, be identified in institutionalist conceptions of political order.

IN MOST CONTEMPORARY THEORIES of politics, traditional political institutions, such as the legislature, the legal system, and the state, as well as traditional economic institutions, such as the firm, have receded in importance from the position they held in the earlier theories of political scientists such as J. W. Burgess or W. W. Willoughby, economists such as Thorstein Veblen or John R. Commons, and sociologists such as Max Weber. From a behavioral point of view, formally organized social institutions have come to be portrayed simply as arenas within which political behavior, driven by more fundamental factors, occurs. From a normative point of view, ideas that embedded morality in institutions, such as law or bureaucracy, and that emphasized citizenship as a foundation for personal identity, have given way to ideas of moral individualism and an emphasis on conflicting interests.

In recent years, however, a new institutionalism has appeared in political

---

This chapter originally appeared in *The American Political Science Review*, 78:3 (1984), 734–749.

science. It is far from coherent or consistent; it is not completely legitimate; but neither can it be entirely ignored. This resurgence of concern with institutions is a cumulative consequence of the modern transformation of social institutions and persistent commentary from observers of them. Social, political, and economic institutions have become larger, considerably more complex and resourceful, and *prima facie* more important to collective life. Most of the major actors in modern economic and political systems are formal organizations, and the institutions of law and bureaucracy occupy a dominant role in contemporary life.

Attention to political institutions has increased in the literature on legis- latures (Shepsle and Weingast, 1983), budgets (Padgett, 1981), public policy making (Ashford, 1977; Scharpf, 1977), local government (Kjellberg, 1975), and political elites (Robins, 1976). It is manifest in studies of the origin of the state (Wright, 1977) and the development of national administrative capacity (Skowronek, 1982), in analyses of the breakdown of democratic regimes (Potter, 1979), and in discussions of corporatism (Berger, 1981; Olsen, 1981; Schmitter and Lehmbruch, 1979). It is reflected in the Marxist rediscovery of the state as a problem in political economy (Jessop, 1977) and of the importance of orga- nizational factors for understanding that role (Therborn, 1980). It is present in studies of formal organizations and particularly in studies of the place of such organizations in the implementation of public policy (Hanf and Scharpf, 1978). It is visible in attempts to link the study of the state to natural science (Masters, 1983) and to the humanities (Geertz, 1980), as well as in a renewed interest in making historical-comparative studies of the state (Evans, Rueschemeyer, and Skocpol, 1983; Hayward and Berki, 1979; Krasner, in press).

In this article we examine some aspects of these developments and their implications for developing a theoretical understanding of how political life is organized. We approach the task from the perspective of students of formal organizations. The argument, however, extends beyond organization theory to a more general view of the place of institutions in politics and the possibilities for a political theory that is attentive to them.

## THEORETICAL STYLES OF
## CONTEMPORARY POLITICAL SCIENCE

Although the concept of institution has never disappeared from theoretical po- litical science, the basic vision that has characterized theories of politics since about 1950 is (a) *contextual*, inclined to see politics as an integral part of society, less inclined to differentiate the polity from the rest of society; (b) *reductionist*, inclined to see political phenomena as the aggregate consequences of individual behavior, less inclined to ascribe the outcomes of politics to organizational structures and rules of appropriate behavior; (c) *utilitarian*, inclined to see action as the product of calculated self-interest, less inclined to see political actors as responding to obligations and duties; (d) *functionalist*, inclined to see history as an efficient mechanism for reaching uniquely appropriate equilibria, less concerned with the possibilities for maladaptation and non-uniqueness in historical development; and (e) *instrumentalist*, inclined to define decision making and the allocation of resources as the central concerns of political life, less attentive to the ways in which political life is organized around the development of meaning through symbols, rituals, and ceremonies.

### *Politics as Subordinate to Exogenous Forces: Contextualism*

Historically, political scientists and political philosophers have tended to treat political institutions, particularly the state, as independent factors, important to the ordering and understanding of collective life (Heller, 1933). Modern political scientists, with few exceptions, have not. The state has lost its position of centrality in the discipline; interest in comprehensive forms of political organization has declined; political events are defined more as epiphenomena than as actions necessary to an understanding of society; politics mirrors its context (Easton, 1968).

The most conspicuous contextual factor cited in recent writing is the social class structure. The social stratification of a modern society with its associated distribution of wealth and income has obvious major effects on political events. Class differences translate into political differences with great reliability across time and across cultures; differences in the organization and ideology of social class seem to lead to predictable differences in political organization and institutions (Tilly, 1978). Other analyses at the same level of aggregation make the structure and process of politics a function of physical environment, geography, and climate; of ethnicity, language, and culture; of economic conditions and development; or of demography, technology, ideology, or religion. Plausible arguments which make political life a derivative of one or more of these broad contextual forces have been developed, and it is not hard to find empirical data to support the arguments. Although there are a number of relatively precise contextual theories, the major theoretical significance of these ideas from the present point of view is less the specific forms of the theories than their general inclination to see the causal links between society and polity as running from the former to the latter, rather than the other way around. It is assumed that class, geography, climate, ethnicity, language, culture, economic conditions, demography, technology, ideology, and religion all affect politics but are not significantly affected by politics.

### The Macro Consequences of Micro Behavior: Reductionism

Historically, political theory has treated political institutions as determining, ordering, or modifying individual motives, and as acting autonomously in terms of institutional needs. In contrast, substantial elements of modern theoretical work in political science assume that political phenomena are best understood as the aggregate consequences of behavior comprehensible at the individual or group level.

Such theories depend on two presumptions. The first presumption is that a political system consists of a number (often a large number) of elementary actors. Human behavior at the level of these elementary actors may be seen as conscious, calculated, and flexible, or as unconscious, habitual, and rigid. In either case, the preferences and powers of the actors are exogenous to the political system, depending on their positions in the social and economic system. The second presumption is that collective behavior is best understood as stemming from the (possibly intricate) interweaving of behavior understandable at a lower level of aggregation. Discovering, or deducing, the collective consequences may be difficult, even impossible; but the central faith is that outcomes at the collective level depend only on the intricacies of the interactions among the individual actors, that concepts suggesting autonomous behavior at the aggregate level are certainly superfluous and probably deleterious.

Within such a perspective, for example, the behavior of an organization is the consequence of the interlocking choices by individuals and subunits, each acting in terms of expectations and preferences manifested at those levels (Niskanen, 1971). The behavior of a market is the consequence of the interlocking choices by individuals and firms, each acting in terms of a set of expectations and preferences manifested at those levels (Stigler, 1952). It is not necessary that the micro processes involve choice, of course. Aggregate behavior in a group can be defined as the consequence of the interlocking of trial-and-error learning occurring at the individual level (Lave and March, 1975). Or the aggregate behavior of an industry can be defined as the consequence of the interlocking of standard operating procedures and accounting rules followed at the level of the individual firm (Nelson and Winter, 1982).

There is nothing intrinsic to a perspective that emphasizes the macro consequences of micro actions which requires that the elementary units be individuals. All that is required is that the behavior of a more comprehensive system be decomposable to elementary behaviors explicable at a less comprehensive level.

In practice, however, in most of the social sciences, the actions of individual human beings are considered to determine the flow of events in a larger social system. Outcomes at the system level are thought to be determined by the interactions of individuals acting consistently in terms of the axioms of individual behavior, whatever they may be. Thus, we make assumptions about individual consumers to understand markets, about voters to understand politics, and about bureaucrats to understand bureaucracies.

The two best-specified theories of aggregate behavior in the social sciences, the economic theory of markets and the ecological theory of environmental competition, exemplify the modern style. Consider the theory of markets. Within this theory we find individual consumers, each attempting to make purchases at the best possible prices considering his or her own preferences and alternatives, and individual producers, each attempting to make production and pricing decisions that result in the best possible return considering his or her own preferences and alternatives. The behavior of the market is assumed to be understandable as a consequence of these individual actors making choices that, in aggregate, fit together into market phenomena. Consider similarly the ecological theory of environmental competition. Within this theory we find individual species, each adapting to an environment through survival, mutation, and reproduction. Selection and changes in population distributions within the environment are assumed to be understandable as consequences of the actions of individual actors that, in combination with the actions of others and the potential capacity of the environment, produce a distribution of types.

## Action as the Making of Calculated Decisions: Utilitarianism

Historically, political science has emphasized the ways in which political behavior was embedded in an institutional structure of rules, norms, expectations, and traditions that severely limited the free play of individual will and calculation (Wolin, 1960). In contrast, modern political science has, for the most part, described political events as the consequence of calculated decisions. Not just in political science, but throughout modern theoretical work in the social sciences, the preeminent vision of human behavior is a vision of choice. Life is characterized as deliberate decision making.

The details of the choice metaphor vary from one treatment to another, but the characteristic form is one that assumes choices stem from two guesses about the future. The first is a guess about the uncertain future consequences of possible current action. Decision theorists recognize that human limitations may restrict the precision of the estimates, that the estimates may be biased, and that the information on which the estimates are based may be costly; but information about probable consequences is assumed to be important to a choice. From this assumption comes an emphasis on the power of information and expertise (Crozier, 1964) and the importance of reliable and unbiased information sources (Nisbet and Ross, 1980). Although numerous psychological experiments have indicated that the guesses of human subjects are biased (Kahneman, Slovic, and Tversky, 1982), it has not been easy to formulate alternatives to the simple notion that the guesses of experienced humans are, on average, accurate. As a result, most theories of choice present decisions as being, on average, sensible. In their political versions, choice theories assume that, on average, voters vote intelligently with respect to their interests; legislators organize sensible coalitions, given their interests; and nation states voluntarily enter alliances that, on average, improve their positions.

The second guess on which intentional, anticipatory choice is based is a guess about a decision maker's uncertain future preferences for possible future outcomes. In any theory of deliberate choice, action depends on the decision maker's values. Since the consequences of interest are to be realized in the future, it is necessary to anticipate not only what will happen but how the decision maker will feel about those outcomes when they are experienced (March, 1978). The complexities of the second guess are largely ignored by theories of choice. In their standard forms, the theories assume that preferences are stable, thus that current preferences are good predictors of future preferences; that preferences are unambiguous and consistent, thus that a choice will be clearly indicated, given the first guess; and that preferences are exogenous, thus that whatever process generates preferences, it precedes choice and is independent of the choice process. In one of the best-developed forms of choice theories, these assumptions about preferences are taken as axioms, and preferences are discovered not by asking decision makers to report them but by defining a "revealed preference" function that satisfies the axioms and is consistent with choices made by a decision maker (Luce and Raiffa, 1957). Although the empirical existence of consistent revealed preferences has been the subject of considerable debate (Becker and Stigler, 1977; Kahneman, Slovic, and Tversky, 1982), the theoretical idea forms the basis of extensive analytical development and empirical exploration.

## The Efficiency of History: Functionalism

Historically, political theory has been ambivalent about the efficiency of history. Like other social scientists, students of political development have been inclined to accept an idea of progress, the more or less inexorable historical movement toward some more "advanced" level. At the same time, political histories have often emphasized the unique significance of a particular sequence of events or choices, the impact of a particular campaign strategy or speech, or the particular tactics of international negotiation. In modern usage, the terminology of progress has been largely replaced by a terminology of survival, but for the most part, in contemporary theoretical political science, institutions and behavior are thought to evolve through some form of efficient historical process.

An efficient historical process, in these terms, is one that moves rapidly to a unique solution, conditional on current environmental conditions, thus independent of the historical path. The equilibrium may involve a stochastically stable distribution or a fixed point, but we require a solution that is achieved relatively rapidly and is independent of the details of historical events leading to it. The assumption of historical efficiency is a standard, although usually not explicit, assumption of much of modern social science. Economic theories of markets and ecological theories of competition, for example, are concerned with the characteristics of an equilibrium, if one exists. They are used to predict differences (e.g., in markets, organizational structures, population, technologies) that will be observed, at equilibrium, in different environments. Similarly, some postwar theories of political parties see party orientation and organization as equilibrium solutions to problems of survival in a competitive political environment (Downs, 1957). The assumption of historical efficiency makes such theories largely indifferent to the behavioral reality of the micro processes that are assumed. For example, competition can be assumed to eliminate action that is inconsistent with the logic of survival. Examples include theories of market equilibria, such as those found in recent ideas of efficient capital markets (Sharpe, 1970); theories of organizational structure, such as those found in recent ideas of industrial organization (Williamson, 1978); and theories of political parties, such as those found in ideas of political economy (Olson, 1965).

History cannot be guaranteed to be efficient. An equilibrium may not exist. Even if there is an equilibrium, historical processes can easily be slow enough relative to the rate of change in the environment that the equilibrium of the process is unlikely to be achieved before the environment, and thus the equilibrium, changes. By assuming quickness, theories of political behavior avoid focusing on transient phenomena that might be less predictable and more subject to effects from the details of the processes involved. For example, when it is predicted that political parties will come to identical positions in an environment of single-peaked voter preferences, it is assumed that party adjustment will be much more rapid than will be changes in voter preferences. Efficiency also requires that the equilibrium be unique and achievable. Processes with multiple equilibria are, of course, easily specified and frequently observed. What makes them unattractive is not their rarity, but their intractability and the indeterminacy of their outcomes. It is no accident that the most common principle of theories in the social sciences is the optimization principle, and that one of the greatest concerns in such theories is showing that a process has a unique optimum that is guaranteed to be achieved.

## The Primacy of Outcomes: Instrumentalism

Historically, theories of political institutions portrayed political decision making primarily as a process for developing a sense of purpose, direction, identity, and belonging. Politics was a vehicle for educating citizens and improving cultural values. Although there are exceptions, the modern perspective in political science has generally given primacy to outcomes and either ignored symbolic actions or seen symbols as part of manipulative efforts to control outcomes, rather than the other way around.

Modern polities are as replete with symbols, ritual, ceremony, and myth as the societies more familiar to anthropological tradition. Politicians announce public support for positions they fail to defend in private (Edelman, 1964). Legislators vote for legislation while remaining indifferent to its implementation (Pressman and Wildavsky, 1973). Administrators solicit public participation in decision making in order to secure public support for policies to which they are already committed. Chief executives advocate reorganization of the public bureaucracy, announce plans for making reorganizations, and regularly abandon the plans (March and Olsen, 1983). Information is gathered, policy alternatives are defined, and cost-benefit analyses are pursued, but they seem more intended to reassure observers of the appropriateness of actions being taken than to influence the actions (Feldman and March, 1981).

In modern discussions of politics, these symbolic actions are characteristically portrayed as strategic moves by self-conscious political actors. Rituals and ceremonies are defined as window dressing for the real political processes, or as instruments by which the clever and the powerful exploit the naive and the weak. The hiring of experts lends legitimacy to policies (Meyer and Rowan, 1977); associating unpopular moves with popular symbols is reassuring (Edelman, 1964). Control over symbols is a basis of power, like control over other resources (Pfeffer, 1981a); and the use of symbols is part of a struggle over political outcomes (Cohen, 1974).

## INSTITUTIONALIST PERSPECTIVES

The new institutionalism is not peculiar to political science. Renewed interest in institutions is characteristic of recent trends in economics, which has discovered law, contracts, hierarchies, standard operating procedures, professional codes, and social norms (Akerlof, 1980). It is also seen in anthropology and sociology, although non-institutionalist visions never succeeded in those fields to the extent that they did in political science and economics. Nor are the institutionalist ideas entirely new. By labeling the collection of ideas "the new institutionalism," we mean to note the fact that there was indeed an "old institutionalism," that cycles in ideas have brought us back to considerations that typified earlier forms of theory in political science. We do not mean to suggest, however, that the new and the old are identical. It would probably be more accurate to describe recent thinking as blending elements of an old institutionalism into the non-institutionalist styles of recent theories of politics.

This new institutionalism can be presented and discussed as an epistemological perspective of profound importance to understanding social science, but for our purposes, it is more useful to define it in terms of a narrow collection of challenges to contemporary theoretical thinking in political science, a small set of relatively technical ideas of primary interest to professional students of political life. The ideas deemphasize the dependence of the polity on society in favor of an interdependence between relatively autonomous social and political institutions; they deemphasize the simple primacy of micro processes and efficient histories in favor of relatively complex processes and historical inefficiency; they deemphasize metaphors of choice and allocative outcomes in favor of other logics of action and the centrality of meaning and symbolic action. The ideas are not all mutually consistent. Indeed, some of them seem mutually inconsistent. For example, ideas based on the assumption that large institutional structures (e.g., organizations, legislatures, states) can be portrayed as rationally coherent autonomous actors are uneasy companions for ideas suggesting that political action is inadequately described in terms of rationality and choice.

### The Causal Position of Political Institutions

Without denying the importance of both the social context of politics and the motives of individual actors, the new institutionalism insists on a more autonomous role for political institutions. The state is not only affected by society but also affects it (Katzenstein, 1978; Krasner, 1978; Nordlinger, 1981; Skocpol, 1979; Stephan, 1978). Political democracy depends not only on economic and social conditions but also on the design of political institutions. The bureaucratic agency, the legislative committee, and the appellate court are arenas for contending social forces, but they are also collections of standard operating procedures and structures that define and defend interests. They are political actors in their own right.

The argument that institutions can be treated as political actors is a claim of institutional coherence and autonomy. The claim of coherence is necessary in order to treat institutions as decision makers. From such a point of view, the issue is whether we wish to picture the state (or some other political institution) as making choice on the basis of some *collective* interest or intention (e.g., preferences, goals, purposes), alternatives, and expectations (Levi, 1981). There is no necessary answer to the question unless we impose one. Whether it makes pragmatic theoretical sense to impute interests, expectations, and the other paraphernalia of coherent intelligence to an institution is neither more nor less problematic, a priori, than whether it makes sense to impute them to an individual (Kahneman, 1982; March and Shapira, 1982). The pragmatic answer appears to be that the coherence of institutions varies but is sometimes substantial enough to justify viewing a collectivity as acting coherently.

The claim of autonomy is necessary to establish that political institutions are more than simple mirrors of social forces. Empirical observations seem to indicate that processes internal to political institutions, although possibly triggered by external events, affect the flow of history. Programs adopted as a simple political compromise by a legislature become endowed with separate meaning and force by having an agency established to deal with them (Skocpol and Finegold, 1982). The establishment of public policies, or competition among bureaucrats or legislators, activates and organizes otherwise quiescent identities and social cleavages (Olsen and Saetren, 1980; Tilly, 1978). Policy experts within the political system develop and shape the understanding of policy issues and alternatives (Heclo, 1974).

Such phenomena are not routinely accommodated by modern political theory, which makes political outcomes a function of three primary factors: the distribution of preferences (interests) among political actors, the distribution of resources (powers), and the constraints imposed by the rules of the game (constitutions). Each of these is treated as exogenous to the political system. That is, preferences are developed within a society and transmitted through socialization, resources are distributed among political actors by some broad social processes, and rules of the game are either stable or change by a revolutionary intervention exogenous to ordinary political activities.

The idea that preferences are produced and changed by a process that is exogenous to the processes of choice is fundamental to modern decision theory. In the "revealed preference" version of the theory, preferences must be stable in order for the theory to be testable. In other versions, preferences can change, but choice itself does not produce a change in preferences. Conventional theories of markets, for example, picture advertising and experience as providing information about alternatives and their properties, not as affecting tastes. Similarly, conventional theories of politics assume that a voter's exposure to and choice of a candidate do not change that voter's preferences for various attributes that a candidate might possess, although they may change a voter's beliefs about which candidates possess which attributes. The new institutionalism, in company with most research on preferences, argues that preferences and meanings develop in politics, as in the rest of life, through a combination of education, indoctrination, and experience. They are neither stable nor exogenous (Cohen and Axelrod, 1984). If political preferences are molded through political experiences, or by political institutions, it is awkward to have a theory that presumes preferences are exogenous to the political process. And if preferences are not exogenous to the political process, it is awkward to picture the political system as strictly dependent on the society associated with it.

The contrast between the two kinds of notions is found most starkly in theories of political leadership. One classic idea of political leadership emphasizes the creation of winning political coalitions among participants with given demands (March, 1970). The leadership role is that of a broker: providing information, identifying possible coalitions, and facilitating side payments and the development of logrolls. Such a view of leadership is implicit in the theory of the political process that has been developed in political science in recent decades. A second conception of leadership emphasizes the transformation of preferences, both those of the leader and those of the followers (Burns, 1978; Selznick, 1957). Leaders interact with other leaders and are co-opted into new beliefs and commitments. The leadership role is that of an educator, stimulating and accepting changing worldviews, redefining meanings, stimulating commitments. Such a view is more conspicuous in the ideas of the new institutionalism.

The distribution of political resources is also partly determined endogenously. Political institutions affect the distribution of resources, which in turn affects the power of political actors, and thereby affects political institutions. Wealth, social standing, reputation for power, knowledge of alternatives, and attention are not easily described as exogenous to the political process and political institutions. Holding office provides participation rights and alters the distribution of power and access (Egeberg, 1981; Laegreid and Olsen, 1978). The policy alternatives of leaders are not defined completely by exogenous forces, but are shaped by existing administrative agencies (Skocpol, 1980; Skocpol and Fine-gold, 1982; Skowronek, 1982). The outcomes of the political process modify reputations for power, which in turn modify political outcomes (Enderud, 1976; March, 1966).

Finally, the third exogenous factor in conventional theories of politics, the rules of the game, is not really exogenous either. Constitutions, laws, contracts, and customary rules of politics make many potential actions or considerations illegitimate or unnoticed; some alternatives are excluded from the agenda before politics begins (Bachrach and Baratz, 1962), but these constraints are not im-posed full-blown by an external social system; they develop within the context of political institutions. Public agencies create rules and have them sanctioned by politicians (Eckhoff and Jacobsen, 1960), and revolutionary changes are ini-tiated and pursued by military bureaucrats (Trimberger, 1978).

## The Causal Complexity of Political History

Theories of politics tend to assume a relatively uncomplicated intermeshing among the elementary units of a political system. There may be many individu-als, groups, or classes involved, but they are relatively undifferentiated and their interactions are relatively simple. Empirical observations of political systems, on the other hand, often stress the institutional complexity of modern states (Ashford, 1977; Scharpf, 1977) and identify a rather complicated intertwining of institutions, individuals, and events. Alternatives are not automatically pro-vided to a decision maker; they have to be found. Search for alternatives occurs in an organized context in which problems are not only looking for solutions, but solutions are looking for problems. Information about the consequences of alternatives is generated and communicated through organized institutions, so expectations depend on the structure of linkages within the system, as well as the ways in which biases and counter-biases cumulate (Simon, 1957a, b). Guesses about future preferences are developed within institutions dedicated to defin-ing and modifying values and the meanings of actions (Cyert and March, 1963; March and Olsen, 1976). There are many such institutions, some nested within others, with multiple, overlapping connections (Long, 1958). National political systems fit into international political systems and are composed of numerous subsystems, some of which extend beyond national boundaries.

If this complexity is not decomposable analytically into smaller systems or susceptible to some relatively simple aggregation techniques, the theoretical problems of understanding social history are not easily accommodated within contemporary theoretical styles. For example, it may be rash to assume that errors in expectations have a normal distribution with a mean of zero. The allocation of attention may be critical to the flow of events. The responsiveness of the political system to environmental pressures may, at least in the short run, depend on the amount of slack in the system, and on the ways in which accounting numbers are produced and fudged. The system may not come close to trying to resolve conflict but simply attend sequentially to the demands placed on it (Cyert and March, 1963). Learning may be superstitious, and fallacious rules of inference may persist for long periods (Nisbet and Ross, 1980). At the limit, the connections between problems and solutions may be less dominated by a logic of causal linkages between means and ends than by the less problematic temporal linkages of simultaneity (Cohen, March, and Olsen, 1972).

Theories of collective behavior most commonly simplify the potential morass of collective complexity by one of two classic routes. The first is statistical aggregation. In its usual guise, aggregation assumes that the factors affecting outcomes can be divided into two groups, one systematic and the other random. Thus, for example, we might assume that in a population of voters there are many factors affecting electoral choice. Some of those factors (e.g., income) have impacts on the vote that are strong and consistent across individuals. Other factors (e.g., specific policy issues) have impacts that are weaker or less consistent or less well understood. If we assume the latter factors can be treated as noise, that is, that they are independent, randomly distributed variables, the systematic factors will be clear in the aggregate results. In this way, conventional assumptions of aggregation impose a statistical order on the results.

The second classical simplification is the assumption of historical efficiency. Although the argument is usually associated with theories of natural selection and best specified in modern theories of population biology, the basic idea of historical efficiency is implicit in many modern theories. Regardless of the complexity or apparent anomalies of human behavior, historical processes are assumed to eliminate rules for behavior that are not solutions to an appropriate joint optimization problem. Thus, a prediction based on solving the optimization problem will correctly predict behavior, regardless of whether the actors involved formulate or solve that problem explicitly (Friedman, 1953). For example, we might predict the outcome of a complicated political negotiation by assuming that the actors are each acting rationally on the basis of complete information about each other and the world, even though we recognize that such assumptions are quite false as a description of individual behavior.

Students of institutions suggest alternative theoretical simplifications for understanding complex political systems, most commonly the assumption of a political structure. By a political structure we mean a collection of institutions, rules of behavior, norms, roles, physical arrangements, buildings, and archives that are relatively invariant in the face of turnover of individuals and relatively resilient to the idiosyncratic preferences and expectations of individuals. In contrast to theories that assume action is choice based on individual values and expectations, theories of political structure assume action is the fulfillment of duties and obligations. The difference is important. In a choice metaphor, we assume that political actors consult personal preferences and subjective expectations, then select actions that are as consistent as possible with those preferences and expectations. In a duty metaphor, we assume that political actors associate certain actions with certain situations by rules of appropriateness. What is appropriate for a particular person in a particular situation is defined by the political and social system and transmitted through socialization.

Political structure simplifies a complex world for the individuals in it. It does not necessarily, however, simplify the problems of the political theorist. The complex intermeshing of rule-driven behavior may be just as difficult to unravel as the complex intermeshing of preference-driven behavior. As a result, there has long been a tendency to combine ideas of political structure with ideas of historical efficiency. If individual behavior is driven by rules within a political structure, then it is possible to imagine that historical experience accumulates over generations of individual experience. The information about that experience is encoded in institutional rules (Nelson and Winter, 1982). This argument is a familiar one to political discourse. It has been a part of conservative doctrine for hundreds of years, forming a basis for defending both traditional rules of behavior and the existing political order.

The advantage to treating behavior as rule driven, in addition to its apparent consistency with numerous observations, is not that it is possible thereby to "save" a belief in historical efficiency; rather, it is that it leads more naturally than does treating behavior as optimization to an examination of the specific ways in which history is encoded into rules, and thus to making the idea of historical efficiency more attentive to the possible limiting conditions for efficiency, and more likely to generate interesting predictions about multiple equilibria or long time paths. In fact, the assumption of efficiency becomes mostly a matter of faith if the joint optimization problem cannot be specified or solved by the observer, or if it is impossible to identify the precise mechanisms by which historical experience is transformed into current action. Unless the process is specified, it is impossible to examine either the likelihood that a particular equilibrium will be achieved or how long it will take.

## Politics as an Interpretation of Life

A conception of politics as decision making is at least as old as Plato and Aristotle. It is reflected in the language and concerns of political thought, from the earliest political philosophers through Bentham to Merriam and Lasswell. Who gets what and how? For the most part, contemporary theory in political science considers politics and political behavior in such instrumental terms. The intent of actions is found in their outcomes, and the organizing principle of a political system is the allocation of scarce resources in the face of conflict of interest. Thus, action is choice, choice is made in terms of expectations about its consequences, meanings are organized to affect choices, and symbols are curtains that obscure the real politics, or artifacts of an effort to make decisions.

Parts of the new institutionalism are challenges to this primacy of outcomes. These challenges echo another ancient theme of political thought, the idea that politics creates and confirms interpretations of life. Through politics, individuals develop themselves, their communities, and the public good. In this view, participation in civic life is the highest form of activity for a civilized person. The ideas find post-Hellenistic voices in J. S. Mill, Pateman (1970), and Lafferty (1981). Politics is regarded as education, as a place for discovering, elaborating, and expressing meanings, establishing shared (or opposing) conceptions of experience, values, and the nature of existence. It is symbolic, not in the recent sense of symbols as devices of the powerful for confusing the weak, but more in the sense of symbols as the instruments of interpretive order.

The primary source of the institutionalist challenge is empirical. Observers of processes of decision making regularly discern features that are hard to relate to an outcome-oriented conception of collective choice. The pleasures are often in the process. Potential participants seem to care as much for the right to participate as for the fact of participation; participants recall features of the process more easily and vividly than they do its outcomes; heated argument leads to decisions without concern about their implementation; information relevant to a decision is requested but not considered; authority is demanded but not exercised (Feldman and March, 1981; March and Olsen, 1976). These observations are often reported as anomalies, as symptoms of some kind of perversity in the systems that were observed, paradoxical. The appearance of paradox, however, is a product of our theoretical presumption that the main point of a decision-making process is a decision. For many purposes, that presumption may be misleading. The processes of politics may be more central than their outcomes.

Politics and governance are important social rituals. In older worlds in which the major causal force producing historical experience was the will of the gods, social rituals were organized around ceremonies by which that will was discovered and influenced. Most contemporary developed societies, being somewhat more secular in their conceptions of causality, believe that experience is produced by a combination of natural laws and intentional human action. In these societies, therefore, social and political rituals are organized around the consultation of expertise and the making of decisions (Olsen, 1970). The procedures of decision that we observe are reflections and reminders of this modern, secular conception of the social order. They are signals and symbols of the appropriateness of events, not in the sense that what happened needs to be viewed as desirable or pleasant, but in the sense that what happened can be viewed as having occurred in the way things happen (Feldman and March, 1981). The usual term is "legitimate"; but legitimacy may denote something narrower than is intended, for what rituals seek to establish is not only the moral virtue of events but also their necessity.

## THEORETICAL RESEARCH
## AND POLITICAL INSTITUTIONS

Human actions, social contexts, and institutions work upon each other in complicated ways, and these complex, interactive processes of action and the formation of meaning are important to political life. Institutions seem to be neither neutral reflections of exogenous environmental forces nor neutral arenas for the performances of individuals driven by exogenous preferences and expectations. As a result, contemporary political theory is probably overly sanguine about the possibilities for a theory of politics that ignores political institutions.

For the most part, however, the relevant theoretical work remains to be done. It is interesting to suggest that political institutions and the society are interdependent, but that statement needs to find a richer theoretical expression. It is appropriate to observe that political institutions can be treated as actors in much the same way we treat individuals as actors, but we need more detailed demonstrations of the usefulness of doing so. There is good sense in noting that history is not necessarily efficient, but it would be of greater help if we were able to show the specific ways by which specific history-dependent processes lead to outcomes that are either non-unique or long delayed under some conditions. It is plausible to argue that politics is filled with behavior that is difficult to fit into a utilitarian model, but the plausibility would be augmented if we could describe an alternative model. And it is provocative to note the importance of symbols, ritual, ceremony, and myth in political life, but we cannot sustain the provocation without a clearer specification of how theories of politics are affected by such a vision.

Moving from the subtle judgments of empirical knowledge to an appropriate theoretical formulation is no easier in the analysis of politics than it is elsewhere. It requires not only further empirical studies but also theoretical research. By theoretical research we mean primarily the development of ideas, concepts, and models based on empirical observations and relevant to a behavioral understanding and prescriptive ordering of political life. The objective is not impossible. Thirty years ago, empirical students of organizations made two major criticisms of the existing theory of organizational decision making. The first criticism was that the theory made extraordinary time and information demands on organizations (March and Simon, 1958; Simon, 1957a, b). Information and time were treated as freely available resources. To ask that all consequences of all alternatives be known precisely seemed unreasonable in the face of empirical evidence that organizations considered only a small number of alternatives, examined only a small number of consequences related to only a subset of organizational goals, and made relatively imprecise estimates.

The second criticism was that the theory assumed that all participants in an organization shared the same goals, or if they did not, that conflict among them could be readily managed through the terms of some prior agreement (Cyert and March, 1963; March, 1962). In the case of a political organization, the agreement was a coalition contract, or constitution, by which all members of a coalition or polity agreed to be bound to the policies specified through bargaining or legislation. Thus, the familiar distinction between "politics" and "administration." In the case of an economic organization, the agreement was an employment contract by which employees, in return for the payment of wages, agreed to act as though they had the same goals as the owner or other legitimate policy maker. Empirical studies seemed to indicate that conflict was endemic in organizations and that it tended to be interminable rather than settled by prior agreements.

These criticisms began to have serious impact on formal theories of organized action when they were translated into useful theoretical statements through the development of information economics and theories of agency. Such theories consider information as a scarce resource subject to strategic action in a world populated by self-interested rational actors. Ideas drawn from organizational studies of bounded rationality and internal conflict permeate modern economic theory in the form of discussions of moral hazard, asymmetric information, agency, signalling, and optimal information strategies (Hirschleifer and Riley, 1979). Most students of organizations would argue that these theories are also incomplete, but it is clear that the earlier empirical criticisms have reformed theoretical thinking.

The new institutionalism would benefit from similar theoretical development if it could be accomplished. Like the early observations about bounded rationality and internal conflict, observations about the importance of institutions have generally taken the form of criticism of existing theoretical ideas rather than the delineation of an alternative set of precise theoretical concepts. Developing a comprehensive theoretical structure for institutional thinking is, of course, a prodigious and pretentious task, not one that will be undertaken here. We can, however, identify a few ideas associated with the new institutionalism that might warrant theoretical attention.

## Institutional Conceptions of Order

Institutional thinking emphasizes the part played by institutional structures in imposing elements of order on a potentially inchoate world. Traditional political theory involved considerable attention to the order produced by political contracts and reflected in constitutions, laws, and other stable rules, or by a community of moral obligation, often inspired and buttressed by religious dogma (Berki, 1979; Waterstone, 1966). For the most part, modern political theory eschews such concerns and focuses on aggregation and historical efficiency superimposed on two other kinds of order: the order imposed by reason and the order imposed by competition and coercion. Reason is recognized in ideas of rationality and intentional action; it finds institutional expression in the hierarchical organization of means and ends (and thus in formally planned institutions). Competition and coercion are recognized in ideas of conflict of interest, power, bargaining, survival, and war; they find institutional expression in elections and policy making. Theoretical research relevant to the new institutionalism would involve elaborating additional notions of political order. We believe it is possible to identify at least six such conceptions on which a modest amount of theoretical work might yield rewards.

### Historical Order

The concept of historical order implicit in contemporary theory emphasizes the efficiency of historical processes, the ways in which history moves quickly and inexorably to a unique outcome, normally in some sense an optimum. An institutional theory would specify how historical processes are affected by specific characteristics of political institutions, and it would provide greater theoretical understanding of the inefficiencies of history, that is, historical processes that do not have equilibria, take extended periods of time, lead to non-unique equilibria, or result in unique but suboptimal outcomes. Theoretical attention to the inefficiencies of history involves a greater concern for the ways in which institutions learn from their experience (Etheredge, 1976) and the possibilities that learning will produce adjustments that are slower or faster than are appropriate or are misguided. It involves trying to specify the conditions under which the sequential branches of history turn back upon each other and the conditions under which they diverge. It involves characterizing the role of standard operating procedures, professions, and expertise in storing and recalling history.

## Temporal Order

In most theories of action, we assume things are ordered by their consequential connections. Means are linked to appropriate ends; causes are linked to effects they produce; consequences are linked to actions that lead to them and to preferences they affect; solutions are linked to problems they solve. Such concepts of order underlie theories of choice. Deviations from consequential order are viewed as interesting aberrations, disturbances of a system otherwise held together by the way wanting something leads to doing something connected to the want, and doing something leads to consequences related to the intention. Temporal order provides an alternative in which linkages are less consequential than temporal. Things are connected by virtue of their simultaneous presence or arrival. In a culture with a strong sense of monthly or yearly cycles or of birth cohorts, we should not be overly surprised by temporal order. In many human situations the most easily identified property of objects or events is the time subscripts associated with them. Thus, students of time allocation in organizations have observed the ways in which attention to problems seems to be determined as much by the time of their arrival as by assessments of their importance. A classic form of temporal order is found in queuing theory, although most discussions of queuing are embedded in a consequential structure in which queues are either indistinguishable or distinguishable only by their processing times.

## Endogenous Order

Much of contemporary theory emphasizes the way order is imposed on political institutions by an external environment. From this perspective, for example, power within a political system is determined by possession of resources in the environment, interests are determined by position in the external world, and coherence within an institution is assured by the exigencies of existence. Thus, order is effectively exogenous to the institution and does not depend on properties of the institution or processes within it. Students of institutions have suggested a number of ways in which internal institutional processes affect things like the power distribution, the distribution of preferences, or the management of control. As a result, they invite theoretical development of models appropriate for understanding the ways in which interests and preferences develop within the context of institutional action, the ways reputations for power evolve as a result of the outcomes of politics, the ways in which the process of controlling purposive organizations produces unanticipated consequences, and the ways in which the course of decision making within political systems systematically, and endogenously, results in illusions of success and failure.

## Normative Order

It is a commonplace observation in empirical social science that behavior is constrained and dictated by cultural dicta and social norms. Although self-interest undoubtedly permeates politics, action is often based more on discovering the normatively appropriate behavior than on calculating the return expected from alternative choices. As a result, political behavior, like other behavior, can be described in terms of duties, obligations, roles, and rules. Such a description has not, however, been translated into any very compelling theoretical form. Some efforts have been made to rationalize normative rules, such as altruism (Kurz, 1978) and reciprocity (Axelrod, 1980), or to specify the conditions for their evolution (Axelrod and Hamilton, 1981; Trivers, 1971). From an institutionalist perspective, such efforts are exemplary, but they tend to limit attention to the comparative statics of individual norms. A broader theoretical examination of normative order would consider the relations among norms, the significance of ambiguity and inconsistency in norms, and the time path of the transformation of normative structures. A theoretical understanding of such conventional norms as those surrounding trust and legitimacy seems likely to be particularly germane to political analysis.

## Demographic Order

It is tempting for students of politics, as for students of other human endeavor, to find order defined in terms of the logic of their particular domain of interest. Thus, students of legislatures imagine that a legislature is best understood in terms of lawmaking, and students of courts imagine that a court is best understood in terms of adjudicating. Alternatively, a human institution can be studied and interpreted as the cross-section of the lives of the people involved. The idea that collective behavior can be understood as a mosaic of private lives links contemporary theoretical thought to similar ideas among qualitative students of human behavior and novelists (Krieger, 1983). A focus on institutional demography combines such a vision of organized life with attention to a property of individual lives that is itself a product of the institutional structure—the individual career (March and March, 1978; Pfeffer, 1981b). The theoretical requirements include useful concepts of the ways in which organizations adapt through turnover, institutions are driven by their cohort structures, and the pursuit of careers and professional standards dictates the flow of events.

## Symbolic Order

Students of formal organizations have called attention to the ordering force of symbols, rituals, ceremonies, stories, and drama in political life (March, 1981; March and Olsen, 1976, 1983; Meyer and Rowan, 1977; Pfeffer, 1981a; Pondy, 1978). Symbols permeate politics in a subtle and diffuse way, providing interpretive coherence to political life. Many of the activities and experiences of politics are defined by their relation to myths and symbols that antedate them and that are widely shared. At the same time, symbolic behavior is also a strategic element in political competition. Individuals and groups are frequently hypocritical, reciting sacred myths without believing them and while violating their implications. The traditional problem with such observations is not doubt about their veracity but about our ability to translate them into useful theoretical statements without excessive damage to their meaning. Theoretical development reflective of an institutional perspective would include an examination of the ways in which the tendencies toward consistency and inconsistency in beliefs affect the organization of political meaning, the ways in which "exemplary centers" (Geertz, 1980) create social order through ceremony, and the ways in which symbolic behavior transforms more instrumental behavior and is transformed by it. In particular, a serious theoretical understanding of myths, symbols, and rituals must include some attention to the dynamics of symbols, to the processes by which symbols shape the behavior not only of the innocent but of the society as a whole.

### Examples of Possible Theoretical Research

Within these six conceptions of order, there are possibilities for theoretical research attentive to the insights of students of institutions. Such research is institutional in two respects: First, it is oriented to one or more of the institutionalist conceptions of order; second, it tries to illuminate how institutional and organizational factors affect political events. As examples, consider the following:

### Example 1: Policy Martingales

Many models of history recognize that specific historical events involve elements of chance. The unique historical happening may be a draw from some probability distribution of possible events. Even in cases where chance, strictly considered, is not viewed as vital, any specific event is seen as the consequence of a complicated interweaving of factors impossible to predict with precision in a single case. In the independent trial version of such models, any specific historical event is subject to various kinds of random fluctuations but, in the long run, unlikely events at a particular time are balanced by different unlikely events at a subsequent time. The specific realizations of the historical process that comprise the events of today are independent of the specific realizations that comprise the events of yesterday. Each specific event of an unfolding history is relatively difficult to predict, but prediction is not improved by knowledge of the history of past realizations of that process.

It is possible to see political policy making as an independent trial process. Suppose we think of policy as the result of bargaining among political actors with prior preferences and resources, but subject to trial-by-trial variation attributable to specific, unpredictable, and uncontrollable factors. Then understanding the short-run outcomes of a policy process would depend on considerable detail of the specific situation. A student of institutions might well observe that the details of the way attention is organized, how alternatives are presented, what information is available, which participants are free from other demands, how institutional memory is consulted, and a host of other factors would affect the specific political policy adopted at a specific time. At the same time, however, such factors are irrelevant (or redundant) to understanding the long-term mix of policies. Such an understanding is possible simply from a knowledge of the underlying political process and any systematic institutional biases.

Not all policy-making processes are independent trial processes. Many of them seem to be more in the nature of martingales (Feller, 1950). Like an independent trial process, a martingale process is subject to chance variation, but the variations accumulate. What distinguishes a martingale is the property that the *expected value* of the process at one time is equal to the *realization* of the process at the preceding time. This property makes the specific path of history important to understanding current historical events. In effect, the chance fluctuations of history change the baselines of the next step of the historical process.

Common descriptions of incremental policy processes make them appear to be in the nature of martingales. The distribution of possible outcomes from a policy process is pictured as resulting from competition and bargaining over incremental adjustments in the current policy; the policy actually adopted is a draw from that distribution. This martingale property of policy making is not independent of institutional factors. Indeed, it seems a prototypic institutional characteristic. Policies, once adopted, are embedded into institutions. They are associated with rules, expectations, and commitments. By affecting attention and aspirations, they affect the future search behavior of political participants.

Martingales diverge more rapidly than do independent trial processes; that is, for a given amount of chance variation in each time period, the variance across possible outcomes after some number of periods will be substantially greater in a martingale. As a result, the precision with which specific realizations of the process can be anticipated is considerably less. Thus, policy martingales are related to, but not identical to, various less precise ideas of forks in history, of critical events that made a difference. There is a sense in which the first step is more important than any subsequent one, but it is a limited sense. In a martingale process all events are forks; the policy paths of two political systems with identical underlying political conditions will be radically different simply because of the way in which (possibly small) perturbations shift the focus of political pressure.

## Example 2: Experiential Learning

It is a frequent observation of institutionalism that institutions accumulate historical experience through learning. The results and inferences of past experience are stored in standard operating procedures, professional rules, and the elementary rules of thumb of a practical person. These elements of historical knowledge have been portrayed both as forms of irrational retrogression and as carriers of wisdom, and it is not hard to specify environmental situations in which either characterization would be appropriate. What is less clear is whether we can model the processes of institutional learning. Although there have been some loose arguments that experiential learning will, in the long run, lead to the discovery and adoption of optimal strategies, little theoretical effort has been devoted to specifying precisely the conditions under which learning from experience leads to optimal behavior, or to relating those conditions to features of institutional structure or life.

Consider the following simple model of learning (Levinthal and March, 1982). A decision-making institution simultaneously learns along three dimensions. First, it modifies its strategy; that is, it changes the likelihood of making one choice rather than another among the alternative activities available to it. Subjective success leads to increasing the chance of repeating a choice; subjective failure leads to decreasing the chance of repeating a choice (March and Olsen, 1976). Second, an institution modifies its competences; that is, it changes the skill it has at the various activities in which it might engage. Competence at an activity increases with experience at it; it decreases with time (Preston and Keachie, 1964). Third, an institution modifies its aspirations; that is, it changes its definition of subjective success. Aspirations move in the direction of past performance (Cyert and March, 1963). It is clear that institutional factors affect several of the key features of such learning. The learning rates associated with the three kinds of learning are partly a function of features of the institution. The degree of loose coupling in an organization affects the precision with which choices are made, outcomes observed, aspirations expressed, and competences realized. Thus, it can be expressed as various forms of noise in the process. Organizational slack affects the degree of centralization in the organization, and thus the linkage among subunits.

The three dimensions of learning obviously interact. For example, learning of aspirations affects the definition of subjective success, and thereby affects the learning of strategies. Learning of competences affects performance outcomes, and thereby affects the learning of both strategies and aspirations. Learning of strategies affects choices, and thereby affects the learning of competences. The model can be explored to discover the circumstances under which it reaches an equilibrium, and, among those the circumstances, those under which it reaches an optimum. It can also be combined into more complicated structures of learning where the choices of one institution affect the outcomes of another (e.g., competition and cooperation), and where the learning institution is itself composed of learning subunits.

## Example 3: Garbage Cans

Garbage-can models of organizational choice have been suggested as a representation of a particular temporal order. In the form most commonly discussed in the literature, the garbage-can model assumes that problems, solutions, decision makers, and choice opportunities are independent, exogenous streams flowing ~rough a system (Cohen, March, and Olsen, 1972). They come together in a ~r determined by their arrival times. Thus, solutions are linked to prob- ~arily by their simultaneity, relatively few problems are solved, and ~made for the most part either before any problems are connected to them (oversight), or after the problems have abandoned one choice to associate themselves with another (flight). This situation of extreme loose coupling, called an open structure in the original discussions of the garbage can, has attracted most of the attention in the literature, and empirical studies have revealed decision processes that appear to approximate such an open structure (March and Olsen, 1976).

Not all decision situations are quite so unstructured, however. We can characterize a choice situation in terms of two structures. The first is the access structure, a relation between problems (or solutions) and choice opportunities. The access structure may require, allow, or not allow a particular problem, if activated, to be attached to a particular choice. The second structure is the decision structure, a relation between decision makers and choice opportunities. This structure may require, allow, or not allow that a particular decision maker participate in the making of a particular choice. Access and decision structures can be imagined in any kind of arbitrary configuration, but two special forms have been considered formally. A specialized structure is one that is decomposed into substructures that are open. Thus, a specialized decision structure is one in which it is possible to divide choice opportunities and decision makers into subgroups and match the two sets of subgroups so that every decision maker in a particular subgroup of decision makers has access to every choice opportunity in the matched set of choice opportunities, but to no other. A hierarchical structure is one that expands access rights as a function of hierarchical rank. For example, in a hierarchical access structure, problems and choices are ordered, and each problem has access to choices of the same or lower rank. The differences made by these structures have been noted both formally (Cohen, March, and Olsen, 1972) and empirically (Egeberg, 1981; Olsen, 1983), but the empirical and theoretical examination of garbage-can processes within access and decision structures that are not completely open is barely begun.

### Subtle Phenomena and Simple Theories

These examples hardly exhaust the list. Empirical observations of reputations for power in politics suggest that such reputations depend heavily on the place of an individual in a political structure and on inferences about the relation between preferences and outcomes. Some simple models of the dynamic relations among reputations for power, institutional position, preferences, and social outcomes would provide a richer understanding of the ways in which power reputations affect politics. Empirical observations of post-decision surprises (i.e., deviations of realized outcomes from expected outcomes) suggest that there are systematic differences between the ways in which individuals experience the consequences of their actions and the ways in which institutions do. Some simple models of institutional expectations, choices, and post-decision assessments would clarify the occasions for expecting positive or negative surprises from deliberate action.

What characterizes all of the examples, as well as the others that might be added, is a relatively simple approach to institutional phenomena. The new institutionalism is often couched in terms of a contrast between the complexity of reality and the simplifications provided by existing theories, but theoretical research from an institutional perspective cannot involve the pursuit of enormous contextual detail. It is constrained by the capacity of human (and artificial) intelligence to cope with complexity, and although that capacity seems to expand with time, the rate of expansion continues to be modest relative to the demands of a fully contextual and institutional theory. From the point of view of theoretical research, consequently, the new institutionalism is probably better viewed as a search for alternative ideas that simplify the subtleties of empirical wisdom in a theoretically useful way.

## CONCLUSION

The institutionalism we have considered is neither a theory nor a coherent critique of one. It is simply an argument that the organization of political life makes a difference. Some of the things we have noted are fragments of ideas; others are somewhat more systematic in developing a theme or reporting a series of observations. They are held together by an awareness of a set of phenomena that are more easily observed than explicated. Insofar as the ideas are consistent, the consistency is sustained partly by ambiguity. Many of the core ideas seem plausible and have been durable, but plausible durability (as numerous students of the history of knowledge have observed) is neither necessary nor sufficient for good sense.

The new institutionalism is an empirically based prejudice, an assertion that what we observe in the world is inconsistent with the ways in which contemporary theories ask us to talk. Like other prejudices in knowledge, it may be wrong-headed or muddle-headed, but it may also be a useful continuation of that gentle confrontation between the wise and the smart that describes much of intellectual history. On the chance that it is the latter, which of course does not exclude the possibility that it is also the former, we have tried to draw some possible implications for theoretical research in political science. They are, at best, theoretical directions suggested by a sympathetic appreciation of a tradition of institutionalise thought. Such an effort is a little like trying to write a useful commentary on Heidegger in the form of a Shakespearean sonnet. If it has virtue, it is in attempting to encourage talking about a subtle body of thought in a way sufficiently naive to entice the technically proficient.

Accepted for publication: December 6, 1983. This research has been supported by grants from the Norwegian Research Council for Science and Humanities, the Norwegian Ministry of Consumer Affairs and Government Administration, the Mellon Foundation, the Spencer Foundation, the Stanford Graduate School of Business, and the Hoover Institution. We are grateful for comments by Julia W. Ball, Michael D. Cohen, Stephen D. Krasner, Martin Landau, Todd LaPorte, W. Richard Scott, and William Siffin.

REFERENCES

Akerlof, G. A. The economics of social customs, of which unemployment may be one consequence. *Quarterly Journal of Economics*, 1980, *95*, 749–775.

Ashford, D. E. Political science and policy studies: Towards a structural solution. *Policy Studies Journal*, 1977, *5*, 570–583.

Axelrod, R. More effective choice in prisoners' dilemma. *Journal of Conflict Resolution*, 1980, *24*, 379–403.

Axelrod, R., and Hamilton, W. D. The evolution of co-operation. *Science*, 1981, *211*, 1390–1396.

Bachrach, P., and Baratz, M. The two faces of power. *American Political Science Review*, 1962, *56*, 947–952.

Becker, G. S., and Stigler, G. J. De gustibus non est disputandum. *American Economic Review*, 1977, *67*, 76–90.

Berger, S. (Ed.). *Organizing interests in Europe: Pluralism, corporatism, and the transformation of politics*. Cambridge: Cambridge University Press, 1981.

Berki, R. N. State and society: An antithesis of modern political thought. In J. E. S. Hayward and R. N. Berki (Eds.), *State and society in contemporary Europe*. Oxford: Martin Robertson, 1979.

Burns, J. M. *Leadership*. New York: Harper and Row, 1978.

Cohen, A. P. *Two-dimensional man: An essay on the anthropology of power and symbolism in complex societies*. London: Routledge and Kegan Paul, 1974.

Cohen, M. D., and Axelrod, R. Coping with complexity: The adaptive value of changing utility. *American Economic Review*, 1984, *74*, 30–42.

Cohen, M. D., March, J. G., and Olsen, J. P. A garbage can model of organizational choice. *Administrative Science Quarterly*, 1972, *17*, 1–25.

Crozier, M. *The bureaucratic phenomenon*. Chicago: University of Chicago Press, 1964.

Cyert, R. M., and March, J. G. *A behavioral theory of the firm*. Englewood Cliffs, N.J.: Prentice-Hall, Inc., 1963.

Downs, A. *An economic theory of democracy*. New York: Harper and Row, 1957.

Easton, D. Political science. In D. L. Sills (Ed.), *International encyclopedia of the social sciences*. Vol. 12. New York and London: Macmillan and Free Press, 1968.

Eckhoff, T., and Jacobsen, K. D. *Rationality and responsibility in administrative and judicial decisionmaking*. Copenhagen: Munksgaard, 1960.

Edelman, M. *The symbolic uses of politics*. Urbana: University of Illinois Press, 1964.

Egeberg, M. *Stat og organisasjoner*. Bergen: Universitetsforlaget, 1981.

Enderud, H. The perception of power. In J. G. March and J. P. Olsen (Eds.), *Ambiguity and choice in organizations*. Bergen: Universitetsforlaget, 1976.

Etheredge, L. S. *The case of the unreturned cafeteria trays*. Washington, D.C.: American Political Science Association, 1976.

Evans, P., Rueschemeyer, D., and Skocpol. T. (Eds.). Bringing the state back in. Report of a conference on research implications of current theories of the state. Unpublished manuscript, 1983.

Feldman, M. S., and March, J. G. Information as signal and symbol. *Administrative Science Quarterly*, 1981, 26, 171-186.

Feller, W. *An introduction to probability theory and its applications*, Vol. I. New York: Wiley, 1950.

Friedman, M. *Essays in positive economics*. Chicago: University of Chicago Press, 1953.

Geertz, C. *Negara: The theater state in nineteenth-century Bali*. Princeton, N.J.: Princeton University Press, 1980.

Hanf, K., and Scharpf, F. (Eds.). *Interorganizational policy making: Limits to coordination and central control*. London: Sage, 1978.

Hayward, J. E. S., and Berki, R. N. (Eds.). *State and society in contemporary Europe*. Oxford: Martin Robertson, 1979.

Heclo, H. *Modern social policies in Britain and Sweden*. New Haven, Conn.: Yale University Press, 1974.

Heller, H. Political science. In E. R. A. Seligman and A. Johnson (Eds.), *Encyclopedia of the social sciences*. New York: Macmillan, 1933 (1957).

Hirschleifer, J., and Riley, J. G. The analytics of uncertainty and information—an expository survey. *Journal of Economic Literature*, 1979, 17, 1375–1421.

Jessop, B. Recent theories of the capitalist state. In *Cambridge Journal of Economics*, 1977, 1, 353–373.

Kahneman, D. Bureaucracies, minds, and the human engineering of decisions. In G. R. Ungson and D. N. Braunstein (Eds.), *Decision making: An interdisciplinary inquiry*. Boston: Kent, 1982.

Kahneman, D., Slovic, P., and Tversky, A. (Eds.). *Judgment under uncertainty: Heuristics and biases*. Cambridge: Cambridge University Press, 1982.

Katzenstein, P. J. (Ed.). *Between power and plenty: Foreign economic policies of advanced industrial states*. Madison: University of Wisconsin Press, 1978.

Kjellberg, F. *Political institutionalization*. London: Wiley, 1975.

Krasner, S. D. *Defending the national interest: Raw materials, investments and the U.S. foreign policy*. Princeton, N.J.: Princeton University Press, 1978.

Krasner, S. D. Approaches to the state: Alternative conceptions and historical dynamics. *Comparative Politics*, in press.

Krieger, S. *Mirror dance*. Philadelphia: Temple University Press, 1983.

Kurz, M. Altruism as an outcome of social interaction. *American Economic Review*, 1978, 68, 216–222.

Laegreid, P., and Olsen, J. P. *Byraakrati og beslutninger*. Bergen: Universitetsforlaget, 1978.

Lafferty, W. M. *Participation and democracy in Norway*. Oslo: Universitetsforlaget, 1981.

Lave, C. A., and March, J. G. *An introduction to models in the social sciences*. New York: Harper and Row, 1975.

Levi, M. The predatory theory of rule. *Politics and Society*, 1981, 10, 431–465.

Levinthal, D., and March, J. G. A model of adaptive organizational search. *Journal of Economic Behavior and Organization*, 1982, 2, 307–333.

Long, N. The local community as an ecology of games. *American Journal of Sociology*, 1958, 44, 251–261.

Luce, R. D., and Raiffa, H. *Games and decisions*. New York: Wiley, 1957.

March, J. C., and March, J. G. Performance sampling in social matches. *Administrative Science Quarterly*, 1978, 23, 434–453.

March, J. G. Bounded rationality, ambiguity, and the engineering of choice. *Bell Journal of Economics*, 1978, 9, 587–608.

March, J. G. The business firm as a political coalition. *Journal of Politics*, 1962, 24, 662–678.

March, J. G. Decisions in organizations and theories of choice. In A. H. van de Ven and W. F. Joyce (Eds.), *Perspectives on organizational design and behavior*. New York: Wiley, 1981.

March, J. G. Politics and the city. In K. Arrow, J. S. Coleman, A. Downs, and J. G. March (Eds.), *Urban processes as viewed by the social sciences*. Washington, D.C.: The Urban Institute, 1970.

March, J. G. The power of power. In D. Easton (Ed.), *Varieties of political theory*. Englewood Cliffs, N.J.: Prentice-Hall, 1966.

March, J. G., and Olsen, J. P. *Ambiguity and choice in organizations*. Bergen: Universitetsforlaget, 1976.

March, J. G., and Olsen, J. P. Organizing political life: What administrative reorganization tells us about government. *American Political Science Review*, 1983, 77, 281–296.

March, J. G., and Shapira, Z. Behavioral decision theory and organizational decision theory. In G. R. Ungson and D. N. Braunstein (Eds.), *Decision making: An interdisciplinary inquiry*. Boston: Kent, 1982.

March, J. G., and Simon, H. A. *Organizations*. New York: Wiley, 1958.

Masters, R. D. The biological nature of the state. *World Politics*, 1983, 35, 161–193.

Meyer, J. W., and Rowan, B. Institutionalized organizations: Formal structure as myth and ceremony. *American Journal of Sociology*, 1977, 83, 340–363.

Nelson, R. R., and Winter, S. G. *An evolutionary theory of economic change*. Cambridge, Mass.: Harvard University Press, 1982.

Nisbet, R., and Ross, L. *Human inference: Strategies and shortcomings of social judgement*. Englewood Cliffs, N.J.: Prentice-Hall, 1980.

Niskanen, W. A. *Bureaucracy and representative government*. Chicago: Rand McNally, 1971.

Nordlinger, E. *On the autonomy of the democratic state*. Cambridge, Mass.: Harvard University Press, 1981.

Olsen, J. P. Local budgeting: Decision making or a ritual act? *Scandinavian Political Studies*, 1970, 5, 85–118.

Olsen, J. P. Organizational integration in government. In P. Nystrom and W. Starbuck (Eds.), *Handbook of organizational design*. Vol. 2. New York: Oxford University Press, 1981.

Olsen, J. P. *Organized democracy*. Bergen: Universitetsforlaget, 1983.

Olsen, J. P., and Saetren, H. *Aksjoner og demokrati*. Bergen: Universitetsforlaget, 1980.

Olson, M. *The logic of collective action*. Cambridge, Mass.: Harvard University Press, 1965.

Padgett, J. F. Hierarchy and ecological control in federal budgetary decision making. *American Journal of Sociology*, 1981, 87, 75–129.

Pateman, C. *Participation and democratic theory.* Cambridge: Cambridge University Press, 1970.

Pfeffer, J. Management as symbolic action: The creation and maintenance of organizational paradigms. In L. Cummings and B. M. Staw (Eds.), *Research in organizational behavior.* Vol. 3. Greenwich, Conn.: JAI Press, 1981(a).

Pfeffer, J. Some consequences of organizational demography: Potential impacts of an aging work force on formal organizations. In S. B. Kiesler, J. N. Morgan, and V. K. Oppenheimer (Eds.), *Aging: Social change.* New York: Academic Press, 1981(b).

Pondy, L. R. Leadership as a language game. In M. W. McCall, Jr. and M. M. Lombardo (Eds.), *Leadership.* Durham, N.C.: Duke University Press, 1978.

Potter, A. L. Political institutions, political decay and the Argentine crises of 1930. Unpublished doctoral dissertation, Stanford University, 1979.

Pressman, J. L., and Wildavsky, A. B. *Implementation.* Berkeley: University of California Press, 1973.

Preston, L. D., and Keachie, E. C. Cost functions and progress functions: An integration. *American Economic Review*, 1964, 54, 100–108.

Robins, R. S. *Political institutionalization and the integration of elites.* Beverly Hills, Calif.: Sage, 1976.

Scharpf, F. W. Does organization matter? Task structure and interaction in the ministerial bureaucracy. In E. H. Burack and A. R. Negandhi (Eds.), *Organizational design: Theoretical perspectives and empirical findings.* Kent, Ohio: Kent State University Press, 1977.

Schmitter, P., and Lehmbruch, G. (Eds.). *Trends toward corporatist intermediation.* Beverly Hills, Calif.: Sage, 1979.

Selznick, P. *Leadership in administration.* Evanston, Ill.: Northwestern University Press, 1957.

Sharpe, W. F. *Portfolio theory and capital markets.* New York: McGraw-Hill, 1970.

Shepsle, K., and Weingast, B. Institutionalizing majority rule: A social choice theory with policy implications. *American Economic Review*, 1983, 73, 357-372.

Simon, H. A. *Administrative behavior.* (2nd ed.) New York: Macmillan, 1957a.

Simon, H. A. *Models of man.* New York: Wiley, 1957b.

Skocpol, T. Political response to capitalist crises: Neo-Marxist theories of the state and the case of the New Deal. *Politics and Society*, 1980, 70(2), 155–201.

Skocpol, T. *States and social revolutions: A comparative analysis of France, Russia, and China.* Cambridge and New York: Cambridge University Press, 1979.

Skocpol, T., and Finegold, K. State capacity and economic intervention in the early New Deal. *Political Science Quarterly*, 1982, 97, 255–278.

Skowronek, S. *Building a new American state.* Cambridge: Cambridge University Press, 1982.

Stephan, A. C. *The state and society: Peru in comparative perspective.* Princeton, N.J.: Princeton University Press, 1978.

Stigler, G. J. *The theory of price* (Rev. ed.) New York: Macmillan, 1952.

Therborn, G. *What does the ruling class do when it rules?* London: Verso, 1980.

Tilly, C. (Ed.). *From mobilization to revolution.* Reading, Mass.: Addison-Wesley, 1978.

Trimberger, E. K. *Revolution from above: Military bureaucrats and development in Japan, Turkey, Egypt, and Peru.* New Brunswick, N.J.: Transaction Books, 1978.

Trivers, R. The evolution of reciprocal altruism. *Quarterly Review of Biology,* 1971, *46,* 35–57.

Waterstone, G. C. *Order and counterorder. Dualism in western culture.* New York: Philosophical Library, 1966.

Williamson, O. E. *Markets and hierarchies.* New York: Free Press, 1978.

Wolin, S. *Politics and vision.* Boston: Little, Brown, 1960.

Wright, H. T. Recent research on the origin of the state. *Annual Review of Anthropology,* 1977, *6,* 379–397.

# CHAPTER 10

# The Institutional Dynamics
# of International Political Orders

JAMES G. MARCH AND JOHAN P. OLSEN

## INTRODUCTION

Students of international organization try to understand how and when international political orders are created, maintained, changed, and abandoned. Many of the key questions belong to a wider class of difficult questions about the dynamics of social order and development. How can order develop out of anarchy? What stabilizes an order? When and how does a stable order fall apart? How does peaceful change occur? Why do peaceful relations sometimes find themselves drawn into less peaceful confrontations? How is the search for order among collectivities linked to the search for order within them?

In this article we address such questions, though our ambitions are considerably less than might be imagined from such an agenda. We consider a few stylized ways of thinking about the history and possible future of international political organization and elaborate one of them, something that might be called an institutional approach to such thinking. The chapter is written from the perspective of students of organizations, thus with deference to, but without pretense of extensive knowledge of, the literature of international political relations.

## CHANGE AND CONTINUITY IN
## INTERNATIONAL ORDERS

The history of political orders is written in terms of changes in domestic and international political relations.[1] At some periods in some areas, political life has been rather well organized around well-defined boundaries, common rules and practices, shared causal and normative understandings, and resources adequate for collective action. At other times and places, the system has been relatively anarchic. Relations have been less orderly; boundaries less well defined;

---

This chapter originally appeared in *International Organization*, 52 (1998), 943–969.

and institutions less common, less adequately supported, and less involved. As political institutions experience their histories, political life achieves or loses structure, and the nature of order changes.[2]

## The Westphalian Order of Nation-States

Although the history of international political order long antedates the seventeenth century, only in the last three or four hundred years has anything approximating a single world order developed. The Treaty of Westphalia (1648) reflected and proclaimed a conception of international political order that gradually extended itself from its European roots to encompass most of the world. It was a conception built around the central importance of a particular type of political actor—the territorial, sovereign state. By the end of the twentieth century, the idea of the nation-state and a world geography defined by national boundaries had evolved to a position of conceptual dominance, as had principles of international relations built upon them.[3] Such principles and the conceptions on which they were based were never all encompassing. Indeed, states are still developing in some parts of the world as the twentieth century draws to its close,[4] and state authority and control have been weakened in other parts. Nevertheless, most contemporary writing portrays the world as partitioned into mutually exclusive and exhaustive territorial units called states.

This Westphalian nation-state order makes a fundamental distinction between domestic political spheres characterized by institutional density, hierarchical relationships, shared interests, and strong collective identities, and an international political sphere characterized by a lack of strong institutions, few rules, conflicting interests, and conflicting identities. The state imposes unity and coherence on domestic society,[5] a coherence based on a national identity that suppresses or subordinates competing identities and belongings and on an elaborate set of rules (laws) and institutions. National identity and other political identities are fundamental to structuring behavior, and rules of appropriate behavior and institutions associated with those identities both infuse the state with shared meaning and expectations and provide political legitimacy that facilitates mobilization of resources from society.

International political life, on the other hand, is seen as much less institutionalized, much more anarchical. Individual states are imagined to act rationally in the service of coherent goals, to form mutually beneficial coalitions with others, to seek understandings that are mutually satisfactory, and to use all available resources to maximize the attainment of separate national objectives. Such attainment is limited primarily not by explicit rules regulating international encounters but by the simultaneous competitive efforts of other states to maximize their own objectives. Although some understandings are common within the international community and some rules are recognized, norms and institutions are weaker, less widely shared, and less taken for granted than they are within individual states. International institutions are generally seen as requiring explicit rationalization in terms of the current interests of current states in order to secure their force and effectiveness.

As a result, many contemporary theories of international politics (like many theories of economic systems of business firms) embrace a two-stage conception of organization. In the first stage, domestic political activities, including political socialization, participation, and discourse, create coherent state actors out of the conflicts and inconsistencies of multiple individuals and groups living within the boundaries of a single state. In the second stage, those coherent systems compete and cooperate, pursuing state interests in international spheres that recognize few elements of collective coherence beyond those that arise from the immediate self-interests of the actors. Political order is defined primarily in terms of negotiated connections among externally autonomous and internally integrated sovereigns. Although such a two-stage conception has frequently been questioned by writers who see domestic and international politics as richly interconnected, it remains the most common approach to thinking about international relations.

### Contemporary Changes in the Nation-State Order

The nation-state order has never been static and is unlikely to become so.[6] According to most observers, in fact, change has accelerated in recent times. The possibility of the emergence of a distinctively different post-Westphalian order is a serious topic for contemporary discussion.[7] Moreover, traditional concerns with formal agreements reflected in treaties are being supplemented by attention to changes in a wide range of practices and relations.[8] In particular, three kinds of changes are commonly noted: First there have been relatively rapid changes in national boundaries, constituting and reconstituting the basic units of the international order. The disintegration of some states and the (re)integration of others are changing state borders. These splits and mergers do not directly challenge the Westphalian order. European nation-state history since 1648 is replete with border changes and state reconstitutions. Still, frequent changes are uncomfortably accommodated within theoretical approaches assuming stable and unitary actors.

Second, many contemporary states seem to be characterized by increasing fragmentation and disintegration. In the last decade, a number of developing countries have lost critical elements of statehood as their central governments have broken down.[9]

Internal (as well as external) processes of differentiation are making the state "centerless" or multicentered. Ethnic, religious, linguistic, regional, functional, and class identities have created solidarities that do not coincide with nation-state boundaries. The state seems to be evolving into a less coherent and less tightly coupled unit.[10] These resurgences of substate and supranational identities have renewed interest in concepts like culture and identity as fundamental to understanding international relations.[11] At the end of the twentieth century, many states show symptoms of incoherence and disintegration somewhat reminiscent of an earlier time when political life involved confusing, overlapping, and conflicting demands on individual allegiances; and when polities were organized around emperors, kings, feudal lords, churches, chartered towns, guilds, and families.[12]

Third, substantial increases in international and cross-national connections and institutions are challenging an international order dominated by monocentric, hierarchical, and unitary states.[13] State autonomy and sovereignty have been compromised in fundamental areas such as security, capital regulation, migration, ecology, health, culture, and language. Institutional barriers to interaction across nation-state boundaries have been weakened or removed, making integration based on voluntary exchange easier. This "negative integration"[14] includes relaxed borders and barriers to exchange. Numerous economic, cultural, and intellectual transnational networks have formed to link individuals across state boundaries,[15] responding to changes in the ease of communication, transactions, and travel across nation-state borders.[16]

At the same time, there has been considerable increase in the number and importance of international institutions, regimes, laws, organizations, and networks[17]; and the Westphalian principle of nonintervention in internal affairs has been eroded by interventions in the name of dispute resolution, economic stability, and human rights.[18] Some rudiments of an international polity seem to be emerging, including instruments of opinion and will formation[19] and institutions for applying rules, making and implementing policies, and *kompetenz-kompetenz,* or the ability to change the scope and character of one's own authority.

Intergovernmental and supranational institutions, including bureaucracies, courts, parliaments, and enduring committees, have elaborated to a point where they are creating their own systems of rules and identities. Institutional complexity and the coexistence of different partial orders, each considered legitimate in its sphere, seem to have become permanent features of the international scene.[20]

These institutions link states (and their components) in structures of shared norms and expectations that impinge on nation-state autonomy and make it hard to maintain sharp distinctions between foreign and domestic politics.[21]

### Understanding and Anticipating Change in Political Orders

Theories of political development are attempts to understand and anticipate such changes in political orders. In part, such theories presume that a political order is reformed by intentional design. Organization is seen as purposeful and the creation of organization as stemming directly from the desires of political actors. In part, the theories assume less intentional mechanisms by which changes in international environments lead to changes in a political order. They trace the organizational consequences of such things as economic and technological globalization, mass migration, changes in material or political power, or changing military capabilities. And, in part, theories of international political development assume that local processes of growth, adaptation, elaboration, cooperation, conflict, and competition within and among political units lead to new political orders. For example, they examine the international consequences of internal state dynamics associated with the long historical development of the West European state.

From the perspective of such theories, it is not at all clear how contemporary changes in the nation-state and relations among them will affect the Westphalian, territorial, nation-state order with which we are familiar. Are we observing only minor modifications of an international order based on sovereign states with exclusive authority over a population within territorial boundaries and interstate relations based on anarchy, intergovernmentalism, balance of power, and hegemony? Or are we witnessing a major transformation of the constitutive principles and practices of international political life and the beginnings of a new form of political order and governance?[22] Although there is no question that the nation-state political order has changed and will change,[23] a reading of recent studies in international relations and comparative government, politics, and law suggests that there is little agreement about the scope and significance of new elements of international order.

There is somewhat more agreement about the historical processes that will be involved in any changes that may occur. Nearly everyone agrees that wars, conquests, and foreign occupations will contribute significantly to the elaboration and modification of the international political order, as they have in the past.[24] And nearly everyone agrees that more peaceful, gradual changes will come about because such changes match the changing interests of powerful political actors and the changing demands of the environment. We do not disagree with such judgments, but we think that these intuitive notions of "interests," "power," and "environmental fitness" require considerable elaboration, qualification, and supplementation to provide much help in understanding international politics.

As a step in that direction, we wish to explore some ideas drawn from an institutional perspective. Research on international institutions became somewhat unfashionable during the 1970s, but recently it has become common to argue that a better understanding of how institutions are structured; how they work; and how they emerge, are maintained, and change may contribute to a better understanding of international political life.[25] In the course of this recent resurrection of a "new institutionalism," the term has acquired somewhat expanded and confusing definitions that strain its linkage with the "old institutionalism,"[26] but there is a core set of ideas that is fairly broadly shared. In the remainder of this article, we examine the main features of one variety of an institutional perspective and illustrate its application to interpreting the dynamics of international order.

## AN INSTITUTIONAL PERSPECTIVE

The term *institutional* has come to mean rather different things in different contexts and disciplines in recent years.[27] In a general way, an "institution" can be viewed as a relatively stable collection of practices and rules defining appropriate behavior for specific groups of actors in specific situations. Such practices and rules are embedded in structures of meaning and schemes of interpretation that explain and legitimize particular identities and the practices and rules associated with them.[28] Practices and rules are also embedded in resources and the principles of their allocation that make it possible for individuals to enact roles in an appropriate way and for a collectivity to socialize individuals and sanction those who wander from proper behavior.[29]

Institutionalization refers to the emergence of institutions and individual behaviors within them.[30] The process involves the development of practices and rules in the context of using them and has earned a variety of labels, including structuration and routinization, which refer to the development of codes of meaning, ways of reasoning, and accounts in the context of acting on them.[31] An institutional approach is one that emphasizes the role of institutions and institutionalization in the understanding of human actions within an organization, social order, or society.

Such definitions are consistent with the general terminology of current discussions in the literature, but they are broad enough to encompass things as varied as collections of contracts, legal rules, social norms, and moral precepts. To narrow the range somewhat, we define the perspective in terms of two grand issues that divide students of the dynamics of social and political action and structures.

## Issue 1: Bases of Action

The first issue concerns the basic logic of action by which human behavior is interpreted.[32] On the one side are those who see action as driven by a logic of anticipated consequences and prior preferences. On the other side are those who see action as driven by a logic of appropriateness and senses of identity. As in most cases of arguments among students of decision making, the argument has both normative and descriptive elements. The normative question is whether one logic leads to a better society than the other. In this spirit, histories of Western democracies have been interpreted as reflecting a tension between the virtues of "bourgeois" calculating and taking care of personal interests and the virtues of "citoyen" service in the name of civic identity.[33] They reflect an argument between those who believe that an exclusively calculative, consequential approach undermines laws and institutions[34] and those who see the durability of laws and institutions as resting on their contribution to the calculated interests of rational actors.[35]

The descriptive question is whether (or when) one logic is more likely than the other to be observed as the basis for actual behavior. It is this descriptive question that primarily concerns us here. The two questions are, of course, not entirely separate, either objectively or in the mind of any particular discussant; but this article is addressed primarily to the descriptive value of two specific logics of action in interpreting the history of international orders.

## Logic of Expected Consequences

Those who see actions as driven by expectations of consequences imagine that human actors choose among alternatives by evaluating their likely consequences for personal or collective objectives, conscious that other actors are doing likewise. A consequential frame sees political order as arising from negotiation among rational actors pursuing personal preferences or interests in circumstances in which there may be gains to coordinated action. Political integration represents a collection of "contracts" negotiated among actors with conflicting interests and varying resources. Whether coordination is achieved and the terms of coordination (for example, who adopts whose system) depend on the bargaining positions of the actors.

In more complicated versions, the actors themselves are coalitions of rational actors and the negotiation goes on at several different levels simultaneously. Within the consequentialist perspective, politics is seen as aggregating individual preferences into collective actions by some procedures of bargaining, negotiation, coalition formation, and exchange.[36] Society is constituted by individuals for the fulfillment of individual ends. The only obligations recognized by individuals are those created through consent and contracts grounded in calculated consequential advantage.

From this perspective, history is seen as the consequence of the interaction of willful actors and is fully understood when it is related to expectations of its consequences and to the interests (preferences) and resources of the actors. Individual actions are "explained" by identifying consequential reasons for them. Foreign policy is "explained" by providing an interpretation of the outcomes expected from it. The behavior of individuals or states is influenced by providing consequential incentives.

The idea that action by individuals, organizations, or states is driven by calculation of its consequences as measured against prior preferences has been subject to numerous criticisms.[37] In particular, presumptions of omniscience in anticipating consequences seem far from descriptive of actual human behavior in actual organized systems.[38] And presumptions of stable, consistent, and exogenous preferences seem to exclude from consideration the many ways in which interests are changing, inconsistent, and endogenous.[39] Theories of bounded rationality and ambiguity have resulted in significant modifications in the classical theory of rational instrumental action;[40] but like the theories they criticize, they assume, for the most part, a logic of consequences.

Theories of consequential calculation tend to ignore problems of exogenous uncertainties by using some variation on an assumption of rational expectations. In some versions, it is assumed that estimates about the future are on average accurate. In other versions, it is assumed that there are differences among actors in their abilities to predict, and competitive pressures eliminate those with lesser abilities until the population is reduced to those with the best abilities.

Similarly, theories of consequential action simplify problems of preference complexity and endogeneity by seeing politics as decomposing complex systems into relatively autonomous subsystems, most commonly by linking them hierarchically. In a hierarchical decomposition, many potential interactions are eliminated, and the problems of preference integration are restricted to relations among hierarchical equals. Thus, an engineering problem can be divided into subproblems, each of which is similarly divided. At each stage in the process, the solution to a prior problem is taken as given. It is a powerful device of problem solving, but one that is known for its failures as well as for its successes.

The equivalent hierarchical organization in international relations involves first integrating the relations of groups of people (for example, nations) and then integrating across groups—what we have called earlier a "two-stage" conception of order. The constitution of the interests of a nation is taken as established before negotiations among nations begin.[41] Thus, the existence of coherent nations is taken as unproblematic in studying relations among states. However, the assumption of nation-state coherence, like the assumption of hierarchical problem structure, is a heroic one. It has been estimated, for instance, that over the last decades there have been more intrastate than interstate armed conflicts, and more people have been killed in such internal conflicts than have been killed in conflicts between states.[42]

A view of action as driven by expectations of its consequences constitutes the most conventional frame in interpretations of international political life. Stories built around such a frame are readily given credence as prima facie believable. Constructing stories of specific historical events within the frame is made easy by its flexibility in fitting events of the past into such an interpretation and by the familiarity and acceptability of such explanations to political actors. From this point of view, the coherence and significance of the nation-state in international relations is explained as the result of efforts of political actors to find structures favorable to their individual objectives. The major elements of the nation-state are assumed to thrive because they serve the interests of key actors. The interests of political actors come first; the interests of nation-states are derived from them. Within such an interpretation, changes in international institutions are the outcomes of local adaptation by political actors pursuing well-defined interests. For example, it is assumed that the European Union will prosper to the extent to which it increases the efficiency of collective decision making and strengthens national governments.[43]

## Logic of Appropriateness

Linking action exclusively to a logic of consequences seems to ignore the substantial role of identities, rules, and institutions in shaping human behavior. Within the tradition of a logic of appropriateness, actions are seen as rule based. Human actors are imagined to follow rules that associate particular identities to particular situations, approaching individual opportunities for action by assessing similarities between current identities and choice dilemmas and more general concepts of self and situations. Action involves evoking an identity or role and matching the obligations of that identity or role to a specific situation. The pursuit of purpose is associated with identities more than with interests, and with the selection of rules more than with individual rational expectations.[44]

Appropriateness need not attend to consequences, but it involves cognitive and ethical dimensions, targets, and aspirations. As a cognitive matter, appropriate action is action that is essential to a particular conception of self. As an ethical matter, appropriate action is action that is virtuous. We "explain" foreign policy as the application of rules associated with particular identities to particular situations. We "explain" behavior by determining the identities that are evoked and the meaning given to a situation. We influence behavior by providing alternative interpretations of the self and the situation.

Like the logic of consequences, the logic of appropriateness is explicitly a logic of individual action. It is specified as a mode of action or justification for an individual actor. Thus, it is as individualistic in structure as is the logic of consequences. In practice, however, the two traditions differ in their treatment of the relation between the premises of action and society. Scholars committed to a consequentialist position tend to see an international system of interacting autonomous, egoistic, self-interested maximizers. Preferences are usually taken as given, and expectations of consequences are taken as determined by the state of the external world and the biases (if any) of the individual.

Scholars committed to an identity position, on the other hand, see political actors as acting in accordance with rules and practices that are socially constructed, publicly known, anticipated, and accepted.[45] They portray an international society as a community of rule followers and role players with distinctive sociocultural ties, cultural connections, intersubjective understandings, and senses of belonging. Identities and rules are constitutive as well as regulative and are molded by social interaction and experience.[46]

## Relationship between the Two Logics

Although there is some tendency for society to be divided into separate spheres, each based primarily on either consequential calculation or rules,[47] the two logics are not mutually exclusive. As a result, political action generally cannot be explained exclusively in terms of a logic of either consequences or appropriateness. Any particular action probably involves elements of each. Political actors are constituted both by their interests, by which they evaluate their expected consequences, and by the rules embedded in their identities and political institutions. They calculate consequences and follow rules, and the relationship between the two is often subtle.

There are four major interpretations of the relationship between the two logics. The first assumes that a clear logic dominates an unclear logic. When preferences and consequences are precise and identities or their rules are ambiguous, a logic of consequences tends to be more important. When identities and their implications are clear but the implications of preferences or expected consequences are not, a logic of appropriateness tends to be more important. In this vein, Geoffrey Garrett and Barry Weingast suggest that ideational factors (such as norms and identities) will be important "the lesser the distributional asymmetries between contending cooperative equilibria and the smaller the disparities in the power resources of actors."[48] The importance of rules may also increase when the consequences of agreements are unclear or relative capabilities difficult to determine.

The second interpretation distinguishes major decisions from minor refinements of them. The argument is that one logic is used to establish fundamental constraints for a decision, and the other logic is used to make refinements within the constraints. One version of this interpretation associates a logic of consequences with big decisions and a logic of appropriateness with refinements. In this version, rules are "weak causes" of human behavior. In order for institutions to affect macro issues, rather than the minor elaborations of them, decisions have to be shielded from "strong causes" of behavior such as personal interests and known consequences.[49] A second version, as might be expected, reverses the roles of the two logics. Rules are seen as the preconditions of calculation and the unfolding of consequential rationality. Only after important sources of contingency have been resolved by rules are the remaining (relatively minor) contingencies susceptible to resolution by deliberate rational calculation of alternatives.[50]

The third interpretation sees the relation between consequential action and rule-based action as a developmental one. As it is usually discussed, the distinction between consequence-based (instrumental) action and rule-based (identity) action is seen as reflecting a stable difference either among actors or among scholars. Alternatively, suppose that the basis of action changes over time in a predictable way. In particular, suppose that action becomes more rule based in a specific situation the greater the accumulated experience in that situation. Rules and standard operating procedures supplant and constrain instrumental-calculative action in a given situation as result of experience. Actors enter into new relationships for instrumental reasons but develop identities and rules as a result of their experience, thus shifting increasingly toward rule-based action, which they then pass on to subsequent actors. By this mechanism, instrumental modes of action can be seen to be self-limiting, whereas rule-based modes are seen to be self-reinforcing.

The fourth interpretation sees either logic as a special case of the other.[51] Students of action who are wedded to a logic of consequences, for example, believe that all action is consequential. They picture rules as instruments resulting from prior consequential negotiation.[52] From this point of view, rules and identities are simply devices that minimize transaction costs in the implementation of consequential action. Students of action who are wedded to a logic of appropriateness, on the other hand, assume that all action involves rule following.[53] They see consequential logic and personal interest calculations simply as rules of a particular form that are associated with specific identities and situations.[54]

Despite these interconnections, we believe that the two logics are sufficiently distinct to be viewed as separate explanatory devices. They involve different explanations for action and different bases for institutional change. This is especially important in the modern era of international relations in which explanations based on a logic of consequences are ubiquitous and explanations based on a logic of appropriateness have been relegated to a considerably less significant role.

## *Issue 2: Historical Efficiency*

The second grand issue that divides students of the dynamics of social and political action and structures is the question of historical efficiency. On the one side are those who see history as following a course that leads inexorably and relatively quickly to a unique equilibrium dictated by exogenously determined interests and resources. On the other side are those who see history as inefficient, as following a meandering path affected by multiple equilibria and endogenous transformations of interests and resources.

### Efficient Histories

For those who see history as efficient, the primary postulated mechanism is competition for survival. Political actors compete for resources and primacy, and the resulting equilibrium eliminates actors who fail to achieve optimal resource allocations and strategies. In one version, mutually satisfactory trades are arranged until the system locates a position on the Pareto frontier. The point that is located depends critically on the initial preferences of the actors and on the initial distributions of resources, although it is not uniquely determined by them. In a second version, coercion is used by dominant actors to impose explicit or implicit agreements that are not (in a meaningful sense) voluntary for weaker actors but stem from differences in initial conditions. In both versions, history is determined by, and predictable from, prior conditions of the environment.

Efficient history perspectives see the outcomes of politics, including the dynamics of political order, as implicit in environmental constraints. Competition for survival is seen as compelling social structures to be consistent with environmental conditions. Different environments dictate different orders. Because optimality is required for survival, predicting the equilibrium order does not depend on any specific knowledge about the actors beyond the initial interests and resources that are imposed on them by the environment. The presumption is that political bargains adjust quickly and in a necessary way to exogenous changes, and changes in orders are explained as stemming from exogenous changes in interests and resources. As a consequence, there is little independent role for institutions. Institutions are simply products of a history that is exogenously determined.

## Inefficient Histories

Those who see history as inefficient emphasize the slow pace of historical adaptation relative to the rate of environmental change, thus the low likelihood of reaching an equilibrium. Even more, they emphasize the existence of multiple equilibria and internal dynamics that make it difficult to escape local optima. Thus, a view of history as inefficient portrays the match between political institutions and their environments as less automatic, less continuous, and less precise than does a view of history as efficient. The pressures of survival are sporadic rather than constant, crude rather than precise, and environments vary in the extent to which they dictate outcomes. Institutions and identities are pictured as sometimes enduring in the face of apparent inconsistency with their environments, sometimes collapsing without obvious external cause. In short, neither competitive pressures nor current conditions uniquely determine institutional options or outcomes.[55] There are lags in matching an environment, multiple equilibria, path dependencies, and interconnected networks for the diffusion of forms and practices.

In such a world, institutional development depends not only on satisfying current environmental and political conditions but also on an institution's origin, history, and internal dynamics.[56] Inefficient history perspectives also place more emphasis on the interactive effects of an ecology of interacting locally adaptive actors. Consider in this regard the tradition of models of majority voting by rational actor citizens. A common focus of such studies is the way in which majority voting schemes lead to outcomes not uniquely determined by prior conditions but also dependent on procedural or institutional factors (for example, the order of voting on alternatives). In that spirit, for example, simple economic and majority vote models have been used to show how the institutions and procedures of a democratic political process might fail to achieve a system of nation-states and boundaries among them that is uniquely implicit in economic exchange considerations.[57]

Environments adapt to institutions at the same time as institutions adapt to environments. Institutions and their linkages coevolve. They are intertwined in ecologies of competition, cooperation, and other forms of interaction. Furthermore, institutions are nested, so that some adapting institutions are integral parts of other adapting institutions. Finally, ideas of inefficient history place a greater emphasis on the ways in which the unfolding results of history transform the premises of action. Identities, resources, values, norms, and rules guide action, but they are simultaneously shaped by the course of history.[58] From this point of view, individual identities and preferences are both premises of politics and products of it,[59] and the development of competencies makes institutions robust against external pressures for change. These features of action and its outcomes form a foundation for a variety of quite different stable equilibria.

The complications tend to convert history into a meander.[60] Rules and institutions become locally stable. Historical branches tend to be irreversible. The direction taken at any particular branch sometimes seems almost chancelike and subject to minor intentions, but the specific direction taken can be decisive in its effect on subsequent history.[61] As a result, the course of history can sometimes be changed by relatively small, timely interventions. The ability to create change, however, does not guarantee either that any arbitrary change can be made at any time, that changes will turn out to be consistent with prior intentions or interests,[62] or that the outcomes will be stable.

## Four Perspectives

These two issues of the logic of action and the efficiency of history divide studies (and to a lesser extent students) of international political dynamics into four relatively distinct groups. The first group of studies emphasizes a view of action based on a logic of consequences and a view of history as efficient (upper-left quadrant of Figure 1). This is the most common perspective in international political studies. Scholars in this group see history as resulting from interactions among consequentialist individuals, groups, organizations, or states, each seeking to realize as much as possible in terms of individual preferences but collectively confronting the fact that not everyone can have everything desired. In the resulting conflict, negotiation, warfare, and debate, outcomes are largely implicit in the environmental conditions that produce them.

This group comprises a number of somewhat different categories of studies. For example, studies by neoliberal institutionalists define international institutions and regimes as stemming from attempts by individual actors to achieve control and counteract the inadequacy of their own resources. Fluctuations in the number or strength of international institutions and regimes reflect the calculations of self-interested actors (primarily states) trying to resolve collective-action problems and gain efficiency through voluntary exchanges, contracts, and treaties. Outcomes depend on the ability to find and implement Pareto improvements, counteract market failures, reduce transaction costs, and overcome conflicts of interest. A core question is how alternative institutions and regimes affect the chances of discovering mutual benefits.[63]

On the other hand, studies by realists portray states as less concerned with Pareto improvements and more concerned with clashing interests, strategic interaction, alliances, coercion, relative power, distributional aspects, and relative gains. States are the important actors, and international institutions are less likely and less important. Because such elements of order reflect the interests of powerful states, they are more likely when power is concentrated in the international system—for instance, when a hegemon or a stable coalition of dominant powers sees an institutional arrangement as maintaining or increasing the ability to exercise power. Changes in order result from changing powers and material capabilities.[64]

While studies in the (neo)liberal institutional tradition and the (neo)realist tradition are often characterized as being in opposition, their differences are relatively narrow. They place different emphases on the role of voluntary exchange and dominance, and they specify utility functions differently, that is, the relative importance of absolute and relative gains.[65] They also locate rationality at a different level. The realist assumption of states as unitary actors is different from the neoliberalist assumption of rational individuals calculating the personal benefits of alternative memberships and policies.

Nevertheless, the two approaches share consequentialist assumptions about action and conceptions of history as efficient. Both traditions account for changes in the international order by describing calculating egoists acting in a history-free world. Actors are opportunistic and always look for individual advantage. They never honor contracts out of a sense of obligation. There are no intrinsically valuable forms of association and cohesion.[66] And although there is some recognition of a possible role of institutions in creating the preference functions of egoists,[67] for the most part, the creation of preferences and interests is seen as exogenous to the politics they affect.

The second group of studies emphasizes a view of action based on a logic of consequences but within an inefficient historical process (lower-left quadrant of Figure 1). This group includes many economic and evolutionary studies of search and local feedback.[68] Outcomes of actions taken at one time depend on factors of attention allocation and probabilistic interaction that are not predictable from environmental conditions. Those outcomes, however, determine subsequent paths of history in a way that makes a consequential history path dependent. In addition, interests and resources evolve from the outcomes of history. The premises of history are not fixed but coevolve with their consequences.

The third group of studies emphasizes a view of action based on a logic of appropriateness and history as efficient (upper-right quadrant of Figure 1). This group includes many works by institutional economists and some by institutional sociologists.[69] For them, action is rule based. Institutions and norms are important. Individual actors seek to fulfill their identities. However, the rules, norms, identities, organizational forms, and institutions that exist are the inexorable products of an efficient history. The principles are the principles of comparative statics. Surviving institutions are seen as uniquely fit to the environment, thus predictable from that environment.

The fourth group includes those studies that emphasize a view of action based on a logic of appropriateness but see history as inefficient (lower-right quadrant of Figure 1). Much of the time, our own work is located within this group.[70] So also is the work of evolutionary economists who emphasize the process of evolution rather than any necessary outcome.[71] The rules, norms, institutions, and identities that drive human action are seen as developing in a way that cannot be predicted from prior environmental conditions. They coevolve with the worlds in which they act. They are subject to local positive feedback that traps them at local optima. Rules are understandable only by understanding their histories.

Studies of international political orders draw from all four of these scholarly traditions to make sense of international organizations and politics, but they do not draw equally from each. The overwhelming inclination of interpreters of international politics is to favor consequentialist, efficient history accounts over accounts that emphasize appropriateness and inefficient histories. This preference is hard to justify strictly from historical observations. Any of the interpretations can claim a certain amount of confirmation in the historical record, but

*Assumed logic of action*

|                          | Logic of consequences | Logic of appropriateness |
|--------------------------|------------------------|--------------------------|
| Efficient history        | Functional rationality | Functional institutionalism |
| Inefficient history      | History-dependent rationality | History-dependent institutionalism |

*Conception of history* (row label spanning both rows)

FIGURE I    Four-fold division of perspectives on the dynamics of international political order

none is unambiguously dominant over the others on that basis. It is not obvious that any one approach is superior to the others in capturing the complexities of change. There are several stories to be told and a necessary humility associated with the telling of any one of them.

Given, however, that recent efforts to understand political orders have emphasized consequential action and efficient histories, either jointly (the upper-left quadrant of Figure 1) or individually (the lower-left and upper-right quadrants), we believe a perspective based on the lower-right quadrant may be useful in identifying otherwise overlooked or underestimated phenomena. Consequently, in this article we emphasize the perspective of the fourth group of studies. We examine some aspects of the inefficient historical processes by which identities, rules, resources, capabilities, and institutions of international political orders develop over time. The approach is not remarkable and provides no extraordinary magic of interpretation, but it may not be entirely foolish.

## COEVOLUTION OF POLITICS AND INSTITUTIONS

If history were efficient, political practice would adjust immediately and uniquely to current, exogenously determined desires and capabilities. We have argued that history is not efficient in that sense; that, indeed, institutions are relatively robust against environmental change or deliberate reform and that desires and capabilities coevolve with the practices that reflect them. As a result, history is path dependent in the sense that the character of current institutions depends not only on current conditions but also on the historical path of institutional development.

Change and stability are linked to definitions and redefinitions of the self and the situation. Those definitions are partly the result of deliberate policies adopted by existing authorities. Our interest, however, is more in the consequences of the ordinary course of political history as individuals, groups, and states act with only incidental concern for grand issues of international organization. Identities and competencies are shaped by political activities and interactions. They arise partly in the context of politics and become embedded in rules, practices, beliefs, and institutions. As illustrations, we consider two mechanisms of historical path dependence in the evolution of political order: the effect of engagement in political activities on the shaping of identities and the effect of engagement on the development of competence and capability.

### Illustration 1: Engagement and the Development of Identities

Students of international politics tell three different exaggerated stories about the effects of political interaction on the premises of politics. In story 1 political identities arise in ways unconnected to political life. They are social products of broader cultures of belief that are beyond the reach of politics.[72] Sociocultural bonds, preferences, identities, internalized principles, codes of appropriate behavior, and political resources are all important, but they are formed outside of politics and prior to political interaction.[73]

In story 2, in contrast, political actors are pictured as malleable within politics. The emergence, development, and spread of understandings, identities, interests, and institutions are shaped by interaction and involvement in political activities.[74] Interdependence, interaction, and communication lead to shared experiences and hence to shared meaning, to a convergence of expectations and policies, and to the development of common institutions. As a result of either calculated strategy, learning, or socialization, actors are induced to act differently from the way they would act in one-time encounters.[75] Long-term contacts create habits of working together, friendships, group loyalties, and knowledge about others. They create convergence, mutual confidence, and positive trust spirals.[76] They alter political competencies, augmenting skills at political compromise.

In story 3, as in story 2 but not in story 1, political actors are seen as created by their political interactions, but contact is portrayed as exacerbating international differences. Contact contributes to exposing and sharpening differences rather than eliminating them and to reinforcing antagonisms, contradictory worldviews, and stereotypes rather than extinguishing them.[77] Whereas ignorance of differences allows cooperation, knowledge of those differences stimulates actions that accentuate them and encourage hostility. Whereas inexperience in international political relations makes political actors cautious about political adventures, experience breeds risky adventures justified by a sense of competence and control. In this view, extensive political involvement, contact, and experience do not facilitate understanding, but rather make conflict more likely.

The mechanisms involved in each of the three stories are well-established ones. The outcomes of each are easily imaginable, and history provides numerous occasions interpretable as consistent with any of them. Each of the stories clearly captures part of observed histories. In particular, we think it is clear that story 2 describes a significant mechanism involved in the development of international orders. The idea that contact and involvement in joint political activities among the individuals of different states will lead to a more stable and inclusive political order needs to be qualified in significant ways to fit history; but understandings, identities, interests, and institutions can mold the behaviors of political actors and through them the outcomes of politics. The nation-state secures much of its coherence from a sense of belonging among citizens that translates into a set of obligations of citizenship. Individuals within a state are sometimes capable of empathy, confidence, trust, goodwill, shared norms, and bonds of cohesion, that is, "civicness" or "social capital."[78] Nation-states secure their legitimacy and permanence from shared conceptions of an orderly rule-based life.[79]

## Creating International Identities Deliberately

Some proponents of international order believe that the processes that sustain national civic identities and thereby reconstitute nation-states can be used deliberately to create some kind of international civic identity. Advocates of the European Union have argued that a common market and federal legal order were "not sufficient to bind the member states and the peoples of Europe together as the EU began to impinge on key attributes of state authority."[80] Europeans are invited to "imagine" a number of different "Europes," to remember some identities and common ties, and to forget identities that tend to create cleavages and conflicts.[81] This emphasis on the importance of a European identity and constitutive belongings tends to be paired with a view of communication, joint reasoning, and argumentation as necessary conditions for international cooperation, civilized conflict resolution, and political order.[82] Hopes for such a transformation are buoyed by the observation that even if genuine identity-related discourse is rare in world politics,[83] pockets of such discourse can be found, for instance, around themes like human rights[84] and environmental sustainability.[85]

Enthusiasm for achieving new identities through political engagement cannot entirely negate either the pessimism about the political molding of human identities that typifies story 1 or the dangers of interaction highlighted by story 3. There are ample grounds for caution in anticipating a sudden burst of global definitions of self. The difficulties involved in trying to develop a European identity, citizenship, and culture deliberately are manifest. Attempts by EU authorities to use cultural and media policies to construct collective identities and a common European communicative space confront highly diverse and conflicting existing identities and allegiances.[86]

The worldviews, values, desires, commitments, and capabilities necessary for more inclusive political orders can be quite inaccessible to political experience and learning, but an elementary fact of the past two hundred years is that humans have civilized their lives within the nation-state context by developing institutions and rules that regulate their relations. They have created identities that often restrain passions and interests, inducing individuals to follow rules of conduct that are both taken for granted and oriented to collective obligations.[87] Whether a similar program can accomplish a similar integration at an international level is certainly in doubt, but when organizations such as the OECD call attention to differences between "leaders" and "laggards" among countries in terms of their willingness and ability to adopt what is defined as a modern, democratic, and economically efficient public sector, they modify the reference groups of national bureaucrats, their aspirations, and their behavior.[88]

## Creating International Identities Unintentionally

The mechanisms of education, socialization, and participation that develop, maintain, and undermine shared identities are obviously more weakly developed at the international level than within individual nation-states.[89] That situation will not change quickly, but it can change gradually without much in the way of conscious intention.[90] To explore how this might happen, consider two mechanisms that contribute to making international institutions and identities imaginable:

First, it is possible that international identities will evolve from a "spillover" of domestic democratic orientations and identities into international politics. The tendency of democratic states to deviate from strictly consequentialist international actions has been noted by students of international relations. Scholars have observed that democracies rarely go to war against each other.[91] In bilateral relations, democracies appear generally to treat each other in a somewhat more rule-based manner than do nondemocratic regimes. Rules of appropriateness are sometimes followed even in critical cases of societies living on "the security knife-edge."[92] For example, the (Norwegian, not British) historian Odd-Bjørn Fure observes that in a war involving an existential struggle, Britain refrained in 1940 from using its sea power against German transportation of iron ore from Northern Norway in Norwegian waters. Such attacks were seen to be against international law, and British authorities apparently acted less from a calculation of military or political consequences than out of concern for what could legitimately be done in international affairs. Fure also observes that similar concerns inhibited Britain from using force in disputes with Norway over sea territory and fishing rights in 1933–36.[93]

Moreover, although they also often calculate consequences, democratic states are likely to import democratic norms and decision-making rules into international encounters, for example, norms of transparency, consultation, and compromise. Since such internal norms and rules tend to be shared among democratic states, their generalization to international relations is unsurprising, although hardly assured in all instances. In turn, experience with shared rules facilitates the development of rule-based international institutions and makes the creation of a collective identity more likely.[94] At the same time, democratic norms are contagious. They spread through international contact to countries with less secure democratic traditions. For example, participation in the EU has been portrayed as contributing to the construction not only of a European identity but also of a domestic democratic political identity in countries such as Greece and Spain.[95]

In these ways, rule-based versions of democratic identities and action, negotiation, and collective behavior have been extended to international institutions. The extension is, however, neither reliable nor assured for the future. In addition to the complications already noted, it should be observed that the idea of political institutions based on democratic rules has been somewhat eroded in modern market-based societies by conceptions that place greater emphasis on consequence-based action and market exchange mechanisms for collective choice, that is, by introducing into politics the basic rules and practices of markets. Thus, the spillover of democratic political identities from domestic politics to international politics is counterbalanced by the spillover of individualistic identities of competitive self-interest in the other direction.

Second, international identities may evolve from the practice of expert cooperation around specific tasks. The tension between expertise and politics has been a familiar theme of democratic political theory since the days of the Greek city-state. Those discussions are primarily concerned with the difficulties that expertise and specialized knowledge create for democratic control over public policy and the difficulties that democratic control create for intelligent use of expertise. Those issues remain in the international sphere, along with the difficulties of defining boundaries between expert and lay domains. Partly because modern democratic processes are primarily organized around and within the nation-state, international political issues tend to be defined as issues of nation-state interests, bargaining, negotiation, and conflict. Some issues are, however, defined as "nonpolitical" in the sense that national interests are not treated as overwhelmingly compelling. In particular, "modernization" emphasizes notions of instrumental performance and efficiency, rather than local traditions or interests. Such issues allow more room for experts, technical considerations, and professionalism. The boundary shifts with changing political pressures, but there is always a domain for expertise and technical problem solving, and this domain tends to be organized along transnational lines.

Concepts of expertise stimulate associations and collaborations that recognize national boundaries but tend to subordinate them to shared professional concerns. These "epistemic communities"[96] and international networks of experts and bureaucrats define problems, construct conceptions of causal knowledge, and create frames for action that integrate across nation-states.[97] Their activities and associations lead to bonds that can develop into international identities. Concepts and codes of appropriate behavior, traditionally the province of local schools and civic education, become a product of international contact, institutions, allegiances, and organizations. As international identities and contacts among experts become more dense and specialized, these linkages contribute to definitions of problems as international in scope and of identities and meaning as cutting across state boundaries.

This mutual reinforcement of associations, identities, and perceptions of problems leads to an elaboration of international connections, making them more pervasive, more overlapping, and more embedded in definitions of expertise.[98] The process can be described simply: stage 1: "non-political," technical issues create occasions for participation across borders; stage 2: frequent and long-term participation in discussing technical issues fosters more general familiarity, shared identities, and mutual trust; stage 3: trust, shared identities, and familiarity encourage further contact, further integration, an expansion of the number of topics viewed as appropriate for discussion and the development of common definitions of problems and appropriate actions.[99]

The resulting order is characterized by functional networks of people often organized around representatives of "sister-institutions," like central banks, professional associations, courts, and bureaucracies operating at the national and international decision-making levels.[100] This pattern of organization stimulates and supports new transnational identities. This suggests that the institutions of expertise associated with the World Bank, UNESCO, OECD, the EU, and other similar organizations have to be seen as creators of meaning in general and more specifically of identities.[101] That is, they are not only decision-making institutions but also institutions for socializing individuals and creating meaning and for promoting specific concepts of the nature and role of the state, markets, human rights, and international organizations.

## Illustration 2: Engagement and the Development of Capabilities

Political actors accumulate experience with existing institutions, practices, and rules as they try to track and adapt to their environments and to changes in them. Capabilities for using institutions, practices, and rules are refined through mundane processes of learning, interpretation, reasoning, education, imitation, and adaptation. As a result, involvement in political activities not only changes identities. It also builds and directs political capabilities.

### Competency Traps and Multiple Equilibria

Political arrangements become more efficient as the rules are refined and as actors become more competent in operating within them. Efficiency, however, easily becomes the enemy of adaptiveness. As particular rules are used repeatedly, political actors become more familiar with them and more competent operating within them, thus encouraging their further use. This local positive feedback[102] produces what has been called a competency trap—the tendency for a system to become firmly locked into a particular rule-based structure by virtue of developing familiarity with the rules and capabilities for using them.[103] These refined capabilities strengthen a system in the short run and make it resistant to change. By developing competence with rules, institutions stabilize their norms, rules, meanings, and resources so that many different procedures can exhibit surprising durability.[104]

The accelerating development of competence with particular institutional arrangements and practices is a major feature of institutional history and is one of the more obvious reasons why history is path dependent. The local optima produced by competence elaboration are resistant to new opportunities. For that reason, they are also potential precursors to long-run obsolescence[105] and to the discontinuous, contested, and problematic change[106] associated with "punctuated equilibria,"[107] "critical junctions,"[108] and "performance crises."[109]

The competency trap is a variation on a standard problem in adaptation: The exploitation and refinement of known technologies, practices, and rules tend to drive out the exploration of possible new ones. As competence grows with established rules and practices, the disadvantage of new rules and practices increases. As that disadvantage increases, experiments with new rules are decreased. And as experiments with new rules decrease, the chance of finding a good new alternative or gaining competence on one that might be superior becomes smaller.

Social, economic, and political systems are all prone to competency traps and to at least moderate jerkiness in fundamental transformations. They typically have difficulty sustaining experimentation. From any immediate perspective, this is not because they are stupidly rigid, but because they are intelligently efficient. For them to pursue new alternatives makes little apparent sense. The returns to exploration tend to be less certain and less immediate than the returns to exploitation. They also tend to be more distant, less localized in their realization to the immediate organizational neighborhood of the exploration. This is partly because new ideas tend to be poor ones, and it is partly because even good new ideas have returns that are more distant in time and space than those realized from current ideas. It is not easy for an organization to justify experimentation that, at least in the short run, does not make sense in terms of immediate local return. What is required is a willingness to engage in experimentation that is unlikely to succeed and particularly unlikely to be rewarding in the temporal and spatial neighborhood of the experiment. Unfortunately, although too little experimentation is likely to be disastrous in the longer run, too much experimentation is likely to be disastrous immediately.

Few organizations do well with the problems associated with balancing exploitation and exploration,[110] and there is little reason to think that international organizations will be particularly clever about it. There is an obvious difficulty in producing a requisite level of exploration in an organizational world dedicated to responding to short-run feedback or maximizing local expected return. It seems very likely that rather little of the experimentation in international organization occurs because of a conscious organizational intent to experiment. It occurs because of identities associated with experimentation, because of conflict, because of ideologies of experimentation, and as an unintended byproduct of instrumental action.[111] For example, some scholars have argued that core democratic identities require that citizens have a "hypothetical attitude" toward existing institutions and forms of life and should seek to restructure the institutions, rules, and manners of living together.[112] This tendency to legitimize change introduces a bias that often seems perverse in the way it overturns functioning practices. For example, democratic politics is sometimes an annoyance to experts in law, who seek coherent and unified legal hierarchies of norms and values.[113] To a limited extent, however, a bias for change is a way by which democracy becomes a source of experimentation in political relations,[114] making continuous processes of integration, disintegration, and reintegration more likely and less dependent on external pressures alone.

Not surprisingly, institutions are particularly likely to be changed when they are seen to fail. On the whole, people are less likely to follow institutional rules if they believe that the rules produce poor results.[115] If institutions miss their targets or aspiration levels, the failure creates a loss of confidence in existing rules and a search for new alternatives.[116] Since experience frequently improves performance, failure would not produce much experimentation in a highly competent system were it not for the fact that definitions of "success" and "failure" are notoriously subject to updating of aspirations, bias, and noise. If success and failure were reliably determined, the development of competence would make institutions more stable than they are. Unreliability in assessment of success and the insatiable character of aspirations are quite likely to lead political institutions to experiment at the right time for the wrong reasons.

### Competence and the Transformation of Objectives

The development of competence in the service of existing institutions and objectives is primarily a stabilizing force. But it also creates foundations for new institutions and new objectives. Organizations not only become better and better at what they do, they also see new things to do. Having the capability of doing new things leads, in turn, to seeing their desirability. Capabilities stimulate recognition of the salience of problems to which they can provide solutions.[117] By transforming capabilities, therefore, competence transforms agendas and goals.

Of particular relevance to present concerns is the way competence is developed in the context of concrete activities and then becomes the basis for expansion of objectives to a wider range of concerns. In their early stages, European states developed competencies as an artifact of solving immediate practical problems and taking care of local interests. Those competencies gradually were transformed into institutions and political practices that used them. Nation-state builders started with instrumental motives, such as winning a war or collecting taxes; over time they discovered that they had built the foundations for strongly institutionalized states.[118] In a similar way, the development of military and economic competencies and institutions using them poses a persistent threat to nonmilitary and noneconomic political institutions. The existence of capabilities is converted into an inclination to discover goals the abilities might serve, perhaps in competition with the political system. Thus, the elaboration of tasks is as much a consequence of competence as a cause of it.

The EU has numerous arenas for interaction, argumentation, and collective problem solving and conflict resolution for bureaucrats, experts, representatives of organized interests, and elected politicians. The process of *engrenage* exposes participants to new arguments, new perspectives, and new identities.[119] More importantly perhaps, it develops capabilities for mutual engagement. Considerable experience with acting together is accumulated, and a significant amount of mutual influence between the EU and domestic institutions and actors is taking place, with no clear-cut borderline between the "national" and the "European."[120] The number of meetings in the context of the EU, together with meetings in the context of other international institutions, during some periods actually make ministers, bureaucrats, and experts interact as much with colleagues from other countries as with their domestic colleagues.[121]

The changes these contacts have produced were neither particularly well anticipated by, nor the result of the will of, any easily identifiable group of political actors.[122] The elaboration of international capabilities is part of a long historical transformation of the West European state, reflecting as well as contributing to the erosion of state autonomy.[123] That transformation continues, and predicting the direction it will take is not easy. For example, the EU is still an unsettled constitutional order, in terms of geographical reach, institutional balance, decision rules, and functional scope. Efforts to deepen European integration and create a European polity, or even society, are balanced against nation-states protecting their autonomy and the potential fragmentary tendencies of enlargement of the EU.[124] Even within expert domains, there are conditions that encourage a balkanization of expertise. Developments occur through learning in small (though not always consistent) ways in many places.

The resulting institutional structure more closely resembles a marble cake than a hierarchy,[125] but it is not the same as it used to be. Involvements in highly instrumental and technical activities in the EU have created organizational capabilities for international collaboration that translate into a more general international institution and make more elaborate international coordination possible. The EU has become the most highly institutionalized international organization in history, in terms of depth as well as breadth, yet without becoming a federal state.[126] Participation in the EU has, indeed, altered the nation-state itself. For example, EU citizens and corporations can, and do, invoke EU law against other

individuals and their national governments. The Europeanization of law and
the increased significance of norms in international politics[127] clearly have compromised the identity of territory and authority[128] in ways that owe much to the
gradual accumulation of experience and the resulting gains in competence.

## A Different Emphasis

The two examples illustrate some differences between a perspective (which we
have called an institutional perspective) that assumes identity-based action and
inefficient history and a more conventional perspective that attributes action to
calculations of consequences and environmental constraints. The latter interprets
changes in an international political order primarily in terms of exogenously
specified interests and capabilities, rational actors, expectations of consequences,
and environmental pressures. The former sees changes in a political order more
as involving the construction and evocation of rules, institutions, and identities, the development of capabilities, and the path-dependent meanders of an
inefficient history.

The illustrations are drawn from a universe that includes others, but they are
not randomly drawn from that universe. Although the illustrations themselves are
brief and incomplete, they are chosen not only to exemplify institutional modes
of thinking in general but also to identify two of the more important specific
contributions to the study of international relations that might be drawn from
institutional perspectives. Understanding the ways in which political identities,
rules, and capabilities evolve within a political order and the ways in which
the evolution of identities, rules, and capabilities serves to create, sustain, or
corrupt an order may be important to understanding histories of international
political order.

## CONCLUSION

The historical processes by which international political orders develop are
complex enough to make any simple theory of them unsatisfactory. An interconnected and interdependent world produces histories in which changes in
environmental conditions are not automatically or unambiguously reflected in
changing political orders and institutional arrangements. Nor is it possible to
describe the evolution of international political orders in terms of any simple
notions of intentionality and design at the nation-state level. History is created
by a complicated ecology of local events and locally adaptive actions. As individuals, groups, organizations, and institutions seek to act intelligently and

learn in a changing world involving others similarly trying to adapt, they create connections that subordinate individual intentions to their interactions. The locally adaptive actions that constitute that ecology are themselves based on subtle intertwinings of rational action based on expectations of consequences and rule-based action seeking to fulfill identities within environments that influence but do not uniquely dictate actions. Expectations, preferences, identities, and meanings are affected by human interaction and experience. They coevolve with the actions they produce.

Such ideas do not encourage aspirations for applying standard experimental design or hypothesis testing in conventional form to the naturally occurring histories of international relations. Nor do they provide justification for expecting to predict specific events such as the end of the Cold War, the fall of the Wall, the ebbs and flows of European integration, or the renewed strength of ethnic nationalism. The study of international relations, like much of social science, is a branch of history, and the history of history discourages grandiose predictive hopes. Historical interpretations of the development of international orders are made difficult by the necessity of learning from small samples of uncontrolled conditions.

We accept the implications of that difficulty and thus the implausibility of proclaiming a bold new direction built on institutional representations of international political orders. Nevertheless, we think it may be useful to consider conceptions of history that build on the lower right-hand quadrant of Figure 1, supplementing ideas of consequential action, exogenous preferences, and efficient histories with ideas of rule- and identity-based action, inefficient histories, and institutional robustness. Used to interpret careful historical observations and descriptions of behavior and events, such a perspective provides a basis for intelligent compromises between simple renderings of history that are inconsistent with reality and complex renderings that are inconsistent with human capacities for comprehension.

The research for this article was supported by the Spencer Foundation and the ARENA program (Advanced Research on the Europeanisation of the Nation-State) financed by the Norwegian Research Council. We are grateful for the help provided by Peter Katzenstein, Robert O. Keohane, Stephen D. Krasner, Helene Sjursen, Arthur Stein, Bjørn Otto Sverdrup, and Arild Underdal in introducing us to the international relations literature and for constructive comments.

### NOTES

1. See Krasner 1983a; Smith 1996; and Remmer 1997.
2. See Dewey 1927; Eisenstadt 1987; and March and Olsen 1995.
3. Hall 1996.

4. Mann 1993.

5. Habermas 1996, 1.

6. See Bendix 1968, 9; and Bull 1995, 21.

7. These were issues to be discussed at the International Conference to Celebrate the 350th Anniversary of the Peace of Westphalia 1648–1998: "From Pragmatic Solution to Global Structure," Münster, 16–19 July 1998. However, part of this conference was cancelled and part of it was moved to Twente, The Netherlands.

8. Stone 1994, 448.

9. See Jackson 1990; and World Bank 1997.

10. See Marin and Mayntz 1991; Luhmann 1982, 253–55; Teubner 1993; Habermas 1996, 393; Ladeur 1997; and Rhodes 1997.

11. Lapid 1996, 3, 5.

12. March and Olsen 1995, 70.

13. Ladeur 1997.

14. Scharpf 1996, 15.

15. See Risse-Kappen 1995b; and Joerges, Ladeur, and Vos 1997.

16. Deutsch et al. 1957.

17. See Krasner 1983a; Keohane 1983a, 1984, 5, 1996; Kratochwil and Ruggie 1986; Haggard and Simmons 1987; Young 1989, 13, 1994, 1996; Mayer, Rittberger, and Zürn 1995, 403; Levy, Young, and Zürn 1995; and Hasenclever, Mayer, and Rittberger 1996, 1997.

18. Checkel 1997.

19. Habermas 1996, 475.

20. Mayer, Rittberger, and Zürn 1995, 401, 405.

21. Lake 1996, 30.

22. See Krasner 1983b; Keohane 1983a, 1984, 5, 1989a, 9; Young 1986, 109, 1996; Rosenau and Czempiel 1992; Krasner 1995a, 150; Mayer, Rittberger, and Zürn 1995, 293–94, 397–98; Risse 1997, 18; Stokke 1997; and Olsen 1997a.

23. See Buzan 1993, 351; and Jepperson, Wendt, and Katzenstein 1996, 74.

24. See Tilly 1975, 1993; and Giddens 1985. But see also Kaysen 1990.

25. See Krasner 1983a, 1988, 1995a, 145; Keohane 1984, 1988, 380, 1989a, 2; Young 1986, 1994, 1996; Stone 1994, 464; and Goldmann 1996.

26. Stinchcombe 1997.

27. March and Olsen 1996, 260, n. 2.

28. DiMaggio 1997.

29. See March and Olsen 1984, 1989, 1995.

30. Olsen 1997a, 159–60.

31. See Weber 1978; and Giddens 1984.

32. See March and Olsen 1989; and March 1994a.

33. See Sabine 1952; and Friedrich 1963.

34. Habermas 1996, xi, 8, 26–29.

35. See North 1981; Shepsle 1989; and Coleman 1990.

36. See Downs 1957; Riker 1962; Coleman 1966; March 1970; Niskanen 1971; and Hechter and Kanazawa 1997.

37. See Elster 1979, 1983; and March 1988, 1994a.

38. See Simon 1955, 1956.

39. See March 1978; and Elster 1986b, 1989c.

40. See March 1992, 1996.

41. See Moravcsik 1991, 1993, 1997.

42. See Heldt 1992; Rummel 1994, 1995; Holsti 1996; and Wallensteen and Sollenberg 1997.

43. See Milward 1992; and Moravcsik 1993.

44. See March and Olsen 1989, 1995.

45. Cerulo 1997.

46. See Ruggie 1983b; Kratochwil and Ruggie 1986; Wendt and Duvall 1989; Young 1989; Thomas et al. 1987; Kratochwil 1989; Buzan 1993; Wendt 1994; Risse-Kappen 1995b; Katzenstein 1996c; Chayes and Chayes 1995; Finnemore 1996a,b; Wæver 1997, 20; Risse 1997; and Hasenclever, Mayer, and Rittberger 1996, 220, 1997.

47. Habermas 1996.

48. Garrett and Weingast 1993, 186.

49. Stinchcombe 1986, 158.

50. Offe 1996, 682.

51. March 1994a, 101–102.

52. See Coleman 1986; and Shepsle 1990.

53. Searing 1991.

54. See Taylor 1985; and Nauta 1992.

55. See North 1981, 1990.

56. See Berman 1983; March and Olsen 1989, 1996; and Olsen 1992.

57. See Alesina and Spolaore 1997; and Bolton and Roland 1997.

58. March 1994b.

59. Sandel 1982, 1984.

60. March 1994b.

61. See Brady 1988; and Lipset 1990.

62. See March 1981; and Rothstein 1992.

63. See Keohane 1983a, 1984; Stein 1983; and Young 1996.

64. See Strange 1983; Grieco 1988; Keohane 1989b, 8; Mearsheimer 1994, 7, 13; Stone 1994, 449; and Krasner 1995a, 115.

65. See Hasenclever, Mayer, and Rittberger 1996, 196, 202, 205, and 1997; and Wæver 1997, 19.

66. Lake 1996, 12, 13.

67. Keohane 1989a, 6.

68. See North 1981, 1990; and Arthur 1989.

69. See Meyer 1980; Thomas et al. 1987; Finnemore 1996a,b; and Jepperson, Wendt, and Katzenstein 1996.

70. See March and Olsen 1989, 1994, 1995, 1996.

71. Nelson and Winter 1982.

72. Cerulo 1997.

73. This mainstream view is discussed and criticized by Wendt 1992, 1994; Risse-Kappen 1996a, 1996b; Buzan 1996; and Wæver 1997. See also Mayer, Rittberger, and Zürn 1995, 424; and Hasenclever, Mayer, and Rittberger 1996, 181, 184.

74. See Mayer, Rittberger, and Zürn 1995; Hasenclever, Meyer, and Rittberger 1996, 211; and Wendt 1992, 1994.

75. See Axelrod 1984; Buzan 1993, 349; Mayer, Rittberger, and Zürn 1995, 394.

76. See Slaughter 1995, 530; and Tonra 1996.

77. Allport 1954.

78. Putnam 1993.

79. See Habermas 1996, 139; and Eriksen and Weigård 1997.

80. Laffan 1997a, 4.

81. Schlesinger 1991, 178, 182.

82. Risse 1997.

83. Risse 1997, 19.

84. Eide and Hagtvet 1992.

85. World Commission 1987.

86. See Schlesinger 1993, 1994.

87. Elias [1939] 1994.

88. Olsen 1997b.

89. See Krasner 1995a, 117; and March and Olsen 1996, 259.

90. See Wendt and Duvall 1989; Buzan 1996, 59; and Wæver 1997, 10.

91. See Doyle 1983a,b; and Gleditsch 1992. This phenomenon, as one might expect, has also been given an interest-based, consequential interpretation. See S. Chan 1997; and McMillan 1997.

92. Keohane 1996a, 470.

93. Fure 1996, 247, 349.

94. See Slaughter 1995; and Risse-Kappen 1996b, 397, 399.

95. See Pérez-Díaz 1993; and Katzenstein 1996c, 520.

96. Haas 1992a.

97. Hill and Wallace 1996, 11.

98. Young 1996, 1, 20.

99. Haas 1958.

100. See Egeberg and Trondal 1997; and Joerges, Ladeur, and Vos 1997.

101. See Finnemore 1993, 1996a,b; and Olsen 1997b.

102. See Arthur 1989.

103. See Levitt and March 1988; and March 1991.

104. See Stinchcombe 1965; and Starbuck, Greve, and Hedberg 1978.

105. Levinthal and March 1993.

106. See Skowronek 1982; and Orren and Skowronek 1994.

107. Krasner 1984.

108. Collier and Collier 1991.

109. March and Olsen 1989.

110. Levinthal and March 1993.

111. March 1994a, 40–54.

112. Habermas 1996, 468.

113. Stone 1994, 442.

114. Shapiro and Hardin 1996, 5–6.

115. Stinchcombe 1986, 166.

116. Cyert and March 1963.

117. See Cyert and March 1963; and Cohen, March, and Olsen 1972.

118. Tilly 1975.

119. See Hill and Wallace 1996, 1; Rometsch and Wessels 1996; and Laffan 1997b, 9.

120. See Rometsch and Wessels 1996, 329; and Jachtenfuchs and Kohler-Koch 1996.

121. See Wessels 1990; and Hill and Wallace 1996, 7, 11.

122. Stone 1994, 425.

123. See Flora 1983; and Wessels 1997, 22–24.

124. Laffan 1997a.
125. Jachtenfuchs and Kohler-Koch 1996.
126. See Hill and Wallace 1996, 12; Haas 1967, 331; Keohane 1996a, 467; and Laffan 1997b.
127. Stone 1994, 473.
128. Krasner 1995a, 134.

REFERENCES

Alesina, A., and E. Spolare. 1997. On the Number and Size of Nations. *Quarterly Journal of Economics* 112:1027–1056.

Allport, G. W. 1954. *The Nature of Prejudice*. Reading, MA: Addison-Wesley.

Arthur, W. B. 1989. Competing Technologies, Increasing Returns, and Lock-in by Historical Events. *Economic Journal* 99:116–131.

Axelrod, R. 1984. *The Evolution of Cooperation*. New York, NY: Basic Books.

Bendix, R., ed. 1968. *State and Society*. Boston, MA: Little, Brown and Co.

Berman, H. J. 1983. *Law and Revolution. The Formation of the Western Legal Tradition*. Cambridge, MA: Harvard University Press.

Bolton, P., and G. Roland. 1997. The Breakup of Nations: A Political Economy Analysis. *Quarterly Journal of Economics* 112:1057–1090.

Brady, D. W. 1988. *Critical Elections and Congressional Policy Making*. Stanford, CA: Stanford University Press.

Bull, H. 1995. *The Anarchical Society. A Study of Order in World Politics*. 2d ed. London: Macmillan.

Buzan, B. 1993. From International System to International Society: Structural Realism and Regime Theory Meet the English School. *International Organization* 47:327–352.

———. 1996. The Timeless Wisdom of Realism? In *International Theory: Positivism and Beyond*, edited by S. Smith, K. Booth and M. Zalewski, 47–65. Cambridge: Cambridge University Press.

Cerulo. K. A. 1997. Identity Construction: New issues, New Directions. *Annual Review of Sociology* 23:385–402.

Chan, S. 1997. In Search of Democratic Peace: Problems and Promises. *Mershon International Studies Review* 41:59–91.

Chayes, A., and Chayes, A. H. 1995. *The New Sovereignty. Compliance with International Regulatory Agreements*. Cambridge, MA: Harvard University Press.

Checkel, J. T. 1997. International Norms and Domestic Politics: Bridging the Rationalist-Constructivist Divide. *European Journal of International Relations* 3:473–495.

Cohen, M. D., J. G. March, and J. P. Olsen. 1972. A Garbage Can Model of Organizational Choice. *Administrative Science Quarterly* 17:1–25.

Collier, R. B., and D. Collier. 1991. *Shaping the Political Arena: Critical Junctures, the Labor Movement, and Regime Dynamics in Latin America*. Princeton, NJ: Princeton University Press.

Coleman, J. S. 1966. Foundations for a Theory of Collective Decisions. *American Journal of Sociology* 71:615–627.

———. 1986. *Individual Interests and Collective Action*. Cambridge: Cambridge University Press.

———. 1990. *Foundations of Social Theory*. Cambridge MA: Harvard University Press.

Cyert, R. M., and J. G. March. 1963. *A Behavioral Theory of the Firm*. Englewood Cliffs, NJ: Prentice-Hall.

Deutsch, K. W., et al. 1957. *Political Community and the North Atlantic Area*. New York, NY: Greenwood.

Dewey, J. 1927. *The Public and its Problems*. Denver, CO: Alan Swallow.

DiMaggio, P. 1997. Culture and Cognition. *Annual Review of Sociology* 23:263–287.

Downs, A. 1957. *An Economic Theory of Democracy*. New York, NY: Harper and Row.

Doyle, M. W. 1983a. Kant, Liberal Legacies, and Foreign Affairs, Part 1. *Philosophy & Public Affairs* 12:205–235.

———. 1983b. Kant, Liberal Legacies, and Foreign Affairs, Part 2. *Philosophy & Public Affairs* 12:323–353.

Egeberg, M., and J. Trondal. 1997. An Organization Theory Perspective on Multi-level Governance in the EU: The Case of the EEA as a Dorm of Affiliation. Working Paper Series, 21. Oslo: ARENA.

Eide, A., and B. Hagtvedt, eds. 1992. *Human Rights in Perspective. A Global Assessment*. Oxford: Blackwell.

Eisenstadt, S. N. 1987. *European Civilization in Comparative Perspective*. Oslo: Norwegian University Press.

Elias, N. 1994 (1939). *The Civilizing Process*. Oxford: Blackwell.

Elster, J. 1979. *Ulysses and the Sirens: Studies in Rationality and Irrationality*. Cambridge: Cambridge University Press.

———. 1983. *Sour Grapes: Studies in Subversion of Rationality*. Cambridge: Cambridge University Press.

———. 1986. *The Multiple Self*. Cambridge: Cambridge University Press.

———. 1989. *The Cement of Society: A Study of Social Order*. Cambridge: Cambridge University Press.

Eriksen, E. O., and J. Weigård. 1997. Conceptualizing Politics: Strategic or Communicative Action? *Scandinavian Political Studies* 20:219–241.

Finnemore, M. 1993. International Organizations as Teachers of Norms: The United Nations Educational, Scientific, and Cultural Organization and Science Policy. *International Organization* 47:565–597.

———. 1996a. *National Interests in International Society*. Ithaca, NY: Cornell University Press.

———. 1996b. Norms, Culture, and World Politics: Insights from Sociology's Institutionalism. *International Organization* 50:325–347.

Flora, P. 1983. *State, Economy, and Society in Western Europe 1815–1975*. Frankfurt: Campus.

Friedrich, C. J. 1963. *Man and his Government*. New York, NY: McGraw-Hill.

Fure, O-B. 1996. *Mellomkrigstid 1920–1940*. Oslo: Universitetsforlaget.

Garret, G., and B. R. Weingast. 1993. Ideas, Interests and Institutions: Constructing the European Community's Internal market. In *Ideas and Foreign Policy: Beliefs, Institutions, and Political Change*, edited by J. Goldstein and R. O. Keohane, 173–398. Ithaca, NY: Cornell University Press.

Giddens, A. 1984. *The Constitution of Society*. Berkeley, CA: University of California Press.

———. 1985. *The Nation State and Violence*. Oxford: Polity Press.

Gleditsch, N. P. 1992. Democracy and Peace. *Journal of Peace Research* 29:369–376.

Goldmann, K. 1996. International Relations: An Overview. In *A New Handbook of Political Science*, edited by R. E. Goodin and H-D. Klingemann, 401–427. Oxford: Oxford University Press.

Grieco, J. M. 1988. Anarchy and the Limits of Cooperation: A Realist's Critique of the Newest Liberal Institutionalism. *International Organization* 42:485–507.

Haas, E. B. 1958. *The Uniting of Europe. Political, Social and Economic Forces 1950–1957*. London: Stevens & Sons Limited.

———. 1967. The Uniting of Europe and the Uniting of Latin America. *Journal of Common Market Studies* 5:315–343.

Haas, P. M. 1992. Introduction: Epistemic Communities and International Policy Coordination. *International Organization* 46:1–36.

Habermas, J. 1996. *Between Facts and Norms*. Cambridge MA: The MIT Press.

Haggard, S., and B. A. Simmons. 1987. Theories of International Regimes. *International Organization* 41:491–517.

Hall, J.A. 1996. *International Orders*. Cambridge: Polity Press.

Hasenclever, A., P. Mayer, and V. Rittberger. 1996. Interests, Power, Knowledge: The Study of International Regimes. *Mershon International Studies Review* 40:177–228.

———. 1997. *Theories of International Regimes*. Cambridge: Cambridge University Press.

Hechter, M., and S. Kanazawa. 1997. Sociological Rational Choice Theory. *Annual Review of Sociology* 23:191–214.

Heldt, B., ed. 1992. *States in Armed Conflict 1990–1991*. Report No. 35. Uppsala: Uppsala University, Department of Peace and Conflict Research.

Hill, C., and W. Wallace. 1996. Introduction: Actors and Actions. In *The Actors in Europe's Foreign Policy*, edited by C. Hill, 1–16. London: Routledge.

Holsti, K. J. 1996. *The State, War, and the State of War*. Cambridge: Cambridge University Press.

Jachtenfuchs, M., and B. Kohler-Koch, eds. 1996. *Europäische Integration*. Opladen: Leske and Budrich.

Jackson R. H. 1993 (paperback ed.). *Quasi-states: Sovereignty, International Relations and the Third World*. Cambridge: Cambridge University Press.

Jepperson, R. L., A. Wendt, and P. J. Katzenstein. 1996. Norms, Identity, and Culture in National Security. In *The Culture of National Security. Norms and Identity in World Politics*, edited by P.J. Katzenstein, 33–75. New York, NY: Columbia University Press.

Joerges, C., K-H. Ladeur, and E. Vos, eds. 1997. *Integrating Scientific Expertise into Regulatory Decision-Making. National Traditions and European Innovations*. Baden-Baden: Nomos.

Katzenstein, P. J., ed. 1996. *The Culture of National Security. Norms and Identity in World Politics*. New York, NY: Columbia University Press.

Kaysen, C. 1990. Is War Obsolete? A Review Essay. *International Security* 14(4):42–64.

Keohane, R. O. 1982. The Demand for International Regimes. *International Organizations* 36:141–171.

———. 1984. *After Hegemony. Cooperation and Discord in the World Political Economy*. Princeton, NJ: Princeton University Press.

———. 1988. International Institutions: Two Approaches. *International Studies Quarterly* 32:379–396.

———. 1989. Neoliberal Institutionalism: A Perspective on World Politics. In *International Institutions and State Power: Essays in International Relations Theory*, edited by R. O. Keohane, 1–20. Boulder, CO: Westview.

———. 1996. International Relations, Old and New. In *A New Handbook of Political Science, edited by* R. E. Goodin and H-D. Klingemann , 462–476. Oxford: Oxford University Press.

Krasner, S. D., ed. 1983a. *International Regimes*. Ithaca, NY: Cornell University Press.

———. 1983b. Regimes and the Limits of Realism: Regimes as Autonomous Variables. In *International Regimes*, edited by S. D. Krasner, 355–368. Ithaca, NY: Cornell University Press.

———. 1984. Approaches to the State: Alternative Conceptions and Historical Dynamics. *Comparative Politics* 16:223–246.

———. 1988. Sovereignty: An Institutionalist Perspective. *Comparative Political Studies* 21:66–94.

———. 1995. Compromising Westphalia. *International Security* 20:115–151.

Kratochwil, F. V. 1989. *Rules, Norms and Decisions. On the Conditions of Practical and Legal Reasoning in International Relations and Domestic Affairs*. Cambridge: Cambridge University Press.

Kratochwil, F. V., and J. G. Ruggie. 1986. International Organization: A State of the Art on an Art of the State. *International Organization* 40:753–775.

Ladeur, K-H. 1997. Towards a Legal Theory of Supranationality—The Viability of the Network Concept. *European Law Journal* 3: 33–54.

Laffan, B. 1997a. The IGC as Constitution-building—What's New at Amsterdam. Unpublished manuscript, University College Dublin, Dublin.

———. 1997b. The European Union: A Distinctive Model of Internationalization? *European Integration Online Papers* 1(018):http://eiop.or.at/eiop.texte/1997018a.htm

Lake, D. A. 1996. Anarchy, Hierarchy, and the Variety of International Relations. *International Organization* 50:1–33.

Lapid, Y. 1997. Culture's Ship: Returns and Departures in International Relations Theory. In *The Return of Culture and Identity in IR Theory*, edited by Y. Lapid and F. Kratochwil, 3–20 (paperback edition). Boulder, CO/London: Lynne Rienner Publishers.

Levinthal, D. A., and J. G. March. 1993. The Myopia of Learning. *Strategic Management Journal* 14:95–112.

Levitt B. and J. G. March. 1988. Organizational Learning. *Annual Review of Sociology* 14:319–340.

Levy, M. A., O. R. Young, and M. Zürn. 1995. The Study of International Regimes. *European Journal of International Relations* 1:267–330.

Lipset, S. M., 1990. *Continental Divide*. New York, NY: Routledge.

Luhmann, N. 1982. *The Differentiation of Society*. New York, NY: University of Colombia Press.

Mann, M. 1993. Nation-states in Europe and Other Continents: Diversifying, Developing, Not Dying. *Daedalus* 122 (3): 115–140.

March J. G. 1970. Politics and the City. In *Urban Processes as Viewed by the Social Sciences*, edited by K. Arrow, J. S. Coleman, A. Downs, and J. G. March, 23–37. Washington, D.C.: The Urban Institute Press.

———. 1978. Bounded Rationality, Ambiguity, and the Engineering of Choice. *Bell Journal of Economics* 9:587–608.

————. 1981. Footnotes to Organizational Change. *Administrative Science Quarterly* 26:563–577.

————. 1988. *Decisions and Organizations*. Oxford: Blackwell.

————. 1991. Exploration and Exploitation in Organizational Learning. *Organizational Science* 2:71–87.

————. 1992. The War Is Over and the Victors Have Lost. *Journal of Socio-Economics* 21:261–267.

————. 1994a. *A Primer on Decision Making*. New York, NY: Free Press.

————. 1994b. The Evolution of Evolution. In *Evolutionary Dynamics of Organizations*, edited by J. Baum and J. Singh, 39–49. New York, NY: Oxford University Press.

————. 1996. Continuity and Change in Theories of Organizational Action. *Administrative Science Quarterly* 41:278–287.

March, J. G., and J. P. Olsen. 1984. The New Institutionalism: Organizational Factors in Political Life. *American Political Science Review* 78:734–749.

————. 1989. *Rediscovering Institutions*. New York, NY: Free Press.

————. 1994. Institutional Perspectives on Governance. In *Systemrationalität und Partialinteresse*, edited by H.U. Derlien, U. Gerhardt and F. W. Scharpf, 249–270. Baden-Baden: Nomos.

————. 1995. *Democratic Governance*. New York: Free Press.

————. 1996. Institutional Perspectives on Political Institutions. *Governance* 9:247–264.

Marin, B. and R. Mayntz, eds. 1991. *Policy Networks*. Frankfurt am Main: Campus.

Mayer, P., V. Rittberger, and M. Zürn. 1995. Regime Theory: State of the Art and Perspectives. In *Regime Theory and International Relations*, edited by V. Rittberger, assisted by P. Mayer, 392–430. Oxford: Oxford University Press.

McMillan, S. M. 1997. Interdependence and Conflict. *Mershon International Studies Review*, 41:33–58.

Meyer, J. W. 1980. The World Polity and the Authority of the Nation-state. In *Studies of the Modern World-System*, edited by A. Bergesen, 109–158. New York, NY: Academic Press.

Mearsheimer, J. J. 1994. The False Promise of International Institutions. *International Security* 19:5–49.

Milward, A. 1992. *The European Rescue of the Nation-State*. Berkeley, CA: University of California Press.

Moravcsik, A. 1991. Negotiating the Single European Act: National Interests and Conventional Statecraft in the European Community. *International Organization* 45:19–56.

————. 1993. Preferences and Power in the European Community: A Liberal Intergovernmentalist Approach. *Journal of Common Market Studies* 31:473–524.

————. 1997. Taking Preferences Seriously: A Liberal Theory of International Politics. *International Organization* 51:513–53.

Nauta, L. 1992. Changing Conceptions of Citizenship. *Praxis International* 12:20–34.

Nelson R. R. and S. G. Winter. 1982. *An Evolutionary Theory of Economic Change*. Cambridge, MA: Harvard University Press.

Niskanen, W. A. 1971. *Bureaucracy and Representative Government*. Chicago, IL: Rand McNally.

North, D. C. 1981. *Structure and Change in Economic History*. New York, NY: Norton.

————. 1990. *Institutions, Institutional Change and Economic Performance*. Cambridge: Cambridge University Press.

Offe. C. 1996. Political Economy: Sociological Perspectives. In *A New Handbook of Political Science*, edited by R. E. Goodin and H-D. Klingemann, 675–690. Oxford: Oxford University Press.

Olsen, J. P. 1992. Analyzing Institutional Dynamics. *Staatswissenschaften und Staatspraxis* 3:247–271.

———. 1997a. European Challenges to the Nation State. In *Political Institutions and Public Policy*, edited by B. Steunenberg and F. van Vught, 157–188. Dordrecht: Kluwer.

———. 1997b. Civil Service in Transition—Dilemmas and Lessons Learned. In *The European Yearbook of Comparative Government and Public Administration*, Vol. III/1996, edited by J. J. Hesse and T. A. J. Toonen, 225–250. Baden-Baden and Boulder, CO: Nomos/Westview.

Orren, K., and S. Skowronek. 1994. Beyond the Iconography of Order: Notes for a "New Institutionalism." In *The Dynamics of American Politics*, edited by L. C. Dodd and C. Jillson, 311–330. Boulder, CO: Westview Press.

Pérez-Díaz, V. M. 1993. *The Return of Civil Society*. Cambridge, MA: Harvard University Press.

Putnam, R. D. 1993. *Making Democracy Work: Civic Traditions in Modern Italy*. Princeton, NJ: Princeton University Press.

Remmer, K. L. 1997. Theoretical Decay and Theoretical Development: Resurgence of Institutional Analysis. *Comparative Politics* 50:34–61.

Rhodes, R. A. W. 1997. *Understanding Governance. Policy Networks, Governance, Reflexivity and Accountability*. Buckingham: Open University Press.

Riker, W. H. 1962. *The Theory of Political Coalitions*. New Haven, CT: Yale University Press.

Risse-Kappen, T., ed. 1995. *Bringing Transnational Relations Back In. Non-state Actors, Domestic Structures and International Institutions*. Cambridge: Cambridge University Press.

———. 1996a. Exploring the Nature of the Beast: International Relations Theory and Comparative Policy Analysis Meet the European Union. *Journal of Common Market Studies* 34:53–80.

———. 1996b. Collective Identity in a Democratic Community. In *The Culture of National Security. Norms and Identity in World Politics*, edited by P. J. Katzenstein, 357–399. New York, NY: Columbia University Press.

———. 1997. "Let's talk!" Insights from the German Debate on Communicative Behavior and International Relations. Unpublished manuscript, European University Institute, Florence.

Rometsch, D., and W. Wessels. 1996. Conclusion: European Union and National Institutions. In *The European Union and Member States*, edited by D. Rometsch and W. Wessels, 328–365. Manchester: Manchester University Press.

Rosenau, J. N. and E-O. Czempiel, eds. 1992. *Governance without Government. Order and Change in World Politics*. Cambridge: Cambridge University Press.

Rothstein, B. 1992. Labor-market Institutions and Working Class Strength. In *Structuring Politics. Historical Institutionalism in Comparative Analysis*, edited by S. Steinmo, K. Thelen, and F. Longstreeth, 33–56. Cambridge: Cambridge University Press.

Ruggie, J. G. 1982. International Regimes, Transactions, and Change: Embedded Liberalism in the Postwar Economic Order. *International Organization* 36:379–415.

Rummel, R. J. 1994. Power, Genocide and Mass Murder. *Journal of Peace Research* 31:1–10.

———. 1995. Democracy, Power, Genocide, and Mass Murder. *Journal of Conflict Resolution* 39:3–26.

Sabine, G. H. 1952. The Two Democratic Traditions. *The Philosophical Review*, 61:493–511.

Sandel, M. J. 1982. *Liberalism and the Limits of Justice*. Cambridge: Cambridge University Press.

———. 1984. The Procedural Republic and the Unencumbered Self. *Political Theory*, 12:81–96.

Scharpf, F. W. 1996. Negative and Positive Integration in the Political Economy of European Welfare States. In *Governance in the European Union*, edited by G. Marks et al., 15–39. London: Sage.

Schlesinger, P. R. 1991. *Media, State and Nation*. London: Sage.

———. 1993. Wishful Thinking: Cultural Politics, Media, and Collective Identities in Europe. *Journal of Communication* 43:6–17.

———. 1994. Europe's Contradictory Communicative Space. *Daedalus* 123 (2): 25–52.

Searing, D. D. 1991. Roles, Rules and Rationality in the New Institutionalism. *American Political Science Review* 85:1239–1260.

Shapiro, I., and R. Hardin. 1996. Introduction. In *Political Order*, edited by I. Shapiro and R. Hardin, 1–15. New York, NY: New York University Press.

Shepsle, K. A. 1989. Studying Institutions: Some Lessons from the Rational Choice Approach. *Journal of Theoretical Politics* 1: 131–147.

———. 1990. *Perspectives on Positive Economy*. Cambridge: Cambridge University Press.

Simon, H. A. 1955. A Behavioral Model of Rational Choice. *Quarterly Journal of Economics* 69:99–118.

———. 1956. Rational Choice and the Structure of the Environment. *Psychological Review* 63:129–138.

Skowronek, S. 1982. *Building a New American State*. Cambridge: Cambridge University Press.

Slaughter, A-M. 1995. International Law in a World of Liberal States. *European Journal of International Law* 6 (4):203–238.

Smith, M. 1996. The European Union and a Changing Europe: Establishing the Boundaries of Order. *Journal of Common Market Studies* 34:5–28.

Starbuck, W. H., A. Greve and B. L. . Hedberg. 1978. Responding to Crises. *Journal of Business Administration* 9 (2):111–137.

Stein, A. A. 1983. Coordination and Collaboration: Regimes in an Anarchic World. In *International Regimes*, edited by S. D. Krasner, 115–140. Ithaca, NY: Cornell University Press.

Stinchcombe, A. L. 1965. Social Structure and Organizations. In *Handbook of Organizations*, edited by J. G. March, 142–193. Chicago, IL: Rand McNally.

Stinchcombe, A. L. 1986. Reason and Rationality. *Sociological Theory* 4:151–166.

———. 1997. On the Virtues of the Old Institutionalism. *Annual Review of Sociology* 23: 1–18.

Stokke, O. S. 1997. Regimes as Governance Systems. In *Global Governance: Drawing Insights from the Environmental Experience*, edited by O. R. Young, 27–63. Cambridge, MA: MIT Press.

Stone, A. 1994. What is a Supranational Constitution? An Essay in International Relations Theory. *The Review of Politics* 56:441–474.

Strange, S. 1983. "Cave! Hic dragones": A Critique of Regime Analysis. In *International Regimes*, edited by S. D. Krasner, 337–354. Ithaca, NY: Cornell University Press.

Taylor, C. 1985. *Philosophy and the Human Sciences*. Cambridge: Cambridge University Press.

Teubner, G. 1993. *Law as an Autopoietic System*. Oxford: Blackwell.

Thomas, G. M. et al. 1987. *Institutional Structure. Constituting State, Society, and the Individual*. Beverly Hills, CA: Sage.

Tilly, C., ed. 1975. *The Formation of National States in Western Europe*. Princeton, NJ: Princeton University Press.

———. 1993. *Coercion, Capital, and European States* (rev. ed.). Cambridge, MA: Blackwell.

Tonra, B. 1996. Dutch, Danish and Irish Foreign Policy in the EPC/CFSP 1970–1996. Ph.D. diss. University of Dublin, Trinity College.

Wallensteen, P., and M. Sollenberg. 1997. Armed Conflicts, Conflict Termination and Peace Agreements, 1989–1996. *Journal of Peace Research* 34:339–358.

Weber, M. 1978. *Economy and Society*. Berkeley, CA: University of California Press.

Wendt, A. 1992. Anarchy Is What States Make of It: The Social Construction of Power Politics. *International Organization* 46:391–425.

———. 1994. Collective Identity Formation and the International State. *American Political Science Review* 88:384–396.

Wendt, A., and R. Duvall 1989. Institutions and International Order. In *Global Changes and Theoretical Challenges: Approaches to World Politics for the 1990s*, edited by E-O. Czempiel and J. N. Rosenau, 51–73. Lexington MA: Lexington Books.

Wessels, W. 1990. Administrative Interaction. In *Dynamics of European Integration*, edited by W. Wallace, 229–241. London: Pinter.

———. 1997. An Ever Closer Fusion. Unpublished manuscript, Universität zu Köln.

Williamson, O. E. 1975. *Markets and Hierarchies: Analysis and Antitrust Implications*. New York, NY: Free Press.

———. 1996. *The Mechanisms of Governance*. New York, NY: Oxford University Press.

World Bank. 1997. *World Development Report 1997. The State in a Changing World*. Oxford: Oxford University Press.

World Commission on Environment and Development. 1987. *Our Common Future*. Oxford: Oxford University Press.

Wæver, O. 1997. Figures of International Thought: Introducing Persons Instead of Paradigms. In *The Future of International Relations. Masters in the Making?*, edited by I. B. Neumann and O. Wæver, 1–37. London: Routledge.

Young, O. R. 1986. International Regimes: Toward a New Theory of Institutions. *World Politics* 39:104–122.

———. 1989. *International Cooperation: Building Regimes for Natural Resources and the Environment*. Ithaca, NY: Cornell University Press.

———. 1994. *International Governance. Protecting the Environment in a Stateless Society*. Ithaca, NY: Cornell University Press.

———. 1996. Institutional Linkages in International Society: Polar Perspectives. *Global Governance* 2:1–24.

# CHAPTER 11

# A Learning Perspective on the Network Dynamics of Institutional Integration

JAMES G. MARCH

## INTRODUCTION

Events of the late twentieth century suggest that an understanding of social, political, and economic institutions requires rethinking some old issues in organization theory. One of the more conspicuous of those issues concerns the factors that lead to different levels and forms of institutional integration. This paper examines a small part of that issue. It considers how networks, a key aspect of integration, might be imagined to evolve.

## THE ISSUE OF INTEGRATION

At least since Aristotle, students of organizations have been trying to prescribe and predict variations in organizational integration and centralization. History provides numerous instances of both the disintegration of previously highly integrated systems and the integration of previously highly disintegrated systems. In recent years, these changes have included the development of new organizational forms, such as international financial markets and the European Union, and the transformation of old forms, such as the Soviet Union and the multidivisional, full-time employment business firm.

Changes in institutions have occurred in parallel with (and not entirely independent of) changes in theories of organization. For much of its history, organization theory has emphasized the dependence of organizational forms on organizational tasks or contexts. Variations in integration have been attributed to variations in functional necessities. The litany has become well known: When integration provides an advantage, organizations are integrated. When lack of

This paper was prepared in celebration of Johan P. Olsen's 60th birthday. It owes a great deal not only to his 30 years of research writings, but also to my 30 years of personal collaboration and friendship with him. In a more mundane way, the research was supported by the Spencer Foundation. It appeared as a chapter in Morten Egeberg and Per Lægreid, eds., *Organizing Political Institutions: Essays for Johan P. Olsen*. Oslo: Scandinavian University Press, 1999.

integration provides an advantage, organizations are not integrated. The mechanisms, though often not specified explicitly, have been assumed to be elementary. Organizations are seen either as choosing forms strategically and rationally or as evolving them through some kind of competitive selection. In either case, the mechanisms are usually assumed to operate with sufficient precision in matching organizational forms to environmental necessities that differences in integration can be reliably predicted from differences in functional demands.

In recent treatments of organizational development, however, conceptions of organizations and organizing have changed from primary emphases on conceptions of coherent rationalization and hierarchical order to ideas of conflict and complexity; from primary attention to contingency theory and comparative statics to greater concern with history-dependent dynamics of change. Organizations are seen less as systems coordinated by structures of hierarchical authority in the service of unitary goals than as complex coalitions and networks coordinated by rules that have evolved through experience with conflict and confusion. They are seen less as products of deliberation than as products of learning and selection.

Learning and selection, in turn, are seen as having multiple local optima. Assumptions of historical efficiency have been questioned in the name of more path-dependent conceptions of organizational adaptation (March and Olsen 1989, 1998). As a result, organizational forms are pictured as less predictable from knowledge of current functional requirements or competitive advantages, and organization theory has become less a theory of comparative statics mediated by rational adjustments and more a theory of imperfect learning and history dependence.

In the past 30 years, these developments have been furthered particularly by the research of Johan P. Olsen. In his studies of organization theory (Cohen, March, and Olsen 1972; Olsen 1972; March and Olsen 1976; Brunsson and Olsen 1998), modern democracy (Olsen 1970, 1981, 1990, 1998; March and Olsen 1995), modern bureaucracy (LLægreid and Olsen 1978, 1984; Olsen 1983, 1986b), bureaucratic reform (Olsen 1976a, 1988, 1996b; March and Olsen 1983; Brunsson and Olsen 1993), institutional change (Olsen 1986a, 1992, 1998), and the development of the European Union (Olsen 1996a, 1997), Olsen has persistently called for theories of organization that are consistent with the complex empirical realities of change and yet clarify the processes underlying the contextual details of institutional history.

This paper is an attempt to move in the same direction. It suggests a small step toward understanding changes in institutional integration. More specifically (and narrowly), it explores learning-based transformations of networks that tie organizations together. Such an approach offers an alternative vision of why organizational forms change over time. It is by no means a comprehensive vision. Understanding the claims of functional necessity is fundamental to interpreting organizational forms. Nevertheless, a learning perspective on networks provides a supplement to attempts to explain differences among organizations or histories of integration exclusively in terms of processes by which history efficiently matches organizational forms to environmental or task requirements.

## The Brunsson and Olsen Challenge

In a 1998 essay (Brunsson and Olsen 1998), Nils Brunsson and Johan P. Olsen argue that research on organizations over the past few decades has dismantled the Weberian ideal of organization, an ideal built around emphases on central coordination, internal differentiation, social legitimacy of organizational authority, efficacious action, organizational malleability, and the rationalization of modern society. The institutions that are described by students of organizations have many Weberian features, but they also have properties that seem to vary significantly from the Weberian ideal.

Many of the specifics of this dismantling of Weber can be described as variations on a simple refrain: Things are not simple. The world of organization is more complicated than a Weberian description seems to suggest. Rejecting the notion that these complexities destroy coherence in organization studies, Brunsson and Olsen propose that recent research can be seen "as enriching the field of organizational research by expanding the range of variation in organizational phenomena and therefore opening up new and exciting directions" (p. 20). They describe the primary challenge for students of organization as being to understand the implications of complexity for organized, cooperative action, to comprehend what they call "the organizational mosaic of current societies" (p. 23). In that spirit, they write:

The challenge, then, is to understand the diversity, complexity and dynamics of contemporary "organizational society". We need better descriptions and analyses of the variety of ways in which individuals and organizations cooperate in a more or less purposeful, unitary, and sustained way. We need better interpretations and explanations of the dynamics of organizational change. Likewise, contemporary societies need normative theories and debates about the alternative ways in which cooperative efforts within or across national borders should be ordered. (p. 22)

They make this challenge more specific by proposing attention to the ways in which organized, cooperative action is achieved, regardless of whether it involves formal organizations. Thus, they call for thinking not only about hierarchies and markets, but also about relations among organizations of varying degrees of structure and permanence. They invite greater consciousness of the intricate interactions among formal organizations, their constituent parts, regulating agencies, standards, and social norms in producing organized social action. Finally, they argue that such attention to the structure of organized action needs to be paired with attention to its dynamics—with a focus on the ways in which organization is transformed through experience and through the diffusion of beliefs and practices.

As an illustration, they propose the nuances of an ancient organizational issue—integration vs. disintegration. They suggest exploring the reasons for variation in integration among organized systems. Why are some systems more integrated than others, and how are we to understand changes in integration? This paper is an attempt at a step in the direction to which Brunsson and Olsen have pointed.

## The Comparative Statics of Integration

Issues of integration and disintegration have been a focus for research by students of many kinds of organized systems. These include studies of political regimes, including many volumes on the rise and collapse of empires, for example, the Roman Empire (Gibbon 1862) and the Incan Empire (Patterson 1991); on the decline of feudalism and the rise of the nation-state (Eisenstadt and Rokkan 1973); on the rise and decline of colonial empires and the destruction of native orders (Madariaga 1947, 1948; James 1994); on the rise and decline of Eastern European communist regimes (West 1994; Fowkes 1995); and recently on the development of the European Union (Jacobsson 1993; Olsen 1997). Other political institutions that have been approached from the point of view of understanding their changing levels of integration include political parties, interest groups, and the nation-state. Beyond the political sector, we have studies of families, personalities, churches, markets, firms, electrical power grids, and neural networks.

## Studies of Integration

Empirical studies of integration and disintegration have generally been highly concrete studies of specific historical contexts, intended to describe and interpret history rather than contribute to or draw from more general theoretical knowledge. They have been relatively rich in detailed contextual information, and relatively modest in theoretical pretensions. The theoretical traditions involved in considering issues of institutional integration are, for the most part, somewhat removed from those studies, and include things as heterogeneous as systems theory, network theory, organization theory, theories of diffusion and institutionalization, and theories of social change.

Nevertheless, it is possible to identify some main theoretical questions that have guided research in the area. The dominant perspectives are, for the most part, variations of comparative statics, efforts to identify the different external conditions that are associated with different levels of integration. Underlying most of these perspectives is an assumption that organizational forms will come to fit environmental imperatives. In some cases, the idea is basically a selection, efficient history conception. In this conception, institutions come to match their environments (i.e., find optimal fits). Institutions change because their environments change. The details of the particular mechanisms by which this happens are treated as being relatively unimportant since competitive selection assures a fit. In other cases, the idea is based on a conception of rational institutions. Institutions are seen as rational actors that seek to maximize their well-being. Their practices, forms, and procedures are chosen so as to make them do better. This leads them to adopt the best practices for their conditions.

In this spirit, contemporary discussions of institutional integration proceed by first specifying changes in the environment and then deriving some implications for short-run adaptations of institutions. In recent years, that has meant identifying changes in world economic conditions, in particular the development of global markets with changes in the flows of capital and rapidly diffused economic turbulence. It has also meant noting the development of information technology with its resulting increase in the permeability of national and institutional boundaries; the increased role of knowledge in institutional survival; the resurgence of deep identity-based solidarities of religion and ethnicity. Change appears to be accelerating and becoming more interconnected across institutions and across countries.

There is little agreement, however, on the effects that such environmental changes have had or will have for the integration of specific institutions. For example, it seems plausible to suggest that information technology will have an impact on organizational forms of the future, but speculations based on that premise exhibit little agreement on the precise effect. Does Royal Dutch Shell or the European system of nation-states or the Chinese state become more or less integrated as a result of the new technology? Indeed, there is little agreement on what we mean by integration or how we might think about the transformation of institutional integration in response to environmental change, or more generally.

## Processes of Integration

The elementary notion underlying talk of integration is a straightforward one. We imagine a world consisting of a set of parts. At the least, integration is gauged by some measure of the density, intensity, and character of the relations among the elements of that set. The literature recognizes three primary criteria for recognizing integration. The first is consistency. The idea is that various actions and beliefs fit together to make sense. They are coordinated or coherent from the point of view of some common objective. The second criterion for integration recognized by the literature is interdependence. In these terms, a system is described not by a set of relations among individuals or tasks, but by the linkages among the variables of a causal system. Integration is associated with relatively small random elements and relatively large off-diagonal elements in the matrix of coefficients. The third criterion for integration in the literature is structural connectedness. This is the criterion associated with sociometric or network visions of integration. It depends on defining a relation existing between two elements of the basic set of parts (i.e., two individuals, two firms, two nations). The number and pattern of such relations can be characterized by a variety of statistics, some of which might plausibly be defined as integration.

These three criteria, of course, yield different results. For example, most markets are more clearly integrated when considered from a connectedness criterion than from a consistency criterion. Moreover, although the concept of integration invites thinking of a single criterion that locates a particular institution on an integration/disintegration continuum, the pattern of integration may be more significant than any overall index. For example, one might imagine measuring integration by the average likelihood of a link between a pair of nodes drawn from the universe under consideration. Such a measure, however, would overlook differences between systems characterized by weak but universal connections, on the one hand, and systems divided into distinct subgroups with tight connections within each group and no connections across groups, on the other.

These difficulties in finding a consensual definition of integration may, however, be less important than trying to go beneath the highly concrete details of specific historical transformations to understand more generally how a system might become more or less integrated over time. Why do we observe the collapse of an integrated set of institutions under some conditions, the rise of an integrated system under other conditions? What are the fundamental processes that produce the variations in integration that we observe, variations across institutions at a specific time and variations across time in a particular institution?

## Puzzles of Integration

The historical record of system integration is filled with puzzles. Systems that appear well integrated and stable sometimes unpredictably collapse or drift into disintegration. Systems that appear rather disintegrated sometimes unpredictably become integrated. Many of the great classics of historical research seek to understand such events (e.g., Gibbon 1862). The search for a plausible explanation of integration and disintegration in social systems may, of course, be forlorn. There is no guarantee that any historical observations will be adequate to identify the mechanisms that produce the historical paths we experience. Nevertheless, students of social integration have a long record of trying to specify those mechanisms. Their search has led them primarily to ideas that link changes in social systems to changes in opportunities or necessities for competitive advantage, for example, those produced by changes in demographics or technologies. Insofar as integration is defined in terms of connectedness, for example, changing technologies of travel, communication, and exchange seem necessarily to have implications for the integration of social systems.

The adaptation of organizations to their environments is, however, not routine. It requires internal organizational processes that may not only be slow or unreliable, but may also introduce systematic "errors" that can be quite large. Among the processes that seem likely to be implicated are processes by which knowledge is developed, certified, and shared (Barth 1990), processes by which rules, forms, standards, and practices change (Brunsson 1998), processes by which solidarities grow and decline (Tilly 1975), and processes by which beliefs in history are socially constructed (Olsen 1976b; March, Sproull, and Tamuz 1991). Any comprehensive treatment of integration in institutions will probably have to attend to all of these processes.

### A LEARNING PERSPECTIVE

One obvious process of interest to students of integration is that of learning. Social institutions learn from their own experiences, and such learning is the focus of many of the things that are written about organizational change. Organizations act, observe the apparent consequences of their actions, and revise their propensities to act in the future in such a way as to make future actions more consistent with what might have been more sensible in the past (March and Olsen 1975). Such experiential learning has been used to describe some features of organizational change, as well as the difficulties of such change (Olsen and Peters 1996).

Institutions also learn from what is known elsewhere. Knowledge, information, practices, and beliefs that are known in one place are transferred to another place. Indeed, most of what we ordinarily describe as "learning," for example, through education, consists in such diffusion. Thinking about integration clearly involves thinking about the ways ideas, practices, beliefs, rules, and information move within populations of individuals, groups, organizations, nations, and societies.

## Integration as a Product of Learning through Diffusion

Preferences, identities, and rules diffuse among institutions. Organizational forms and practices, as well as beliefs, spread from one site to another. When preferences, identities, practices, and rules diffuse, it becomes more likely that activities in one part of the world will be consistent with activities in other parts. Diffusion is notoriously subject to limits on its capabilities for achieving institutional integration, but it is a major instrument of the spread of information, knowledge, practices, beliefs, and policies.

Students of the spread of things in, and among, organizations, like students of diffusion and epidemiology more generally, distinguish between two broad kinds of diffusion processes (Lave and March 1975; DiMaggio and Powell 1983). The first process involves the spread of something from a single source to possible "users." The standard metaphor is that of a radio broadcast. The rate and pattern of diffusion depends on the connection of potential users to a particular broadcast source. The second process involves the spread of something from one user to another. The standard metaphor is that of word-of-mouth rumor transmission. In practice, of course, most diffusion involves a mix of contact with sources outside the target population and within the population. A typical structure is one in which some fraction of a population is exposed to external sources and provides the initial impetus for spread within a population (Coleman, Katz, and Menzel 1957).

Classical theories of diffusion seem ill-suited to studies of organizational or institutional development (Brunsson 1998). In particular, they have, for the most part, been built on two critical assumptions that are questionable (Bailey 1975). The first is the assumption of reproductive reliability. Objects of diffusion (information, ideas, technologies) are assumed to spread through a population without themselves being changed. The second is the assumption of network exogeneity. The relationships that affect the process of diffusion are assumed to be unaffected by it.

The assumptions are useful, frequently valid, but ultimately problematic. The assumption of reliable reproduction is sometimes approximately fulfilled by virtue of some conspicuous properties of the diffusion process. For example, the diffusion of knowledge through education involves extensive efforts to assure reliable cloning of knowledge as it passes from one person to another. When knowledge is transferred from a teacher to a student, a major part of the process is establishing that what the student knows is an accurate reproduction of what the teacher knows. Similarly, in many instances of information diffusion (for example, in exchanges between air traffic controllers and pilots), the sender and receiver of information ensure the reliability of the process by repeating the signal as heard or seen; and elaborate training procedures are dedicated to the same end.

In most cases of interest to students of organization, however, diffusion processes do not reproduce reliably. The knowledge diffused from one person to another or from one organization to another is different from the knowledge received and transmitted to another. Many of the problems in reproductive reliability are considered in treatments of the "implementation" of new technologies, policies, or reforms (Pressman and Wildavsky 1973; Bardach 1977; Abrahamson 1991; Olsen and Peters 1996; Brunsson and Olsen 1993). The tendency for organizations to change the meaning of new innovations in the course of adopting or implementing them has been well documented (Westphal, Gulati, and Shortell 1997; Czarniawska and Joerges 1998).

New innovations are transformed, in part, because of conflict of interest between those introducing the innovations and those using them (Mayntz 1979). They are transformed, in part, because of disparities in the knowledge between those transferring the innovation and those copying it (Cohen and Levinthal 1990). They are transformed because they have been made ambiguous in order to facilitate adoption (Baier, March, and Sætren 1986). They are transformed by the patterns of discourse that they stimulate or accompany (Brunsson 1998).

The spread of ideational impulses through organizations may be as complex as free associations in the mind. The spread of technologies through a population of organizations may be as complex as the contexts into which they are introduced. At the very least, knowledge as it is reproduced in an organization is a joint product of the knowledge that is diffused and the knowledge that is already held. These problems of recombination suggest an analogy between diffusion processes and processes of sexual reproduction which, while (almost) precisely reproducing the genetic code, simultaneously produce an extraordinarily rich variety of combinations. The analogy is misleading in several ways, but it is instructive in that it calls attention to the difficulty of dealing with unreliable reproductive processes without a precise theory of the transformations involved.

Network exogeneity is similarly doubtful, but it has attracted less attention from students of organizational learning. Many simple models of diffusion make an assumption of random exposure, presuming that contacts between sources and recipients are essentially chance-like. It is obvious that such assumptions do not fit most situations of diffusion in social systems. The rates and patterns of diffusion within and among social systems depend on the patterns of linkages within the populations and on propensities to utilize them. This pattern is what is normally described as the network structure of a system.

A network in these terms is a collection of points (individuals, organizations, or parts of organizations) connected by relations. The relations are usually defined in terms of connections between pairs of individuals such as "is a friend of," "regularly communicates with," "reports to," or other similar things, or connections between pairs of organizations such as "belongs to the same association," "has overlapping board membership with," or "does business with," or other similar things. The resulting system is frequently described in terms of a square matrix in which the off-diagonal entries reflect the existence or strength of links among pairs.

In most treatments of diffusion, the network structure is taken as given. Most studies assume that networks are stable, or if they change that they change as a result of exogenous forces. Recent empirical work on organizational networks, for example, has emphasized developing a taxonomy of measures on contact matrices and associating features of the structure or position in the structure with features of the spread of knowledge, information, practices, or beliefs. Recent theoretical work on networks has sought to extend earlier ideas about stable and complete network structures. Ideas that have grown out of, but have developed considerably beyond, graph-theoretic elaborations of the early balance notions of Heider (1958) and others (Flament 1963).

Insofar as it is concerned with variations in networks, most of the literature on organizational networks is, broadly speaking, "functional" in the sense that it sees networks as arising, growing, and collapsing in response to some exogenous functional advantage or disadvantage that particular structures provide. Thus, hierarchical networks are usually explained by citing advantages that they offer in a competitive environment. Within such a functional, comparative statics approach, networks are explained by rationalizing them, by seeing them as optimal (in some sense) solutions to some kind of joint maximization problem. Networks are seen as moving inexorably to forms dictated by an exogenous environment and as changing primarily in response to changes in that environment.

This assumption of network exogeneity and rationalization, like the assumption of reproductive reliability, is subject to considerable question. It seems clear that networks change endogenously as well as exogenously. A network structure simultaneously affects the spread of things and is affected by them. Experience within a network is both determined by the network that exists and serves to change that network. Consciousness of this endogeneity of network development is sustained in part by contemporary enthusiasms for coevolution (Giddens 1991; Baum and Singh 1994).

The fundamental coevolutionary idea is that at the same time that structures shape experience, experience also shapes structures. Social structures are nourished or decayed by experience with their use. Ideas about the coevolution of networks and their environments can be seen in some recent efforts to understand the ebb and flow of political or economic integration (for example, the nation-state and globalization of economic markets) and in efforts to understand how the use of contacts in a population of organizations affects the structure of contacts.

## Network Development through Experiential Learning

A conception of integration as a product of diffusion through networks is a learning conception in two senses. First, insofar as theories of learning emphasize learning from others, they are essentially indistinguishable from diffusion theories. It is largely through diffusion, imitation, and appropriation from others that knowledge, practices, ideas, preferences, identities, and rules spread within a population and create a basis for integration. The system consequences of learning from others depend on network structures. Second, the network structures of diffusion are themselves modified by experience. Links in a network are the consequence of learning from past experience with them. Links that are, in some sense, rewarding tend to be strengthened. Links that are unrewarding atrophy. From this perspective, networks that contribute to "integration" are seen as not so much imposed by plan as they are developed through experience.

A social network is normally seen as a collection of bilateral relations that collectively arrange themselves in ways that provide much of the structure to organized life. In particular, the bilateral relations may be connected so as to produce segregated groups, isolated nodes, dense or sparse connectivity, and a variety of other features well known to the literature on networks (Marsden 1982; Håkansson 1987; Knoke 1990; Axelsson and Easton 1992; Powell and Smith-Doerr 1994). We ask whether it is possible to imagine a process by which these connections change, when an existing link will be strengthened or weakened.

There are several ideas about understanding such changes. For example, it is possible to see changes as making a structure more coherent through filling "holes" in the structure (Burt 1983) or eliminating inconsistencies (Flament 1963). The strategy is one of identifying some equilibrium states and predicting that structures will move from disequilibria toward equilibria. It is a strategy that has led to indispensable contributions for understanding networks as well as for understanding institutions more generally (North 1981, 1990).

A learning conception of network development is not inconsistent with such approaches; but it is somewhat more oriented to specifying the processes of change and deriving the outcomes from the processes, rather than from an assumed structural equilibrium. The idea is that each node in a network learns locally from local experience, thereby adjusting the local linkages. The aggregate properties of the evolution of a network are produced by the effects of local learning at the various nodes, rather than any global rationality—either deliberate or evolved. Local learning depends on local judgments about the "success" or "failure" of experience with particular local links.

The primary engine of this learning-based development of structure is what might be called the basic mutual learning multiplier. There is a strong positive feedback loop by which jointly favorable experiences lead to further jointly favorable experiences, and jointly unfavorable experiences lead to further jointly unfavorable experiences. Each successful experience with a link increases the likelihood of a subsequent successful experience, and each unsuccessful experience increases the likelihood of a subsequent unsuccessful experience. The idea is a variation of a very general feature of positive feedback loops in social relations (Homans 1950, 1961; Simon 1957).

A key feature of any such conception is the idea of "success." There are numerous possible definitions of success in experience with linkages in a network. Many of those definitions depend on characterizing an outcome that follows from the utilization of a link. For example, utilization of a business partnership or military alliance might lead to favorable performance outcomes, or it might not. Linkages that result in favorable outcomes would be reinforced.

The strategy here is somewhat different. Suppose that every utilization of a bilateral link involves a double veto in the sense that it requires both an initiation on the part of one member of a pair and an acceptance by the other. If either is absent, the linkage fails. Then the jointly successful result occurs only when there is both an initiation and an acceptance. When such a jointly successful event occurs, the likelihood of future initiations by the same initiator toward the same target, as well as the likelihood of acceptances of those initiations, increases. On the other hand, when no initiation is made, or when an initiation is not accepted, the likelihood of each decreases. Thus, we imagine a pattern of initiations followed by acceptances or rejections that slowly build networks linking nodes that are mutually attracted and eliminate links between those not mutually attracted in a world in which the attractions themselves are changing as a result of experience.

## A LITTLE MODEL

To illustrate the effects of the mutual learning multiplier in a social network setting, we can model a network that changes as a result of learning. The model is conservative with respect to the classical assumptions of diffusion models. It retains the assumption of reproductive reliability while relaxing the assumption of network exogeneity.

The model focuses on paths of diffusion. A diffusion path is a connected sequence of transfers. It plays somewhat the same role in theories of diffusion that genealogical paths play in theories of reproductive inheritance. In this case, however, we assume that each location on a path strictly reproduces the object of diffusion received from a prior node. We consider a population of "nodes" and a sequence of paths of diffusion through that population by which an object of diffusion is spread.[1]

Each effort to introduce a new object of diffusion generates a sequence of paths. Each path begins with some node having contact with the outside world. The spread of an object of diffusion to each subsequent node on a path requires an "initiation" by one node directed to another and an "acceptance" by that other. The target of an initiation made by any particular node is a node drawn from the population of other nodes. The probability of a particular node choosing any particular other node is a changing function of experience. Initially, all other nodes are equally likely to be chosen. The initiation has a changing probability of being accepted. Initially this probability is the same for all targets and all initiators in the population. If an initiation is accepted, then the path is extended to the new node, and the process is repeated. A path ends when a transfer attempt is rejected or when it reaches a maximum length.

Thus, each path can be described as a sequence of nodes. The same node may appear more than once in a path, but not consecutively (i.e., we exclude a step in a path in which node i passes an object of diffusion to itself directly, but we do not exclude a path that goes from i to j and back to i). Each introduction of a particular object of diffusion has a fixed number of original initiators (nodes connected to the outside), each initiator initiates a fixed number of paths, and all paths have the same upper limit in length. When all of the paths for one introduction have been completed, a new introduction is begun. The model explores what happens to the path structure and the spread of objects of diffusion over a sequence of successive introductions as experiences with attempts to transfer objects of diffusion lead to modification in the network structure. The structure of the network emerges from the history of these paths.

The main features of the model revolve around two critical probabilities involved in the extension of paths of diffusion: (1) The probability, $p_{i,j,t}$, that node i, having received an object of diffusion, will initiate a transfer attempt to individual j at time t. Unless the path has already attained the maximum length, every receipt of an object of diffusion leads to an attempt to extend the path and transfer the object to some other node. The probability that a particular i will direct that attempt to a particular j varies from one i,j pair to another and changes over time in response to experience. The sum of the probabilities over all j for each i is 1. (2) The probability, $r_{i,j,t}$ that node j will accept an initiation from node i if it occurs at time t. This probability varies from one i,j pair to another and changes over time in response to experience.

In particular, these two probabilities are shaped by realized experience with transfer attempts. If an initiation is attempted and accepted, it increases the likelihood of such an initiation and such an acceptance in the future. On the other hand, If an initiation is made and not accepted, it decreases the likelihood of such an initiation or such an acceptance in the future.[2] In both cases, the new likelihood is a mix between the old likelihood and L(L < 1) in the case of a successful transfer and $(1-L)$ in the case of an unsuccessful initiation. Thus, L defines the learning limits for success directly and for failure indirectly. The rate of learning after a success is controlled by a parameter **a1**, the weight on L in a mix with the previous probability that defines the new probability. The rate of learning after a rejected initiation is controlled by a similar parameter **a2**, the weight on $(1-L)$ in a mix with the previous probability. Since the sum of the $p_{i,j,t}$, over i, must equal 1, any change in a particular $p_{i,j,t}$, necessitates a subsequent normalizing change in the probabilities. Those changes are assumed to maintain the proportional relations among the probabilities.

Learning processes often appear to be not unlike this in structure, particularly when they involve mutual learning (the learned adjustment of two learners to each other) or the simultaneous learning of what to do and how to do it well. As is well known, the chances of being rewarded for doing something in these situations are likely to increase with the frequency of doing it. The joint effect is to reduce the occurrence of probabilities that are far from the learning limits. The present model explores that phenomenon in the context of network development.

## RESULTS

Through monte carlo simulations, the model generates a set of paths for objects of diffusion, thus also both patterns of diffusion and network structures. The diffusion patterns and the network structures change over time. The changes are produced by elementary experiential learning and by the probabilistic structure of the model, not by any exogenous forces. Thus, they provide a minor existence proof for the proposition that substantial variation in network integration can be produced without variation in functional necessity.

The following general characteristics of the process are revealed by the model:

1. The path histories observed within the model produce substantial fluctuation in the "integration" of the system from replication to replication and from trial to trial. The same environment may produce quite different networks. And without any exogenous shocks, a network system moves rather naturally through quite different integration patterns.

2. Histories of paths show that paths tend to become semi-stable. That is, each initiator (i.e., node with contact outside) develops a path of diffusion that connects certain nodes in the system. Paths grow by finding willing partners and reinforcing both the finding and the willingness, thus beginning a cycle of positive feedback. Subject to some probabilistic variation, each node on a path learns to attempt to pass knowledge to a small set of other nodes (quite often only one) that will accept it and those nodes, in turn, learn to accept it. These paths, once stabilized, are used repeatedly. Over time, each initiator strengthens connections to a particular subset of nodes and weakens connections to others.

3. The path structure is not completely stable. There is some chance that a link in a path will break. When that happens, an initiator looks for a new partner, a process that is chancy since most potential partners have had either no experience or bad experience with the initiator. After a time, the broken path may reconnect to some fragment of an earlier one, leading to some irregular fluctuations of long and short paths. These irregular fluctuations can produce occasional major transformations by which parts of the system move from being very central to being very peripheral.

4. The length of each path initiated by an individual initiator can vary from a length of 1 to a length as long as is allowed. At one extreme, all paths are of length 1, and there is no diffusion to the rest of the population. At the other extreme, all paths are as long as is allowed. In the latter case, paths may vary in the degree of their "diffusion efficiency" (i.e., the number of distinct individuals represented on the path divided by the length of the path).

5. The ease of establishing paths and maintaining them and the spread of the object of diffusion through the population of nodes depend on the learning parameters, but not (in the long run) on the initial value (common to all $j,i$ pairs) of $r_{j,i,0}$. Generally, fast learning from success and slow learning from failure lead to longer paths on average, a higher fraction of the population receiving the initiation, a lower rejection rate for initiation attempts that are actually made, and a higher variance over $i$ of $p_{i,j,t}$, and over $j$ of $r_{j,i,t}$, than do slower learning from success and faster learning from failure.

6. When learning is slow, or when learning from failures is substantially faster than learning from success, the process leads to gradual disintegration in the sense that the fraction of the population receiving a particular object of diffusion decreases over successive introductions, and the likelihood of an initiation meeting with acceptance declines.

7. Learning parameters that lead to an increase in integration in the short run often lead to a decline later. If we begin with an undifferentiated population (as above), the proportion of the populations obtaining whatever objects of diffusion have been introduced first increases and then gradually decreases. The proportion of the population that is isolated decreases at first, then gradually increases over time.

A representative sample of these basic results is displayed in Figure 1. None of the results is surprising, and their connections to features of the model are transparent. If there is significance in the results, it lies in demonstrating how some very simple learning processes can produce some relatively striking integration results. The models suggests some reasons from suspecting that in this domain as in many others that have been explored by scholars who emphasize institutions (e.g. Olsen 1992), the historical development of social integration and disintegration may not be completely understandable as a consequence of adaptation to environmental change, but may be sensitive to intra-institutional phenomena as well.

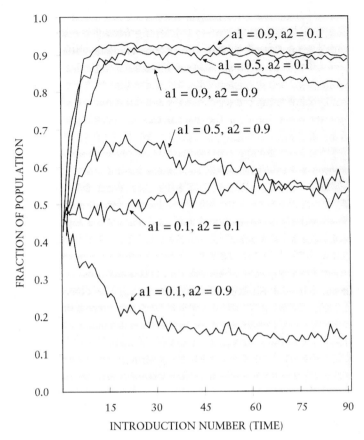

FIGURE I    Fraction of population receiving an object of diffusion over time (introduction number) for several values of **a1** and **a2** ($r_{i,j,0}$ = 0.5; L = 0.95; number of nodes = 100, number of initiators = 10, number of paths per initiator each introduction = 5, maximum path length = 10).


## LEARNING AND INTEGRATION

Suppose we measure system integration by a network's effectiveness in diffusing new objects of diffusion through the population. The model sketched above tells a simple story about how a system that initially is partly integrated develops over time in a predictable way. Low levels of integration are associated with two features of the network liking participants: First, the pairwise likelihoods of initiating diffusion attempts and accepting them tend to be relatively low. Second, the likelihoods tend to be undifferentiated (i.e., they have small variability across pairs of nodes).

Beginning with an undifferentiated, loosely linked but generally receptive population, a learning process of the sort described here systematically
changes both features. If learning from successes is slow and learning from
failures is fast, the system gradually becomes less integrated, though some
small clusters of linkages can exist. Initiators keep looking, with decreasing
success, for nodes that will accept their initiations. Local learning reduces
linkages and diffusion.

On the other hand, if the parameters for learning associated with success are
large enough, the system becomes more integrated in the sense that more linkages are formed and an object of diffusion spreads to more nodes. At the same
time, the system becomes more differentiated as some links are strengthened and
others are weakened. More and more initiation attempts are successful because
they are directed at nodes that have previously responded favorably, and parts
of the population become cut off from flows of objects of diffusion. This differentiation effect limits the increase in integration over time and can result in
such a focusing of the network that it actually produces a decline (i.e., a decline
in the number of nodes receiving the object of diffusion). Learning transforms
weak ties either into very strong ties or into even weaker ties, and thereby slows
or reverses the development of integration.

Thus, institutional integration can be furthered by experiential learning as
networks transform themselves through the experience of being used. If a pairwise transfer in a network increases the tightness of the link, networks develop.
However, the same learning processes that build networks can also lead to their
destruction or crippling. This can happen in two ways. First, if the system learns
more rapidly from failures than from successes, it occurs immediately. Learning
produces a withering of the network structure that previously existed. Second, if
the system learns more rapidly from successes than from failures, it occurs after
a period of increasing integration. Learning of the kind described here tends to
extend and strengthen a network, but it also tends to focus a network so that a
small number of nodes becomes more and more tightly connected to each other
and less and less connected to others. This process of focusing makes some links
easier and stronger, but it reduces system capabilities for spreading objects of
diffusion broadly through the population.

Network development (in the model) tends to convert the population into
segregated groups, each group consisting of nodes that receive all objects of
diffusion that are introduced into the system (provided their initiator receives
them). Quite frequently, however, many of these "groups" contain only one node.
They are isolates and receive objects of diffusion only if they are connected to

NETWORK DYNAMICS OF INSTITUTIONAL INTEGRATION          291

an outside source. If the learning limits are close to 1 and 0, this process in the long run tends to produce a quite stable segregated system. Lower learning limits introduce restrictions on the effectiveness of learning that make the system less stable and the groups less segregated.

Networks that grow in roughly this way from local feedback will evolve in an understandable way, but there is no assurance that the networks that develop will satisfy any particular external optimality requirements. On the contrary, the model suggests that powerful learning mechanisms may make optimal integration relatively difficult to achieve, if optimality requires persistent experimentation both by initiators looking for possible new places to which to send knowledge and by receivers looking for possible new places from which to gain knowledge. Since it is intermediate probabilities that provide experimentation, learning processes of this kind are at risk of sacrificing long-run viability for short-run efficiency. Even if returns realized from connections between pairs were different for different pairs, and the network developed in response to such feedback to favor links that provided higher returns, the learning process would not assure favorable connections would be found. It would be quite possible for the discovery of favorable links to be quite haphazard and incomplete, dominated by the historical path of learning.

The results here show, as might be expected, that path development is dependent on the learning rates (**a1** and **a2**), but not (in the long run) on the initial level of shared propensities to respond favorably to initiations. In general, although there are some interactions, higher values for **a1** and lower values for **a2** produce greater integration (in the sense of a more inclusive spread of the object of diffusion). Along the way, higher values for **a1** and lower values for **a2** also produce greater differentiation in the probabilities of initiating and accepting an initiation, that is, greater differentiation in the network. Collections of learners (nodes) that learn faster from local successes than from local failures would be likely to develop more elaborate network structures more quickly than would those who learn faster from failures than from successes, but might ultimately become vulnerable to a breakdown of integration resulting from a focusing of networks on segregated groups.

Those effects invite speculation about what might affect the learning parameters. In general, as we have seen, the differences between parameters that lead to increased integration and those that lead to decreased integration are not simply differences in learning rates. It is not true that rapid learning leads to integration and slow learning leads to disintegration, or vice versa. Slow local learning leads to only small changes in integration or disintegration. Fast local learning leads to relatively rapid and substantial changes, but those changes sometimes result in increases in system integration and sometimes result in decreases. Understanding the ways attributes of the nodes affect changes in integration, therefore, does not involve understanding why some nodes learn more rapidly than others as much as it does understanding why there are differences in the relative rate of learning after success and failure. What makes local learning relatively rapid after success and relatively slow after failure?

Perhaps the most obvious speculation is that expectations might affect learning rate. What is less obvious is how expectations shape the learning rate. There are two plausible scenarios. On the one hand, perhaps expectations of failure make it harder to observe successes and therefore easier to interpret events that are successes as failures. Similarly, perhaps expectations of success make it harder to observe failures and therefore easier to interpret events that are failures as successes. These biases in interpretation are equivalent to biases in learning rates since they result, in the first instance, in applying the failure learning rate more often than is appropriate and, in the second instance, in applying the success learning rate more often than is appropriate. Such speculations would suggest that social networks would become integrated through learning more rapidly when participants are relatively optimistic about local network linkages than when they are relatively pessimistic.

On the other hand, perhaps expectations of failure would make success a greater surprise than failure and therefore a more significant learning event. Similarly, perhaps expectations of success would make failure a more significant learning event. Expectations are themselves learned, so we might speculate that experiences of success would encourage expectations of success, and thus a discounting of the learning rate from success and an augmentation of the learning rate from failure. Experiences of failure would encourage expectations of failure, and thus encourage a discounting of the learning rate from failure and an augmentation of the learning rate from success. Such speculations would suggest that social networks would become more rapidly integrated through learning when participants are relatively pessimistic about local network linkages than when they are optimistic, and that they would be relatively pessimistic when they have had poor experiences in the past.

There is no easy way to choose between the two sets of speculations, and others could undoubtedly be added. The intent here is not to settle any argument between these two ideas or to provide additional ideas, but simply to observe that the present analysis suggests that a local learning perspective on network development not only casts some possible light on the story of integration, but also provides a reason for focusing less on institutional rates of learning generally than on the relative rates of learning after success and failure.

## CONCLUSION

The present analysis ties institutional integration to network structure, where a network is defined in terms of two probabilities associated with a pair of nodes (individuals, groups, organizations, nations): the probability of initiating a contact and the probability that such an initiation will be accepted. It is assumed that such networks change by changing the two probabilities. Changes in the two probabilities undoubtedly will reflect calculation of expected returns that are omitted in the present model, but they also reflect local learning from experience. The latter has been examined here.

The process specified here is very general, as are the outcomes. Local learning is a two-edged sword for integration. By strengthening links that are used, learning leads to differentiation in a population of pairs. Over time, the variances of the two probabilities across the population of pairs increase as the probabilities connected to each pair move toward either the upper or lower learning limit. By reinforcing links that have experienced successful transfers and extinguishing those that have failed to make a connection, learning sorts nodes into groups. It strengthens the ties within groups and weakens the ties between groups. As a result, it can ultimately interfere with integration in the population as a whole, even while strengthening the internal integration of subgroups.

The model explored here is a very limited one, but the basic phenomenon is not. One of the major concerns of students of European integration, for example, has been to understand how opportunities for the creation of cross-national networks and experience in initiating and accepting or rejecting transfers within the networks will affect political, social, and economic integration (Olsen 1992, 1996a, 1997). Simple linear predictions of an increasing integration of European social systems seem not to describe what has happened or is likely to happen in the future. In particular, predicting the future of group solidarities within a union of states has seemed to require a different set of mechanisms from those used in predicting the development of European integration. Although it would be an heroic overstatement to suggest that a local learning perspective on network development provides overpowering insight into such complex problems, it may perhaps offer a small clue to the possibility that the same local learning mechanisms that can produce relatively rapid increases in integration can also produce a slowdown or decrease in integration.

## NOTES

1. The discussion below adopts the convention of talking about the spread of "objects of diffusion" among "nodes" in order to keep the language general. The "nodes" could be individuals, or organizations or nations. The "objects of diffusion" could be anything (e.g., information, knowledge, beliefs, rules, practices, standards) that involves an initiation and the acceptance of an initiation.

2. Note that an alternative assumption might be that the rejection of a transfer initiation by the intended node increases the propensity to accept a later one.

## REFERENCES

Abrahamson, E. 1991. "Managerial Fads and Fashions: The Diffusion and Rejection of Innovations." *Academy of Management Review* 16: 586–612.

Axelsson, B. and G. Easton (eds.). 1992. *Industrial Networks: A New View of Reality.* London: Routledge.

Baier, V. E., J. G. March and H. Sætren. 1986. "Implementation and Ambiguity." *Scandinavian Journal of Management Studies* 2: 197–212.

Bailey, N. T. J. 1975. *The Mathematical Theory of Infectious Diseases.* New York: Hafner Press.

Bardach, E. 1977. *The Implementation Game.* Cambridge, MA: MIT Press.

Barth, F. 1990. "The Guru and the Conjurer: Transactions in Knowledge and the Shaping of Culture in Southeast Asia and Melanesia." *Man 25:* 640–653.

Baum, J. and J. Singh (eds.). 1994. *The Evolutionary Dynamics of Organizations.* New York: Oxford University Press.

Brunsson, N. 1998. "Homogeneity and Heterogeneity in Organizational Forms as the Result of Cropping-up Processes," in N. Brunsson and J. P. Olsen (eds.): *Organizing Organizations.* Bergen: Fagbokforlaget.

Brunsson, N. and J. P. Olsen, 1993. *The Reforming Organization.* London: Routledge.

Brunsson, N. and J. P. Olsen. 1998. "Organization Theory: Thirty Years of Dismantling, and Then . . . ?" in N. Brunsson and J. P. Olsen (eds.): *Organizing Organizations,* pp. 13–43. Bergen: Fagbokforlaget.

Burt, R. S. 1983. *Applied Network Analysts.* Beverly Hills, CA: Sage.

Cohen, M. D., J. G. March and J. P. Olsen. 1972. "A Garbage Can Model of Organizational Choice." *Administrative Science Quarterly* 17: 1–25.

Cohen, W. M. and D. A. Levinthal. 1990. "Absorptive Capacity: A New Perspective on Learning and Innovation." *Administrative Science Quarterly* 15: 128–152.

Coleman, J. S., E. Katz and H. Menzel. 1957. "The Diffusion of an Innovation among Physicians." *Sociometry* 20: 253–270.

Czarniawska, B, and B. Joerges. 1998. "Winds of Organizational Change: How Ideas Translate into Objects and Actions," in N. Brunsson and J. P. Olsen (eds.): *Organizing Organizations.* Bergen: Fagbokforlaget.

DiMaggio, P. J. and W. W. Powell. 1983. "The Iron Cage Revisited: Institutional Isomorphism and Collective Rationality in Organizational Fields." *American Sociological Review 48:* 147–160.

Eisenstadt. S. N. and S. Rokkan (eds.). 1973. *Building States and Nations,* Vols. 1 and 2. Beverly Hills, CA: Sage.

Flament, C. 1963. *Applications of Graph Theory to Group Structure.* Englewood Cliffs, NJ: Prentice-Hall.

Fowkes, B. 1995. *The Rise and Fall of Communism in Eastern Europe.* 2nd ed. Basingstoke, Hampshire: Macmillan Press.

Gibbon, E. 1862. *The History of the Decline and Fall of the Roman Empire.* London: J. Murray.

Giddens, A. 1991. *The Consequences of Modernity.* Oxford: Polity Press.

Håkansson, H. 1987. *Industrial Technological Development: A Network Approach.* London: Croon Helm.

Heider, F. 1958. *The Psychology of Interpersonal Relations.* New York: Wiley.

Homans, G. C. 1950. *The Human Group.* New York: Harcourt, Brace.

Homans, G. C. 1961. *Social Behavior: Its Elementary Forms.* New York: Harcourt Brace and World.

Jacobsson, B. 1993. "Europeisering av forvaltningen." *Statsvetenskaplig Tidsskrift 96:* 113–137.

James, L. 1994. *The Rise and Fall of the British Empire.* London: Little, Brown.

Knoke, D. 1990. *Political Networks: The Structural Perspective.* New York: Cambridge University Press.

Lægreid, P. and J. P. Olsen. 1978. *Byråkrati og Beslutninger.* Bergen: Universitetsforlaget.

Lægreid, P. and J. P. Olsen. 1984. "Top Civil Servants in Norway: Key Players on Different Teams," in E. N. Suleiman (ed.): *Bureaucrats and Policy Making.* New York: Holmes and Meter.

Lave, C. A. and J. G. March. 1975. *An Introduction to Models in the Social Sciences.* New York: Harper and Row.

Madariaga, S. 1947. *The Rise of the Spanish Empire.* London: Hollis and Carter.

Madariaga, S. 1948. *The Fall of the Spanish Empire.* New York: Macmillan.

March, J. G. and J. P. Olsen. 1975. "The Uncertainty of the Past: Organizational Learning under Ambiguity." *European Journal of Political Research 3:* 147–171.

March, J. G. and J. P. Olsen. 1976. *Ambiguity and Choice in Organizations.* Bergen: Universitetsforlaget.

March, J. G. and J. P. Olsen. 1983. "Organizing Political Life: What Administrative Reorganization Tells Us About Government." *American Political Science Review 77:* 281–297.

March, J. G. and J. P. Olsen. 1989. *Rediscovering Institutions: The Organizational Basis of Politics.* New York: Free Press/Macmillan.

March, J. G. and J. P. Olsen. 1995. *Democratic Governance.* New York: Free Press.

March, J. G. and J. P. Olsen. 1998. "The Institutional Dynamics of International Political Orders." *International Organization 52:* 943–969.

March, J. G., L. S. Sproull, and M. Tamuz. 1991. "Learning from Samples of One or Fewer." *Organization Science 2:* 1–13.

Marsden, P. V. 1982. *Social Structure and Network Analysis.* Beverly Hills, CA: Sage.

Mayntz, R. 1979. "Public Bureaucracies and Policy Implementation." *International Social Science Journal 31:* 632–645.

North, D. C. 1981. *Structure and Change in Economic History.* New York: Norton.

North, D. C. 1990. *Institutions, Institutional Change and Economic Performance.* Cambridge: Cambridge University Press.

Olsen, J. P. 1970. "Local Budgeting: Decision-Making or a Ritual Act?" *Scandinavian Political Studies 5:* 85–118.

Olsen, J. P. 1972. " 'Voting,' 'Sounding Out,' and the Governance of Modern Organizations." *Acta Sociologica 15:* 267–283.

Olsen, J. P. 1976a. "Reorganization as Garbage Can," in J. G. March and J. P. Olsen (eds.):
*Ambiguity and Choice in Organizations,* pp. 314–337. Bergen: Universitetsforlaget.

Olsen, J. P. 1976b. "The Process of Interpreting Organizational History," In J. G. March
and J. P. Olsen (eds.): *Ambiguity and Choice in Organizations,* pp. 338–350. Bergen:
Universitetsforlaget.

Olsen, J. P. 1981. "Integrated Organizational Participation in Government," in P. C.
Nystrom and W. H. Starbuck (eds.): *Handbook of Organizational Design,* Vol. 2,
pp. 492–516. New York: Oxford University Press.

Olsen, J. P. 1983. *Organized Democracy.* Bergen: Universitetsforlaget.

Olsen, J. P. 1986a. "Foran en ny offentlig revolusjon." *Nytt Norsk Tidsskrift 3:* 3–15.

Olsen, J. P. 1986b, "Privatisering og forvaltningspolitikk." *Norsk Statsvitenskapelig
Tidsskrift 1:* 51–57.

Olsen, J. P. 1988. "Administrative Reform and Theories of Organization," in C. Campbell and B. G. Peters (eds.): *Organizing Governance, Governing Organizations,* pp.
233–254. Pittsburgh, PA: University of Pittsburgh Press.

Olsen, J. P. 1990. *Demokrati på svenska.* Stockholm: Carissons.

Olsen, J. P. 1992. "Analyzing Institutional Dynamics." *Staatswissenschaften und Staatspraxis 2:* 247–271.

Olsen, J. P. 1996a. "Europeanization and Nation-State Dynamics," in S. Gustavsson and
L. Lewin (eds.): *The Future of the Nation-State,* pp. 245–276. London: Routledge.

Olsen, J. P. 1996b. "Norway: Reluctant Reformer, Slow Learner—or Another Triumph
of the Tortoise?" in J. P. Olsen and B. G. Peters (eds.): *Lessons from Experience. Experiential Learning in Administrative Reforms in Eight Democracies,* pp. 180–213.
Oslo: Scandinavian University Press.

Olsen, J. P. 1997. "European Challenges to the Nation-State," in B. Steunenberg and
F. van Vught (eds.): *Political Institutions and Public Policy,* pp. 157–188. Dordrecht: Kluwer.

Olsen, J. P. 1998. "Institutional Design in Democratic Contexts," in N. Brunsson and J. P.
Olsen (eds.): *Organizing Organizations,* pp. 203–229. Bergen: Fagbokforlaget.

Olsen, J. P. and B. G. Peters. 1996. "Learning from Experience?" in J. P. Olsen and B. G.
Peters (eds.): *Lessons from Experience. Experiential Learning in Administrative Reforms in Eight Democracies,* pp. 1–35. Oslo: Scandinavian University Press.

Patterson, T. C. 1991. *The Inca Empire: The Formation and Disintegration of a Pre-
capitalist State.* New York: St. Martin's Press.

Powell, W. W. and L. Smith-Doerr. 1994. "Networks and Economic Life," In N. J. Smeiser
and R. Swedberg (eds.): *Handbook of Economic Sociology.* Princeton, NJ: Princeton
University Press.

Pressman, J. L. and A. Wildavsky. 1973. *Implementation.* Berkeley, CA: University of
California Press.

Simon, H. A. 1957. *Models of Man.* New York: Wiley.

Tilly, C. (ed.). 1975. *The Formation of Nation-States in Europe.* Princeton, NJ: Princeton University Press.

West, R. 1994. *Tito and the Rise and Fall of Yugoslavia.* London: Sinclair-Stevenson.

Westphal, J. D., R. Gulati and S. M. Shortell. 1997. "Customization or Conformity? An
Institutional and Network Perspective on the Content and Consequences of TQM
Adoption." *Administrative Science Quarterly 42:* 366–394.

PART IV

# EXPLORATIONS IN THE MODERN HISTORY OF ORGANIZATION STUDIES

## *An Introductory Essay*

MIE AUGIER

T HIS SECTION PRESENTS ARTICLES by James March related to the evolution of ideas in general, and the evolution of ideas in organization studies in particular. As a short introduction, I shall discuss a few aspects of some of the themes covered in these articles, as relates to history, history of ideas, organization studies as a field, and as a field within business education.[1]

As current scholars in the field know, March's own work has played a central role from the beginning. As part of what is sometimes called "the Carnegie School" (Earl, 1992), March worked, along with Herbert Simon and Richard Cyert, to build much of the foundations for the field of organization studies in general, and behavioral perspectives on firms, organizations, and decision making in particular. At that time, both fields (organization studies and behavioral science) were very much in their infancy. They borrowed and extended and integrated ideas from the more mature fields of economics, political science, sociology, and social psychology. The emergence and the early development of the field went hand in hand with the creation of another interdisciplinary field, behavioral social science, and also with an increasing focus in the disciplines (at least within economics) on behavioral ideas on decision making and the evolution of institutions (Day, 1964; Winter, 1964), as well as some significant changes in U.S. business schools and management education (Gordon and Howell, 1959; Pierson, 1959).

Looking back at these developments it is clear that these were at least in part overlapping in terms of the central people involved (as well as the results of collaborative efforts). As March notes in the article "Scholarship, Scholarly Institutions, and Scholarly Communities" (Chapter 16 in this volume), scholarship is a collective activity, and often involves overlapping individuals and institutions. For example, Herbert Simon, central to the early development of organization theory, also served as advisor to the first foundation programs on behavioral social science, and was also actively involved in reforming business education. Similarly, March's own early work became central to the fields of organization sciences and behavioral science; he, too, was at a business school and was an early fellow at the then newly established Center for Advanced Study in Behavioral Science (CASBS).[2] It is also clear, in looking back, that key to making these developments possible in the first place was the support, intellectual backing— not to say funding—of a few key Cold War developments and institutions, in particular the RAND Corporation and the Ford Foundation.[3] In their search for research that was interdisciplinary, fundamental, yet empirically motivated and more realistic than many previous academic traditions, RAND and the Ford Foundation provided institutional and financial support to the fields of organization studies and behavioral social science, while at the same time providing legitimacy by building and supporting institutions that could further help these emerging fields mature (notably, in addition to CASBS, also, the Graduate School of Industrial Administration at, then, the Carnegie Institute of Technology). Within those, the researchers had considerable freedom to do what they found interesting and ultimately central to building better theories and frameworks that could help us understand certain elements in the world better.

The institutional importance of this history is the fundamental reason for the central role of business schools for the development of the field of organization studies (see Augier, March, and Sullivan, Chapter 14 in this volume, in particular pp. 352–357), and vice versa. One of the core areas in most business school research and teaching is organization studies (sometimes called organizational behavior or organization theory); and other core business school areas such as strategy and finance also build on research pioneered in business schools. This raises some interesting questions. For example, given the interrelatedness of scholars, ideas, and institutions, how much of what we see today in the field has been formed by this coevolution? What if March, Simon, and Cyert had not been at GSIA, but had stayed in disciplinary departments instead; would the early organization studies have had a less interdisciplinary flavor, and would later developments have taken as firm a root as we see today within business education, with the associated journals, handbooks, and professional societies that later became important institutional and professional focal points for scholars in the field as well as for the "professionalization" of organization studies as a research program? What if Cyert, March, and Simon had decided not to study organizations, but only individual decision making? What if they had written the early contributions within a distinct rational choice framework—how would that have influenced the developments that we see today in behavioral economics, in theories of the firm, strategy, and in organization studies?[4] What if Hitler had not been born, would the field have developed differently (or at all) if it didn't have the migration of social scientists from Germany and Central Europe, and Cold War environment and enthusiasm and funding as background?

Such counterfactual questions/lines of thought might be useful intellectual exercises for contemporary scholars in organizations, who might find insights and ideas from past developments that did (or did not) happen that resonate, contradict, support, or even anticipate modern contributions, or perhaps just may help us understand the modern mosaic of the field better. The roads not taken are part of the map, too. March captures this spirit in his article "Hopes *for* the Past and Lessons *from* the Future" (my emphasis), Chapter 12 in this volume.

In addition to March's own contributions to the field's history (several of the central pieces included in this volume as well as in his earlier collection of articles), his articles in this part all have a distinct historical character—talking about the field, its geographical diffusion, roots, disciplinary specialization, and other matters. Now, history itself is a field, a discipline, a serious set of ideas with different "schools of thought" and perspectives on "what is history" and "what constitutes good historical research," ranging from doxography to rational reconstructions to counterfactual reasoning to deconstruction and critical theory and even social construction. For example, those who argue that past events are best understood by studying those events in terms of what actually happened are in contrast (and evoke arguments with) those who see history less as a record of past facts and events and more like an "invention" or construction—a creation more than an interpretation and understanding—of the past.[5]

Scholars interested in the history of the field of organization studies may not need to be experts on historical disciplines and perspectives, but some of the same arguments that are present in that literature may be useful, because there are additional controversies about the role and status of studying history in any field. As anyone with a serious interest in the history of ideas will know, scholars (in particular young scholars) are often discouraged from engaging in historical studies. They are sometimes confronted with questions such as "Why don't you just *do* [organization] theory?" or "Aren't you fifty years too young to study the history of thought?" Such attitudes neglect the fact that an examination of past ideas can often help one to understand current developments better and is also essential to the future progress of a field, at least, for the following reasons.

First, arguing against the history of ideas in a field sometimes implicitly or explicitly implies that all that is of value in past research is reflected in current contributions. In other words, the "market" for ideas in any particular area is "efficient" and incorporates the "real" theoretical value of older contributions (Stigler, 1969).[6] But the market for ideas, and the history of thought, is inefficient (Vaughn, 1993). It is filled with imperfections such as forgotten or neglected ideas, forgetful scientists, and organizational inefficiencies that result in imperfections due to the internal nature of adaptation processes (March, 1994). Researchers and scholars forget; they have biases and make mistakes, and those create additional imperfections and lack of knowledge, compared to what an efficient market would. The incompleteness of information in the research market is not necessarily bad. As Whitehead (1938) famously argued: "Great advances in thought are often the result of fortunate errors." But given this state of affairs with adaptive and informational inefficiencies present in the history of ideas in organization studies, historical research may actually help improve this situation. Uncovering and discussing past developments and knowledge helps this knowledge to become embedded and reflected in current and future research, and in the field itself. Therefore, from the point of view of traditional efficiency arguments, historical research becomes of value because of its contributions to efficiency because of the presence of inefficiencies in the field and market for ideas.

Second, knowledge in and of any field and subject is largely historically determined (Kuhn, 1962; March, 1994; Whitehead, 1938). What we know about how certain organizations (or mechanisms within or between organizations) work today is not something that is just the result of the most recent issues of the *Academy of Management Review* or the *Administrative Science Quarterly*; it is also the sum of all the ideas, inefficiencies, thoughts, insights, mistakes, and reinterpretations of past works in the field. The use (and abuse) of history in scientific evolution has been recognized since at least Nietzsche (1873) and Kuhn (1962). And, as a result of the path-dependent nature of intellectual activities, any attempt to understand a contemporary idea in the field—and the future of any idea of field—should include an examination of the origin and development of that particular idea. Or, in March's terms (Chapter 14 in this volume and March, 1994), we base our understanding of the past on the basis of combining exploration and exploitation, and we draw lessons for the future of the field at least in part on the basis of our understanding of its past(s).[7]

So for these (and other) reasons, the history of ideas as a field of research in organization studies has other and more important goals than keeping researchers with antiquarian interests busy. Through our investigation of the past, we can rediscover and reuse the insights from the past, which can supply new ways of looking at a particular problem in contemporary and future studies in organization.

## THE (UN)DISCIPLINARY FOUNDATIONS
## FOR ORGANIZATION STUDIES

While some intellectual roots of the field have existed since Plato, much of what we recognize today as "organization studies" has been developed in the last five decades (see Chapters 14, 15, and 16 in this volume). March's reflections on the past and the future(s) of the field offer insights into both its context and its content. His discussions emphasize the changing (inter/non)disciplinary foundations and biases of the field. Many ideas emerged out of behavioral social science and at certain institutions; and some of these developments, in turn, are embedded in the history of modern business schools, which may have influenced again the development of the field of organization studies in direct as well as indirect ways. For example, he argues in "The Study of Organizations and Organizing since 1945" (Chapter 15 in this volume) how the politics of the Cold War and the subsequent fall of the Soviet Union may have had unintended consequences for the field of organization studies. Given the institutional change in nations and politics, leading to issues such as rapid immigration of eminent scholars to the United States in the years immediately before and after the World War II (Craver, 1986), organization studies, in building on those ideas, naturally emerged mostly in the United States. And later, with the 1960s and 1970s movements, more methodological open ideas entered the field, particularly in Europe (see Chapter 15 in this volume).

Thus, a theme for current and future studies and scholars in organizations concerns the (un/non/multi)disciplinary foundations for the field, and perhaps we might learn or get inspiration from previous generations. For today, despite the centrality of organizations in modern life, when young scholars begin to study organizations, they will immediately observe that the field is in serious disarray. We see this manifested in the diverse approaches from rational choice theory and game theory, over institutional and evolutionary theory, and to post-feminism and social constructivism; they all appear to be part of the modern organization scholar's tool kit. Quite frequently, textbooks and survey articles characterize the field precisely by its methodological and theoretical open-endedness, appealing to interdisciplinarity and multidisciplinarity at the same time. On closer examination, almost all early work in organization theory was based on disciplines, and what appears as multidisciplinary early work is actually using insights from several disciplines. The early generation of "organization theorists" such as March, Herbert Simon, Philip Selznick, Peter Blau, Alex Bavelas, and Richard Cyert were all trained in disciplines (in particular political science, sociology, psychology, and economics). They attempted to contribute to disciplines, while also branching out to find value in other disciplinary tools and ideas. Indeed, the study of organizations, or organization science/studies, was born as a stepchild of the then emerging field of the behavioral sciences. It borrowed from them all without following any one of them closely, and thus it did not immediately have a unique home in a discipline world. In particu-lar, it aspired to be interdisciplinary, rather than disciplinary in the traditional sense. To single-minded disciplinary trained economists, sociologists, or psy-chologists, this might have seemed an unnecessarily broad program, and one moreover that depended excessively on the development of a new conceptual apparatus for studying organizations. For early researchers in organization studies, however, the intellectual advantages of being interdisciplinary seemed obvious. Any other conception of the study of organization would necessarily contain the seeds of its own destruction in the sense that there would be unexploited research areas (on how to study organizational behavior) within the disciplines, which, once exploited, would break the disciplinary boundaries. For the early organization scholars, these issues were not fatal, for it was more important for them to establish the agenda, and provide empirically relevant theory of organizational behavior and decision making, than it was to worry about disciplinary boundaries.

Nevertheless, early organizations scholars were still speaking the language of the disciplines, publishing their research in disciplinary journals, and trying to get the disciplines to think about organizations in an interdisciplinary way. Thus, there are many miles from the early interdisciplinary vision to today's multidisciplinary and (at times) eclectic approach; and perhaps the most important feature missing today is, paradoxically, the discipline of the disciplines (Augier, March, and Sullivan, Chapter 14 in this volume). For prior generations, one had first to be disciplined (and trained in at least one discipline), then interdisciplinary. Today, most organization scholars are interdisciplinary before becoming (if at all) certified within a traditional social science discipline. Interdisciplinarity or multidisciplinarity is not necessarily bad, but it does make it more difficult to provide a common language among the different camps of organization studies. A common language, or at least a set of (more or less) agreed on concepts might make it more likely that modern scholars use those concepts, tools, and languages to develop a better understanding of the central issues in real organizations; and less likely that they get stuck in discussions that might appear less intelligible to people outside the field on issues, such as the influence of critical theory on new organizational forms, or the significance of postmodern capitalism on organizational epistemology (no, I am not making up these topics; in fact, I heard them discussed at a recent conference). Regardless of the perceived importance of such debate among contemporary scholars in organization studies, an admirable quality of earlier generations is their ability to contribute significantly not only to academic debate but also to science, scholarship, and even practice.[8] Central to this influence seem to be the ability to develop central concepts (such as bounded rationality and organizational slack), hypotheses and insights and the application of those to real world firms, and issues present in real world organizations, or the observation of certain behaviors in firms and organizations (for instance, on routines, or pricing behavior) and the use of these to modify, revise, or develop new theory.

This does not mean that they aspired to be "relevant" in a narrower sense of the term. For, as March argues in "The Pursuit of Relevance in Management Education," Chapter 17 in this volume), there was less a focus on criteria of usefulness and relevance than there is today; and more focus on scholarship, ideas, and educational values that could provide frameworks and tools for thinking about complex problems (also see Bach, 1958; Cyert and Dill, 1964; Simon, 1967). In other words, the focus in management education was more on teaching people *how* to think, not *what* to think.

The problems of being empirically motivated and contributing to science as well as to understanding the real world, without focusing on fixing current problems and trying to be "relevant," seem related to the problems of being interdisciplinary, but in a disciplinary way. Not losing sight of the disciplinary roots and tools that can be useful to study interdisciplinary problems and to revise theory could again become central to organization studies. As March argues, the instinct to balance knowledge of the discipline with the need to be interdisciplinary that was central to early works in the field arose at least in part out of certain developments in behavioral social science, which provided the context for the early contributions. Thus, any attempt to reconstruct the success of past developments might be informed by understanding also the context for these developments. Significant with regard to the early development of organization studies in this respect is GSIA (now the Tepper School) at Carnegie Mellon University, and the simultaneous developments in behavioral social science and business education.

## BEHAVIORAL ORGANIZATION STUDIES AND CARNEGIE

As pointed out in "Notes on the Evolution of a Research Community" (Chapter 14 in this volume), much of the funding for the early works in the field of organization studies came from the Ford Foundation's program in behavioral and social science. And in keeping with March's observation on the social quality of research, this funding was undoubtedly influenced by the close connections between the Ford Foundation and the early Graduate School of Industrial Administration (GSIA) where this early work was being done. For example, at the time when the behavioral science area was developed and executed, the dean at GSIA, Lee Bach, was an important advisor to the foundation; and Herbert Simon later became advisor to the behavioral science area. Simon also knew many of the central people from the RAND Corporation, and served on many of the committees advising the foundation on how to encourage interdisciplinary collaboration among the sciences (and the scientists). In addition to these personal connections, the interdisciplinary spirit of the early GSIA fitted the Ford Foundation vision well, and quickly the research at Carnegie became the role model for the Ford Foundation initiatives, both with regard to the development of behavioral social science (and organization theory) and as an overall model for business education.[9]

It was a very special place with an intellectually stimulating atmosphere as well as a remarkable collection of individuals. Researchers there counted innovative economists and others who could combine mathematics and quantitative techniques with organizational sociology and social psychology; and after a few years, Bach and Simon were joined at GSIA by scholars such as Richard Cyert, Harold Leavitt, Charles Holt, and Merton Miller, James G. March, Harold Guetzkow, Franco Modigliani, Richard Nelson, Allan Newell, and Harrison White. The group at Carnegie soon consisted of many talented young scholars who were all eager to contribute to this newly formed vision of behavioral science. The spirit (if not always the reality) at Carnegie was that everybody interacted with everybody else, discussing each others' research and science. So, collaborative teams worked together as well as across each other's projects. Consisting of different people with different interests, these teams worked effectively together, despite their origins in different disciplines. It was, as March notes in "Scholarship, Scholarly Institutions, and Scholarly Communities," "the Vienna circle of its time."

One of the most well known early projects at Carnegie was the "inventory" of organization theory funded by the Ford Foundation, which led to the book *Organizations*. It was here (and in follow-up projects) that the behavioral vision was realized, and important seeds to the field of organization studies were planted. In addition to filling a need in the establishment of the behavioral sciences, research on organizations became the emergent discipline of business school education, bringing together different disciplines in the study of decision making and behavior in organizations. *Organizations* was an inventory of organization theory that used insights from organization theory and social psychology, while also praising mathematical and statistical tools. It also emphasized the idea of organizations as social institutions in society and the role of organizations in constraining decision making. "The basic features of organization structure and function," March and Simon wrote, "derive from the characteristics of rational human choice. Because of the limits of human intellective capacities in comparison with the complexities of the problems that individuals and organizations face, rational behavior calls for simplified models that capture the main features of a problem without capturing al its complexities" (March and Simon, 1958, p. 151).

Beginning in 1957, the Ford Foundation also supported a larger project on behavioral theories of organizations elaborating ideas from articles published beginning in 1955 by Richard Cyert and James March. They (along with their students, including Julian Feldman, Edward Feigenbaum, William Starbuck, and Oliver Williamson) sought to investigate how the characteristics of business firms as organizations affect important business decisions. Integrating theories of organizations with existing (mostly economic) theories of the firm, they developed an empirical theory rather than a normative one, and focused on classical problems in economics (such as pricing, resource allocation, and capital investment) to deal with the processes for making decisions in organizations. The resulting book, *A Behavioral Theory of the Firm* (Cyert and March, 1963), extended the earlier ideas, particularly by elaborating concepts of organizational slack, adaptive aspirations, organizational learning, and the role of rules and routines. The book furthermore addressed a major dilemma of organization studies: the choice between a realistic, but unmanageable theoretical model of organization, and a simple, manageable model. Cyert and March used computer simulations that provided a relatively realistic description of actual processes while retaining a modicum of the predictive power so essential to empirical testing (Cyert, Feigenbaum, and March, 1959).

These two major early works were foundational for the field of organization studies, and many of the central concepts in today's contributions were conceived or developed in those early books (Williamson, 2002; Argote and Greve, 2007; Augier, Cohen, Dosi, and Levinthal, 2003). The unique research environment at Carnegie made the interdisciplinary character of the research possible. It was a business school, but it was a business school where ideas mattered. As the dean, Lee Bach noted:

I want to stress as strongly as I can my own belief that *fundamental* research is a major responsibility of every leading business school, especially those which offer graduate work. It is parallel in importance to the teaching responsibilities, which tend to blanket most of our institutions. I mean by fundamental research development of analytical tools and models, application of old and new tools to business problems at a level where the search for useful generalizations is involved, and attempts at depth of understanding—all in contrast to mere description of best prevailing business practice. We need to know what best prevailing business practice is. But I hold no brief for any leading business school that is content with describing such practice in its research, and with teaching only such practice in its classrooms. *The function of the university is to be ahead of best practice, not to be trailing a few steps behind the operating business world.* (Bach, 1958: 363–364; emphasis added)

This is an issue that is as relevant today as it was fifty years ago. March's own discussions of the need for research and ideas in business education are discussed in this part and elsewhere (March, 2006; March and Sutton, 1997). They reflect his awareness of some of the institutional and organizational mechanisms that, on a broader level, influence research in business education; and by influencing the *context* for much of the field of organization studies, also the *content* and the *future* of this field. The important point to emerge from this discussion is not only of substance (relating to the need to focus less on relevance and more on ideas, and to be interdisciplinary, but in a disciplined way). But if the future of the field of organization studies as well as of business education might benefit from reaching back to some of the fundamental ideas and ways of doing research (as some have indicated, see Reed, 2006 for instance), then we need to know the institutions involved, the interests, the people, the ideas, and the interplay of those on how history did (and did not) unfold. In the articles that follow, March discusses aspects of some of this history and context (as well as content) of business schools, organization studies, ideas, and institutions.

## NOTES

1. The desperately brief summary/discussion that follows touches on history, organization studies, and business school research, and March's contributions to these topics, but does justice neither to the role of March's work in the history of the field (or his work in general) nor to the sophistication and almost poetic qualities of his work. I also focus on his early (and late) work, to the exclusion of other themes in his scholarship, such as his work on political institutions, learning, models, and organizational change. For more complete discussion of his works, see Argote and Greve (2007); Augier, Cohen, Dosi, and Levinthal (2003), and others. I am grateful to the John and Cynthia Reed Foundation for support of research for writing this introduction.

2. The Center for Advanced Study in Behavioral Sciences was established in 1954 and intended to provide an institutional structure for scholars doing interdisciplinary work in the disciplines such as economics, sociology, political science, and psychology. The idea and the model was invented and supported by the Ford Foundation, in particular its then innovative president, Rowan Gaither, and Bernard Berelson who became the director of one of the five program areas at the foundation, focused on behavioral social science. For some discussion of the early vision of the center (and the field of behavioral science), see Tyler (1963), Merton (1963), and Berelson (1963).

3. The RAND Corporation was established in 1946 as an Air Force think tank, and in 1948 reorganized as an independent organization. In the immediate postwar years, researchers at RAND contributed significantly to developments in decision making, organizational behavior, linear programming, and game theory. The Ford Foundation existed before RAND but became infused by the spirit and ideas (and people) who had been at

RAND, when the former chairman of the RAND board, Rowan Gaither, became the man behind the Ford Foundation's new mission statement—and later president of the foundation. He wrote a report (known as "The Gaither Report") laying out future research areas for the foundation, which became the intellectual basis on which both the push in behavioral social science and the reorganization of business schools were built.

4. For some discussion on the influence of the early behavioral ideas on theories of the firm, in particular evolutionary economics and transaction cost theory, see Nelson and Winter (2002) and Williamson (2002); and on the influence on the field of strategic management, see Rumelt, Schendel, and Teece (1994).

5. I shall not go into the details about the status of truth and facts in (theories of) history, but the issues are quite interesting and perhaps more relevant to the field of organization studies that one might expect. For some discussion, see Carr (1961) and Evan (1999).

6. This discussion comes from Stigler's article on "Does Economics Have a Useful Past?" in which the author presents both arguments for and against historical research. He ends with a typical economics argument about whether or not to do intellectual history: "Economics, I . . . believe, has a useful past, a past that is useful in dealing with the future. Many commodities and services are not produced in a society because they are worth less than they cost; it remains the unfulfilled task of the historians of economics to show that their subject is worth its cost" (pp. 229–230); thus defending the use of history if it leads to more efficiency in markets for research (Vaughn, 1993).

7. This is a variation of a theme, prominent in March's work, on the need for both exploration and exploitation of ideas. As he notes in a famous article: "[Researchers] that engage in exploration to the exclusion of exploitation are likely to find that they suffer the cost of experimentation without gaining many of its benefits. They exhibit too many undeveloped new ideas and too little distinctive competence. Conversely, [researchers] that engage in exploitation to the exclusion of exploration are likely to find themselves trapped in suboptimal stable equilibria" (1991, p. 71).

8. Several of the early contributors to organization studies won scientific medals and were members of the National Academy of Science; I haven't done comparison to how many current stars in organization theory will be in the NAS, but I doubt it is anywhere near the earlier generations.

9. It was also the Ford Foundation that commissioned Gordon-Howell report, which became important in the reorientation of U.S. business schools toward a more research-oriented model.

## REFERENCES

Argote, L. and H. Greve. 2007. A behavioral theory of the firm—40 years and counting. Introduction and impact. *Organization Science* 18 (2, March/April): 337–349.

Augier, M., M. Cohen, G. Dosi, and D. Levinthal. 2003. Institutions and organizations: Introduction to special issue in honor of James G. March. *Industrial and Corporate Change* 12(4): 647–652.

Bach, G. L. 1958. Some observations on the business school of tomorrow. *Management Science* 4(4): 351–364.

B. Berelson. 1963. Introduction to the behavioral sciences. In B. Berelson (ed.), *The Behavioral Sciences Today*. New York: Basic Books.

Carr, E. 1961. *What Is History?* New York: Vintage.

Craver, E. 1986. The immigration of the Austrian economists. *History of Political Economy* 18(1): 1–30.

Cyert, R. and W. Dill. 1964. The future of business education. *Journal of Business* 37(3): 221–237.

Cyert, R. Edward A. Feigenbaum, and James G. March. 1959. Models in a behavioral theory of the firm. *Behavioral Science* 4: 81–95.

Cyert, R. M. and J. G. March. 1963. *The Behavioral Theory of the Firm*. Englewood Cliffs, NJ: Prentice Hall.

Day, R. 1964. Review of "A Behavioral Theory of the Firm." *Econometrica* 3(3, July): 461–465.

Earl, P. 1992. *Microeconomics for Business and Marketing*. Aldershot, U.K.: Edward Elgar.

Evans, R. 1997. *In Defense of History*. London: Granta Books.

Gordon, R. A., and J. E. Howell. 1959. *Higher Education for Business*. New York: Columbia University Press.

Kuhn, T. 1962. *The Structure of Scientific Revolutions*. Chicago: University of Chicago Press.

March, J. G. 1991. Exploration and exploitation in organizational learning. *Organization Science* 2: 71–87.

March, J. G. 1994. *A Primer on Decision Making*. New York: Free Press.

March, J. G. and H. A. Simon. 1958. *Organizations*. New York: Wiley.

March, J. and R. Sutton. 1997. Organizational performance as a dependent variable. *Organization Science* 8: 697–706.

Merton, R. 1963. The mosaic of the behavioral sciences. In B. Berelson, 1963, *The Behavioral Sciences Today*. New York: Basic Books

Nelson, R. and S. G. Winter. 2002. Evolutionary theorizing in economics. *Journal of Economic Literature* 16(2): 23–46.

Nietzsche, F. 1873. The use and abuse of history for life. In Nietzsche, F. 1874. *Untimely Observations*. Cambridge: Cambridge University Press.

Pierson, F. 1959. *The Education of Businessmen*. New York: McGraw Hill.

Reed, J. 2006. *Interview*. In M. Augier, 2006. Making management matter: An interview with John Reed. *Academy of Management Learning and Education* 5(1): 84–100.

Rumelt, R., D. Schendel, and D. Teece. 1994. Introduction. In *Fundamental Issues in Strategy*. Harvard Business School Press: Boston.

Simon, H.A. 1967. The business school: A problem in organizational design. *Journal of Management Studies*: 1–17.

Stigler, G. 1969. Does economics have a useful past? *History of Political Economy* 1(2): 217–230.

Tyler, R. 1963. Institutional organization of the behavioral sciences. In B. Berelson (ed.), *Behavioral Sciences Today*. New York: Basic Books.

Vaughn, K. 1993. Why teach the history of economics? *Journal of the History of Economic Thought* 15(2): 174–183.

Whitehead, A. N. 1938. *Adventures of Ideas*. New York: Free Press.

Williamson, O. E. 2002. Empirical microeconomics: Another perspective. In M. Augier and J. G. March (eds.), *The Economics of Choice, Change and Organization: Essays in Honor of Richard M. Cyert*. Cheltenham, UK: Edward Elgar.

Winter, S.G. (1964). Review of "A Behavioral Theory of the Firm." *The American Economic Review* 54 (2, Part 1): 144–148.

# CHAPTER 12

# Research on Organizations

## *Hopes for the Past and Lessons from the Future*

### JAMES G. MARCH

This paper considers the problems of balancing exploration and exploitation in research on organizations, particularly the problem of generating new ideas and persisting in them. It develops an argument based on three propositions. The first proposition is that long time perspectives for the future stimulate exploration of new ideas. Both the generation of new ideas and persistence with them are more favored by long future time horizons than by short ones. The second proposition is that long time perspectives for the past encourage long time perspectives for the future. Scholarly traditions that recognize their long pasts are more likely to look ahead to their long futures. The third proposition is that perceptions of the past have to involve a particular structure. Long perspectives of a past and future connected by a conception of continuity stimulate exploration of slowly developing ideas. The paper embraces a particular version of historical interpretation as contributing both to the long forward time horizons that facilitate imaginative exploration of new ideas and to a conception of scholarship that resists existential doubt. It argues that hopes for the past are a basis for learning from the future.

## INTRODUCTION

Conventional wisdom proclaims the importance both of incorporating the lessons of past experience into present actions and of maintaining hopes for the potentials of the future. Scholarship, for example, is seen as extracting knowledge from the past and aspiring to a future of new discoveries and new comprehension. The wisdom is innocuous enough, but it may conceal an element of truth lurking in a somewhat different proposition: Learning from the future is made easier by hope for the past, and it is hope for the past that organizes the past in a particular way. It is a proposition that leads into some basic issues in thinking about adaptation, history, life, and research.

---

This chapter originally appeared in *Nordiske Organisasjonsstudier*, 1 (1999), 69–83.

The argument begins with the unsurprising premise that scholarship requires both novel ideas and the elaboration and refinement of established ideas (Kuhn, 1962; March, 1991). A classical problem is to avoid an emphasis on either that atrophies the other (Arthur, 1989; Cohen and Levinthal, 1989). The problem is characterized this way in a recent article:

Social, economic, and political systems . . . have difficulty sustaining experimentation. From any immediate perspective, this is not because they are stupidly rigid but because they are intelligently efficient. For them to pursue new alternatives makes little apparent sense. The returns to exploration tend to be less certain and less immediate than the returns to exploitation. They also tend to be more distant, less localized in their realization to the immediate organizational neighborhood of the exploration. This is partly because new ideas tend to be poor ones, and it is partly because even good new ideas have returns that are more distant in time and space than those realized from current ideas. It is not easy for an organization to justify experimentation that, at least in the short run, does not make sense in terms of immediate local return. What is required is a willingness to engage in experimentation that is unlikely to succeed and particularly unlikely to be rewarding in the temporal and spatial neighborhood of the experiment. Unfortunately, although too little experimentation is likely to be disastrous in the longer run, too much experimentation is likely to be disastrous immediately. (March and Olsen, 1998, pp. 964–965)

Friedrich Nietzsche said it somewhat more poetically:

Anyone who deviates from tradition becomes a victim of the extraordinary; anyone who remains within tradition is its slave. In either case, he will be destroyed, (Nietzsche, 1996, p. 275)

Research domains are not exempt from such dilemmas. They frequently suffer from lock-ins in which persistence in elaborating and refining what is familiar and understood works to the detriment of new discoveries. Correcting such tendencies would be relatively easy were it not for the fact that new ideas in research, like new ideas in general, are more frequently poor ideas than they are good ones. Scholarly communities consequently can rather easily fall into patterns of endless change in which they flit from one new idea to another. These tendencies toward repeated turnover in unrewarding novelty are encouraged by difficulties in developing interesting ideas. Even those novel ideas that are, in fact, good ones are likely to be initially unproductive, thus to require persistence in pursuing them if they are to have their potential realized. Not only must a research domain maintain a balance between exploring new ideas and exploiting old ones, it must also maintain a precarious enthusiasm for rejecting the old but not the new in situations in which, since the old will, on average, be better than the new, precisely the opposite inclination is likely (March, 1995).

Consideration of the nuances of these trade-offs between exploitation and exploration, on the one hand, and between the abandonment of and persistence with apparently unrewarding new ideas, on the other, is a central topic for theories of adaptation. The ambition here is not to provide a comprehensive treatment but to explore one small aspect of those issues—the relation between the past and the future. The argument is a simple one based on three propositions about exploration, time perspectives, and histories in research.

PROPOSITION 1: *Long time perspectives for the future stimulate exploration of new ideas.*

The first proposition is that the pursuit of new ideas is favored by long future time horizons. The attractiveness of exploration relative to exploitation and the attractiveness of persistence with new ideas relative to abandonment of them both increase as the time horizon lengthens. The argument is a simple one based essentially on presumptions about risk taking and intertemporal comparisons in action. Returns to the exploration of new ideas and to persistence in them, are, on average, less certain than are returns to exploitation. That is, the variance of the probability distribution over future returns stemming from new ideas tends to be large relative to that of returns stemming from established ideas. Moreover, new ideas often require a longer time to develop, and when they develop, they have a greater variance (thus, in that sense, are more risky) than do ideas that require less time. Good new ideas are likely to be hard to distinguish from bad new ideas, and the greater the long-run impact of an idea, the longer it is likely to be before it can be developed enough to have its potential reliably recognized. Since the costs of exploration are ordinarily not similarly problematic or delayed, both the generation of new ideas and persistence in them become more attractive as the intertemporal weight given to immediate gratification declines. One way in which this can happen is by lengthening the forward time horizon. The further ahead a decision maker looks, the more relevant are the distant returns of exploration relative to the immediate returns of exploitation.

The proposition that long time horizons provide more support for persistent exploration than do short time horizons is well known from the literature on rational adaptation. Probably the most powerful set of theorems from the analysis of search decisions (so-called bandit problems) is a set that ties optimal investment in search for new alternatives, rather than consumption of returns from currently known alternatives, to the time horizon of the decision maker (Chernoff, 1972). The shorter the future time horizon, the smaller the amount of resources that should be devoted to search by a rational actor. Similarly, the advantages to be gained from variation in a variation/selection model depend on the future time perspective. The longer the perspective, the greater the level of variability that is desirable.

Thus, any research endeavor is left with an obvious problem. Research requires new ideas and persistence with them in order to sustain long-run development. However, new, slowly developing ideas are unlikely, on average, to be good ones, particularly when assessed in the short run. The long-run interests of a field in generating new risky ideas and pursuing them with persistence conflict with the short-run interests of individual scholars and their patrons in achieving results quickly. From such a perspective, it is not surprising that organizational research emphasizes cross-sectional analyses, retrospective data gathering, and comparative statics. Complaints about the absence of longitudinal studies and the relative reluctance to use contemporaneous archival sources in both quantitative and qualitative modes are as legendary as are the failures to respond significantly to the complaints. Programs involving the sustained development and elaboration of ideas (e.g., population ecology, comparative statics of structure) fall in and out of fashion within a generation. And there are very few examples in organizations research of sustained individual commitment to scholarly projects involving very long delays in completion and highly uncertain returns. About the only successful recent example that occurs to me is John Padgett's work on the development of the Florentine political system (Padgett and Ansell, 1993; Padgett, 1998).

Increasing the flow of new ideas and the persistence with which they are pursued, probably requires extending the time horizons of research institutions and individual scholars involved in research on organizations. The search for instruments that encourage long time perspectives is a search common to many kinds of students of human development. Theorists of financial and managerial incentives worry about encouraging long-run concerns in financial markets and business decisions. How are the long-term interests of future organizational stakeholders made relevant to current organizational actors (Jacobs, 1991; Siegel, 1998)? Democratic political theorists worry about representing the long run in democratic elections and deliberations. How does a democratic political system, which is responsive to present citizens, attend to the legitimate concerns of the unborn (March and Olsen, 1986; Elster, 1992)? Psychological students of self-control worry about individual propensities to discount the future. How is it possible to induce ordinary humans to delay gratification or to reject immediate pleasures that have long-run adverse consequences (Shefrin and Thaler, 1992; Mischel et al., 1992)?

This concern about inadequate attention to the long run is derived from empirical observations of human bias, not from any theorem about the necessary primacy of effects in the long future for current action. Indefinitely long future time perspectives are not necessarily desirable. Defining optimal action for the present involves attending to the long run, but it also involves recognizing that the long run is realized through a series of short runs, each of which must be negotiated successfully. However, there is a clear human bias militating against attention to the long run. The evidence from psychological and economic studies is overwhelming in substantiating a general human and other animal tendency to favor the present over the future. This occurs despite considerable evidence that a short time horizon is not an immutable trait of human beings. As Lens and Moreas observe:

There is no doubt that human beings are cognitively able to foresee a very distant future, extending much beyond their individual life time and that of their children. Even motivationally they are sometimes able to anticipate and take into consideration goals in a very distant future. (Lens and Moreas, 1994, 35)

Nevertheless, most people most of the time favor the present over the future. Similarly, the evidence from studies of organizations is overwhelming in substantiating a general organizational tendency to favor the present over the future. Although it is possible to find occasional sacrifices of the present for the future in organizations, ordinarily the demands of the present seem to be distinctively more compelling than the demands of the future. Concerns about long-run adaptability are likely to be subordinated to concerns about short-run efficiency (March, 1994). The reasons for this bias at both individual and organizational levels are not understood in great depth, but they are almost certainly tied to the immediacy and accessibility of the present, relative to the future.

It would be surprising, indeed, if a similar bias were not also characteristic of scholarship. There are numerous well-known reasons why time perspectives tend to be short in organizational research. In particular, two are commonly noted. First, there is a pervasive, almost ritualized, mantra proclaiming that the rate of environmental and organizational change is accelerating (March, 1995; Clegg and Hardy, 1996). Volatility in history seems to make the past irrelevant and the future unpredictable, thus encourages a focus on the immediate present. Second, research incentives do not seem to support attention to the long run. Competition among scholars for short-run reputations and among the patrons of scholars for immediate material returns make long perspectives tied to the long-run development of the field individually dysfunctional (March and Sutton,

1997). Ambitions for immediate effects seem to produce short time horizons (Loewenstein and Elster, 1992), and short time horizons seem to diminish persistence in experimentation.

Incentives for research and the volatility of the world of organizations are important contributors to time horizons in organizational research, but there is another reason for short time perspectives. It is the alienation of the individual scholar from a sense of belonging to an endeavor and a community that extends forward in time, the idea that research done now contains seeds of a long future that will unfold in a continuous, orderly way. Within the consequential logic of individual motivation that is shared widely within western society, long time perspectives require identification with a future that extends beyond an individual's immediate concerns and life (Tocqueville, 1945 [1835], Vol. II, Second Book, Chapter 17, 149–150).

Families, communities, and cultures are primary sources of a sense of a long-term future. When members of a current generation subordinate their personal well-being to provide for their children, it is presumably with some kind of belief that their sacrifices will allow their children (and carriers of their genetic inheritance) to live a better life than they have lived, even as they have been served by the long time perspective of their parents, and even as their children's intergenerational perspectives will, in turn, serve subsequent generations (and thus their genetic legacy). These beliefs in connectedness are embedded sometimes in rational calculations and sometimes in cultural rules, but in either case they tie individuals to a conception of life as extending forward beyond any single life.

Contemporary alienation from the future stems partly from elements of a broader social loss of community, for example in the decay of the extended family and academic communities; but it also stems partly from pervasive pessimism about links to the future. Contemporary cosmologies, social organization, and ritual all disassociate living actors from their afterlives. Mortality is defined in individual more than systemic terms. Out of this comes a persistent tendency to imagine that time is short, that problems must be solved immediately, that ideas must be connected to their immediate practical implications in order to claim a right to be supported, articulated, or exchanged. Much of the pressure for well-defined relevance of scholarship in modern society stems from the profound alienation of current research sponsors and researchers not only from the long-run future of organizations and populations of organizations but also from the long-run future of scholarship, knowledge, and communities of citizens and scholars.

PROPOSITION 2: *Long time perspectives for the past encourage long time perspectives for the future.*

The first proposition was that long time horizons lead to exploration, and that modern research in organizations is oriented overwhelmingly to short time horizons. The second proposition is that long time horizons for the future are encouraged by long time horizons for the past. It is hard to imagine a long future without confidence in a long past. Long future time perspectives are associated with imagining that one is part of an historical process that will continue. Those connections across history provide a feeling of continuity, and the sense of continuity and development over the past provides a basis for expecting similar continuity and development in the future. A connection to the past facilitates a connection to the future, and alienation from the past leads to alienation from the future.

Fifteen years ago, Omar El Sawy did a study of time perspectives among CEOs in the Silicon Valley (El Sawy, 1983). He found that there was a positive correlation between past time horizons and future time horizons. The further an executive looked into the past, the further that executive looked into the future. Moreover, El Sawy found this relationship to be one way. Looking first into the future did not affect the time horizon for looking into the past, but executives who looked first into the past had a future time horizon that extended about 80 percent further into the future than those who looked into the future without first considering the past.

In the context of his study, it was natural for El Sawy to interpret this result primarily as reflecting an eliciting bias induced by the order of asking about past and future horizons. The phenomenon is, indeed, a potential complication for researchers interested in eliciting and measuring time horizons; but it is more than that. The effect of a time horizon for the past on a time horizon for the future is an important human bias in life. Involvement in the past leads to concern about the future, thus to being more likely to invest in activities with long-term returns, rather than short-term returns. In the same study, for example, El Sawy found that although the willingness to delay gratification in order to achieve future returns (what he called "tenacity") was significantly lower among executives than among a comparison group of non-executives, gratification delay among executives was positively correlated with the length of time an executive looked backward. The further into the past they looked, the more they were willing to sacrifice present advantage for future benefits.

In a similar way, contributions to the future of research depend on delayed gratification in the present. And delayed gratification in the present is made more likely by a sense of hope for the past. Research on organizations finds traces of its origins in the writings of the earliest Chinese and Greek philosophers and men of affairs. The problems of getting organized are not uniquely modern problems, and knowledge about organizing did not begin with Henri Fayol. It is not hard to construct a compendium of comments on organizations that extends over a long period of history. It is harder to describe that history as forming a stream of interrelated projects that can be connected by a coherent story.

Thirty years ago, in the introduction to the *Handbook of Organizations*, I contrasted an historical chronology of ideas in organization studies with a "pedigree," a series of ideas that were connected in a causal chain by which earlier ideas were elaborated and built upon. The argument was that the study of organizations could claim a chronology but not a pedigree (March, 1965, p. ix). In wry confirmation of that proposition, two of the editors of a subsequent handbook, Stewart Clegg and Cynthia Hardy, observed that changes in organizations and organization studies in the three decades since 1965 made comparison between the two handbooks impossible (Clegg and Hardy, 1996, p. 24–25n). Although a reasonable case can be made for some integration of studies of organizations at a particular time, the field exhibits little sense of integration across time. The styles of scholarship in organization studies are not cumulative. On the contrary, for the most part, contemporary conventions of scholarship considerably glorify an individual scholar's current work and remove that work from its long historical context in order to establish its independent significance and uniqueness.

Having once experienced much of the past as the present, we who have lived through it are likely to think the past more relevant than it is. The point, however, is not that the past is relevant for its own sake, or for what can be learned from it directly. Rather, it is that an effective research tradition requires an extended forward time horizon, and a sense of connection with the future is intimately linked to a sense of connection with the past. For example, counter to what might be expected and is sometimes postulated, time horizons (except for personal life expectancies) do not appear to vary negatively with age (Nurmi, 1994, Fig. 4; Bouffard et al., 1994). Consciousness of the future feeds on consciousness of the past. Those who believe their pasts are irrelevant to them cannot expect that they will be relevant to their futures.

PROPOSITION 3: *Long perspectives of a past and a future connected by a conception of continuity stimulate exploration of slowly developing ideas.*

The first proposition was that the generation of new ideas and persistence in pursuing them are stimulated by long time perspectives for the future. The second proposition was that long time perspectives for the future are facilitated by long time perspectives for the past. Simple knowledge of the past, however, is not enough. Thus, the third proposition is that conceptions of the past have to have a particular structure to encourage patient exploration. Scholars have to imagine that there is a coherent history of research on organizations and that current involvement in research flows out of the contributions of that history and will flow into the contributions of the future. They have to see the past and the future as having direction and to represent accumulation of knowledge, what students of time perspective sometimes call "temporal integration" (Nuttin, 1985). When long histories and long futures are intertwined by a sense of continuity and development, they stimulate the pursuit of new ideas.

As anyone who has attended even slightly to controversies in historical interpretation can attest, there are two kinds of historical stories told about the development of an institution or society. In the first version, history is seen as coherent. Current action is pictured as embedded richly in the past and projecting sensibly into the future. It is the usual story of the history of great empires, such as the Chinese, Roman, or Incan. It is also the usual story of technologies or fields of science. The second version of historical development sees history as a meander of local wanderings without aggregate directionality. History is fortuitous. Current actions are embedded only lightly in the past and project only dimly into the future. It is the usual story told of the development of art, poetry, and aesthetic taste, and the story of jewelry.

Similarly, there are two readings possible of the history of scholarship on organizations. One reading is a history of development, with new ideas building on old ones and gradually reducing ignorance. It involves a conception of knowledge, a research task, and a scholarly tradition all of which extend backward into the past and forward into the future. For example, such a story can be told of the evolution of the idea of organizations as collections of self-interested and conflicting actors, a story that cumulates over the contributions of Aristotle, Hobbes, Madison, Bentham, Pareto, Michels, Barnard, von Neumann and Morgenstern, Coase, and Kreps. A similar story can be told of the development of the idea of rationality.

A second possible reading of the history of research on organizations is a story of transitory enthusiasms. New ideas replace old ideas and then are replaced in turn without accumulation or systematic development. Such a reading is commonly associated with changing fads in scholarly epistemologies and methodologies. It is also used to characterize changing fashions in ideas of consciousness or in theories of history. By this characterization, the history of organizational research since the Second World War seems to reflect more a wandering history of changes in fashion than a history of cumulative development.

These stories can be seen as alternative ways of describing the past; and although a reasonable judge of the history of research on organizations might well give as much credence to the second story as to the first, organizational research will be able to realize its possible future only when it can portray a past in which early ideas became enriched and modified by subsequent ones in a process that left those earlier ideas detectable but transformed in a way that improved them in a meaningful sense. If ideas in Aristotle or Ibn Khaldoun seem fully relevant today, they are not connected to a cumulative history. If the history of scholarship can be seen as a collection of thoughts by disconnected, independent observers some of whom can as easily be regarded as authorities as can their successors, contemporary scholars cannot expect that their own ideas will be elaborated and augmented by some future scholars. At best, they may hope to be "rediscovered" at some later time. Thus, their ideas must be complete in their own time and not merely initiated. If scholarly endeavor is seen as organized around the specific individual lives of specific scholars, research perspectives are, at most, only as long as individual lives, and hopes for a vision of a community of ideas that endures and develops are forlorn. If the past of scholarship is seen as futile or as a collection of non-cumulative and non-social brilliances and fads, then the future will be seen as similarly futile, non-cumulative, non-social, and faddish.

On the other hand, if it is possible to believe that ideas evolve over a long history of scholarship, that the history of scholarship is cumulative, that ideas at one time are transformed and elaborated, rather than ignored or rediscovered, then it is possible to see kernels of ideas generated at present as becoming the basis for later elaborations through which those kernels are developed. In a cumulative history, the ideas of an Aristotle or an Ibn Khaldoun will have been vital to the development of subsequent ideas, and will be honored for that role, but knowledge would now go beyond them and make "rediscovery" of them of only ancillary use. From this point of view, any historical focus on individual scholars, however distinguished, is misguided. The proper history of organizational research is a history of evolving ideas, not of the individual scholars who have been temporary vessels for components of those ideas.

If we want to sustain patient exploration in organizational scholarship, we cannot be neutrals with respect to theories of knowledge and history. Without some form of a commitment to the cumulative nature of knowledge, there can be little basis for long time perspectives in scholarship. Unless it is possible to imagine that ideas develop, so that the implications of an initial idea unfold as the idea is elaborated and are not wholly implicit in the original formulation, there is very little point in exploring new ideas whose fruition might take a long time. If Weber, Commons, Gulick, Simon, and Levi-Strauss do not speak to contemporary scholars through a chain of developments that have elaborated and refined their ideas, then surely the scholars of today can have little reason to expect that they will speak to those who follow them except insofar as they may be from time to time briefly "rediscovered." In order to participate now in activities that have a return only in the distant future and only after their elaboration by others over a long future, scholars need to be able to imagine that there is some sense in which the future will build upon the present and go beyond it.

There is a word for such a conception, and the word is progress. It is a stigmatized word. A distinctive feature of modern social science and organizational research is its rejection of the notion that each step of the research endeavor builds on previous steps and goes beyond them in a way that expands knowledge. Conceptions of progress have been forcefully deconstructed by prominent voices of the humanities and social sciences. The history of organization studies, for example, is portrayed, for the most part, as a history of contending seekers for power. As a result, a remarkable number of quite different writers in the field portray their individual contributions, or those of a small coterie of supporters, as distinctive revolutionary approaches doing battle with powerful forces of the establishment. They are inclined to see parallel disputes among others as minor quarrels within a hegemonic order that seeks to subjugate them (Clegg and Hardy, 1996). From this perspective, knowledge is contested, not in the directional sense of the struggle between youth and maturity but in the circular sense of the struggle among the seasons of the year.

The proposition that progress is a socially constructed myth is now rather generally taken as obvious, and those who speak of directionality in history or ideas are viewed as either naive or agents of the current political, social, and intellectual establishment. In modern theories of meaning, historical stories are arbitrary social conventions without inherent order or extralinguistic validity. In modern theories of adaptation, the path of history has no clear direction, and the evolution of scholarship consists of endless cycles of conversational disagreements. Scholars who work to elaborate old ideas are likely to be listed as old-fashioned, and those who see scholarship as making modest, anonymous contributions to a long history of slow progress in knowledge are likely to be treated as retarded.

Such deconstructions, however compelling and particularly because they can be quite compelling, undermine research endeavors. Social science and organization studies can, of course, be seen as consisting in independent essays written by autonomously brilliant essayists. In such a spirit, major contributions are timeless in the sense that there is no link between the validity of any particular essay and the date of its appearance. Timeless essays are an important part of the social science tradition. The observations of a Tocqueville, Tolstoy, or Vico are still rewarding. This timelessness, however, as well as conceptions of the research endeavor as a directionless meander or a pursuit of fashion by unconnected individuals, undermine a long time perspective in research. To justify a commitment to research that will come to fruition in the distant future, if it ever does, scholars need to conceive the pursuit of knowledge to involve the gradual improvement of ideas as they evolve through generations of individual scholars and scholarly communities, each building on those who went before and providing a base for those who follow.

History is a choice. It is a choice constrained by historical evidence, but it is a choice. Recently, an official in the French Ministry of Culture responded to an acrimonious dispute over the appropriateness of a controversial new public sculpture in Paris by saying, "We are going to re-create a continuity that has always existed for a very long time." As the American writer who quoted this comment in the *New Yorker* observed, *"It was a perfect French ministerial sentence, a sentence you could walk around and admire from every angle, like a statue in the park"* (*The New Yorker,* Vol. 74, no. 7, April 6, 1998, p. 63). It is, indeed, a charming sentence, but it is also a profound one. It recognizes the essential character of history: The links among the past, the present, and the future by which human history is established are only partly given by events. They are also created by willful human choice.

We can have, if we choose, a history of organizational thought that interprets current work within a long history of related efforts that have built on each other, that sees gains in comprehension over time, fitful gains perhaps but nonetheless gains. We can, in the words of the French minister, "re-create a continuity that has always existed for a very long time." The choice of such a past is not without costs, but it also has benefits. When isolation from the past is reduced by recognition of the links of present research to earlier research, a sense of discipline and continuity is created. When the future is seen as extending beyond individual studies and the past is seen as filled with interconnected and cumulative research, a temporal context is provided for individual contributions to organizational scholarship. Because research on organizations has a past, it has a future. Because it has a future, current research directions are less dictated by current rewards and current fashions. Because the germination time of ideas is extended into the future by anticipations of patient gardeners, slowly germinating ideas can be planted and fertilized, including ideas that will flower under new gardeners in new gardens.

## CONCLUSION

The argument advanced here is not complicated. The conclusion is elementary. Organizational scholarship needs to stimulate exploration of new ideas. Both the generation of new ideas and persistence with them are encouraged by long future time horizons. Long future time horizons, in turn, are facilitated through conceptions of a long past connected to a long future by a sense of continuity and progress. As a consequence, a better future history of research on organizations is made possible if the present is connected to the past in a way that is consistent with a vision of progress. The choice of such a history creates a richer future for those who follow. If scholarship is seen as cumulating over time and over scholars in a way that makes past work a foundation, but not a substitute, for current work, individuals are more likely to undertake the risky, long-term projects that will contribute to such a dream.

Such a conception of history is not self-evident, and some esteemed scholars believe that it is naive to imagine progress and muddle-headed to advocate it. They proclaim a catechism according to which commitment to progress has to be justified by a belief in it, and belief in progress has to be justified by its unambiguous historical demonstrability. The present apostasy stems neither from ignorance of the argument nor from lack of appreciation of its force but from a recognition that how contributions are made to history depends on how history is conceived and how scholars think of themselves. Ultimately, a scholar's commitment to progress in scholarship is a matter of faith. It goes to the essence of a scholarly life, is reaffirmed by identification with a multi-generational tradition of scholarship, and is immune to existential doubt.

The development of such a faith and the construction of such a history is the responsibility of those of us who are committed to the long-run development of human knowledge. We can invite our skeptical colleagues to share that faith and discover the benefits and beauties of being connected to a boundless past of cumulative scholarship that can anticipate a boundless future in which the ideas of today mature and develop into complex wonders of future knowledge. And whether we put greater emphasis on the contributions of such a faith to sustaining exploration in ideas, or on the beauties of such a faith in fulfilling a vision of scholarship, we will have chosen a history that ennobles our craft and embeds our individual lives in a grander scheme. By discerning hopes for the past, we build a basis for learning from the future and for achieving grace as minor figures in a modest history.

This paper was originally presented at the Scandinavian Consortium for Organizational Research Conference on "Samples of the Future," at Stanford University, September 20, 1998, celebrating the tenth anniversary of the creation of Scancor, so it is particularly appropriate that it was included in the inaugural issue of *Nordiske Organisasjonsstudier*. I am grateful for the comments of Mie Augier and Johan P. Olsen. The research has been supported by the Spencer Foundation.

## NOTES

1. "On va recréer une continuité qui a toujours existé depuis longtemps."

## REFERENCES

Arthur, W. Bryan (1989). "Competing Technologies, Increasing Returns, and Lock-in by Historical Events," *Economic Journal*, 99: 116–131.

Bouffard, Léandre, Etienne Bastin, and Sylvie LaPierre (1994). "The Personal Future in Old Age," pp. 75–94 in Zaleski, Zbigniew, ed. (1994). *Psychology of Future Orientation*. Lublin: Towarzystwo Naukowe KUL.

Chernoff, H. (1972). *Sequential Analysis and Optimal Design*. Philadelphia, PA: Society for Industrial and Applied Mathematics.

Clegg, Stewart R., and Cynthia Hardy (1996). "Introduction: Organizations, Organization and Organizing." Pp. 1–28 in Stewart R. Clegg, Cynthia Hardy, and Walter R. Nord (eds.), *Handbook of Organizational Studies*. London: Sage.

Cohen, Wesley M., and Daniel A. Levinthal (1989). "Innovation and Learning: The Two Faces of R&D," *Economic Journal*, 99: 569–590.

Dahl, Robert A., and Charles E. Lindblom (1953). *Politics, Economics, and Welfare*. New York: Harper.

El Sawy, Omar (1983). "Temporal Perspective and Managerial Attention: A Study of Chief Executive Strategic Behavior." Ph.D. dissertation, Stanford University.

Elster, Jon (1992). "Intertemporal Choice and Political Thought," pp. 35–53 in Loewenstein, George, and Jon Elster, eds. (1992). *Choice over Time*. New York: Russell Sage Foundation.

Jacobs, Michael T. (1991). *Short-term America: The Causes and Cures of Our Business Myopia*. Boston, MA: Harvard Business School Press.

Kuhn, T. S. (1962). *The Structure of Scientific Revolutions*. Chicago: University of Chicago Press.

Lens, Willy, and Marie-Anne Moreas (1994). "Future Time Perspective: An Individual and Societal Approach," pp. 23–38 in Zaleski, Zbigniew, ed. (1994). *Psychology of Future Orientation*. Lublin: Towarzystwo Naukowe KUL.

Loewenstein, George, and Jon Elster, eds. (1992). *Choice over Time*. New York: Russell Sage Foundation.

March, James G. (1991). "Exploration and Exploitation in Organizational Learning." *Organization Science*, 2: 71–87.

March, James G. (1994). *Three Lectures on Efficiency and Adaptiveness.* Helsinki: Svenska Handelshögskolan.

March, James G. (1995). "The Future, Disposable Organizations, and the Rigidities of Imagination." *Organization,* 2: 427–440.

March, James G., ed. (1965). *Handbook of Organizations.* Chicago, IL: Rand McNally.

March, James G., and Johan P. Olsen (1986). "Popular Sovereignty and the Search for Appropriate Institutions," *Journal of Public Policy,* 6: 341–370.

March, James G., and Johan P. Olsen (1998). "The Institutional Dynamics of International Political Orders," *International Organization,* 52: 943–969.

March, James G., and Robert I. Sutton (1997). "Organizational Performance as a Dependent Variable," *Organization Science,* 8: 697–706.

Mischel, Walter, Yuichi Shoda, and Monica L. Rodriguez (1992). "Delay of Gratification in Children," pp. 147–164 in Loewenstein, George, and Jon Elster, eds. (1992). *Choice over Time.* New York: Russell Sage Foundation.

Nietzsche, Friedrich (1995). *Human, All Too Human, I.* Stanford, CA: Stanford University Press.

Nurmi, Jari-Erik (1994). "The Development of Future-Orientation in a Life-Span Context," pp. 63–74 in Zaleski, Zbigniew, ed. (1994). *Psychology of Future Orientation.* Lublin: Towarzystwo Naukowe KUL.

Nuttin, Joseph (with the collaboration of Willy Lens) (1985). *Future Time Perspective and Motivation: Theory and Research Method.* Leuven (Belgium): Leuven University Press.

Padgett, John F., and Christopher K. Ansell (1993). "Robust Action and the Rise of the Medici, 1400–1434." *American Journal of Sociology,* 98: 1250–1310.

Padgett, John F. (1998). "Organizational Genesis, Identity and Control: The Transformation of Banking in Renaissance Florence." Unpublished paper, Department of Political Science, University of Chicago, Chicago, IL.

Shefrin, Hersh M., and Richard H. Thaler (1992). "Mental Accounting, Saving, and Self-Control," pp. 287–330 in Loewenstein, George, and Jon Elster, eds. (1992). *Choice over Time.* New York: Russell Sage Foundation.

Siegel, Jeremy J. (1998). *Stocks for the Long Run: The Definitive Guide to Financial Market Returns and Long-term Investment Strategies,* 2nd ed. New York: McGraw-Hill.

Tocqueville, Alexis de (1945 [1835]). *Democracy in America.* Vols. 1 & 2. New York: Alfred A. Knopf.

CHAPTER 13

# Parochialism in the Evolution of a Research Community
## The Case of Organization Studies

JAMES G. MARCH

The organizations research community is a multidisciplinary, multinational, and multilingual association of scholars with all the paraphernalia of international exchange. Nevertheless, it is a community that is organized in a geographically fragmented way, with linguistic, national, cultural, and regional boundaries separating relatively autonomous scholarly communities. Although this fragmentation limits the integration of organization studies, it serves an adaptive role in making the resistance of deviant ideas to the homogenizing tendencies of dominant scholarly groups easier. The effective use of such differentiation, however, requires linkages among the fragmented parts of the field. We consider some ways of thinking about how research boundaries can be both sustained and violated, with particular attention to the emergence of Chinese scholarship in the study of organizations.

ONE OF THE PERSISTENT ASPIRATIONS of social science is to create multidisciplinary, multinational, and multilingual associations of scholars that profit from exchanges of ideas across disciplinary, national, and linguistic boundaries. Proclamations of the need for such communities are part of the standard mantra of contemporary scholarly life, stimulated by perceived needs of both scholarship and public policy. Many problems of modern social science, for example those focused on the processes and dilemmas of adaptation, appear to demand integration across multiple disciplines and to profit from attention across multiple nations, cultures, and languages. Many problems of contemporary societies, for

This paper is based in part on remarks made in August 2003 at the Academy of Management meetings in Seattle and in October 2001 at the University of Poitiers (Godelier, 2003) and appeared in *Management and Organization Review*, 1 (2004), 5–22. I am grateful for the comments of Mie Augier, Marshall Meyer, Johan P. Olsen, Bilian Ni Sullivan, and two anonymous reviewers. The work has been supported by the Spencer Foundation.

example the design of resilient social institutions, involve complex combinations of knowledge and perspectives. Moreover, in an era fascinated with intellectual property rights and the role of knowledge in social change, the organization of the flow of ideas is a strategic issue. Demands for multidisciplinary, multinational, and multilingual research communities are encouraged by concerns about possible competitive disadvantages that may accrue to individual disciplinary, national, or linguistic groups as a result of exclusion from vital knowledge that is known by others.

Since World War II, barriers to cross-disciplinary and international research exchange have become less formidable. Thanks to modern transportation technology, physical contact among scholars has become easier. Simultaneously, thanks to modern communication technology, direct physical contact has become less essential to collaboration and exchange of ideas. As a consequence, integration across disciplines, nations, and languages has increased in contemporary organization studies, as it has throughout the social sciences. Nevertheless, organization studies remains a scholarly field that is organized in a fragmented way, with disciplinary, linguistic, national, cultural, and regional boundaries separating relatively autonomous scholarly communities (Pfeffer, 1993; Whitley, 1984; Zammuto and Connolly, 1984). This paper examines the role of geographic fragmentation in the evolution of a scholarly field and suggests some ways of thinking about organizing a multidisciplinary, multinational, and multilingual community. The immediate context is the development of an organizations research community in China, but the argument and the observations are intended to be relevant also to a more general set of issues.

## GEOGRAPHIC FRAGMENTATION
## IN ORGANIZATION STUDIES

The organizations research community is organized into geographically concentrated enclaves. The enclaves are connected in important ways, but their substantial isolation from each other is easily documented. To a considerable extent, geographic fragmentation can be attributed to the geographic distribution of language groups. Relatively few students of organizations outside of China or Japan read journals or books in Chinese or Japanese, and relatively few students of organizations outside of the Francophone world regularly read journals or books in French. Although presumably many scholars who study organizations are able to read some languages other than their own, most of the references found in publications written in any language are references to books or journals published in that language. In principle, the translation of books and articles into other languages might reduce the linguistic barriers; but in practice it does so only to a limited extent. There is only a modest amount of translation of books into languages other than the one in which they are first published, and there is no translation service for journal articles that is readily available to the general scholarly community. Because of the cross-language linkages that exist, there are useful connections among scholars operating in different languages; but the resulting diffusion of ideas might more properly be called "idea seepage" than "idea flow."

To be sure, the pervasive use of English in the contemporary scholarly world has reduced barriers to discourse among separate linguistic communities. English language journals specializing in organization studies exist in many parts of the world, and English is the standard language of international conferences. However, this focus on English leaves large parts of the research community (and even larger parts of the potential research community) poorly connected. Moreover, although this sharing of a language has greatly facilitated exchange across the geographic barriers associated with language differences, it creates a bias in favor of Anglophone experience, researchers, and worldviews, a bias that both contributes to and is reinforced by a North American hegemony in organization studies and has to some extent become institutionalized by rules requiring English-language publications imposed on scholars in other parts of the world. The bias undermines the effectiveness of scholarly development and the fairness of scholarly competition (Engwall, 2002, chaps. 8, 10), and thereby threatens the long-run position of English as the unique international language of scholarly exchange. It is not clear that such a position will be sustained in a future world of scholarship less dominated by North American research. It may be well to remember that French was once the international language of discourse.

The extensive use of English reduces fragmentation, but it does not eliminate it. Even in the English-language relations between North America and Western Europe, where international contact is almost certainly the easiest and most dense in the world, the geographic separation of intellectual discourse is nonetheless conspicuous (Engwall, 2003). A minor illustration of the point can be made by looking at four recent issues of each of four leading North American journals of the field (*Academy of Management Journal, Academy of Management Review, Administrative Science Quarterly, Organization Science*) and four leading European (English-language) journals (*Journal of Management Studies, Organization, Organization Studies,* and *Scandinavian Journal of Management*). Table 1 shows, for all eight journals, the proportions of the members of the editorial

TABLE 1    North American presence in eight organizations studies, English-language journals

| | Journal | | | | | | | |
| | North American | | | | European | | | |
| | AMJ | AMR | ASQ | OS | JMS | O | OS | SJM |
|---|---|---|---|---|---|---|---|---|
| Editorial boards | 0.94 | 0.93 | 0.93 | 0.76 | 0.73 | 0.31 | 0.25 | 0.15 |
| Authors | 0.80 | 0.77 | 0.85 | 0.90 | 0.23 | 0.04 | 0.14 | 0.02 |
| References | 0.95 | 0.92 | 0.94 | 0.93 | 0.73 | 0.45 | 0.72 | 0.72 |

boards who are currently employed in North America, the proportions of the articles that are authored by North Americans and the proportion of references that cite pieces published in North America.

In a fully integrated world, the fraction of North American editors, contributors and references would be the same in both North American and European journals. They are not. Even though all eight journals share a common language, the North American journals are considerably more North American in their editorial boards, contributors, and references than are the Western European journals. As would be expected from differences between North America and Europe in the scale of the research efforts, North American editors, authors, and references are much more likely in European journals than are non–North American editors, authors, and references in North American journals. For any plausible estimate of the fraction of all research that is North American, editorship, authorship, and citations are all biased in a geographically parochial way in both the North American and the European journals.

Even in the West, despite a long history of substantial contact and exchange between Anglophone scholars of North America and those of Western Europe, the centrifugal forces of regionalism, nationalism, and cultural pride divide English-language organizational scholarship into parochial communities. It is easy to observe that fragmentation is even more pronounced in the relations across languages in the West and between organizations research in the Western world and organizations research in Asia or Latin America. Although there are some connections between individual scholars in the Western Anglophone world and individual European scholars who publish in other languages or scholars in Asia and Latin America, there is little direct scholarly discourse involving the different research communities.

## FRAGMENTATION AND THE EVOLUTION
## OF RESEARCH COMMUNITIES

In an echo of more general theories of adaptation (Holland, 1975; Mayr, 1976), theories of the adaptation of a scholarly field describe a process involving struggles between a core establishment committed to a relatively coherent conception of truth and various peripheral challengers to that conception. The struggles reflect a necessary tension between the development, refinement, and exploitation of existing knowledge and methods and the exploration of possible new directions (Crane, 1972; Knudsen, 2003a; Kuhn, 1970; Lakatos, 1970; Wagner, Wittrock, and Whitley, 1991). A hallmark of effective knowledge refinement and exploitation is a tight network among researchers. Such networks thrive on easy communication, and communication thrives on unified understandings. Consensus on the fundamentals is essential. Exploration, on the other hand, involves the examination of numerous possibilities, many of them dubious. It thrives on diversity and deviance. Because the efficiencies of coherence are useful immediately, they dominate local adaptive processes of learning. However, they are invitations to long-run stagnation. Without exploratory diversity, disciplines, cultures, and languages turn in upon themselves. Thus, the emphasis in adaptive theory on maintaining a mix of both exploitation and exploration (March, 1991).

Although the necessity of a mix is reasonably clear, there is no general answer to the optimal allocation of effort between exploitation and exploration. Quite aside from the manifest difficulties in estimating future returns from either, the optimum balance between exploitation and exploration is known to depend critically on the time and space perspectives chosen (March, 1994, chap. 6). Moreover, a productive balance between exploitation and exploration is continually threatened by two well-known dynamics. The first dynamic involves accelerating attention to the purification and refinement of existing ideas with emphases on maintaining agreement on fundamentals of knowledge and on tightening the enforcement of shared standards for scholarship. This dynamic drives a field toward exquisite barrenness (Mirowski, 1992). The second dynamic involves accelerating attention to innovation, the multiplication of novel ideas and the glorification of the new to the detriment of the development of the old. This dynamic drives a field toward cascades of triviality (Donaldson, 1995; Mone and McKinley, 1993). These insatiable instincts of refinement and imagination continually threaten balanced attention to both in a scholarly community.

Students of adaptation have noted particularly that processes of adaptation themselves make it difficult for adaptive systems to persist in new ideas long enough to discover the truly good ones among them (Denrell and March, 2001). Adaptive processes are myopic in the way they respond locally to local feedback (Levinthal and March, 1993). Since the returns to new ideas are systematically less certain and more distant in time and space than are the costs, learning (and other adaptive processes) are generally biased against them. New ideas can be encouraged by introducing incentives or identities favoring novelty, but often the same incentives and identities also discourage persistence with any specific new idea. As a result, there is a tendency for adaptive processes to generate either too few new ideas or too rapid cycling through a multitude of new ideas.

Fragmentation within a scholarly field is implicated in this story of adaptation (Knudsen, 2003b; Whitley, 1984). Regional, national, and disciplinary loyalties, beliefs, identifications, and the like are all instruments for controlling the rate and locus of convergence in knowledge and belief. They build communities of faith and social support within which ideas and styles that differ from those sanctified in other regions are sustained and refined. This feature of fragmentation forms the basis of one of the more important intellectual (as opposed to political) justifications for decentralization and diversity in political and economic organization (Flora, Kuhnle, and Urwin, 1999; Hirschman, 1991, p. 168; March and Olsen, 1995, pp. 168–173). As in other forms of organization, parochialism in research communities supports experimentation. For example, the business school parochialism of early organizations scholarship in economics helped to protect behavioral ideas about the economics of the firm from premature sacrifice to the hegemony of economic theory (Augier, 2003; Williamson, 2003). And the European parochialism of critical organization studies helped to protect subjectivist ideas from premature sacrifice to the hegemony of North American logical positivism (Westwood and Clegg, 2003).

The benefits of fragmentation come, however, with costs. Small enclaves risk both abandoning the discipline of the larger community in enforcing quality and losing talented researchers to more-established research perspectives. For individual members of a regional community, parochialism limits adaptation to the core knowledge community and thereby limits both the acquisition of conventional knowledge and access to standing within that community. The most talented scholars gravitate to the conventional and the paradigmatic where their talents lead to reliable success. Talented individual scholars who, either by choice or by necessity, identify with a regional fragment become unwitting altruists, sacrificing their clearest chances for recognition in order to participate in unlikely exploratory gambles that serve the field more than themselves.

Lastly, the same fragmentation that sustains local ideas through a sense of common identity, language, and worldview also inhibits the extension of those ideas to others. A missionary group that isolates itself from society in order to protect its distinctiveness maintains its purity but finds itself handicapped in its efforts to penetrate that society with its message. The isolation in business schools that protected ideas of behavioral economics in their early development probably also made their integration into economic theories of the firm more difficult. And the geographic isolation that protected subjectivist organization studies in their early development probably made their integration into a broader community of organizations scholarship more difficult.

The current structure of geographic fragmentation in the social sciences is a product of the last 50 years of the twentieth century. Prior to World War II, North American social scientists who aspired to intellectual leadership often went to Europe to do their studies; they read European journals and books; and they tried to cement collaborative relations with major European scholars. After the war, the balance of scholarly trade shifted. North American social science experienced a massive expansion in human and financial resources, an expansion that far eclipsed parallel growth rates in the rest of the world. North American scholars (including many who were refugees from Europe) built a new research community that was international in scope and intention but based in Anglophone North America. The history of the organizations research community in North America was part of that social science story. In the last half of the twentieth century, it was transformed from a small cluster of researchers scattered among several different disciplines and nations into a large quasi-discipline with its own journals and concentrated in North American schools of business (Augier, March, and Sullivan, 2004).

Growth and institutionalization made the North American organization studies community largely autonomous and self-sustaining. Links between North American scholarship and work in the rest of the world were characterized, for the most part, by individual non-American scholars becoming associated with some part of the North American research community, doing work within that tradition and style and being accepted as part of that community. Some non-American centers became closely connected to American scholarship; other centers did not. Communities based on languages other than English tended to maintain independent, but localized, presences, as did some English language centers in the United Kingdom and the Commonwealth nations.

History also influenced the enthusiasms of scholars in different parts of the world. The North American expansion of the number and variety of institutions of higher education and research immediately after World War II came at a time of great optimism for science and the extension of scientific method to social science. European and Asian expansions came later and were associated with different elements of intellectual ferment. Increases in European invest-ment in organization studies and social science generally coincided more with a scholarly temperament that put less emphasis on science and more emphasis on ideology, social criticism, and literature. These differences between Europe and North America were reinforced by the way European traditions of social science were more firmly anchored to traditions of philosophy, law, and history than were parallel developments in North America. These intellectual, economic, political, and social histories have produced organizational research communities in Europe, parts of which have become closely linked to the North American community and parts of which have established themselves as European English language alternatives to American scientism.

Developments in Asia, like those in North America and Europe, have been shaped both by traditions specific to the individual regions and by the particular academic enthusiasms current at the times of growth. The recent expansions of Asian attention to organization studies and social sciences have coincided with a period of fascination with information technology and bio-engineering, and with a shrinking role of the state in regulating enterprises. These associations with a different set of intellectual excitements, along with the different traditions of Asian cultures, suggest that Asian organizations scholarship will probably differentiate itself in important ways both from the current North American core and from its European challengers.

As the history of any field of study unfolds, its trajectory depends on the re-lation between the rate of adoption of new ideas by the establishment (change) and the rate of adoption of old ideas by challengers (stability). If challengers adapt too rapidly relative to the adaptation of the establishment, experimenta-tion is extinguished. If the establishment adapts too rapidly, scholarship cycles endlessly among new ideas without developing any of them. In order to move forward, a scholarly field needs to avoid both extremes. Disciplinary, linguis-tic, and geographic fragmentations interfere with the consolidation of a clear paradigm, but they encourage both experimentation and persistence with new ideas. Differentiated enclaves of knowledge simultaneously resist the homog-enizing tendencies of dominant groups and sustain new beliefs against further originality long enough to explore them fully. In this way, new ideas of rel-evance for the study of organizations have been nurtured in places somewhat insolated from the dominant North American organizations research establish-ment. Provided those buffers are, in the end, permeable, the field can adopt the new initiatives that appear to offer good results (Anacona and Caldwell, 1992; Postrel, 2002).

Consider, in this light, the advantages for the evolution of organization studies stemming from the disciplinary, linguistic, and geographic distance between the Anglophone North American organizations research community and potentially relevant, but distant, scholars such as Nils Brunsson, John Child, Michel Crozier, Barbara Czarniawska, Erhard Friedberg, Anthony Giddens, Jürgen Habermas, Anthony Hopwood, Håkon Håkonsson, Bruno Latour, Johan P. Olsen, Claude Riveline, and Jean-Claude Thoenig. Individual scholars and scholarly communities that have been separate from, but not totally disconnected from, the North American establishment have protected new ideas from the guardians of respectability long enough to elaborate defensible new perspectives. One example is the elaboration of subjectivist ideas about organizations in European scholarly enclaves surrounding journals such as *Accounting, Organizations, and Society* and *Organization Studies.*

Just as there is no general specification of the optimal allocation between exploration and exploitation, there is no general specification of the optimal fragmentation of a field. Nevertheless, the regional fragmentation and differentiation of organization studies and the elements of mutual isolation of North America, Europe, Asia, and Latin America in recent decades, though often costly for would be architects of a coherent field, seems to have served the field reasonably well. Thus, it has been argued that:

the peripheral position of the Nordic countries in the last half of the 20th century created . . . a distinctive variant nurtured by being peripheral and by the unintendedly benign neglect of the establishment . . . Nordic organization scholarship has been remote enough to evade the paradigm police, connected enough to influence the more vulnerable elements of the non-Nordic research community. (Czarniawska and Sevón, 2003, pp. 414–415)

It is an old story, told for example about the development of American social science as derivative of, but distinct from, its German and British antecedents; and of the English language literature in India and Spanish language literature in Latin America as both elaborating older continental literary traditions and innovating new forms, rather than following closely the contemporary fashions of writers in Europe.

It is an old story, but it is not a foreordained story. At first blush at least, adaptive systems seem more likely to fall into extremes of exploitation or exploration than into a balance between them. The long history of human civilization includes numerous examples of isolated systems of knowledge that disappeared before they spread to other systems. Western conceptions of truth have been largely isolated from conceptions that evolved, thrived, and disappeared in parts of the Middle East, Asia, Africa, and America. Western conceits tend to view these systems of knowledge as inferior and to treat their failure to survive as evidence of that inferiority, but scholars of the Middle East, Asia, Africa, and America are less confident of that assessment. A fruitful balance between fragmentation and integration in organization studies is not assured, but arguably it has happened. It has not been planned by anyone, nor is it the result of any wise public policy. It has come about in large part through the fortuitous conjunction of contending ambitions combined with the interventions of a relatively large number of scholars blessed with ambivalence.

## CHINESE ORGANIZATIONS SCHOLARSHIP WITHIN A LARGER RESEARCH COMMUNITY

Chinese efforts to increase exposure to the rest of the world and to experiment with new forms of enterprises have been characteristic of the last 20 years of exceptional economic growth in China. Chinese enterprises have become major participants in the global economy. The Chinese political-economic system has engineered a transformation in economic activities while maintaining relative political stability. Chinese political and economic organization has managed to reconcile the ideology of the market with the ideology of Marxism and to balance the established forces of the Party, the army, and local interests with emerging forces empowered by economic growth. The rise of China as an economic and political power has stimulated research interest in Chinese enterprises and, at the same time, made such research feasible. Li and Tsui (2002) identified 226 articles reporting research on Chinese enterprises in 20 leading English language journals during the period from 1984 to 1999. Seventy percent of the articles appeared during the last half of the period. A growing population of organizations scholars in China and in the Pacific Rim countries heightens the prospects for China-oriented organizations research in the next few decades.

There are two vital contributions that a Chinese organizations research community can make to international organizations scholarship. The first is a delineation of the Chinese context. The Chinese context includes both a specific set of institutional arrangements and a set of cultural understandings, both embedded in a distinctive history (Li and Tsui, 2000). The institutional arrangements involve the state, laws, economic system, and political organization, indeed the whole fabric of Chinese organized society. The cultural understandings include the values, beliefs, frames, and practices that are associated with being Chinese. In their study of 226 articles, Li and Tsui (2002, p. 97) found that "most of the topics in the PRC studies are unique to the context. These topics include the influence of market transition and reform on the firm, the issue of organization structure and change, cross-cultural analysis and adjustment, influence of culture on behavior and values as well as occupational mobility." Understanding these institutional arrangements and cultural understandings in their unique twenty-first century manifestations are essential to comprehending contemporary Chinese enterprises. Since organization studies seeks to say something about organizations wherever they are observed, whatever contributes to understanding Chinese organizations contributes to that goal (Malinowski, 1922; Pike, 1967).

Studies in the Chinese context are also crucial to the identification and elaboration of a context-free set of ideas. While conceding the overwhelming importance of context, most students of organizations aspire to a more general understanding of organizations, an appreciation of how the contextual factors affecting organizations intersect with context-free sets of ideas about human behavior, institutions, history, and society. Research in the Chinese context plays a role in clarifying context dependencies. It helps to expose the limitations of ideas that are accepted as context-free but that reflect a particular political or cultural history. Every new context that is added clarifies the way context affects organization and thereby contributes to the identification and elaboration of more nearly context-free ideas. For example, it seems likely that Chinese conceptions of "strategy" will be less focused than most Western conceptions on the ways in which individual enterprises can improve earnings and shareholder value and more focused on relations with the institutional, particularly political, environments and survival (Marshall Meyer, personal communication) and on policies for industrial or national economic health.

Although the early decades of the twenty-first century in Chinese organizations research will undoubtedly be heavily influenced by a propensity toward North American training and orientation, it seems inevitable that the passage of time and the dynamics of growth will accentuate pressures toward parochialism. The distinctiveness of Chinese languages, history, and organizations, the geographic distance of China from North America and Europe, the size of the country and its population, and the logic of cultural pride all dictate differentiation, particularly since organization studies depend heavily on institutional contexts and on ideas that are not easily viewed as politically or ideologically neutral and that are refined and communicated primarily through natural language, rather than through mathematics. By providing a pocket of scholarship partially protected from the strictures of other pockets and drawing upon philosophical, literary, legal, and scientific traditions that differ from those of other regions, the Chinese organizations research community can provide a source of deviant ideas for the Western establishment. As it has historically, geographic parochialism can encourage both the development of new alternatives and re-examination of old ideas that have been abandoned too rapidly by the guardians of received truth.

What is less clear is whether the inevitable parochialism of Chinese organizations scholarship will be combined with effective contact with the rest of the organizations research community to the benefit of both the wider community and Chinese scholarship. For the benefits to be realized, Chinese scholarship must be disciplined and accessible. All significant scholarly activities are based on disciplined knowledge communities. They exhibit the rigor, precision, and commitment to quality that are characteristics of well-constituted specialties, unified cultures, and shared, precise languages (Cole, 1983; Pfeffer, 1993). The maintenance of a differentiated structure of beliefs and practices within a small, homogeneous community enforces standards and yields the elegance of a refined domain of knowledge. However, such cohesion is potentially self-destructive. As a community develops loyalty toward its own members it encourages a conflation of familiarity with quality. The same sense of community that brings refinement and consensus also brings an in-group bias. All research communities suffer from this bias, but deviant groups—in their consciousness of and in defence of their distinctiveness—are particularly prone to defending the incompetent among them in the name of group solidarity.

A community enforcing an insistence on quality is vital, but it has to be combined with access from the outside. Disciplined experimentation with new ideas within a fragmented field serves the general organizations community only if good, new ideas are accessible to scholars other than their initial enthusiasts. Other organizations research communities, and particularly those of North America, Europe, and East Asia, need to be able to and willing to pay attention to their Chinese colleagues. Such attention within a multidisciplinary, multinational multilingual field requires a point of view about the ways in which scholars deal with the heterogeneity around them—the cacophony of claims of truth and beauty. Many years ago, an art critic told me how he approached the problem of commenting on many different styles of paintings. The spirit of his formulation was:

There are two questions a critic should ask of a painting. The first question is "Is the game the artist has chosen to play a game worth playing?" The second question is "How well does the artist play the game?" A good art critic almost always subordinates the first question to the second. The primary issue in art is quality, not genre.

The formulation is not totally satisfactory, of course. There is always some ambiguity about the interaction between the two questions, and the definition of "quality" is always contested in ways that confuse it with genre. Nevertheless, it is a good formulation—not only about painting but also about scholarship. Improving scholarship is more a function of improving the quality of research within a worldview and tradition than it is of choosing a worldview. A scholar will almost always learn more from another talented scholar who embraces quite different disciplinary, epistemological, cultural, or linguistic convictions than from a colleague who shares prejudices but executes them less well.

### CREATING A MULTIDISCIPLINARY, MULTINATIONAL, MULTILINGUAL COMMUNITY

The relatively small return that has been realized from many decades of proclaiming the need for crossing boundaries suggests that utilitarian reasons for interaction across disciplines, nations, and languages, however frequently they may be cited in post hoc explanations, are unlikely to become major causal factors in creating diverse communities of scholars. Exchanges among scholars are governed by two crucial propositions. The first is a proposition about contact. Scholars, like other humans, prefer most of the time to associate with people who are similar to themselves, people who share their histories, experiences, language, and worldviews (Schelling, 1978). These preferences generate a social structure built around differentiated, coherent, and unified subgroups (Baum, Shipilov, and Rowley, 2003). The second proposition is about the development of inter-subjective knowledge. Although to a substantial extent it is what scholars share that makes discourse possible, it is what they do not share that makes it valuable. Scholars associate primarily with others whom they understand well, those who are, by virtue of their familiar knowledge and beliefs, people from whom they can learn relatively little.

These basic features of social life and social exchange cannot be ignored by those who want to create new elements of integration within a research community. North American organizations researchers will continue, in general, to talk about research with other North American researchers rather than with others who do not share the same terminology, framework, and knowledge. Chinese-speaking scholars will talk to other Chinese-speaking scholars; English-speaking scholars will talk to other English-speaking scholars. For the most part, Russian psychologists and Japanese anthropologists do not come together. If they do, it is initially less out of a passion for talking about the connections between psychology and anthropology than by virtue of some other reasons.

As a first approximation, scholarly communities that violate disciplinary, national, and linguistic boundaries are created largely by arbitrary physical proximity, isolation, and irrelevant social facilitation. A French sociologist talks to a Thai economist when they are stranded together in an unfamiliar city, there is wine, and they are attracted to each other. The process is not mysterious. Ultimately, a scholarly community requires serious talk and a serious meeting of minds; but it does not have to begin there. When some social basis for interaction exists across disciplines, cultures, or languages, those boundaries will often be ignored. In an echo of the history of links between North America and Western Europe, links between Asian scholars and English-speaking scholars of the West have become easier in recent decades with the greater involvement of the Anglophone parts of the Pacific Rim (Australia, New Zealand, India, The Philippines, Western Canada, Western United States), with substantial Asian immigration to English-speaking countries, and with the participation of ethnically Asian scholars domiciled in the West with scholars in the countries of their family origins.

These facilitators of geography and genealogy are augmented by appropriate attention to the role of wine, flirtation, and play. Among strangers, wine can often usefully antedate talk, play can often usefully antedate work, and meetings of the heart can often usefully antedate meetings of the mind. The grim Puritanism of scholarly work has often been intolerant of such frivolity. As a result, scholarly institutions are often designed incorrectly. Conferences are filled with research papers and commentaries, to the exclusion of bottles of wine and opportunities for casual interaction. Offices are filled with desks, computers, and straight-backed chairs, to the exclusion of refrigerators, games, and pillows. And stories of successful collaboration are filled with rationalizations for it, to the exclusion of records of the vintages consumed.

The irrelevant facilitators of association provide bases for warm social interaction and thus, ultimately, for scholarly exchange and collaboration (Hollingshead, 1998; Wegner, Erber, and Raymond, 1991). In the end, however, scholarship requires the exchange not only of cordiality and affection but also of ideas. And therein lies a second complication of multidisciplinary, multinational, and multilingual research. The exchange of ideas involves words; words involve interpretation; and interpretation transforms meaning (Czarniawska and Joerges, 1996; Nord and Connell, 1993; Scott, 2003). Scholarship is both victimized and ennobled by trying to communicate what is known, victimized by the extent to which the interpretation of words reflects inadequately the thoughts behind them, ennobled by the extent to which words communicate more than their author knows.

Writers appear, most of the time, to be more conscious of the victimization than the ennoblement. They regularly claim privileged access to the meanings of their writings and bemoan the perverse interpretations and translations invented by others (Baudelaire, 1961, pp. 155–6; Kundera, 1996). The reproductive unreliability of ideas produced by the fecundity of writing and its comprehension is noticeable even within a single discipline, culture, or language; but disciplinary, national, or linguistic differences accentuate it. Blatant misinterpretations and perverse misunderstandings are conspicuous features of scholarly life. Consciousness of the genuine difficulties of intellectual exchange can, however, easily lead to an exaggerated longing for transparency of meaning, to an ambition that scholarly messages will mean to a reader unambiguously what their writers intended them to mean, nothing more and nothing less.

Although the spread of ideas is vital to enriching disciplines, cultures, and languages and to shielding them from their tendencies to become self-contained, the enrichments of scholarly exchange come only partly from transparency, from being able to borrow ideas reliably. They also come partly from imaginative misunderstandings introduced through the use of words and compounded by the diffuse effects of disparate languages, cultures, and disciplines. The openness of meaning found in the written word allows creative interpretations (as well as nonsense), particularly on the boundaries of distinct disciplines, nations, and languages. It was the differentiation of other languages from Latin that made translation of the Judaic-Christian bible into those languages a heretical act in the fifteenth and sixteenth centuries and rescued Christianity from itself. It is the specialization of economics and sociology that makes translation between them a source of heresy and creativity for both and may save each from itself (Gibbons, 2003).

It is the distinct linguistic character of Chinese and English that empower each in imputing new meanings to ideas originally expressed in the other. When the distinguished Japanese writer Yasunari Kawabata accepted the Nobel Prize for Literature, he said that he was quite sure that no one in the Swedish Academy had read his novels in the language in which he wrote them. As a result, he was not sure whether the prize should properly go to him or to his translator. It was the words of his translator that led to the prize, not the Japanese characters that Kawabata had originally written. In this elegant way, he acknowledged a fundamental feature of human discourse—the inescapable linkage between the transfer of meaning and its transformation. Translation—whether across languages or within a language—is fundamentally a creative act, a primary source of meaning in scholarship. A writer's words and the language connecting them are not simply vessels of intended meaning; they evoke meaning unanticipated by the writer.

As a result, part of the genius of written scholarship lies in amplifying those echoes through a deliberate use of evocative ambiguity. Clarity is usually a virtue; precision is usually a necessity; but one of the joys of scholarship is contemplating the ways that words, metaphors, and models elaborate meanings outside the control of their author. The American poet and essayist, T. S. Eliot, once commented on the analysis of a critic who tried to understand Eliot's poem "A Love Song of J. Alfred Prufrock." Eliot said: "the analysis of 'Prufrock' . . . was an attempt to find out what the poem really meant—whether that was what I had meant it to mean or not. And for that I was grateful" (Eliot, 1961, p. 126). For Eliot, the essence of poetry was the stimulation of meanings more interesting than those of which the poet was fully conscious in writing the words.

Social scientists are all, in Eliot's sense, poets. They write within an interpretive community of scholars. As their ideas travel within that community, or outside of it, they carry meanings that owe much to the nuances of language and culture. Within a relatively closed scholarly community, nuances are shared and meaning tends to be conserved; but the exchange of knowledge across disciplines, nations, and languages is a source of change in meaning, a risky activity for those who seek the safety of established conventions, straightforward problems, and unambiguous words (Westney, 1987). Willful misinterpretation is a corruption of scholarship; the notion that words can mean anything is an atrocity; and no scholarly community can be sustained without a determined thrust toward clarification. Nevertheless, for those who see the creative beauty generated by the wanderings of ideas, the magic and mystery of language is a wonder of intellectual discourse. Scholars celebrate the evocation of new meanings that arise when others discover, not exactly what they thought they meant when they wrote their words or characters but rather what the words or characters themselves might be imagined to mean. That evocation of meaning is a natural product of crossing disciplinary, cultural, national, and linguistic boundaries.

## CHINESE SCHOLARSHIP AND THE FUTURE OF ORGANIZATIONS STUDIES

The creation of a new international journal specializing in research on Chinese organizations provides a ritual occasion for speculating about the coming decades, but invitations to provide forecasts of the future should be accepted only cautiously and with trepidation. The paths of history are inevitable only in retrospect, and major changes in the contexts of organizations studies will produce major changes in their content in the next 100 years. The expansion and elaboration of the European Union, the development of organizations research in China, combined with that country's size and economic power and the future decline of the American Empire all presage substantial changes in the context of research that will shape the way the international community of organizations scholars will evolve over the coming decades. It would be foolish to try to anticipate or dictate the details of those changes or of the ways in which the changing contexts of life will affect the development of organizations scholarship.

Forecasts are foolish, but the future of a scholarly field is connected to its past and to the social context of its development. During the last 50 years of the twentieth century, organizations scholarship in Anglophone North America created a history of its past and thereby created a basis for its future (Augier, March, and Sullivan, 2004; March, 1999). In connected but distinct ways, organizations scholars in other parts of the world also created senses of history that provide bases for related futures (Brunsson and Olsen, 1998; Clegg, Hardy, and Nord, 1996; Czarniawska and Sevón, 2003). Although those histories and their linkages are fragile and the future is uncertain, a foundation for the future of the field has been laid. It is a foundation that is consistent with many different future paths, but it will shape the way organizations research is constructed over the coming years. The future of organizations scholarship, like its past, seems likely to be filled with substantial regional differences, incoherence, and fragmentation, as well as calls for greater coherence. It seems likely to continue to struggle with the dilemmas of exploitation and exploration, resolving them with not much greater elegance than in the past. It will confront the future with the advantages and disadvantages of a quasi-discipline built over the past 50 years, a field with greater structure and greater autonomy than it might have had with a different twentieth-century history. And it will try to maintain a viable alignment between the organization of scholarship and the changing geopolitical organization of the world.

In the midst of all this context and complexity, any calls to action on the part of individuals must be viewed as quixotic—more derivative of a sense of self than of a sense of the future. The future, like the past, will be produced less by plan or coordinated action than by the uncoordinated and inconsistent actions of ambivalent scholars. In that spirit, it is imaginable that future organizations scholars may come to embrace a dream of a research community that recognizes the exploratory advantages of fragmentation into enclaves of high but differentiated quality at the same time as it endorses the multidisciplinary, multinational, and multilingual contacts that exploit those advantages in the service of a more inclusive vision of knowledge. With the coming development of the Chinese organizations research community, such a dream would be rash as a prediction, but perhaps sustainable as a hope.

## REFERENCES

Ancona, D. G. and 'Caldwell, D. E (1992). "Bridging the boundary: External process and performance in organizational teams." *Administrative Science Quarterly*, 37, 634–65.

Augier, M. (2003). "The evolution of behavioral economies." Unpublished manuscript, Stanford University.

Augier, M., March, J. G., and Sullivan, B. N. (2004). "The evolution of a research community: Organization studies in Anglophone North American, 1945–2000." Unpublished manuscript, Stanford University.

Baudelaire, C. (1961). *Les Fleurs du Mal*. Garden City, NY: Doubleday.

Baum, J. A. C., Shipilov, A. V., and Rowley, T. J. (2003). "Where do small worlds come from?" *Industrial and Corporate Change*, 12, 697–725.

Brunsson, N. and Olsen, J. P. (1998). "Organization theory: Thirty years of dismantling and then . . . ?" In Brunsson, N. and Olsen, J. P. (Eds), *Organizing Organizations*. Bergen, Norway: Fagbokforlaget.

Clegg, S., Hardy, C., and Nord, W. R. (Eds) (1996). *Handbook of Organizational Studies*. London, UK: Sage.

Cole, S. (1983). "The hierarchy of the sciences." *American Journal of Sociology*, 89, 111–39.

Crane, D. (1972). *Invisible Colleges: Diffusion of Knowledge in Scientific Communities*. Chicago, IL: University of Chicago Press.

Czarniawska, B. and Joerges, B. (1996). "Travels of ideas." In Czarniawska, B. and Sevón, G. (Eds), *Translating Organizational Change* (pp. 13–48). Berlin: de Gruyter.

Czarniawska, B. and Sevón, G. (Eds) (2003). *The Northern Lights: Organization Theory in Scandinavia*. Copenhagen, Denmark: Copenhagen Business School Press.

Denrell, J. and March, J. G. (2001). "Adaptation as information restriction: The hot stove effect." *Organization Science*, 12, 523–38.

Donaldson, L. (1995). *American Anti-management Theories of Organization: A Critique of Paradigm Proliferation*. Cambridge: Cambridge University Press.

Eliot, T. S. (1961). *On Poetry and Poets*. New York, NY: Noonday.

Engwall, L. (2002). *Managing Mercury*. Uppsala, Sweden: Uppsala Universitet.

Engwall, L. (2003). "On the origin of the Northern Lights." In Czarniawska, B. and Sevón, G. (Eds), *The Northern Lights: Organization Theory in Scandinavia* (pp. 395–411). Copenhagen, Denmark: Copenhagen Business School Press.

Flora, P., Kuhnle, S., and Urwin, D. (Eds) (1999). *State Formation, Nation-Building and Mass Politics in Europe: The Theory of Stein Rokkan*. Oxford: Clarendon.

Gibbons, R. (2003). "Team theory, garbage cans and real organizations: Some history and prospects of economic research on decision-making in organizations." *Industrial and Corporate Change*, 12, 753–87.

Godelier, E. (2003). *James March: Penser les Organisations*. Paris: Hermes Science/ Lavoisier.

Hirschman, A. O. (1991). *The Rhetoric of Reaction*. Cambridge, MA: Harvard University Press.

Holland, J. H. (1975). *Adaptation in Natural and Artificial Systems*. Cambridge, MA: MIT Press.

Hollingshead, A. D. (1998). "Communication, learning, and retrieval in transactive memory systems." *Journal of Experimental Social Psychology*, 34, 423–42.

Knudsen, C. (2003a). "The essential tension in the social sciences: Between the "unification" and "fragmentation" trap." In Jensen, H. S., Richter, L. M. and Vendelø, M. T (Eds), *The Evolution of Scientific Knowledge*. Cheltenham: Edward Elgar.

Knudsen, C. (2003b). "Pluralism, scientific progress and the structure of organization studies." In Tsoukas, H. and Knudsen, C. (Eds), *Oxford Handbook of Organisation Studies: Meta-theoretical Perspectives*. Oxford: Oxford University Press.

Kuhn, T. S. (1970). *The Structure of Scientific Revolutions*. Chicago, IL: University of Chicago Press.

Kundera, M. (1996). *Testaments Betrayed* (trans. Linda Asher). New York, NY: Harper Collins.

Lakatos, I. (1970). "Falsification and the methodology of research programmes." In Lakatos, I. and Musgrave, A. (Eds), *Criticism and the Growth of Knowledge:* 91–6. Cambridge: Cambridge University Press.

Levinthal, D. A. and March, J. G. (1993). "The myopia of learning." *Strategic Management Journal*, 14, 95–112.

Li, J. T and Tsui, A. S. (2000). "Management and organizations in the Chinese context: An overview." In Li, J. T, Tsui, A. S., and Weldon, E. (Eds), *Management and Organizations in the Chinese Context* (pp. 9–32). London: Macmillan.

Li, J. T. and Tsui, A. S. (2002). "A citation analysis of management and organization research in the Chinese context: 1984–1999." *Asia Pacific Journal of Management*, 19(1), 87–107.

Malinowski, B. (1922). *Argonauts of the Western Pacific*. London: Routledge & Sons.

March, J. G. (1991). "Exploration and exploitation in organizational learning." *Organization Science*, 2, 71–87.

March, J. G. (1994). *A Primer on Decision Making: How Decisions Happen*. New York, NY: The Free Press.

March, J. G. (1999). "Research on organizations: Hopes for the past and lessons from the future." *Nordiske Organisasjonsstudier*, 1, 69–83.

March, J. G. and Olsen, J. P. (1995). *Democratic Governance*. New York: Free Press.

Mayr, E. (1976). *Evolution and the Diversity of Life*. Cambridge, MA: Harvard University Press.

Mirowski, P. (1992). *More Heat than Light: Economics as Social Physics, Physics as Nature's Economics*. Cambridge: Cambridge University Press.

Mone, M. A. and McKinley, W. (1993). "The uniqueness value and its consequences for organization studies." *Journal of Management Inquiry*, 2, 284–96.

Nord, W. R. and Connell, A. E (1993). "From quicksand to crossroads: An agnostic perspective on conversation." *Organization Science*, 4, 108–20.

Pfeffer, J. (1993). "Barriers to the advance of organizational science: Paradigm development as a dependent variable." *Academy of Management Review*, 18(4), 599–620.

Pike, K. L. (1967). *Language in Relation to a Unified Theory of the Structure of Human Behavior*. The Hague: Mouton.

Postrel, S. (2002). "Islands of shared knowledge: Specialization and mutual understanding in problem-solving teams." *Organization Science,* 13, 303–20.

Schelling, T C. (1978). *Micromotives and Macrobehavior.* New York, NY: W. W. Norton.

Scott, W. R. (2003). "Institutional carriers: reviewing modes of transporting ideas over time and space and considering their consequences." *Industrial and Corporate Change,* 12, 879–94.

Wagner, P., Wittrock, B. and Whitley, R. (Eds) (1991). *Discourses on Society: The Shaping of the Social Science Disciplines.* Dordrecht: Kluwer Academic Publishers.

Wegner, D. M., Erber, R. and Raymond, P. (1991). "Transactive memory in close relationships." *Journal of Personality and Social Psychology,* 61, 923–9.

Westney, D. E. (1987). *Imitation and Innovation: The Transfer of Western Organizational Patterns to Meiji Japan.* Cambridge, MA: Harvard University Press.

Westwood, R. and Clegg, S. (2003). The discourse of organization studies: Dissensus, politics, and paradigms. In Westwood, R. and Clegg, S. (Eds), *Debating Organization: Point-Counterpoint in Organization Studies* (pp. 1–42). Oxford: Blackwell.

Whitley, R. (1984). "The development of management studies as a fragmented adhocracy." *Social Science Information,* 23, 125–46.

Williamson, O. E. (2003). "Examining economic organization through the lens of contract." *Industrial and Corporate Change,* 12, 917–42.

Zammuto, R. F. and Connolly, T. (1984). "Coping with disciplinary fragmentation." *Organizational Behavior Teaching Review,* 9, 30–7.

# CHAPTER 14

# Notes on the Evolution
# of a Research Community

## *Organization Studies in Anglophone*
## *North America, 1945–2000*

MIE AUGIER, JAMES G. MARCH, AND BILIAN NI SULLIVAN

Since the Second World War, the field of organizations studies has grown substantially in the number of researchers, number of publications, and amount of research produced. It has moved from being a combination of established disciplines to becoming a quasi-discipline of its own, with its own journals and professional associations. It has established a standardized set of ancestors, a stylized history. It has solidified an academic home in business schools. This history has implications for understanding both the future of organizations research and the social dynamics of the development of scholarly communities.

THE HISTORY OF ORGANIZATION STUDIES has sometimes been written to reflect origins as distant as the earliest systematic human writings and extended to include distinguished writers of later years: Thomas Aquinas, John Locke, Jean-Jacques Rousseau, Jeremy Bentham, Vilfredo Pareto, Adam Smith, and the authors of the *Federalist Papers* among many others. More conventionally, the history has been written to include major contributors of the last half of the nineteenth century and the first half of the twentieth: Marx, Pareto, Weber, Durkheim, Taylor, Fayol, Commons, Follett, Mayo, Gaus, Roethlisberger and Dickson, Gulick and Urwick, Barnard, Merton (for some excursions into the history, see March 1965, pp. ix–xvi; Pfeffer 1982, pp. 1–40; Westwood and Clegg 2003, pp. 2–4; Scott 2004).

Despite this long heritage, the contemporary field of organization studies is primarily a creation of a shorter and more parochial history created in the

---

This chapter originally appeared as an article in *Organization Science*, 16 (2005), 85–95.

last half of the twentieth century in Anglophone North America.[1] The focus on North American scholarship is not to overlook the substantial twentieth century contributions from other parts of the world. European scholars such as Tom Burns, Ronald Coase, Michel Crozier, David Hickson, Edith Penrose, Derek Pugh, Claude Riveline, George Stalker, and Joan Woodward were major figures in the middle of the century, as were scholars such as Nils Brunsson, Lex Donaldson, Giovanni Dosi, Alfred Kieser, Bruno Latour, Johan Olsen, Andrew Pettigrew, and Jean-Claude Thoenig in the latter part. Scholarly fields often bury their early and geographically distant contributors through some combination of ignorance, localized ambitions for recognition, and convenient conceptions of progress; and the field of organization studies in North America clearly exhibits such myopia. However, there are special features of twentieth century history that shaped the development of the organizations research community after 1945 in such a way as to lead to a relatively autonomous genealogy.

## I. AN EMBEDDED HISTORY

The history of the study of organizations is truncated by the decisive reality of 1945. Before the Second World War, American scholars who sought to be in the forefront of scholarship characteristically went to Europe to study. They sought close collaboration with European scholars who were recognized as leaders in their fields. After the Second World War, particularly in the social sciences, American scholars (many of them refugee immigrants from Europe) began to build a new community of scholarship. It was a community that was clearly international in its intentions and range, but it was based in North America. Important scholars survived the war in Europe and new scholars were educated in Europe and Asia in the years following the war, but the scholarly center of gravity moved toward North America.

In 1945, Great Britain was exhausted; continental Europe and countries in Asia were beginning a period of recovery and reconstruction that would take two or three decades to complete, and the United States was beginning a period of unprecedented power, prosperity, and growth. American universities and the research associated with them were about to expand at an extraordinary rate, both in size and in quality. In the decades after the war, the more important research sites were increasingly found at American universities; the more important journals were increasingly likely to be published in North America and to be edited by North Americans, and scholars throughout the world increasingly looked to North America for training and leadership.

The knowledge community associated with the study of organizations in

North America was a product of that time and that history (Smiddy and Naum 1954, Churchman 1956). The immediate postwar period was an era that glorified science (Leslie 1993, Zachary 1999). The social and behavioral sciences became more quantitative, more analytical, and more committed to the principles of modern science. The impact was somewhat different in the different fields of anthropology, economics, history, political science, psychology, and sociology, but the impact was profound. As the years passed, the preeminence of science and the sacred position of logical positivism were challenged, but the idea of research-based knowledge and the role of academic institutions in generating and teaching such knowledge were taken as given.

In the first decade or two after the war, organization studies attracted the attention of a quite heterogeneous group of scholars. Subsequently, it absorbed several waves of substantive and methodological enthusiasms. Soon after the Second World War, it was shaped considerably by a group of scholars who sought to vitalize scholarship in the field through adopting the methods of science, the techniques of mathematics, and a commitment to systematic empirical observation (Thompson 1956, Berelson 1963). This urge was in parallel with an enthusiasm for statistical conceptions of the analysis of data, and particularly multivariate statistics (Festinger and Katz 1953, Lazarsfeld 1955). Part of the impetus came out of operations research and related conceptions of organization design (Helmer 1958); part of the impetus came from postwar hubris about the possibilities for improving social, political, and economic life through social science (O'Connor 2001); and part of the impetus came from the disciplines—from psychologists interested in groups (Cartwright and Zander 1953), sociologists interested in institutions (Merton 1949), economists interested in the firm (Baumol 1959), and political scientists interested in the problems of bureaucratization (Truman 1951).

In keeping with most of the rest of social science, students of organizations during the first few decades after the Second World War were primarily students of comparative statics, seeking to identify the conditions under which particular organizational structures survived and thrived. The emphasis was on the ways in which the efficiency of structures (their functionality) could be inferred from, or used to predict, their endurance or proliferation (Lawrence and Lorsch 1967, Pugh and Hickson 1976). The presumption was that survival and efficiency were fairly closely linked, therefore the precise mechanisms by which efficient forms were selected to survive did not need to be specified or understood. As time passed, this perspective was complemented by perspectives that devoted more attention to trying to comprehend the processes underlying the shape and functioning of organizations and human understanding of them (Padgett and Ansell 1993, Cohen and Sproull 1996).

As the field developed, it generally adopted a conception of human behavior in organizations that was broadly consequentialist (March 1996). It portrayed action as generated by choice, choice as based on consideration of alternatives in terms of expectations of their consequences, and expectations as shaped by personal experience and social settings (Flood 1955, Shubik 1958). This conception gradually was supplemented by a conception of human behavior in organizations that saw action as generated by rule following—rules as based on processes of domination, learning, variation, selection, and diffusion within complex social networks that assume many structures in addition to the familiar hierarchies; rules as organized into institutions that endure; and rule-based systems as heavily ecological in character (Burns and Flam 1987; March and Olsen 1989 1995).

This latter conception fostered variants of evolutionary theory (Nelson and Winter 1982, Dosi 2000) and theories of complexity (Kauffman 1995, Axelrod and Cohen 1999), as well as methods of history and ethnography that emphasized the ways in which the historical and social contexts of organizations make a difference (Barley and Orr 1997, Hodgson 2001), a point of view that also provided an opening (as did the earlier ideas about the social basis of expectations) for notions that emphasized the social construction of meaning and the extent to which life is better understood, not as action, but as interpretation (Weick 1969, 1995; Martin 1992).

Meanders similar to those found in organization studies are characteristic of the intellectual landscape of the entire Anglophone North American study of human behavior and institutions in the last half of the twentieth century (National Research Council 1988). Organizations studies in North America has been more affected by some ideas than by others, more receptive to some ideas than to others, but it has developed in the same general temporal, social, and intellectual context that shaped the rest of social science. The main ebbs and flows of enthusiasms within the field have involved responses both to major external forces that affected scholarship very broadly and to the diffusion of ideas among students of individual and social behavior. This intertwining of the history of organization studies with the more general economic, social, political, and intellectual climate of the times is true at several levels. Not only are the specific enthusiasms of social science echoed in organization studies, but many of them can also be tied fairly easily to some broad historical trends, particularly the triumph of capitalism, the sanctification of individual and group self-interest, the proliferation and elaboration of organizations, the extension of American hegemony, and the creation of a computer-based information technology. The field grew to maturity in a particular era of western history and bears the marks of that era, both in its substance and in its institutions.

## 2. CREATING A SCHOLARLY IDENTITY

All modern thinking about intellectual history has been shaped decisively by the contributions of T. S. Kuhn (Kuhn 1970), in particular by his characterization of paradigms and paradigm shifts. The Kuhnian emphasis on the struggle between new ideas and established ideas is obviously relevant to the development of organization studies during the last half of the twentieth century, but insofar as organizations studies can be described as a field, it has a paradigm only at a level of abstraction that makes it indistinguishable from the rest of nineteenth and twentieth century social science. We describe a history that certainly encompasses change in the standing of ideas, even elements of changes that might be identified as moving in some temporarily consistent directions, but in a broad sense the history is more similar to the history of philosophy than it is to the history of physics.

In the 1950s, different scholars speculated about the process by which organization studies could and would evolve. Boulding (1958) argued that although from the beginning the field of organization studies was trying to separate itself from the parent disciplines (sociology, economics, psychology, and political science), it was fundamentally dependent on developments in the disciplines themselves for a successful take-off. While Boulding and others were searching for a general theory of organizations, others focused on the difficulties in establishing a new discipline. Litchfield (1956) noted: "Our confusion of terminology makes it difficult to speak accurately to one another within any one field, let alone across fields and across cultures" (p. 6). Also, there was substantial agreement that although a general theory of organizations was something worthy of effort, the field had a long way to go. As Helmer (1958, p. 172) noted:

There has been a lot of talk in the last decade or two about organization theory as the up-and-coming thing. Yet the trouble with organization theory to date is its continued nonexistence. This is true despite the fact that numerous sporadic efforts in this general area have succeeded in providing a variety of insights into the mechanism of all kinds of organizations.

Robert Merton expressed similar concerns with regard to the early evolution of the behavioral sciences (Merton 1963).

From that beginning, the field has experienced the gradual creation of a knowledge domain, a knowledge community, and a scholarly identity. This process is revealed by two conspicuous features: First, the field of organization studies has constructed a history of itself, a set of loosely connected stories. Although there is considerable chaos in the history, with numerous enthusiasms finding relatively short-term popularity and a strong tendency to claim novelty (Pfeffer 1993), there has been some development of a canon. One indication of the development is a change in the age distribution of references. For example, whereas the median age of a reference in a well-known early book (March and Simon 1958) was 5 years, the median age in a well-known book that came later (Scott 1998) was 18 years. This particular difference unquestionably reflects differences in the styles of those specific authors, but it also is symptomatic of a change in the field. North American organization studies has come to exhibit a sense of a somewhat shared intellectual history, a history that has been constructed with a first generation, by now only dimly seen and vaguely remembered, that is pictured as more or less immaculately conceived in the first two decades after 1945.

Second, the domain of organization studies has increasingly differentiated itself from other fields and from the social science disciplines. Although citations in books and articles dealing with organizations are to a very large number of journals, the concentration of citations has increased over time as the field has come to identify a few primary outlets, many of which were created in the last half of the twentieth century. This increased concentration has occurred in parallel with increased differentiation from the journals of the major social science disciplines. The picture varies from subfield to subfield. For example, work on organizational demography maintains relatively frequent references to sociological journals; work on institutional approaches to organizations maintains relatively frequent references to economic, political science, and sociology journals; work on cognitive aspects of individual behavior in organizations maintains relatively frequent references to psychological journals. Overall, however, there appears to have been a substantial increase in references to organizations journals and a substantial decrease in references to disciplinary journals. For example, Table 1 shows the changing distribution of citations to journals across three handbooks in the field (March 1965, Nystrom and Starbuck 1981, Baum 2002) over a period of almost forty years. Although some features of the changes are undoubtedly attributable to idiosyncrasies of the editors, it seems clear that organization studies in Anglophone North America has increasingly differentiated itself from other fields.

From a time in which references were to a diffuse set of disciplines and academic frames, the field has become organized around a relatively distinct set of

TABLE 1    Number and fraction of citations in three handbooks, by discipline

| | 1965 | | 1981 | | 2002 | |
|---|---|---|---|---|---|---|
| Discipline | Number of citations | Fraction | Number of citations | Fraction | Number of citations | Fraction |
| Anthropology | 38 | 0.027 | 35 | 0.013 | 4 | 0.003 |
| Economics | 109 | 0.076 | 319 | 0.123 | 156 | 0.099 |
| Political Science | 152 | 0.107 | 124 | 0.048 | 12 | 0.008 |
| Psychology | 291 | 0.204 | 312 | 0.120 | 41 | 0.026 |
| Sociology | 382 | 0.268 | 392 | 0.151 | 324 | 0.205 |
| Organizations | 249 | 0.174 | 731 | 0.281 | 834 | 0.527 |
| Business | 51 | 0.036 | 179 | 0.069 | 100 | 0.063 |
| Other academic | 149 | 0.104 | 440 | 0.169 | 91 | 0.057 |
| Popular | 6 | 0.004 | 59 | 0.023 | 4 | 0.003 |
| Unclassified | 0 | 0.000 | 13 | 0.005 | 17 | 0.011 |
| Total | 1,427 | 1.000 | 2,604 | 1.000 | 1,583 | 1.000 |

journals, which in turn have become increasingly specialized to the community of organization researchers. It has also become more specialized with distinct micro and macro subdivisions, as well as more narrowly defined specialties, each with a distinct canon and pattern of predecessor acknowledgment. The micro part of the field retains linkages to psychological journals; the macro part retains linkages to sociological journals; but both parts have become to a significant degree independent of their disciplinary cousins. Indeed, in the handbook published in 2002 (Baum 2002), which is strongly tilted toward macro perspectives, over 50 percent of the citations are to articles published in just five journals (*Administrative Science Quarterly, American Journal of Sociology, Strategic Management Journal, Organization Science, American Sociological Review*), only two of which are associated with a traditional academic discipline.

The knowledge story was part of a broader development—the development of a scholarly identity. In the early periods of this history, a scholar's identity as a member of the organizations community was weak compared to identity as a member of some discipline community. Over time, it became stronger. By the year 2000, it had become socially meaningful for a scholar to identify with the organization studies field, to publish in journals of that field, to cite other scholars of that field who published in journals of that field, to belong to professional associations connected to that field, to attend professional conferences for that field, and to have a professorial title that identified that field. At the same time, the disciplinary identification of organizations scholars appears to have weakened, as has the importance of the field as a source of ideas and concepts in the various disciplines.

The developments in North America were parallel to, but not much influenced by, the elaboration of the field in Western Europe and Asia. As the field differentiated itself from other disciplines in North America, it maintained its isolation from scholarship outside of North America. One count of four recent issues of four leading North American journals (*Academy of Management Journal, Academy of Management Review, Administrative Science Quarterly, Organization Science*) showed that, in each of the journals, over 90 percent of the citations were to books or articles published in North America (March 2004). This parochialism was exhibited during the same period in which important journals outside of North America (e.g., *Organization Studies, Journal of Management Studies, Scandinavian Journal of Management, Revue Française de Gestion, Industrial and Corporate Change*) became increasingly robust outlets for papers reporting research on organizations.

### 3. FINDING A HOME

Early in the postwar period, the study of organizations in North America had multiple academic homes. Philip Selznick and Peter Blau were sociologists. Dorwin Cartwright and Alex Bavelas were psychologists. Herbert Simon and James March were political scientists. W. F. Whyte and Leonard Sayles were anthropologists. William Cooper and West Churchman were operations researchers. Richard Cyert and Jacob Marschak were economists. By the end of the twentieth century, disciplinary outposts for organizational studies remained in most of the social science disciplines, but the bulk of the research in the field was found in business schools, concentrated in departments describing themselves as being concerned with "organizational behavior" and "strategic management."

### 3.1. *The Context*

This history can be understood as reflecting important characteristics of the character and history of both American business schools and American universities. With respect to the latter, four major features of academic social science in postwar North America may be noteworthy. First, there was growth (Hodgkinson 1971). Spurred first by the GI Bill, which offered university education to millions of veterans, later by the maturation of baby boomers, and throughout by an increased economic demand for university-educated labor, academic social science thrived. Second, there was optimism (Lazarsfeld et al. 1967). The idea that social science could be made more scientific and could contribute to solving social and economic problems permeated not only the ranks of social scientists, but also social and political leadership. Third, there was enthusiasm among policy makers and among many important social scientists for the idea of interdisciplinary research (Sherif and Sherif 1969). Social problems and cutting-edge research questions seemed to cut across the academic disciplines, and the successful experience during the war with interdisciplinary projects in science suggested that the future of social science might involve significant interdisciplinary efforts. Fourth, among academics, the disciplines were primary (Clark 1995). Academic excellence depended on and sustained the autonomy of the major academic disciplines. The organization of social science in universities was profoundly an organization of separate disciplines. And the status of departments and individuals within disciplines was determined by the disciplines, not by outsiders.

These features of academic social science interacted with, and to some extent produced, a transformation of university business schools in North America. University-based business education had existed in North America for some time, but its link with the core of the universities was tenuous and often contentious. In the early twentieth century, business education was established at the undergraduate level, and in 1916 business educators established their own professional association, the American Association of Collegiate Schools of Business (AACSB) (Schlossman et al. 1994, p. 4).

The first North American graduate degree in business was given in 1900 from Dartmouth College, and in 1908 the Northwestern University School of Commerce and the Harvard Graduate School of Business Administration were established. Other universities followed, but only a few hundred American MBAs were awarded annually prior to the Second World War.

Early business schools in North America defined their role primarily in terms of codifying and communicating good business practice, as exemplified by business-case writing and teaching. Many early faculty positions were filled with experienced businessmen rather than young scholars, and the distinction between managerial consulting and managerial research was hazy. Despite the efforts of some deans and faculty to push them toward more academic pursuits, business schools emphasized practical, not theoretical, courses; applied, not basic, science; and the contributions of faculty were more often published in journals focusing on detailed descriptions of business techniques than in academic journals.[2] Because of these choices, North American business schools had difficulty establishing legitimacy in the academic core. Whatever virtues they had, they were, for the most part, not considered by most of the rest of the academic community as serious participants in the world of academic scholarship and intellectual pursuits. Herbert Simon, who witnessed and contributed to the transformation of business education, reflected in his autobiography:

Accurately or not, we perceived American business education at that time as a wasteland of vocationalism that needed to be transformed into science-based professionalism, as medicine and engineering had been transformed a generation or two earlier. (Simon 1991, p. 138)

### 3.2. The Transformation of Business Schools

The postwar period provided an opportunity for university presidents, academically oriented business school faculty, and visionary business executives to combine with external forces to impose academic respectability on the business school community. Although some major business schools were content to be successful in the business world without achieving substantial academic standing, for most of them the postwar period provided an opportunity to improve their previous low status within the academic community. They sought a new approach to business education and an invigoration of fundamental interdisciplinary research in accounting, finance, operations research, microeconomics, and organizations.

The transformation of business schools involved a classic combination of money, institutional power, organization, opportunistic self-interest seeking, and visionary leadership. In particular, it involved the Ford Foundation. The Ford Foundation had at that time formulated a program for "the study of man" (which became known as "the behavioral science research area"), the specific objective of which was stated as follows: "The Ford Foundation will support scientific activities designed to increase knowledge of factors which influence or determine human conduct, and to extend such knowledge for the maximum benefit of individuals and of society."[3] Research had to be scientific; embodied in the Ford Foundation's understanding of the behavioral science concept was "its emphasis upon the scientific approach to problem solution" (p. 4). Also, it had to be practical, to some extent at least, given the foundation's interest not in knowledge per se, but in "knowledge which promises at some point to serve human needs."

To justify a major initiative in business schools, the Foundation commissioned the Gordon-Howell Report in 1959, which described the limited scientific foundation for American business education (Gordon and Howell 1959). This led to Foundation expenditures of $35 million over a little more than a decade. A key part of the initiative was stimulating an increased focus on the disciplines (particularly economics, but not limited to economics) and disciplinary-like research. What evolved in business schools was a strategy of pursuing disciplinary-like research in domains that were slighted by the disciplinary department—domains of applied economics and multidisciplinary fields such as organizations. The Foundation effort was a key part of a massive and successful effort to transform business schools into academic institutions somewhat comparable in scholarly standing to other university units (Schlossman et al. 1987). The effort was supplemented by more modest expenditures to provide support for similar efforts in Europe (e.g., the establishment of the European Institute for Advanced Studies in Management—EIASM—in Brussels).

The reform of business schools in North America was made feasible by financial strength. The improvements stimulated by the Ford Foundation combined with the economic prosperity experienced in North America to increase the fiscal autonomy of business schools. The fiscal improvements were used to create both substantial research support for individual faculty members that did not depend on applications to external foundations or governmental agencies, and also a major difference between what a research-oriented academic could earn as a faculty member in a business school compared to what could be earned by the same person as a faculty member in a disciplinary department. To a significant extent, business schools bought their way into academic respectability. The largess of the Ford Foundation stimulated the change, but the indispensable precondition was that the primary product of the business schools—the MBA—became, despite occasional doubts (Pfeffer and Fong 2001), highly valued in the labor market.

It was under these social, political, and economic circumstances that the field of organization studies migrated into business schools. The migration was natural, but it was perhaps not entirely foreordained. From the perspective of 1945, it would have been hard to anticipate the elaboration of a quasi-discipline of organization studies based primarily in business schools. Even as late as 1970, a listing of major North American publications in organizations during the preceding two decades would have listed primarily works from researchers found in disciplinary departments, works such as Lindblom (1959), Blau and Scott (1962), Olson (1965), Stinchcombe (1965), Tullock (1965), Katz and Kahn

(1966), Downs (1967), Thompson (1967), Hirschman (1970), Allison (1971), and Perrow (1972).

By 1970, however, the migration of organization studies to business schools and to publication outlets closely linked to business schools was well underway in North America. The migration is illustrated by, and was to some extent influenced by, the role of the Graduate School of Industrial Administration at the Carnegie Institute of Technology. In a brief period in the 1950s and early 1960s, the organizations group at Carnegie executed a research program the results of which became anointed over the ensuing decades as a partial prolegomena to a field (March and Simon 1958, Cyert and March 1963). The works from "the Carnegie School," along with a few others during this period (for example, Lawrence and Lorsch 1967, Weick 1969) were particularly important in defining the study of organizations as a research responsibility of business schools, as were the works of students who were products of that school during this period—for example, Oliver Williamson, Louis Pondy, William Starbuck, and Arie Lewin. Similar things were happening at the same time in other business schools, for example, at the Massachusetts Institute of Technology, the University of Chicago, and the University of California (Berkeley).

By 1970, organizations studies would be graced by a handbook (also a product of the Carnegie group) and a set of professional associations closely linked to business school faculties. These included the Academy of Management (originally established in 1936 but considerably reinvigorated in the 1950s and 1960s), the Operations Research Society of America (established in 1952), and the Institute of Management Science (in 1954). This invigoration of professional associations also led to new journals, including the *Journal of Operations Research Society in America,* initiated in 1952 and changed in 1956 to *Operations Research; Management Science* initiated in 1954; and the *Journal of the Academy of Management,* initiated in 1958 and changed in 1962 to the *Academy of Management Journal.* These outlets, together with other journals such as *Administrative Science Quarterly* and later *Organization Science,* encouraged publication by scholars in organization studies.

By 1980, a field had been defined. It had helped legitimize business schools as serious academic institutions, and the center of gravity of organization studies had moved decisively to a business school locale. This home had some effects on the emphases in the field, for example, moving them closer to economics and further from political science. In addition, because the home was created in the context of a specific transformation of business schools, organization studies absorbed some of the characteristic ideology of that transformation, in particular the emphasis on fundamental research. From the point of view of the short-run development of the field, however, the more important thing was that the business school home provided a stable base less affected by the vagaries of disciplinary department enthusiasms. It provided a financial base and a student base. It provided a doctoral program independent of the disciplines. It granted control over academic appointments and promotions to the field.

Finally, the migration of the field to business schools tied organization studies more to the private sector and to issues of performance, and led to the development of a link between students of organizations and other students of decision making and strategy in a domain that came to be called "strategic management." The story of the sociological and intellectual dynamics of the creation of the field of strategic management remains to be told in its full detail (Schendel and Hofer 1979, Hambrick 1990, Rumelt et al. 1994, Hoskisson et al. 1999), but the business school locale both of that development and of organization studies is clearly implicated in that story. An earlier business school teaching field of business policy, which was largely the province of the least research-oriented parts of business schools, was transformed into a new field dominated by an uneasy coalition of micro economists, decision theorists, game theorists, behavioral students of organizational decision making, and students of organizational history, evolution, and demography. The ties and tensions between the new field and economics on the one hand, and organization studies on the other, are products, in part, of the distinctive business school location of the effort.

## 4. IMPLICATIONS

The story we have told is obviously linked to a particular period and (in large part) to a particular region of the world. Its implications are limited by those contexts. Nevertheless, it may be instructive to ask whether anything can be learned from such a history for the future of organization studies or for understanding the development of scholarly communities. The future of organization studies will undoubtedly reflect the multicontinental and multilingual nature of scholarship in the twenty-first century, and the brief period of Anglophone North American hegemony and isolation will end. Nevertheless, understanding the 1945–2000 period in the North American history of organization studies may be useful in anticipating and shaping the coming decades.

The development of a knowledge community among students of organizations in Anglophone North America involved the intertwining of history, time, place, and agency. The story is one of history dependence, and ecological interaction. Some elements of the story are shared with many other fields of social science during the same period. This is particularly true of the development of ideas. As we try to think more generally about the development of scholarly communities, these elements discourage any notion of uniqueness in the history of any particular community. Other elements of the story seem less universal, but are driven largely by external forces impinging on the study of organizations. These elements discourage any notion of autonomy in the development of a scholarly community. In addition, some details of the story seem neither universal nor necessary, but appear to have been influenced by relatively chancelike meanders and deliberate actions taken by particular individuals and institutions. These elements suggest a possible role for chance and agency.

## 4.1. The Future of Organization Studies

In the last 55 years of the twentieth century, the field of organization studies grew enormously in Anglophone North America. It grew in terms of the numbers and prestige of scholars, number and reputation of journals and publications, and the number and quality of students. It is a history of expansion, recognition, standardization, differentiation, localization, and legitimization. At the start of the period, organization studies was an ill-defined, small interdisciplinary combination of established disciplines. By the end of the period, the boundaries of the field remained somewhat fluid and the breadth of its inclusiveness somewhat in dispute, but it was a large quasi-discipline of its own, with its own journals, professional associations, and identities. It had solidified an academic home within business schools. To a modest extent, it had established a stylized history and a relatively agreed-upon set of ancestors, most of them dating from the 20-year period beginning in 1945.

Although this history of growth, consolidation, and localization considerably tightened professional institutionalization and identities within the field, it did so by creating a loose canon, history, identity, and locale, rather than a paradigm (Pfeffer 1993, van Maanen 1995). Thus, it also created opportunities for exclusion, autonomous development, and quarrels over techniques and worldviews. Moreover, differentiation, elaboration, and institutionalization left disciplinary remnants (e.g., public administration, organizational economics, organizational psychology, organizational and economic sociology) in the disciplines. These remnants developed in different ways in different disciplines, but they all became somewhat isolated (both intellectually and institutionally) from the American business school–based group, as the latter did from them.

The main institutionalization also proceeded, for the most part, in a geographically and linguistically parochial way. Many European and a few Asian and Latin American scholars were well integrated into the North American group. However, as organizations scholarship grew outside of North America toward the end of the twentieth century, some relatively autonomous clusters of European and Asian scholars established themselves, stimulated in part by the growth and increasingly academic and increasingly independent orientation of European and Asian business schools (Garel and Godelier 2004).

The elaboration of the field during the last half of the twentieth century was a considerable accomplishment, and it sowed the seeds of future harvests. Future generations of scholars will find the intellectual soil easier to till and the markets for ideas more accessible. At the same time, however, the unfolding of history has left the field with several important features that are likely to affect its future development in a less homogeneously benign way. The first feature is the separation from the social science disciplines. Virtually all research on organizations involves concepts and methods of social science; virtually all organizational researchers consider themselves social scientists. The creation of an independent quasi-discipline tends to separate the field from the salutary discipline of the disciplines. This separation from the disciplines has implications for the balancing of exploration and exploitation required for the long-run adaptation of the field (Holland 1975, March 1991). It makes the field more open to novelty (exploration), but less persistently rigorous (exploitation).

The second feature that will affect the future is the parochialism of the North American community. The last half of the twentieth century provides a classic instance of the inattention of the large and powerful to the small and weak. North American scholars appear to be consistently less conscious of European and Asian research than European and Asian scholars are of North American research. As European and Asian centers of organizations scholarship continue to develop, this parochialism will become increasingly dysfunctional. American imperialism is one form of scientific universalism, but it is a form that is likely to encounter increasing resistance from European and Asian scholars and could leave their North American colleagues dangerously isolated.

The third feature of the history that will affect the future is the migration to business schools. The business school home of organization studies is a natural and productive one, but it produces systematic intellectual biases. It brings an overwhelming focus on the private sector, reducing the attention to the public sector that characterized much early work in the field. It brings relatively close contact with ideas from economics that might be relevant, but makes contact with ideas from the sciences, psychology, sociology, or political science somewhat less routine. It brings an emphasis on the audience of practitioners, on finding the correlates of organizational performance rather than other organizational phenomena. It brings an orientation to the problems and possibilities of individual organizations (firms) and less attention to populations of organizations. It focuses on organizational strategies, rather than societal strategies. It brings pressure for relevance and reduces emphasis on fundamental research and knowledge.

The future of organization studies will be as context and history dependent as its past. It is easy to predict that the course of world political, social, economic, and intellectual history will shape organization studies decisively. Because it is foolish to try to predict that course in any detail, it is foolish to try to predict its derivative, the history of organization studies. The 55-year history that began in 1945 was a period that made scholarship associated with Anglophone North America central to the development of the field. The next century will certainly witness a decline in the unique importance of the North American linguistic and geographic enclave. As that history develops, the cacophony of multiple languages, disciplines, and regions may well make some wish for the "good old days" when there was a reasonably defined field located in a reasonably stable place, when there was a somewhat shared sense of history and a shared location, but the unusual combination of circumstances that shaped scholarly communities in the last half of the twentieth century will give way to a new combination.

## 4.2. The Development of Scholarly Communities

There were two critical things that happened in this history: The rudiments of a knowledge story were created, and a home was found. In the early periods, the field had a weak sense of its own place and history. As the community developed, it distinguished itself from other communities and connected the community to itself over time. To a limited extent, it created its own genealogy. At the same time, the organizations research community found a home for itself in business schools. This location was to some extent fortuitous, but the effects of the migration were significant for the subsequent development of the field.

Both the creation of a history and the location of a home are history dependent in two senses. First, the particular historical context affects the course of history. The particular history of organization studies that was constructed in Anglophone North America in the last half of the twentieth century bears the clear imprint of that era and place. A business school was a natural home for organizations studies at that time in a way that it would not have been earlier or perhaps later. Second, the particular branches of history that are taken at a particular time affect the future unfolding of history. If organizations studies had located itself in engineering schools, rather than business schools, its subsequent development would almost certainly have been different. Some idea of what might have been expected can be deduced from the work of engineering-based organizations scholars in Anglophone North America, individuals such as Stephen Barley, Kathleen Eisenhardt, Raymond Levitt, and Robert Sutton. In a similar way, the fact that computer science developed as a research community at a particular time shaped its own history; and the fact that computer science located itself in engineering and science schools, rather than in business schools, was important to the development of that field.

The story we have told is a story of success. Anglophone North American business school organization studies created a relatively distinct quasi-discipline with its own community, its own institutions, its own standards, and its own language. It discovered an intellectual, institutional, and geographic location that isolates, nurtures, and protects it. Each of these successes contains a warning about the natural history of adaptation. They portend, and to some extent exhibit, variations on a single theme of success—the inclination to persist in a successful course, refining it and extending it, rather than to explore new possibilities (Cyert and March 1963, Denrell and March 2001). Exploitation drives out exploration. As a scholarly field solidifies and exploits its successes, its efforts to exercise control over scholarship improve the average quality of research, but at the same time threaten the long-run health of the field by limiting variation. New ideas that stray from established conventions or have weak links to recognized field "ancestors" are likely to be rejected before they can be explored.

The comfortable bleakness of that pessimism requires some qualification, however. On the one hand, the gains realized from exploitation are not to be underestimated. Ideas are refined; methods are honed; knowledge is codified. As we have noted, a new field cut off from the stabilizing forces of the disciplines is quite likely to suffer from an excess of exploration. Moreover, success—particularly rapid success—unleashes the aggravating rashness, brashness, imagination, arrogance, and persistence of the upwardly mobile. As late arrivals to academic legitimacy, business schools suffered from the anxieties of the nouveau riche. As a late arrival to disciplinary legitimacy, organization studies suffered from disciplinary envy. As a late arrival to cultural legitimacy, North America suffered from fears of cultural inferiority. Anxieties, envies, and fears stimulate imitative silliness, but they also stimulate the edginess, risk taking, and ambition associated with the illusions of winners and with consciousness of the fragility of newly acquired status. The resulting explorations and adventures undoubtedly generate more junk than jewels, but revolutions are produced neither by contentment nor by despair, but by the ambitions and illusions unleashed by the first derivative of success (Brinton 1965, Kahneman and Lovallo 1993).

It seems plausible to suggest that the development of almost any scholarly community will involve both creating a history and finding a home. The creation of an identity (and the definition of a knowledge story associated with it) and the finding of a home are implicated in similar descriptions of the evolution of nations (Bendix 1964, Eisenstadt et al. 1970), organizations (Pettigrew 1985, Lincoln and Kalleberg 1990), and religions (Weber 1922–1923, Oberoi 1994). The contemporary term is likely to be consciousness; and the differentiation, solidification, and glorification of a particular research community is not remarkably different from the differentiation, solidification, and glorification of the nation state, the corporation, or the religious sect. Knowledge and scholarship are social phenomena. Their claim to a special relationship to empirical truth affects the development of knowledge communities in important ways, but the communities are social and their development is analogous to the development of other social communities.

Our portrayal of the 1945–2000 history of organization studies in North America suggests a picture of the development of scholarly fields as involving the history-dependent construction of histories, identities, and homes and the dynamic cycling of adaptive exploration and exploitation. That portrayal is, however, incomplete in at least one major way. The evolution of any particular field is embedded in the evolutionary ecology of many fields. A standard observation is that every entrance is an exit somewhere else. A similar thing might be said about the development of a scholarly community. Every new community that is created changes old communities that previously tied scholars together and kept them apart, and thereby changes the ways in which knowledge develops.

Although both the original observation and its present corollary are subject to some important qualifications, they suggest a fundamental feature of social evolution. The processes of integration and disintegration are closely linked (Lawrence and Lorsch 1967, March 1999). New loyalties are built on the undermining of old ones; new homes characteristically imply the abandonment of old ones. As the organizational research community constructed a new home, history, and identity, it affected not only itself but other research communities. Any true history of the structure of social science scholarship in the last half of the twentieth century would have to address the question of what might have happened to organizational economics, public administration, organizational psychology, and organizational sociology under a different scenario of the development of organizations studies.

## ACKNOWLEDGMENTS

This research has been supported by grants from the Spencer Foundation. Earlier versions of parts of this paper were presented at a conference in honor of W. Richard Scott (2002), at the 2004 Organization Science Winter Conference, and at the 2004 Academy of Management Meetings. The authors are grateful to these audiences, and to Arthur Bedian, Giovanni Dosi, Robert Gibbons, Arie Lewin, John S. Reed, W. Richard Scott, Olav Sorenson, Bill Starbuck, Marc Ventresca, Oliver Williamson, and two anonymous reviewers for their comments.

## NOTES

1. We use the term "organization studies" to include various forms of research and speculations on organizations occurring under labels such as "organization theory," "administrative theory," "management theory," "organizational economics," "organizational psychology," and "organizational and economic sociology."

2. Business schools in Europe had histories and social positions that were different, but European schools (many of them called Handelshochschule or equivalent) were similar in being substantially removed from the core of academic research located in the universities.

3. "The Ford Foundation Behavioral Science Program: Proposed Plan for the Development of the Behavioral Sciences Program," 1951. Herbert A. Simon Papers, Carnegie Mellon University Library.

## REFERENCES

Allison, G. T. 1971. *Essence of Decision: Explaining the Cuban Missile Crisis*. Little, Brown, Boston, MA.

Axelrod, R. M., M. D. Cohen. 1999. *Harnessing Complexity: Organizational Implications of a Scientific Frontier*. Free Press, New York.

Barley, S. R., J. E. Orr, eds. 1997. *Between Craft and Science: Technical Work in U.S. Settings*. IRL Press, Ithaca, NY.

Baum, J. A. C., ed. 2002. *Companion to Organizations*. Blackwell, Malden, MA.

Baumol, W. J. 1959. *Business Behavior, Value and Growth*. Macmillan, New York.

Bendix, R. 1964. *Nation-Building and Citizenship: Studies of Our Changing Social Order*. University of California Press, Berkeley, CA.

Berelson, B., ed. 1963. *The Behavioral Sciences Today*. Harper & Row, New York.

Blau, P., W. R. Scott. 1962. *Formal Organizations*. Chandler, San Francisco, CA.

Boulding, K. 1958. Evidences for an administrative science: A review of the *Administrative Science Quarterly*, Volumes 1 and 2. *Admin. Sci. Quart.* 3(1), 1–22.

Brinton, C. 1965. *The Anatomy of Revolution*. Vintage Books, New York.

Burns, T. R., H. Flam. 1987. *The Shaping of Social Organization: Social Rule System Theory with Applications*. Sage, Beverly Hills, CA.

Cartwright, D., A. Zander, eds. 1953. *Group Dynamics, Research and Theory*. Row, Peterson, Evanston, IL.

Churchman, W. 1956. Management science—Fact or theory. *Management Sci.* 2(2), 185–194.

Clark, B. R. 1995. *Places of Inquiry: Research and Advanced Education in Modern Universities*. University of California Press, Berkeley, CA.

Cohen, M. D., L. S. Sproull, eds. 1996. *Organizational Learning*. Sage, Thousand Oaks, CA.

Crozier, M. 1964. *The Bureaucratic Phenomenon*. University of Chicago Press, Chicago, IL.

Cyert, R. M., J. G. March. 1963. *A Behavioral Theory of the Firm*. Prentice Hall, Englewood Cliffs, NJ.

Denrell, J., J. G. March. 2001. Adaptation as information restriction: The hot stove effect. *Organ. Sci. 12, 523–538.*

Dosi, G. 2000. *Innovation, Organization and Economic Dynamics: Selected Essays*. Edward Elgar, Cheltenham, UK.

Downs, A. 1967. *Inside Bureaucracy*. Little, Brown, Boston, MA.

Eisenstadt, S. N., R. B. Yosef, C. Adler, eds. 1970. *Integration and Development in Israel*. Praeger, New York.

Festinger, L., D. Katz, eds. 1953. *Research Methods in the Behavioral Sciences*. Holt, Rinehart and Winston, New York.

Flood, M. 1955. Decision making. *Management Sci. 1*(2), 167–169.

Garel, G., E. Godelier. 2004. *Enseigner le management*. Lavoisier, Paris, France.

Gordon, R. A., J. E. Howell. 1959. *Higher Education for Business*. Columbia University Press, New York.

Hambrick, D. C. 1990. The adolescence of strategic management, 1980–1985: Critical perceptions and reality. J. W. Fredericksen, ed. *Perspectives on Strategic Management*. Harper and Row, New York, 237–261.

Helmer, O. 1958. The prospects of a unified theory of organizations. *Management Sci. 4*(2), 172–176.

Hirschman, A. O. 1970. *Exit, Voice, and Loyalty*. Harvard University Press, Cambridge, MA.

Hodgkinson, H. L. 1971. *Institutions in Transition: A Profile of Change in Higher Education*. McGraw-Hill, New York.

Hodgson, G. M. 2001. *How Economics Forgot History: The Problem of Historical Specificity in Social Science*. Routledge, London, UK.

Holland, J. H. 1975. *Adaptation in Natural and Artificial Systems*. MIT Press, Cambridge, MA.

Hoskisson, R., M. Hitt, W. Wan, D. Yiu. 1999. Theory and research in strategic management: Swings in a pendulum. *J. Management 25*(3) 417–456.

Kahneman, D., D. Lovallo. 1993. Timid choices and bold forecasts: A cognitive perspective on risk taking. *Management Sci. 39,* 17–31.

Katz, D., R. L. Kahn. 1966. *The Social Psychology of Organizations*. Wiley, New York.

Kauffman, S. A. 1995. *At Home in the Universe: The Search for Laws of Self-Organization and Complexity*. Oxford University Press, New York.

Kuhn, T. S. 1970. *The Structure of Scientific Revolutions*. University of Chicago Press, Chicago, IL.

Lawrence, P., J. Lorsch. 1967. *Organization and Environment: Managing Differentiation and Integration*. Graduate School of Business Administration, Harvard University, Boston, MA.

Lazarsfeld, P. F. 1955. *Mathematical Thinking in the Social Sciences*. Free Press, Glencoe, IL.

Lazarsfeld, P. F., W. H. Sewell, H. L. Wilensky, eds. 1967. *The Uses of Sociology.* Basic Books, New York.

Leslie, S. 1993. *The Cold War and American Science.* Columbia University Press, Columbia, NY.

Lincoln, J. R., A. L. Kalleberg. 1990. *Culture, Control, and Commitment: A Study of Work Organization and Work Attitudes in the United States and Japan.* Cambridge University Press, Cambridge, UK.

Lindblom, C. E. 1959. The "science" of muddling through. *Public Admin. Rev. 19,* 79–88.

Litchfield, E. 1956. Notes on a general theory of administration. *Admin. Sci. Quart. 1*(1), 3–29.

March, J. G., ed. 1965. *Handbook of Organization.* Rand McNally College Publishing Company, Chicago, IL.

March, J. G. 1991. Exploration and exploitation in organizational learning. *Organ. Sci. 2,* 71–87.

March, J. G. 1996. Continuity and change in theories of organizational action. *Admin. Sci. Quart. 41*(2), 278–287.

March, J. G. 1999. Learning perspective on some dynamics of institutional integration. M. Egeberg, P. Lægreid, eds. *Organizing Political Institutions: Essays for Johan P. Olsen.* Scandinavian University Press, Oslo, Norway, 129–155.

March, J. G. 2004. Parochialism in the evolution of a research community. *Management Organ. Rev. 1,* 5–22.

March, J. G., J. P. Olsen. 1989. *Rediscovering Institutions: The Organizational Basis of Politics.* Free Press/Macmillan, New York.

March, J. G., J. P. Olsen. 1995. *Democratic Governance.* The Free Press, New York.

March, J. G., H. A. Simon. 1958. *Organizations.* Wiley, New York.

Martin, J. 1992. *Cultures in Organizations: Three Perspectives.* Oxford University Press, New York.

Merton, R. K. 1949. *Social Theory and Social Structure.* Free Press, Glencoe, IL.

Merton, R. K. 1963. The mosaic of the behavioral sciences. B. Berelson, ed. *The Behavioral Sciences Today.* Basic Books, New York, 247–272.

National Research Council Committee on Basic Research in the Behavioral and Social Sciences. 1988. *The Behavioral and Social Sciences: Achievements and Opportunities.* National Research Council, Washington, DC.

Nelson, R. R., S. G. Winter. 1982. *An Evolutionary Theory of Economic Change.* Harvard University Press, Cambridge, MA.

Nystrom, P. C., W. H. Starbuck, eds. 1981. *Handbook of Organizational Design.* Oxford University Press, Oxford, UK.

Oberoi, H. 1994. *The Construction of Religious Boundaries: Culture, Identity, and Diversity in the Sikh Tradition.* University of Chicago Press, Chicago, IL.

O'Connor, A. 2001. *Poverty Knowledge: Social Science, Social Policy, and the Poor in Twentieth Century U.S. History.* Princeton University Press, Princeton, NJ.

Olson, M. 1965. *The Logic of Collective Action: Public Goods and the Theory of Groups.* Harvard University Press, Cambridge, MA.

Padgett, J. F., C. K. Ansell. 1993. Robust action and the rise of the Medici, 1400–1434. *Amer. J. Sociology 98,* 1250–1310.

Perrow, C. 1972. *Complex Organizations: A Critical Essay.* Random House, New York.

Pettigrew, A. M. 1985. *The Awakening Giant: Continuity and Change in Imperial Chemical Industries.* Blackwell, Oxford, UK.

Pfeffer, J. 1982. *Organizations and Organization Theory.* Pitman, Boston, MA.

Pfeffer, J. 1993. Barriers to the advance of organizational science: Paradigm development as a dependent variable. *Acad. Management Rev. 18*(4), 599–620.

Pfeffer, J., C. Fong. 2001. The end of business schools? Less success than meets the eye. *Acad. Management Learn. Ed. 1*(1), 78–95.

Pugh, D. S., D. J. Hickson. 1976. *Organizational Structure in Its Context.* Saxon House, London, UK.

Rumelt, R. P., D. E. Schendel, D. J. Teece. 1994. Introduction. R. P. Rumelt, D. E. Schendel, D. J. Teece, eds. *Fundamental Issues in Strategy.* Harvard Business School Press, Boston, MA, 9–24.

Schendel, D. E., C. W. Hofer. 1979. *Strategic Management.* Little Brown, Boston, MA.

Schlossman, S., M. Sedlak, H. Wechsler. 1987. The "new look:" The Ford Foundation and the revolution in business education. *Selections 14*(3), 8–28.

Schlossman, S., R. Gleeson, M. Sedlak, D. Allen. 1994. *The Beginnings of Graduate Management Education in the United States.* Graduate Management Admission Council, Santa Monica, CA.

Scott, W. R. 1998. *Organizations: Rational, Natural, and Open Systems,* 4th ed. Prentice Hall, Englewood Cliffs, NJ.

Scott, W. R. 2004. Reflections on a half-century of organizational sociology. *Annual Rev. Sociology 30*, 1–21.

Sherif, M., C. W. Sherif, eds. 1969. *Interdisciplinary Relationships in the Social Sciences.* Aldine, Chicago, IL.

Shubik, M. 1958. Studies and theories of decision making. *Admin. Sci. Quart. 3*(3), 289–306.

Simon, H. A. 1991. *Models of My Life.* MIT Press, Cambridge, MA.

Smiddy, H., L. Naum. 1954. Evolution of a "science of managing" in America. *Management Sci. 1*(1), 1–31.

Stinchcombe, A. 1965. Social structure and organizations. J. G. March, ed. *Handbook of Organizations.* Rand McNally, Chicago, IL, 142–192.

Thompson, J. 1956. On building an administrative science. *Admin. Sci. Quart. 1*(1), 102–111.

Thompson, J. 1967. *Organizations in Action.* McGraw-Hill, New York.

Truman, D. B. 1951. *The Governmental Process.* Knopf, New York.

Tullock, G. 1965. *The Politics of Bureaucracy.* Public Affairs Press, Washington, DC.

Van Maanen, J. 1995. Style as theory. *Organ. Sci. 6*, 132–143.

Weber, M. 1922–1923. *Gesammelte Aufsätze zur Religionssoziologie.* Mohr, Tübingen, Germany.

Weick, K. E. 1969. *The Social Psychology of Organizing.* Random House, New York.

Weick, K. E. 1995. *Sensemaking in Organizations.* Sage, Thousand Oaks, CA.

Westwood, R., S. Clegg. 2003. The discourse of organization studies: Dissensus, politics, and paradigms. R. Westwood, S. Clegg, eds. *Debating Organization: Point-Counterpoint in Organization Studies.* Blackwell, Oxford, UK, 1–42.

Zachary, G. P. 1999. *Endless Frontier: Vannevar Bush, Engineer of the American Century.* MIT Press, Cambridge, MA.

# CHAPTER 15

# The Study of Organizations and Organizing since 1945

## JAMES G. MARCH

The history of organization studies is embedded in its times and the ways those times affect different regions differently. In particular, significant features of the field were molded by the moods and prejudices associated with academia after three critical events in 20th-century history: (1) the Second World War, (2) the social and political protest movements of the late 1960s and early 1970s, and (3) the collapse of the Soviet Empire and the triumph of markets. Speculating about the unfolding of the events of the future that will have similar impacts is discouraged by an awareness that neither their timing nor the severity of their impacts can be specified with any precision. In any event, our task is not to join any particular wave of the future, but to make small pieces of scholarship beautiful.

MY STATUS AS AN HONORARY MEMBER of European Group for Organizational Studies (EGOS) is a status that I treasure, as I do the invitation to speak to the EGOS community and to pose as a European. I am especially grateful for your tolerance of me since the last March of my family to have been born in Europe came to America almost 400 years ago. My intention is to take advantage of your invitation and your tolerance to provide one man's impressions of the last 60 years of organization studies. They are the impressions of an affectionate enthusiast who has the advantages and disadvantages of having lived through those years. I would not want to underestimate the disadvantages. I learned early to be skeptical about the words of aged scholars. Now that I have become one of them, I am even more skeptical. Age generates self-indulgence more reliably than it generates wisdom.

---

This chapter was originally a keynote address delivered at the 2006 EGOS Colloquium, Bergen, Norway and was published in *Organization Studies*, 28:9 (2007), 9–19. I am grateful for the comments of Mie Augier and Johan P. Olsen.

## INTRODUCTION

The field of organization studies is a large, heterogeneous field involving numerous enclaves having distinct styles, orientations, and beliefs. It is integrated neither by a shared theory, nor by a shared perspective, nor even by a shared tolerance for multiple perspectives. It retains substantial intellectual, geographic, and linguistic parochialism, with separate enclaves persisting in their own worlds of discourse and forming a common field only by a definition that overlooks the diversity.

## The Myth of Organization Studies

And, yet, EGOS exists. EGOS was originally conceived, I believe, as a kind of intellectual social movement within organizations scholarship, defending, developing, and extending a particular scholarly point of view and producing, augmenting, and proclaiming European resistance both to the hegemony of North American scholars and to the glorification of quantitative analysis and other symptoms of scholarly testosterone. It has, however, increasingly positioned itself as a broad association of scholars brought together by the myth of organization studies, by the idea that such a thing exists (or might exist), and by the idea that we are, however uncomfortably, united in a common endeavor. This myth of a distinct field of organization studies cannot easily be sustained by a contemplation of either our teachings, our writings, or our research. It is sustained by our hopes.

In the spirit of those hopes and that myth, I ask what the history of organization studies since the Second World War can tell us about the processes by which the field of organization studies refines old ideas and introduces new ones. Given the variety of our commitments, it is a hopeless task, made only somewhat manageable by gross simplification.

## A Simple Model

The story I will tell neglects those aspects of intellectual history that involve ideas competing for acceptance on the basis of evidence or other forms of gradual scholarly winnowing. Such things certainly exist and are important, but they are subordinated here to a simple story of diffusion. I imagine that ideas, frameworks, and worldviews invade a scholarly field and, if successful, reproduce from scholar to future scholar and so on through generations with reliability that declines over generations. Ideas, frameworks and worldviews also migrate from one part of a field to another and from one enclave to another and are modified in the course of migration. The observed distribution of scholarly commitments over time and over geographic and linguistic regions is generated by this interaction of invasion, reproduction, migration, and transformation.

To explore such a model of the history of a field thoroughly would require a more precise specification of the enclaves and the parameters of invasion, reproduction, migration, and transformation, as well as their interaction. I do not propose to provide such a specification today. I want, however, to call attention to one aspect of such a process—the way the history of a scholarly field is embedded in its times and the way those times affect different regions differently. In particular, significant features of the field of organization studies were molded by three critical events in 20th-century history: (1) the Second World War, (2) the social and political protest movements of the late 1960s and early 1970s, and (3) the collapse of the Soviet Empire and the triumph of markets. The invasions of ideas associated with the aftermaths of these three events have produced a community of scholars with strong generational imprints.

The story is obviously considerably complicated by the reproduction of worldviews through the education of new scholars by old ones. Each generation reproduces scholars at a rate dependent on the number of old scholars still active and the opportunities for employment of new scholars. These new scholars and their own progeny extend the impact of earlier invasions. In addition, ideas travel, leading to their spread and modification within the field. These complications are important, but generational imprinting is a striking feature of the intellectual history of organization studies. Moreover, since the three waves of ideas arose during times of different rates of growth in universities in different parts of the worlds, the temporal imprints of ideas have tended to become geographic imprints.

## THREE INVASIONS

Although it is possible to point to precursors of organization studies in Asia and Africa, written contributions to organizational scholarship had their Western origins in the writings of Aristotle and developed in Europe after the Renaissance and Reformation and up through the 1930s, primarily as elements of the fledgling disciplines of social science and human engineering. The early contributors to the field were few, scattered among the disciplines, and primarily European.

The easily recognizable ancestors of modern organizations scholarship include such notable European social scientists as Emile Durkheim, Alfred Marshall, Robert Michels, Gaetano Mosca, Vilfredo Pareto, Adam Smith, and Max Weber. They were supplemented by early European organizations engineers such as Henri Fayol and Lyndall Urwick.

Some North American writers, such as Luther Gulick, Elton Mayo (actually an Australian for most of his life), John Dewey, Mary Parker Follett, and Frederick Taylor were pioneers, but the field's pre–Second World War origins were primarily European.

## The Second World War

The Second World War changed things. The massive material, intellectual, and economic devastation of Europe, including the decimation of the German, Austrian, Italian, and Eastern European scholarly communities, made the reconstruction of European scholarly strength a relatively slow process. Although there were significant European scholars working on studies of organizations earlier in the postwar period, it was not until well into the 1970s that European studies of organizations achieved a scale adequate to reassert itself as an important force.

In contrast, economic recovery in North America was relatively fast and contributed to the postwar economic and political expansion of North American institutions. A significant factor both in the recovery of North American scholarship and in the directions that recovery took was the extraordinary immigration of scholars to North America from Germany, Austria, and the rest of Central Europe during the 1930s. These scholars, who were born as Jews in Central Europe and came to the United States to escape persecution, included some of the more distinguished subsequent contributors to North American academic concern about organizing. Peter Blau, Fritz Heider, Leo Hurwicz, Kurt Lewin, Fritz Machlup, Jacob Marschak, Oskar Morgenstern, Anatol Rappoport, Joseph Schumpeter, Alfred Schütz, Friedrich A. von Hayek, Ludwig von Mises, and John von Neumann, among others. In many ways, the greatest single benefactor of North American social science and organization studies in the mid-20th century was Adolf Hitler.

Because of the rapid peacetime recovery and the massive growth of American higher education in the years immediately after 1945, the most obvious feature of the history of organization studies in North America after the Second World War, and a major factor in the invasion and reproduction of post–Second World War ideas, was growth in the size of the scholarly community. Although the magnitude of that growth in North America is difficult to assess precisely, it seems to have been on the order of at least 100-fold.

The field did not grow as a response to exciting new discoveries, findings, or theories, nor as a response to a clear, overwhelming demand for knowledge on the part of society. It grew as a function of the rapidly increasing supply of scholars. The demand that led to the increase in scholars was not a demand for scholarship, but a demand for teachers to teach the increasing numbers of university students. As the number of scholars increased, so also did the number of papers produced. As the number of papers increased, so also did the number of journals to publish them.

In 1965, Rand McNally published a *Handbook of Organizations*. The field that that handbook described was focused on a variety of institutions as much as it was on general principles. Nine of the chapters dealt with specific institutional spheres (e.g., unions, public bureaucracies, political parties, military units, hospitals, schools). The field was also based in the disciplines. Of the contributors to the handbook, 60 percent held appointments in disciplinary departments when the handbook appeared. They had different degrees and lived in different scholarly communities, but they shared a diffuse worldview and a vision of scholarship. They were a postwar North American generation of social scientists. They were—every one of the 30 contributors to the 1965 handbook—American, white, male, and young. About two-thirds of them were less than 40 years old in 1965.

The generation represented by the handbook contributors was a postwar generation and was profoundly influenced by, indeed intertwined with, the development of a scientific behavioral science in North America. The postwar era in the United States was one that saw the election of the first social scientists to the National Academy of Science, and the inclusion of social science as a division of the National Science Foundation. It saw the conversion of economic theory into a workable mathematical form. It saw the development of mathematical models in psychology, sociology, economics, geography, political science, and anthropology. It saw an extensive elaboration of techniques for the gathering and multivariate analysis of quantitative data in economics, psychology, political science, and sociology.

The postwar North American contributors to the study of organizations included a long list of scholars, not only refugees from Central Europe but also such other academics as Alex Bavelas, Richard M. Cyert, Robert Dubin, Alvin W. Gouldner, Mason Haire, Harold H. Kelley, Charles E. Lindblom, Seymour M. Lipset, Robert Merton, John Meyer, Roy Radner, Leonard R. Sayles, W. Richard Scott, Philip Selznick, Martin Shubik, Herbert A. Simon, William H. Starbuck, Arthur L. Stinchcombe, James Thompson, Karl E. Weick, Harrison White, and William F. Whyte. For the most part, they identified with, and were viewed as part of, the effort to make postwar studies of human behavior and institutions more scientific. The attitudes of this generation of scholars were strengthened by, and gave strength to, the simultaneous effort to make North American business schools more explicitly academic, to increase the role of academic knowledge and methods, and to reduce the role of experiential knowledge and methods in management education.

## The Protests of the 1960s and 1970s

The European story is similar in many respects to the North American. In the first two decades after the Second World War, a number of distinguished European scholars interested in organizations established themselves: for example, Sune Carlsson, Michel Crozier, Walter Goldberg, David Hickson, Knut Dahl Jacobsen, Edith Penrose, Derek Pugh, Claude Riveline. The Aston Group and the Tavistock Institute produced both research and new scholars. However, the European story differed from the North American in one important respect. Because the negative economic and political impact of the war was much greater in Europe than it was in North America, postwar economic recovery, and consequently scholarly recovery, was slower. As a result, the major European expansion of organization studies was delayed. It not only occurred in a different place; it occurred at a different time.

By 1970, European universities had largely recovered from the ravages of the Second World War and had started to experience the same kind of exceptional growth that had profoundly affected North American universities 20 years earlier. During the 1970s and 1980s, numerous vigorous research centers emerged, and numerous scholars interested in organizations became visible: for example, Mats Alvesson, Nils Brunsson, John Child, Stewart Clegg, Barbara Czarniawska, Lars Engwall, Erhard Friedberg, Anthony Hopwood, Håkon Håkonsson, Alfred Kieser, Cornelius J. Lammers, Bruno Latour, Nikolas Luhmann, Renate Mayntz, Johan P. Olsen, Andrew Pettigrew, Jean-Claude Thoenig.

The re-emergence of European organizations scholarship followed different paths in different countries, particularly across different linguistic groups. Like their North American colleagues, many European organization scholars found homes in business schools at a time when business schools were increasing in size, importance, and research emphasis. There were other patterns, however. For example, the early prominence of political scientists in the development of organization studies in North America was replicated in Norway and Sweden where Johan P. Olsen and Nils Brunsson created substantial communities of scholars dedicated to research on public organizations and to an institutional perspective. Michel Crozier and his associates in France created a tradition that was based in political sociology and focused particularly on issues of bureaucracy and power.

European organization studies, like North American organizations studies, developed a scholarly identity and canon; but there was a striking difference between the intellectual mood of the 1970s and 1980s, when organization studies expanded rapidly in Europe, and the intellectual mood of the 1950s and 1960s, when organization studies—along with other social and behavioral sciences—expanded rapidly in North America. European organization studies were influenced deeply by the fact that expansion occurred in the decades following the protest and counterculture movements of the 1960s and 1970s.

These movements created a distinctive intellectual setting in universities throughout Europe. The setting combined:

- Opposition to American involvement in Vietnam and more generally to American hegemony
- Support for a feminist sensibility, rhetoric, and historical perspective
- A radical (primarily Marxist) critique of society and social science
- A poststructuralist, postmodern, social constructivist worldview
- A romantic enthusiasm for "flower power" and other accoutrements of countercultures

In contrast to the mood of the 1950s, which was optimistic about social science and its possibilities for becoming a science that served an enlightened society through rational analysis and social engineering based on systematic quantitative research, the later mood was pessimistic. It was likely to portray the apparatus of social science as an instrument of white, male, capitalist oppression. Adam Smith and Max Weber were displaced by Michel Foucault and Anthony Giddens.

Although important parts of European organization studies developed and retained the commitments that were characteristic of the earlier period, the timing of European growth in higher education produced an intelligentsia that had, compared to the immediate postwar group, substantially less positive attitudes about the academic establishment, about business, about science, about mathematics and numbers, about males and the intellectual prejudices attributed to them, about the older generation, about progress, and about things associated with North America, but most of all about the quantitative methods and the mathematical theoretical forms that were hallmarks of the earlier period.

Most strikingly perhaps, this era in organizations studies produced a major change in the gender composition of the community of scholars. From being an almost exclusively male domain, the field of organization studies was transformed into a field with a substantial female presence. The change was unmistakable in North America but it was—because of the timing of growth in Europe—even more visible there. By the end of the period, women scholars represented at least 25 percent and in some areas more than 50 percent of the community.

Both the Second World War and the protest movements are, of course, fading from memory now and are hardly recognized by scholars who have entered the field in the last 25 years; but their intellectual progeny and artifacts still litter the field and form barriers to subsequent invasions both in North America and in Europe. The first period's effects are found particularly in such things as quantitative research on institutional diffusion in populations of organizations, organizational demography, decision making, information processing, networks, learning, evolution, and comparative structures. The second period's effects are seen particularly in such things as qualitative research on culture, gender, sense making, social construction, and power.

### THE TRIUMPH OF MARKETS

When the Soviet Empire collapsed in 1991 after almost a decade of gradual disintegration, it signaled the triumph of capitalism both as an economic system and as an intellectual basis for social thought. That event reverberated through North American and European universities because of the special importance of oppositional and particularly Marxist positions in social science. A central traditional feature of university culture, more conspicuous in schools of humanities and social science than in schools of business or engineering, was the oppositional role of the university. For most of the 20th century, the conventional basis for opposition in university cultures—both in North America and in Europe—was Marxism. This relatively stable ideational and acculturation system in universities fell apart when the Soviet Empire collapsed. Marxism as an instrument and a symbol of opposition to the establishment lost appeal. Insofar as Marxism was replaced in university oppositional enthusiasms, it tended to be replaced by a new program of social reform that emphasized competitive markets and a much reduced role for government. The economic ideas of the Austrian School became fashionable among young students.

In Europe and North America, the result in organization studies, as in many other domains of social science, was twofold. The first was an effect on the cohort of organization scholars recruited to organization studies during the 1970s and 1980s and the scholarly commitments they had reproduced in their students. Assertions that what was believed was not what was true, which had been buttressed by a Marxist portrayal of the real truth, were transformed into assertions that nothing was true, that scholarship could not involve the pursuit of truth because truth in the sense intended by most traditional scholars did not exist.

The second result of the triumphs of markets in Europe and North America was an effect on young radical scholars. The new radicals were libertarian liberals, and markets became the preferred revolutionary mode of organizing, in the public sector as well as the private. The preeminence of markets was taken for granted, and discovering the factors contributing to individual or organizational success within a market system, or discovering new uses of markets as instruments of organizing, became prototypic forms of research in organization studies. Just as young scholars entering the field in the 1950s had been drawn to science and young scholars in the 1970s had been drawn to the humanities, young scholars in the 1990s were drawn to markets. They became fascinated by the excitements and rewards of market competition. Leadership, mergers and acquisitions, outsourcing, and entrepreneurship became major topics of research.

These third-wave invaders faced a situation that, on the one hand, was made more difficult by the fact that the scholarly world was no longer growing rapidly in either North America or Europe. Organization studies had become less vulnerable to invasion by virtue of its location in relatively stable institutions both in North America and in Europe. On the other hand, the situation was made more favorable for the third wave both by the gradual dissipation of the reproduced scholarly residue of the postwar and post-protest invasions, and by the way the third wave resonated with a business school emphasis on immediate relevance.

The revolution in business schools that occurred in the 1950s and 1960s in North America and later in Europe had made the schools more academic and research oriented. This contributed to, and was promoted by, the first two invasions into organization studies. In the 1980s and 1990s, this revolution was challenged by a counterrevolution, led by the business press. This counterrevolution threatened to alienate and isolate the scholars of the revolution and their heirs but opened the schools to the post-1985 invasion.

Although it clearly exists and is important in North America and Europe, the third wave seems likely to be even more prominent in Asia. The rapid expansion in the number of scholars that was experienced in North America in the decades after the Second World War and in Europe in the decades after the protest movements of the 1960s characterized most Asian countries in the decades after the fall of the Soviet Empire.

This growth is likely to move China, India, and other Asian countries to leading positions not only in terms of their educated workforces, economies, and political power but also in terms of their research. Because of the timing of Asian expansion, the kinds of organization studies that will be carried out and the kinds of scholarship that will be reproduced are likely to reflect a greater degree of concern for understanding and fostering the success of enterprises in a market-based world than is currently found in North America and Europe with their legacies of earlier invasions and expansions.

## THE FUTURE

Forecasting the future is a fool's conceit. There is no reason to expect the next 60 years of organization studies to unfold in a way that is any more predictable from the perspective of today than the last 60 years would have been from the perspective of the end of the Second World War.

### The Sources of Novelty

There are, however, elements of the post–Second World War history that seem to cast light on the generation and persistence of novelty in organization studies. First, a primary source of novelty in organization studies has been importation from outside. Both after the Second World War and after the protests of the 1960s and 1970s, new ideas entered the field from other fields, particularly from the behavioral sciences and natural sciences in the former and from the humanities and feminist studies in the latter.

Second, novelty is facilitated by growth. When a scholarly community is growing rapidly, the instruments of socialization that are essential to exploitation and resistance to novelty are less effective. Turnover facilitates the entry of new ideas. Scholarly communities that grow at different times are likely to be invaded by different ideas.

Third, novelty and variety are sustained by parochialism. The mutual isolation of European scholars and North American scholars has been extensively documented. This isolation has allowed separate scholarly communities to thrive and to develop different ideas and prejudices. The mutual isolation of Asian and Western communities is likely to produce a similar situation in which Asian ideas are protected from socialization into the conventions of dominant groups in North America and Europe.

Does this demonstrate that by some magic we have discovered the optimal mix of exploitation and exploration? Not at all. The fact that there appear to be as many voices describing the level of novelty and diversity in organization studies as too high as there are describing it as too low does not demonstrate that it is exactly right. What the present story suggests is not that history is efficient in locating optimal paths but that some features of the history of organizations studies have affected the mix of exploitation and exploration in the field without any conscious intent to do so, and that the future mix as well as the level of diversity in organization studies that it fosters are likely to be similarly affected.

## The Future of the Present

There are many conspicuous features of the present that may have implications for the future:

- The movement toward global economic, political, and cultural linkages
- The continuing elaboration of information and biological technologies
- The reduced economic, political, and cultural centrality of Europe and North America
- The changing distribution of wealth
- The rising tide of fundamentalist religious belief in Judaism, Christianity, and Islam
- The earth's declining tolerance for the human species

In one form or other, each of these seems inexorable; and each of them will affect organization studies in ways that, although they are not easy to predict precisely now, are likely to be substantial. Future invasions of the field will reflect critical events of the future, just as past invasions have reflected critical events of the past. Speculating about the unfolding of these trends is, however, discouraged by an awareness that neither their timing nor their magnitudes can be specified with any precision.

## The Business School Locale

There is, however, one feature of the context within which the future of organization studies apparently will be realized that may be worth noting—the business school location of much of the research. For the last few decades, business schools have provided stable financial and occupational bases for organization studies and many of the scholars who consider themselves students of organizations have secured both their training and their employment in business schools. The business school context is not a neutral one:

- It encourages the mutual isolation of business school scholars of organizations and disciplinary scholars.

- Insofar as it encourages contact with the disciplines, it makes contact with ideas from economics more likely, and contact with ideas from the sciences, psychology, sociology, or political science less likely.
- It focuses research on the private sector, reducing the attention to institutions of the public sector that characterized much early work in the field.
- It brings an emphasis on the audience of practitioners, on finding the correlates of organizational performance rather than other organizational phenomena.
- It brings an orientation to the problems and possibilities of individual organizations (firms) and less attention to populations of organizations or to "organizing."
- It stimulates an emphasis on organizational strategies, rather than societal strategies.

The implications of the business school context for research are not so clear that they can be asserted with enormous confidence, but they appear to cast doubt on the long-term future of some programs of research congenial to scholars of the first two waves and their progeny. Most of the time in the history of business schools, business school locales have been less welcoming to fundamental research than to applied research, less welcoming to critiques of the market/hierarchical orders than to research that accepts or extols them. A business school culture is not normally supportive of excursions into such things as philosophies of science, mathematical social science, interpretive social science, complexity theory, postmodern sensibilities, organizational demography, or critical theory. Those excursions often maintain postures of intellectual disdain for discourse comprehensible to others and typically provide little immediate, demonstrable utility. The pressures in business schools toward immediate relevance and practical comprehension seem to point in different directions. It may be seen as ironical that programs of organizations scholarship rooted in science and programs of organizations scholarship rooted in antipathy for science are not only out of step with each other; they are both out of step with important elements of the modern mood and with business schools.

Unless organization studies can re-create the academic ambitions that permeated North American business schools in the 1950s and 1960s and European business schools in the 1970s and 1980s, those parts of organization studies that trace their origins to either the aftermath of the Second World War or to the aftermath of the protests of the 1960s are likely to become less welcome in business schools.

## A Scholar's Job

The future, like the past, is destined to be shaped by invasions of ideas and by growth in the numbers of scholars. In a real sense, however, the fact that the intellectual future will be at the mercy of historical happenings over which we have little control is not relevant to those of us who are practicing scholars. Our task is not to discern the future in order to join it; nor even to shape it. Our task is to make small pieces of scholarship beautiful through rigor, persistence, competence, elegance, and grace, so as to avoid the plague of mediocrity that threatens often to overcome us. If we do that, we may not protect scholarship from future historical waves of renewed enthusiasms; but neither will we disgrace it.

# CHAPTER 16

# Scholarship, Scholarly Institutions, and Scholarly Communities

## JAMES G. MARCH

Scholarship is less an individual than a collective activity. The history of *A Behavioral Theory of the Firm* illustrates two key aspects of the collective nature of scholarship. The first aspect is the dependence of scholarship on the institutions of scholarship. For a period of about 10 years beginning around 1954, the Graduate School of Industrial Administration at the Carnegie Institute of Technology was an extraordinary incubator of ideas, the "Vienna Circle" of its time. The second aspect is the cooperative interdependence of communities of scholars. Ideas take form and reproduce through an intergenerational, international pyramid of promiscuous and acrobatic intellectual intercourse.

WHEN DICK CYERT WAS PRESIDENT of Carnegie Mellon University, he was often asked to open conferences at the university with the customary presidential platitudes of welcome. On at least one such occasion, at a conference on organizational economics, when it came time for Dick to make his harmless presidential welcoming remarks, he delivered an hour-long professional paper, complete with equations, theorems, and results. It was a performance that seriously upset the scheduling of the conference; but it awed, amazed, and pleased his colleagues. I suspect if Dick were living and were asked to write something on this occasion, he would do something similar. I cannot duplicate him, either in style or in content, but I hope that anyone who reads the collection of papers in this Special Issue will reflect on what a remarkable person Dick Cyert was (Augier and March 2002).

### INTELLECTUAL HISTORY

Intellectual history is a perilous activity at best, and particularly perilous when pursued by people who might imagine they were part of the history. I would

---

This chapter was originally published in *Organization Science*, 18:3, 2007, 537–542.

not want to claim any special protection from the peril, nor any intention to do more than make a few minor comments on *A Behavioral Theory of the Firm* and its history. Those comments are elementary ruminations on one fundamental feature of scholarship: Scholarship is less an individual than a collective activity. The rewards, accolades, and prizes of scholarship are often individual; the work is not.

The history of *A Behavioral Theory of the Firm* illustrates two key aspects of the collective nature of scholarship. The first is the dependence of scholarship on the institutions of scholarship. Great scholarship thrives on combinations of scholars brought together under institutional conditions that stimulate and support them. For much of modern history, those conditions have been associated with universities. Traditions of great universities, including academic freedom and the support of intellectual discourse, fundamental research, and the unconditional and unremitting pursuit of excellence are the foundations of contemporary scholarship. Universities vary in the degree to which they foment scholarly creativity and rigor, and there are many universities that make negligible contributions to scholarship, but in modern times major scholarship has been overwhelmingly associated with institutions of higher learning. When universities and their patrons, their schools, their institutes, and their departments sustain the institutional qualities essential to scholarship, scholarship thrives. When they fail to do so, scholarship withers.

The second aspect is the cooperative interdependence of communities of scholars. Concepts of intellectual property and the awarding of honors and prizes, with their pretenses of allocating responsibility for ideas to individuals, are inconsistent with the real processes of scholarship. Stories of genius, like stories of heroes, are attributable more to the mythic expectations of listeners than to the realities of history. There are great scholars, and they should be honored, but the greatest of them is embedded in an intergenerational and international community. The continual flow of ideas, interpretations, and elaborations within the scholarly community makes it an exercise in fabrication to isolate any one contribution or contributor as separable from many others.

## AN EXCEPTIONAL INSTITUTION

*A Behavioral Theory of the Firm* was published in 1963 (Cyert and March 1963), with a second edition published in 1992 (Cyert and March 1992). The research that culminated in the book began around 1954, and the papers underlying the book were published over the five years beginning in 1956. The research overlapped in time, place, and authorship with the simultaneous work that led to another well-known organization studies piece of the period by March and Simon (1958, 1993).

The research and writing were carried out[1] at the Graduate School of Administration (GSIA) of the Carnegie Institute of Technology in Pittsburgh.[2] GSIA was an exceptional place for scholarship during the 1950s and 1960s. If we use Google Scholar to list all of the social science books and articles published in the 10 years from 1955 through 1964 that are recorded as having 1,500 or more citations, we secure a list of 22 pieces.[3] In terms of citations, these are the idols of social science scholarship from the period. They are some of the more influential pieces written after the Second World War. By far the majority of these 22 citation-anointed publications were written by scholars who were resident at major American universities (e.g., Harvard, Yale, Princeton, Columbia, MIT, Chicago, California [Berkeley], Stanford).[4] Virtually the only pieces on the list that did not come from a handful of top universities emanated from a single small faculty group at a young school (GSIA) improbably located at the Carnegie Institute of Technology.

More precisely, five of the 22 publications came from GSIA:

1955: H. A. Simon, "A Behavioral Model of Rational Choice," *Quarterly Journal of Economics;*

1958: J. G. March and H. A. Simon, *Organizations;*

1958: F. Modigliani and M. Miller, "The Cost of Capital, Corporation Finance and the Theory of Investment," *American Economic Review;*

1963: R. M. Cyert and J. G. March, *A Behavioral Theory of the Firm;*

1964: V. Vroom, *Work and Motivation.*

Moreover, among all articles and books published in the social sciences and management, the single most frequently cited work in each of 3 of the 10 years between 1955 and 1964 was an article or book that was done at GSIA (Simon 1955, March and Simon 1958, Cyert and March 1963, respectively). GSIA played a role that far exceeded what would have been expected from a small faculty at a young school.

These publications were only part of the story. During the same period at GSIA, Abraham Charnes and William W. Cooper published a series of articles (also highly cited, but not reaching the 1,500 mark for any one) that shaped the development of operations research (Charnes and Cooper 1957), as did the work of Charles Holt (Holt et al. 1960). John Muth (Muth 1961) and Robert

Lucas (Lucas 1972) formulated the ideas underlying the later explosion of rational expectations economics. Oliver Williamson, as a doctoral student, began to formulate his contributions to transaction cost economics (Williamson 1967). Edward Prescott, another doctoral student, began to formulate an approach to the role of rules in economic policy and business cycles (Lovell and Prescott 1968, Kydland and Prescott 1977). William Starbuck, another doctoral student, began his work on organizational growth and development (Starbuck 1965). Edwin Mansfield began his pioneering work on the economics of technology and innovation (Mansfield 1968). Harrison White developed his ideas about networks and vacancy chains (White 1970). Richard Nelson worked on ideas about evolutionary theories in economics that he later published with Sidney Winter (Nelson and Winter 1973, 1982). Edward Feigenbaum, Julian Feldman (Feigenbaum and Feldman 1963), Allen Newell (Newell et al. 1958), and Herbert Simon (Simon and Barenfeld 1969) began a pursuit of the fundamentals of cognitive psychology and artificial intelligence that profoundly influenced work in those fields.[5]

For a period of about 10 years beginning around 1954, GSIA was an extraordinary incubator of ideas, the "Vienna Circle" of its time. Testimony about GSIA as a place for scholarship is readily available from the recollections of several of those who were there (e.g., Starbuck 1993; Leavitt 1996, pp. 289–290; Williamson 1996; Modigliani 2001, pp. 85–86; Ijiri 2004, p. 110). The faculty was small; it grew from a total of about 30 in 1955 to about 50 in 1964. It included a group of distinguished social scientists doing the work that made them distinguished, but before they had become icons. Ultimately, Lucas, March, Modigliani, Newell, Simon, White, and Williamson were elected to the National Academy of Sciences; Feigenbaum was elected to the National Academy of Engineering; March, Simon, Starbuck, Vroom, and Williamson all received the Scholarly Contributions to Management Award from the Academy of Management; and Lucas, Miller, Modigliani, Prescott, and Simon all received Nobel Prizes in Economics.

*A Behavioral Theory of the Firm* was written within this remarkable research milieu. It was a culture of intense collaboration and competition, immense intellectual arrogance, major messianic inclinations, and an unremitting work ethic. It was a setting in which individual scholars fed on each other and built on each other. I will not attempt to identify the precise components of administrative skill, entrepreneurial risk taking, ordinary smarts, intellectual combustion, and good luck that made GSIA, for a decade or more, an exceptional institution. The central leadership of the Carnegie Institute of Technology deserves part of the credit. They had the tolerance to support the development of a bastion of social science and management education in an engineering school at a time when the opportunities for growth in new fields of engineering were immense. However, most of the kudos must go to a handful of leaders at GSIA. If scholarly institutions of the 1950s and 1960s had granted options on institutional revenues as rewards for contributing to institutional successes, G. Leland Bach, William W. Cooper, Franco Modigliani, and Herbert A. Simon would have become much richer than they did.

## THE ENDURANCE OF IDEAS

*A Behavioral Theory of the Firm* has persistently maintained a high citation rate through a history of change in scholarly prejudices and across substantial geographic and disciplinary distances. Citation records are notoriously inadequate criteria for assessing the scholarly impact of ideas. High citation rates can be more symptomatic of scholarly fashion or networks of friends than of scholarly distinction, thus likely to be sources of embarrassment as well as pride. There is a long-term upward movement of citation rates that makes comparisons across time difficult. Citations are, however, the currency of scholarly evaluation and can be used to trace the life cycles and geographic diffusion of attention to individual pieces of work (Engwall and Danell 2002).

The Cyert and March book was written at a particular time, the 1950s and early 1960s, and in a particular part of the world, North America. During this time, North American universities grew rapidly, whereas European universities and scholarship were still recovering from the Second World War. North American social science expanded in scale and importance in conjunction with the growth of universities. The prejudices of the time were exercised and embedded in North American institutions as they grew to prominence. It was a time and place of considerable optimism about the possibilities for a scientific social science, for the uses of mathematics and quantitative analysis in scholarly work, for the creation of new interdisciplinary specialties for research (e.g., organization studies, operations research), and for the role of fundamental knowledge and analysis in guiding social and organizational policies. Although there were other voices, those enthusiasms dominated North American social science scholarship for two decades after the Second World War. It was also a time in which the leaders of the various social sciences knew each other. They saw each other at meetings and on committees. They thought of themselves as, and functioned as, a relatively integrated scholarly elite that encompassed all of the major social science disciplines and extended into applied mathematics and the fledgling domain of computer science.

That time passed. By 1975, the North American social science establishment had grown to a point that greatly diminished the awareness of colleagues across disciplines and the enthusiasm for the cross-disciplinary diffusion of ideas. Increasing scarcity in resources had led to increasing conflict over them, to slower growth, and to a preference for research that was largely isolated within a single discipline. European centers had started to grow rapidly and had formulated perspectives that deviated in important ways from North American perspectives. Enthusiasm for science had been muted by sentiments that emphasized the subjective character of experience and knowledge, the limitations of formal and quantitative analysis, the symbolic content of information and choice, and the role of ideas in ideological and political struggles. Subsequently, of course, those enthusiasms also waned, to be replaced by a fervor for markets, presumptions of self-interest, and the analysis of implicit and explicit pricing mechanisms (March 2007).

The endurance of *A Behavioral Theory of the Firm* through these waves of changes in intellectual enthusiasms is undoubtedly due, in part, to the reproduction of scholars (Engwall and Danell 2002). Ideas are handed down from vigorous teachers to vigorous students; and anyone who has been as durable and opportunistically eager to propagate ideas as Dick or I scatters a lot of seeds among future planters. I can count more than 100 doctoral and postdoctoral students with whom I have worked closely who have gone on to academic careers, not to mention another 100 or so who have done other productive things. Dick Cyert had a similar list. Our lists include the names of numerous people doing research in fields far removed from *A Behavioral Theory of the Firm* and over whom the book had little observable influence. They include the names of numerous people who have chosen to have relatively short publication lists and who have not themselves been much engaged in educating new scholars. However, the lists also include the names of a significant number of people who have become distinguished scholars in fields connected to the book and who have reproduced and continue to reproduce their own student progeny.

It is conceivable that the durability of ideas also has some connection to the character (quality?) of the ideas. It is a speculation that flourishes among successful scholars without enormous evidence to support it and despite the patent (and probably justified) skepticism of their less successful brethren. Such a hope leads to the obvious question: What qualities of the ideas in *A Behavioral Theory of the Firm* might have facilitated their endurance? I accept the fable that the survival of ideas is, to some degree, connected to their truth, thus that the endurance of the book reflects some elements of truth in its formulations.

The conceit exposes underlying enthusiasms not only for the ideas expressed in the book, but also for the concept of truth and for imagining the possibility of progress toward comprehending it.

Enthusiasms for truth and the possibility of scholarly progress, however, do not preclude a fascination with the obvious fact that the processes of scholarship result in citation rates that do not always seem to be correlated perfectly with scholarly elegance, beauty, or demonstrated validity. Among the many factors other than truth, beauty, and justice that contribute to citations are some obvious ones that reflect time and place. *A Behavioral Theory of the Firm* was written in English (more or less) and published in North America at a time when English was rapidly becoming the most common language of scholarly discourse and North America the largest purveyor of scholarly writings. Had the book been written in Farsi and published in Teheran, it might not have fared as well.

Among the many features of the book, aside from its truth-value, its language, and its locale, which might have affected its citation rate, I will mention only two. The first is the advantage provided by a large sample size of speculations. For a relatively short book, *A Behavioral Theory of the Firm* has a fairly large number of ideas. Survival of the book does not require that all of the ideas subsequently were found to be of value, only that some of them were.

Nor does survival require that all scholars found the same ideas to be of use at the same time. Some of the ideas in the book appealed more to some scholars than to others; some appealed more at some times and in some disciplines and in some regions of the world than at other times or in other disciplines or other regions. The idea that a firm is a political coalition resonated with many, but not all of those who agreed with the coalition formulation had equal enthusiasm for the idea that a coalition is held together by exploiting the shifting attention of coalition members so that coalitions are more stable than policies and decisions. The idea that organizations adapt over time to local search and feedback on the relation between performance and aspirations was a welcome one for many; but the implications for traveling on a rugged terrain, for superstitious learning, for competency traps, and for risk avoidance were not equally compelling to all. The idea that organizational slack serves to dampen fluctuations in performance and to provide a form of search that is less constrained by relevance became fundamental to some subsequent scholars of innovation and change, but not to all. The idea that preferences are ill defined, unstable, and endogenous found several enthusiastic audiences; but each saw those ideas through a prior lens that led to different implications. The idea that organizations attend to things sequentially and locally, rather than simultaneously and globally, and consequently exhibit inconsistencies over time and place was more easily accommodated by some theories than by others. The idea that organizations follow rules and standard operating procedures struck many people as fundamental, but there were many different views about where rules arise, how they are followed, and how they change.

A second factor giving a possible advantage for the survival and diffusion of ideas from the book is evocative ambiguity. Ideas are forms of art that invite (or discourage) elaboration and appreciation over time and thereby contribute to their endurance. A combination of precision and ambiguity leaves the meaning of ideas and other objects of art resistant to frivolous interpretation, but open to new elaborations of meaning. In the hands of others, evocative ideas evolve to become richer and retrospectively more interesting.

I have no basis for speculating that Cyert and March consciously sought to use evocative ambiguity to enlist subsequent scholars in the task of finding *A Behavioral Theory of the Firm* worthy of citation. To the best of my knowledge, they did not. However, it is instructive to compare the way they themselves summarize and interpret the ideas of the book in 1963 (first edition, Chapter 6) with the way they do so in 1992 (second edition, Epilogue). The two summaries are consistent with each other, but they are not the same. The summary in the second edition increases focus on the book's use of a history-dependent, adaptive conception of the firm relative to the book's use of an expectation-dependent, decision-making conception. Over time, both authors have drawn a wide variety of implications from the book (Cohen and March 1974; Cyert and DeGroot 1975, 1987; March 1988, 1994, 1999; March and Olsen 1976, 1989, 1995; March et al. 2000). The authors' understandings of the ideas were modified by their own and others' experience with them.

Moreover, in a world of thousands of citations, the authors' interpretations are only a small part of the story. What the ideas in *A Behavioral Theory of the Firm* might be imagined to be was shaped by the articles that sought to use them. The book as seen through the lenses of political decision making (Allison 1971), political institutions (March and Olsen 1989), or political discourse (Brunsson 1989) was notably different from the book as seen through the lens of transaction cost economics (Williamson 1975); and all of those were different from the book as seen through the lens of business decision making (Bower 1970), the lens of evolutionary economics (Nelson and Winter 1982), the lens of organizational learning (Cohen and Sproull 1996), the lens of innovation and change (Greve 2003), the lens of scarce attention (Kingdon 1984) and temporal sorting (Cohen et al. 1972), or the lens of behavioral decision theory (Ungson and Braunstein 1982). With brilliant imagination and persistent altruism, later scholars made Cyert and March look good.

Interpretive imagination of ideas is both stimulated by and constrained by the frequency of their citation. It is stimulated by the signal that frequent citation provides, a signal that suggests there might be something of interest, or at least acceptability, in a reference. At the same time, imaginative interpretation is constrained by the gradual molding of a conventional interpretation through the accumulated citation history. Just as Cyert and March were embedded in a prior intellectual history as recorded in their citation genealogy, their successors are embedded in a history that includes not only the original text of *A Behavioral Theory of the Firm,* but also interpretations of that text as recorded in its citations. I have not read the contributions to this Special Issue, but I am confident they can be used to document both the evocative ambiguity of the ideas and the subtle (and useful) tensions that exist among the legitimacy of a reference, its relevance, and its meaning.

### INTELLECTUAL HISTORY: REPRISE

Scholarship is a collective, not individual, enterprise. It depends critically on the institutions of scholarship and on the community of scholars. *A Behavioral Theory of the Firm* would not have been written without a supportive and demanding institutional context. It would not have thrived in subsequent years without an imaginative and vigorous scholarly community. I doubt that either Dick Cyert or I realized at the time what an unusually fertile institution GSIA was in the 10 years from 1955 to 1964. We thought the GSIA of that period was a stimulating place, but it was only in retrospect that we realized how extraordinary it was. It was not unique, and doubtless its role can be exaggerated, but that decade of institutional history is a reminder that institutions capable of creating cultures of first-class scholarship are international treasures.

Dick and I were somewhat more aware of our dependence on our contemporary colleagues and on those who went before us for the ideas that we massaged. We lived in a community in which ideas were sustenance, and we realized that we were nourished not only by our colleagues but also by a history of scholarship. What we did not appreciate fully, and only came to recognize over the years following, was our dependence on generations of later scholars trying to imagine what our words might be constructed to mean to make them interesting. Ideas take form and reproduce through an intergenerational, international pyramid of promiscuous and acrobatic intellectual intercourse. We enjoyed and profited from it all.

For all of these reasons, Dick Cyert and I owe a substantial debt to our colleagues and to the institutions and groups of which we were a part. We are grateful for the institutions and the many ways they have made our work possible. We are grateful for the scholarly communities that have welcomed us, for the numerous contributions they have made to our field within the behavioral tradition, and for the ways they have honored us with their attention and affection over the years. Our debt is increased by this issue of *Organization Science*. In particular, Linda Argote, Mie Augier, Henrich Greve, Daniel Levinthal, and Michael Prietula have our warmest thanks for their toil as editors and for our years of friendship.

## ACKNOWLEDGMENTS

The fact that if he had lived Dick Cyert would certainly have coauthored this little essay should not obscure the fact that he probably would not agree with all of it and should not be held posthumously responsible. The research has been supported by the Reed Foundation. The author thanks Mie Augier, Henrich Greve, and Johan P. Olsen for their comments.

## NOTES

1. March also worked on the research during a year (1955–1956) at the Center for Advanced Study in the Behavioral Sciences, Stanford, California.

2. In 1967 the Carnegie Institute of Technology merged with the Mellon Institute to form Carnegie Mellon University. The Graduate School of Industrial Administration became the Tepper School of Business in 2004.

3. This ignores books that deal with disciplines (including statistics) other than the social sciences and management, or that represent new editions of earlier master works (e.g., Dewey, Schumpeter). Because of the errors and multiple listings in Google Scholar citation counts, it is possible that a few works with more than 1,500 citations have been overlooked. It is unlikely, however, that any of the 22 works identified by this procedure have fewer than 1,500 citations.

4. The authors include Gordon Allport, Kenneth Arrow, Gary Becker, Benjamin Bloom, Ronald Coase, Anthony Downs, Leon Festinger, Jay Forrester, Milton Friedman, Erving Goffman, Thomas Kuhn, George Miller, and Robert Solow. Because the journal coverage of Google Scholar tends to inflate the records of works in economics relative to other fields, the list does not include important works written during this period by luminaries from other fields, such as Howard Becker, D. E. Broadbent, James Coleman, Robert Dahl, Clifford Geertz, George Homans, V. O. Key, Charles Lindblom, Seymour Martin Lipset, David McClelland, Robert Merton, Hans Morgenthau, Talcott Parsons, and B. F. Skinner. An expanded list that included such names would confirm the point that almost all high-citation works come from scholars at a small number of major institutions.

5. A few others who were at GSA during the 1955–1964 period and who had distinguished academic careers were: Albert Ando, Igor Ansoff, Kalman Cohen, Dwight Crane, J. Patrick Crecine, William Dill, Jacques Drèze, Harold Guetzkow, Yuji Ijiri, Alfred Kuehn,

Harold Leavitt, Arie Lewin, Michael Lovell, Takehiko Matsuda, Timothy McGuire, Allan Meltzer, Dale Mortensen, Bertil Näslund, Louis Pondy, William Pounds, Dick Ramström, and Eric Rhenman.

## REFERENCES

Allison, G. T. 1971. *Essence of Decision: Explaining the Cuban Missile Crisis.* Little, Brown, Boston, MA.

Ando, A., F. Modigliani. 1963. The "lifecycle" hypothesis of saving: Aggregate implications and tests. *Amer. Econom. Rev. 53* 55–84.

Augier, M., J. G. March, eds. 2002. *The Economics of Choice, Change and Organization: Essays in Memory of Richard M. Cyert.* Edward Elgar, Cheltenham, UK.

Augier, M., J. G. March, eds. 2004. *Models of a Man: Essays in Memory of Herbert A. Simon.* MIT Press, Cambridge, MA.

Bower, J. L. 1970. *Managing the Resource Allocation Process.* Harvard Business School Division of Research, Boston, MA.

Brunsson, N. 1989. *The Organization of Hypocrisy: Talk, Decisions, and Actions in Organizations.* Wiley, New York.

Chames, A., W. W. Cooper. 1957. Management models and industrial applications of linear programming. *Management Sci. 4* 38–91.

Cohen, M. D., J. G. March. 1974. *Leadership and Ambiguity: The American College President.* McGraw-Hill, New York.

Cohen, M. D., L. S. Sproull, eds. 1996. *Organizational Learning.* Sage Publications, Thousand Oaks, CA.

Cohen, M. D., J. G. March, J. P. Olsen. 1972. A garbage can model of organizational choice. *Admin. Sci. Quart. 17* 1–25.

Cyert, R. M., M. H. DeGroot. 1975. Adaptive utility. R. H. Day, T. Groves, eds. *Adaptive Economic Models.* Academic Press, New York, 223–246.

Cyert, R. M., M. H. DeGroot. 1987. *Bayseian Analysis and Uncertainty in Economic Theory.* Rowman and Littlefield, Totowa, NJ.

Cyert, R. M., J. G. March. 1963. *A Behavioral Theory of the Firm.* Prentice-Hall, Englewood Cliffs, NJ.

Cyert, R. M., J. G. March. 1992. *A Behavioral Theory of the Firm,* 2nd ed. Blackwell, Oxford, UK.

Day, R. H. 1964. Book review: A behavioral theory of the firm. *Econometrica 32* 461–465.

Engwall, L., R. Danell. 2002. The behavioral theory of the firm in action. M. Augier, J. G. March, eds. *The Economics of Choice, Change and Organization: Essays in Memory of Richard M. Cyert.* Edward Elgar, Cheltenham, UK, 27–47.

Feigenbaum, E. A., J. Feldman. 1963. *Computers and Thought.* McGraw-Hill, New York.

Greve, H. R. 2003. *Organizational Learning from Performance Feedback: A Behavioral Perspective on Innovation and Change.* Cambridge University Press, Cambridge, UK.

Holt, C. C., F. Modigilanl, J. Muth, H. A. Simon. 1960. *Planning Production, Inventory and Work Force.* Prentice-Hall, Englewood Cliffs, NJ.

Ijiri, Y. 2004. Interdisciplinary reasoning and Herbert Simon's influence. M. Augier, J. G. March, eds. *Models of a Man: Essays in Memory of Herbert A. Simon.* MIT Press, Cambridge, MA.

Kingdon, J. W. 1984. *Agendas, Alternatives, and Public Policies*. Little, Brown, Boston, MA.

Kuhn, T. S. 1962. *The Structure of Scientific Revolutions*. University of Chicago Press, Chicago, IL.

Kydland, F. E., E. C. Prescott. 1977. Rules rather than discretion: The inconsistency of optimal plans. *J. Political Econom.* 85 473–491.

Leavitt, H. J. 1996. The old days, hot groups, and managers' lib. *Admin. Sci. Quart.* 41 23–47.

Lovell, M. C., E. Prescott. 1968. Money, multiplier accelerator interaction, and the business cycle. *Southern Econom. J.* 35 60–72.

Lucas, R. E. 1972. Expectations and the neutrality of money. *J. Econom. Theory 4* 103–124.

Mansfield, E. 1968. *Industrial Research and Technological Innovation*. Norton, New York.

March, J. G. 1988. *Decisions and Organizations*. Blackwell, Oxford, UK.

March, J. G. 1994. *A Primer on Decision Making: How Decisions Happen*. Free Press, New York.

March, J. G. 1999. *The Pursuit of Organizational Intelligence*. Blackwell, Oxford, UK.

March, J. G. 2007. The study of organizations and organizing since 1945. *Organization Studies 28* 9–19.

March J. G., J. P. Olsen. 1976. *Ambiguity and Choice in Organizations*. Universitetsforlaget, Bergen, Norway.

March, J. G., J. P. Olsen. 1989. *Rediscovering Institutions: The Organizational Basis of Politics*. Free Press, New York.

March, J. G., J. P. Olsen. 1995. *Democratic Governance*. Free Press, New York.

March, J. G., H. A. Simon. 1958. *Organizations*. John Wiley, New York.

March, J. G., H. A. Simon. 1993. *Organizations*, 2nd ed. Blackwell, Oxford, UK.

March, J. G., M. Schulz, X. Zhou. 2000. *The Dynamics of Rules: Change in Written Organizational Codes*. Stanford University Press, Stanford, CA.

Modigliani, F., M. Miller. 1958. The cost of capital, corporation finance and the theory of investment. *Amer. Econom. Rev.* 48 261–297.

Muth, J. 1961. Rational expectations and the theory of price movements. *Econometrica 29* 315–335.

Nelson, R. R., S. G. Winter. 1973. Toward an evolutionary theory of economic capabilities. *Amer. Econom. Rev.* 63 440–449.

Nelson, R. R., S. G. Winter. 1982. *An Evolutionary Theory of Economic Change*. Harvard University Press, Cambridge, MA.

Newell, A., J. C. Shaw, H. A. Simon. 1958. Elements of a theory of human problem solving. *Psych. Rev.* 65 151–166.

Simon, H. A. 1955. A behavioral model of rational choice. *Quart. J. Econom.* 69 99–118.

Simon, H. A., M. Barenfeld. 1969. Information-processing analysis of perceptual processes in problem solving. *Psych. Rev.* 76 473–483.

Starbuck, W. H. 1965. Organizational growth and development. J. G. March, ed. *Handbook of Organizations*. Rand McNally, Chicago, IL, 451–533.

Starbuck, W. H. 1993. "Watch where you step!" or Indiana Starbuck amid the perils of academe. A. Bedeian, ed. *Management Laureates: A Collection of Autobiographical Essays*, Vol. 3. JAI Press, Greenwich, CT, 63–110.

Ungson, G., D. Braunstein, eds. 1982. *Decision Making: An Interdisciplinary Inquiry.* Kent Publishing Company, Boston, MA.

Vroom, V. 1964. *Work and Motivation.* Wiley, New York.

White, H. C. 1970. *Chains of Opportunity.* Harvard University Press, Cambridge, MA.

Williamson, O. E. 1967. Hierarchical control and optimum firm size. *J. Political Econom.* 75 123–138.

Williamson, O. E. 1975. *Markets and Hierarchies.* Free Press, New York.

Williamson, O. E. 1996. Transaction cost economics and the Carnegie connection. *J. Econom. Behav. Organ.* 31 149–155.

Winter, S. G. 1964. Book review: A Behavioral Theory of the Firm. *Amer. Econom. Rev.* 54 144–148.

# CHAPTER 17

# The Pursuit of Relevance in Management Education

MIE AUGIER AND JAMES G. MARCH

Throughout the 20th century, university-level business schools in North America were forums for argument over the appropriate character of management education, how to think about the structures and programs of such education, and what kind of schools such thinking suggests. The conflict extended to questions of staffing, organization, curriculum, and research programs. It shows no signs of abating at the start of the 21st century.

Persistently through the history, two contending exaggerations have framed the debates. The first proclaims that management education has sacrificed relevance to the esoterics of academic purity. The second bemoans the subordination of fundamental knowledge and research to the limited perspectives of immediate problems. These proclamations may often have been overly dramatic, but they have reflected an enduring dispute in professional schools that is manifest also in the histories of schools of medicine, engineering, law, education, and public policy and administration.[1]

## Practical Experience and Scholarship

All of these schools exhibit tensions between "experiential" knowledge and "academic" knowledge.[2] Experiential knowledge is derived from practical experience in the field. It is stored in the wisdom of experienced practitioners and is communicated by them. Its hallmark is direct and immediate relevance to practice. Academic knowledge is derived from scholarship. It is stored in the theories of academics and is communicated by them. Its hallmarks are an aesthetic of ideas and abstraction from practice.

---

We are grateful to Markus Becker, Robert Gibbons, Michael Hay, Michael Jacobides, Thorbjørn Knudsen, Andrew Marshall, William Pounds, John Reed, and Sidney Winter for comments and conversations on the topic, and to referees for their helpful suggestions. The research on the history of management education has been supported by grants from the Sloan Foundation and the Cynthia and John Reed Foundation. Parts of the paper are based on talks given at the Copenhagen Business School and York University, and the chapter was published in *California Management Review*, 49:3 (2007), 129–146.

The dichotomy oversimplifies the relationship. Experiential knowledge and academic knowledge are in many ways better seen as intertwined than as in opposition. Experience is interpreted within frames that reflect academic sensibilities, and the research on which academic knowledge is based is deeply affected by the observations and understandings of experience. However, at least from the time when Aristotle undertook to teach Alexander the Great, concerns about the relation between the knowledge gained from experience by skilled practitioners, on the one hand, and the knowledge gained from scholarship by skilled academics, on the other, has shaped the formal training of practitioners. Knowledge derived from practical experience tends to emphasize immediacy and applicability in a specific context. It is ordinarily more focused in time and space than is academic scholarship. Conversely, the academic perspective tends to emphasize the timelessness and generality of its relevance. As a general rule, the longer the time horizon and the broader the scope, the greater the comparative advantage of academic knowledge.

The prototypic response to tensions between the two forms of knowledge is to call for some form of "balance" or "integration." The idea is to determine the appropriate mix of experiential and academic knowledge by invoking an analysis in which the costs and benefits of alternative investments are assessed from the point of view of some conception of the common or collective good over time, or to find a conception of knowledge that integrates what is generated through practical experience with what is generated through academic research. Much of the discourse over business education tacitly accepts some version of such a formulation. There is widespread obeisance to the mantras of "balance" and "integration."[3]

In particular, the ideas of "balance" and "integration" as solutions to conflict are understandable predilections of leaders. They long for some kind of institutional coherence, with conflict resolved through reference to some higher aspirations. One early president of the American Collegiate Schools of Business proclaimed:

The future of collegiate education for business lies wholly within our ability to integrate successfully the work of a professional school and the basic academic disciplines that underlie that work.[4]

Similar sentiments can be found in the pronouncements of many other leaders of the effort to transform business schools in the 1950s and 1960s,[5] as well as in essays by writers who are skeptical about that transformation.[6]

One common vision was that by doing research driven by real-world problems but aimed more at understanding than at solving those problems in a specific context, business schools and researchers in management education would both help define and frame practical problems—*and* help advance the disciplines from which they draw. The "balance" and "integration" problems were reduced or "solved" by declaring them potentially nonexistent.

These longings and formulations have shaped the ways in which the debate has been framed. Talk of balance and integration is obligatory. However, the pursuits of balance and integration generally do not lead to them. Although almost everyone may agree that a balanced mix of experiential and academic knowledge is essential, there is little agreement on the current mix, the optimal mix, or the criteria by which the optimum might be determined. Debates over balance are engaged without any significant chance of being resolved by data or by derivation from shared assumptions. A few stylized "facts" are presented from time to time and some crude empirical summaries are put forth, but the conclusions turn less on facts than on perspectives and prior prejudices.

Similarly, although almost everyone may agree that experiential knowledge and academic knowledge need to be integrated, there is little agreement on strategies for strengthening that integration or even for ways to describe the level of integration desired or achieved. As a result, there is little or no dissent from the desirability of integrating experiential and academic knowledge, but little consensus on what that means in terms of educational practice.

As business schools and their constituencies have struggled with the problems, the discussion has often been characterized more by rhetorical ripostes from contending advocates than by thoughtful engagement. Thus, a critique of business schools as intellectually shallow and academically second rate[7] is counterposed to a critique of the schools as far removed from managerial reality, thus irrelevant to, or destructive of, good management practice.[8]

Both sides see themselves as disadvantaged in the struggle. In the perceptions of the advocates of academic knowledge, the advocates of experience have an enormous advantage in American business schools stemming from the way the schools are embedded in a system of business firms and business careers and from the control of the advocates of experience over the flows of financial resources essential to the schools. Faculties of business schools sometimes become anti-academic, pursuing careers as consultants to, or adulators of, business practitioners. As a result, advocates of academic knowledge believe that business school education and research, responsive to such imbalances in power, is inattentive to the limitations reflected in the time and space horizons manifested in experiential conceptions of relevance.[9]

In the perceptions of the advocates of experiential knowledge, on the other hand, American business schools are impervious to outside pressures. They are run by faculties for the benefit of themselves and academic knowledge. Although business schools secure a substantial part of their financial resources from the business community, they are seen as using those resources largely to pursue their own agendas of irrelevant research. As a result, advocates of experience believe that business school education, responsive to such imbalances in power, becomes devoid of knowledge that can be used to address the real problems of business managers or firms.[10]

## Recent History

The history of business schools in North America and Europe has been explored by a number of scholars.[11] From the present point of view, they tell a fairly consistent story. During the first half of the 20th century, business schools worked to be useful to students seeking careers within the business community. As an early study of business education put it:

The primary aim of the university school of commerce is to prepare its students for successful and socially useful careers in business.[12]

The research scholarship component of academic life was, for the most part, not a conspicuous part of business schools. Some business schools had doctoral programs, but those programs contributed relatively little to the training of research scholars. Some business schools had research programs, but the research was rarely viewed as distinguished or fundamental within the scholarly community. Business schools hired experienced executives as professors and tried to replicate experience through the teaching of cases, the involvement of faculty in consulting, and the linking of course work with temporary employment of students in business firms. They sought to become the carriers of "best practice."[13]

The effort to be useful to business was, to a significant extent, successful. The success was achieved, however, at a cost. It left North American business schools (all of the important ones, which were formally associated with universities) with only modest legitimacy in academe. Even the Harvard Business School, probably the best-known North American business school prior to the Second World War, was not always enthusiastically embraced by Harvard disciplinary departments.

Reasonable people differ on the extent to which the inconsequential standing of business schools in the halls of academe reflected accurate assessments of their academic performance or stemmed from envy of business school affluence; but there was little question that North American business schools suffered from reputations for mediocre academic capabilities.[14] Although the data did not always consistently support the stereotype, students enrolled in business curricula were generally viewed as weaker than students enrolled in most other curricula. Although there were outstanding scholars on business school faculties, faculty in business schools were generally viewed as less distinguished academically than other faculty.[15] Herbert Simon, whose training was exclusively in academic disciplines but who held an appointment in a business school, reflected on the standing of business schools in his autobiography:

Accurately or not, we perceived American business education at that time [i.e., immediately after the Second World War] as a wasteland of vocationalism that needed to be transformed into science-based professionalism, as medicine and engineering had been transformed a generation or two earlier.[16]

Although a careful documentation of the extent and nature of the changes has not, to our knowledge, been published, it is widely believed and reported that management education experienced a change of some magnitude during the 1950s and 1960s. According to the reports of observers, most North American business schools were transformed by coalitions of deans, faculties, foundations, and business executives who sought to augment the role of academic knowledge in the education of managers.[17] They searched for programs of research that might lead to improvements in practice, not so much through diffusion of "best practice" as through changes in fundamental knowledge. They emphasized knowledge generated through research, closer links with the disciplines, more rigor, including the greater use of mathematical models and the research findings of psychology and economics, and the substitution of formal analysis for rules of thumb.

The transformation was heralded by a well-known report written for the Ford Foundation by Aaron Gordon and James Howell.[18] Their report observed:

The general tenor of our recommendations was that the business schools (and departments of business) need to move in the direction of a broader and more rigorous educational program, with higher standards of admission and student performance, with better informed and more scholarly faculties that are capable of carrying on more significant research, and with a greater appreciation of the contributions to be made to the development of business competence by both the underlying . . . disciplines and the judicious use of . . . materials and methods.[19]

The champions of these changes in management research and education portrayed the goal of management education as being two-fold:[20]

- *First*, business schools were seen, particularly at the graduate level, to be responsible for the education of future teachers and researchers of management, and for research that was both relevant to management and respected in the underlying disciplines.

- *Second*, at all levels in the education of managers—undergraduate, graduate, and executive programs alike—the proper training of future practitioners of management was seen as based on the foundational disciplines of economics and of behavioral science as well as the quantitative disciplines—for much the same reasons that it was important to the schools and practice of medicine to be based on biology, physiology, and chemistry.

Cyert and Dill declared:

The student of management . . . is expected to learn enough about mathematics, statistics, and the computer to be able to understand and use decision models from the management sciences and operations research. He is expected to understand the theoretical and research underpinnings on which economists base their advice to corporations and governments. He is expected to know the main findings and hypotheses about human behavior from psychology, sociology, and political science.[21]

The efforts of the reformers were successful. In the space of two decades, the culture and practice of most leading North American business schools were changed substantially. Curricula became more analytical and demanding. The quality of students relative to the quality in other university programs was improved. New faculty, particularly those drawn from the disciplines, became more important and more demanding of a significant research presence in the schools. Graduate programs became more important relative to undergraduate programs. Graduate students were drawn increasingly from serious undergraduate disciplinary programs at major universities. The various fields represented in business school faculties became quasi-disciplines with academic research journals and professional associations.[22] In the process, many North American business schools sought to become and, in fact, did become academically respectable. The success was made easier by the fact that business schools were undergoing dramatic growth in students, faculty, and resources. Many new faculty were recruited from disciplinary training. It was a time of optimism about the potential for contributions to management from scientific research.

In subsequent years, North American business schools found confirmation of these changes in their apparent successes at restructuring business practice. For example, academic operations research (e.g., linear and dynamic programming, queuing theory) transformed business practice in the management of operations; academic financial economics transformed business practice in financial management; and academic organizations studies transformed practice in personnel and human resource management. As academic enthusiasms shifted over time, business schools were led into the seemingly exotic wonders of game theory, chaos theory, evolutionary theory, graph theory, theories of cognition, literary theory, and the nuances of cultural differences, some of which seemed—at least to some observers—to contribute similarly useful ideas to management practice.

The post-WWII revolution in North American management education was followed by a counter-revolution that began in the 1980s and 1990s. The counter-revolution was supported by the business press and by elements of the business school community (including faculty members), particularly but not exclusively in and around those schools and parts of schools whose relative position had declined in the 1950s and 1960s. With claims that North American business schools had become too academic and too removed from practice, these groups undertook to take charge of the evaluation and character of business schools. They spoke against a business school emphasis on the disciplines and the abstractions of academic knowledge. The business press was successful in placing the rankings of business schools under their control and in imposing criteria that subordinated the exhibition of academic prowess to the exhibition of business experience, consultation, and market value.

Such pressures, in combination with the increasing dependence of business schools on financial support from business firms and business executives, the economic advantages for professors from participating in the market for consultation, the softening of labor market demand for business school graduates, and the vociferousness of business school students in their roles as "customers," led business schools to seek greater immediate relevance by increasing the emphasis on experiential knowledge in their research and in their teaching, and by decreasing the emphasis on academic knowledge.

As was true in the "revolution," the contending groups cut across academic/business lines. Many business school faculty arrayed themselves on the "practical experience" side of the argument. For example, in an article published in a leading popular business journal, Warren Bennis and James O'Toole, both well-known business school professors with considerable academic and consulting experience, declared:

During the past several decades, many leading B-schools have quietly adopted an inappropriate, and ultimately self-defeating, model of academic excellence. Instead of measuring themselves in terms of the competence of their graduates, or by how well their faculties understand important drivers of business performance, they measure themselves almost solely by the rigor of their scientific research.[23]

At the same time, many leading business executives located themselves on the "academic" side. For example, John Reed, former CEO of Citicorp and Citigroup, argued:

In general, I believe it is very important for business practice to be shaped by basic research and basic knowledge. Research that draws from the academic disciplines (but in an interdisciplinary way) serves the important function of creating a framework that allows managers and management practitioners to understand the context and content of the specific problems they are dealing with. So, clearly, the interaction between the academic community and management practice is important—and management theory need to not worry so much about immediate relevance as to providing the basic framework for understanding managerial problems.[24]

It seems likely that the next fifty years of the history of business schools will witness similar debates over relevance. Future advocates will be as noble, as self-interested, as thoughtful, as insistent, as eloquent, and as blind to history as past advocates have been. The history will include periods of relative quiet in which a semi-permanent understanding will be viewed as having established a new regime; but the quiet will give way to a new burst of debate. It seems unlikely that either the academic proclivity for the argument or the difficulty of resolving it will disappear.

## Reasons and Interests

Not surprisingly given the academic arena, most descriptions of the history of the pursuit of relevance in management education have been couched primarily in the relatively antiseptic terms of intellectual debates. Although individual and group interests have obviously been implicated in relevance discussions, the terms of discourse have usually not been explicitly personal or group interest-centered. There are those who demand that business schools be instruments of the business community, that they be bastions of consulting, that they tie intelligence to practical problems, and that their speculations lead to practical implications. They emphasize the general individual and social value of such arrangements. They speak in terms of strengthening management education, not in terms of serving interests. Similarly, there are those voices that demand that business schools be institutions of fundamental scholarship, that they be bastions of research, that they embrace autonomous intellectual curiosity, and that they treat questions of immediate relevance as pernicious. They link their preferences to conceptions of general value. Like their brethren on the other side, they present themselves as advocates for improving management education, not for serving special groups.

The implicit conception has been one of a history that evolved through a more or less reasoned conversation over policies couched in words and defended within philosophies. Such an understanding is obviously an incomplete one. It confuses the political reality of the development of a living institution with the tactical articulation of reasons by its denizens. A suppression of interests in developing the story makes business school history appear to be driven exclusively by a discourse on relevance. Like all such framings of history, it treats conflicts of interests as encapsulated in the arguments ornamenting them. It subordinates uncertainties with respect to whose interests are served to uncertainties with respect to what argument makes sense. A focus on discourse largely omits more brutal questions from political philosophy concerning whose interests should count and how the conflicting interests (welfare) of the various participants in a society (and future society) should be weighted in taking action. Who should be more relevant than whom? What should be more relevant than what?

We make no serious apology for assuming words are important. It is what academics do. However, it may be useful to recognize that individual and group interests are also implicated in, and lurk behind, the contending arguments. A 20th century history of North American business schools that was more interest-based might well treat the debates over relevance as minor rhetorical frosting for a serious political contest over control of business schools and management education. It would observe that relevance issues are masks for issues of political power and that the obscuring of interests and their importance is not innocent in a struggle among interests. It gives advantages to some and disadvantages to others. At the most obvious level, advocates for experiential knowledge tend to be those with a comparative advantage in a world built around experience; and advocates for academic knowledge tend to be those with a comparative advantage in a world built around academic knowledge. There is no mystery in that, and the list of interests affected by business school choices is a long one.

Despite a recognition of the force of the argument, we persist in imagining that any characterization of words as epiphenomenal probably underestimates their significance, particularly in a political process in which academics are key players. In contemporary discussions of the role of words and ideas in history,[25] we should be recorded on the side of those who think their effects are sometimes perceptible. Moreover, even if the content of the debate over relevance were of minor importance to the outcomes of business school history, it would be of major importance to the humanizing of that history. Reality is not always kind to the advocates of reason and discourse, but a commitment to reason and discourse is a hallmark of the romance of educated human existence.

## THE CRITERION OF USEFULNESS

Debates about the design of management education exhibit the extent to which schools of management are creatures of a utilitarian morality. The time and resources devoted to the creation, retention, and transfer of knowledge are generally justified in instrumental ways, in terms of the contributions of management education and research to individual and collective needs and desires. The undisputed criterion—shared across a wide variety of actors, interests, contexts, and commentators—is usefulness.

### A Utilitarian Morality

Investments in the development, refinement, and reproduction of knowledge are rationalized by the returns they are expected to generate for individuals and for society. Knowledge activities are seen as having value by virtue of the ways they improve either the outcomes that can be achieved, the likelihood of achieving them, or the choices among alternatives. This broad utilitarian vision is embraced by the overwhelming majority of those discussing the future of management education.[26]

In its application to business schools, the catechism is quite familiar: Curricula should be relevant to students' needs and desires. Skills of graduates should be relevant to the needs and desires of employers and thereby to the needs of graduates. Skills of faculty should be relevant to the needs and desires of organizations interested in employing them as consultants or their students as managers. Scholarship should be directed toward generating knowledge relevant to improving individual success, organizational efficiency, and economic growth. For example, in the past few decades, business education—like education more generally—has become "commodified" and "marketized" through a sanctification of market-based allocations of resources. The bedrock of contemporary enthusiasms and concerns over the introduction of markets to educational products is this utilitarian morality.

A utilitarian orientation is, however, broader than a market orientation. Market formulations postulate that things should be useful to customers, but the conception of usefulness is pointedly subjective. Utility is determined by the user. Many participants in the educational debate would extend the idea of utility to include "objective" or "social" usefulness (as difficult as those are to specify), thus they would see a market implementation of usefulness as incomplete or misleading. Nevertheless, these critics of markets and the "commodification" of education are most commonly thoroughly utilitarian in their opposition to markets. They deny the usefulness of markets but accept the criterion of usefulness.

As in other discussions within a utilitarian world, the definition of "utility" is often quite elastic when applied to management education. Relevance may reflect social as well as individual values, hedonistic as well as practical values, and short-run as well as long-run values. The dominance of a utilitarian morality induces efforts to provide utilitarian justifications, not only for such obviously practical items as bookkeeping but also for classical icons of literature, art, music, religion, and metaphysics. On occasion, the morality has been twisted into such convoluted specifications of usefulness as to become operationally meaningless. As a result, it often becomes a language of argument more than a language of judgment.

## Ambiguity and Myopia

The idea of "utility" suggests some kind of metric that, in combination with a measure of likelihood, can yield a measure of expected value by which various alternatives can be compared. The search for a basis by which such a cardinal utility function might be imagined to underlie human choice has occupied choice theorists for many years, but the results have been mixed. The values that humans profess appear often to be less consistent, less simple, less clear, and less precisely measured than expected value calculations demand.

Indeed, the utilitarian frame for the pursuit of relevance suffers from two widely noted complications that threaten to make the pursuit unrewarding. *First, the definition of relevance is ambiguous, its measurement imprecise, and its meaning complex.* Most of the significant values involved in education are extraordinarily hard to measure and predict. We value graduates who have developed a knowledge basis for lifelong capabilities, but there is little agreement on how to assess current students (or study programs) in those terms. We value knowledge that has a long-run impact on understanding, but there is little agreement on how to assess current research in those terms. The result is that utilitarian arguments can easily degenerate into little more than variations of word games. "Costs" and "benefits" come to include abstractions not susceptible to calibration or comparison. Moreover, there is a well-known tendency to conflate measurability with significance, to assume that things that are difficult to measure can be ignored.[27]

Advocates of fundamental research and scholarship have to concede that the return from such work is not only more distant, but also more uncertain. The probability distribution over possible future outcomes has a relatively high variance. This makes investments in scholarship not only more "risky" in terms of the variance over possible outcomes but also more subject to biased errors of estimation. On average, scholars probably overestimate and managers probably underestimate the possible returns from fundamental research, and this disparity in estimation probably increases as the distance from the predicted outcomes increases.

*Second, the pursuit of relevance is often myopic in practice.* Although the concept of usefulness can be interpreted to include distant considerations, the ambiguities of relevance are ordinarily resolved in a way that favors consequences that are near in space or time over those that are more distant. For example, any teacher in a modern business school is aware that although faculty and students may share a common utilitarian morality, the implicit space and time horizons of business students can be notably narrower and shorter than the implicit space and time horizons of scholarship.

There is no easy way to determine the best spatial or temporal horizon. Reasonable people can easily disagree about either. Consider the appropriate spatial focus: What is useful to top managers or society leaders is not necessarily useful to actors in the immediate neighborhood of the action. To what extent should a business school be relevant for workers, middle management, or top management? For stockholders? Or political leaders? To what extent should a business school be relevant for its students? Its donors? Firms? The global economic/political system? The society? The easy answer is that the school should be relevant for all of those; and to some extent contemporary business schools manage to be. However, as a code word, "relevance" usually denotes attention to the concrete, practical concerns of immediate, local actors rather than more distant, less tangible, and more theoretical concerns.

Consider similarly the appropriate time perspective for relevance: Relevance carries a time subscript. Useful when? To what extent should a business school seek relevance in the near term? In the long run? Are managers to be educated for tomorrow, or for the decades to come? Are the things that matter in the long run different in important ways from the things that matter in the short run? Or is it true that the long run is merely a long string of short runs, thus that the long run will take care of itself if the short run is controlled? The issues are complicated by differences in certainty about consequences. Outcomes that are distant in time are systematically harder to predict than are outcomes that are near.

Concern about excessive attention to the short run was conspicuous in the arguments of the architects of the 1950s reform of North American business schools. G. Leland Bach (founding dean of the Graduate School of Industrial Administration at the Carnegie Institute of Technology) wrote:

My central proposition is both trite and revolutionary. It is that business education should be focused on training not for the business world of today but for that of to-morrow—for 1980 not for 1958. . . . surely anything we can do to develop flexibility of mind, openness and receptivity to new and changing ideas, habitual skills in learning for one's self, and other such mental characteristics must promise more use to the individual and to society over the quarter century of change ahead, than would comparable attention to descriptive information about today's institutions and today's best business practice.[28]

Similar comments were common among educational and business leaders of the time.

Confidence that fundamental knowledge will ultimately yield practical return is characteristic of advocates of academic knowledge. For example, Simon noted:

When tests of relevance are applied, it is essential that they be applied by people who understand the tortuous, many-step process by which fundamental knowledge may gradually be brought to bear on management problems.[29]

However, the evidence for the belief in the inexorability of practical return from fundamental scholarship is characteristically more anecdotal than systematic. Miner analyzed 32 established organizational science theories in terms of their rated importance, validity, and usefulness.[30] She found little evidence of any consistent relationships among these three attributes.

## Myopic Adaptation

Myopia has been explored theoretically in the analysis of experience-based human adaptive processes, such as problem solving, learning, evolution, and political competition.[31] In problem solving, consequences in the long run are ignored or discounted relative to consequences in the short run. In learning, the mechanisms of learning from experience respond to local and immediate experience. In evolution, differential rates of survival and reproduction respond to local and immediate conditions. In political competition, groups advocating courses of action promising immediate usefulness generally command greater resources and attention than do groups advocating actions promising usefulness that is more delayed. There is a systematic bias against activities that provide benefits at some temporal distance from the point at which adaptation takes place.

Because of the way they tend to ignore things that are distant in time and space in order to attend to things that are near, instrumentally adaptive processes are potentially self-defeating. Alternatives providing long-run, uncertain, distant, and abstract benefits are at a disadvantage in competition with alternatives providing more immediate, more certain, nearer, and more concrete benefits. This disadvantage leads to pursuing a course that reduces long-run gains in order to capture short-run gains. Exploitation tends to drive out exploration.[32] Although it is possible that an adaptive process will move too far toward exploration in pursuing a balance between exploitation and exploration, it is more likely that it will move too far toward exploitation.

This problem is well known. It has led to an extensive literature on two problems of experience-based adaptation that stem from the way experiential learning involves the endogenous, sequential sampling of possible experience and, therefore, the undersampling of alternatives for which early experience is poor.[33] The first problem is the problem of encouraging *altruism* in the face of spatial myopia. The second problem is the problem of encouraging *self-control* in the face of temporal myopia. These are problems implicit in any form of adaptation to experience. They are problems in the pursuit of relevance.

It is an old story. Not always (but often enough to be worrisome), the explicit, calculated, fast-responding pursuit of a goal may reduce the likelihood of reaching it. An explicitly "short-run" approach to pursuing self-interest may undermine longer-run credibility and trust. The repeated short-run mobilization of adrenaline for a "fight or flight" response may undermine memory and learning. Pressure to respond quickly to feedback may undermine the patience essential to learning. The adverse consequences have been noted in child rearing, business strategy, economic policy, politics, and war. Similar propositions have been pronounced about many other important pursuits in life: the pursuit of virtue, the pursuit of love, and the pursuit of glory. History offers copious evidence both for the ubiquity of the problem and for its intractability.

## Implications for Business Schools

The relevance criterion exalts the importance of early consequences for students, faculty, administrators, donors, and alumni of a particular school and diminishes the importance of later consequences or consequences for those same groups in other schools and for more distant groups and individuals or broader concerns. The myopia of relevance favors teaching over research, teaching of interviewee technique over theories of information exchange, research on business problems over models for problem solving. It favors concrete knowledge over abstract knowledge. It favors business cases over analytical models. It favors consideration of strategies for firms over strategies for public policy.

Experiences in business schools, as well as an understanding of the myopia of adaptation, appear to support the idea that the pursuit of relevance in management education will be systematically biased against forms and practices having returns that are uncertain, indirect, or delayed. This feature of the pursuit suggests a utilitarian reason for caution about relevance. Although it is possible that concerns about relevance will move schools of business too far toward emphasizing academic knowledge, it is more likely that such concerns will move the schools too far toward experiential knowledge with its claim of immediate and local relevance.

## THE PURSUIT OF MEANING AND BEAUTY

The argument within and around North American business schools is thoroughly Benthamite. Not everyone agrees with that basis. As John Stuart Mill pointed out in his famous critique, Jeremy Bentham had "the completeness of a limited man." Mill wrote:

Man is never recognized by [Bentham] as a being capable of . . . desiring for its own sake, the conformity of his own character to his standard of excellence, without hope of good or evil from other source than his own inward consciousness.[34]

According to Mill, Bentham failed to comprehend or represent a range of fundamental human sentiments that stem less from concerns about the usefulness of human institutions and practices than from demands that those institutions and practices identify, honor, and reproduce key elements of the human spirit.

### Alternative Moralities

To some participants in the business school debate, a discussion limited to considerations of relevance, even if broadly defined, is incomplete. The pursuit of relevance and the utilitarian morality on which it is based overlook or reject traditions and moralities that emphasize education as an object of faith and beauty and its connection to humanity and human identities. Within such traditions, relevance is, for the most part, irrelevant. They emphasize questions not about the usefulness of education and research but about their essential nature as components of a proper human existence, about the definition and meaning of scholarly identities, and about contemplating and improving the beauties of scholarly life.

Such questions seem strange in a discourse organized around a utilitarian worldview, but they are at least as familiar in human history. Rather than Bentham and Mill, they conjure the voices of Kant, Kierkegaard, Kundera, Nietzsche, Plato, and Whitehead. The discussion is oriented not to what is useful but to what is "essential." What is it that is essential to education and research, without which it fails to fulfill the fundamental nature of a human existence? In this view, education and research can be seen as organized to provide grace, meaning, delicacy, and elegance to human life, not because those attributes can be shown to yield competitive advantage but because they are basic elements of an educational faith. A commitment to education can be seen as derived from a commitment to a philosophic conception of humanity and an aesthetic conception of beauty more than from a calculation of consequences.

Any claim of the legitimacy of such issues in discussions of management education is necessarily a challenge to the dominant utilitarian argument, a challenge that is different from the arguments about the ambiguity and myopia of "relevance." Questions of faith and beauty require conversations that differ from conversations over utilitarian questions. In the end, they are linked to a sense of identity and aesthetic quality. What is essential to being human? What brings beauty to human life? And how are the essential nature of education and its beauty reflected in an institution and its practices? The answers turn not on relevance in anything like its usual sense but on an appreciative comprehension of humanness and life and their manifestation in education and research in universities. A condition for such an examination is a commitment to glorifying the human estate and through that a commitment to sustaining grace and beauty in education and research.

### Essences and Beauty

From the point of view of those who pursue the meaning and beauty of education, rigid insistence on a utilitarian framework for educational design, despite its enormous appeal and unquestioned value, is a mistake. At the same time, however, it must be recognized that questions about what constitutes the essence of education and what constitutes its beauty are not easy questions to answer. In the guise of mundane questions about educational policy, they introduce a subtle combination of historical consciousness and philosophical elegance. Quixote said, "I know who I am." For management educators to know who they are, they would have to uncover what is essential to the aesthetics of a scholarly life. Presumably, knowledge achieves its beauty through precision of expression, through the simplification of complexity, through the generation of intellectual surprise. It augments the other beauties of life by providing interpretations of them. It glorifies consciousness and choice as indispensable conceits of human existence.

The words are brave (or foolish), but they are not easily made meaningful in any concrete way. At most, it is possible to imagine some crude guidelines for thinking about management education. First, it is possible to think of research and education as preeminently concerned with exposing, contemplating, and rejoicing in the beauties of ideas. The "winner's curse" has turned out to have some very practical uses, but it is the aesthetic of the idea that makes it particularly significant for management education. Second, it is possible to respect the aesthetics of competence. Bluster, chutzpah, and self-indulgent illusions of exceptional capabilities all have their place, but management honors the grace of the elementary skills that make an organization a work of art: the letters that are written with style; the pipes that are connected with delicate attention to fit; the motors that are tuned precisely; and the abilities that are polished beyond all added usefulness. It is possible to introduce an artistry of elegance to the artifacts of efficiency—the opera of balance sheets and the sculpture of business plans. Third, it is possible to think of managers and management as icons of aspirations for humanity. The dilemmas of leadership can be seen as instances of the dilemmas of life and their human resolution in management as models for achieving humanness in life.

Such a perspective sometimes borders on mysticism, and there is ample potential for pretentiousness in the invocation of meaning and beauty in a discussion of management education, as well as abundant dangers of nonsense. There are risks of forgetting the elementary requirements of education—that books be read, that curricula be specified, that papers be graded, that standards be imposed, and that toilets and computers work. It is not only hard to deny that consequences matter, it is also stupid.

Those who emphasize seeking to realize the "essence" of education and to glorify its beauty match the catechism of utilitarianism with a catechism of their own: Ideas are not only instruments of purpose; they are objects for contemplation. Conversations about management contribute not only to the implementation of intentions; they are explorations of the beauties of words and their meanings. Education is not only a device for augmenting individual and social utilities; it is a sacred element of the human spirit. The essential manifesto: In the end, we are all dead and the species is extinct; it is only the grace and beauty of the decoration that we provide to the realization of those outcomes that distinguishes us.

From the point of view of these advocates, business schools, like other educational institutions, create themselves through the persistence and imagination of their attempts to elaborate a sense of themselves that ennobles the human condition and glorifies the mind. They picture the performances and scripts of management education as refining the routines of reason into objects and instruments of beauty worthy of human aspirations. In such a world, it might be bearable to them if business schools were also occasionally useful, but that is a lesser aspiration.

## CONSTRUCTING MANAGEMENT EDUCATION

We have described a short, incomplete history of argument over management education. It is a history of rhetoric, of attempts to provide elegant reasons for mundane actions. The rhetoric is often overblown and the arguments often inconclusive, but they reflect a persistent desire to find justification for educational practice and institutions.

Nothing in the history either of business schools or of the rhetoric about management education suggests progress toward resolution of the issues posed by the tension between experiential knowledge and academic knowledge. The histories are distinguished by their tendencies to cycle through shifting phases of emphases.

It is easy to despair at this cycling of argument in the pursuit of relevance and meaning for management education. It is natural to wish for some decisive resolution. It is, however, unreasonable to expect such an outcome. The implicit function of the unending debate between the believers in experience and the believers in scholarship is not to yield definitive answers but to encourage the keepers of institutions of management education to be cautious about embracing simple solutions stemming from glib presumptions that embrace either without attention to the other.

The argument, moreover, is not merely an argument between experience and scholarship; it is also an argument over the proper criteria by which to assess both. There is nobility in a utilitarian morality; there is nobility in a morality of identity and aesthetics; and there is nobility in weaving them together to create management education. In the best of all worlds, the unresolvable dialectic between the claims of experiential knowledge and the claims of academic knowledge provides an opportunity for making management education and business schools both more useful and more meaningful and beautiful as well. That happy result is not likely to be produced by some magical wand that eliminates conflict, but by unending confrontation of the inconsistent voices of a demanding soul. In the process, the management education that is constructed reflects both managers and educators, and the arguments they develop to justify that education define the kind of people they wish to imagine themselves to be.

## NOTES

1. For schools of medicine, see W. Rothstein, *American Medical Schools and the Practice of Medicine: A History* (New York, NY: Oxford University Press, 1987). For schools of engineering, see T. Reynolds, *The Engineer in America* (Chicago, IL: University of Chicago Press, 1991). For schools of law, see J. Hurst, *The Growth of American Law: The Law Makers* (Boston, MA: Little, Brown, 1950). For schools of education, see D. Labaree, *The Trouble with Ed Schools* (New Haven, CT: Yale University Press, 2004). For schools of public policy and administration, see T. Haskell, *The Emergence of a Professional Social Science: The American Social Science Association and the Nineteenth Century Crisis of Authority* (Urbana, IL: University of Illinois Press 1977).

2. Parts of this section draw freely from J. G. March, "Experiential Knowledge and Academic Knowledge in Management Education," in G. Garel and E. Godelier, eds., *Enseigner le Management* (Paris: Lavosier, 2004), pp. 13–17.

3. F. Vermulen, "On Rigor and Relevance: Fostering Dialectic Progress in Management Research," *Academy of Management Journal,* 48/6 (December 2005): 978–982.

4. M. W. Lee, "It's Good To Be in a Business School," *Business Horizons,* 3/2 (Summer 1960): 4–19, at p. 10.

5. G. L. Bach, "Some Observations on the Business School of Tomorrow," *Management Science,* 4/4 (July 1958): 351–364; H. A. Simon, "The Business School: A Problem in Organizational Design," *Journal of Management Studies,* 4/1 (February 1967): 1–17; R. M. Cyert and W. Dill, "The Future of Business Education," *The Journal of Business,* 37/3 (1964): 221–237; T. Carroll, "Education for Business: A Dynamic Concept and Process," *The Accounting Review,* 33 (1958): 3–10.

6. J. Behrman and R. Lewin, "Are Business Schools Doing Their Job?" *Harvard Business Review,* 62/1 (January/February 1984): 140–147.

7. R. Gordon and J. Howell, *Higher Education for Business* (New York, NY: Columbia University Press, 1959); H. Mintzberg, *Managers, Not MBAs* (San Francisco, CA: Berrett-Koehler Publishers, 2004).

8. S. Ghoshal, "Bad Management Theories Are Destroying Good Management Practices," *Academy of Management Learning and Education,* 4/1 (2005): 75–91; W. Bennis and J. O'Toole, "How Business Schools Lost Their Way," *Harvard Business Review,* 83/5 (May 2005): 96–104; "Comment and Analysis: Shredded Credibility?" *Financial Times,* April 29, 2005; "A Rank Offence to Business Schools?" *Business Week,* August 10, 2005.

9. H. A. Simon, *Models of My Life* (Cambridge, MA: MIT Press, 1991); J. Thompson, "On Building an Administrative Science," *Administrative Science Quarterly,* 1/1 (June 1956): 102–111.

10. D. Hambrick, "What if the Academy Actually Mattered?" *Academy of Management Review,* 19/1 (January 1994): 11–16; Bennis and O'Toole, op. cit.

11. F. Kast, "Management Education in Europe," *The Academy of Management Journal,* 8/2 (June 1965): 75–89; R. Edelfelt, "U.S. Management Education in Comparative Perspective," *Comparative Education Review,* 32/3 (1988): 334–354; L. Engwall, *Mercury Meets Minerva* (Oxford: Pergamon Press, 1992); A. Kieser, "The Americanization

of Academic Management Education in Germany," *Journal of Management Inquiry,* 13/2 (June 2004): 90–97.

12. J. Bossard and J. Dewhurst, *University Education for Business* (Philadelphia, PA: University of Pennsylvania Press, 1931), p. 55.

13. Gordon and Howell, op. cit.

14. Ibid.

15. F. Pierson, *The Education of American Businessmen* (New York, NY: McGraw Hill, 1959); Gordon and Howell, op. cit.

16. Simon, op. cit., p. 138.

17. Bach, op. cit., pp. 363–364.

18. Gordon and Howell, op. cit.

19. Ibid., p. 426.

20. Bach, op. cit.; Cyert and Dill, op. cit.; Simon, op. cit.

21. Cyert and Dill, op. cit., p. 223.

22. M. Augier, J. G. March, and B. Ni Sullivan, "Notes on the Evolution of a Research Community: Organization Studies in Anglophone North America, 1945–2000," *Organization Science,* 16 (2005): 85–95.

23. Bennis and O'Toole, op. cit., p. 98.

24. M. Augier, "Making Management Matter: An Interview with John Reed," *Academy of Management Learning and Education,* 5/1 (2006): 84–100.

25. P. Hall, *The Political Power of Economic Ideas* (Princeton, NJ: Princeton University Press, 1989); J. Goldstein and R. Keohane, eds., *Ideas and Foreign Policy* (Ithaca, NY: Cornell University Press, 1993); M. Blyth, *Great Transformations: Economic Ideas and Institutional Change in the Twentieth Century* (Cambridge: Cambridge University Press, 2002).

26. Hambrick, op. cit.

27. D. Halberstam, *The Best and the Brightest* (New York, NY: Random House, 1972).

28. Bach, op. cit., pp. 351–352.

29. Simon, op. cit., p. 10.

30. J. Miner, "The Validity and Usefulness of Theories in an Emerging Organizational Science," *Academy of Management Review,* 9/2 (April 1984): 296–306, at p. 296.

31. J. Denrell and J. G. March, "Adaptation as Information Restriction: The Hot Stove Effect," *Organization Science,* 12/5 (September/October 2001): 523–538.

32. J. G. March, "Exploration and Exploitation in Organizational Learning," *Organization Science,* 2/1 (February 1991): 71–87; L. Marengo, "Knowledge Distribution and Coordination in Organizations: On Some Social Aspects of the Exploitation vs. Exploration Trade-Off," *Revue Internationale de Systémique,* 7/5 (1993): 553–571.

33. J. G. March, "Learning to be Risk Averse," *Psychological Review,* 103/2 (1996): 309–319; J. Denrell, "Why Most People Disapprove of Me: Experience Sampling in Impression Formation," *Psychological Review,* 112/4 (2005): 951–978.

34. J. S. Mill, "Bentham," in *Mill on Bentham and Coleridge* (London: Chatto and Windus, 1862 [1950]), p. 66

# PART V

# EXPLORATIONS IN ORGANIZATIONS THROUGH LITERATURE

## An Introductory Essay

ELLEN S. O'CONNOR

*[W]e now find ourselves from the very start in the midst of a dialogue between nature and man, a dialogue of which science is only one part, so much so that the conventional division of the world into subject and object, into inner world and outer world, into body and soul, is no longer applicable and raises difficulties. For the sciences of nature, the subject matter of research is no longer nature in itself, but nature subjected to human questioning, and to this extent man, once again, meets only with himself.*

—Heisenberg in Huxley 1963: 76.

THE FOLLOWING THREE ESSAYS—their inclusion in this volume, as well as their content—make a case that literature adds something vital to the study of organizations. This case has been made before, but not in the same ways or with the same stakes; in fact, March's essays suggest significant reorientations not only of the field's past and present relationship to literature but also of its relationship to itself as an institutional work in progress.

In a very broad sense, this introduction takes up what typically appear in Western traditions as opposites: sciences versus humanities, nature versus artifice, objectivity versus subjectivity, mind versus heart. How can man, the human, and human experience be known? An adequate treatment of the relationship between literature and the study of human organization would cover histories and philosophies of science, aesthetics, and epistemology dating to Plato's banishing of the poets from his republic and to Aristotle's distinctions among logos, pathos, and ethos in rhetorical discourse. Nor are these debates merely philosophical or about knowledge and inquiry as ends in themselves: They take institutional form, play out in political arenas, and have material consequences. Similarly, then, an adequate treatment would cover histories of institutions.

This introduction focuses on the relationship between literature and organization studies (OS) as a formal institutional field per Augier et al. (2005). Institutionalizing in a formal management academy and in the university-based business school, OS has been a U.S.-based project for legitimation relative to the natural and social sciences academies (Goodrick, 2002), to other professional schools (Gleeson et al., 1995; Schlossman et al., 1998), and to sciences-research funding policy (Klausner and Lidz, 1986). At the same time, the humanities academy has pursued its own course of institutionalization, also with consequences for the OS-literature relationship.

This introduction argues that institutionalization has rarified the OS-literature relationship, and it introduces March's essays as expansive moves in OS's institutionalization and in its collaborations with literature. It also suggests that March's work may signal or even help to establish that the management-academic institution is now sufficiently legitimized such that the field may engage with literature per his examples.

Specifically, March's essays do several things together that no single literature-OS collaboration has done: They move away from a relationship based on literary criticism, hermeneutics in particular, to a relationship with human life and experience through literature. They move away from organizational scholarship in the institutional sense of ritualized, habitual practices that have taken on a life or death of their own and go to literature for what is otherwise unavailable. In words and deeds both, March moves outside of a field trapped in myths of its own making. Literature is a remedy or way out, not as escape, but as exploration and what it entails: discovery and renewal. Subversively, he reverses the commonsense logic: a scientific field with presumably explanatory power is not up to the task. One turns to literature, the imaginary, and merely symbolic representations of highly complex phenomena, to understand organizations as human and to understand human experience generally.

This introduction attempts to address both moves relative to each other. It argues that OS's relationship with literature is intertwined with its institutionalization. The analysis begins with OS's pre-institutionalization, the 19th-century Western European origins of social science. It shows that OS's institutionalization led to a highly circumscribed relationship with literature. It then examines the trajectory of the OS-literature relationship and March's specific moves therein. It concludes by discussing the implications of these moves: renewed and renewing literature-OS collaborations.

## SOCIOLOGY AND LITERATURE: 19TH-CENTURY BRITAIN, FRANCE, AND GERMANY

Lepenies (1988) shows how 19th-century men and women of letters and general publics took a great interest in science as it related to technological and industrial advancement and to associated national and public policies. Considerable public debate ensued around the idea of progress: Was it good for the state, for society, for individuals; and who was to say, how was one to know, and what were the practical implications? Men and women of society and letters—intellectuals, philosophers, literary writers—conducted and influenced social critique about economic advancement and its costs, educational reform relative to industrial development, and the effects of industrialization on national culture. These debates affected and engaged the general public as well as policy makers. They were integral to literary movements and to the founding and early development of sociology.

In Britain, France, and Germany, social science was an ideal according to naturalism, a movement that applied natural-sciences empirical practices and logics to study and advance society. The French novelist Honoré de Balzac wrote a social botany comparable to the work of a natural historian or zoologist (Lepenies, 1988: 144). An early title of his Human Comedy series was Etudes Sociales, or "Social Studies." Henry James placed Balzac in an intermediary role between natural history and sociology (Lepenies, 1988: 5). Marx and Engels claimed that they learned more from Balzac than from all the professional economists and historians they knew (Lepenies, 1988: 5). Over a half century later, the sociologist Karl Mannheim praised the French novelist:

[A] character in Balzac will acquire the insight that in modern society one can rise to the top only when one has studied with the closest attention the laws of the society in which one intends to rise. Balzac's novels themselves are an attempt to produce such a sociological natural history of bourgeois society . . . in addition to this they have a sense of the visions and vagaries which, in spite of all its rationality, or precisely within this element of rationality, are to be found in this society's actual existence. (Lepenies, 1988: 323)

Zola's experimental novel was a "practical sociology"; a contemporary critic called it the "novel with scientific intent" (Lepenies, 1988: 7, 86). In his study of suicide, Durkheim drew from all three literary genres in citing extensively from Goethe, Musset, Lamartine, and Chateaubriand. In Britain, Wordsworth pursued "a science of the feelings" through his precise descriptions of subjective experience. Herbert Spencer did not consider George Eliot's work as fiction; and H. G. Wells founded and led a professional association, journal, and intellectual circle where novelists practiced "sociology" and wrote literary works inspired by naturalism. Wells stated, "The modern novel . . . is the only medium through which we can discuss the great majority of the problems" of "our contemporary social development" (Lepenies, 1988: 153).

Appeals to a general and unified science of society became battles for disciplinary, collegial, and individual-scholarly superiority or imperialism. Comte, for example, envisaged sociology taking over history, political economy, and psychology; Marx's "scientific history" aimed to replace "old" history and economics together (Lepenies, 1988: 116). These two choices, bipolar opposition or takeover, would characterize the literature-science relationship—as it does today (see below).

Lepenies takes John Stuart Mill as a case study. Mill struggled to integrate the tendencies of utilitarianism and aestheticism, logic and emotion, and distance and empathy in his philosophy and in his life (Lepenies, 1988: 93–111). Juxtaposing Bentham and Coleridge, Mill identified two distinct temperaments, one scientific and politically progressive, the other poetic and conservative. Mill criticized Bentham for his limited view of human nature; the utilitarian's empiricism was that of "one who has had little experience" (Lepenies, 1988: 104). For Mill, common humanity trumped identity as a scientist or poet. In taking office as rector of University of St. Andrews, Mill argued that universities had to pursue intellectual, moral, and aesthetic goals all at once (Lepenies, 1988: 164).

In the famous "two cultures" debates between Matthew Arnold and Thomas Huxley in the late 19th century, which C. P. Snow and F. R. Leavis repeated in the mid-20th century, consensus on social progress was again the storm center. Huxley, known as "Darwin's bulldog" for his passionate advocacy of evolutionary theory, argued for educational reform emphasizing "the laws of nature" so that the nation's minds would be "ready, like a steam engine, to be turned to any kind of work." Industrialists sided with Huxley (Lepenies, 1988: 165). Arnold—in a letter to a "working man"—argued that science did not address the whole man even under utilitarian logic: "[A]s to useful knowledge, a single line of poetry, working in the mind, may produce more thoughts and lead to more light, which is what man wants, than the fullest acquaintance . . . with the processes of digestion" (Lepenies, 1988: 172). Arnold argued that any social reform had to be cultural reform and that science was part of culture, not outside of it. At heart was the very organizing principle of social life—again posed in bipolar terms: Should action trump thought and feeling, or vice versa? Arnold posited these as literally cultural choices—"Hebraic" versus "Hellenic." In the Snow/Leavis debate, the former took Huxley's side and the latter, Arnold's. Snow saw science as a means to factual consensus for social progress, but Leavis feared a "systemization" of social theory that would subsume the individual (Lepenies, 1988: 183). Trilling (1962), Oppenheimer (1962), and Huxley (grandson of Thomas) (1963) later weighed in on the two cultures debates; and, like Mill, they argued for balance. In social science, the Gulbenkian Commission and Burawoy's response provide a recent example of the debates (Burawoy, 2005).

## U.S. INSTITUTIONALIZATION

These debates and their intertwining of literature, social critique, and politics do not appear in historical accounts of U.S. sociology. Nineteenth-century U.S. academics pursued differentiation over integration with Western European thinkers and philosophy; and the idea of industrial progress evidently enjoyed greater consensus in the United States compared to Europe. However, U.S. sociologists briefly aligned with social movements protesting industrialization through the Social Gospel, which was also a Christian-revival movement and a status move to defend the dominant New England aristocracy (Morgan, 1969; Hofstadter, 1956; Church, 1974). Accounts of the history of U.S. sociology stress its enthusiastic embrace of "the natural science model" and break from the "humanistic disciplines and the arts" (Reiss, 1968), particularly its pursuit of objectivity and of freedom from "values" (Bannister, 1987; Ross, 1991; Furner, 1975). Interestingly, the accounts acknowledge a break with philosophy but not literature

(Oberschall, 1972a); even philosophers' accounts of this history acknowledge only a break with the cultural-sciences constructs such as Weber's *verstehen* and Husserl's phenomenology (Natanson, 1953). They play up the field's ties to mathematics, statistics, and quantitative analysis (Oberschall, 1972b). These historical accounts were written when U.S. sociologists aligned with the natural sciences to access unprecedented levels of federal research funding (Klausner and Lidz, 1986; Turner and Turner, 1990: 188–194). Even the subsequent argument for a "poetics of sociology" showed no trace of revitalizing Durkheim's literary sensibilities; they were already deleted from the record (Brown, 1977).

The prospects for integrating sociology and literature in the United States lessened through a compounding effect: the social sciences institutionalized within business schools that were, themselves, institutionalizing. In the Cold War environment that gave birth to OS, legitimacy building for both institutions focused on the natural sciences academy, macroeconomic policy makers and planners, industrialists, and computer scientists. Combining, they had promising techniques and technologies as well as generous funding and access to advance their models and methods. This legitimacy campaign reached an apotheosis in business schools and the management academy through the Carnegie plan (Gleeson and Schlossman, 1995), also known as the "business school revolution" (Schlossman et al., 1998).

In sum, U.S. social science's and business schools' compounded institutionalization have helped shape and have been shaped by a highly focused, intensive legitimacy-building campaign that involved breaking from and deleting ties to social, political, and philosophical traditions in which literature and literary writers figured prominently. At the same time, the humanities academy was also separating, exaggerating the divide (see below). The pre-institutionalized field with ties to literature and to social critique became contemporary OS without them.

## Contemporary OS and Literary Criticism

So far this introduction has focused on the centrifugal tendencies of OS's institutionalization. However, there are also centripedal tendencies; and they have to do with the extent to which scholars identify with and invoke philosophical traditions. Legitimation requires theory building, which involves positioning in a tradition. In OS, Weber continued through Parsons and figures in contemporary institutional theory; Schütz continued through Berger and Luckmann and figures in social-construction theory; Dilthey continued through hermeneutics, which was combined with American pragmatism (O'Connor, 1997); and Durkheim, *sans* literature, continued through Mayo (O'Connor, 1999). However, OS literature reviews generally dispense with the linguistic, cultural, and historical complications of intellectual traditions; in this way, they perpetuate the centrifugal tendencies outlined previously.

The business school and management academy institutionalized as the U.S. university, itself, did so. The natural science, social science, and humanities academies institutionalized separately and relative to each other within this overarching process. Formed in a colonial religious tradition, the U.S. university accomplished a "revolution in higher education" by professionalizing per the German university model (Oberschall, 1972a: 192). The model was particularly influential in the social sciences (Shils, 1979: 119–121). The first U.S. academic social scientists completed their doctoral training in Germany, including those who entered the first U.S. business schools (Sass, 1982).

The humanities also institutionalized relative to the social sciences. Gumbrecht describes Dilthey's resolution of a tension between "an experimental school of research, based on measurement and other scientific methods of investigation" and "a philosophical approach that relied on the traditions and intuitions of understanding" (2004: 43). Rejecting "the idol of science," Dilthey pursued an independent knowledge system for the humanities and for the arts. This model had to include "psychic life" as integral to social relations (Lepenies, 1988: 236–239). Dilthey blocked Hermann Ebbinghaus's appointment at the prestigious University of Berlin on account of the psychologist's scientific and empirical methods and his "transgressions" into physiology. Dilthey successfully led a formal institutional separation between the Geisteswissenschaften, or cultural disciplines, that took interpretation as their principal practice, and "scientific" research. This "cultural" knowledge system held that all interpretation would "ultimately uncover the immediacy of lived experience . . . under layers of meaning." Dilthey and his colleagues believed this formulation offered "the key to complete and final knowledge. . . . All that had to be done was to interpret everything known in light of this new knowledge" (Ben-David, 1971: 115).

The situation was different in France or Britain, which admitted greater ties to "the natural sciences and to empirical social thought" and where "the subjectivity of cultural values seemed to preclude an objective philosophical approach" (Ben-David, 1971: 115). Correspondingly, the literary movements of these two countries oriented around the realistic novel; but in Germany, poetry dominated (Lepenies, 1988: 204–205, 214–220). In Germany, Dilthey and his colleagues succeeded in uniting literary and social science movements under the overarching theme of subjectivity. Nationalist, as well as aesthetic and epistemological, interests figured in this move: German scholars considered sociology "too French"

(Lepenies, 1988: 235). Germany's defensive or competitive reaction to the emerging discipline led to a distinctively different formulation: "a new speculative philosophy that extolled an ascientific idea of a [superior] nationalistic philosophical, literary, and historical culture" (Ben-David, 1971: 116). In these intellectual and institutional traditions both, "all social science had to adopt the principle of the 'subjective point of view' privileging the interpretation of the action and its settings in terms of the actor" (Schütz, 1963: 333). Natanson called intersubjectivity the "cardinal philosophical problem of the social sciences" (1963: 280) in accordance with "the intentional character of human life."

The price that the humanities paid for this move was "the loss of any non-Cartesian, any non-experience-based type of world-reference" (Gumbrecht, 2004: 43).

In Anglo-American schools, I. A. Richards led a similar institutionalization in the humanities (Gumbrecht 2004: 45). The OS-literature relationship follows this tradition, pursuing interpretation as a tool to access inherent, and inherently problematic, subjective meaning.

In OS, business schools have intermingled continuously with the pre-institutionalized and Western European social science traditions by recruiting faculty from the social sciences. In particular, the organizational culture and symbolism movements of the 1980s turned squarely to these traditions (Van Maanen and Schein, 1979: 255). They engaged not only the German interpretive-sociological and hermeneutic traditions but also the textual-analytical and ethnographic methods presumed to access and articulate culture. However, these movements did not engage with the literary artifact as such but again with hermeneutics and criticism. Prasad (2005) reviews these collaborations, reformulated as an OS subfield, "qualitative research methods," which translates the German idealist traditions into techniques.

Combined with the work on culture in the subfield of organizational behavior, this collaboration led to a prolific body of research that continues to thrive. The study of culture in organizations and cultural constructs to study it corresponds to "interpretive," "linguistic," and "narrative" turns in social science and to the humanities reformulated as "cultural studies" (O'Connor et al., 1995: 121). In OS, this category entails the analysis of discourse (Putnam and Fairhurst, 2004). The organization and acts of organizing thus afford problematic textual data for expert interpretation according interpretive-sociological and hermeneutic traditions as influenced by American pragmatism and symbolic interactionism (O'Connor, 1997).

This line of work has been limited in two ways. First, the relationship has not been with literature in the literal sense of literary artifacts but with literary theory, particularly hermeneutics, and with criticism, particularly textual interpretation. In this sense, OS and the humanities have in fact unified under the legitimation imperative of expertise and the German interpretive and hermeneutic traditions (Prasad, 2005: 5). Hermeneutics presumes a meaning only provisionally approachable through such means. Textual interpretation, "the only game in town" for literary scholarship (Fish, 1980, cited in Miall, 2006: 24) has become the same in OS.

This point of view has dominated literary criticism and is now associated with the status quo intellectual and social order of the humanities. It has led one scholar to locate himself critically in the institution and even to risk ostracism—with palpable trepidation as he invokes metaphors of heresy and terrorism—by seriously entertaining "substantialism" and something "beyond meaning" (Gumbrecht, 2004: 51–90). This point of view has also dominated the OS-literature collaborations. March in fact does for OS what Gumbrecht does for the humanities academy. Together, they show some affinity with Sontag's assessment that "interpretation is the revenge of the intellect upon art" (1983: 98).

Second, when organizational scholars have engaged with the literary artifact as such, they have positioned OS as a subfield of literary criticism. Grey calls this the "postmodern critique"; that is, "all texts must be regarded as rhetorical and . . . the difference between scientific and non-scientific texts is 'only' one of the rhetorics which they deploy, not of truth value" (1996: 64). Scholars have extended this logic to the very construct "organization"; that is, it is a text (Phillips and Zyglidopoulos, 1999: 594). Parker et al. introduced their readings of science fiction through Feyerabend and the "attack on the primacy of scientific rationalism" (1999: 584). For Grey, realist fiction is useful "to understand management and organization" but one must quickly dispense with the naive idea that the novel might mirror reality (Grey, 1996: 62–63).

In fact, this move continues Dilthey's debates with his colleagues and his institution building. Intellectually, it counters the privileging of one logic or system with that of another. If a single field, organization studies, is to be posited, then it finds itself in a fight with itself; it is trapped not only in the logic of differentiation but also of competition. Although Waldo (1968) wrote his pioneering work on administration and literature well before the advent of postmodernism in OS, he too identified and reified a two-cultures rift but personalized it as "literary" versus "organization man." The gap was as much social as intellectual: Novelists did not take organization men seriously. But Waldo limited his vision to the "administrative novel."

Outside of OS theory building and research, a further collaboration with literature deserves mention—that with pedagogy. Literature is used extensively in business ethics (e.g., Williams, 1997) and in juxtaposition to the case method (Czarniawska-Joerges and Guillet de Mouthoux, 1994), which is limited by the U.S.-cultural limits of OS (Liang and Wang, 2004). The classroom use of literature, as well as film and popular culture, continues a long tradition of liberal arts education and moral philosophy.

### MARCH'S MOVES

March's essays propose new possibilities for relating literature to organization studies. These moves expand the field beyond its institutionalized limits and practices to recover relationships to longer historical and to wider cultural traditions as sketched in this introduction. First, he disassociates himself from literary theory and conducts an independent, idiosyncratic reading of literature. He presents "a disclaimer of Ibsen-competence": "There must be several hundred serious Ibsen scholars in the world. I am not one of them." He engages with literature not only as a scholar of organization but also as a lay reader; for example, commenting on Yeats, "The readers of the poem are enjoined to remember the heroes as much-loved members of the family." He refers to general readers who will understand Yeats as they understand their families—in human, not literary terms.

Second, March implicitly changes the theoretical commitment in reading literature away from hermeneutics to correspondence-with-reality (or play-along-with-correspondence-of-reality) premises: He accepts a truth value for the literary text. According to mimetic theory (which is not necessary to know in order to use; it is the premise of lay reading; Miall, 2006), literature may correspond with empirical reality in three ways: by depicting the empirical world, by creating a fictive world that reveals something of the empirical world, or by showing an actual person's inventions (Halliwell, 2002). In contrast to hermeneutics, which posits the text as a veil to be penetrated by the expert interpreter, this theory privileges the literal level. March, however, does not theorize the move but rather just executes it.

Third, March expands the focus from organizations and organizing to human experience, to social order or disorder, and to "critical issues of life more generally." Fourth, March invites the reader to engage personally with these issues: to understand the truths expressed in literature "involves experiencing the social, personal, and intellectual pains" associated with them. Fifth and finally, March invites the reader to read literature for no reason whatsoever.

## *"Literature" as a Resource*

March does not define "literature"; but his references to Yeats, Cervantes, Ibsen, and others show that he values all three principal literary genres—the novel, poetry, and plays. Or better put, he does not privilege one over the other. This is noteworthy because most collaborations have used the novel (Grey, 1996; Czarniawska-Joerges and Guillet de Monthoux, 1994; Waldo, 1968; Parker et al., 1999; Alvarez and Merchán, 1992; Patient et al., 2003). His further references to "great literature" and to "masterpieces" suggest that he is particularly interested in the category of the classical, the value of which has been eloquently stated by Calvino (1999: 3–9).

However, whereas OS offers a stable definition for this introduction (Augier et al., 2005), "literature" does not. Moreover, the matter remains unsettled as to whether "literature" is a "fundamental category of discourse with distinctive properties" or a relatively recent "cultural formation" resting on social conventions (Miall, 2006: 89). Theorists from literary criticism, rhetoric, discourse, linguistics, philosophy, and aesthetics have weighed in on this matter, which will not be settled here. Rather, it is viewed relative to March's moves, which provoke a rethinking of the OS-literature relationship.

Following reader-response theory (Iser, 1978), reading literature is a "communicative relationship" characterized by openness and indeterminacy (Gumbrecht, 1985: 475). The relationship and process accommodate wide access and enable diverse experiences. The institutionalized humanities readings and the OS-literature collaborations are one way of reading and of relating to literature. "Literature," be it absolute or relative, needs beholders; and literary readings generously accommodate them.

According to correspondence theories of truth and mimetic theories, organizational researchers would treat literature as any other empirical resource; that is, they would go to literature just as they go to "the field." Although this approach has been suggested (Philllips, 1995), it has not had much resonance in OS (but see Patient et al., 2003); it has been used extensively in political philosophy (e.g., Whitebrook, 1992; Negash, 2004; Zuckert, 1990; Horton and Baumeister, 1996). It has also been used in action theory (e.g., Livingston, 1991). In this context, literature clarifies and develops theory. Whitebrook uses the novel to elaborate concepts such as responsibility, freedom and order, obligation and commitment, and the integration of public and personal selves (1995). For those seeking practical guidance, as well as for "ordinary" students of politics seeking to understand "the field," literature provides a fruitful place to turn through its capacity not only to "illustrate real situations" but also "to present in their own right articulations of theoretical positions as they apply to real lives." It depicts "moral complexity, possibilities of choice, the way that theory works out in practice—for 'real individuals'" as represented by fictional characters (1995: 28–29). Similarly, Fishman finds in literature the "concrete human implications" of theories such as "Lockean egoism" (1992: 166). The novel in particular has been identified as the quintessential genre for studying the relationship of the individual to society and to environments. "Modern novels suggest . . . the link between self-identity and the taking on of responsibilities"; they cross the individual, moral, political, and social levels (Whitebrook, 1996: 43, 48). Furthermore, they address the experiential and emotional consequences of these relationships to individuals, a theme neglected in OS (Chanlat, 2003).

Livingston reads literary texts to refine hypotheses: Comparing the literary work and a theory's explanatory models brings out inadequacies. "Actions and attitudes evoked by the work" may challenge the theory, or the theory may not account for "details and circumstances evoked by the work" (Livingston, 1991: 83).

March proposes something similar for organizational scholars. He models three ways to relate to literature: as specialists expanding the field's limits, as academic generalists pursuing greater expanse and depth of knowledge, and as human beings living ordinary lives and pursuing heightened or more diverse experience—or nothing particular whatsoever.

### Specialists Expanding Management-Academic Limits

March's essays say that organization theory oversimplifies its subject. It believes in clear causal relations, proofs of effectiveness, and instrumental logic. It also ostracizes some subjects because it has difficulty accommodating them. Literature not only takes on these subjects but also does so in deep and enduring ways. It does justice to its subjects through nuance. It offers "psychological, philosophical, and moral subtlety" that "exercises and clarifies" complexity and is able to sustain a relationship with complexity, meaning it forces no closure. This is due to the literary genres' "more profound realization" as to what must be seen "as intractable dilemmas rather than as problems to be solved." Like the heroes in Yeats's poem, organizational scholars must pursue "an intelligent comprehension of the complexity of real human experience." For example, for March, Ibsen is "a student of rule-based action." Ibsen's characters allow theory development that is otherwise not possible in mainstream organization theory, specifically to develop ideas about "reactions to conflicts among values" from a rule-based point of view.

## Academics Expanding Disciplinary Limits

Organization theory and research is subsumed in a larger category—no longer literary criticism but human behavior. "[R]ational theories of choice and incentive theories of motivation are incomplete." Leadership "entails a passion that rejects justification in utility." March uses Ibsen's plays to develop not organization theory but social theory about a powerful, encompassing system of lies. Ibsen's plays enable observation of the lie multiplier in the first place; furthermore, they help "identify more clearly the conditions for the spiral" and clarify "the mechanisms that keep it from exploding." This exploration includes the human costs at the emotional level, particularly individual suffering. Mainstream organizational research does not access the level of subjective experience, for example, "the sense of personal torment that is part of human choice." March extends the analysis from Ibsen's characters to the "objects of organizations research" to "organizations scholars themselves."

## Organization Studies Expanding Its Own Limits

Literature's ability to accommodate complexity, subtlety, and contradiction and to sustain these without resolution is a life skill that may transfer to the reader of literature. The issues that complicate leadership, such as private/public, cleverness/innocence, diversity/unity, ambiguity/coherence, are unresolvable. As such, one can only learn to live with them. Literary environments permit sustenance of these dilemmas. March suggests that by reading literature, individuals leading their lives may be better equipped to live with these dilemmas. Blindly confining themselves to the limits of the field, organizational scholars will fall far short in the pursuit of knowledge, with emotional costs to themselves and to their readers.

### Theory, Pleasure, and Love

March introduces himself and his own motives in these writings more generously than in his other writings. He becomes more human to his readers. He states that he is a "Norwegian groupie." His unabashed "amateur" status recalls the Latin derivation of amateur—"lover." "A human commitment to the masterpieces of literature, like a commitment to leadership, is itself a transcendental act . . . The passionate consumption of a great text by a leader" is not unlike "the glory of an arbitrary enthusiasm for the pains and pleasures of being human." Sidestepping the instrumentalist logic that constrains mainstream organizational scholarship, March sees the engagement with literature as foolish, unjustifiable or at least not requiring any justification, or "the point" being "to be foolish without justification." In other words, the field, in relating to literature, may enjoy freedom from having to be "rational or boundedly rational."

## OS and the Ordinary

Paradoxically, of course, March sees literature as an opportunity to access the ordinary. Through the repetitive and perhaps calcified practices of institutionalization, organizational scholars have removed themselves from the ordinary, which is too mundane or bothersome for real scientists: "My chief enjoyment and sole employment throughout life has been scientific work; and the excitement from such work makes me for the time forget, or drives away, my daily discomfort. I have therefore nothing to record during the rest of my life [from the time he moved to Down in 1842], except the publication of my several books" (Darwin, cited in Hagstrom, 1965: 3). "[The] essential in the being of a man of my type lies precisely in what he thinks and how he thinks, not in what he does or suffers. Consequently, [this autobiographical essay] can limit itself in the main to the communicating of thoughts which have played a considerable role in my endeavors" (Einstein, cited in Hagstrom, 1965: 3).

Likewise, one scholar reflected on his experiences with OS institutionalization in the mid-1950s. Citing his changing role from "social scientist" to "research entrepreneur," he noted not only a new type of intellectual organization but also a new type and way of life for himself and his colleagues: that of a businessman in a scientific environment (Bennis, 1955: 47). The researcher was becoming as ordinary as the objects of his study! The tone of his essay is one of overwhelm; he sees the required reconciliations as "a gigantic task." Yet this is still the opportunity before the field: to handle the ordinary, to be ordinary, amid trajectories and tendencies toward the rarified. Perhaps literature can help the field live with—itself.

## Renewed and Renewing Relationships with Literature

March's essays suggest two potentially fruitful directions for the field's collaborations with literature.

### Revisit Ongoing Work

March invites the field to identify problems and to use literature to address them, and to read literature with these problems in mind. For example, March identified rule-based logic as one of the field's shortcomings. Similarly, Waldo identified knowledge of informal organization as one of these areas, particularly as it relates to formal organization (1968: 40).

A collaboration with literature could help the field reconnect to practice, particularly by revisiting its *own* classics in this new light (Stinchcombe, 1982). In institutionalizing, OS rejected most practitioner writings as anecdotal (March and Simon, 1958: 33). The field knows Chester Barnard, for example, primarily through Simon, who translated Barnard to an institutionalizing OS (Simon, 1991: 73, 86–88). Barnard was a theorist, but he theorized based on his extensive executive practice as head of New Jersey Bell Telephone; and Simon, lacking such experience, was unable to incorporate this element of Barnard (Wolf, 1995). Barnard worried particularly about the prospects for leadership in an increasingly complex environment (Barnard, 1938: 272–274; 1948: 81–110). He found that the physical and emotional strain of leadership was too harsh for most people because of their inability to reconcile conflicting moral codes; and he held that management education was not up to the task. A promising literature-OS collaboration might study the problem Barnard identified. It could combine March's observations on the need to sustain paradox and ambiguity with Barnard's point about the difficulty of reconciling moral codes.

Barnard also held that status systems were fundamental in organization, but his outline was strictly theoretical (Barnard, 1948: 205–244). Literature could illuminate this aspect; for example, Tom Wolfe has said that he considers himself a theorist of status (McNamara, 2002). A final example is decision making. March himself suggested elsewhere that decision making might best be understood as "a cross-section of lives" and as an intermingling with "the complexities of ordinary lives." He suggested a contextual perspective that would involve "fit[ting] the decision into the life of each participant" (1981: 229–230). Literary texts offer solid prospects for pursuing such an understanding.

## Build New Theory

The field might follow March's example with Ibsen, Girard's use of literature to develop social theory (1966), and Weick's (1993) use of Maclean's (a literature professor) *Young Men and Fire* to build sensemaking theory. McGuire (1973) noted that a neglected area in research is "the creative, hypothesis formation stage" relative to the "hypothesis-testing stage." McGuire enumerated several methods to tackle this challenge—case study, paradoxical incident, analogy, hypothetico-deductive method, functional analysis, rules of thumb, conflicting results, accounting for exceptions, and straightening out complex relationships. He did not identify literature, but literature could be added to the list as a new item or an overarching category containing McGuire's suggested approaches.

In March's own terms, literature could serve as a rich exploration site. One potentially highly fruitful way to do this would be to read what authors say about their works. Many authors have addressed the social theory accompanying their works. In American literature, some examples are Mamet (Kane, 2001), Miller (1971: 1–6), and Wolfe (Scura, 1990). As previously shown, Balzac, Zola, Wells, and others discussed their work as social study. The field could profit from using such writings as a resource.

## Exercise Different Thinking to Access Knowledge

Barnard cited Bateson's reference to the eidological aspects of group behavior, or how people think about things, such as the "dichotomous" Aristotelian logic that "seems to govern our thinking about ordinary affairs," according to which "we think in terms of existence or nonexistence and exclude intermediates." Barnard rejected this type of thought for situations involving numerous interdependent variables for which measures were not readily assignable. He cited organizational life as the prime example of such a situation. Quantitative and deductive processes failing, to understand such situations "has to be a matter of judgment almost aesthetic in character" (Wolf and Iino, 1986: 117–119). Literary readings permit, and may develop, ways of thinking that access and accommodate complexity, especially circular and qualitative relations (Follett, 1924).

### SYNTHESIZING THE INTRODUCTION AND THE ESSAYS: DESIGNING READINGS AS RELATIONSHIPS

March describes his readings of literature as informed by his scholarship, amateur status, and foolishness. This introduction has discussed OS and the OS-literature relationships as institutions. Reading, too, is an institution. March's ways of reading provoke reflection on how scholars design their reading of literature. Literature "implies a relationship between the author and the reader of a more egalitarian and less authoritarian cast than most orthodox philosophical or political modes of writing" (Horton and Baumeister, 1996: 24–25). Orwell, for example, crossed the fictional and nonfictional domains; and he used literature to change the relationship between his works and his readers. "The kind of relationship implied by the author as the 'wise man,' the authority, imparting his superior knowledge to the ignorant was too close to that imperialist relationship that he believed to be so corrosive of the values of decency and human fellow-feeling, the absence of which makes the soil fertile for forms of cruelty and inhumanity" (Horton and Baumeister, 1996: 24–25). March, writing on literature, implicitly alters his own historic relationship with OS, with his readers, and with organizational inquiry. Doing so, he expands the institutionalized OS-literature relationship. Subversively, he deinstitutionalizes OS by playing out the effects of dehabituation and defamiliarization that literary reading affords (Miall, 2006: 145–153, 190–191, 200–202).

March's relationship with literature might best be described as independent, experimental, and creative. He acknowledges the existence of literary scholarship, which he chooses to disregard. He demonstrates the utility of literature, which he is equally content to ignore. And he is drawn in, not in fully logical or rational ways, through an enthusiasm for other cultures and eras as well as for no particular reason whatsoever. In other words, March suggests his own unique approach to reading and invites his colleagues to find theirs.

This proposition coincides with recent empirical studies of reading (Miall, 2006) suggesting the diverse personal ways in which individuals relate to reading. It also connects reading to living and leading one's life. Some approaches have emphasized reading as an exercise of the imagination (Alvarez and Mechán, 1992; Whitebrook, 1995: 35). Another approach sees reading not as straightforward consumption of the literary artifact but as research design for shaping one's experience of "going to the field." Merely theoretically inclined readings risk "critical estrangement" (Costa Lima, 1985: 463). Reading may be designed, or it may be an emergent process, relative to concerns from prior experiences or current dilemmas (Miall, 2006: 107). "Ordinary" (non-academic, non-theoretically focused) readings work in a non-rule-gathering way (Miall, 2006: 167) and may afford freedom from constraint. OS, as a field, as an academy of scholars, and as a human community, may exercise considerable discretion and intelligence in designing new and renewing relationships with literature. These relationships will limit or expand the scope and depth of what is discovered (Hatchuel, 2000, 2005).

"We surrender / The pleasures of freedom / To gain the comforts of security—/ Until they stifle us, / And we revolt" (March, 2005: 35). March's essays invite experimentation with the openness and closure of institutionalization, as in living with our own Frankensteins, both literal and figurative—business schools and the management academy; disciplines and their relations; reading as inquiry into and experience of life in its ordinary as well as extraordinary manifestations. In the end, March takes up choice, his signature topic, once again with feeling, and this time with a boundless enthusiasm that—with any luck—will be contagious.

REFERENCES

Alvarez, J., and C. Merchán. 1992. The role of narrative fiction in the development of imagination for action. *International Studies of Management and Organization* 22(3), 27–45.

Augier, M., J. March, and B. Sullivan. 2005. Notes on the evolution of a research community: Organization studies in Anglophone North America, 1945–2000. *Organization Science* 16(1), 85–95.

Bannister, R. 1987. *Sociology and Scientism: The American Quest for Objectivity, 1880–1940.* Chapel Hill, NC: University of North Carolina Press.

Barnard, C. 1948. *Organization and Management.* Cambridge, MA: Harvard University Press.

Barnard, C. 1938. *The Functions of the Executive.* Boston, MA: Harvard University Press.

Ben-David, J. 1971. *The Scientist's Role in Society: A Comparative Study.* Englewood Cliffs, NJ: Prentice-Hall.

Bennis, W. 1955. The social scientist as research entrepreneur: A case study. *Social Problems* 3(1), 44–49.

Brown, R. 1977. A Poetic for Sociology. Cambridge, UK: Cambridge University Press.

Burawoy, M. 2005. Provincializing the social sciences. G. Steinmetz, ed. *The Politics of Method in the Human Sciences: Positivism and its Epistemological Others.* Durham, NC, and London: Duke University Press, 508–525.

Calvino, I. 1999. *Why Read the Classics?* New York: Pantheon, (tr. by M. McLaughlin).

Chanlat, J.-F., ed. 2003. *L'individu dans l'Organisation: Les Dimensions Oubliées,* 6th ed. Quebec and Montreal : Les Presses de l'Université Laval et les Editions ESKA.

Church, R. 1974. Economists as experts: The rise of an academic profession in the United States, 1870–1920. L. Stone, ed. *The University in Society: Europe, Scotland, and the United States from the 16th to the 20th Century,* v.2. Princeton, NJ: Princeton University Press, 571–609.

Costa Lima, L. 1985. *Social representation and mimesis.* New Literary History 16(spring), 447–466.

Czarniawska-Joerges, B., and P. Guillet de Monthoux. 1994. *Good Novels, Better Management: Reading Organizational Realities in Fiction.* Chur, Switzerland: Harwood Academic.

Fishman, E. 1992. Images of Lockean America in contemporary American fiction. M. Whitebrook, ed. *Reading Political Stories: Representations of Politics in Novels and Pictures.* Lanham, MA: Rowman and Littlefield, 165–184.

Follett, M. 1924. *Creative Experience.* New York: Longmans, Green.

Furner, M. 1975. *Advocacy and Objectivity: A Crisis in the Professionalization of American Social Science, 1865–1905.* Lexington: University Press of Kentucky.

Girard, R. 1966. *Deceit, Desire, and the Novel: Self and Other in Literary Structure.* Baltimore, MD: Johns Hopkins University Press.

Gleeson, R., and S. Schlossman. 1995. George Leland Bach and the rebirth of graduate management education in the United States, 1945–1975. *Selections* 11(3), 8–37.

Goodrick, E. 2002. From management as a vocation to management as a scientific activity: An institutional account of a paradigm shift. *Journal of Management* 28(5), 649–668.

Grey, C. 1996. C. P. Snow's sociology of management and organizations. *Organization* 3(1), 61–83.

Gumbrecht, H. 2004. *Production of Presence: What Meaning Cannot Convey*. Stanford, CA: Stanford University Press.

Gumbrecht, H. 1985. History of literature—Fragment of a vanished totality? *New Literary History* 16(3), 467–479.

Hagstrom, W. 1965. *The Scientific Community*. New York: Basic Books.

Halliwell, S. 2002. *The Aesthetics of Mimesis: Ancient Texts and Modern Problems*. Princeton, NJ and Oxford, UK: Princeton University Press.

Hatchuel, A. 2005. Towards an epistemology of collective action: Management research as a responsive and actionable discipline. *European Management Review* 2, 36–47.

Hatchuel, A. 2000. Quel horizon pour les sciences de gestion? Vers une théorie de l'action collective. A. David, A. Hatchuel, and R. Laufer, eds. *Les Nouvelles Fondations des Sciences de Gestion: Elements d'Epistémologie de la Recherche en Management*. Paris: Librairie Vuibert, 7–43.

Hofstadter, R. 1956. *The Age of Reform*. New York: Macmillan.

Horton, J., and A. Baumeister. 1996. *Literature and the Political Imagination*. London and New York: Routledge.

Huxley, A. 1963. *Literature and Science*. New York: Harper & Row.

Iser, W. 1978. *The Act of Reading: A Theory of Aesthetic Response*. Baltimore, MD: Johns Hopkins University Press.

Kane, L., ed. 2001. *David Mamet in Conversation*. Ann Arbor, MI: University of Michigan Press.

Kay, C. 1988. *Political Constructions: Defoe, Richardson, and Sterne in Relation to Hobbes, Hume, and Burke*. Ithaca, NY: Cornell University Press.

Klausner, S., and V. Lidz, eds. 1986. *The Nationalization of the Social Sciences*. Philadelphia: University of Pennsylvania Press.

Lepenies, W. 1988. *Between Literature and Science: The Rise of Sociology*. Cambridge, UK: Cambridge University Press( tr. by R. Hollingdale).

Liang, N., and J. Wang. 2004. Implicit mental models in teaching cases: An empirical study of popular MBA cases in the United States and China. *Academy of Management Learning and Education* 3(4), 397–413.

Livingston, P. 1991. *Literature and Rationality: Ideas of Agency in Theory and Fiction*. Cambridge, UK: Cambridge University Press.

March, J. 2005. *Footprints*. Palo Alto: Bonde.

March, J. 1981. Decisions in organizations and theories of choice. A. Van de Ven, W. Joyce, eds. *Perspectives on Organization Design and Behavior*. New York: Wiley, 205–244.

March, J., and H. Simon. 1958. *Organizations*. New York: John Wiley.

McGuire, W. 1973. The yin and yang of progress in social psychology: Seven koan. *Journal of Personality and Social Psychology* 26(3), 446–456.

McNamara, C. 2002. Men and money in Tom Wolfe's America. C. Henderson, ed. *Seers and Judges: American Literature as Political Philosophy*. Lanham, MA: Lexington Books, 121–136.

Miall, D. 2006. *Literary Reading: Empirical and Theoretical Studies*. New York: Peter Lang.

Miller, A. 1971. *The Crucible* (32nd ed.). New York: Bantam.

Morgan, J. 1969. The development of sociology and the Social Gospel in America. *Sociological Analysis* 30(1), 42–53.

Natanson, M. 1963. *Philosophy of the Social Sciences: A Reader.* New York: Random House.

Natanson, M. 1953. A study in philosophy and the social sciences. M. Natanson, ed. *Philosophy of the Social Sciences: A Reader.* New York: Random House, 271–285.

Negash, G. 2004. Art invoked: A mode of understanding and shaping the political. *International Political Science Review* 25(2), 185–201.

Oberschall, A. 1972a. The institutionalization of American sociology. A. Oberschall, ed. *The Establishment of Empirical Sociology: Studies in Continuity, Discontinuity, and Institutionalization.* New York: Harper & Row, 187–251.

Oberschall, A., ed. 1972b. *The Establishment of Empirical Sociology: Studies in Continuity, Discontinuity, and Institutionalization.* New York: Harper & Row.

O'Connor, E. 1999. The politics of management thought: A case study of the Harvard Business School and the Human Relations School. *Academy of Management Review* 24, 117–131.

O'Connor, E. 1997. Telling decisions: The role of narrative in organizational decision making. Z. Shapira, ed. *Organizational Decision Making.* New York: Cambridge University Press, 304–323.

O'Connor, E., M. Hatch, H. White, and M. Zald. 1995. Undisciplining organizational studies: A conversation across domains, methods, and beliefs. *Journal of Management Inquiry* 4(2), 119–136.

Oppenheimer, J. 1962. On science and culture. *Encounter* 19(4), 3–10.

Parker, M., M. Higgins, G. Lightfoot, and W. Smith. 1999. Amazing tales: Organization studies as science fiction. *Organization* 6(4), 579–590.

Patient, D., T. Lawrence, and S. Maitlis. 2003. Understanding workplace envy through narrative fiction. *Organization Studies* 24(7), 1015–1044.

Phillips, N. 1995. Telling organizational tales: On the role of narrative fiction in the study of organizations. *Organization Studies* 16(4), 625–649.

Phillips, N., S. Zyglidopoulos. 1999. Learning from *Foundation*: Asimov's psychohistory and the limits of organization theory. *Organization* 6(4), 591–608.

Prasad, P. 2005. *Crafting Qualitative Research: Working in the Postpositivist Traditions.* Armonk, NY: M.E. Sharpe.

Putnam, L., and G. Fairhurst. 2004. Discourse analysis in organizations: Issues and concerns. F. Jablin, L. Putnam, eds. *The New Handbook of Organizational Communication.* Thousand Oaks, CA: Sage, 78–136.

Reiss, A. 1968. Sociology: The field. D. Sills, ed. *International Encyclopedia of the Social Sciences*, v. 15. New York: Macmillan, 1–23.

Ross, D. 1991. *The Origins of American Social Science.* New York: Cambridge University Press.

Sass, S. 1982. *The Pragmatic Imagination: A History of the Wharton School, 1881–1981.* Philadelphia: University of Pennsylvania Press.

Schlossman, S., M. Sedlak, and H. Wechsler. 1998. The "new look": The Ford Foundation and the revolution in business education. *Selections* 14(3), 8–28.

Schütz, A. 1963. Concept and theory formation in the social sciences. M. Natanson, ed. *Philosophy of the Social Sciences: A Reader.* Princeton, NJ: Princeton University Press, 231–249.

Scura, D. 1990. *Conversations with Tom Wolfe.* Jackson, MS: University Press of Mississippi.

Shils, E. 1979. The order of learning in the United States: The ascendancy of the university. A. Oleson and J. Voss, eds. *The Organization of Knowledge in Modern America, 1860–1920*. Baltimore, MD, and London: Johns Hopkins University Press, 19–47.

Simon, H. 1991. *Models of My Life*. New York: Basic Books.

Sontag, S. 1983. *Against interpretation. A Susan Sontag Reader*. Harmondsworth, UK: Penguin, 95–104.

Stinchcombe, A. 1982. Should sociologists forget their mothers and fathers? *American Sociologist* 17(1), 2–11.

Trilling, L. 1962. Science, literature and culture. *Commentary* 33 (Jan.–Jun.), 461–477.

Turner, S., and J. Turner. 1990. *The Impossible Science: An Institutional Analysis of American Sociology*. Newbury Park, CA: Sage.

Van Maanen, J., and E. Schein. 1979. Toward a theory of organizational socialization. B. Staw, ed. *Research in Organizational Behavior*. Greenwich, CT: JAI Press, 209–264.

Waldo, D. 1968. *The Novelist on Organization and Administration: An Inquiry into the Relationship between Two Worlds*. Berkeley, CA: Institute of Governmental Studies.

Weick, K. 1993. The collapse of sensemaking in organizations: The Mann Gulch disaster. *Administrative Science Quarterly* 38(4), 628–652.

Whitebrook, M. 1996. Taking the narrative turn: What the novel has to offer political theory. J. Horton and A. Baumeister, eds. *Literature and the Political Imagination*. London and New York: Routledge, 32–52.

Whitebrook, M. 1995. *Real Toads in Imaginary Gardens: Narrative Accounts of Liberalism*. Lanham, MD, and London: Rowman & Littlefield Publishers.

Whitebrook, M., ed. 1992. *Reading Political Stories: Representations of Politics in Novels and Pictures*. Lanham, MD: Rowman & Littlefield Publishers,.

Williams, O., ed. 1997. *The Moral Imagination: How Literature and Films Can Stimulate Ethical Reflection in the Business World*. Notre Dame, IN: University of Notre Dame Press.

Wolf, W. 1995. Barnard's post–1947 comments on decision processes. *Journal of Management History* 1(4), 100–111.

Wolf, W., and H. Iino., eds. 1986. *Philosophy for Managers: Selected Papers of Chester I. Barnard*. Tokyo: Bunshindo.

Zuckert, C. 1990. *Natural Right and the American Imagination: Political Philosophy in Novel Form*. Savage, MD: Rowman & Littlefield.

CHAPTER 18

# Literature and Leadership

JAMES G. MARCH

THE FUNDAMENTAL ISSUES OF LEADERSHIP—the complications involved in becoming, being, confronting, and evaluating leaders—are not unique to leadership. They are echoes of critical issues of life more generally. As a result, they are characteristically illuminated more by great literature than by modern essays or research on leadership.

Consider, for example, this small handful of central issues:

*Private lives and public duties.* Leaders have private lives from which they draw emotional balance and human sustenance, though they often find their official lives systematically more rewarding. Leadership can destroy both the privacy and the quality of personal life. The importance of position undermines authenticity in personal relations. Self becomes inseparable from standing, thereby making love and hate equally suspect. Leadership also attracts curiosity and gossip, compromising privacy. Followers claim a right to knowledge about a leader's personal life on grounds of its relevance to assessing character and establishing rapport. Finally, private lives complicate the responsibilities of leadership. Personal motives and relations affect the actions of leaders. Personal jealousies and loyalties bend a leader's judgment. Interpersonal trust contributes to, yet corrupts, organizational actions. What are the possibilities for combining a rich personal life with life as an organizational leader? How are personal feelings to be reconciled with organizational responsibilities?

*Cleverness, innocence, and virtue.* Commentators on leadership are ambivalent about sophistication and cleverness. On the one hand, leaders are often portrayed as astute manipulators of resources and people, praised for their use of superior knowledge and adroitness. They are frequently described as intelligently devious and secretive, as wily experts in maneuver and misdirection. We honor their superior abilities to outsmart others. On the other hand, leaders are often pictured not as sophisticated in the usual sense but as possessing an

Originally published as "Littérature et leadership," *Revue Économique et Sociale* (Lausanne), 59 (2001), 301–308.

elemental innocence that overcomes the fatuous convolutions of clever people and goes instinctively to the essentials. This capability for simplification is associated not with education, intelligence, and propriety but with an ability to connect, in some uncomplicated way, to the fundamentals of life. In this spirit, leaders are often praised for their naiveté and openness, and for their ability to use honesty as a basis for inspiring and extending trust. What is the place of cleverness and innocence, intelligence and ignorance in descriptions of, or prescriptions for, leadership?

*Genius, heresy, and madness.* Great leaders are often portrayed as geniuses. They are said to see further and more accurately than others. Because of this visionary capability, they dare to take risks that others dare not. They transform organizations through their imagination, creativity, insight, and will. These descriptions of great leaders seem, however, to portray greatness as being associated with heresy, thus to be at variance with the needs of organizations for safer, more reliable behavior. The needs are not perverse. Though heresy sometimes proves, retrospectively, to be the basis for desirable change, most bold new ideas are foolish and properly ignored. They are more likely to destroy an organization than to lead it to new heights of achievement. Thus, great leaders are characteristically heretics who are associated with a transformation of orthodoxy, but most heretics would be disasters as leaders. What are the relations among genius, madness, and leadership? How do we recognize great leaders among the crazies? How do we nurture genius if we cannot recognize it before history does?

*Diversity and unity.* In everything from problem solving to personnel policies to ideologies, leaders make trade-offs between diversity and unity, between variety and integration, between convergence and divergence. Organizations are collections of individuals and groups often having quite diverse attitudes, backgrounds, religions, aspirations, training, identities, ethnicities, experiences, social ties, and styles. Leadership frequently involves finding ways to minimize the problems of diversity through recruitment from a common background, experience, or education, or through the use of persuasion, bargaining, incentives, socialization, and inspiration to mold multiple talents and backgrounds into a common culture. Such a vision of leadership as forging a unity of harmonious purpose and commitment clashes, however, with an alternative vision of leadership as stimulating and nurturing diversity as a source of organizational innovation and social strength. How do leaders choose between building unity and building diversity? Can they have both? To what extent is unity at one level in an organization a necessary precondition for diversity at another?

*Ambiguity and coherence.* Leadership is generally seen as a force for coherence, as contributing to effective organizational action by eliminating contradictions and preventing confusions. Future leaders are taught to remove inconsistencies, ambiguities, and complexities through precise objectives and well-conceived plans. The modern prototype in a business firm is the idea of business strategy and the development of a "business plan." However, inconsistency and ambiguity have a role in change and adaptation, and the compulsion toward coherence could be an incomplete basis for understanding or improving leadership and life. In general, effective leadership implies an ability to live in two worlds: the incoherent world of imagination, fantasy, and dreams and the orderly world of plans, rules, and pragmatic action. How do we sustain both ambiguity and coherence? Both foolishness and reason? Both contradiction and resolution? To what extent are talents to do so related to artistic, literary, and poetic imagination?

*Power, domination, and subordination.* Many modern ideologies treat inequalities in power as illegitimate. Yet, we pursue power and are fascinated by it. We equate personal power with personal self-worth, and powerlessness with loss of esteem and identity. We write history and describe progress in terms of changing patterns of domination and subordination. As a result, we see power as both central to leadership and a complication for it. We recognize a tension between hierarchy and participation, between power and equality, and between control and autonomy. Power is often said to corrupt the holder of it, to transform normally honorable people into monsters. It is also said to condemn, to undermine the ordinary pleasures of honesty in interpersonal relations. At the same time, power is often described as elusive, more a story-telling myth than a reality. Insofar as leaders have power, how do they use it? What are its limits? What are its costs? How does a person with little power function in a power-based institution? What are the moral dilemmas of power?

*Gender and sexuality.* Gender and sexuality are well-recognized factors in modern biology, sociology, and ideology. They affect a wide range of behaviors, and interpretations of behaviors, in organizations. In virtually all societies, leadership is linked to questions of sexual identity and gender equality. Historically, most leaders have been men; and the rhetoric of leadership has been closely related to the rhetoric of manliness. Changes in gender stereotypes with respect to leadership interact with the ways women and men are interpreted to have (or not have) distinctive styles, characters, beliefs, or behaviors, as well as with our understandings of their relations, not only outside hierarchical organizations but also within them. Moreover, leadership appears to be intertwined with sexuality.

Being a leader and being seen as having power are components of sexual appeal and sexual identity. Sexual relations and accusations of sexual misconduct are endemic around leadership. How do the manifest elements of sexuality and gender in leadership affect the ways we understand, become, and act as leaders?

The proper texts for discussing these fundamental issues of leadership are drawn from Shakespeare, Molière, Ibsen, Tolstoy, Cervantes, Mann, Goethe, Akhmatova, Schiller, Stendhal, Kawabata, Shaw, James, Dostoevsky, Balzac, and others of similar stature. Great literature engages these questions in a deeper and more enduring way than other texts. This greater engagement stems from a more profound realization that the issues are to be seen as intractable dilemmas rather than as problems to be solved. They deal with what the great Danish physicist, Niels Bohr, called "profound truths"—recognizable by the fact that their opposites are also profound truths. Because the struggles with these truths have no resolution, they create enduring inter- and intra-personal conflicts; and understanding them involves experiencing the social, personal, and intellectual pains of those conflicts.

To document the power of literature in identifying and clarifying the dilemmas of leadership is beyond the possibilities of a short essay and the capabilities of the present author, but it may perhaps be illustrated briefly by considering a final fundamental issue of leadership:

*Great actions, great visions, and great expectations.* In the ideology of leadership, action is seen as intentional and instrumental, driven by an evaluation of its expected consequences. Costs are paid because benefits are anticipated. Within such an ideology, leaders need to have expectations of great consequences to justify the great commitments demanded of them. They need to believe they can make a difference. We ask whether this is an adequate description of leadership behavior or an adequate moral foundation for it. In particular, we wonder about the implications of justifying great actions by great hopes in a world in which causality is obscure and effectiveness problematic. Within an ethic of consequentiality, how do we sustain commitment in the face of adverse or ambiguous outcomes? How do an organization and a society maintain illusions of efficacy among its leaders? What are the consequences? Are there alternatives?

Innumerable treatises on incentives, rationality, and leadership portray great actions as sustained by hopes for great consequences. The mythic tales of leaders portray them as heroically instrumental. Leaders are routinely induced to sacrifice themselves by anticipations of great individual and social consequences.

They, their supporters, and their opponents all imagine that the actions of leaders make a difference. In the world of leader motivation, the great man theory of history is king.

As Tolstoy reminds us, however, there is a conspicuous problem with justifying great action by expectations of consequential significance. Our mythic tales are not, in general, consistent with ordinary experience, except as we make them so by our acceptance of the myths. Life does not provide consistently persuasive confirmation of the possibility of achieving great consequences through willful action. The chaos and complexity of organizations, like the chaos and complexity of the Battle of Borodino, frustrate our efforts to establish unambiguous understandings of the causes of success and failure or to influence them reliably.

Thus, the existential problem of commitment: How can we sustain great action by intelligent leaders in the face of ordinary experience that denies the possibility of grand significance? Ibsen's Dr. Relling (*The Wild Duck*) provides one classical answer. In the play, Dr. Relling argues for sustaining the illusions (life-lies) of people. Take away their hopes for consequences, he says, and you take away their happiness. Pirandello's Liola (*Liola*) echoes the same sentiment by saying "Pretending is virtue, and if you can't pretend, you can't be king." The mythic tales of leadership that we find in every part of human life reflect a Relling or Liola response to the dilemmas of absurdity: Create a mythic life-lie that leads people to make great commitments.

This insistence on tying actions to hopes, even dubious ones, is a hallmark of modern motivation. Actions are assumed to be based on expectations of positive outcomes. The implicit social strategy is to use myths to produce a large pool of people who imagine great possibilities. When experience undermines that hope in particular individuals, the disillusioned are replaced by the naive. The innocent pursue a logic of consequences and invent fantasies of possibilities to justify heroic commitment. Modern students of economics talk of incentives, and modern students of psychology confirm that, under some circumstances, false beliefs in efficacy sometimes leads to better performance than realistic knowledge of one's prospects for success.

Our inclination to build hopes on lies in order to sustain commitment is, however, both dangerous and unnecessary. It is dangerous because hopes based on lies are more persuasive to the foolish than to the wise and more enduring in the short run than in the long run. A life based on hopes for heroic achievement is a life condemned to disappointment or delusion. As Unamuno (*Tragic Sense of Life*, 106) reminds us, skepticism and uncertainty are "the position to which reason, by practising its analysis upon itself, upon its own validity, at last arrives." Leaders of intelligence and perceptiveness recognize the limits of their capabilities and the threat of absurdity in their lives. Because they see the inconsistency between the realities of limited control and the demands for heroic hopes, they are in danger of succumbing to cynicism or withdrawal, leaving only the less intelligent and less perceptive willing to persist in the commitments demanded by leadership.

Building hopes on lies is dangerous. It is also unnecessary. Great actions need not depend on expectations of consequences. In an exquisite scene from Cervantes' masterpiece (I, 4), Don Quixote confronts a group of traders from Toledo. He demands that the traders affirm "that in all the world there is no maiden fairer than the Empress of La Mancha, the peerless Dulcinea del Toboso." The traders ask Quixote to show them this remarkable lady. "If she is of such beauty as you suggest," one of them says, "with all our hearts and without any pressure we will confess the truth that you have required of us." In reply, Quixote proclaims, "If I were to show her to you, what merit would you have in confessing a truth so manifest. The essential point is that without seeing her you must believe, confess, affirm, swear, and defend it."

It is a superb declaration of the glory of arbitrary vision, the vital human talent of discovering a basis for action that does not depend on the realities and justifications of a consequential life, indeed is compromised by them. Comprehending, developing, and harnessing that talent for fantasy is an integral part of the psychology of leadership, as well as of the moral, aesthetic, and pragmatic conundrums of being or contemplating leaders.

Quixote's proposition that belief justified by reality warrants no particular honor contradicts our precepts of sanity, yet is a crucial element of leadership in a world in which reality is partly socially constructed, life is often absurd, and morality is confused with rationality. A talent for a certain kind of self-deception is both an essential ingredient of leadership and a source of its terror, and Cervantes provides a better basis for examining the dilemmas, possibilities, and costs of self-deception than do books that deal explicitly with leadership.

Quixote acts not in the name of consequences but in the name of an identity. "Yo sé quien soy," he says, "I know who I am." To Don Diego de Miranda (II, 17) he says, "All knights have their special parts to play . . . As it has fallen to my lot to be a member of the knight-errantry, I cannot avoid attempting all that to me seems to come within the sphere of my duties." And later (II, 32) he explains to the duke and duchess that "I am in love for no other reason than that it is an obligation for knights-errant to be so."

The struggle between a Benthamite logic of consequences and a Quixote logic of appropriateness is a central struggle in the psychology of leadership.

The struggle is pursued in Dostoevsky (*The Idiot*), Shakespeare (*Hamlet, King Lear*), Stendhal (*Le Rouge et le Noir*), and innumerable other literary works with a psychological, philosophical, and moral subtlety that exercises and clarifies the issue without fully resolving it.

These works of literature do not provide easy answers. Quixote, for example, is not a paragon; he often hurts the people he seeks to help. These complex treatments of human motivation in literature, however, challenge leaders to recognize that there is an issue, that modern rational theories of choice and incentive theories of motivation are incomplete, that action may depend more on an identity than on anticipated rewards, and properly so. Leadership entails instrumental probity, a fine sense of how to make things work; but it also entails a passion that rejects justification in utility. It affirms life through the unreasoning discovery and embedding of an individual identity within an appreciation of the history and destiny of humanity.

The glories and sorrows of such an orientation are exhibited with impressive force and delicacy in literature, and reading literary masters may easily be justified for that reason. However, any justification that sees works of great literature as helping leaders cope with particular issues of leadership is incomplete. A human commitment to the masterpieces of literature, like a commitment to leadership, is itself a transcendental act, beyond instrumental justification. The passionate consumption of great text by a leader, like the passionate commitment to being a leader, confirms the glory of an arbitrary enthusiasm for the pains and pleasures of being human. And although it may sensibly be said that leadership is too prosaic an activity to sustain such a lofty ambition, it may also be argued, with Quixote (I, 25) that "for a knight-errant to make himself crazy for a reason merits neither credit nor thanks; the point is to be foolish without justification."

CHAPTER 19

# Poetry and the Rhetoric of Management

## *Easter 1916*

JAMES G. MARCH

> An exploration of William Butler Yeats's poem *Easter 1916* as an illustration of
> the proposition that poetry is a natural medium for expressing and contemplating
> doubt, paradox, and contradiction—features of life, well known to experienced
> managers, but normally banished, perhaps with reason, from the public language
> of management.

POETRY EXPOSES MOMENTARY GLITTERS of transcendent humanness in
the beauty of a mind. Anything else is extra. In a utilitarian culture, however,
poems are sometimes validated by claiming practical uses for them. This article
is in such a spirit, exploring a possible utilitarian justification for poetry in the
life of organizational managers. It uses one of the better known poems by William Butler Yeats, *Easter 1916* (Yeats, 1996), as an illustration of the proposition that poetry is a natural medium for expressing and contemplating doubt,
paradox, and contradiction—features of life, well known to experienced managers, but normally banished, perhaps with reason, from the public language
of management.

*Easter 1916* is a short poem of some 430 words arrayed in 80 lines. It is a
song of exquisite lyricism with sounds and rhythms and rhymes that would deserve recitation and incite admiration even if the lines were devoid of meaning.
There is music in the words.

> I have met them at close of day
> Coming with vivid faces
> From counter or desk among grey
> Eighteenth-century houses.

I am grateful for the comments of Ted Buswick, Dennis Gioia, Daniel Newark, and Marty Tarshes. This
chapter was originally published in *Journal of Management Inquiry*, 15 (2006), 70–72.

There is music in the words, and that is reason enough to enjoy the poem; however, *Easter 1916* also evokes a cascade of meanings. In particular, it illustrates the epigram (attributed to W. H. Auden) that poetry is "the clear expression of mixed feelings." The poem is an exploration of ambivalence and paradox, of the possibility of feeling simultaneous sentiments that seem contradictory, of living in multiple worlds and experiencing multiple feelings, and of recognizing the role of ugliness in the creation of beauty.

*Easter 1916* celebrates the Dublin insurrection of 1916, a failed-but-inspirational cameo in the history of Irish independence. The poem honors the visionary leaders of an ultimately successful revolution, paying tribute to the martyrs of the Easter insurrection and their "terrible beauty."

> MacDonagh and MacBride
> And Connolly and Pearse
> Now and in time to be,
> Wherever green is worn,
> Are changed, changed utterly:
> A terrible beauty is born.

The readers of the poem are enjoined to remember the heroes as much-loved members of the family,

> To murmur name upon name,
> As a mother names her child.

However, the admirable qualities found in the martyrs of 1916 are not derived as much from their characters as from the dramaturgical requirements of the Irish revolutionary story. Their beauty is, in modern terms, a socially constructed beauty. Their actions and their natures were purified and sanctified by the executions of 1916 and the subsequent independence of Ireland; however, the poem is unabashedly ambivalent about the individuals. One is viewed as distracted by the insurrection from his true literary potential; another as a strident rabble-rouser; and another as an egocentric bastard.

> A drunken, vain-glorious lout.
> He had done most bitter wrong
> To some who are near my heart.

*Easter 1916* is a eulogy in which the heroes of 1916 are extolled and reproached; and the admiration and condemnation are too closely connected to be considered separate sentiments. The poem invites an awareness that the leaders involved in radical change are saints only by subsequent reconstruction; that battles lost and won in life are often fought in a muck of human lunacy; that although lives are lived in a public world of decisions, revolutions, collective goals, speeches, and history, they are also and simultaneously lived in the daily episodes of private lives and private thoughts that are filled with ambitions, envies, sentiments, fears, and sorrows; and that the demands of history may conflict with the demands of decency. The implicit claim of the poem is that ambiguities, contradictions, and ambivalences are not errors to be purged from consciousness. They are components of any intelligent comprehension of reality. Confidence has its doubts; love has its hates. Every virtue has its vice, and every vice its virtue.

Such a sense of life as filled with unavoidably mixed feelings matches the experience and understanding of many experienced managers; however, it conflicts with standard rhetorical imperatives for managerial talk. The rhetoric of management is a rhetoric of decisiveness, certainty, and clarity. Managers are usually expected to represent confusions as clarified, contradictions as resolved, estimates as certain, and doubts as driven out. Although the confusions and contradictions of life are often obvious to them, managers generally avoid the public expression of perplexed perceptions, mixed feelings, private images, and the torments of ambivalence. They often articulate a fantasy world that is simpler than the world in which they live and that they know from experience.

This rhetorical fantasy serves a purpose. There is ample evidence that confidence and certainty, even when unfounded, create conditions for decisive action; and decisiveness is often a prerequisite for effectiveness. Effective managers frequently seek to absorb ambiguities and doubts so that they do not spread to others in the organization or reduce commitment to action. Leaders often make things simple and unambiguous to mobilize followers (and themselves) for coordinated actions involving substantial personal commitment.

The paradox that it is often the simplicity, stubbornness, single-mindedness, and blindness of leaders, not their subtle perceptiveness and flexibility, that foster organizational change is well known. Simplemindedness is an instrument of change; and, in moments of change, adaptive organizations often exhibit rigid leaders. As *Easter 1916* observes,

> Hearts with one purpose alone
> Through summer and winter, seem
> Enchanted to a stone.

Rather than flexible instruments adapting to life's natural course, committed leaders are obstructions to it—stones in a river, stubbornly inert "to trouble the living stream."

*Easter 1916* is a tribute to fanatical visionaries for their contribution to Irish independence; however, it is also a reminder of the social and human costs involved. In particular, the poem observes that leaders are quite likely to be (or become through the process) something less than unconditionally attractive as human beings.

> Too long a sacrifice
> Can make a stone of the heart.

The heroes portrayed by the poem have been led by the sacrifices they have made to substitute an ugly confidence in their own simple faith for an intelligent comprehension of the complexity of real human experience. They contribute to beauty and flexibility without being beautiful or flexible themselves.

Is there an alternative? Can managers sustain an awareness of the contradictions, paradoxes, ambiguities, and ambivalences of life (as intelligence, human beauty, and learning require) while espousing a rhetoric of simplicity, clarity, consistency, and certainty (as managerial norms and practice require)? A passion for poems such as *Easter 1916* is not essential to maintaining such a duality, but it helps. Poems claim exemption from the rules of coherence and resolution of dilemmas that managerial discourse imposes. They exhibit "the clear expression of mixed feelings." At the same time, not only by virtue of their tolerance of contradiction but also because they are rhetorically private, poems help to sustain a consciousness of complexity. By reinforcing an awareness of life's confusions without requiring that that awareness be reflected in managerial talk, poems protect intelligent comprehension from the simplifying necessities of managerial life.

Poetry is a voice of an incoherent truth. It reminds managers and their advisors that life is gloriously chaotic and endlessly confusing, that contradictions of feelings and comprehensions bring a bittersweet, but essential, enrichment to life, and that although the rhetoric of management is exquisitely disconnected from managerial reality, that disconnection itself is part of the panoply of paradoxes that protects the beauty of human existence.

### REFERENCE

Yeats, W. B. 1996. Easter 1916. In A. Norman Jeffares (ed.), *Yeats's Poems*. London: Macmillan, 287–289.

# CHAPTER 20

# Ibsen, Ideals, and the Subornation of Lies

JAMES G. MARCH

Henrik Ibsen wrote his first play in 1850 and wrote three plays in verse, *Love's Comedy* (*Kjærlighedens Komedie*)(1962), *Brand* (1866), and *Peer Gynt* (1867), before he began the cycle of twelve prose plays written from 1877 to 1899[1] that assured his fame. The intent in this essay is to explore the implications for students of organizations of some of Ibsen's observations of the human condition. The comments focus particularly on an issue that is more conspicuous in *Love's Comedy, Brand, Peer Gynt,* and the earlier part of the cycle of twelve prose plays than it is in the later part of the cycle.

Are there lessons in these plays for students of organizations? Surely on the occasion of a conference in Norway, the answer to that question must be "yes." My elaboration of that answer must, however, be prefaced not only by a confession of bias—I am a long-time Norwegian groupie—but also by a denial of Ibsen competence. There must be several hundred serious Ibsen scholars in the world. I am not one of them.

## IDENTITY IDEALS

As an observer of human behavior, Henrik Ibsen is an institutional theorist, a student of the way humans seek to act in ways appropriate to their identities. Ibsen's characters try to fulfill the identity ideals by which they and their positions in society are defined. These ideals take the form of the obligations of being a community leader, wife, husband, minister, public official, etc.

For the most part, Ibsen's characters view any world bereft of identity ideals as a world of little attraction. Thus, in *A Doll House* (Act III) Torvald Helmer attributes his wife's behavior to an absence of ideals. He proclaims:

> All your father's flimsy values have come out in you. No religion, no morals, no sense of duty.[2]

I am grateful for the comments of Daniel Newark, Johan P. Olsen, and Åse Vigdis Ystad. This chapter was originally published in *Organization Studies*, 28 (2007), 1277–1285.

And in Act IV of *Rosmersholm,* when Johannes Rosmer asks Ulrik Brendel whether he can help him in any way, the resulting exchange suggests the despair of a life short of ideals:

> Brendel: Can you let me have a loan?[3]
> Rosmer: Yes, willingly.[4]
> Brendel: Can you spare me an ideal or two?[5]

This pursuit of identity ideals is vital to a proper life. Hjalmar Ekdal speaks for most Ibsen characters when he says in Act IV of *The Wild Duck:*

> There are certain claims—what shall I call them?—let me say claims of the ideal—certain obligations, which a man cannot disregard without injury to his soul.[6]

Even Rebekka West in her revolt against the ideals of the Rosmer family observes in Act IV of *Rosmersholm* that a way of life that emphasizes living up to ideals kills happiness, but it is a noble way of life.[7]

### THE VIRTUE GAP

Individuals pursue ideals, but they habitually fail to live up to them. They experience a virtue gap—a disparity between their hopes for their lives and their experience. For example, in an exchange with Pastor Manders in Act I of *Ghosts,* Mrs. Alving records her assessment of the virtue gap in her life:

> Manders: Do you mean the whole of your marriage—all those years together with your husband—were nothing more than a hollow mockery?[8]
> Mrs. Alving: Not a crumb more.[9]

The problems posed by this gap between ideals and reality are particularly difficult in situations where the ideals are especially demanding, for example, in situations involving people holding positions of social importance and in societies with strongly held and widely shared norms (for example, Norway in the last half of the 19th century).

According to standard conceptions of rational action, individuals seek happiness and virtue by evaluating alternatives in terms of their expected costs and benefits, calibrated in comparable units. Conflicts among wants or between wants and capabilities, such as those reflected in the virtue gap, are converted into calculations of expected value and trade-offs. As Ulrik Brendel observes to Johannes Rosmer in Act IV of *Rosmersholm* in a description of Peder Mortensgård, such a conversion makes choices easier. He says:

> Peder Mortensgård never wants anything more than what he can do. Peder Mortensgård is wholly capable of a life without ideals. And that, you see—that,

essentially is the great secret of action and success. It's the sum of all worldly wisdom.[10]

Brendel describes Mortensgård as a man for whom regrets over things foregone are subordinated to recognition that all actions involve costs. Such a course removes moral pain and its effects from action. When the identity-based commandment "Thou shall not kill" is converted into its decision theory substitute "Thou shall kill only when the marginal expected benefit exceeds the marginal expected cost," a claim on the self is transformed into a tractable decision rule. Any sense of personal torment is removed.

Personal torment inhabits Ibsen's plays. The Peder Mortensgård described by Ulrik Brendel is not a typical Ibsen character. Most of the characters are acutely conscious of the claims of duty and the obligations of their identities. They exhibit anguish over the sacrifice of ideals to other exigencies or over the sacrifice of self to the ideals. The virtue gap is experienced less as a necessary cost than as a source of anguish. In Act IV of *The Wild Duck,* Hjalmar Ekdal cries out:

> In certain cases, it is impossible to disregard the claim of the ideal. . . . But . . . the human being in me also demands its rights.[11]

Such torment is obvious not only in Hjalmar Ekdal but also in many of Ibsen's other principal characters, including Brand (*Brand*), Nora Helmer (*A Doll House*), Mrs. Alving (*Ghosts*), Karsten Bernick (*Pillars of Society*), Johannes Rosmer (*Rosmersholm*), Ellida Wangel (*The Lady from the Sea*), Mrs. Stockmann (*An Enemy of the People*), Hedda Tesmann (*Hedda Gabler*), and Arnold Rubek (*When We Dead Awaken*).

## REDUCING THE VIRTUE GAP

The Ibsen characters seek to reduce the virtue gap through two principal tactics. The first is the course adopted by many of the most honored of the characters. They renounce the life they have led and the identities and ideals within which they have tried unsuccessfully to live and substitute others. These characters include Mrs. Alving in *Ghosts,* Dr. Thomas Stockmann in *An Enemy of the People,* Rebekka West and Johannes Rosmer in *Rosmersholm,* Hedda Tesmann in *Hedda Gabler,* Maja and Arnold Rubek in *When We Dead Awaken,* and Nora Helmer in the *A Doll House.* In the famous scene from Act III of *A Doll House,* Nora denounces her life as a wife and child:

> Our home's been nothing but a playpen. I've been your doll-wife here, just as at home I was Papa's doll-child.[12]

Since the disavowal of an identity cannot easily be made unilaterally, these characters suffer from their attempts to withdraw from the obligations of an identity that they have been unable or unwilling to fulfill. In the Ibsen world, identities are social and cannot be arbitrarily chosen or abandoned by individuals without penalty. Nor is the triumph clearly a spiritual one as spirituality is defined by the Ibsen spokespeople of religiosity. Pastor Manders, in a lecture to Mrs. Alving in Act I of *Ghosts*, scorns the abandonment of an identity ideal in the name of happiness:

> But this is the essence of the rebellious spirit, to crave happiness here in this life. What right have we human beings to happiness? No, we must do our duty, Mrs. Alving![13]

The second major response to a virtue gap is to invent stories in which actions inconsistent with ideals are concealed or rationalized, that is, to lie. Ibsen's characters are concerned with gaining self-respect and the respect of others by securing and maintaining a reputation for having fulfilled the ideals of their identities. In the face of the difficulty of satisfying the ideals, they lie about their business relations, their family life, their political beliefs, and their sexual relations.

The result is a set of social institutions that are constructed around ideals and the lies that both mock them and sustain them. Consider, for example, the institution of friendship. In the *Pillars of Society* a somewhat grateful Karsten Bernick asks Lona Hessel why she came back to goad him into admitting the lies on which his reputation has been built. In a cruel allusion to rusting boats, she replies:

> Old friendship does not rust.[14]

The vision evoked by Lona's statement is one of the enduring obligations of friendship. Ibsen, however, complicates such a vision with a recognition that friendship often depends on deceptions. In Act II of *John Gabriel Borkman*, Borkman talks with Vilhelm Foldal:

> Borkman: . . . we've practiced mutual deception on each other. And perhaps deceived ourselves—both of us.[15]
>
> Foldal: But isn't that the very basis of friendship, John Gabriel?[16]
>
> Borkman: Quite so. To deceive—is friendship. You're right in that.[17]

The lies that support social institutions and beliefs are not resisted but fomented by the representatives of society, who insist on and collaborate in the lies, punishing those who refuse to protect the ideal by lying. In Act III of *Pillars of Society*, Karsten Bernick describes his awareness that the respect in which he is held by the community depends on maintaining the illusion of virtue:

> You've forgotten this community of ours, or else you'd know that that [i.e., a
> confession of his deviation from the ideals] would totally and utterly crush me.[18]

It is in such terms that Dr. Stockmann attacks the majority in Act IV of *An
Enemy of the People:*

> The most insidious enemy of truth and freedom among us is the solid majority.
> Yes, the damned, solid, liberal majority—that's it![19]

The instruments of society, such as the media, join in protecting the lies. In Act
III of *An Enemy of the People,* when Petra accuses the newspaper editor, Hovs-
tad, of knowing very well that he is publishing lies, he agrees with her:

> You're perfectly right; but then an editor can't always do what he might prefer.[20]

### THE DYNAMICS OF HYPOCRISY

Ibsen's characters live in worlds that encourage them to lie in order to conceal
deviations from the ideals. Moreover, the plays are populated with explicit advocates for such hypocrisy, characters who enjoin others to maintain the fiction
that they fulfill the ideals. When, in Act II of *Rosmersholm,* Headmaster Kroll
lectures Johannes Rosmer about his relationship with Rebekka West, he advocates a systematic strategy of hypocrisy.

> If this madness has to go on, then think and believe and trust in anything you
> want, for God's sake—anything. But keep your beliefs to yourself.[21]

To modern ears, most of the articulate hypocrites are unattractive voices (e.g.,
Headmaster Kroll [*Rosmersholm*], Pastor Manders [*Ghosts*], Mayor Stockmann
[*An Enemy of the People*]). Among the proponents of hypocrisy, however, there
is one who is less concerned with maintaining the moral order than with making
life tolerable. He is Dr. Relling in *The Wild Duck.* For Dr. Relling, the aspirations of ideals are impossible to achieve except through lies, so lies and ideals
are inextricably connected. Lies are suborned by ideals.

When, in Act V, Gregers bemoans Ekdal's loss of his youthful "ideals" to
Relling:

> Relling: Don't use that foreign word ideals. We have, you know, the good native
> word—lies.[22]
>
> Gregers: Do you mean that the two are related to each other?[23]
>
> Relling: Yes, about like typhus and the fever of putrefaction.[24]

By constructing lies as unavoidable, Relling makes them a necessary part of happiness for ordinary people. In Act V, in one of the best-known Ibsen quotations, he exclaims:

> Take the life-lie away from an ordinary man and you take happiness away from
> him as well.[25]

In the long run, as Dr. Relling seems to argue, the thrust for ideals and the lies that they stimulate jointly produce not only torment for the individuals involved but also corruption for the society. The torment is reflected in the guilt expressed by characters such as Karsten Bernick in *Pillars of Society* and Mrs. Alving in *Ghosts*. In Act II of *Ghosts*, Mrs. Alving castigates herself for her efforts to maintain a public illusion about her marriage:

> I felt it was my duty and obligation—so year after year, I've gone on lying to my
> own child. Oh, what a coward—what a coward I've been![26]

The societal corruption comes from a positive feedback loop that escalates lies and demands for virtue—the lie multiplier. Every lie offends the defenders of the faith and stimulates their concern for the society and the individual. These defenders of the faith include characters such as Brand (*Brand*), Lona Hessel (*Pillars of Society*), Gregers (*The Wild Duck*), and Dr. Stockmann (*An Enemy of the People*). Their demands make the aspirations of the code more rigidly demanding, thus inducing more lies.

Karsten Bernick in *Pillars of Society* indicts society for its contribution to the multiplication of lies. In Act III, he says:

> Is it not society itself that makes us devious?[27]

And again in Act IV:

> We are the puppets of society, no more no less.[28]

The accelerating spiral of demands for virtue and the resulting lies makes society unattractive. In the *Pillars of Society*, Lona Hessel, seemingly unaware of her own complicity in the process, denounces the result:

> . . . of what consequence is it whether such a society be propped up or not? What
> does it all consist of? Show and lies—and nothing else.[29]

## RELEVANCE FOR ORGANIZATION STUDIES

The Ibsen plays provide a structure for thinking about the social dynamics of lying and hypocrisy in organizations and in organizations scholarship. A model inferred from the Ibsen characters can be expressed in four simple propositions.

1. Social and individual norms and ideals are generally inconsistent with human capabilities. As a result, humans persistently fail to achieve them.

2. Faced with a gap between the ideals and their capabilities, individuals lie. They portray a false world in which the ideals are fulfilled.

3. The lies that preserve the ideals and protect an individual's reputation produce, at the same time, moral torment and guilt in the individuals involved.

4. The more individuals lie, the more resolute and vigorous become the guardians of ideals in enforcing them, which in turn induces more lies. The result is an accelerating spiral of demands for virtue and lies, accompanied by a rising crescendo of individual anguish.

This Ibsen model of hypocrisy and the lie multiplier resonates with the work of students of performance measures and agency who have discussed the incentives to lie in organizational life, and the work of Nils Brunsson in his explorations of the organization of hypocrisy. In contrast to most of the work on lying in organizations studies, however, the primary Ibsen basis for falsehood is not a consequential incentive for lying but a threat to a sense of self, arguably a basis that is both more powerful and more emotional.

The Ibsen treatment also focuses attention on a positive feedback multiplier for lying by which lying and the enforcement of ideals are enmeshed in an armaments race of mutual stimulation. Lies stimulate demands for moral purity, which stimulate more lies. As with all such multipliers, this one requires more investigation of the mechanisms that keep it from exploding. For, as Dr. Relling says at the end of Act III of *The Wild Duck*:

> Oh, yes, it [moralistic fever] is a national disease, but it only breaks out now and then.[30]

For example, human societies have concepts of "half-truths" and "white lies," as well as of the humanness of imperfection, that recognize the impossibility of achieving ideals. Not everything that is true is appropriately said. Not every failure to achieve virtue is grounds for damnation. Not every lie is defined as a lie. As a result, the dynamic multiplier of lies and prudery does not necessarily explode into an epidemic of both.

The Ibsen formulation is relevant to organizations scholars in at least two ways. First, managers, the objects of organizations research, are likely to be caught in the Ibsen dilemma. The myths of management require executives to exhibit certainty, consistency, single-mindedness, and clarity in a world of ambiguity, ambivalence, paradox, and confusion. These aspirations are inconsistent with the capabilities of managers in the worlds in which they live. So they lie. They lie to the world. They lie to themselves. And they lie to scholars studying them. They try to engage scholars in the construction of ideal-satisfying fantasies about managerial life.

Second, scholars of organizations are themselves likely to be caught in the Ibsen dilemma. The myths of scholarship are inconsistent with the realities of scholarship. Scholars live in a world in which their livelihood and reputations depend on declaring results even when there are no results, and proclaiming relevance for practice even when the relevance of what is known is obscure. So scholars produce stories that conceal their failures and cater to the expectations of their readers. In *Hedda Gabler,* the scholar Eilert Løvborg describes his book as being not very good. When his audience complains that the book has been very well received, Løvborg comments:

> That was exactly what I wanted. And so I wrote a book everyone could agree with.[31]

When business leaders falsify their accounts, or political leaders lie about their information or intentions, or scholars invent stories inadequately supported by evidence, they are exposed to moral censure that translates into a personal sense of guilt. That censure seems eminently reasonable, but it should not obscure the extent to which a society or organization that insists strongly on virtue will become a society or organization based on lies and one that risks becoming entangled in an escalation of lying and prudery. In his influential book *Moral Man and Immoral Society*, published in 1932, Reinhold Niebuhr described hypocrisy as "an inevitable by product of all virtuous endeavour." He might easily have drawn implications for organizations scholarship. Any theory of organizations is necessarily also a theory of hypocrisy, a theory of the role of lies in sustaining human institutions and commitments to ideals, and a theory of the emotional response to involvement in a system of lies.

An understanding of the power of such phenomena and the elements of human nature from which they stem is a possible contribution to be drawn from the plays of Henrik Ibsen.

## NOTES

1. Those twelve included (in order) *Pillars of Society (Samfundets støtter), A Dollhouse (Et dukkehjem), Ghosts (Gengangere), An Enemy of the People (En folkefiende), The Wild Duck (Vildanden), Rosmersholm (Rosmersholm), The Lady from the Sea (Fruen fra havet), Hedda Gabler (Hedda Gabler), The Master Builder (Bygmester Solness), Little Eyolf (Lille Eyolf), John Gabriel Borkman (John Gabriel Borkman), When We Dead Awake (Når vi døde vågner).* The original Norwegian words corresponding to the English translations found in the text are shown in the footnotes to each quotation.

2. Alle din fars lettsindige grunnsetninger har du tatt i arv. Ingen religion, ingen moral, ingen pliktfølelse.

3. Kan du yde meg et lån?

4. Ja, ja, så gjerne det!

5. Kan du avse et ideal eller to?

6. Der er visse krav—. Hvad skal jeg kalde de krav? Lad mig sige—ideale krav,—visse fordringer, som en mand ikke kan sætte til side, uden at han tar skade på sin sjæl.

7. Actually, she said it the other way around: Det rosmerske livsyn adler. Men det dreper lykken.

8. Hele Deres ekteskap—hele dette mangeårige samliv med Deres mann skulle ikke være annet enn overdekket avgrunn!

9. Ikke en smule annet.

10. Peder Mortensgård vil alrdi mer enn han kan. Peder Moretnesgård er kapabel til å leve livet uten idealer. Og det—ser du,—det er just handlingens og seierens store hemmelighet. Det er summen av all verdens visdom.

11. I visse tilfælde er det umuligt at sætte sig ud over de ideale krav.... Men ... mennesket i mig kræver også sin ret.

12. Vårt hjem har ikke vært annet enn en lekestue. Her har jeg vært din dukkehustru, liksom jeg hjemme var pappas dukkebarn.

13. Det er just den rette opprørsånd å kreve lykken her i livet. Hva rett har vi mennesker til lykken? Nei, vi skalgjøre vår plikt, frue!

14. Gammelt vennskap ruster ikke.

15. Vi har bedradd hinannen gjensidig altså. Og kanskje bedradd oss elv—begge to.

16. Men er da ikke det i grunnen vennskap, John Gabriel?

17. Jo, det å bedra—det er vennskap. Det har du rett i.

18. Du kjenner ikke vårt samfunn lenger, ellers måtte du vite at dette ville knuse meg i bunn og grunn.

19. Sannhetens og frihetens farligste fiender iblant oss, det er den kompakte majoritet. Ja, den forbannede, kompakte, liberale majoritet,—den er det.

20. De har så fullkommen rett; men en redaktør kan ikke alltid handle som han helst ville.

21. Når galt skal være, så tenk og men og tro i Herrens navn alt hva du vil—både i den ene retning og i den annen. Men behold bare dine meninger for deg selv.

22. Bruk ikke det utenlandske ord: idealer. Vi har jo det gode norske ord: løgne.

23. Mener De at de to ting er i slekt med hinannen?

24. Ja, omtrent som tyfus og forråtnelsesfeber.

25. Tar De livsløgnen fra et gjennomsnittsmenneske, så tar De lykken fra ham med det samme.

26. Jeg var under plikten og hensynene, derfor løy jeg for min gutt år ut og år inn. Å, hvor feig—hvor feig jeg har vært!

27. Er det ikke samfunnet selv som tvinger oss til å gå krokveie?

28. Vi er samfunnets redskaper, hverken mer eller mind.

29. Hva makt ligger der på om et slikt samfunn støttes eller ikke? Hva er det som gjelder her? Skinnet og løgnen—og intet annet.

30. Jaha; det [rettskaffenhetsfeber] er en nasjonal sykdom; men den opptrer kun sporadisk.

31. Det var nettopp det jeg ville. Og så skrev jeg boken så at alle kunne være med på den.

# Contributors

MIE AUGIER is a social science research associate at Stanford University. She is also a research consultant for the Director of the Office of Net Assessment, Office of the Secretary of Defense. She has coauthored several papers and co-edited books with James G. March. Her research is on the history of ideas in organization studies, the history of North American business schools and management education, behavioral social science, strategic thinking, and related topics. Mailing address: 70 Cubberley, Stanford University, Stanford, CA 94305-3096. Email: augier@stanford.edu

DANIEL LEVINTHAL is the Reginald H. Jones Professor of Corporate Strategy at the Wharton School, University of Pennsylvania. His research interests focus on issues of organizational adaptation and industry evolution, particularly in the context of technological change. Mailing address: 2000 Steinberg-Dietrich Hall, Wharton School, University of Pennsylvania. Philadelphia, PA 19104-6370. Email: Levinthal@wharton.upenn.edu

ELLEN O'CONNOR teaches at the University of Paris Dauphine, DRM-CREPA, Research Center in Management and Organization, CNRS UMR 7088. She studies the relationship between the humanities and organization studies. She has published in leading academic journals including Academy of Management Review, Journal of Applied Behavioral Science, Organization Studies, and Hispanic Review. She is currently researching how the institutionalization of organization studies affected the field's relationship to its classics. Mailing address: 510 Panchita Way, Los Altos, CA 94022. Email: *Ellen.Oconnor@dauphine.fr*

JOHAN P. OLSEN is professor emeritus in political science at ARENA, Center for European Studies, University of Oslo. He has coauthored three books and several articles with James G. March. His most recent books are *Europe in Search for Political Order* (Oxford University Press, 2007) and *University Dynamics and European Integration* (coauthored with Peter Maassen, Springer, 2007). Mailing address: Holmenveien 14, 0374 Oslo, Norway. Email: j.p.olsen@arena.uio.no

ZUR SHAPIRA is the William Berkley Professor of Entrepreneurship and Management at the Stern School of Business, New York University. His publications include the following books: *Risk Taking: A Managerial Perspective* (1995), *Organizational Decision Making* (1997), *Technological Learning: Oversights and Foresights* (1997), and *Organizational Cognition* (2000). Mailing address: New York University, 40 W 4th St. #7-06, New York, NY 10012. Email: zshapira@stern.nyu.edu

# Index

Academy of Management, 356, 383

*Academy of Management Journal*, 327, 352, 356

*Academy of Management Review*, 301, 327, 352

*Accounting, Organizations, and Society*, 333

Action Theory, 423

Adaptation, 6, 108–115; competitive selection and reproduction, 126–134; experiential learning, 119–126; feedback-based, 172–75; memory of, 139–40; precision of, 136–39; as sequential sampling, 117–19; speed of, 134–36. *See also* Evolutionary theories; Exploitation; Exploration; Hot stove effect; Intelligence; Learning; Mimetic theories; Risk

*Administrative Science Quarterly*, 301, 327, 351–52, 356

Agency theory, 24, 58–60, 65, 81, 219

Akhmatova, Anna, 437

Alchian, Armen, 58, 155

Alexander the Great, 394

Allison, G.T., 356

Allport, Gordon, 389n4

Altruism, 41, 46, 110, 112, 114, 175, 222, 406

Ambiguity, 31, 35, 45, 443–44; of choice, 19; and coherence, 436; of history, 85–87, 89, 138; of managerial life, 21; and myopia, 403–5; of preferences, 24, 28–29, 41, 61–63, 81, 138, 171. *See also* Evocative ambiguity; Logic of appropriateness; Logic of consequences

*American Journal of Sociology*, 351

*American Sociological Review*, 351

Ando, Albert, 389n5

Ansoff, Igor, 389n5

Appropriateness, logic of. *See* Logic of appropriateness

Aquinas, Thomas, 345

Aristotle, 169, 217, 273, 318–19, 369, 394, 414, 428

Arnold, Mathew, 417

Arrow, Kenneth, 182, 389n4

Aspirations, 7, 27, 93, 120–21, 226, 258. *See also* Satisficing; Targets

Asset specificity, 57

Attention: allocation, 8, 28–30, 36–37, 69–70, 221, 224–225, 249; mosaics, 69–70; sequential attention to goals, 8, 28, 30, 79, 199

Auden, W.H., 442

Augier, Mie, 414

Avesson, Mats, 372

Babcock, Linda, 27

Bach, G. Leland, 304–6, 384, 405

Balzac, Honoré de, 415–16, 428, 437

Bandit problems, 9, 108–9, 174, 312

Barnard, Chester, 318, 345, 427–28

Bateson, Gregory, 428

Bavelas, Alex, 302, 352, 371

Beauty, 13, 21, 22, 408–10, 441–42, 444

Becker, Gary, 29, 389n4

Becker, Howard, 389n4

Behavioral economics, 16, 299, 331

*A Behavioral Theory of the Firm*, 11, 25–26, 52, 72, 306, 380–88

Bennis, Warren, 399–400

Bentham, Jeremy, 169, 217, 318, 345, 407–8, 416, 439

Berger, Peter, 418

Berle, Adolf, 24, 58

Björkman, Ingmar, 86–87

Blau, Peter, 302, 352, 355, 370

Bloom, Benjamin, 389n4